The Settlers' War

The Struggle for the Texas Frontier in the 1860s

The Settlers' War

The Struggle for the Texas Frontier in the 1860s

Gregory Michno

Caxton Press
Caldwell, Idaho
2011

Hardcover - ISBN 978-087004-503-5
Paper - ISBN 978-087004-494-6

Library of Congress Cataloging-in-Publication Data

Michno, Gregory, 1948-
The settlers' war : the struggle for the Texas frontier in the 1860s / Gregory Michno.
p. cm.
Includes bibliographical references.
ISBN 978-0-87004-503-5 (hardcover) -- ISBN 978-0-87004-494-6 (pbk.)
1. Pioneers--Texas--History--19th century. 2. Frontier and pioneer life--Texas--History--19th century. 3. Indians of North America--Wars--Texas. 4. Indians of North America--Wars--1815-1875. 5. Texas--History--19th century. I. Title.

F391.M63 2011
976.4'05--dc22

2011014019

Cover
By Jim D. Nelson
www.jdnelsonportraits.com

Lithographed and bound in the United States of America

CAXTON PRESS
Caldwell, Idaho
180395

Table of contents

Part 6: 1864

Part 7: 1865

Part 8: 1866

Part 9: 1867

Part 10: 1868

Part 11: 1869

Illustrations

Maps

Preface

Over the past half-century a good number of histories have been written about the Indian Wars in the American West. Many of them span several decades of time, cover many geographic regions, and concentrate on the military campaigns. Such a broad canvas of time and space naturally limits the details. Confined in this respect, authors focused on the prominent incidents and popular themes to paint a picture of a juggernaut of white expansion, usually with a ruthless military on the cutting edge, overwhelming peaceful Indian tribes and conquering the West.

This Course of Empire version was popular for decades, while today, Clash of Culture is more often seen as the explanation of Western History. A likely reason is because many of us can view the past only in terms of our own experiences. The Indian Wars, however, were quite real and germane in an earlier era—probably the defining experience of our nation—but it is often with difficulty that we can separate current emotional responses from an interpretation of history that might seem ancient and irrelevant.

Unlike the general surveys with much of their guilt-ridden transference of sensibilities, are the monographs, where the focus is usually on a single incident or battle. In these, much detail is provided, but a broader view is often lacking. These studies generally paint bloody scenarios of savagery and heroism. They are the colorful, inspiring sinews of history that novelists and moviemakers are attracted to. *The Settlers' War* attempts to synthesize the approaches without moralizing or portraying the protagonists as good or evil. The characters' actions will define them.

The main focus is on the non-combatant Anglos and Hispanics on the Texas frontier—the settlers. Texas was chosen because, although its experience somewhat echoed events elsewhere, it was also unique. I concentrate on a north-south band about 200 miles wide through central Texas, which remained the frontier for 50 years. During the decades from 1820 to 1870 the frontier line expanded 2,000 miles across the trans-Mississippi west; in Texas the frontier line expanded about 200 miles. The supposedly irresistible European force met a nearly immovable Native American resistance and a contest for possession of Texas' hills and prairies ensued for decades. The struggle was down and dirty.

In Texas in the 1860s there were no large scale battles between the army and the Indians. The Comanches, Kiowas, and Apaches attacked only when they had the advantages of numbers and surprise, for that was usually the only way they could win. With the tribes almost always avoiding a pitched battle, a tenacious pursuit and surprise was also the only way the army could win. Indians had to be followed, found, and caught unawares in order to bring them to battle. On the other hand, the Indians had an advantage: their targets—usually the homesteaders on the Texas frontier— were sitting ducks. Almost every successful fight for both sides was the result of a surprise attack, and in surprise attacks, there is a great chance that non-combatants will die.

Retaliation also played a large part in the story. When either side was bloodied, it often took revenge on the most convenient target it could find—almost always an innocent victim. In Texas the non-combatants bore the brunt of the warfare, losing far more than the soldiers who were supposedly there to protect them. There were several notable massacres by soldiers upon Indians during these decades, and although tragic, their numbers pale in comparison to the Anglo and Hispanic non-combatant deaths. It is in the frontier settlements where the tragedy of the Indian wars is found. The majority of killings were done by Indians on unsuspecting white families. They bore the brunt of the conflict, but their story is seldom told—a tale of white victims is not a popular one today. The conflict in Texas had the trappings of a "modern" guerrilla war in which non-combatants suffered because of the inability of most chiefs, soldiers, and politicians to find a diplomatic path to peace. It was hell on the home front.

A major source used in this study is the Indian Depredation Claims; a goldmine of mostly untapped primary reports of Indian attacks. The depredation claims provide a fascinating slice of pioneer life with details that illuminate the life-and-death struggle of survival on the frontier. At the National Archives I photocopied about 300 Kiowa and Comanche depredation claims out of Record Group 123. There are more than 2,200 of them, with perhaps 1,200 occurring in the 1860s. I randomly picked out about one in every four. There was only enough space to directly cite about 250 of them. If the reader is overwhelmed with the amount of raiding, killing, and thefts detailed here, he can be thankful that all are not included. Multiply my sample times four or five to get a more complete picture of the sheer magnitude of the raiding.

Many attacks and killings are detailed, but there were also many more that occurred that do not have enough solid information to pinpoint them geographically or temporally. Accounts that might say, "John Doe was killed sometime in 1868," for instance, are omitted.

Most of the sources are taken from white men's documents. That is where the preponderance of evidence rests and that is the nature of the beast. I choose to call Indians "Indians," because many times the name of the tribe is not given or is uncertain, and because that is what they were called in the 19th Century. As is usual with research, one sometimes discovers things he is totally unprepared for; things that may be pleasing to some and distasteful to others. So be it. The conclusions were arrived at with no particular ax to grind.

The 1860s was the bloodiest decade in the Western Indian wars. Most of the blood, however, came from those who should have been allowed to remain on the sidelines while the main adversaries battled to a conclusion. It wasn't to be. Soldiers and Rangers were largely ineffective. The war on the Texas frontier was fought by the settlers.

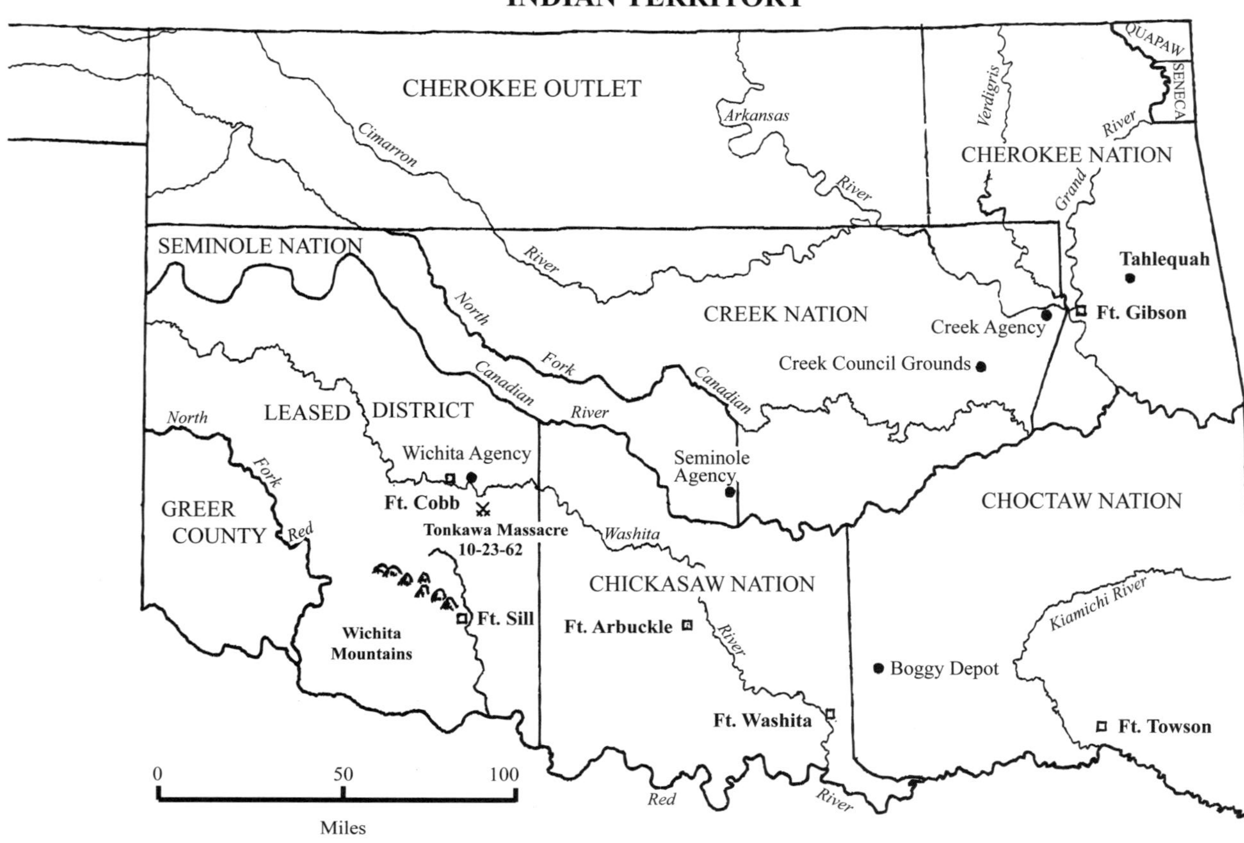
INDIAN TERRITORY
CHEROKEE OUTLET
Cimarron
Arkansas
River
QUAPAW
SENECA
Verdigris
River
CHEROKEE NATION
Grand
SEMINOLE NATION
River
Tahlequah
North
Ft. Gibson
CREEK NATION
Creek Agency
Creek Council Grounds
Fork
Canadian
Canadian
North
LEASED DISTRICT
River
Wichita Agency
Fork
Seminole Agency
Ft. Cobb
GREER COUNTY
Red
CHOCTAW NATION
Tonkawa Massacre 10-23-62
Washita
CHICKASAW NATION
Kiamichi River
Ft. Sill
Ft. Arbuckle
River
Wichita Mountains
Boggy Depot
Ft. Washita
Ft. Towson
0
50
100
Miles
Red
River

TEXAS INDIAN RESERVATIONS

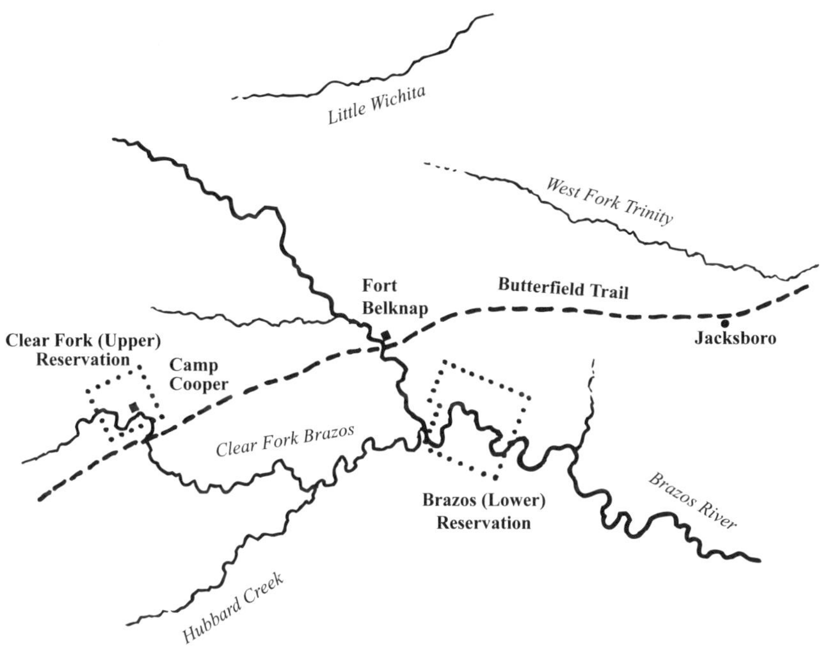

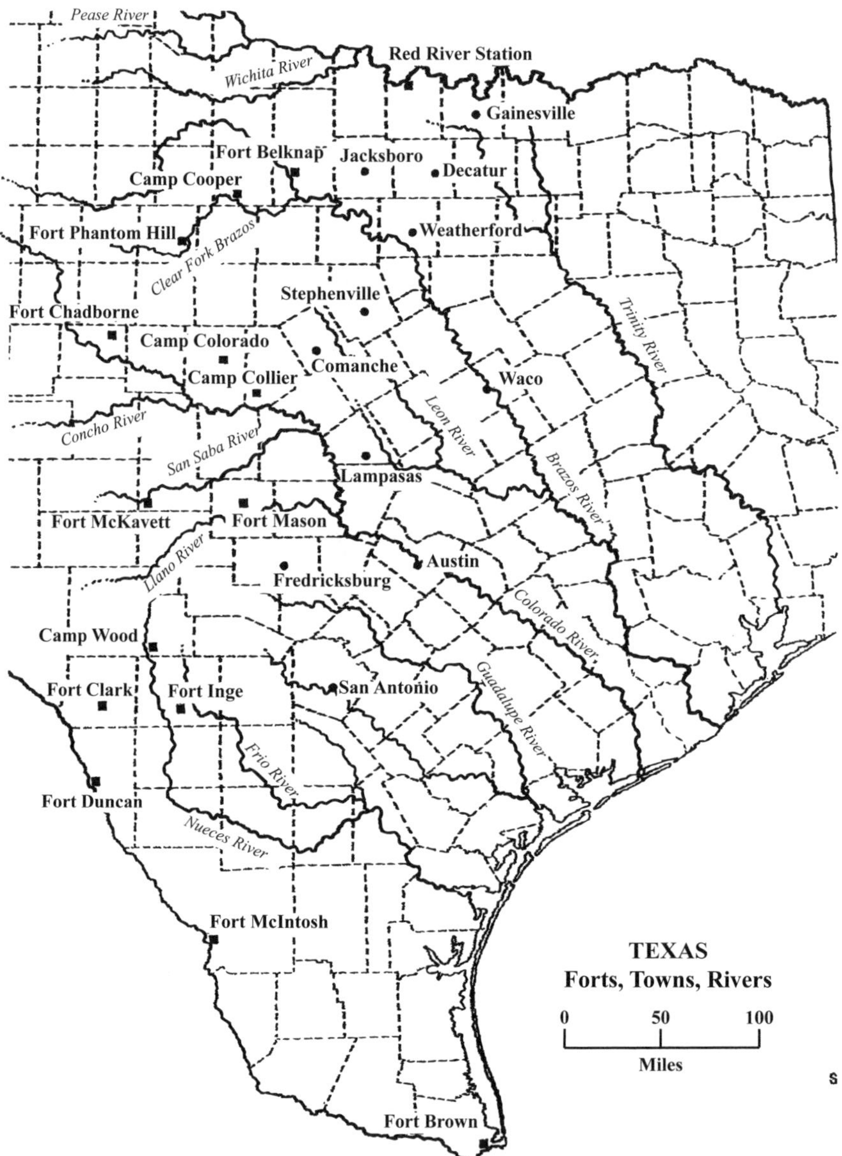
Pease River
Wichita River
Red River Station
Gainesville
Fort Belknap
Jacksboro
Decatur
Camp Cooper
Fort Phantom Hill
Weatherford
Clear Fork Brazos
Stephenville
Fort Chadborne
Camp Colorado
Comanche
Camp Collier
Waco
Trinity River
Leon River
Concho River
San Saba River
Lampasas
Brazos River
Fort McKavett
Fort Mason
Llano River
Austin
Fredricksburg
Colorado River
Camp Wood
Fort Clark
Fort Inge
San Antonio
Guadalupe River
Frio River
Fort Duncan
Nueces River
Fort McIntosh
TEXAS
Forts, Towns, Rivers
0
50
100
Miles
Fort Brown

Part 1: Before the Bloody Decade.

1 "By Naked Conquest."

The westward movement was central to the white American experience. Emigrants traveled toward the setting sun for about 270 years, from the Atlantic to the Pacific, until 1890, when the Census Bureau declared the frontier was officially closed. Westering seemed to be in the peoples' blood. In the 1890s, historian Frederick Jackson Turner crafted what became his legacy out of the simple idea that the West shaped Americans while Americans shaped the West, building something unique and eternal. His paean to our collective imagination painted us a scene at Cumberland Gap, watching the procession of civilization pass by in single file—the buffalo, the Indian, the fur-trader, the cattleman, and the farmer. He bade us to stand again at South Pass in the Rockies a century later and watch the same pageant of civilization. The image Turner painted, however, was not new. Thomas Jefferson had presaged the panorama of empire building seven decades earlier, when in 1825, he wrote of the same "progress of man," seeing the march of civilization advancing from his Virginia seacoast and "passing over us like a cloud of light" as barbarism receded before it.[1]

Turner's thesis notwithstanding, the frontier never was a sharp line of advancing settlements inexorably pushing west like the tide. The progression was more complicated, especially in Texas, which was settled from the Southern and Border states and filled with people who first moved to the coastal regions before pushing onto the prairie. This migration occurred two and three decades before the great emigrant exodus of the 1840s and 1850s. Actually, Europeans were in the present-day boundaries of Texas before their future adversaries, the Comanches. The Spanish noticed them about 1743, when this aggressive horse-mounted tribe rode past San Antonio de Bexar looking for Apaches to fight.[2]

The Comanches arrived in Texas 175 years after Spaniard Cabeza de Vaca first crossed the region. Although they were comparative late-comers, other Indians were in Texas before the Europeans: Lipans, Karankawas, Tonkawas, Kichai, Bidai, Caddos, and Wichitas, among others. The Spanish had alternately fought, traded, and peacefully co-existed with them. When Mexico won independence from Spain in 1821, the authorities decided they needed a buffer between threatening European powers and the Plains tribes to the north, and they allowed Americans to colonize lands north of the Rio Grande. The more aggressive Americans soon began to kill or drive out the local tribes.

If the Spanish, French, and Americans were intruders in the lands of the Texas coastal tribes, the Comanches and Kiowas were invaders in a like manner. Europeans were living in present-day Texas for nearly 100 years before the Comanches arrived. Many Native Americans today cite prior occupancy as an argument that the United States unjustly took their lands. If the argument is valid, then these wandering newcomers had no claim at all to Texas. The argument is specious, however. All of the Indian tribes on the Great Plains had taken over lands from other tribes before them. Conquest was a fact of life.

Of the major players in the Great Plains wars of the 1860s, all were comparative newcomers to the area, and almost all of the tribal wanderings and power shifts were influenced by a few major factors. Disease was foremost. The sporadic appearances of smallpox, cholera, and measles devastated tribes, caused some to relocate, and altered established power structures, creating vacuums and opening avenues for exploitation by other tribes. Trade was another factor. Europeans brought life-altering devices, and their desire for animal resources, such as beaver or bison became a blessing and a calamity for many tribes. Some of the most influential factors in changing life styles were the introduction of the horse and the gun. The spread of firearms generally emanated from the French and English out of the north and east, while the horse originated with the Spanish and ranged out of the south and west. As each tribe incorporated the gun or horse, it gave them advantages over tribes that lacked one or the other. When the two patterns overlapped, there developed the archetypal armed, mounted warrior.

The Comanches, who called themselves Numinu (the people), moved out of present Wyoming in the late 1600s. They acquired guns and were able to push aside tribes who had no firearms. When they ran into Apaches who had horses but no guns, there was a tentative standoff. The Pawnees, who had acquired horses and guns, pressured the Apaches from the northeast. When the Comanches got horses sometime in the 1720s and applied the squeeze from the northwest, the Apaches had no chance. They tried allying with the Spanish to fight the foes coming down from the north, but to no avail.[3]

The Kiowas first entered the historic record in what is today western Montana. A tribal feud caused part of the people to move east to the land of the Crows where they made their first alliance, probably about 1700. They moved to the Black Hills area and were still friends with the Crows in 1765. They got horses in the 1740s, and later, the appearance of the Cheyenne and Sioux forced them south. They made peace with the Comanches about 1790, and in 1805 they were on the North Platte River.[4]

After the end of the War of 1812, extensive expansion of American trade throughout the west effectively eliminated the horse and gun frontier. All the Great Plains tribes had access to both, and metamorphosed into the classic nomadic warrior culture that clashed head on with the encroaching Americans, with a culture seeped in traditions of sedentary cultivation. The stage was set for a collision that had been occurring for thousands of years, the clash between the nomad and the farmer.

How did the Indians acquire the territory they "owned" at the time of the great American migrations during the mid-nineteenth century? "Quite simply," in the words of historian Donald Worster, they got their lands "by force of arms—by naked conquest."[5] Native American took their lands from other Native Americans. The European "Americans" took it from them, and they will own the land until it is taken by another conqueror of the future. The United States is the temporary landlord. Whether this is fair or not is endlessly debatable but irrelevant. It is simply a part of the historical scheme.

In the 1850s and 1860s, Indians and whites were both moving across the plains—whites generally on an east-west trajectory, and Cheyennes, Arapahos, Lakotas, Kiowas, and Comanches generally on a north-south axis. They moved with the weather, with the seasons, and to trade and visit. The bison also followed north-south migratory patterns. The Southern Plains were harsh lands of few viable rivers and little timber, where scarce resources were at a premium. The Indians were in a land where a successful existence was tentative and food sources, once seemingly endless, were fast dwindling. People and scarce resources teetered on an unstable fulcrum. There had to be a reason. There had to be someone to blame.

As thousands of emigrants and settlers entered the picture, the chance of conflict between the two races and cultures, each ethnocentrically assured that it was in the right, was greatly increased. The Anglos entered the Trans-Mississippi West fully assured that their superiority was divine and not an accident of place and time. Prior to 1800 the iconic frontier settler image was not central to the American imagination. During the 19th Century settler explosion, perhaps ten million people moved west, and, as the popular Revolutionary War tune went, *The World Turned Upside Down*. As one historian of the settler revolution expressed it, "growth itself was the economy's main game." The most subversive theme was the idea blossoming in Anglos' minds that there was a great abundance of resources and money to be made with little work. Emigrants came seeking dreams, not only cheaper lands. They wanted a life as well as a living, and they were "boomers" in the extreme.[6]

When the settlers and Indians met, it appeared that conflict was likely, but it was not inevitable. There were forces shaping destinies, but they were still in control of man, with his freedom and wisdom to rise to the challenges or succumb to the temptations.

Thomas Fitzpatrick, the first U.S. agent for the Indians on the southern plains, had negotiated a treaty with the Kiowas and Comanches in 1853.

They had been raiding for years but Fitzpatrick hoped that a sufficient annuity would buy their cooperation. He was astute and knew the options: "The policy must be either an army or an annuity. Either an inducement must be offered to them [the Indians] greater than the gains of plunder, or a force must be at hand able to restrain and check their depredation." He went on to explain that a compromise would not work because it would "neither create fear nor satisfy avarice."[7]

This was a conundrum that had confounded diplomats both in tails and buckskin throughout nearly three centuries, and would continue into and beyond the Cold War of the 20th Century: should the United States use the carrot or the stick approach; should it spend millions for defense, but not one cent for tribute? The version of the dilemma in the West of the 1860s was, is it cheaper to feed the Indians or fight them?

During the 1853 treaty negotiations, Fitzpatrick commented upon the "keen intelligence" of the Indians. He believed that they knew exactly what they were bargaining for. They granted the right of the United States to make roads through their territory, to make reservations, and to establish military posts. They promised not to molest the whites using the road and to cease raiding into Mexico. In return, the government promised to pay an annuity of $18,000 in goods annually.[8]

The assumption that Indians did not know what they were signing, were unsophisticated, and were tricked by unscrupulous whites does not stand up to evidence. Two recent studies of Comanches and Kiowas in particular, show that those tribes were very politically coordinated and perspicacious, knowing quite well what deals they were making, and also quite Machiavellian in their responses to changing political and economic situations. They could adhere to a treaty as well as the white men—or break it just as easily if it was to their advantage. The Comanches agreed to stop raiding in Mexico, but not because the United States wished them to stop: raids in Mexico were already declining because recent cholera epidemics had killed hundreds of warriors; the market for stolen cattle was increasing and it was difficult to drive slow cattle out of Mexico when other sources were closer; and there was increasing danger on their northern frontier from the people rushing to California. The Comanches and Kiowas already had reasons to cut their Mexican raids—they figured they might as well agree to the treaty stipulation and get paid for it.[9]

The Fort Atkinson Treaty failed because neither side saw that it was to their advantage to honor it. What the U. S. commissioners did not realize was that by insisting that the Comanches and Kiowas stop raiding in Mexico, they would simply shift their focus to Texas. One scheme to solve the Indian "problem" was begun in 1854, when two reservations were created for the Texas Indians. Both were located on the Brazos River. The lower one was 12 miles southeast of Fort Belknap and became home to about 2,000 Caddos,

Anadarkos, Wacos, and Tonkawas. About 45 miles to the northwest on the Clear Fork Brazos was the smaller Comanche Reservation, home to less than 500 Penetekas.

The reservation plan failed. There was no clear jurisdiction between Federal and State authority. The Comanches were never good at farming and their agricultural efforts were unsuccessful. The tribes on the Brazos Reserve did better, but Texas authorities and the U.S. Army persistently hired them to act as scouts against warring tribes. This did not please the Comanches or Kiowas. It didn't please many Texans either. When warriors from the north raided in Texas, they often stopped at the Comanche Reservation for succor, implicating the Penetekas who tried to mind their own business. They also went to the Brazos Reserve and threatened the other tribes with destruction if they kept aiding the soldiers.[10]

In every year since the Treaty of 1853, the Kiowas and Comanches got their annuities and promptly went down to Texas to raid. In 1857 they fought the army in ten battles. Although the soldiers had their fights, it was the settlers who felt the worst stings. One particularly heinous foray occurred on April 18, 1858, in Jack County in a little community known as Gertrude. That morning, Indians and several white bandits murdered James B. Cambren and his sons, Luther and James Jr., who were working in their field. The raiders captured Mrs. Mary Cambren and her other children. Half a dozen raiders went to Tom Mason's home, killed Tom Mason and his wife, Mary, but left their two small children alone.

The raiders robbed Cambren's cabin and dragged along Mary and her children. When Mary and her youngest boy began crying, they shot her and speared the child, riding off and leaving behind seven-year-old Mary Cambren and her younger brother, Dewitt. The children walked back home.

Isaac Lynn, father of Mrs. Mason, decided to visit his daughter the next day. He was horrified to discover her and her husband slaughtered and the children crawling in their mother's blood. He went to the Cambren house and discovered a similar scene, finding Mary and Dewitt hiding in a corner.

Lynn took the two Cambren children and his two Mason grandchildren back to his home. While at his daughter's cabin he found a letter she had recently written, but had not yet posted. It was to her brother and sister. She dismissed any fears they had for her safety, saying she was not afraid of the Indians. "Let me tell you I dread them no more than I do the citizens of Tyler. They come to see us often; they are well behaved and sociable and friendly."[11]

The Gertrude Massacre galvanized the surrounding counties as few other raids had done. Charles Goodnight, who lived nearby, said, "Since this was the first bad Indian murder that had occurred on that frontier for many years, it created an unusual excitement because those settlers were not originally frontier people. They were not accustomed to such horrible occurrences, which, a year or two later, would have attracted very little attention."[12]

Chapter 1 notes

1 Turner, *Frontier and Section*, 44; Stegner, *Marking the Sparrow's Fall*, 35; Horsman, *Race and Manifest Destiny*, 84.
2 West, *Contested Plains*, 64; Kavanagh, *Comanches, A History*, 79.
3 West, *Contested Plains*, 47, 64; Secoy, *Changing Military Patterns*, 81-82.
4 Mooney, *Calendar History of the Kiowa*, 153-62, 166.
5 Worster, *Under Western Skies*, 121.
6 Belich, *Replenishing the Earth*, 5, 40, 65, 87, 146, 159, 163, 221.
7 Hafen, *Broken Hand*, 311.
8 Hafen, *Broken Hand*, 310; Kappler, *Indian Treaties*, 600-02.
9 DeLay, *War of A Thousand Deserts*, 117, 119, 141, 144, 305; Hamalainen, *Comanche Empire*, 7, 12.
10 Webb, *Handbook of Texas I*, 210, 364; Richardson, *Comanche Barrier*, 108-12.
11 Huckabay, *Jack County*, 35-39; Marshall, *A Cry Unheard*, 80.
12 Haley, *Charles Goodnight*, 24. Goodnight said the Cambrens and Masons shared a double log cabin.

2 "Your Troubles and difficulties will not cease."

Tired of being on the receiving end of these raids, Texas Governor Hardin R. Runnels authorized Capt. John S. "Rip" Ford, to take 102 Texas Rangers on a punitive expedition. Accompanied by 113 friendly Tonkawas, Anadarkos, Wacos, and Caddos from the Brazos Indian Reserve, under the leadership of Agent Shapley P. Ross, Ford led the column north. On May 11, 1858, they hit a Comanche camp in the Antelope Hills of Indian Territory. The Texans and Ross's Indians killed 76 Comanches, took 18 prisoners, and captured 300 horses, while losing only four killed and wounded.[1]

The Battle of Antelope Hills may have showed the Comanches that they were not safe north of Red River, but it did not stop the raiding. Kiowa Chief Little Mountain, told his agent, Robert C. Miller: "The white chief is a fool.... His men are not strong—too few to contend against my warriors.... [He] threatens to send his soldiers. I have looked for them a long time, but they have not come. He is a coward."[2]

The white soldiers obliged the Indians soon enough. In October, Capt. Earl Van Dorn led his cavalrymen against the Comanches. Van Dorn took 225 men of the 2nd U.S. Cavalry, a detachment of 1st U.S. Infantry, and 135 Reserve Indian auxiliaries out of Fort Belknap, Texas. They found a Comanche village under Chiefs Quo-ho-ah-te-me and Buffalo Hump near Rush Springs, Indian Territory. Not knowing that the Comanches had just finished peace talks with Fort Arbuckle commander, Capt. William Prince, Van Dorn attacked the camp at dawn on October 1, 1858. In a bloody fight, the soldiers lost four killed and 11 wounded, while two civilians were wounded. Van Dorn was wounded so badly he nearly died. They captured 300 horses. The Comanches lost 70 people, a significant number of them women and children. The soldiers said that the women fought with the men and could not be distinguished from the males. Buffalo Hump escaped and vowed to take his revenge.[3]

The Indians had been in Texas stealing and killing people, whom, for the most part, had never lifted a finger in anger against an Indian. Van Dorn went after the marauders and certainly killed innocent women and children who had never fought against the whites. Men on both sides were not strong enough to rise above their desires for revenge. The Comanches were irate, and the Texas frontier would feel their wrath.

Many bands from north of Red River raided Texas, but the depredations were invariably attributed to the Indians on the nearby reservations even as some of them served as army scouts. An inflammatory weekly newspaper called *The White Man*, published in Jacksboro by J. A. Hamner, generally fanned the flames with essays of racial hatred. Hamner's friend, John R. Baylor, often played the role of rabble rouser to incite the locals. Baylor, born in Kentucky in 1822, moved to Texas in 1839 and served in several ranger expeditions against the Comanches. He was Comanche agent in 1855, but Superintendent Robert Neighbors complained that he couldn't handle the Indians and accused him of theft. After being fired in 1857, Baylor became the Indians' nemesis. To his contemporaries he was generally characterized as an upstanding patriot, while today he is more often portrayed as a scoundrel and racist.[4]

As Baylor helped organize citizen resistance in north Texas, in December 1858, about 17 Anadarkos and Caddos from the Brazos Reservation under their leader, Choctaw Tom, received permission from the agent to graze their horses south in Palo Pinto County. They were peacefully camped on the evening of December 26, when 40 men hunting thieves found them. The white hunters, led by Peter Garland, killed eight men, women, and children while they slept in their blankets, as the others ran for their lives. Suddenly concerned about the senseless deed, many whites feared the Indians would retaliate and about 200 of them gathered to do battle.[5]

Superintendent Neighbors learned the names of the Erath County men who had attacked Choctaw Tom, but no indictments could be made. Texas Rangers were sympathetic with the white civilians and the Federal troops stood in between, but were of little help.

Raids and counter-raids continued through 1859. Recovered from his wounds, Van Dorn again went after the Indians. Reinforced with 58 Indians from the Brazos Reservation, he led nearly 500 men of the 2nd U.S. Cavalry north of Red River and all the way into Kansas, where they found a camp on upper Crooked Creek. On May 13, 1859, they trapped the Comanches in a tangled copse of timber and brush. Van Dorn said "they fought without giving or asking quarter until there was not one left to bend a bow." No one escaped. Forty-nine warriors were killed and five were wounded, while 32 women and five men were captured. The soldiers lost two officers wounded, two enlisted men killed and 13 wounded, and four Indian allies killed or mortally wounded. Van Dorn marched home.[6]

Even with all the military efforts, a mob of disgruntled citizens in north Texas took over in May 1859. John R. Baylor charged that the Comanches of Clear Fork were committing the outrages. About 300 men gathered in Jacksboro, under the command of Baylor, Peter Garland, and Allison Nelson. They planned to attack Camp Cooper on the Clear Fork and kill the Indians or drive them out of Texas. The armed citizens did not get beyond the lower agency when a confrontation erupted on May 23, to be called the "Reservation

War." Capt. Innis N. Palmer of the 2nd Cavalry stated that it was his duty to defend the Indians on the reserve. Baylor threatened the Federals, but he was unwilling to make the first move. When Baylor retreated to consult with his lieutenants, his men killed an Indian woman working in her garden, captured an old Indian man who had gotten too near, dragged him away with a rope, and killed and scalped him.

This spurred an attack by 50 or 60 Indians who had been following the Texans and a running fight began. James "Buck" Barry said it took place over several hours, "carried on in regular savage style by both parties, each putting to death all the prisoners taken." Barry lamented that the Texans could not follow through because of the army. Nonetheless, the fight lasted until dark, with about five Texans and one or two Indians killed. The old Tonkawa Chief Placido lamented that it was the first time he had ever fought the whites. The battle proved, if anyone had any doubts, that there could be no peaceful co-existence between Indians and Texans.[7]

The Indians would be removed. The U.S. leased a portion of southwestern Indian Territory from the Choctaw and Chickasaw tribes on which to establish an agency for the Texas Indians. Governor Hardin R. Runnels had issued a proclamation as early as March 12, 1859, warning the citizens to beware of what they wished for. "With the forcible breaking up of these reserves, your troubles and difficulties will not cease…." he declared. "They will have only begun; for, with such an additional number of savages thrown upon the frontier, who will be enraged and exasperated by a sense of wrong, who can doubt the result? Will you then expect the State to expend as many more thousands in defending you from the consequences which your own rash and revolutionary action has brought you…?"[8]

Runnels's caveat was prescient; the situation only deteriorated. Nevertheless, Neighbors worked hard to move the Indians out as soon as possible. On July 31, Indians from both reservations, escorted by U.S. cavalry and infantry, made their exodus out of Texas and to the Leased District. Texas State troops under Capt. John H. Brown followed behind, just to see that there was no mischief. Records showed 1,182 Indians left the Brazos Reserve and 384 vacated the Clear Fork. The Comanches lost or abandoned animals worth about $15,000.

Even as the Indians were moving north, warriors went south to raid. In July 1859 they stole horses from the ranch of William L. Williams in Brown County. In Comanche County in the middle of the night they crept up near Elisha H. Barcroft's ranch on Mercer Creek eight miles south of the village of Comanche, and cut loose three hobbled horses worth $300. All Barcroft found the next morning were moccasin tracks in the dirt.[9]

The Indians would more than make up for the stock they lost by stealing tens of thousands of horses, mules, and cattle during the ensuing years. Agent

Neighbors, meanwhile, was working hard to get his charges safely across Red River, but he did not appreciate the Texas troops watching his every move. When he got them into Indian Territory, he commented: "I have this day crossed all Indians out of the heathen land of Texas and am now out of the land of the Philistines. If you want to have a full description of our exodus, see the Bible, where the children of Israel crossed the Red Sea."[10]

Neighbors turned over the Indians to Samuel A. Blain at the Wichita Agency on August 16, and returned to Texas, stopping at Fort Belknap. He had made many enemies. On September 14, as Neighbors stood in the street talking, a man named Edward Cornett walked up behind him and shot him dead.[11]

The Texans may have gotten some good Indian land that they coveted, but it would not be safe for them to live there. The "children of Israel" would return to smite Egypt. War was kicking into high gear on the Texas frontier.

The Kiowas and Comanches of the Southern Plains were on the horns of a dilemma. Certainly they had signed a treaty promising to allow establishment of posts and ceasing to harass travelers, but that was in 1853, and the situation was no longer the same. In any case, both sides broke treaties whenever their provisions no longer served a purpose. Agent William Bent explained the tribes' situation: "These numerous and warlike Indians, pressed upon all around by the Texans, by the settlers of the gold region, by the advancing people of Kansas, and from the Platte, are already compressed into a small circle of territory, destitute of food, and itself bisected athwart by the constantly marching line of emigrants. A desperate war of starvation and extinction is therefore imminent and inevitable, unless prompt measures shall prevent it."[12]

Bent described the circumstances in dichotomous terms that historians of the 20th and 21st Centuries still struggle with. There was an impending sense of an inevitable clash of cultures, yet a possibility that politics or diplomacy would solve the problems. Today, it appears that "clash of cultures" has become the buzzword to describe the white-Indian conflict in the West, however, it is too simple an explanation. Cultures don't battle each other. Cultural differences do cause dissonance, but by themselves they do not make war inevitable. Poor personal and political decisions made by all parties during America's course of empire caused the clash. Unfortunate choices and accidents set the sparks. Neither side was borne along on a predetermined tide of destiny. Suggesting different cultures will inevitably clash is a cynical, hopeless explanation. A few good men from both sides might have made a difference.

Had any white civilians on the frontier foreseen what was in the cards for the upcoming decade, they might have packed up and gone east, and Indian women and children may have voluntarily accepted the comparative safety of reservation life. The frontier settlers had experienced years of Indian raids that they considered intolerable and they bemoaned the seeming lack of protection by Federal troops, state militia, and Rangers. It would get worse. No one dreamed that when the bells rang for New Year's Day celebrations on January 1, 1860, that they were to experience the bloodiest decade in all the Western Indian wars and possibly the most sustained and destructive assault by Indians on a frontier population. The classic imagery we have of Plains Indian warfare, with warriors flashing by on painted ponies armed with bows and arrows, and the charging cavalry with carbine and saber, were romantic metaphors, painted in oils, printed in novels, and shown on the silver screen. It is true that there were clashes in that classic mode, but for the most part in the forthcoming fighting it was safer to be a warrior or a soldier than to be a non-combatant. It would be hell on the home front.

Chapter 2 notes

1 Michno, *Encyclopedia of Indian Wars*, 62.
2 Mooney, *Calendar History of the Kiowa*, 176.
3 Webb, *Texas Rangers*, 154-58; Nye, *Carbine & Lance*, 19-24.
4 Webb, *Handbook of Texas I*, 124, 210; Webb, *Handbook of Texas II*, 898; Anderson, *Conquest of Texas*, 270, 291, 312.
5 Richardson, *Comanche Barrier*, 128; Winfrey and Day, *Texas Indian Papers III*, 312; Huckabay, *Jack County*, 49.
6 Utley, *Frontiersmen in Blue*, 133-35; Nye, *Carbine & Lance*, 25-26.
7 Wilbarger, *Indian Depredations*, 442; Arnold, *Jeff Davis's Own*, 254-56; Winfrey and Day, *Texas Indian Papers, III*, 328-29.
8 Winfrey and Day, *Texas Indian Papers, III*, 319.
9 Depredation Claims: William L. Williams #4739; Elisha H. Barcroft #5292.
10 Huckabay, *Jack County*, 59.
11 Richardson, *Comanche Barrier*, 131; Winfrey and Day, *Texas Indian Papers III*, 338-39.
12 Hafen, *Relations with the Indians*, 187.

Part 2 1860

3 "I tried that Virginia back heel on him."

The fighting in the 1860s first started on the Texas frontier. It should not have been any surprise; the conflict on the Southern Plains had been almost constant since 1758 when Comanches first destroyed the Spanish mission at San Saba. Fighting intensified as more settlers entered the region while Spain and Mexico were the overseers, continued during the Texas Republic years from 1836 to 1845, and long after Texas became a part of the United States.

There were few places on the American frontier where conditions exacerbated potential suffering as they did in Texas. The "normal" Turnerian frontier, with its progression of trappers, traders, and soldiers did not apply. The Anglo and Hispanic frontier in Texas was one of settlers, of farming families and stock raisers, with men, women, and children colliding with a nomadic warrior culture. There were no buffers and there was no break-in period. The isolated farms and ranches were prime targets. The settlers were not mountain men or frontiersmen. The rules for some of the first colonies banned anyone with an occupation as a hunter, and allowed no drunkards, gamblers, cursers, or idlers. Many of the early colonists were literate and educated. Most of them came from the Trans-Appalachian South, seeking economic opportunity and cheap lands. They came and settled in colonies begun by Austin, Dewitt, De Leon, Robertson, Peters, and Castro, among others. The Texas frontier was being populated with families who were not well-armed, and who were more concerned with making a living—and a profit—than with being an Indian buffer.[1]

The general impression of antebellum Texas is of a land of many cotton-growing slaveholders and poor upland whites. The poor whites got bad press from the 1850s when northerners described them as lazy and physically and morally stunted, beginning a "hillbilly" stereotype that is still difficult to dispel. Texas was called a "default frontier," populated by bankrupt people who could not survive elsewhere. Yet, it is also argued that the upland Texans were "born capitalists" and contributed more to the gross national product than did the small number of cotton-growers. It is said that horses were associated with vibrant boom times and mules were linked to a torpid cotton-growing economy. In Texas there were relatively few mules, but tens of thousands of horses. Horses, hogs, hides, and cattle fueled a Texas boom that lasted from 1846 to 1857. Texas almost tripled its population in the 1850s, from about 200,000 to 600,000. Most of the people, small-time farmers, ranchers, and tradesmen, pushed to the frontier for cheap lands. Although Europeans had preceded the Comanches in eastern Texas, farther west the newcomers were encroaching in places occupied by the Comanches for a century.[2]

At this time there were 13 Comanche bands in five major divisions. Although they were spelled many different ways and sometimes coalesced and separated, the Penetekas, or Hois, known as "honey-eaters" and "timber people," were the ones to follow the buffalo farthest south and were concentrated on the Edwards Plateau when the first serious conflicts erupted with the Texans. North of them were the Nokonis, called "those who turn back," and they roamed from the Texas Cross Timbers west into New Mexico Territory. Next, were the Kotsotekas, the "buffalo-eaters," who were concentrated in today's western Oklahoma. North of them, and extending to the Arkansas River, were the Yamparikas, the "eaters of the yap root." Out on the barren Llano Estacado were the Quahadi, called the "antelopes," or "sun shades on their backs," because they made buffalo-skin umbrellas. They were the smallest of the five, but considered the most aloof and fierce.[3]

The Comanches and their Kiowa allies made Texas a very dangerous place. The farmers and ranchers whose homesteads abutted hard against Indian land had called for years for more protection, which waxed and waned in the form of local militia, Rangers, and the U. S. Army.

In Texas, the year began much as the old one had finished. Capt. Kirby Smith, 2nd Cavalry, with about 60 men and 150 horses, went to Camp Colorado on Jim Ned Creek in present eastern Coleman County. At midnight on January 14, 1860, a settler rode in to report Comanches stealing horses and mules. Lt. Fitzhugh Lee, a nephew of Robert E. Lee, volunteered to take out a patrol in pursuit. With 22 men of Smith's Company B, Lee rode out into the night during a howling norther.

At daybreak they arrived at the ranch where the stock was stolen and Lee followed the trail despite the snow. In mid-afternoon of January 16, the patrol caught up with the Indians who were herding the stolen stock up Pecan Bayou, south of Baird in present Callahan County. Lee ordered his men to draw pistols and charge.

The surprised Comanches scattered into the trees while the two slowest ones were caught at the rear of the herd. A trooper shot one, while the other loosed arrows at Lee and his bugler, Jack Hayes. Lee and five other troopers tracked the warrior for a few miles through snow-covered, wooded hills. The warrior then laid down his red blanket where his pursuers would be sure to see it, and concealed himself over a ledge several yards away.

Lee found the blanket and immediately caught on. He leapt over the ledge and the two men were face to face. The Comanche shot an arrow that struck Lee's carbine stock. He dropped the weapon and the two began wrestling. Lee hit the Indian with his revolver, while the warrior jabbed into Lee's thick overcoat with his knife. Finally both men lost their weapons and wrestled each other to the ground. Lee, holding on to his larger opponent, quickly thought of a trick he had learned wrestling with the boys back home. He figured, "if I tried that Virginia back heel on him I would get him." It worked. Lee had his adversary pressed tight against the ground. "Here was I on top" he said, "holding down, breast to breast, a live Camanche, and a very slippery one, with nothing to kill him!"

Jack Hayes then arrived and helped restrain the warrior while Lee grabbed his revolver and shot the Indian twice. When he checked himself for wounds, he found his outer garments slashed to ribbons but he was otherwise unharmed. He gathered up the warrior's shield, headdress, and weapons, which he later displayed with great pride. Lee's men killed two Comanches and recovered 25 horses.[4]

In January 1860, Indians stole horses from the Beaver Creek settlers in southeast Mason County. On January 19, they shot a Mr. Winkle twice and stole his horses. Settlers went to Fort Mason to ask for help and Sgt. Robert H. Chapman, with a squad of men from Company A, 2nd Cavalry, complied. While they were out, Indians appeared on Comanche Creek, only eight miles from the post, stealing more horses. The settlers complained again, but Capt. Richard W. Johnson had no more men to send.

One of the locals, George W. Todd, who would have his wife killed and daughter captured in nearly the same spot five years later, wrote to the newspaper, stating that it seemed impossible for anyone to catch or stop the Indians "for this simple reason: they have no horses and I cannot see how it is possible for them to have, when the Indians are constantly scouring the country, and stealing every horse they find."

Todd posted his letter from Fort Mason on January 24. Two days later, Sgt. Chapman had some success. Accompanied by three civilians, Chapman trailed the Indians for 100 miles before finding a Comanche camp on Kickapoo Creek in Concho County. They attacked, killed four Indians, wounded several more, and captured 13 horses. Four soldiers and one civilian were wounded.[5]

On January 30, Sgt. Alex Craig and 14 men of Company C, 2nd Cavalry, guided by seven civilian volunteers, rode out of Camp Lawson looking for Comanche raiders who had stolen horses from a Mr. Berry on the Leona River. They found and attacked the Indians on the Frio River. Two soldiers were wounded, but they killed four warriors, wounded two, and recovered 21 horses.

On February 12, at the Head of Concho Station, either Mescaleros or Comanches stampeded the mules of the Overland Mail Company and chased Steve Darret and a man named Morris from Mason County. J. N. Helm, an Overland employee, said Darret was on a good horse and got away, but "Morris was overtaken and killed dead."

Capt. Richard W. Johnson led men of Companies A and F, 2nd Cavalry, out of Fort Mason along the Colorado River to the Concho. On February 13, Johnson found a Comanche camp near Kickapoo Creek where Chapman had fought in January. The Indians took a position in a small thicket and held their ground from mid-afternoon until dusk. Johnson held them down but could not drive them out. It was reported "The Captain offered fifty dollars apiece for scalps, but there was none willing to charge the bush." Johnson pulled back at nightfall. He believed they killed one Indian and wounded two, while one soldier was wounded. The paper noted that "The spoils in this engagement amounted to fifteen old broken down ponies and mules," and concluded that "fights as these make the Indians more bold and daring in their depredations," and that they "were in no dread of chastisement by the U. States troops."[6]

Montague County in north Texas kept records. It showed that in January 1860, Indians stole horses from Wade Hudson, Hugh Ivy, and John McGrew. They also took a fine horse worth $250 from William T. Brumley. They may have also taken Brumley, for the report said, "he has not been heard of since." In February, the county recorded stock losses for Pendleton Porter, R. C. Porter, Daniel P. Brumley, John Morriss, Hiram Williams, and John Womble. Peter R. Sherwood also lost a horse, and the register had a note, "there was moccasin tracks seen about the tree where he was tied."[7]

Stock thefts were a nuisance, but they were only one aspect of the conflict. Governor Runnels' warning the previous year was borne out in shocking terms in February 1860, with the first big raid of the new decade proving to be a harbinger of things to come.

Chapter 3 notes

1 Fehrenbach, *Lone Star*, 135, 138, 141-42.
2 Belich, *Replenishing the Earth*, 240-42.
3 Fehrenbach, *Comanches*, 142-45. Kavanagh, *Comanches, A History*, 4, lists scores of variations of names and divisions.
4 Arnold, *Jeff Davis's Own*, 281-84; Brown, *Indian Wars and Pioneers*, 111-12.
5 *State Gazette* (Austin), February 11, 1860; Smith, *Old Army in Texas*, 146; Vincent, *Vincent's United States Register*, 60.
6 Smith, *Old Army in Texas*, 146; Vincent, ed., *Vincent's United States Register*, 64-65; *State Gazette* (Austin), March 10, 1860.
7 Winfrey and Day, *Texas Indian Papers, IV*, 56-62.

4 "They Held Their Bibles."

The war party that splashed across the cold Red River about the first of the month was likely Peneteka Comanche. The leader of the war party likely had a vision or a dream that he interpreted in ways that would determine where and when the raid should take place. He gathered his friends to discuss the matter. If there was sufficient encouragement he put on his war paraphernalia and at sundown the followers paraded through the village announcing the war dance to be held that night. The objective might be for revenge, for spoils, or for war. The leader announced its purpose and he and the warriors danced and narrated their past exploits. Before the sun rose, the warriors would slip away and meet at a rendezvous point.

Their faces were painted black, the death color, and they danced and left in the darkness, for years ago a war party once left during the daylight and all were killed. The lesson was never forgotten. The route was planned out in detail, the lines of travel, camping places, meeting places, who would scout, cook, get water, how the booty was to be divided, and where they would retreat to if necessary. One or two scouts rode a half-day ahead of the main party. They traveled in the daytime when possible and, when in enemy territory, camped halfway up a hillside whenever one was available. They made no fires, ate dried meat, and endured heat and cold with discipline. The war party was similar to a raiding party, the final objective making the distinction. Otherwise, a raiding party that was probably seeking horses would fight an enemy if necessary, and a war party would not pass up a chance for booty if the opportunity was right. A revenge party was resolute in its mission to kill and scalp and it would stay its course until the leader declared his vengeance was satisfied. Whoever the hapless victims were, they could expect little mercy. There were no rules. Depending on the whim of the assailant, the victim could be slaughtered, raped, tortured, taken captive, or set free.

Once across Red River, the raiders moved down the edge of the Western Cross Timbers, an irregular hilly and wooded region dividing grasslands on both sides and extending south through Montague, Wise, Jack, Parker, Hood, Erath, and Comanche counties. The Cross Timbers' trees and broken topography expedited stealth. Now in enemy territory, the raiders moved by moonlight and holed up during the day.[1]

They first struck about February 6, 1860, a full moon, along the Eastland-Erath County lines near the Allen, Stuart (Stewart), and Lauder (Lowder) homes. The weather had broken, the sun was melting the snow, and all were going about their daily chores. William M. Allen was only 20 years old, but

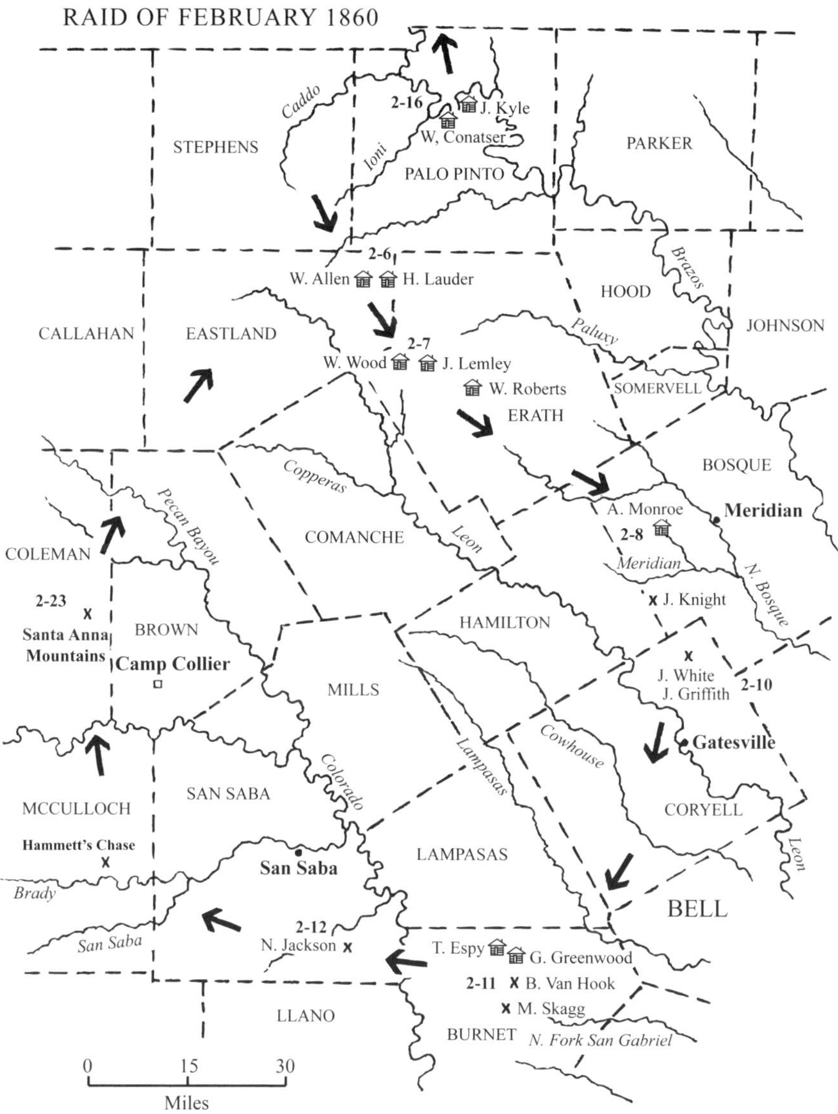
RAID OF FEBRUARY 1860
STEPHENS
Caddo
2-16
J. Kyle
W, Conatser
Ioni
PALO PINTO
PARKER
2-6
W. Allen
H. Lauder
HOOD
Brazos
CALLAHAN
EASTLAND
2-7
W. Wood
J. Lemley
Paluxy
JOHNSON
W. Roberts
SOMERVELL
ERATH
BOSQUE
Copperas
Pecan Bayou
A. Monroe
Meridian
2-8
COLEMAN
COMANCHE
Leon
Meridian
N. Bosque
J. Knight
2-23
Santa Anna Mountains
BROWN
Camp Collier
HAMILTON
J. White
J. Griffith
2-10
MILLS
Cowhouse
Gatesville
Lampasas
Colorado
MCCULLOCH
SAN SABA
CORYELL
Hammett's Chase
San Saba
LAMPASAS
Leon
Brady
BELL
2-12
N. Jackson
San Saba
T. Espy
G. Greenwood
2-11
B. Van Hook
M. Skagg
LLANO
BURNET
N. Fork San Gabriel
0
15
30
Miles

was in charge of his brothers and sisters since their parents had died. He, Sam, and Joe had been target shooting and were molding new bullets when 18 Indians arrived in the field. The three boys bluffed them by going outside and pointing their empty rifles at them. The Indians went away, but not before stealing six horses and a mule.

At the next cabin, Jim Stuart was away clearing underbrush with neighbors Mack Allen and Bethel Strawn. Stuart's wife and Emmaline and Martha Allen were working the spinning wheel when they saw about 20 Indians in the yard. Mrs. Stuart barred the door, grabbed a gun, poked the muzzle out a crack in the door, and said, "Now girls, let's keep cool."

"Yes, and our scalps, too," said Emmaline Allen.

Mrs. Stuart soon said, "Girls, I'm going to shoot," but Emmaline said, "Don't! Wait until they try to get in!" Wisely, she didn't shoot, and the Indians didn't assault the cabin, but plundered the property outside.

Nearby, Mrs. Hannah Lauder, William Allen's oldest sister, saw the Indians from her window. She rang the dinner bell to warn her husband and others working in the fields. When they came running they saw the Indians at Stuart's, and yelling, "Charge boys, charge!" they chased the Indians off with only one of John Lauder's horses in tow.[2]

The Allen boys quickly finished molding new bullets and joined the other men to follow the Indians' trail. They thought the Indians would head out of the area through a gap in the hills near the headwaters of the North Fork Palo Pinto, but when they reached there, the Indians had not followed expectations—they had continued their raid to the south. The Comanches next appeared in Erath County along the Paluxy River, and then northwest of the present town of Lingleville near the head of Rush Creek. They struck again on the night of February 7—a full Comanche moon.

John Lemley and William Wood were some of the first settlers to move to the territory north of Parker County in 1854. Two years later, only about 200 people lived there, but it was enough to organize the area into Jack County. Living on the edge of settlement with Indian raids common was a dangerous existence, and horrible murders such as the 1858 massacre of the Cambren and Mason families convinced them to relocate. The Lemleys moved south to Palo Pinto County for a short time, and even farther south to Erath County in January 1860. William Wood had also recently arrived, building his house about a mile from Lemley.

The two men, still constructing their homes, probably figured they had put a large enough barrier between them and the Indians to the north. John and William had gone to the Leon River for timber and their families had gotten together while the men were gone. Wood's wife, 16-year-old Lucinda Wood, was staying at Lemley's place. Mrs. Lemley had taken her baby, John Jr., to Matt Tucker's house to spend the evening, and later in the afternoon, her daughter, Dallie Lemley, joined them. Left behind at the Lemley house were Lucinda Wood, and the three sisters, Liddie, Nancy, and 19-year-old Hulda Lemley.

The Indians attacked without warning, and before the women could take any defensive measures, the warriors captured all four of them. The raiders carried them a few miles to where Lingleville would later be built. There, with reasonable assurance that they would not be interrupted, the warriors beat and raped the women. At dusk they released Lucinda Wood and Liddie Lemley, and motioned to them to go home. The Indians had just begun their raid and apparently there was disagreement among them as to the merits of taking the women or killing them. A few warriors quickly made up their minds. They rode back down the trail, found Lucinda and Liddie, shot them in the back with arrows and lanced them with spears. Lucinda, with a full head of light golden hair, was scalped, but Liddie's thin head of hair was left behind.

Nancy and Hulda Lemley made little protest about their treatment and sought the protection of an older warrior who seemed more kindly disposed to them. At least they were still alive. The Indians placed them on horses and they rode away under the light of a full moon. They stopped about three miles southwest of Stephenville and Nancy and Hulda were raped during the night. In the morning, warriors stripped the last of their clothing and the women probably assumed they were going to be raped again, and perhaps killed. Instead, the warriors motioned for them to head home, just as they had done to Lucinda and Liddie. In the freezing February morning, the two terrified women headed down the trail in the direction the Indians had pointed, certain that they would be killed. When out of sight of the Indians, however, they veered off the trail and headed back toward Stephenville. The Indians did not go after them, but continued on their raid, with two less white women to be concerned about. Nancy and Hulda staggered to the home of Will "Turkey" Roberts one mile from town. Soon, townswomen brought them clothing and they related the story of what had happened.

Lauder, Stuart, and the Allen boys arrived a short time later, passing Wood's destroyed house on the way. Farther on they found the mutilated bodies of Lucinda Wood and Liddie Lemley and located the families to tell them of their grisly discovery. Lucinda and Liddie were buried in the West End Cemetery near Stephenville. Nancy and Hulda had been abused so badly that Dr. I. P. Vollintine of Weatherford had to treat them for several weeks before they recovered. John Lemley was so distraught that he could no longer stay in the area and moved the remaining members of his family back to Jack County. The girls both lived many years after the incident, Hulda marrying Jesse Reasoner and remaining in the area. She was still alive in 1926 when she related her story.

William Wood, had he thought about it, may have felt the great irony of the situation. One "W. Wood" was listed as a member of Peter Garland's 40-man force who attacked Choctaw Tom's peaceful band just 14 months earlier. Another member of Garland's posse was W. T. L. Lauder. If these were the same men, both of them, and particularly William Wood, may have felt the grief and anger that Choctaw Tom assuredly felt after his wife was killed for no apparent reason.[3]

The Comanches continued southeast. From Erath County they split into several smaller parties and headed further into the settlements. On February 8, they were in Bosque County. Brothers Angus (49) and Colin (or Copeland) (36) Monroe, from North Carolina, were splitting rails on Spring Creek eight miles west of Meridian. The Comanches killed them both, leaving one "stripped to the drawers," and the other with only shirt and drawers. One of the bodies had seven arrows in it and the other had 13. Reportedly the Comanches left a one hundred dollar bill lying next to one of the bodies, not knowing its value. The bodies were taken to the Bosque County courthouse in Meridian where onlookers viewed them. One of them, William H. Parsons, wrote, "may my eyes never again witness such a spectacle of horror…."

Parsons made the same point that hundreds of settlers made: if there was no protection, "the frontier counties will be speedily abandoned." Furthermore, there didn't appear to be any frontier. "Meridian," Parsons wrote, "is a hundred miles within the long line of outer settlements, and the boldness with which the Indians have advanced so far into the interior…is an indication of the audacity of the foe." Parsons estimated that 5,000 horses had been stolen in the past three years and there didn't seem to be any end in sight. He was right.

The Comanches were not finished with the current raid. They moved south and later the same day or the next, found James Knight (22) on Neils Creek about four miles south of present-day Cranfills Gap on the Bosque-Hamilton County lines. Knight was cutting timber for John Pancake and William Babb who lived on Neils Creek. The Indians killed Knight and continued south.[4]

The next day the raiders stole horses in Coryell County in the Leon Valley ten miles above Gatesville. On February 10, two Baptist preachers, Jesse J. Griffith, and John C. White, had the misfortune to stumble upon the Indians. Griffith, from Alabama, arrived in Hamilton County in 1855 and started a school in his home on the banks of the Leon River in Hamilton. White, also from Alabama, had only arrived in Coryell County in January 1860. When White learned that there was another Primitive Baptist preacher in the adjoining county, he made arrangements to meet him. Griffith and White were soon on their way to a Primitive Baptist Church in northeastern Coryell County where Turnersville is today. A few miles west of their destination they rode into a herd of about 80 horses and stopped to count them, not realizing the implication of such a large herd seemingly in the middle of nowhere. Within minutes the Comanches were on them. One account says White was armed with a six-shooter, and another says they were unarmed—when they were told to carry weapons, "they held up their Bibles" instead.

This time there was no fable about being saved by a "Holy Book" that turned away a potentially fatal arrow. The preachers fled, with their long, frock-tailed coats flapping in the wind. The warriors overtook White and shot him in the back, while putting six arrows into Griffith. The preachers still managed to escape, crawling off into the brush and reaching the home of Green Buchanan that night. The nearest doctor, J. S. O'Bryan, was in McClennan County. He came as soon as he could, but believed that both men, with lungs punctured, would soon die. Griffith died nine days later, but White, carrying the arrowhead in his back, lived until 1884.[5]

The Comanches veered southwest and were in Burnet County on Saturday February 11. About ten in the morning they found Kentuckian Benjamin Van Hook (47) herding horses on the headwaters of the North Fork San Gabriel a few miles southeast of present Lake Victor. They murdered him. Riding southwest another five miles they found Meshac S. Skagg alone hunting stock. They charged him and chased him several miles before catching and killing him. A third man named Hardy was missing and presumed dead. The Comanches added some of Skagg's horses to their herd and swung north toward Lampasas.[6]

In northern Burnet County they swept up ten horses worth $1,450 belonging to Joseph J. Greenwood. About eight miles south of Lampasas they hit Garrison A. Greenwood's place, stealing another dozen or so animals. Garrison Greenwood was on the range hunting loose stock when he found three of his horses shot with arrows. As he quickly rode to spread the word, the Comanches were hitting Thomas H. Espy's ranch less than a mile away. They got ten of what Espy called "winter horses" which were only in fair condition and worth about $400.

Espy had been on a trip up to Parker County. As he rode south, he passed through areas that had just been hit by the raiding Indians, and the word was that there were about 100 warriors divided into eight parties of about a dozen men each, thus enabling them to cover so much ground and seeming to be everywhere at once. Espy got home about the time that his neighbors were gathering a posse at his house. Garrison Greenwood got a hired hand and they went to Espy's that night, riding broken down and abandoned Indian ponies because the best horses were stolen. As they crossed through his range after nightfall, Greenwood heard his bell mare being led away and Indians whistling to each other. They stopped in their tracks, realizing they had ridden right in among the warriors leading their horses away in the darkness. The two men slowly backed off and rode home.

Meanwhile, a posse consisting of Joe Greenwood, Tom Espy, James Espy, Jonathan Burleson, George Weldy, Dr. Hillary Ryan, W. D. Bean, and Tilford Bean left early in the morning from Espy's house, tracking the Indians who had turned west. About three miles down the trail they found one of Joe Greenwood's horses with an arrow in its shoulder. Further on was a dead horse partly eaten by the hurrying Indians. The posse continued across the Colorado River and went another 12 miles before losing the trail.[7]

The marauders next stole horses in Llano County, chased but failed to catch Parson Chadwick's son, and attacked Newton Jackson near the head of Fall Creek on the Llano-San Saba County lines as he rode in a wagon from Austin to San Saba. He bluffed them with his gun and got away into the brush. They plundered the wagon, getting, among other goods, some government rifles that were being delivered to Ranger Capt. William B. Davis in San Saba.

Now driving upwards of 500 stolen livestock, some of the Comanches called it quits and headed north. A number of civilian posses were on their trail, along with Rangers under Lt. Washington Hammett. Hammett could only find a small band of about six Indians on Brady Creek in McCulloch County. They chased the Indians nearly two miles but could not catch the fleeter ponies. Another retreating war party was not as lucky as it led a large herd through a pass in the Santa Anna Mountains in eastern Coleman County. About February 13, Rangers caught them, killed two warriors, and rounded up a number of horses. Among the recovered horses were those belonging to R. H. Chrisman, R. B. Wells, and Pat Gallagher, who resided in Coryell County and had a running fight with some of these same warriors the previous month.[8]

Some of raiders were not quite finished. On the way back to Indian Territory, a band passed through central Palo Pinto County and could not resist the temptation of rounding up a few more horses from ranchers living near Eagle Creek north and west of the county seat. On February 16, 1860, they hit James H. Chick and got eight horses and one mule worth $750 from him on the open range just west of town. Chick knew they were Penetekas because he and neighbor J. M. Kyle used to trade with them while they were at the Brazos Reservation. "Belknap Indians" is what they called them. Chick saw a few ponies left behind that the Indians had run nearly to death, all with the split ears typical of the Penetekas.

The Indians stole seven horses from A. G. Crawford, and then went north of Palo Pinto toward Kyle Mountain, named after Kyle's family, who were some of the first white settlers in the area. With word out that Indians were in the area, several ranchers took extra precautions; William and Jack Conatser, G. W. Slaughter, and Kyle rounded up their stock, picketed or hobbled them, and stood guard all night. Jack Conatser hid in a cedar crib in the center of his

Author's collection

Sam Houston, governor of Texas from December 1859 to March 1861.

corral. About two in the morning, Indians crept in to steal his 25 horses. Jack sprang up and began firing, while Bill Conatser and employee, George Dodson, came out of the house to help him. The raiders had most of the horses out when bullets from either Jack Conatser or Dodson brought down a warrior.

"Oh Lordy!" the Indian cried in plain English as he tried to get away crawling on hands and knees. Bill Conatser took hold of him and shook him.

"You sure you don't want to try to steal some more horses?" Conatser sarcastically asked. The warrior, however, died in a few minutes. The next morning, they put him in a wagon and took him over to Kyle's place, where several men had gathered to discuss their losses. They identified the dead warrior as one they had seen several times at Fort Belknap. The fleeing Indians had gone past Kyle's the night before and shot his father's dog and a cow. Kyle, Chick, a man named Farris, and a few others trailed the Indians for a few miles, finding another exhausted split-eared pony before calling it quits. The Indians were gone, back north of Red River.[9]

While the raid was still in progress, citizens of Weatherford organized a committee, which included J. H. Prince, Ezra Mulkin, and John R. Baylor, and sent a resolution to Governor Sam Houston. They blamed the former reserve Indians for the outrages and stated that "from the course of Gov. Houston, we feel that the frontier has been abandoned to merciless savage foes." They accused the government of "feeding and arming the very Indians who are ruthlessly butchering helpless women and children and desolating our frontier, and that until those Indians are taught that *bullets* are to be substituted for *blankets*, there will never be peace on our borders." They stated that they did not wish to be disrespectful to the governor, but they "are determined not to let *his love for the red man*, or his peculiar notions of frontier policy, break up our friends and endanger their lives and property."[10]

One big raid was over, with at least nine settlers killed, several wounded, and two captured and abused, but marauders were still overrunning the frontier counties. On February 19, 1860, Indians killed Thomas S. Milligan, ex-sheriff of Mason County. They shot him down in his cow lot next to his house less than two miles from the county seat of Mason. Mrs. Milligan barred the door as the Indians menaced her all night and she could not get to her husband until the next morning. He was dead and his ears were cut off. Mrs. Milligan and her many children were left destitute.

On February 27, Indians attacked Henry Wood and W. D. C. Wood on Richland Springs Creek about ten miles from San Saba. The settlers ran, and the Indians pursued them to Henry Wood's cabin, where they shot six arrows into W. D. C. Wood and killed him.[11]

The February raids made the news across the country. In the village of Gettysburg, Pennsylvania, three years before it became famous as the site of the greatest battle ever fought on American soil, *The Adams Sentinel* reported: "Indian War in Texas. Houston, March 10—The Indians are depredating in Bosque Co., and have killed seventeen families. There is great alarm there. A company of volunteers left Waco on the 7th to defend the inhabitants."[12]

The number of deaths was exaggerated, but the perception was valid. In Texas, complaint letters and petitions poured in to Governor Houston, who had taken office on December 21, 1859, after defeating Hardin Runnels by 9,000 votes. Runnels, a hard-line Democrat and state's rights planter who endorsed reopening the African slave trade, lost because he had none of Houston's charisma or personal popularity, because his radicalism invited northern interference, and because voters believed he neglected protecting the frontier. Voters assumed Houston would do better.

One letter writer, R. B. Wells of Coryell County, asked Houston on February 16, 1860, "Must we abandon our homes, or will the state protect us?" Wells explained that they also asked the question of ex-Governor Runnels and were told that he was doing all he could. But, Wells said, "Enough of us 'knew better,' to get a tried friend of the frontier in his stead.... They...now tauntingly ask us 'where is the protection to our property and the safety of our families you promised us if Houston was elected?'"[13]

J. H. Chrisman of Coryell County wrote on February 11, that "for the last six years I have taken many a hard ride to rescue property from the hands of the Red Skins my friends and neighbors has been murdered by the midnite assassins we sent Petition after petition to Gov. Runnels and he treated us with contempt...." Chrisman wanted more minutemen "to rainge duering the lite moon" and go after the Indians or he claimed that they would have to abandon the country.

Thomas Espy wrote to Houston on February 15, saying that more Rangers were not enough; what was needed was another regiment or two. He figured the only way to win "is to carry on a devastating war into the Comanche Nation...."[14]

Both the State and Federal government had tried that before, but it didn't seem to work.

Nevertheless, spring was coming and there was always the hope that this year it would be different. One of the first things the new legislature passed was a new frontier protection act, authorizing Houston to raise a ten-company regiment of mounted men for frontier duty. Each company was to consist of 83 men who were to patrol from Red River to the Rio Grande. Houston personally helped select stations for each company, dividing them into camps and directing that they should scout from camp to camp. The legislature was full of grand ideas, but it never had the finances to pay for them; money problems forced Houston to cut company size down to 60 men. Since the potential patrol area stretched about 450 miles, an allocation of one man every seven and a half miles was not going to make a bit of difference; they might just as well have all stayed home and protected their farms.

More pleas for help arrived, and Houston authorized 23 frontier counties to organize a "Minute detachment" of 15 men per county. That plan had poor results too. Houston then wrote to President James Buchanan and Secretary of War John B. Floyd, pleading for a treaty with the wild tribes. He believed that peace was the only way to resolve the issue. In the first three months since Houston took office, the army on the Texas frontier killed about one dozen Indians. About ten soldiers were wounded. On the other hand, Houston estimated that 51 civilians had been killed, with many more wounded, and about 1,800 horses stolen.[15]

It was a disturbing pattern. The U.S. Regulars and Texas Rangers and militia could not seem to find an effective response to Indian raids in Texas. Perhaps other army expeditions would have better results.

Chapter 4 notes

1 Wallace and Hoebel, *Lords of the South Plains*, 240, 250-59; Fehrenbach, *Comanches*, 72-77.

2 The story of this raid is a composite from William M. Allen, Depredation Claim #4605, McConnell, *West Texas Frontier*, Langston, *Eastland County*, Wilbarger, *Indian Depredations*, and Winfrey and Day, *Texas Indian Papers, IV*, all of which give slightly different details.

3 Huckabay, *Jack County*, 49; Winfrey and Day, *Texas Indian Papers, V*, 308.

4 Winfrey and Day, *Texas Indian Papers, IV*, 3-6; Wilbarger, *Indian Depredations*, 441; McConnell, *West Texas Frontier*, 318, 319; *State Gazette* (Austin), February 25, 1860; "Death Records," http://surnamearchive.com/records/records054.htm

5 Winfrey and Day, *Texas Indian Papers, IV*, 6-8; Wilbarger, *Indian Depredations*, 441, 484; McConnell, *West Texas Frontier*, 320; "First Pioneers from Hamilton County," http://hamiltongazeteer.wordpress.com/2008/10/09/first-pioneers-from-hamilton-county/. Wilbarger incorrectly places the event in 1858.

6 Winfrey and Day, *Texas Indian Papers, IV*, 8; McConnell, *West Texas Frontier*, 321.

7 Depredation Claims: Joseph J. Greenwood #2759; Thomas H. Espy #4410. Greenwood's and Espy's claims were denied because the Comanches were not in amity with the U. S. at the time.

8 *State Gazette* (Austin), March 3, 1860; Winfrey and Day, *Texas Indian Papers, IV*, 8, 13-14, 19; Wilbarger, *Indian Depredations*, 485-87.

9 James H. Chick, Depredation Claim #5019.

10 *State Gazette* (Austin), February 25, 1860.

11 Winfrey and Day, *Texas Indian Papers, IV*, 19; McConnell, *West Texas Frontier*, 322, 323; *State Gazette* (Austin), March 10, 1860; Bierschwale, "Mason County," 390.

12 *The Adams Sentinel* (Gettysburg, Pennsylvania), March 19, 1860.

13 Fehrenbach, *Lone Star*, 334-35; McCaslin, *Tainted Breeze*, 28; Winfrey and Day, *Texas Indian Papers IV*, 11.

14 Winfrey and Day, *Texas Indian Papers, IV*, 3-4, 9-10.

15 Smith, *Frontier Defense*, 17-19.

5 "A drought of such continued severity was never known before."

By 1860 it was clear to the authorities that the Comanches and Kiowas were out of control and a severe chastisement by the military was necessary to bring them to their senses. Plans were made for a three-pronged campaign, out of Kansas, Texas, and New Mexico Territory, to converge on the Indians and force them into battle. In charge of the Department of New Mexico, Col. Thomas T. Fauntleroy was organizing his resources for an expedition against the Navajos when, in February 1860, he received a directive to begin operations against the Comanches and Kiowas "as early in the spring as the grass will permit."

The weather refused to cooperate, however, for a severe drought for the past year meant local corn crops were not available and the grass was very poor. In mid-April, Fauntleroy sent a strike force of six companies of the Mounted Rifles under Maj. Charles F. Ruff against the Indians. Colonel Edwin V. Sumner, commanding the Department of the West, explained to his commanders: "As the three columns that are to move upon the plains have been made independent, no instructions can be given for any cooperation, but the government would undoubtedly expect, and rightly too, that the Commanders would act in concert…."[1]

It was pure double-talk—no means will be given to you for cooperation, but cooperate anyway. Such planning was a recipe for disaster. The reason there was no catastrophe in 1860 was because the Indians avoided battle. As so many army commanders would learn to their frustration, it would be hard as hell to catch and fight Indians who didn't want to fight.

Major Ruff gathered his men and supplies at Alexander Hatch's Ranch south of Fort Union where there was better grass for the horses. On June 1, he moved out, but soon his horses began breaking down, many suffering from malnutrition and what was termed "black tongue," a disease that infected their mouths and made it nearly impossible for them to eat even the poor grass. Ruff moved south down the Pecos, getting more frustrated because the tips given him by Comancheros as to the whereabouts of the Indians always proved false. He returned to Hatch's Ranch after 69 of his horses died. If it would only rain, some grass might appear and they could continue the expedition.[2]

The drought affected settlers and Indians across the Central and Southern Plains. It was said that in Nebraska the rain stopped in June 1859 and did not fall again until November 1860. The earth dried and broke open in great cracks. Hot, desiccating winds blew in from the southwest. Fall wheat in

1859 did not come up until the following spring, and then it withered and died. The prairie grass dried and turned brown. Ruined crops exacerbated the economic distress that followed the Panic of 1857.

In Kansas the drought was said to have brought on "an unprecedented period of hardship." Springs and wells dried up and there was no water in the creeks. Granaries were exhausted. When the wheat failed, people planted corn; when the corn failed, they sowed buckwheat; that failed and they tried turnips, which also died. One-third of the settlers were said to be destitute and thousands packed up and fled east to a wetter climate.[3]

In Texas, newspapers constantly spoke of the dry conditions. In June 1860, the Austin *State Gazette* indicated that Texas was not alone in its misery. "We learn that a heavy drought prevails in several portions of Louisiana, Mississippi, and Arkansas." In August the paper bewailed the "long, dreary, and blasting drought…more consuming than the fire of the Lord, sent to reprove Ahab and all Israel for following after Baalim." When the occasional thunderstorms did come, they were also seen in Biblical proportions. One such storm hit south central Texas, eliciting the comment, "the floodgates of Heaven open, as on a former time, when Elijah had finished the good work of slaying the prophets…and on the 7th of August, 1860, and after many months of drought, the rain poured down upon the drooping crops and awoken everything to renewed life and vigor, causing the farmer and planter to smile gratefully at this gracious boon of the Almighty." Such a rain, the paper stated, "has not occurred for the last eight years." A week later, things were back to "normal." In Kaufman County they said, "Everything is suffering from want of rain, and if the present drought continues many weeks longer, our county will be ruined." In San Antonio in September, it was said, "Truly, a drought of such continued severity was never known before. Will it ever rain here?"[4]

The drought on the Central Plains continued five more years. In Texas it was already a serious problem. The wet years of the 1830s changed to a cycle of drought by the mid-1840s and the Southern tribes were adversely affected. The grass range shrank. What little crops they grew withered and died, and they had to kill more bison to trade for agricultural products, yet they would not cut their horse herds which competed for the same grass as the bison. The Comanches were losing their trading empire and by the start of the 1860s, only the Comancheros, generally Hispanic New Mexicans who made their living by trading with the Indians, remained to supply them as a conduit for their stolen horses.[5]

In July, Major Ruff continued his expedition with only 225 men. They went down the Canadian River and this time, on July 15, his guides led him directly to a camp of about 300 Comanches at Canada de los Penavetitos. The Comanches saw the soldiers and escaped easily, and Ruff's poor horses could not chase them. They rode to Adobe Creek to the ruins of Bent's old trading post, where Ruff, becoming too ill to continue, turned back. Fauntleroy's abortive Comanche Expedition was all but finished.

The other columns had nearly as bad luck. Maj. John Sedgwick fought drought while marching through Kansas and had a skirmish with the Kiowas at Blackwater Spring in Colorado Territory in July. Captain Samuel D. Sturgis battled the same blistering heat and waterless trails across Indian Territory and Kansas, finally chasing down a band of Comanches and Kiowas in southern Nebraska in August, where he claimed to have killed 29 Indians. For the most part, the summer's expeditions were failures. Many Indians did not want to fight and simply sidestepped the soldiers at will. Most of them never even knew the soldiers were out looking for them.[6]

Regardless of the provocations, the Comanches avoided attacking their Mexican allies. This association had old antecedents and would be the cause of hundreds of killings and thefts in the coming years. As far back as 1786, Spanish Governor Juan Batista de Anza and Comanche Chief Ecueracapa made an agreement in which the Comanches could move closer to the Spanish settlements if they remained peaceful, and both parties would participate in "free trade and fairs" to exchange goods and services for all.[7]

The Comanche Peace lasted for about six decades, sustained by the Spanish and Mexican realization that both sides would keep the treaty if it was to their advantage. This meant that in addition to free trade, gift giving was also a significant factor, and the idea that giving food and presents was cheaper than fighting became firmly established. In 21st Century terms, the Indians were being paid protection money, but by whatever label used, the system worked—at least until the Americans burst upon the scene.

With the Comanche Peace, enterprising New Mexicans beat paths onto and through the seemingly impassable Llano Estacado (Staked Plains). There were several major routes, with the southernmost being along the Pecos River; the next trail to the north crossed the Llano to the Double Mountain Fork Brazos; the next route went along the Agua Frio and Tule Creek, down the Valley of Tears to Quitaque; a fourth route followed the headwaters of Palo Duro Creek and branched to Quitaque or to the present Amarillo area; the northernmost trail generally followed the Canadian River.[8]

Comancheros generally traded manufactured goods to the Comanches in exchange for furs, robes, horses, mules, and later, cattle. The traders changed less over two centuries than did peoples' conception of them. At first they were thought to be harmless brokers making a living trading innocuous items for the benefit of all concerned. Spanish-Mexican-Comanche bonds grew through trade, as well as in trafficking in human captives. As the traders found more connections with the Indians to the east, they dealt less with Mexico City. When the Americans arrived, imposing their conventions and interfering with the old customs, guns and whiskey began to be introduced into the equation. Prices went up. Indians were induced to steal more stock in Mexico and Texas, as well as take captives. The Mexicans were not happy with the meddling Americans, who would not abide by human exchange, yet when they paid good money to rescue captives it only gave more incentive for the Comanchero and Comanche "businessmen" to continue the cycle. Captured humans and livestock moved north out of Mexico and Texas, and manufactured goods, weapons, ammunition, and whiskey passed to the Indians.[9]

It did not take the Comanches long to realize that peace with the tribes moving in from the east and with the Cheyennes and Arapahos to the north, would open up new markets for them. Instead of having to fight their northern neighbors and guard their villages, leaving less warriors to raid in Mexico, peace would allow them to fully concentrate on stealing tens of thousands of horses and become the middlemen and main suppliers for customers across the length and breadth of the land.

The game changer came in 1840 when the Comanches and Kiowas made peace with the Cheyennes and Arapahos in a great ceremony on the Arkansas River. The peace had far reaching consequences. The contested plains east of the Rockies, which had been a no-man's land because of the warfare, had been a bison haven. After 1840, the land was open to all, which resulted in the exploitation of the bison. Bison robes became the hot, new trade item. The Bent Brothers became prime beneficiaries as middlemen for the Cheyennes and Arapahos as those tribes began the remarkably quick process of hunting the animals toward extinction. The Comanches and Kiowas, on the other hand, cared less about the bison as a marketable item, but could now turn their full attention south into the rich horse regions of northern Mexico. "Peace" sent the buffalo on the road to extinction in one region and led to increased conflict in another.[10]

Much of the fighting that would escalate during the 1860s was less an "Indian" war than it was a business war over turf and control of scarce resources. Horses and captives could buy almost anything and few wanted to upset the applecart. The Comanches and New Mexicans had long-established kinship and trade ties since the peace of 1786. One reason the Comanches generally left the New Mexicans alone was because they owned few horses. Estimates placed horse ownership at only three thousand, while three million sheep roamed the New Mexican plains. The Comanches didn't want sheep, and consequently used New Mexicans as trade partners. In contrast, the department of Durango alone was said to possess about 150,000 horses and mules. The Comanches would remain at peace with New Mexico as long as the economics of the deal suited their needs. Old Mexico and Texas could be exploited instead. [11]

Chapter 5 notes

1 Oliva, *Fort Union and the Frontier Army*, 165-67; Hafen, *Relations with the Indians*, 198.
2 Oliva, *Fort Union and the Frontier Army*, 167-69.
3 Dick, *Great American Desert*, 326; Gambone, "Economic Relief in Kansas," 149-51.
4 *State Gazette* (Austin), June 16, 1860, July 14, 1860, August 11, 1860, August 25, 1860; San Antonio *The Daily Ledge and Texan* (San Antonio), September 11, 1860.
5 Hamalainen, *Comanche Empire*, 296, 298, 301.
6 Oliva, *Fort Union and the Frontier Army*, 170-73; *New York Times*, August 31, 1860; Kenner, *Comanchero Frontier*, 129, 131-32; Michno, *Encyclopedia of Indian Wars*, 77-79.
7 Kenner, *Comanchero Frontier*, 23, 51-52.
8 Kenner, *Comanchero Frontier*, 53, 55; Morris, *El Llano Estacado*, 183-189.
9 Brooks, *Captives and Cousins*, 6, 30-31, 198, 201, 258, 291-92; Kenner, *Comanchero Frontier*, 96-97.
10 DeLay, *War of a Thousand Deserts*, 40, 60, 80, 84, 88; West, *Contested Plains*, 77, 80, 192.
11 DeLay, *War of a Thousand Deserts*, 109.

6 "This knife will take off my scalp before I get home."

Brigadier General David E. Twiggs had been department commander in Texas since 1857, but in the winter of 1860, he took sick leave and went home to Georgia. Replacing him was Lt. Col. Robert E. Lee. Lee was promoted to lieutenant colonel of the 2nd Cavalry in 1855 and spent some time with the regiment on the Texas frontier. Lee took over in February 1860. Troubles with Mexicans led by Juan Cortina had caused turmoil in the lower Rio Grande valley for months, and Lee kept four of his ten companies on the southern border, making for a thin line in the north. The Texans wanted army protection on all fronts, and when units moved to one border, citizens on the other side complained. Lee's performance was lackluster, as he sent his companies hither and yon, chasing down Indian and Mexican raiders.[1]

After the great raid of February 1860, newspapers railed for more protection and individuals sent missives to Governor Houston. Inquiries went to Agent Samuel A. Blain at the Wichita Agency in Indian Territory, asking if his Indians had anything to do with the raids. Blain insisted they had not. In a series of letters to Houston in April, Blain said that "no Indian belonging to this Reserve has ever crossed Red River into Texas" unless they were scouting with the army. In fact, Blain said his Indians had been chasing hostile Comanches and Kiowas who came through the reservation. Blain was angry that his Indians were "to be made the scape goat upon whom is to be thrown all the crimes committed on your frontier." On May 10, Blain wrote to Houston that his Indians had chased a Kiowa band 40 miles before catching and killing six of them. "This is ten scalps in the last month" that his Indians took, wrote Blain. "Only let your troops be as active as these Indians and it will not be three months until the Indians of the frontier will recoil and return howling to their dens."[2]

Blain's Indians may have been innocent, but marauders were coming from somewhere. While Comanches drove stolen stock out of central Texas, Kickapoos crossed Red River and raided Cooke and Montague counties, and about February 16, stole horses from Henderson B. Haven and men named Myers, Porter, and McGuire. The ranchers went from Sadler's Bend to Spanish Fort to try and find some Rangers to help them, but no Rangers were around. Near Head of Elm, present-day Saint Jo, they found wounded and dead horses, one of which had its ears cut off and stuck on sticks. Such cruelty to a poor horse left an impression on Haven.[3]

A larger band of raiders hit Comanche County beginning on March 1, 1860. Elisha Barcroft, who had lost stock in July 1859, was hit again when

Indians took four horses worth $390 from his place on Mercer Creek south of Comanche. Warriors also hit Kenneth McKenzie's place on Indian Creek about five miles east of Comanche, stealing one horse. The news brought out several neighbors, among them Bailey Marshall, Wallace Foreman, Jim Wilson, and brothers Kenneth and James E. McKenzie, who congregated in town to figure what action to take. They trailed the Indians and found an abandoned camp that the Indians certainly planned to return to, for there were 12 hobbled horses, shelters, hides, 40 pounds of cured beef, and a good rifle. The men took what they could and drove the horses into the town of Comanche.

That night, feeling good about their exploits, "the boys" did a little talking and a little drinking, and in a short time were probably filled with more bluster than ability. Near midnight, eight of them decided to go back to the camp and secure more of the goods. Only half a mile outside of town they rode into 15 Comanches who were undoubtedly going to pay the citizens a visit. The whites charged and the Indians fell back, drawing them on until they were strung out, when the Indians abruptly spun around and charged. As townsman William H. Kingsbury described it, "one good *turn* deserved another," and the boys "made a precipitate flight to town, leaving the Indians the masters of the field." It is not known if any warriors were hit, but several of the settlers' horses were shot, Kenneth McKenzie was mortally wounded, and James McKenzie was badly wounded and crippled. Kenneth died the next day, and was buried on Saturday, March 3. After the raids, Kingsbury speculated that there were not "a dozen horses in the county fit for service."

That weekend was hell for several neighboring families. Gid Foreman, who lived on the South Leon, was in the village of Cora about six miles from his home in the southeast corner of the county. Hearing of the raids, he expressed his concern about getting home safely. As Tom Mathes honed Foreman's butcher knife on a grindstone, Foreman said, "This knife will take off my scalp before I get home this evening." Foreman walked home and was joined for a time by Dave Merchant and Calvin Lester who were on horseback. Where the trail branched, the riders took one fork while Foreman took the other. He had not gone 300 yards when Indians jumped him. Foreman was short of cash, but had chosen a bad time to sell his pistols, because he only had his knife when the Indians appeared. He tried to run, but they were on him in an instant, killing, stripping, mutilating him, and taking a great scalp of his bright red hair. Merchant and Lester heard the commotion and rode back in time to see the Indians scalping Foreman—possibly with his own knife. They left only a sock and shoe on his left foot.

The Indians went further up the Leon to Baggett Creek near the present-day town of Hazeldell. In the afternoon of March 3, they came to the Baggett home. John Baggett had gone to town for supplies and Mrs. Baggett was there with her nine children. When she saw the Indians approaching, she succeeded in getting seven of the children inside, and then asked Sarah (14), where the others were.

"Ma, they are in the thicket below the cow-pen; the Indians will kill them!" she cried. Mrs. Baggett climbed on a chair to look through a crack above the door and she heard Joe (12) scream, but could not see him. She saw warriors bring Bettie (10) out into the open and one of them pushed an arrow between her ribs. They tortured the children in front of the house, probably hoping to induce whoever was inside to come out and try to rescue them. They lanced Joe until he fainted, and then scalped and killed him, leaving only his left sock and shoe. Mrs. Baggett had two guns, but would not shoot unless Indians actually broke into the cabin.

Bettie was stripped and stabbed with arrows five times, but not enough to kill her. Instead they sent her bleeding and staggering to the house, hoping that the door would open and they could rush in. Although she cried, "Open the door!" Mrs. Baggett dared not open it, but told her to go around the back. The Indians, not sure who was inside and getting impatient, stole what they could and rode off. Mrs. Baggett dressed Bettie's wounds and went out to get Joe's body, as the hogs were coming in. "The hogs were very bad to tear up anything they found," she said.

John Baggett and his brother, Joel, got home about ten that night, not having heard a thing about what was happening. John was devastated. Seeking vengeance, the next morning he rode into Cora and gathered a posse of 17 men. They trailed the Indians northwest of Comanche, finding a dead horse and a campground with several pictographs drawn on a rock, showing what appeared to be a fight between Indians and white men. The raiders, however, appeared to have gotten clean away.[4]

Shortly after the killings in Comanche County, possibly the same raiding party moved north into Eastland County. In mid-March at the tiny settlement of Mansker's Lake, which became Alameda, about eight miles northwest of present Desdemona, Indians ran off several of Henry Mansker's horses, shot arrows at J. L. Ellison, and killed several hogs. Mansker, his son, Tom, William Cross, and eight others took up the Indians' trail. They went east into Erath County and either on Flat Creek or Armstrong Creek they ran into 14 Comanches. Henry and Tom Mansker's horses were killed and the others dismounted to fight, but the Indians had the better position. They killed Billy Cross and pressed the survivors so closely that they abandoned their horses and jumped over a high bluff to escape in a ravine. Some of them ran into a camp of militia under Lt. Dixon Walker. Walker, who styled himself "Lewtenant Comnd Bosque County Raingers," wrote to Sam Houston on April 5, that 14 of his boys "started to the sean of blud arrived in the night carried the ded body to a hous skelpt and stript of all but his shirt and socks."[5]

In March, marauders hit Palo Pinto County and stole horses from Thomas Matthews. On March 3, near the San Saba-Brown County border, brothers Richard and Aaron Robbins and their brother-in-law John Jones ran into a war party. They put up quite a fight, but Richard Robbins was killed and the other two were badly wounded. Robbins, "scalped and cut open," was buried the next day, leaving behind a wife and four children.

Also on March 3, raiders farther south in San Saba County hit R. W. Vaughn's ranch on Cherokee Creek and stole a mule and four horses. He got his neighbors, John and Isaac Williams, Matthew Kuykendall, Milton Hannah, and Edmund More, and pursued. Late that day they caught up to the eight Indians at the head of Cherokee Creek and had a sharp fight that lasted until nightfall. One warrior was left dead on the ground when the Indians pulled out, and there was evidence that a couple more were wounded. John Williams's horse was shot out from under him and a bullet pierced his coat and his provision sack, but none of the whites were otherwise hurt. The whites recovered six horses and Williams believed they had stopped the Indians who "intended to attack some house that night."[6]

Another band raided on the Bosque-McLennan County lines on March 5, reportedly killing members of six families on Hog Creek, 25 miles from Waco. The stage from Waco to Burnet was held when the news arrived. T. Moore wrote from Burnet to the Austin *State Gazette* that on the same day "a negro belonging to John S. Proctor was shot in the head with an arrow," while another belonging to Mrs. Allen was shot in the arm. He appealed to the people of Austin for help: "Give us your aid! Our Governor fails to do so. Remember, if Burnet falls, Austin comes next...." A national report stated that "The Indians are indeed coming down almost into the lower country. The people will have to turn *en masse* to the frontier to repulse them."

The raiders then moved a dozen miles south to Coryell Creek near Gatesville and stole horses from Louisa Haynes. Her neighbors formed a posse and pursued for three days to no avail. Even the soldiers occupying the outer posts were not immune. On March 15, the San Antonio *Ledger* reported that Indians had raided Camp Cooper on the Clear Fork Brazos and stolen 60 head of government mules.[7]

In the south, Indians, probably Lipans, were all over Uvalde and Medina counties. Brothers Joseph and Peter Conrad lived two miles below Castroville in Medina County. On March 13, they went into a live oak thicket and found one of their horses dead and another wounded by arrows. With some neighbors they formed a search party and found another horse running loose with an Indian's lariat on it. One of the posse, Mr. Volmer, had lost horses the previous day. They soon ran into a party of Indians driving about 25 stolen horses and a brief running fight ensued. The posse captured the horses, and lost them again when the Indians counterattacked. Joe Conrad could hear some of the warriors swearing at them in Spanish. He drew bead on a female warrior who he could plainly see shooting arrows at them from behind a tree. One of her arrows went under his brother's arm. Joe tried several times, but the hammer of his rifle would not snap. The woman shifted position and Conrad lost his chance; he later realized that the hammer had only been at half-cock. One of the posse, a German, was struck by a bullet.

The Indians moved southeast into Atascosa County and ran into two young men from Castroville. Vincent Bilhartz and John Youngman (Jungman) (21) had left town on March 15 to hunt oxen. Both were unarmed. When they failed to return home, a search party went out and on Saturday, March 17, their bodies were found at Black Hill, in the extreme northern tip of Atascosa County. From the position of the bodies it appeared that one of them had been knocked off his horse while riding. Both were filled with arrows and bullets and Bilhartz, who had long, curly hair, was scalped.[8]

The same war party was probably back in Medina County about March 21, when they killed an old man named Schroon outside D'Hanis. Twelve Indians attacked him while he was unarmed and hauling wood. He left a wife and three children. John Reinhart, who had a ranch nearby, saw the Indians but they did not pursue him; they were on foot, and Reinhart figured they were planning to remedy the situation by stealing horses.

Reinhart circled back home, meeting Jack Wolf and advising him to go home with him because Indians were about. The next morning the Indians caught a Mexican named Anisette (19), who worked for Ross Kennedy, and shot him through the heart while he was out hunting stock. Kennedy found him a little later and took his body back to his house. Kennedy's wife urged him to get some men and find the killers.

The Indians moved along Seco Creek stealing horses and suddenly became much more of a threat. John Reinhart and Jack Wolf went to Alexander Hoffman's ranch on the Little Seco in Medina County, to get Wolf's brother, Sebastian (20), who worked for Hoffman (38). Hoffman joined the party and the four of them went back to where Reinhart first saw the Indians. They trailed the Indians down the Seco to D'Hanis. While Reinhart and Jack Wolf went into town, Sebastian Wolf and Hoffman trailed the Indians west to the Sabinal River.

The Lipans were waiting for them on the morning of March 23, in the brush along the river about eight miles north of the town of Sabinal. They ran down and killed the whites, but not before they killed at least one warrior. The next day, a posse of men including Ross Kennedy, William "Seco" Smith, W. B. Knox, W. A. Crane, and several others, found the dead men. Wolf's throat "was cut from ear to ear" and his body was lying about 20 feet from Hoffman's. They also found a dead Indian, rolled in a blanket, and placed in the forks of a live oak tree, with his shield, bow, and arrows placed near it.

They followed the Indians' trail which led up Little Blanco Creek in Uvalde County. The Indians were camped in a little glade by the creek when the posse charged into them. Their horses stampeded right into their camp, however, alerting them to the presence of the whites and allowing them to escape into a dense cedar brake. The posse did recover almost all of the Lipans' equipment, supplies, and 46 stolen horses. They also recovered what they thought was a white woman's scalp, which proved to be the long, curly hair of Vincent Bilhartz. They sat down to dine on a fat yearling which the Indians had just finished barbecuing, and rode back to Sabinal. The next day they came back to bury Hoffman and Wolf in the same grave. The raid resulted in the deaths of another six settlers.[9]

In late March 1860, Indians in Bosque County killed a Mr. Freeman and the son of Mr. Ragget, while spearing Ragget's little daughter. Citizens under a Captain Wilson, and Messrs. Gilifillan, Anderson, Allen, Renfro, and Kells, chased the raiders and intercepted them in a mountain gap, killing three, and taking their scalps. The Indians, identified as Caddos, had blankets marked "U.S." As one of them lay wounded he cried, "Don't shoot, me plenty sick." The citizens surprisingly desisted, but when they began to move on, the wounded Caddo shot and killed Gilifillan's horse, prompting him to blast the wounded man and make him "somewhat 'sicker.'" The angry citizens sarcastically wrote to Governor Houston that if he would be so kind to ride over on his new "Spanish pony…he can have all his doubts about the depredations and murders of Indians, removed by ocular demonstration."[10]

In March, J. J. Keener was killed by an Indian in Titus County in northeast Texas, apparently an isolated incident and not as part of a raid. Late in the month, raiders swept through Wise and Jack counties stealing horses. They attacked three men working on the West Fork Trinity and killed Jess Clemens. A posse formed up and buried the murdered man, but could not overtake the Indians. Posse member, W. W. O. Stanfield, wrote to Governor Houston that he had lived in Texas since 1834, and believed that his section of the country was in as great a turmoil as back in the days of the Runaway Scrape in 1836.[11]

Bombarded with complaints, Houston and government officials adopted resolutions demanding compensation for citizens' losses due to the "shocking enormity of Indian massacres, robberies, and thefts" that had been occurring for years. On March 24, Houston acknowledged the "bleeding and suffering" citizens and offered evidence that Lipans and other tribes based in Mexico "committed their depredations on our frontier inhabitants, and pass beyond the Rio Grande with their booty with impunity because our troops and citizens are not at liberty to pursue and chastise them on Mexican soil."[12]

Chapter 6 notes

1 Harwell, *R. E. Lee*, 93, 104; Smith, *Frontier Defense*, 19.

2 Winfrey and Day, *Texas Indian Papers, IV*, 27, 30, 34.

3 Henderson B. Haven, Depredation Claim #1879.

4 Wilbarger, *Indian Depredations*, 456-59, says this incident occurred in 1857; McConnell, *West Texas Frontier*, 325, says it happened in 1861; Deaton, *Indian Fights on the Texas Frontier*, 86-90, says it happened in 1860. Claimants, family members, and witnesses in Elisha H. Barcroft, Depredation Claim #5292, Mary A. Jenkins (McKenzie), Depredation Claim #10571, and *The Daily Ledger and Texan* (San Antonio), March 8, 1860, indicate the incidents all happened between March 1 and March 3, 1860. The story is a compilation of these sources. Bettie Baggett recovered and went on to marry Isaac Kuykendall.

5 Winfrey and Day, *Texas Indian Papers, IV*, 26; McConnell, *West Texas Frontier*, 326; Langston, *Eastland County*, 24.

6 Thomas Matthews, Depredation Claim #347; Vincent, *Vincent's United States Register*, 161; *State Gazette* (Austin), March 24, 1860.

7 Greer, ed., *Buck Barry*, 120; *State Gazette* (Austin), March 10, 1860; Vincent, *Vincent's United States Register*, 168; Louisa Haynes, Depredation Claim #5310; *The Daily Ledger and Texan* (San Antonio), March 15, 1860.

8 Sowell, *Early Settlers*, 117-18; *The Daily Ledger and Texan* (San Antonio), March 19, 1860.

9 McConnell, *West Texas Frontier*, 328; Wilbarger, *Indian Depredations*, 652-54; Sowell, *Early Settlers*, 118, 197-98; *The Daily Ledger and Texan* (San Antonio), April 2, 1860; "Death Records." http://surnamearchive.com/records/records054.htm.

10 *The Daily Ledger and Texan* (San Antonio), April 2, 1860.

11 "Death Records." http://surnamearchive.com/records/records054.htm; Winfrey and Day, *Texas Indian Papers IV*, 23-24. The Runaway Scrape referred to the chaos in Texas during the time of the Alamo fight, the advance of Santa Anna's Mexican Army, and the Texans' flight.

12 Britten, *Lipan Apaches*, 218.

7 "Eating twice their own weight in beef."

There was no let up of raiding in April. Indians stole horses from William Jenkins in the eastern corner of Mills County, just east of present Center City. On the morning of April 15, Jenkins and neighbor John Willis went after the thieves. Traveling eight miles northeast into the Lampasas Mountains, they surprised the warriors in camp and charged them. The whites fired, but when Jenkins tried to re-load his rifle, the ball jammed part-way down the barrel. The men fought with revolvers, hitting a few of the warriors. When they fired all their rounds, the Indians counter-charged, but Jenkins had picked up a shotgun in the camp and turned it against them. The Indians fell back and Jenkins said it was time to get out fast. Willis, however, had somehow gotten his horse's bridle tangled in the undergrowth and he called for Jenkins to help him. The delay was fatal. As Willis got free, Jenkins killed another Indian with the shotgun, but he took an arrow right through his chest. The two rode away and Jenkins, evidently in an adrenalin-rush, did not even realize what had happened, believing only that he had been slightly wounded.

"Oh," he said to Willis, "it is nothing and will soon be well." In a short time, however, the shock and pain set in and Jenkins nearly collapsed. Willis helped him home where he died two days later.[1]

To the north in Erath County, Nicholas Lee worked for James H. Swindells, who had the mail delivery contract in the area. Lee rode the Stephenville to Palo Pinto to Jacksboro route up and back, once a week. One April morning, Lee, riding a mule, made it 14 miles northwest of Stephenville when Indians shot him in the back from ambush.

In April 1860, Comanches or Kiowas were in Parker County, stealing five horses worth $700 from Lemuel C. Barton. They also rode into Palo Pinto County and hit L. M. Currant's place three miles from Santo. Currant lost horses, as well as did David White, who resided with him. The Indians took two of White's horses worth $250. Currant, White, and others formed a posse and trailed the Indians northwest, through the old Brazos Reservation and beyond Fort Belknap, but the Indians were well on their way to their sanctuary north of Red River. White figured it was too dangerous and moved north to Jack County. The relocation would later prove to be a big mistake.[2]

In April, Indians attacked Mountain Pass Station in the Abercrombie Range on the Butterfield Mail route, about 30 miles southwest of old Fort Phantom Hill. They killed and scalped the station keeper, two employees, and a Mexican sheep herder. On May 11, 1860, the *Milwaukee Daily Sentinel*

Auithor's photo

The ruins of Fort Phantom Hill, Texas.

reported the incident, stating that "five persons were killed, mules belonging to it were driven off, and cattle slaughtered." Just who was killed and where is uncertain.

The United States Register reported that on April 12, 1860, William Lambshead, James Hamby (15), and Shadrach Styer were killed at Mountain Pass Station, when 14 Indians attacked them 300 yards from the station house. Styer and Hamby were shot and scalped and Lambshead was last seen running away, but his body was never found. The unnamed employee left to defend the station fired at the Indians, who left his door peppered with arrows before they rode away. Shortly after, Styer came stumbling to the station, "scalped and dripping with gore." He lived only ten more minutes.

Other information, however, places James Hamby working for Englishman, Thomas Lambshead (53), William's older brother, at Clear Fork Station just downriver from Camp Cooper on the Clear Fork Brazos, near the mouth of Lambshead Creek. Thomas Lambshead ran a large ranch in the area, and apparently ran Clear Fork Station for a time. Waterman Ormsby, one of the first passengers to use the Butterfield Overland route in 1858, mentioned a Lambshead running Mountain Pass Station, as well as the next one at Valley Creek (Lambshead also had a brother named John). A black woman who fixed Ormsby's breakfast was said to have been killed by Indians the next year. Hamby, perplexingly, was said to have been killed at Mountain Pass, and also on the headwaters of the Elm, just north of Thomas

Lambshead's ranch in Throckmorton County. All the Lambshead brothers seem to disappear from the record about this time, leading one to speculate if they all were killed or moved away from a very dangerous frontier.[3]

Beset by citizens' complaints about a lack of protection, Governor Houston, on April 14, 1860, sent a dispatch to the War Department. He said that the U.S. Regulars were "useless in fighting the Indians" for they detested the service and were not trained for it. Houston still wanted a regiment of Texas volunteers in ten companies, to be placed at ten posts along the frontier from Red River to the Rio Grande, and patrols made between the posts. He believed the Indians could not pass through the lines without being discovered and caught. Houston estimated that "the Texas Rangers are not only superior to any other class of troops for the service, but more economical." The Rangers were supposedly smarter, tougher, excellent horseman, inured to hardships, and acquainted with Indian habits and haunts. Houston said that on that very day he had word of five more Texans killed by Indians, who were raiding within 30 miles of San Antonio and 40 miles of Austin, stealing horses, and shooting cattle. Houston wanted Rangers, but he wanted the Federal government to foot the bill.[4]

It was a familiar litany. After the Confederate government took over in 1861, Texas governors still wanted the same non-payment deal. In addition, there appeared to be a lack of imagination in military planning. Houston's idea to place the troops at scattered posts and ride patrol between them was nothing new. It had been tried off and on since the Texas Revolution in 1836—it was not effective before and it would not prove effective in the future. Neither regulars nor Rangers could effectively check Indian marauders.

Raids continued unabated in May. On April 7, Sgt. Thomas G. Dennin and men of Company K, 1st Infantry, were escorting an army wagon train to Fort Lancaster. Indians, who could have been Comanches or Apaches, attacked them at Howard's Well, stealing horses, mules, and oxen. The Indians reportedly had two wounded while one civilian teamster was wounded.[5]

On May 10, Conrad Newhouse (Neuhaus) and his Mexican employee named Martinez (60), who often worked freighting between San Antonio and Fort Belknap, were working at Newhouse's ranch about ten miles northwest of the fort in Young County. The two were rounding up loose stock along Elm Creek only 200 yards from the ranch house when a band of Indians rode up from the creek bottom and charged. Newhouse always carried two pistols—except this day. Not only was he unarmed, he didn't even saddle up his horse. The shouting warriors spooked the horse, which reared up and threw Newhouse to the ground. Newhouse ran toward the house and Will Newhouse and Parker Johnson heard his cries and came running, but they were too late. The warriors killed Martinez and put arrows and a lance into

Newhouse's back. Newhouse was carried to the ranch but died the following night.[6]

Governor Houston finally reacted to these raids by authorizing an expedition into Indian Territory, comparable to those led by John Ford and Earl Van Dorn. Col. Middleton T. Johnson was authorized to take seven companies of Rangers, about 400 men, north to recover stolen horses and punish the Indians.

Johnson had not even started before citizens expressed their misgivings. On April 30, 1860, Rev. F. G. Faucett of Jack County wrote that his county tried to comply with the call for minute companies in accordance with Houston's instructions. They signed up the men and elected J. A. Hamner lieutenant, but Houston refused to commission him, using what Faucett called the language of "a street bully." Hamner and some of Baylor's other cronies were thought to be part of a horse-theft ring and blaming it on the Indians. Houston was not about to legitimize a man he considered as contributing to the border turmoil. Faucett, however, assumed that Houston blindly accepted reports of the innocence of the Indians from his agents, such as Sam Blain, instead of his own citizens. Faucett was certain that the same Reserve Indians who had troubled Texas for years were still the culprits and not the "wild" Comanches farther north.

Before Conrad Newhouse died, he was said to have remarked that the Indians who shot him were Reserve Indians, because he knew them well. To make matters worse, Faucett railed, Colonel Johnson and Shapley Ross recruited 20 "murdering, thieving Caddoes" to spy for them. "Does any man expect Col. Johnson's expedition to give peace to our distracted frontier?" he asked. "No, it will but encourage the wild Indians" and likely make them join the others to wage war on Texas. Faucett said that Houston's incomprehensible actions abused the confidence and forfeited the respect of the people.

Colonel Johnson left Fort Belknap on May 23, and rode all the way to the Kansas border and back without finding any Indians. The Weatherford *White Man* trashed Governor Houston and the seeming incompetence and graft that led to the failed expedition. The citizens wanted protection, but both the State and Federal government "displayed a cold blooded indifference to our condition." Houston gave Colonel Johnson a regiment "which proved to be the most stupendous sell [out?] ever practiced on the frontier people." Their great expectations resulted only "in eating twice their own weight in beef at 11 cents a pound...." The paper railed that the expedition cost the state half a million dollars, but "resulted in no good; without killing or even finding a single Indian." The excursion was caustically labeled "the beef campaign" and left the people "in a worse condition than we were before."[7]

The same day that Johnson left Belknap, citizens of Llano County gathered to improve a road between Llano and Austin, where it ran along Honey Creek through the rough country west of Packsaddle Mountain. Methodist Rev. Jonas Dancer (54) was one of the earliest settlers in the county, arriving about 1852 at a beautiful, secluded spot at Honey Creek Cove. Dancer was early for work that morning, and went alone to the site. Unarmed, he was busily engaged with shovel and ax when five Indians appeared around him. Dancer fled into a deep ravine but the warriors stayed on the bluff above and shot arrows down into him. He crawled up on a flat rock and died, whereupon the warriors scalped and mutilated the body. Searchers found and buried him the next day.[8]

Lipan Apaches were likely the culprits along the Rio Grande. In May they attacked a Mexican wagon train west of Fort Clark and killed many of the cattle. Nearby at Johnson's Ranch on the San Felipe (Del Rio) they killed two Mexicans working in the fields. When troops from Fort Clark reached the area the next day, they followed the Indians' tracks to the banks of the Rio Grande where they disappeared across the river.

In mid-May, Indians attacked a Mr. Magoffin's Train camped in Johnson Draw in northern Val Verde County halfway between Camp Hudson and Howard's Well. Magoffin had his horses close and well-hobbled and the raiders failed to stampede any of them, but there was a 15-minute fight. The train's defenders claimed to have wounded three Indians and five of their horses. Troops from Camp Hudson had visited Magoffin's camp only one hour before the Indians attacked, declaring that the area was secure and no raiders were about. It was the third train attacked along Johnson Draw on the Lower Military Road in three weeks. A civilian at Camp Hudson inquired, "What is the reason that the Government took all the cavalry from this road?"

Farther downriver Lipans killed Francisco Zapeda (22) as he herded cattle north of Laredo in Webb County. Bookkeeper Ignacio Chavis (60) was unlucky enough to be caught and killed near Zapata. Lipans killed stock keeper Masadonia Lindon (20) in Zapata County, and herdsman Silvester Delos Santos (21) farther downriver near Rio Grande City in Starr County. On June 3, raiders hit a sheep camp near Laredo, reportedly killed five men, took a boy prisoner, plus a man, Juan Escoba, who had previously been a captive for years. On June 4, 14 Indians, said to be Comanches, hit another sheep camp, drove off the animals, and took two shepherd boys prisoner. The report said, "This country is suffering dreadfully for want of protection."[9]

In June, Lipans were raiding along the Frio and Leona Rivers in Zavala and Frio counties, stealing horses from John Burleson, Bill Walker, Dan Williams, Ben Slaughter and others. A Mr. Gowan lost 100 head. Raiders hit Joel Walker's ranch on June 10, and captured a Mexican herder who worked for him. He tried to escape by jumping from his horse into the chaparral, but they shot him seven times. It was estimated that 300 horses were stolen. About 25 citizens chased them but they headed straight for the Rio Grande and got away.

Peter Tumlinson once commanded a company of Rangers in the area, but it had been disbanded, and the locals complained to Governor Houston, saying that had the Rangers been active they could have prevented the raid or recovered the stock. *The Daily Ledger* aired their concerns, printing "this governor of ours, while professing to protect the frontier, is in reality throwing it open to the ravages of the murderous Indian by disbanding the Rangers…" Yet, it caustically predicted, Houston will run for office again, and "Oh yes! Certainly in common gratitude for his efforts in their behalf, the frontier people will *doubtless* support him to a man."[10]

Chapter 7 notes

1 McConnell, *West Texas Frontier*, 327; Wilbarger, *Indian Depredations*, 481-82; Vincent, *Vincent's United States Register*, 265. Wilbarger places this event on a Sunday in 1866; McConnell says it occurred in March 1860; Vincent places it on April 15, 1860, which was a Sunday.

2 McConnell, *West Texas Frontier*, 329; Depredation Claims: Lemuel C. Barton #4607; David White #6316.

3 Greene, *900 Miles on the Butterfield*, 51-52; *Milwaukee, Daily Sentinel*, May 11, 1860; Vincent, *Vincent's United States Register*, 288; Ormsby, *Butterfield Overland*, 48, 51-52; Holder, *Lambshead Before Interwoven*, 25-26.

4 Vincent, *Vincent's United States Register*, 290-91.

5 Smith, *Old Army in Texas*, 147; Webb, *List of Engagements*, 21.

6 Wilbarger, *Indian Depredations*, 545; McConnell, *West Texas Frontier*, 331; "Death Records." http://surnamearchive.com/records/records054.htm. Wilbarger places the incident on April 30.

7 *Galveston Weekly News*, June 5, 1860; Anderson, *Conquest of Texas*, 328; Smith, *Frontier Defense*, 19; *The White Man* (Weatherford), September 15, 1860.

8 Wilbarger, *Indian Depredations*, 630-31; McConnell, *West Texas Frontier*, 332. Wilbarger believes the incident took place in 1859.

9 *The Daily Ledger and Texan* (San Antonio), May 24, 1860; *Galveston Weekly News*, June 5, 1860; "Death Records." http://surnamearchive.com/records/records054.htm; Vincent, *Vincent's United States Register*, 499.

10 *The Daily Ledger and Texan* (San Antonio), June 21, 1860.

8 "Glorious news —Nine scalps taken."

In June 1860, Apaches hit W. A. Cavitt's place in Live Oak County, stealing two mules. A more noteworthy incursion occurred that month in northern Stephens County, as Comanches swept up stock along the Clear Fork Brazos. William Browning and family lived at the mouth of Hubbard Creek near its junction with the Clear Fork, in the present-day Crystal Falls area. Five miles up Clear Fork was the ranch of John R. Baylor, who had been so prominent in closing down the two Brazos Indian reservations the previous year. Because of Indian depredations, however, Baylor had moved his family to Weatherford. About June 11, John Baylor, his brother George, his sons Walker and Jack, and several other cowmen were back in the area rounding up strays.

Unknown to them, the two adult sons of "Uncle Billy" Browning were also nearby rounding up stock. It was very hot, and Frank (32) and Josephus (22) had gotten off their horses to rest under a shade tree. Joe had hobbled his horse, but Frank figured they wouldn't be there long and let his graze free. No sooner had they stretched out when a half dozen Comanches galloped in. The brothers jumped on their horses; Josephus had no time to unhobble his mount and tried to ride with the horse's legs restricted. The Indians soon caught up, killed, scalped, and mutilated him. Frank got farther before Indians were on both sides of him. When they grabbed his bridle reins he fired his pistol several times at point blank range and hit two or three warriors. They dropped back, but not before they filled him and his horse with arrows.

Frank jumped his horse into Hubbard's Creek and swam him across. The water was deep and the Indians gave up the chase. On the other bank, Frank fell, and the horse continued home. William Browning saw the horse run in with arrows sticking in it and immediately knew what happened. He rode back to the creek, found Frank and brought him home. William set Frank down in the covered "dog run" between the double log cabins. He had 17 arrow wounds, but, incredibly, he was still alive and described what happened. William and some neighbors rode out and brought in the remains of Josephus.

Messengers went out to alert the surrounding homesteads. One of them found the Baylors hunting cattle and they rode to Browning's place. George W. Baylor saw Frank propped against a wall because he could not breathe while lying down. George, just a few years older than Josephus, viewed the mutilated body and remarked how he must have tried to defend himself against the Indian's knives, as his hands were all sliced to pieces. He remembered Josephus as "an amiable, brave, manly, handsome young fellow, full of life and fun."[1]

John and George Baylor paid their respects, grasped "Uncle Billy's" hand, and promised him that they would get revenge by taking many Indian scalps. A posse formed up at Browning's place and the elder Baylor was elected captain. John knew Indian ways, and realized that warriors were likely watching to see if anyone was coming after them. He chose to wait two days to let things cool down, and then took up the trail. The posse consisted of John and George Baylor, Barber Reynolds, Elias Hale, Minn Wright, and John Dawson.

They trailed the raiders to the northwest, finding some of their camps. At one, George found Josephus' scalp on the ground, probably dropped by a careless warrior. After four days, they came upon a camp on a small stream, and discovered a stock of fresh meat hidden in a ravine. John Baylor was sure the Indians had stored it while they raided elsewhere, planning to return later. He had his men hide in the brush, surround the camp, and wait.

The next day, two Indians approached, but divined that their hiding place had been discovered and turned around. Baylor's men chased after them. John went after the faster of the two warriors, while George zeroed in on the slower one. George and the warrior rode, dodged, maneuvered, and fired. Finally the Indian jumped off his horse and loosed arrows that hit George's belt and grazed his back. George dismounted and pulled the trigger, but the cap had fallen from the gun and it would not fire. He fumbled for another cap while the warrior nocked another arrow. Just then the other posse members rode up and the warrior made a run for it. George finally knocked him down with a shot and the others finished him off. John Baylor wrote "I am certain he was a Wichita Indian." John couldn't catch the other warrior. He got off his horse, took careful aim with his rifle, fired, and the Indian went down. The posse took two scalps and rode back to the Indian camp where they found and killed two more warriors. Figuring they had avenged Josephus, they headed for home.

About June 28, on Paint Creek in southern Haskell County they surprised a small band of seven Comanches, killing and scalping six of them. It did not bother them that one of their victims was a woman, since they figured that Indian women were usually crueler to white captives than the warriors were.

The posse headed south to the Clear Fork of the Brazos and then east toward home when they spotted another six Comanches driving 35 stolen horses. The two parties halted within earshot of each other, not quite knowing what to do. John Baylor, who learned some Comanche from his days as agent, heard one warrior tell his comrades that they should whip the whites and take their horses, but in the fight that followed, it was the Comanches who were whipped, and Baylor and his men had several more scalps. They recovered the horses, and an elaborate war shield decorated with the auburn hair of a white woman. They also got an elaborate silver hair ornament that the two brothers made into belt buckles.

The posse returned to Browning's, boasting that they had killed 12 Indians and recovered 55 horses. John Baylor gave William Browning his son's scalp and said he had been avenged; the posse had nine Comanche scalps to show for their efforts. The men were given a heroes' welcome in Young County, and were guests during the Fourth of July celebration at Palo Pinto. In Weatherford, the posse members were honored at a great barbecue and ball at the courthouse. On a rope stretched across the room they hung captured shields, headdresses, weapons, and the nine scalps. George called the late night festivity a "regular scalp dance." Not all the people of the area were pleased with the carrying-on. That summer persons unknown burned J. A. Hamner's printing presses and shut down operation of *The White Man* for a few months.[2]

Despite the Baylors' success in Haskell County, other warriors were raiding in Palo Pinto County at the same time. On June 15 they stole four horses from Mr. Daily and the next day took ten head from Mr. Cochrane. On the 18th they stole 40 horses from several people and on the 19th got 21 head from Mr. Carter.

An Austin newspaper decried the thefts and celebrated the vengeance: "Glorious News—Nine scalps taken… Browning's scalp recovered…Hurrah for Capt. Baylor and his little band!!" Parker County also rejoiced in the affair, but when word of the celebration reached the east coast, newspapers condemned the Weatherford townsfolk as "barbarians." In turn, the settlers of Parker County thought the easterners were ignorant of conditions on the frontier and knew nothing about Indians other than what they read in James Fenimore Cooper novels. Baylor took his war trophies to towns across north Texas where the citizens congratulated him on a job well done and encouraged him to keep up the good work. The attitude was commonplace. Wise County cattleman H. H. Halsell said that at picnics and reunions white men often displayed Indian scalps to admiring crowds.

Public celebration for victories over the Indians was not a new occurrence. Frontier people had felt the sting of Indian attacks for more than two centuries, and when the original 13 Colonies were adjacent to Indian country, many people entertained similar feelings. For instance, in the French and Indian War in October 1759, Maj. Robert Rogers led his Rangers on a raid into Canada to the Abenaki village at St. Francis. Having found hundreds of white scalps on display, Rogers's men slaughtered many Indians, most of them women and children in numbers estimated from 30 to 200, and took many scalps. In New England, Rogers and his men were considered heroes and celebrities, and were given many thanks for a job well done.[3]

In the southwest, scalping was practiced from the early days of Spanish expansion in the 17th Century. The Indians scalped, but the cousins of Don Quixote were also lifting and paying for Indian hair at the same time they were attempting to convert the "barbarians" to Christianity. When American frontiersmen learned that Indians were in great fear of losing their scalps because they would not be allowed all the pleasures of paradise, they were inclined to take as many scalps as they could, thinking, incorrectly, that it would deter Indian attacks. In 1837, Mexico issued permits to hunt Indians, and bounties of $100 per scalp were offered. Before that time, ears were generally offered as proof of a dead Indian. Americans such as James Kirker and Joel Glanton got involved in the "business," and made quite a name for themselves in the 1830s and 1840s, taking Apache and Comanche scalps—Mexican scalps too, it was alleged, because there was little way to tell the difference. Kirker often used Delawares and Shawnees to help him kill and scalp other Indians, and Mexico sometimes paid Comanches to take Apache scalps, and Apaches to take Comanche scalps. In North America, bounties for scalps were paid on and off for 274 years, from 1617 to 1891. For all the bounty proclamations, however, relatively few were paid. There was plenty of rhetoric that fueled hatreds, but thankfully, little action.[4]

Local newspapers played a large role in fanning the flames. In the East, where the immediacy of Indian War had passed them by, the papers still generally viewed Indians as "Noble Savages," but it was a concept that could be embraced or rejected as needs changed. In the West, the press was more likely to depict Indians as ruthless barbarians. Today, one historian argues that the Indian is once again the "Noble Savage." The media defined our social world and created our myths, and news couldn't be evaluated against an outside reality. Even if it was a culturally constructed product, it was still reality.[5] By 1860, time and space had mellowed Easterners' viewpoints and many looked upon the Texans' attitudes as savage and uncivilized. On the frontier there was always a thin line between "savagery" and "civilization" and whites and Indians became inured to the killing.

The 2nd Cavalry continued to shuffle its companies to and fro, but its attempts to stop the raids appeared to be in vain. The Chapman Family had moved from Tennessee to Parker County, Texas, in 1854, and a short time later, moved to the extreme frontier in Jack County about nine miles north of Jacksboro. Joe Chapman said that the Indians raided almost every full moon and they had to keep their horses locked with trace chains to trees in the yard. Joe's father was hunting close to their house in July 1860.

"I heard his gun fire," Joe said, "and we all thought he was shooting a deer." After Mr. Chapman failed to return home, neighbors searched the next morning and found the body. "He had been shot eighteen times with arrows," Joe said, "scalped, and his clothing taken." His rifle was broken off at the breech, indicating there must have been a hand-to-hand struggle before he died.

Just previous to this, Indians murdered Chapman's neighbor, a man named Cooley, who lived three miles away. Coupled with the Browning killing, it was enough to convince the Chapmans to move back to Parker County—hardly a safer place.[6]

In Coleman County it mattered little that 2nd Cavalrymen were posted nearby. Company B operated out of Camp Colorado during the summer of 1860, but Indians boldly raided the area nevertheless. On July 10, Isaac Chrisman was living right near the camp, employed at burning charcoal for the army, when Comanches rode in and stole horses from Chrisman and his neighbor, Conrad Gryder. The men asked the soldiers to help them recover their horses and a scout went out the next morning, traveling about 100 miles without overtaking the raiders. Civilians had better luck. They caught the Indians, had a brief fight, and forced them to abandon several horses, including one of Gryder's.[7]

The next month Cpl. John Rutter took a detachment of Company B out from Camp Colorado, a post located on Jim Ned Creek in northeast Coleman County. It had rained heavily for two days and Rutter was able to follow Indian pony tracks in the soft ground. On August 28, they swam their horses across the swollen Sabana River in southern Eastland County and found themselves almost inside the Indian camp. In the ensuing melee most of the soldiers' soaked weapons would not fire and the warriors, perceiving their difficulty, blasted them with several volleys and escaped. The soldiers were probably lucky that only one trooper, Pvt. James Cunningham, was killed.[8]

At this time Maj. George H. Thomas commanded a small contingent of 2nd Cavalry and operated out of Camp Cooper, a post on the Clear Fork of the Brazos in southwest Throckmorton County where the Comanche Reservation was previously located. He left on July 23 for a scout to the headwaters of the Concho and Colorado. The same day, Indians were 170 southeast of him in the settlements, stealing 100 horses and riding within five miles of Burnet. Thomas Nobles, who lost 30 head, was called "a hard working and industrious citizen, and can little bear so great a calamity." The locals, as usual, had to chase the Indians by themselves.

Also on July 23, Indians were 160 miles southwest of Major Thomas on the Butterfield Overland, attacking Head of Concho Station. Mr. Shepherd, the station keeper, was with a Mexican employee bringing in the mules when the Comanches appeared. The Mexican, said to have acted on the principle "that a good run was better than a bad stand," ran away. Shepherd had a rifle and a Colt pistol and made a good stand that had a bad ending, being shot down, scalped, and stripped.[9]

Back at Camp Cooper, Major Thomas was looking for more soldiers, and he recruited 13 members of the regimental band to join his detachment of Company B. On the march, Lt. Fitzhugh Lee with part of the company and Capt. Richard Johnson with men of Company F joined him.

With about 100 men, Thomas scoured the area for a month but found no Indians. He split the command to cover more ground as they headed back to Camp Cooper, and sure enough, Thomas's detachment cut an Indian trail. They followed the tracks for 60 miles to the head of the Clear Fork Brazos when, on August 26, one of the Delaware scouts located an Indian camp of about one dozen warriors. An intervening ravine forced Thomas to negotiate a single-file buffalo track to get across. By that time the Comanches fled, but their stolen horses slowed them enough to let Thomas catch up after a four-mile chase.

One brave warrior dropped back and dismounted, offering himself as a sacrifice to slow the pursuing soldiers. Perhaps a commander with more experience would have detailed a few men to dispatch the lone warrior and continued after the others; instead, the entire command attacked the defiant warrior. He rapidly loosed many arrows, mortally wounding Pvt. William Murphy and wounded four others, including two band members. One arrow actually hit Thomas in the chin and pinned his jaw to his chest! The soldiers could not get near the Indian. The Delaware scout shouted to him to surrender.

The warrior answered, "No never! Come on, Longknives!"

The soldiers closed in, wounding the Comanche several times, but he held them back with his lance, wounding two more troopers before he dropped. He had absorbed about 20 bullets. The rest of the Indians got away, but if it was any consolation, Thomas recovered 28 horses. Perhaps embarrassed by the situation, Thomas called off the chase and returned to Camp Cooper on August 30. Killing even one Indian could be an expensive proposition.[10]

Chapter 8 notes

1 Cavitt, W. A., Depredation Claim #2765; Marshall, *A Cry Unheard*, 67-68; McConnell, *West Texas Frontier*, 333.

2 Marshall, *A Cry Unheard*, 69-72; Grace and Jones, *History of Parker County*, 69; Smythe, *Historical Sketch of Parker County*, 138-40; *State Gazette* (Austin), September 22, 1860.

3 *State Gazette* (Austin), July 7, 1860, July 21, 1860; Marshall, *A Cry Unheard*, 72-73, 116; Brumwell, *White Devil*, 202, 240-41.

4 Marshall, *A Cry Unheard*, 112, 114-15; Smith, *Borderlander*, 68, 71, 104-05 122, 234; Silver, *Our Savage Neighbors*, 161.

5 Coward, *Newspaper Indian*, 5-11, 61. One might speculate if it is valid to argue against using modern viewpoints to assess 19th Century actions, when those in the 19th Century were also using "modern" viewpoints to assess what had transpired before them. They might be as "wrong" in their interpretations as we are in ours. All being relative, perhaps there is no right or wrong side.

6 Hunter, *Trail Drivers of Texas, I*, 413-14.

7 Isaac Chrisman, Depredation Claim #4168.

8 Arnold, *Jeff Davis's Own*, 287-88; Smith, *Old Army in Texas*, 147.

9 *State Gazette* (Austin), July 28, 1860; August 4, 1860.

10 Arnold, *Jeff Davis's Own*, 289-90; Webb, *List of Engagements*, 22.

9 "I am going home to die no more."

Soldiers had brushes with the Indians, but not on the scale experienced by the settlers. By 1860, it appeared that the Kiowas and Comanches were as deeply involved in the "stock business" as the horsemen and cattlemen. Legendary Texas cowman Oliver Loving had driven several herds north, and in 1858, had even taken one as far as Illinois. Moving Longhorns that potentially carried "Spanish fever" through stock ranges in Kansas and Missouri was dangerous for the local cattle as well as for the cowboys who drove them, as angry ranchers sometimes resorted to violence to stop the traffic across their ranges.

To avoid trouble, in August 1860, Loving and his associates gathered 3,000 steers on the upper Brazos and headed for a new market. They trailed north and west through Indian Territory to western Kansas, moved up the Arkansas River and wintered near Pueblo, Colorado Territory. In the spring of 1861, Loving moved his herd to Denver. The sale was lucrative, but the Civil War had just begun, and, as a Southern sympathizer, Loving was thrown in jail. Reportedly his friend, "Kit" Carson, bailed him out.[1]

Loving had avoided hostile ranchers and farmers, but the drive through Kiowa and Comanche land was not any safer. He would seek yet another route, but not until after the Civil War was over and Texas cattlemen could once again trail their Longhorns to northern markets. The close of one market for the Texans was exploited by the Kiowas and Comanches who increasingly stole horses to sell or barter in New Mexico Territory, Indian Territory, and Kansas. In reality, the Texans were comparative newcomers to the trade; the Comanches had been taking Spanish stock and driving it north for two centuries.

Indians from Mexico also raided stock. In August 1860, they hit Medina County and stole animals from several ranches, some from John Wernette right outside of Castroville. Ten men formed a posse and pursued the raiders but could not catch them. The same month B. F. Watkins and J. H. Richardson were traveling to Uvalde, Texas, from their homes on the upper Frio River. They camped on the Frio about eight miles northeast of town when Indians caught them sleeping early one morning. When their stripped and mutilated bodies were found, there were dozens of arrows in them and scattered on the ground nearby.[2]

Farther south in Laredo, a citizen wrote to the newspaper that his area had experienced few raids of late. "Our frontier is quiet at present," he penned. "We have had no Indians for about six weeks, I suppose entirely owing to the drought, but during their absence the thieves do their work most admirably."[3] The correspondent touched on a truth that was not fully evident to many: the Indians raided more when the grass was good and there was water in the streams.

On September 1 and 3, Indians were in the Hill Country, stealing horses within six miles of Fort Mason. Six locals, all of them 21 years old or younger, mounted up and chased the raiders west. They rode for nearly 24 hours before catching the Indians resting about 15 miles above the head of Brady Creek in southeast Tom Green County, nearly 90 miles from where they started. After that long ride, the boys were not about to go back without a fight, and the Indians obliged them for nearly an hour. When the warriors pulled out, taking about 25 horses with them, they left John M. Bolt dead, Henry Morris wounded in the leg, George Morris wounded in the foot, and Scott Jones wounded in the arm and head. One of their horses was killed and the other five wounded. It was a long journey back to Mason County.

Major Van Dorn took out elements of the 2nd Cavalry and met the wounded men on their return. From their directions he hurried to the head of Brady Creek and picked up the Indians' trail again, but it led far west into the caprock of the Llano Estacado and scattered. Van Dorn returned with nothing to show but broken down horses. Mason County resident George Todd and three of his neighbors tried to follow but were too far behind. "While this party was out," Todd wrote, "there came in more Indians and cleared up nearly all the horses on Willow Creek," which was only a few miles from Fort Mason. The soldiers based there, Todd said, "are a public nuisance, and are not worth shucks." Rumors were that the fort was to be abandoned and Todd said, "In the name of Peace, let them go, for they are no protection to this neck of woods."[4]

In early September, Kiowas or Comanches were in Palo Pinto County and stole nearly 100 horses, and "a negro man, the property of Mr. Craven, was killed by Indians in sight of the town of Palo Pinto," reported *The White Man*. "The present condition of the frontier is truly alarming."[5]

In September, Lipans killed Sostines Alagrid (22) in Zapata County near Laredo. Comanches hit Thomas Matthews again in Palo Pinto County, stealing fours horses worth $575. In Burnet County in October, Indians visited Thomas Espy a second time, taking 13 fine horses worth $1,300. The same month Indians stole horses from Martin V. Parmer in Jack County, and swung south to Oliver Loving's range in northwestern Palo Pinto County.[6]

In early October 1860, Indians were in Kendall and Kerr counties. Samuel Lane, who lived near the county lines just west of Comfort, was riding up the Guadalupe River to visit John Conner in Center Point. No matter how dangerous the frontier had proved to be, there was always the settler who went about unarmed, believing that tragedies always happened to someone else. Lane rode along without a weapon, munching on pecans, when Indians rose up out of a thicket and shot an arrow into his breast. He tried to escape but they filled his back with arrows. When Lane failed to come home, his family inquired at Conner's if he had ever arrived and learned he did not. Searchers found Lane's body three days later. Clasped tightly in one hand were pecans and hulls and in his teeth, pieces of pecan kernels.[7]

Farther west, Lipans or Mescaleros attacked the Pecos Springs Station on the Lower Military road, 14 miles beyond Fort Lancaster. They killed two men of Mr. Dempsey's wagon train and ran off 250 livestock from the station, "of which they made great slaughter."[8]

James H. Chick, who had lost horses in the February 1860 raid, was now working for Joel McKee, whose spread was in Dark Valley, three miles north of the Brazos, in the same area that Loving had grazed the cattle that he was currently driving to Denver. On October 25, 1860, Chick and three other employees had just come in to breakfast and hobbled their horses 300 yards from the house. Before they could finish eating, about 30 Comanches cut loose their horses, and with the herders on foot, proceeded to leisurely run off almost all of McKee's stock of 130 brood mares, saddle horses, stallions, and colts worth $14,200. Chick and the others procured horses from neighbors and went after the Indians. Northwest about ten miles, Bolin L. Kutch and his brother W. C. Kutch were herding their own stock when the Indians came by driving hundreds of animals. The Kutchs rode to the nearest settlement to raise the alarm and on the way they saw another band of Indians surrounding a lone wagon driving across the prairie. They hurried to town, got a posse, took the trail, joined up with Chick and his party, and now with 15 men went after the Indians.

They first went to the lone wagon they had seen, which was driven by John Bultoff (Bottorff). He lived by the Brazos River near Fort Belknap and was going to the mill in Weatherford. Bultoff often traveled unarmed, and his neighbor, William Marlin, cautioned him to take a weapon. Bultoff carried a small caliber six-shooter with him that day, but it was not enough. The Indians caught him at the edge of Dillingham's Prairie in southwestern Jack County and easily killed him. When the posse reached the wagon they found Bultoff dead on the ground, "face down and freshly scalped; and the tail of one of the oxen cut off." They placed Bultoff's body in his wagon and the next day other settlers buried him in a coffin made of scrap boards. The posse doggedly pursued the Indians for three days and nearly 100 miles. On the way they found two abandoned Comanche ponies, identified because the Comanches always split the ears of their horses. The tracks went nearly to Red River, when they merged with a buffalo trail and all trace was lost.[9]

Some of these same Comanches may have continued up the Brazos River and late in October, attacked the Harmonson-Duncan place northwest of Fort

Belknap. Zerrill J. Harmonson and his wife, Ruth Duncan Harmonson, had moved from Alabama and Arkansas to California Creek, only six or seven miles from the fort. Some of Ruth's sisters and brothers, including William B. Duncan, his wife, Sarah, and their four children, stayed with them, as did John C. Duncan, recently married to a divorcee, Martha A. Hester. Mrs. Harmonson's sister, Eveline Matthews and her husband, Robert, also lived in one of the small clusters of cabins being built near the creek.

It was evening and almost everyone was back at the cabins after a long day's work. Only three were out: Bill Duncan and Bob Matthews were driving in their milk cows and Lindy Harmonson, a black woman working for Cole Duncan, carried a bucket to the creek to get water. When the Comanches swept in, Lindy was first in their path. When she left the cabin, Martha Duncan heard her singing, "I am going home to die no more."

Within minutes, the Indians filled her with arrows. Bill Duncan and Bob Matthews ran for the cabins, and when Cole Duncan ran outside, shouting and waving his hat, he caused the Comanches to hesitate, giving the men enough time to escape. The Indians stole some stock and continued north toward Red River. Lindy Harmonson was buried near California Creek 200 yards from the cabins.[10]

The Indians were finding Texas bountiful grounds for their own stock enterprises.

Chapter 9 notes

1 Gard, *Chisholm Trail*, 34-36; Adkins-Rochette, *Bourland in North Texas I*, 126.
2 John Wernette, Depredation Claim #6208; Sowell, *Early Settlers*, 787.
3 *State Gazette* (Austin), August 18, 1860.
4 *State Gazette* (Austin), September 22, 1860; October 6, 1860.
5 *The White Man* (Weatherford), September 15, 1860.
6 "Death Records," http://surnamearchive.com/records/records054.htm; Thomas Matthews, Depredation Claim #347; Thomas H. Espy, Depredation Claim #4410; Martin V. Parmer, Depredation Claim #5818.
7 Sowell, *Early Settlers*, 649. McConnell, *West Texas Frontier*, 396, states this occurred in 1862.
8 *The Daily Ledger and Texan* (San Antonio), October 8, 1860.
9 Joel McKee, Depredation Claim #829; Wilbarger, *Indian Depredations*, 545; McConnell, *West Texas Frontier,* in www.forttours.com/pages/bottorff.asp
10 McConnell, *West Texas Frontier*, 342; "Duncans in Young County," http://homepages.rootsweb.ancestry.com/~dobson/tx/txyoung.htm.

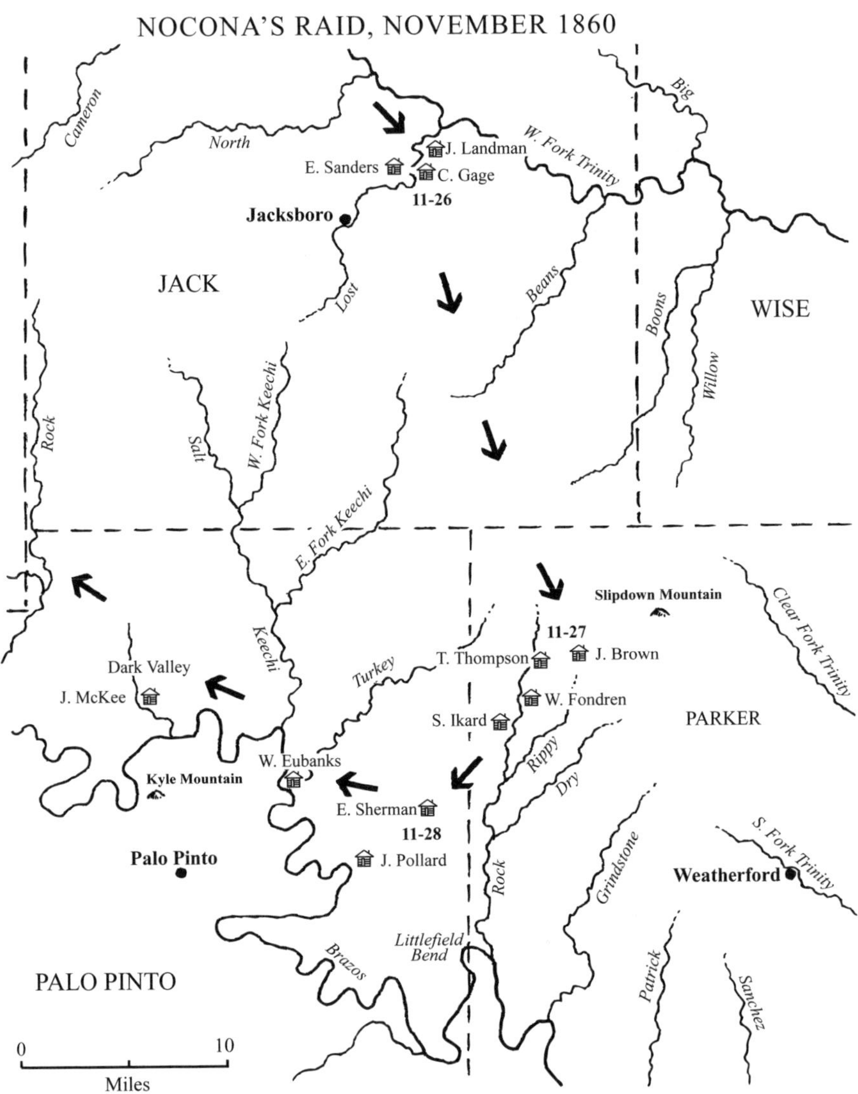
NOCONA'S RAID, NOVEMBER 1860
Cameron
North
Big
W. Fork Trinity
J. Landman
E. Sanders
C. Gage
11-26
Jacksboro
JACK
Lost
Beans
Boons
WISE
Willow
Salt
W. Fork Keechi
Rock
E. Fork Keechi
Slipdown Mountain
Clear Fork Trinity
Keechi
11-27
T. Thompson
J. Brown
Dark Valley
J. McKee
Turkey
W. Fondren
S. Ikard
PARKER
Rippy
W. Eubanks
Kyle Mountain
Dry
E. Sherman
11-28
S. Fork Trinity
Grindstone
Palo Pinto
J. Pollard
Rock
Weatherford
Littlefield
Bend
Brazos
Patrick
Sanchez
PALO PINTO
0
10
Miles

10 "Me Cincee Ann!"

As a result of this latest series of raids, in late October citizens of Palo Pinto and adjacent counties formed a company of 41 men, elected Jack Cureton as captain, and headed out in search of the Indians. They rode far west up the Double Mountain Fork Brazos when the weather turned cold and provisions and water grew scarce. Cureton decided to turn south toward the Colorado River in the vicinity of Fort Chadbourne. With their food gone, some of the men became mutinous, and about ten of them elected George Greer as captain and split off on their own. Curteon's men continued south until they ran into a small band of Comanches on a stream they identified as Wolf Creek, likely in present-day Nolan County.

The Indians were shooting prairie dogs and were surprised as the Texans charged them. Their resistance was brief, and they quickly scattered into the timber by the creek. A few Comanches were hit, and one was seen to hide in some thick brush by the stream. Cureton, Tom Stockton, Wiley Peters, Bud Strong, John Lasater, and James Lane surrounded the wounded warrior. Cureton cautioned them, but Lane tired of the game of hide-and-seek and went into the brush, when an arrow pierced his gut and lodged in his spine. Cureton recovered the badly wounded Lane and broke off the fight. A soldier pulled the arrow from Lane, but the point broke off inside him. The Rangers believed they had killed four Indians. They captured nine horses, saddles, buffalo hides, shields, bows and arrows and one rifle and headed for Fort Chadbourne about one day's ride south.

The soldiers at the post could offer little help. Lane was too weak to travel so Wiley Peters and William McGlothen volunteered to stay behind while Cureton returned to the settlements. A day later, Captain Greer and his party passed the fight site, discovered two dead Comanches, and rode to the fort. The citizen Rangers took the old Butterfield Stage route back east. Peters and McGlothen waited with Lane, who lingered for nine days before he died. After they buried him, the post commander issued the two men provisions enough to get back to the settlements.[1]

Cureton and Greer had been on the trail nearly one month. It was late November before they arrived back in Palo Pinto County hungry and exhausted. There would be no time for rest, however, because a devastating raid had just occurred while they were gone. For both whites and Indians on the southern plains, the year of 1860 would end on a bad note. The tragic episode had its antecedents 24 years earlier, when, on May 19, 1836, several hundred Comanche, Wichita, Kichai, and Caddo Indians attacked Parker's

Fort. Brothers Silas M. and James W. Parker established the private fort in 1834, on the headwaters of the Navasota River in today's Limestone County, Texas. The wooden stockade protected eight or nine families of the extended Parker clan. Despite Indian warnings, the gate was left open that morning when the men went to work in the fields. The raiders were only a quarter mile from the fort when the shout, "Indians," went out. It was too late. When it was over, five of the Parker clan were dead and five were captured. The prisoners, Rachel Plummer Parker and her son James, Elizabeth Kellogg, and John and Cynthia Ann Parker all had their personal ordeals to endure.[2]

Ten-year-old Cynthia Ann Parker, arguably the West's most famous Indian captive, was taken by a Comanche. The first days after her capture were terrifying. She had seen her relatives butchered, and she was beaten and abused. She witnessed the rape of her cousin Rachel, and Rachel's Aunt, Elizabeth Kellogg. Captives were chattel property and their captors could do with them as they pleased—torture, death, sexual abuse, or love and protection depended on individual whim. If a girl captive was young and compliant, the owner might choose to keep her around and eventually marry her.[3]

Cynthia Ann survived and was adopted into the tribe. Sightings of her over the years tantalized the public and kept her relatives' hopes alive that she might one day be rescued. But by then Cynthia Ann no longer wanted to be rescued. She received the name Naduah, which meant, "She carries herself with grace." She married Puhtocnocony, called Peta Nocona by the whites, and gave birth to several children, one of them being Quanah Parker, later to become a Quahadi chief.

She roamed with the Penetekas for a time, and then with her husband's band. By then Naduah, was very likely contented with her new life and family, however, the very thought that she could happily exist as a Comanche "squaw" could not be tolerated on the Texas frontier. Soldiers who saw her in the hands of the Comanches chafed at not being allowed to attack the Indians and attempt a rescue. The fact that the Indians could take white women and force them into "a fate worse than death," and that some would not care to return to white society, stoked the underlying racial and sexual tensions of the frontier folk.[4]

Naduah sometimes went on raids. This raid was led by Peta Nocona, a war chief about 40 years of age who was born into the Nokoni band but later joined and fought with the Quahadis. Almost everyone in Comanche society, including women and children, participated indirectly in a raid logistically or socially in the very important ceremonial dances. Women also joined raiding parties to help manage the camps and assist in carrying off spoils, and women warriors occasionally participated directly in the fighting and killing.[5] Naduah was on the raid, but whether she actually lifted the scalping

Author's photo

A replica of Parker's Fort, near Groesbeck, Texas, where Cynthia Parker was captured in May 1836.

knife or remained in camp in a supporting role is not known. Naduah never told what she did during the raid, or if she did, it was not recorded.

The status of Naduah's raid participation and the involvement of other women and children come into question: were they passive bystanders or active accomplices? A similar query can be made as to the status of white frontier settlers. Some of them hunted Indians while others never did, but did the non-combatants aid and abet the soldiers and Rangers when they sold or gave them supplies, provided sustenance, or cared for their wounded? It is endlessly debatable. In a guerrilla war, however, there are no guilty and innocent; there are no rules and everyone is a potential target.

Peta Nocona's band invaded north Texas in late November 1860. They first struck in Jack County, about four miles northeast of Jacksboro, at the home of James Landman. On November 26, Landman and his stepson, Will Masterson (14), were cutting wood about one mile from the cabin when the Indians arrived. At the house were Mrs. Landman and her son, Lewis (6), her baby, John, and her children from a previous marriage, Jane (12) and Catherine Masterson (15). The Comanches murdered Mrs. Landman, plundered the house, and carried off Jane and Catherine who were visiting the Landmans. Catherine's captor threw her on a horse, but Jane was roped and dragged as they rode away.[6]

The raiders traveled less than a mile to the banks of Lost Creek, where they cut loose Jane's battered and bleeding body, shot her with five arrows, and left her. Nearby was the cabin of Calvin Gage, who had been living on Lost Creek since 1856. At Gage's that day were Anna Gage, her son, Jonathan (5), and daughter, Polly (1). Three Fowler children of Anna's previous marriage also lived with them: Joseph (16), Mary Ann (10), and young Hiram. Joseph was searching for stray oxen about a mile from the house.

Elick Sanders lived close by. He was away, but his mother, Catherine Sanders (Anna Gage's mother) was home, along with her granddaughter, Matilda Gage (14), who was living with the Sanders.[7]

About one in the afternoon the Indians—Matilda Gage estimated their number at 250—engulfed both homesteads. Old Katy Sanders tried to defend the house, but warriors quickly killed her. They ransacked the place, taking household goods, kitchen items, and clothing, and caused about $700 in damages. They grabbed Matilda Gage and threw her on a pony. About the same time, warriors descended on the Gage cabin. They beat Anna senseless and shot her with arrows several times, leaving her for dead. She recovered, but died of complications from her wounds a few years later. They took little Polly and threw her high into the air several times, letting her smash onto the ground. They shot and wounded Mary Ann Fowler and Jonathan Gage.

Tiring of this sport, Nocona and his warriors took what property they could carry and rode south, taking Matilda Gage, Catherine Masterson, and Hiram Fowler with them. Only a short distance away, some of the warriors stopped, stripped Matilda and Catherine, "savagely abused" them, and let them go. The two girls walked in a daze toward the cabin. When they heard a tinkling sound they walked toward it, finding Joseph Fowler coming in with the bell ox. The naked and embarrassed girls told Fowler what had happened and the three of them cautiously returned home to discover the terrible scene. At first, Joe Fowler could not comprehend what had occurred; with a cold north wind and all the mattress feathers blowing about he thought it was snowing. When he came to his senses, Fowler rode to neighboring houses and spread the news.[8]

Meanwhile, J. A. Hamner rode from Jacksboro to the Gage place where he found Jane Masterson in the woods, still alive. The frightened girl told him what had happened, showed him the five wounds in her body where she had pulled out arrows, and pleaded with him for protection and to help the other members of her family. Then she died from loss of blood.[9]

The attack shocked the people of a country who had thought they were fairly inured to Indian depredations. W. W. O. Stanfield wrote to Governor Houston on December 9, stating "this day a week ago we buried five that was killed in the most savage like manner that I have ever herd of." There was a 65 year-old lady "shot through with an arrow" and the others were children aged one through 12 "murdered withe a lance and beat withe rocks some of them cut in as high as 14 different places." Mrs. Gage, Stanfield said, is "the worst bruised human being I have ever saw."[10]

Nocona led his band south into Parker County. One might speculate about Naduah/Cynthia Ann's role in these events as well as her state of awareness. Did she realize the great irony of the episode? Parker County, established in 1855, was named for her own family, and now she rode as the wife of the raid leader currently terrorizing its residents and making captives of children much as had happened to her 24 years earlier.

Just before daylight on November 27, a messenger reached the home of John Brown, about 16 miles northwest of Weatherford. Brown gave the man his best horse so he could continue with his Paul Revere-like ride, while Brown saddled an old cow pony and went to warn his neighbors. Two hours later, Nocona and about 50 Indians appeared. A slave woman called Aunt Harriet saw them coming and told Mary Brown. The old woman hid in the orchard and Mary gathered her children and the slave's son, Anthony (14), in the half-story loft of the cabin. To her horror, Mary realized one of her little girls, Annie, was still in a kitchen outbuilding. Anthony ran to get her and got her in the house just as the Indians appeared in the yard. While Mary Brown pulled everyone else up the trapdoor stairs to the attic, Anthony grabbed an ax and took a stand at the door. Surprisingly, the Indians didn't molest them, but appeared content to steal the horses.

Finally, Anthony went up the stairs and Mary Brown pulled him up and shut the trap door. After a time it seemed that the Indians left, and Mary stepped out on the porch above. Just then, two Indians on horseback in the yard, loosed arrows at her, one of which glanced off her head and cut off a swath of her hair. She slammed the door and the Indians finally rode off. The Comanches encountered John Brown on his cow pony only half a mile from the house. They lanced and scalped him, then cut off his nose. Neighbors found his body under a cover of snow in a post oak thicket the next morning. All he had for a weapon was a pocket knife, still in his hand. Mary Brown buried him in the corner of her yard. Her two oldest children who died during the next few years were buried next to their father.[11]

The raiders stole 18 horses from Brown and rode to T. E. Thompson's place two miles away on Rock Creek. Mrs. Thompson and her children saw about 60 Indians approach. One of Thompson's daughters said that "they came very near and like they were going to kill us all but on second thought they turned and left taking all our horses." The raiders operated on a whim; instead of slaughtering people as at the Landman, Gage, and Sanders' cabins, this time they watched the Thompsons run off and were content to take eight fine breeding mares worth $1,200. Mrs. Thompson and her children traveled about ten miles, warning the neighbors and stopping to fort up at William Fondren's house.

Elsewhere along Rock Creek in northwest Parker County, Nocona's men killed a Mr. White who was on his way to Mr. Kauts's place when he was caught on the open prairie. White had a pistol and shotgun, and neighbors heard his shotgun fire twice. They found him "naked and dead, and most brutally mangled with arrows and spears." Nearby, Comanches killed John Branen as he returned home from a neighbor. He "was shot with two rifle balls, his nose cut off, his body cut to pieces and scalped." It was also reported that the Comanches captured the wife and two children of Seaborn Ikard.[12]

Apparently finished in Parker County, Nocona cut southwest into Palo Pinto County. November 28, Wednesday, was a full moon, but it was not to be seen because of the miserable rainy weather. On Stagg's Prairie just northeast of present-day Mineral Wells, they came upon the home of Ezra and Martha Sherman. Martha's maiden name was Johnson. She had lived earlier in Parker County and was previously married to a Mr. Cheairs. When she wed Ezra (some papers called him Sylvester) Sherman they moved to Palo Pinto County. The Shermans had just sat down for dinner when six Indians burst in the door. They were taken by surprise, but Martha cautioned them not to show any fear. Seven-year-old William H. Cheairs was playing outside, saw the Indians coming, and ran behind the house and hid in an oak thicket.

The youngest child started to cry, but Martha grabbed his arm and squeezed it. Ezra tried to talk to a big warrior with his face painted in black and scarlet. He tried to indicate they had nothing to feed them, and no liquor, only molasses. He tried to indicate that he could give them molasses. Martha used a different tactic, stood up, pointed to the door and said, "Git!"

"Hambre," the Indian said in Spanish, rubbing his belly.

"No you ain't," Martha said, as she picked up her broom and tried to swat him with it. Some of the warriors laughed and one touched her long chestnut hair. Martha pulled back and the Indians talked among themselves.

One of the children then noticed the hair of one of the "Indians." "That's red hair," he said. Martha noticed it too, and realizing that he was probably a white renegade made her more fearful, although she tried her best not to show it.[13]

Finally, one of the warriors said, "Vamoose," and pointed to the door. There was little else the Shermans could do. Ezra and Martha took the two remaining children, Mary Cheairs and one-year-old Joe Sherman, and began hurriedly walking east toward the Potts' home, their nearest neighbor on Rock Creek. It was cold, gray, and snowing lightly and they did not have proper clothing, but they walked fast, without running, to get away before something dreadful happened.

They only got half a mile away when Indians rode up to them. This time they ordered Ezra to continue walking, and grabbed Martha by the hair. Ezra protested, but a lance pointed at his chest convinced him. He hurried away with the children as the Indians dragged Martha back toward the cabin and raped her. One of them pushed an arrow under her shoulder blade. They scalped her and rode their horses over her and left her, no doubt believing she was dead. Other warriors ransacked the house, drank up the molasses, tore up the feather beds and, for whatever reason, stole the family Bible. Then they rode off. William Cheairs watched it all from the thicket.[14]

The raiding Comanches were not finished. Parties scattered out and hit John B. Pollard's farm on the Brazos to the southwest, where they got 26 head of horses worth $2,100, all with their "P" brand on the left shoulder. Others attacked William Eubanks's ranch near the mouth of Turkey Creek at the Brazos, about six miles west of present-day Mineral Wells. Living at Eubanks's was Solomon B. Owens, a 20-year old who had just moved to Texas from Illinois and married one of Eubanks' daughters. While riding toward Turkey Creek, the Comanches drove nearly 300 stolen horses through Owens' wheat field, destroying the entire crop. It was dusk. Neither Eubanks nor Owens were home, but Eubanks' three daughters smartly donned men's clothing and hats and took position behind a fortified picket. When Mary Eubanks accidentally fired, the Indians figured the defiant defenders would be too tough to fight and rode away, but not before stealing all their horses plus those of M. B. Lock, who ran his stock on the same range.

The Indians headed north toward Keechi Creek. Will Eubanks was riding home in the late evening in weather described as "an intolerably cold norther, wind, and rain," when he suddenly found himself among the huge herd of stolen animals. He removed his hat, slumped over, and rode slowly in the same direction. As the night grew darker he sidled away and escaped.

The marauders did the same. They crossed Keechi Creek and turned west, passing through Dark Valley, which was virtually empty of stock following the raid in October. With a herd of more than 300 horses they finally headed out of the settlements.[15]

John B. Pollard and his three brothers Richard W., James T., and Green Pollard first knew that Indians were stealing their stock when a couple of their black slaves ran in with the news that they had seen the Indians. The Pollards rode north toward Staggs Prairie when they saw the large trail right near the Sherman place. Ezra Sherman had already made it to Potts' house, borrowed a gun, and hurried home. The Pollards got to the house first.

James Pollard testified, "They saw feathers flying over the yard and went in the house and saw blood and everything tore up." They went outside and hollered, when Billy Cheairs answered them from the thicket. He came out and told them what he knew. He saw the Indians bring his mother back. Pollard: "The little boy said he could hear her screaming and hollering for an hour and the last he saw of her, her hair was tied to the tail of a pony and they dragged her out on the prairie."[16]

Martha Sherman tried to drag herself to the cabin to get out of the freezing weather. Ezra arrived just after the Pollards, and he found Martha, but there was little he could do. She related all the horrible things the Indians did to her, and how hard it was for them to remove her scalp, sawing and hacking at it for the longest time. Over the next couple of days neighbors came to see her, and one, Henry Belding, could not get the "fearful" sight of her erased from his memory even 50 years later. Martha lingered four days, delivering a stillborn child before she died. Ezra took her body to Weatherford, where it was shrouded in a casket and laid out in a cabin for all to view. Naturally, the people of the county were outraged and the papers reported that what the Indians did to her "is too revolting to be read. May Heaven's bitterest curses rest upon them forever!" Martha Sherman was buried in Willow Spring Cemetery, eight miles east of Weatherford.[17]

Some of the Eubanks, Owens, Lock, and Pollard boys followed the Indians. They found several dead horses that had dropped from exhaustion. Owens said that at one point they found moccasin tracks, a quirt, a "cross mark," and other signs, "which was meant as a dare to [us] to follow them." After two days they gave up.[18]

Nocona's raid convinced some settlers that the area was too dangerous to live in, and many packed up and headed closer to the coast or forted up with other families. According to Ida Lasater Huckabay, the murders "so enraged the settlers that the cavalrymen and Rangers became determined to pursue the Indians to their own doors of the Texas plains."

Ranger Capt. Lawrence "Sul" Ross had been scouting in the northwest counties when the raid occurred. As bits of information came in, he realized he was dealing with more Indians than he could handle. He would have plenty of help, however, as nearly 100 civilian volunteers gathered at Loving's Valley, including many of the tired men who had hardly recuperated from their month-long trek out to Fort Chadbourne. The civilians elected Jack Cureton as captain and Richard W. Pollard as first lieutenant. The volunteers included locally notable families such as the Balls, Blevens, Bakers, Chicks, Eubanks, Coffees, Wells, Deatons, Slaughters, Robertsons, Vollintines, and Pevelers. A 21-man detachment of Company H, 2nd Cavalry, under Sgt. J. W. Spangler, arrived from Camp Cooper. The force moved to Fort Belknap where additional recruits joined up. On December 14, the force of nearly 140 men and Tonkawa scouts rode out. Using Charles Goodnight as a guide, who had discovered the raiders' trail, they marched west to the Pease River.[19]

As Ross, Cureton, and Spangler left Fort Belknap to chase Nocona, other Indians were still in the settlements. Steve Brannon lived on the North Fork Palo Pinto a couple of miles west of Strawn in southwestern Palo Pinto

County. Brannon's wife had been sick for the past few days and on December 15 Steve decided he would go to Mrs. Cohen's to see if she had any remedies. Brannon left his four grown boys to watch their mother. Brannon rode the five miles and found Mrs. Cohen willing to help. She climbed up behind Brannon and they rode home. About half way there Brannon heard an arrow pass by his head and saw it stick into a tree in front of him. Looking back they saw about 20 Indians and Brannon whipped his horse into a gallop. As they twisted along the path, arrows whizzed by, while Mrs. Cohen held her arms around Brannon and leaned left and right to the most dangerous side.

"My God!" Brannon realized. "She is shielding me!" Brannon angled side to side, getting off several shots with his pistol, and believing he had wounded a few pursuers. Mrs. Cohen, in the meantime, had done her job well.

"I am shot Steve," she said. He told her to hold tight and raced ahead. In a short while she said, "Steve, my back is full of arrows: I am killed already. Think of your sick wife, and drop me and save yourself."

Brannon would have none of that. In another mile he reached his farm and called out to his boys, who came out of the house with guns, shouting and shooting and raising such a ruckus that the pursuing Indians halted in their tracks and rode off to the south. Brannon was hit a couple of times, but Mrs. Cohen had taken seven arrows in her back. Brannon recovered, and remarkably, all the arrows were extracted and Mrs. Cohen also survived.[20]

As the soldiers and Rangers continued following Nocona's trail northwest, the war party behind them moved from Palo Pinto to Eastland County. John Flannagan, his wife, and four children lived a few miles south of the present town of Ranger near the North Fork Palo Pinto. Later in the same day that they attacked Brannon and Cohen, the Indians were near Flannagan's. Joe Smith and "Bad" Reese, who worked for Flannagan, were out turkey hunting when they heard people moving through the woods near them. Certain they were Indians, the men ducked down and froze until they had passed. When they crept back to the ranch they reported what happened. Flannagan, his son, Golston, and Ral Smith laughed at their fright.

Thinking nothing of it, the next day, December 16, Gols Flannagan (19) and Joe Smith (20) left to ride 15 miles southeast to C. C. Blair's ranch near present-day Desdemona. Only a mile from home, Flannagan believed he saw the horns of a deer rising above some thick brush.

"Do you see that buck?" he asked Smith. Just then, the "buck" turned into 15 or more Comanches. An arrow slammed into Smith's knee. "I'm shot!" he shouted, as he was knocked backwards into the wagon. Flannagan jumped or fell out and the Indians shot and lanced him. The oxen ran, pulling Smith away, while the Indians converged on Flannagan. The wagon finally overturned and Smith crawled into the brush and escaped back to Flannagan's house. "Bad"

Reese and Ral Smith rode back to the scene and brought back Flannagan's scalped and mutilated remains for burial. Smith pulled an arrowhead out of his knee and recovered. In 1886, 25 years after the incident, the point of another arrowhead broke through the skin behind his knee and he pulled it out. Smith believed he had been hit with a double-headed arrow. [21]

While the Indians were raiding behind them, "Sul" Ross followed Nocona's trail to the junction of Mule Creek and the Pease and on December 19, found the raiders' camp. For young Hiram Fowler, captured in Jack County, they were one day too late. The night before, the rebellious boy was proving to be too much trouble. The Indians murdered him and left his body behind. His bones were found about one year later. Just before Ross moved to attack, Charles Goodnight found a pillowslip on the trail and picked it up. Inside was a little girl's dress and a Bible with Martha Sherman's name on the inside cover. They had caught the guilty Indians—at least some of them.[22]

The Indian camp on Pease River did not contain the entire war party. The raid was over and many individuals went their own ways. Even Peta Nocona had left two days earlier, taking his boys Quanah and Peanut on a hunt with him. Many of the warriors were gone, and the women and children were gathering hackberries. They had killed a skunk and eaten it for breakfast. No longer participating as a female warrior, Naduah joined the other women in the mundane task of taking down the lodges in anticipation of moving. Suddenly she saw white men on horseback come over a hill and ride towards them.

Ross saw the Indians about the same time they saw him. It looked liked the women and about 25 warriors were frantically trying to pack up and flee. Ross had outmarched Cureton's volunteers, but there was no time to wait. While Ross charged ahead, Sergeant Spangler led the cavalry detachment around some sand hills to cut them off. They fled right into him, and Spangler trapped some of the women, many of whom were riding heavily laden horses and were too slow to escape. Spangler caught them, said Goodnight, "and killed every one of them, almost in a pile."

Naduah managed to grab a pony, and with her young daughter, Toh-Tsee-Ah, she mounted, threw a buffalo robe around them, and rode off. "Sul" Ross and Lt. Tom Kelliher chased them. After a mile, Ross was close enough to pull his pistol and shoot, but before he did, his prey turned, held out the child, and shouted, "Americano! Americano!"

Ross called to Kelliher to hold the captive while he rode after the others. He got within 20 yards of the warrior and fired, hitting his passenger, who turned out to be a girl. The bullet also struck the warrior and they both fell from the horse. The warrior got up and loosed some arrows at Ross; one hit his horse, which caused it to rear and buck. An inadvertent lucky shot by Ross hit the Indian's elbow and when his horse calmed down, he put two more bullets into the Comanche. Even so, he was still alive, and Ross watched him crawl off and sing his death song.

When Ross got back to Kelliher, he found the captured woman giving Kelliher all sorts of trouble and he was ready to shoot her when Ross noticed something strange.

"Why, Tom," he said, "this is a white woman! Indians don't have blue eyes." They had found Cynthia Ann Parker.[23]

The Pease River fight cost the Comanches 14 killed, including several women and children. Ross' men were unscathed. No one was certain at first, just who the white woman was. It was either late that night around the campfire, when Jonathan Baker mentioned that she might be one of the Parker children who was carried off years ago, or it might have been after Ross took the command back to Camp Cooper, and Isaac Parker was summoned to identify the woman. In any case, when the name "Cynthia Ann" was mentioned in front of the woman, she finally recognized the sound, stood up, patted herself and said:

"Me Cincee Ann."[24]

James T. Pollard knew it. Riding with the volunteers, he was too late to participate in the battle, but was there when the camp was destroyed and the captives gathered up. The woman looked familiar. He had seen her a few times in 1857 and 1858 on the Comanche Reservation when it was located on the Brazos. He was there when annuities were issued and the beeves were let loose. He saw how the men rode down and shot the cattle like buffalo, and watched how "the squaws would skin them." He noticed one woman's light hair that looked odd for an Indian, but never realized who she was until now. As Cynthia Ann tried to communicate partially in Comanche, English, and sign, Pollard believed she made motions to show that she knew him too.[25]

The ride back to Camp Cooper was not a triumphal return for Cynthia Ann. Several times she tried to escape. She carried her young daughter but had left behind her two boys and was despondent. Her uncle, Isaac Parker, came to take her "home." Word spread of her return, and Cynthia Ann became a minor celebrity. The Texas legislature granted her a pension of $100 per year for five years, plus a league of land (about seven square miles).

She was still unhappy and tried to run away several times. Her brother, Silas Parker Jr., took her to his home in Van Zandt County, and then she went to live with her younger sister Orleana, who was married to R. J. O'Quinn. Here, Cynthia Ann learned to weave, spin, and sew, and began speaking English again. In late 1864, her daughter, called Prairie Flower, caught pneumonia and died. Cynthia Ann went into a deep depression, wasted away, and died in 1870.[26]

The Nocona Raid resulted in nine white settlers killed and five wounded. The Pease River fight resulted in the deaths of about five warriors and nine women and children, and the capture of three women and children. No soldiers or Rangers died. Counting other raids in Texas during the last two months of 1860, about 23 civilians had been killed.[27]

Two compilations of army casualties indicate that either seven or nine soldiers died in combat across the entire West in 1860.[28] In Texas alone, a very conservative estimate shows that at least 78 civilians died. If this was war, it was the non-combatants who bore the brunt. Those who grumbled about lack of protection had a legitimate complaint. The U.S. Army had accomplished little and the civilian ranging companies had not done much better. If the Texans felt vulnerable with the army on the scene, they would feel defenseless and abandoned when the army pulled out and left them to face the Indians alone.

Chapter 10 notes

1 McConnell, *West Texas Frontier*, 338; Wilbarger, *Indian Depredations*, 583-84; *State Gazette* (Austin), October 20, 1860.

2 Exley, *Frontier Blood*, 53; Webb, *Handbook of Texas* 1, 630. For a detailed discussion of their experiences, see Michno, *A Fate Worse Than Death*.

3 Wallace and Hoebel, *Lords of the South Plains*, 241, 261-62; Fehrenbach, *Comanches*, 286-89.

4 Exley, *Frontier Blood*, 138-39; Fehrenbach, *Comanches*, 290, 375.

5 DeLay, *War of a Thousand Deserts*, 120-21.

6 Marshall, *A Cry Unheard*, 135; Huckabay, *Jack County*, 60; McConnell, *West Texas Frontier*, 346. McConnell says that Lewis was also killed, but Huckabay says he was unharmed.

7 Huckabay, *Jack County*, 5; McConnell, *West Texas Frontier*, 346; Marshall, *A Cry Unheard*, 29, Elick Sanders, Depredation Claim #1894.

8 McConnell, *West Texas Frontier*, in forttours.com/pages/tocnocona; Huckabay, *Jack County*, 60; Depredation Claims: Elick Sanders #1894; Mary Catherine Bunch #833. Mary Catherine Masterson survived and later married John Bunch, a neighbor who was one of the first on the scene after the raid. She said that a great number of the raiders were Kiowas.

9 Marshall, *A Cry Unheard*, 135-36.

10 Winfrey and Day, *Texas Indian Papers, IV*, 44.

11 Marshall, *A Cry Unheard*, 30-31; Huckabay, *Jack County*, 61-63. Author Ida Lasater Huckabay was the daughter of the little Annie that Anthony had saved from the kitchen.

12 Grace and Jones, *History of Parker County*, 67; William H. Thompson, Depredation Claim #2756; *State Gazette* (Austin), December 8, 1860. One of Ikard's freed slaves, Bose Ikard, later became a companion of Charles Goodnight and Oliver Loving, and was portrayed by Danny Glover as Josh Deets, in the film *Lonesome Dove*.

13 McConnell, *West Texas Frontier*, 349; Marshall, *A Cry Unheard*, 32-33. A slightly fictionalized account of this episode is found in Graves, *Goodbye to a River*, 132-38.

14 Marshall, *A Cry Unheard*, 32-34, 79; Wilbarger, *Depredations*, 516-17; McConnell, *West Texas Frontier*, in forttours.com/pages/tocnocona.

15 Marshall, *A Cry Unheard*, 34; Huckabay, *Jack County*, 63-64; McConnell, *West Texas Frontier*, 350; Depredation Claims: John B. Pollard #6320; Solomon B. Owens #170.

16 Solomon B. Owens, Depredation Claim#170.

17 Marshall, *A Cry Unheard*, 33-34; Wilbarger, *Depredations*, 516-17; McConnell, *West Texas Frontier*, in forttours.com/pages/tocnocona; *State Gazette* (Austin), December 8, 1860.

18 Solomon B. Owens, Depredation Claim #170.

19 Huckabay, *Jack County*, 60, 64-65.

20 McConnell, *West Texas Frontier*, 352; Langston, *Eastland County*, 30-33.

21 McConnell, *West Texas Frontier*, 353; Langston, *Eastland County*, 34-37; Wilbarger, *Indian Depredations*, 503-04. Wilbarger incorrectly places this incident in 1858.

22 Exley, *Frontier Blood*, 146-53; Haley, *Charles Goodnight*, 52-54; Marshall, *A Cry Unheard*, 43-44.

23 Exley, *Frontier Blood*, 153-58; Ramsay, *Sunshine on the Prairie*, 86-89; Haley, *Charles Goodnight*, 55-57; Robinson, *Men Who Wear the Star*, 119-20. There are many versions of this event. It is sometimes said that it was Peta Nocona who Ross killed. Goodnight claims Ross killed a chief named Nobah.

24 Exley, *Frontier Blood*, 161; Haley, *Charles Goodnight*, 57-59.

25 Solomon B. Owens, Depredation Claim #170.

26 Exley, *Frontier Blood*, 166, 169-79; Webb, *Handbook of Texas* 2, 335, 337; DeShields, *Border Wars*, 165-66; Ramsay, *Sunshine on the Prairie*, 91-93.

27 Exley, *Frontier Blood*, 145; Haley, *Charles Goodnight*, 52.

28 Webb, *List of Engagements*, 21-23; *Adjutant General's Office*, 20-22.

Part 3. 1861

11 "We will swoop down upon him at night."

As 1861 began there did not appear to be any new resolutions to break with past habits. Keeping the routes open to the California and Colorado goldfields was always of more concern to the government than raids on Texas settlers. Initially, one of the primary routes west went along the Butterfield Overland Trail in a sweeping southern arc from Missouri to Texas and west to California. Congressmen and supplicants argued for years about changing to a shorter central route, but sectional differences made compromise difficult. Not until 1860, when the line through Texas had been devastated, with stations burned, vehicles destroyed, horses and mules stolen, and ten drivers killed, was a route change finally accepted. As the slavery and sectional crises deepened and southern states seceded from the Union, Southern opposition mattered little. In March 1861, the Post Office Appropriation bill directed that the southern route be shifted to a central route.[1]

Another factor to facilitate the transition was the new treaty made with the Cheyennes and Arapahos. At Fort Wise, Colorado Territory, on February 18, 1861, the two tribes agreed to accept a reservation and grant passage of roads in exchange for gifts, money, and future annuities. Only a handful of chiefs signed and the majority of the tribes were opposed to the treaty, but the government officials were optimistic. The treaty seemed to indicate that the Cheyennes and Arapahos were pacified, there was a lull in troubles with the Lakotas to the north, and even the Comanches and Kiowas, at least a few western bands, appeared willing to come to the bargaining table. Government agents and army officials held a conference with the Comanches on May 10 at Alamo Gordo Creek, a tributary of the Pecos River. New Mexico Superintendent of Indian Affairs James L. Collins and Capt. Robert A. Wainwright, accompanied by two companies of Mounted Riflemen, made a deal with Comanche chiefs Esaquipa, Pluma de Aguilar, and Paracasqua. In return for peace, they promised to stop raiding settlements in eastern New Mexico, stay away from travelers on the Santa Fe Trail, and stop depredations. For the first time in a long while, it seemed that there might be a lasting peace on the plains.[2]

It would not happen, for there were not enough magnanimous, visionary leaders on either side to pull it off. Furthermore, additional complications in the West developed from events in the East. On April 12, 1861, about two thousand miles away in South Carolina, Confederate cannons opened fire on Union troops in Fort Sumter. The American Civil War had begun, and it would have immediate repercussions in the West, not in instant battles, but in the decisions that the soldiers had to make. Would they remain in the United States Army, resign, desert, or join the Confederacy?

The U.S. Army had its largest losses in Texas. When Confederate forces under Ben McCulloch swarmed into San Antonio on February 16, Gen. David E. Twiggs surrendered all Federal property. Most of the 2nd U.S. Cavalry and 3rd U.S. Infantry got out, but the majority of the 8th Infantry, garrisoning some of the distant forts, was taken prisoner. In Arkansas and Indian Territory the 1st U.S. Cavalry evacuated Forts Smith, Gibson, Washita, Cobb, and Arbuckle and marched north to Fort Leavenworth. Companies of 2nd Infantry at Fort Kearny and artillery at Fort Randall left Sioux country for Leavenworth. The 7th and 10th U.S. Infantry Regiments were sent east, while most companies of the 5th and 9th U.S. Infantry and the 3rd Artillery spent the war years in the west.[3]

When the last of the regulars were gone, the western states and territories would need volunteers to defend themselves and to keep supply and communication routes open. At the far ends of the supply lines, the territories may have been lacking in arms and equipment, but it would have seemed that Texas, an independent republic from 1836 to 1845, and a state since then, would have been sufficiently armed. In the early American colonies it was required that every head of household possess a firearm for militia duty. In six colonies there were laws requiring at least one person in each family to bring a gun to church or other public meetings. By the mid-19th century, however, as the Indian frontier passed beyond the pale of time and space in the east, such laws were either removed or ignored. Even in the west many men did not own weapons and if there was a war to be fought, they would have to be supplied. The majority of Texan settlers were no longer Davy Crocketts or Jim Bowies, if they ever were.[4]

Once they collected enough men, weapons, and supplies, the Confederacy had plans to conquer the western territories. Southern leaders believed they held four aces. They assumed that the Mormons in Utah would gladly accept an alliance with the Confederate States; they believed that one-quarter of Colorado's population would actively support a Confederate invasion; President Jefferson Davis was told that with six regiments assisted by Indians, they could capture Forts Laramie, Wise, and Union; and it appeared that the Confederacy would make alliances with the Indian tribes.[5]

None of the South's cards proved to be aces, but the fact that they were trying to assemble a winning hand caused the North a great deal of consternation. Mormons did not join the Confederacy; the territories did not rebel against the North—in fact, the New Mexicans dislike of Texans almost assured that they would not; the disappearance of Federal troops was more than matched by the recruitment of volunteers; and the Indian tribes did not wholeheartedly join the Rebel cause. The Indian factor, however, did play a role throughout the war.

Before the Civil War had even begun, Texas sent a commission to recruit the Cherokees, Chickasaws, Creeks, Choctaws, and Seminoles for the Confederate cause. Commissioners James E. Harrison, Charles A. Hamilton, and James G. Bourland visited the tribes in March 1861. They found the Creeks, Choctaws, and Chickasaws with Southern sympathies, but the Seminoles and Cherokees to be split. They believed those tribes would raise 20,000 men for the Southern cause. The commissioners had grandiose plans for their allies. "Lincoln may haul his big guns about over our prairies in the daytime," they wrote, "but we will swoop down upon him at night from our mountains and forests, dealing death and destruction to his army."[6]

The commissioners were concerned that during their travels they met more than 120 wagons filled with people from counties in north Texas who were leaving for Kansas. While Texas was voting to secede from the Union, north Texas counties had substantial numbers of people with abolitionist leanings. Split loyalties would lead to suspicion, hatred, and killing in the near future. The settlers in north Texas would have as much to fear from their neighbors as they did from the Indians.

Governor Sam Houston was not even sure this secession business would work and he refused to take the oath of allegiance to the Confederacy. The legislature removed him from office and elevated Lt. Gov. Edward Clark to the position. Now Clark had to figure out how to protect the frontiers. Confederate Secretary of War Leroy P. Walker asked Ben McCulloch to raise a regiment, while Texas congressmen believed they had a better idea. The troops required for frontier duty were required to "be brave, good horseman, acquainted with the country, and able to perform the most fatiguing service."[7] They believed that Rangers would be the answer.

Governor Clark wanted two regiments, and he wanted the Confederacy to arm and equip them. Secretary Walker, however, figured the Indian threat was overblown, "merely predatory and incursional," and carried out by only a few roving bands. He agreed to a second regiment, but it was to be used along the Rio Grande border. Clark wanted to keep the regiments in Texas while the Confederacy wanted the option to move them beyond the borders. It was a sore point throughout the entire war.

Earl Van Dorn, now a Confederate colonel, returned to command the Department of Texas with the same plan as Secretary Walker. Henry E. McCulloch, Ben's younger brother, was appointed colonel of the 1st Texas Mounted Rifles, which took the northern sector, while Col. John S. Ford commanded the 2nd Texas Mounted Rifles in the south.

Before official C.S.A. commissioners could get to Indian Territory, Ben McCulloch was there trying to obtain the Indians' friendship. He figured that if he could make peace with the Comanches and Kiowas, Confederate forces could be free to concentrate on the Federals. McCulloch and Maj. Edward Burleson left the Wichita-Caddo Reservation in early July, taking five companies, Charles Goodnight as a guide, and some Tonkawa scouts, and rode to the Antelope Hills area where John Ford battled the Comanches three years earlier. They met with Red Bear and Eagle Chief of the Comanches, and Lone Wolf, Satank, and Satanta of the Kiowas, but the parley was a failure. According to Goodnight, the Comanches "flatly refused to join the Confederacy." They said that the Texans were "heap rich in cattle and horses, and that they preferred to fight us and steal from us and trade to Mexico." Goodnight said negotiation would not work. They were there a day and a night, and "there was no use staying with the buggers."[8]

Author's collection

Confederate Gen. Henry E. McCulloch commanded the Northern Sub-District during the Civil War.

McCulloch's attempt to treat with the Indians only confused matters, for Albert Pike, Confederate Commissioner to the Indian Nations, was on the same mission. Pike was truly the Indians' friend. Born in Boston in 1809, he moved west as a youth and became a journalist, poet, planter, and lawyer. Pike learned several Indian tongues. He was physically imposing, weighing about 300 pounds, was independent, free-thinking, and controversial, and when he donned his moccasins, leggings, and feathered headdress, he was quite a sight. As an attorney, he had won settlements for several tribes. In May 1861, he climbed aboard a buggy leading a wagon train loaded with food, wine, and assorted goods for the Indians. Pike was authorized to spend up to $100,000 to convince the tribes to sign treaties with the Confederacy.[9]

Formal negotiations between the Confederate States and Indian tribes was hardly consistent with the Southern position since President Andrew Jackson's time, nor was it consonant with states' rights doctrine, but the need for political and military expediency was a hard reality. Andrew Jackson believed that making treaties with Indians was absurd, and said that Congress had the right to dispose of Indian lands as it saw fit. Yet, bribery, cajolery, and gift giving in the guise of friendship would go a long way in lieu of military coercion. In fact, it was wise for the South to send emissaries to the Indians and rather foolish for the North not to.[10]

Pike traveled across Indian Territory from May to August, trying to get the tribes to join the Confederate cause. Previously he wrote to Confederate Secretary of State Robert Toombs: "We shall have no difficulty with the

Creeks, Seminoles, Choctaws, and Chickasaws, either in effecting treaties or raising troops." The problem would be in arming them, for Pike believed that "not one in ten" Indians owned a gun. There were no revolvers to be obtained at any price. Despite being bereft of arms, the Indians were portrayed as finicky when Pike emphasized they must have rifles, for they "would not pick up a musket if it lay in the road."[11]

Pike got the Creeks, Choctaws, and Chickasaws to sign treaties in July. The Seminoles signed a treaty on August 1. It took until October for Pike to get treaties with the Osage, Seneca, Quapaw, and finally, the Cherokees. Political and military exigencies forced the South to concede more than Andrew Jackson ever would have. Needing alliances and assistance, the Confederacy granted the Indians justice; something it never would have granted in normal times. The Confederacy did not want Indian Territory, but it wanted the tribes to remain true to the slaveholding South. The North negotiated in the traditional way, by giving trinkets and promises for Indian neutrality or military assistance, while all the time hungrily eyeing Indian Territory. Both North and South used the Indians for their own purposes, just as the Indians took advantage of both of their supplicants.[12]

If the Confederacy believed that the Indians were capable of self-government they should have been able to conduct their own trade, but no manner of reform could break this custom. Handing out trade licenses for favors or kickbacks was a lucrative practice. The chance to make an easy dollar would beat altruism any day.

Just how avaricious agents and traders could be is shown in the remarkable statement by Douglas H. Cooper. Cooper was the U.S. agent to the Choctaws and Chickasaws before his defection to the Confederacy. While he was in U.S. employ in the spring of 1861, he was also raising troops for the Confederate Army. Cooper's plans are exposed in his letter to Elias Rector, who also left the Federal service to become the Confederate superintendent of Indian affairs. On May 1, Cooper wrote to Rector that he decided to act on Rector's suggestion that they collaborate on absconding with the money meant for the Choctaws.

"If we work this thing shrewdly we can make a fortune each," he penned, "satisfy the Indians, stand fair before the North, and revel in the unwavering confidence of our Southern Confederacy. My share of the eighty thousand in gold you can leave on deposit with Meyer Bro. Subject to my order. Write me soon."[13]

Petty, small-minded, greedy men were more responsible for Indian wars than a clash of cultures ever was.

In addition to the treaties with the above tribes, Pike also drew up a similar document for the Yamparika, Kotsoteka, and Nokoni Comanches, and the Tenawas, thought to be a branch of the Nokonis. Articles stated that all hostilities between the Comanches and the Texans were to be ended, "forgotten and forgiven forever." The tribes would give up their roaming life on the prairies and Staked Plains, settle down on the reservation, and both sides would deliver up all prisoners—except for Mexicans. Twelve Comanche chiefs signed the agreement. Every Comanche band except the Quahadi was now allied with the Confederacy, on paper at least. Whether or not the tribes understood what they were signing was probably not as important at the time as it was to get in on the distribution of goods that the fat white man was giving away.

Author's collection

Albert Pike, Confederate Commissioner to the Indian Nations and a true friend of the Indians.

There were two articles in each of the treaties that may have convinced some of the Indians to sign, but were later struck out by the legislature before ratification in December 1861. One clause said that the Confederate States would furnish every warrior with a rifle and ammunition; the other said that all Texas troops would be withdrawn south of the Red River and would never again set foot in the Leased District.[14]

The treaty also offered the same deal to the Kiowas if they would atone for their recent "murders and robberies" and agree to settle down. The Confederate government may have been as naïve as the Union when dealing with Indians, but it did make an attempt to be practical and genuine. There was no way, however, that it was going to arm the Comanches or stay out of their territory. As for the Comanches, there was no way that they were going to stop raiding in Texas, give up their lifestyle, or turn in their captives.

At best, the treaties were temporary stop-gap measures, enacted as much for conscience as legitimacy. If they prevented the Comanches from raiding for a time, good, and if they actually joined the Confederacy to fight the Union it was all the better. At worst, the treaties were a farce. Few on either side believed the agreements would last. The signatory Comanches and non-signatory Kiowas were likely pleased now that the crazy white men were fighting each other. They could understand that. It was not unlike their own tribal warfare that had been going on as far back as they could remember.

The chiefs of the Plains tribes could be as Machiavellian as any European or American politicians; play one side against the other; promise anything to gain an advantage; shop around. Because Indians felt superior to white men, most of them viewed treaties or peace offers as signs of weakness. One historian contends that when an Indian signed a treaty, it was done only to gain time to build up his forces, get gifts, or placate the whites. In any case a treaty was no more than a subterfuge.[15]

Within two months following their treaty with the C.S.A. the Comanches were at Fort Wise in Colorado Territory trying to find out what kind of deal the Union would offer. In early October, Agent Albert G. Boone indicated that "eight Texas Comanches came to this post bearing a United States flag, and asking to be received into this agency and a country assigned them." It was evident, Boone wrote, that the Texans "have been tampering with them," but he was satisfied that they were "devoted to the Union" and could act as spies to report on Texan movements. The Comanches were as devoted to the Union as Pike believed they were devoted to the Confederacy.

Nearly 600 lodges of Comanches eventually camped near Fort Wise and Boone talked with the chiefs. The Yamparika, Bis-te-va-na, who had signed Pike's treaty, showed Boone a letter of recommendation Pike gave him. The letter was a legitimate note of good character and a request for "protection and safe conduct" for the bearer. The Comanches, Boone said, "were much astonished" when he told them that the treaty they made was with enemies of their great father in Washington. The chiefs told Boone the old treaty should be destroyed, and they wanted to make a new deal with him. Boone complied, framing a preliminary new agreement and passing out the remnant of his supplies.[16]

Poor, naïve Boone, like Pike, had given away his goods for Comanche promises. They took them, smiled, and went back to raiding.

Chapter 11 notes

1 Hafen, *Overland Mail*, 213-14; Moody, *Stagecoast West*, 197-98, 201-02.
2 Kappler, *Indian Treaties*, 807-10; Oliva, *Fort Union and the Frontier Army*, 177-78; Kenner, *Comanchero Frontier*, 136.
3 Utley, *Frontiersmen in Blue*, 212-13; Oliva, *Fort Union and the Frontier Army*, 242; Josephy, *Civil War in the American West*, 35; Smith, *Frontier Defense*, 23-24.
4 Cramer, *Armed America*, 7-9.
5 Colton, *Civil War in the Western Territories*, 9; *WR:* S.1, V.3, 578-79.
6 Adkins-Rochette, *Bourland in North Texas I*, 111-13; *WR:* S.4, V.1, 324.
7 Smith, *Frontier Defense*, 28-29.
8 Haley, *Charles Goodnight*, 64; Smith, *Frontier Defense*, 33-34.
9 Josephy, *Civil War in the American West*, 323-24; Webb, *Handbook of Texas II*, 377.
10 Abel, *American Indian as Slaveholder*, 83, 132; Remini, *Andrew Jackson and his Indian Wars*, 35, 44, 107, 118-19.
11 *WR:* S.4, V.1, 360.
12 Adkins-Rochette, *Bourland in North Texas II*, A-441; Abel, *American Indian as Slaveholder*, 17-18, 67, 157-66.
13 Abel, *American Indian as Slaveholder*, 186-87.
14 *WR:* S.4, V.1, 548-54; *WR:* S.4, V.1, 813.
15 Danziger, *Indians and Bureaucrats*, 67.
16 *Commissioner of Indian Affairs 1861*, 103-06.

12 "He would not killey me."

As Albert Pike traversed Indian Territory making treaties, Henry McCulloch was charged with restraining the "wild" tribes of the Territory, but was restrained himself by the Confederate government for he was not allowed to chase raiders north of Red River. Pike protested McCulloch's proximity to the border and he had to pull back his companies. McCulloch complained to Maj. Edward Burleson that "General Pike has blocked the game on us as far as Indian operations are concerned," but if any Indians came into Texas he wanted Burleson to "follow them no odds where they go, and if you can come up with them, whip them."[1]

Neither McCulloch's men, nor the many other state companies did much whipping. In February 1861, Indians raided in Llano County, stealing a number of livestock, including three saddle horses worth $180 from Joseph D. Cady. Cady and his neighbors unsuccessfully rode after the Indians, finding only moccasin tracks and dead stock shot full of arrows.[2]

Indians also splashed across Red River in February 1861 to hit the northern counties. A party of Rangers, among them Capt. D. M. Tackett, David Stinson, Bud Slover, John Slover, and others were on a scout a dozen miles north of Jacksboro. The Rangers had stopped for their noon meal when the Indians charged them, but quick work with their six-shooters drove the warriors away. The Rangers chased the Indians south, but their fleeter ponies allowed them to escape. The raiders made their next appearance in northwest Parker County, which had barely recovered from Nocona's Raid only three months earlier. The Indians came across William Youngblood who was half a mile from his cabin splitting wood, caught him off guard, and quickly killed and scalped him.

William B. Fondren lived nearby on Dry Creek. That evening, his dogs were restless and began to bark. Fondren investigated and flushed out a few Indians who were hiding behind some grapevines near the house. They put an arrow into one of the dogs and exchanged shots with Fondren before riding away. Fondren gathered a small posse and trailed the Indians west into Palo Pinto County. The raiders had arrived in an area where there was plenty of activity, for there was to be a wedding that day between Pleas Price and Bertha Parmer and neighbors were gathering for the festivities. The Indians first rode by Hugh Van Cleve's place on East Keechi Creek where Price and his friend Milton Lynn had stopped on their way to Parmer's. The Indians tried to steal Van Cleve's horse, but when they cut him loose he ran to the stable. Shots were exchanged and the Indians rode away. Price and Lynn chased them for a short time until an arrow came out of nowhere and lodged into Lynn's saddle, convincing the two men to wait for reinforcements.

The Indians next passed Isaac Lynn's place and briefly exchanged more shots before continuing to Parmer's, five miles away. In the meantime, the small posse from Parker County, with Fondren, William Lowe, and a few other settlers, arrived at Parmer's. It was about three in the afternoon according to R. D. "Dan" Richardson, who was one of the wedding guests, when four men rode up and asked "if we wanted an Indian fight." The proposition, Richardson later wrote, "of course we redaly accepted." The Parker County men rode off while the wedding guests hastily tried to get their horses that were grazing in the wheat pasture. The venture took some time, said Richardson, because "you know how it is when one wants to catch his horse quick."

The Parker posse caught up to the Indians as they tried to cross East Keechi Creek, and the Indians, seeing only four pursuers, decided to turn to fight. A brief battle ensued when suddenly the Palo Pinto wedding guests, including Tobe Parmer, John Curry, Price, Lynn, and Richardson, rode in and quickly tipped the scale. They chased the Indians into the timber, where Richardson said, "we was all mixed up together." Two Indians went down with wounds, and the others tried to escape. Richardson and Parmer rode after one. Richardson figured he would shoot the last two loads from his pistol and give up the chase, when the Indian turned and charged as if to give the others time to retreat. Richardson said that suddenly "all the fear & caution left me & I was determined to kill him or die myself." He said his second shot brought him down, but Parmer had dismounted and was also shooting at the charging warrior.

The two approached the warrior, who was only wounded. The Indian was now "in favor of peace," Richardson said, and in broken English, told Richardson "he would not killey me if I would no killey him," because he was a good Waco. As Parmer remembered it, the warrior said, "No shoot, no shoot, Waco Waco."

"Hell was full of such good Wacos," Richardson said, as he put another load in his pistol and shot him again. He was still alive when the other settlers rode up. Richardson told Parmer "to shoot his brains out & this ended the fight."

Richardson scalped him and took his bow and quiver. Another settler rummaged through the dead man's shot pouch and found William Youngblood's scalp. The dead Indian was propped up against a tree on the Palo Pinto-Jacksboro Road and there the body remained a long time until it disintegrated. Pleas Price tore his wedding clothes while chasing through the timber, but was nevertheless married that evening. Richardson and others took Youngblood's scalp back to his father-in-law, William Fondren, at his home in Parker County. They arrived just in time for the funeral. Richardson placed the scalp back on Youngblood's head before they put him in the ground. As a parting gift, Richardson said, "I gave his wife part of the Indian scalp."[3]

Because of such raids the newly organized state troops tried to take the war to the Indians, but generally had little luck. A group called the "Red River Company," seeking to "prevent the red face from satiating his long settled, deadly hate...and committing...daily depredations" moved to Weatherford to join John R. Baylor, who took charge of several companies going to hunt Indians. The informant named "Cloud," didn't particularly care to join Baylor, but since he controlled the provisions, the Red River Company joined Baylor's "outstretched wings." From that point on, "Cloud" found little to recommend. The 250-man expedition left the Belknap area on February 16, went up the Brazos, over to the Wichita, over to the Pease, upstream to its head and then down to the Double Mountain Fork, back to the Clear Fork, and down to Camp Cooper. "Cloud" was not impressed with Baylor and said that "had we been led by a skillful Indian fighter, and an expert woodsman, that we perhaps [would] have met with more success."

Baylor traveled "in no order, and without spies." When they did discover an Indian camp, Baylor charged, but neither took nor caused any casualties. The warriors, "Cloud" said, "managed to rally, and diddle the Col. until the squaws and papooses could escape unharmed, leaving nought to mark their resting place, save three vacant tents, and chattels of no earthly value: this I believe covers our success. So much for the grand Buffalo hunt." "Cloud," holding the minority view, believed that not one-third of the depredations reported were ever committed, and that white men "are sole instigators" of most of the trouble.[4]

Most Texans would beg to differ. Far to the west near Fort Davis, Mescalero Apaches were creating havoc for George H. Giddings and his San Antonio and San Diego Mail Company. About February 12, they attacked a Giddings's train loaded with copper and stole 100 mules. W. B. Knox's train was attacked in the same area, but the Indians were repelled. Mail coaches were held up back at the Pecos until the Indians left. A stage coming east from El Paso was hit, and the driver, named Lyons, and the conductor were both shot.[5]

In south Texas, Lipans were raising hell. In late February 1861, they crossed the Rio Grande in the vicinity of Laredo and headed east across Webb and Duvall counties, attacking spreads along the isolated San Gertrudis Creek as far east as Jim Wells County and causing concern all the way to Corpus Christi. Riding northwest into Frio County about March 8, they hit several ranches along the Leona River. Leonard Eastwood, John Spears, and Julius Sanders had finished breakfast at Eastwood's place and then separated.

Sanders went upriver. Eastwood and Spears went downriver on business and later in the day, ran into the Indians. Leonard Eastwood, who had only been married the previous Sunday, was caught and killed, while Spears took an arrow but escaped. He made it to Levi English's ranch, where the sight of an arrow sticking out of his back made an indelible impression on young Edward English. A Mr. McFarland was also murdered, and then the Lipans continued north into Medina County and killed a Mr. McElemon on the Hondo River. One of the victims was said to have been "lassoed and dragged to the Indian Camp, and then brutally tortured to death." Local settlers along the Leona forted up at English's for two weeks and then most of them left, going to Atascosa County or San Antonio.

The raiders next appeared in Zavala and Uvalde counties, stealing one horse from Mr. Bates, one from L. P. Herd, two from William M. Evans, and one from A. J. Grimes. They went right inside the town limits of Uvalde and took three horses from William H. Pulliam, staked right at his door. The Indians apparently ignored the troopers at Fort Inge, where Lt. William C. Adams could do little with only ten men. Locals speculated that the Lipans raided because of the withdrawal of Federal troops, but most likely the Lipans didn't know they were gone and didn't care about the political leanings of those remaining.[6]

About this time, 16 Lipans, said to be led by a red-headed man, met up with Julius Sanders. Sanders, who lived on the Frio east of Uvalde and had several days earlier eaten breakfast with the now deceased Leonard Eastwood, was catching wild mustangs on the Leona south of Uvalde when the Indians murdered and scalped him and took his big gray horse.

The Lipans left Uvalde and went north on the Nueces River. About March 13, 1861, they attacked Henry M. Robinson and Henry Adams as they traveled between Uvalde and Camp Wood on the Nueces River. The warriors jumped them as they stopped to make coffee under a pecan tree at a landmark called Chalk Bluff. They were dead before they had a chance to use their guns. The warriors then came upon Robinson's house, about seven miles from the scene of the attack. Mrs. Robinson was visiting a nearby neighbor when she saw Indians chasing her children. George W. Robinson (16) got a gun and fought, wounding two Indians before an arrow hit him in the arm. At the Kelsey (Casey) camp, the Indians lanced and scalped a Kelsey girl (14), who miraculously survived after being carried to Fort Inge for medical care. Mrs. Robinson ran to her children and began hurling rocks at the warriors. Perhaps the Indians admired her courage, for they left her unharmed and went to plunder the house. After ransacking the place they took Henry Robinson's picture from the wall, laid it on the ground, and placed one of his socks on it that they had stripped from his body. Weeks later, on June 12, Rangers operating out of Camp Wood found Robinson and Adams's mutilated and scalped bodies—one man's heart was cut out and laid on his chest.

Late in March the same war party was in Kerr County, stealing horses on the Guadalupe River upstream from Kerrville. James Paul took ten Rangers from Camp Verde, met with eight men of the Kerr County "Minute" company, and followed the Indians' trail. The Lipans had probably ended their raid and were heading back toward the Rio Grande, for the tracks turned southwest back into Bandera County. On Monday, April 1, the citizens reached a recently abandoned campsite on the upper Medina River and found four broken down horses and one mule, three saddles, and a variety of abandoned articles. Paul reported, "I am satisfied these Indians were part of the band who killed Messrs. Adams & Robinson." They picked up the fleeing Indians' tracks again and followed them five more miles before reaching a rocky patch where all trace was lost. The raiders made it back to Mexico. A Mexican captain reported seeing a red-headed man riding a gray horse, possibly the one owned by Julius Sanders.[7]

Chapter 12 notes

1 Smith, *Frontier Defense*, 37.

2 Joseph D. Cady, Depredation Claim #650.

3 Winfrey and Day, *Texas Indian Papers, IV*, 455-57; Grace and Jones, *History of Parker County*, 68; Wilbarger, *Indian Depredations*, 521-22; Marshall, *A Cry Unheard*, 115-16; McConnell, *West Texas Frontier*, 360.

4 *The Standard* (Clarksville), March 30, 1861.

5 *The Daily Ledger and Texan* (San Antonio), February 25, 1861.

6 Sowell, *Early Settlers*, 567; *Galveston Weekly News*, March 19, 1861; *The Daily Ledger and Texan* (San Antonio), April 2, 1861.

7 Wilbarger, *Indian Depredations*, 654-55; Sowell, *Early Settlers*, 787; McConnell, *West Texas Frontier*, 358; Galloway, *Dark Corner of the Confederacy*, 104; *The Daily Ledger and Texan* (San Antonio), April 15, 1861. The dates for this raid range from 1860 to May 1861, with most of the particulars slightly different. This reconstruction is the most logical geographically and chronologically.

13 "They are afflicted with the disease known here as the 'Indian Grab.'"

As was the case in many instances, the civilians bore the brunt of the action, but the soldiers did get their chances. Typical frontier operations of the state troops are illustrated in the experience of Capt. James B. "Buck" Barry's Company C, 1st Texas Mounted Rifles. Barry organized his company in March 1861, and was based at Camp Cooper on the Clear Fork Brazos. They alternated instruction, drill, and on-the-job-training, as Barry conducted four scouts in April without encountering any Indians. The first fatality came not from a battle, but when Pvt. Benjamin F. Fuller drowned in the Clear Fork on May 2. They found no Indians, but the Indians found them, when about 200 Comanches appeared on a hilltop about one mile north of camp, enough, said Pvt. Frank Wristen, "to afford more military glory than we had bargained for."[1]

The Comanches were not sure of the size of the Texan force below them. Barry got all his stock into the corral, formed a defensive perimeter and waited. They stayed on guard all night but the Indians did not molest them, likely leaving to seek an easier target.

Raiding parties rarely stayed in a compact body. This one broke into smaller parties and fanned out. In mid-May, some were in southwestern Palo Pinto County near Strawn, where they stole a few horses from S. B. Strawn. William M. Allen, whose place was the first hit in the big raid of February 1860, was visited again while camped on Palo Pinto Creek two miles west of Strawn as he drove a small herd of cattle. Comanches cut the hobbles of four of his horses while Allen and others slept. Next morning they trailed the Indians a few miles but could not overtake them.

On the night of May 14, a raiding party entered the town of Palo Pinto and stole 17 horses, hobbled or picketed close to several houses. N. H. McLain was up early, discovered his horses were gone and saw moccasin tracks all around. He roused his neighbors and followed the trail 20 miles, coming upon a Ranger camp under Jack Cureton. They joined together and gained on the thieves when Cureton saw signs that the horses had splashed across a small creek and wet bushes and grass pointing in the direction the Indians had taken.

"Boys," Cureton said, "the infernal rascals are close by—look to your arms and be ready for a chase; by grit, I'll have those horses!" Within half a mile they found the Indians making camp and took them by total surprise. They hopped on horses and fled, but Cureton chased them and succeeded in killing one. As the Texans scalped the dead warrior they found another scalp in his possession, supposedly to be that of a "Mr. Phillips, lately killed near Weatherford." They did recover almost all of the stolen horses.[2]

One of these raiding bands attacked Thomas Killen and William Washington in Parker County. Both were about 24 years old and resided on Grindstone Creek west of Weatherford. Along with a man named Sowell, they were looking for loose stock on Poe Prairie north of Millsap when the Comanches caught them. Killen and Washington received serious wounds, but all three got away. Killen, however, died about six weeks later.[3]

The raiders went south to the Comanche-Hamilton County lines. J. C. Deaton and Nat Tatum lived along Waring Creek where, at sunset on May 20, 1861, the raiders crept into the area intent upon stealing horses. Deaton and his wife were at the cow pen when Deaton heard some peculiar "birds" calling. He told his wife to get the baby inside, and once in the house he checked his weapons and asked his wife to mould some more bullets. Deaton had hobbled his horses near the house and in the twilight saw the Indians creeping in. Several shots drove them back, but they shot his dog before they left.

"It was a dreadful night for me and mine," Deaton said. About two in the morning the Indians went a mile to Tatum's cabin and stole his horses. Deaton rode there at sunup and told Tatum what happened before he was even aware that 40 of his horses were gone. They both moved their families to a neighbor's house and formed a posse to hunt the thieves. The trail went northwest but all they found were the remains of horses that the Indians had ridden to death.[4]

Late in May the raiders were in Lampasas and San Saba counties, stealing horses and killing anyone who got in the way. About May 25, 1861, on the San Saba River they murdered Allen Goans and wounded Burrell Nators. On June 5, Indians were still in the area. Levi and Polly Harkey had a place about four miles north of the town of San Saba, when thieves came right up to the house and cut loose five hobbled horses worth $450. Levi, his brother Riley, I. C. McDaniel, and a few other neighbors rode after the raiders. On the trail the pursuers found one of Harkey's colts badly injured from a lance thrust, and a dead calf that the Indians had stolen from another farm. They took one pony that the Indians had abandoned.

In their need to strike hard and ride fast, most Indian raiders drove their horses to and beyond the breaking point. When a pony broke down from exhaustion, they would either kill it or leave it behind, switching to a fresher, recently stolen mount. White pursuers commented many times on the horrible condition of "dropped" Indian ponies. Comanches split the ears of their ponies as a mark of ownership, but when whites found an abandoned one they could immediately tell if it was a Comanche pony even if the ears were not split. Said Riley Harkey, "You could tell a horse the Indians had been riding from the fact that he had a fearful back on him; they hurt the back of everything they rode." The Harkeys did not catch the raiders.

Writing from Lampasas County on June 1, "T.P" complained that the recent raids had left him and his neighbors nearly all afoot. "The range is splendid;" he wrote, "stock of every description are doing finely, excepting horses. They are afflicted with the disease known here as the 'Indian Grab,' which prevails to an alarming extent in this portion of the 'Lord's' vineyard." The correspondent continued, "We hear nothing of McCulloch and his Rangers; they are much needed on the frontier just now. The Minute Company system adopted by the Legislature is a miserable substitute for frontier protection; it has proved a positive failure."[5]

While the Indians slashed through the Texas Hill Country, McCulloch's troopers seemed ineffectual. Captain Barry and Company C did not have their first fight until July 26, 1861. McCulloch ordered Barry to send an escort for a band of Tonkawa Indians and a supply wagon going to Red River Station and Barry selected Cpl. Thomas J. Ercanbrack and ten men. The outward trip was uneventful, but on the return Ercanbrack got eight miles south of Willow Springs, a station halfway between Camp Cooper and Red River, when about 50 Indians attacked. Ercanbrack was caught on the open prairie and the warriors divided on two sides, as if to keep them from going back to Willow Springs or forward to Camp Cooper. Ercanbrack chose to push forward since there was a small camp of soldiers on Fish Creek about 15 miles south and the terrain was better for defense. Private Wristen said, "As the men would charge upon the line in front of them the Indians would disperse, form a new line and confront the men at another point." Ercanbrack charged through the Indians a dozen times in ten miles.

Three men were badly wounded and could barely stay in the saddle. When Pvt. James McKee took an arrow in the back and fell from his horse, Ercanbrack hopped from his horse to pick him up, but his mount broke free and ran. With four wounded, Ercanbrack sent one man ahead for help while the rest of them made their stand. The horse ran right to the Fish Creek camp where seven soldiers caught it, saw the mailbags shredded by arrows, and quickly divined what had happened. The sergeant in charge sent one man to Camp Cooper and with the remaining five, headed north, meeting Ercanbrack's messenger on the way.

Regardless of the odds, they rode back to the little knot of soldiers fighting for their lives. Either the warriors were out of ammunition and arrows, or believed the relief force was larger than it was, because they fled. Four of Ercanbrack's horses were dead and four men were seriously wounded, but they doubled up on the remaining horses and made it to Fish Creek. At nightfall, two men went to Camp Cooper for a surgeon. Next morning the doctor and a 25-man relief force arrived, but Private McKee died overnight.

Back at Camp Cooper, Captain Barry reported that seven men were wounded and one was killed, while only two warriors were killed. He said that the Indians had "Minnie and Sharp's rifles," and were better armed than his men were—an assessment different from Pike's, who believed that not one Indian in ten owned a gun.[6]

Barry took his company after the raiders. On July 29, in the vicinity of where Ercanbrack had his fight, Barry and 32 troopers were strung out on the trail when about 70 Kiowas and Comanches struck the pack mules following in the rear. In a flash they killed three men: Pvts. "Tips" Connelly, Thomas Weatherby, and "Bud" Lynn (Lane). Barry raced back and caught the Indians before they could escape, shooting one old warrior from his horse. Corporal Ercanbrack and Pvt. C. K. Hackworth stopped, and while Hackworth held their horses, Ercanbrack got out his knife and knelt by the warrior.

"I watched him take off his topknot," Hackworth said. He also had a bone whistle in his hair and a beautiful beaded necklace. Barry later got them as souvenirs. They chased the Indians for nearly 15 miles, shooting about a dozen, but having seven troopers wounded in the process. Late in the day they returned to the scene of the initial attack and dug one big grave with their butcher knives to bury the bodies of the three dead soldiers.[7]

Lieutenant Colonel Thomas C. Frost took a large contingent of 1st Mounted Rifles on a scout up Pease River in late July, but all they did was wear out their horses. In early August the Indians noticed Frost's weary mounts and attacked. Frost killed two warriors, but Capt. Green Davidson and Private Carter were also killed in the clash. Frost tried to pursue, but the Indians led him onto an open prairie and turned to fight. Frost noticed he was outnumbered, pulled up, buried his dead, and backtracked to camp. Learning of the affair, McCulloch wrote, "this cannot be regarded as one of those brilliant achievements" that his Rangers could usually boast of.[8]

Despite the efforts of the soldiers, Indians continued to slip past the outposts. In the summer of 1861, young Samuel Kuykendall and another young man named Splann (Strawn) left their homes along Resley Creek near the Erath-Comanche County lines searching for stray cattle. They went down into Hamilton County, found many of them on Honey Creek, and were returning home when the Indians struck. Despite living in dangerous territory, only Splann carried a gun. He got off his mule, used it as a barrier, and waved his weapon at the charging Indians. The warriors made the safe choice and went after Kuykendall, who tried to outrun them on his horse. Sam unfortunately ran his mount into a bog at the present-day location of Carlton and was mired down; the Indians easily caught up, filled him with arrows, stripped and scalped him. Splann escaped.[9]

The 1st Mounted Rifles continued to hunt for marauders, but had no luck until November 1. Captain Barry marched 25 of his company up the Clear

Fork Brazos to its headwaters where they collided with about 60 Comanches. As before, the Indians hit the pack mules and cut them to pieces, destroying most of Barry's supplies. Barry chased the Indians north and ran into their recently abandoned village, where in turn, he destroyed their equipage and spent the night feasting on the Indians' buffalo meat. The next morning Barry continued the chase and soon ran into more Indians who were likely returning to see what had happened to their camp. Barry pursued in a running battle for several miles, and then went into the bluffs at the edge of the Staked Plains. In the confusion, six troopers engaged about 20 warriors in a hand-to-hand fight, with six-shooters ringing, according to C. K. Hackworth, "like a hot skillet full of popcorn."

In the end, the troopers prevailed. Pvt. John Hardigree was shot in the arm and Pvt. Frank Wristen was shot in the neck with an arrow, but Barry reported that they wounded several warriors and counted ten bodies of "good Indians" after the fight. Colonel McCulloch called it the regiment's "first decided victory."[10]

Chapter 13 notes

1 Adkins-Rochette, *Bourland in North Texas II*, A-221; Greer, ed., *Buck Barry*, 134.
2 William M. Allen, Depredation Claim #4605; *Galveston Weekly News*, June 11, 1861.
3 Adkins-Rochette, *Bourland in North Texas II*, A-205; Grace and Jones, *History of Parker County*, 68; Smythe, *Historical Sketch of Parker County*, 145.
4 Deaton, *Indian Fights on the Texas Frontier*, 127-29.
5 Polly Harkey, Depredation Claim #5251; *Galveston Weekly News*, June 18, 1861.
6 Greer, ed., *Buck Barry*, 133-36.
7 Greer, ed., *Buck Barry*, 137-39.
8 Smith, *Frontier Defense*, 38; McConnell, *West Texas Frontier*, 364.
9 Wilbarger, *Indian Depredations*, 501-02; Deaton, *Indian Fights on the Texas Frontier*, 118-19.
10 Smith, *Frontier Defense*, 38-39; Greer, ed., *Buck Barry*, 137-39, 141-42; *WR:* S.1, V.4, 35.

14 "One of the most daring and extensive raids ever known"

Such minor victories were few, and they didn't stop Indian incursions. After a brief occupation of Forts Cobb, Arbuckle, and Washita, the Confederacy's need for manpower drew the Texas State troops to other theaters. By the fall of 1861, the posts were virtually abandoned, with a token presence remaining at the Washita Agency near Fort Cobb to administer to the ex-Texas tribes. These Indians were still a concern. Colonel William C. Young wrote to Confederate Secretary of War Judah P. Benjamin on November 3, that nearly 3,000 Indians were being administered there, Indians who "are susceptible of being made the most disagreeable and destructive enemies to our northwestern frontier…and are unable to protect themselves against the depredations of the combined Comanches and Kiowas."

Young thought the forts should be re-occupied to protect the Indians and prevent them "from being trifled with by the Federals." The war had denuded the frontier of able-bodied men, Young wrote, and "There is a very considerable dread amongst our people on Red River on this account, as it might be justly said that we are now without any power intervening between Texas and the Creek Nation, and none between us and the wild Comanches except the reserve Indians, who will stampede at the first approach of the enemy."[1]

Young's warning of trouble at the agency would prove prophetic. While he called for help, and while McCulloch patrolled in the north, Colonel John Ford and his 2nd Texas Mounted Rifles tried to keep watch on the southern border. Down in Webb County near Laredo, Lipan Apaches were generally the culprits, sneaking across the Rio Grande to raid as far north and east as San Antonio, and driving their stolen stock back to Mexico. One settler who reported a depredation was Ross Kennedy, when Lipans got four of his horses worth $400 in September 1861.[2]

South of the Nueces River, settlers sometimes blamed Lipans when the marauders could be Mexican bandits, possibly men following leaders such as Juan Cortina, considered a revolutionary and bandit by many whites, and a freedom fighter by most Mexicans. Throughout much of the 1850s, Cortina had rustled cattle on both sides of the river and had many brushes with the law. In July 1859, when Brownsville Marshal Robert Shears arrested one of Cortina's men, Cortina rode into town, shot and wounded Shears and took the prisoner back to Mexico.

In September, Cortina raided Brownsville and freed more than 40 men from jail. From then on, American soldiers and civilians battled Cortina and

THE "BIG RAID" OF OCTOBER, 1861

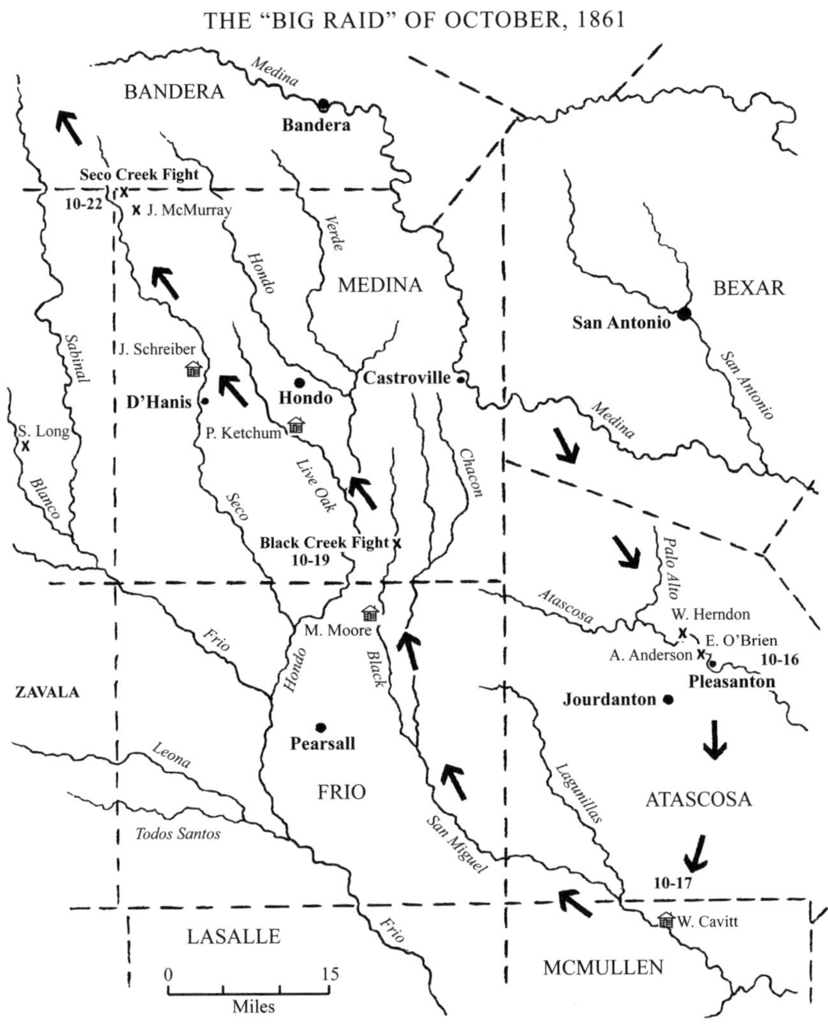

his "freedom fighters." When John Ford and his Rangers defeated Cortina in February 1860, Cortina ceased operations in the area for a year. In May 1861, he was back, invading Texas at Carrizo and Roma. Unsuccessful in his incursions, Cortina concentrated on cattle rustling, and in 1864 declared himself governor of Tamaulipas, making deals with both Union and Confederate forces.[3]

In the early 1860s, Colonel Ford was much too occupied with Cortina and problems on the lower Rio Grande to send his men chasing Lipans. Colonel Van Dorn, however, had another job for Ford. Concerned with Union troops advancing south in New Mexico Territory and buoyed by visions of a sympathetic populace and easy pickings, Van Dorn assigned Ford the tasks of patrolling the Rio Grande and securing New Mexico. How Van Dorn or Confederate officials could believe that the New Mexicans would be well-disposed to a Texan occupation is incomprehensible. Ford, nearly overwhelmed trying to control the lower river, ordered his second in command, Lt. Col. John R. Baylor, to direct affairs on the upper river.

It was just the thing Baylor needed. Dismissed as Indian agent and having a hand in closing down the Texas reservations, he ranched for a time and then dabbled unsuccessfully in state politics. The Civil War gave him a new career. Now, as lieutenant colonel of the 2nd Texas Mounted Rifles, his assignment to secure New Mexico was a grand opportunity to restore his reputation and gain military glory. By mid-June, he was on his way with Companies A, B, D, E, and an artillery battery, and by July 1, he had secured Fort Bliss in west Texas. By August, Baylor had taken possession of the southern quarter of New Mexico Territory. With only 350 men of his 2nd Texas he took Fort Fillmore on the Rio Grande, declared martial law, proclaimed establishment of the Territory of Arizona under the Confederate States of America, named Mesilla as its capital, himself as governor, and waited for help.[4]

Baylor felt cut off. There were nearly 600 miles of road between him and San Antonio. In January, Comanches destroyed Howard's Well Station and attacked Pecos Station. From March through May, Apaches destroyed several stages and killed passengers across southern New Mexico and Texas; thirty civilians were dead, six coaches destroyed, and 146 horses and mules stolen. In June, Indians destroyed Eagle Springs Station.

Baylor was frustrated by the frequent attacks on his communications line. The mails were robbed, he said, and "in one or two instances the passengers were found hanging up by the heels, their heads within a few inches of a slow fire, and thus horribly roasted to death." Baylor wrote to Van Dorn requesting assistance, "as I can't hold the United States troops in check and operate against the Indians with the limited number of men under my command."[5]

It never was safe on the Upper and Lower Military Roads from San Antonio to El Paso, nor in the surrounding countryside. Depredations were frequent, but it was not often that the soldiers could catch up with the raiders. On October 11, 1861, Sgt. W. Barrett and 17 men of Company A, 2nd Texas Mounted Rifles, left Fort Inge in pursuit of a band of Lipan Apaches that hit the settlements to the east. Following leads from civilians, they went between the Nueces and Leona Rivers before discovering a fresh trail heading south toward old Fort Ewell. On the third night, four mules and ponies came into their camp with arrows sticking in them.

Barrett followed the tracks the next morning heading west toward the Rio Grande, however, an incessant rain obliterated much of the trail. They went up what Barrett called "Baresite Creek" (probably El Barrosa Creek) near today's Carrizo Springs, getting bogged in the muck and soaking themselves and their ammunition. When they attempted to camp in a small clearing that evening, the Lipan Apaches struck. The Texans tried to shoot, but with their wet firing caps, Barrett said, "not one in a half dozen would go off."

The men who could not fire made a saber charge and there was a hand-to-hand fight in the gloomy thicket. After a half hour of confused battle, Barrett thought the Indians were receiving reinforcements, and he called a retreat. They quickly mounted up and headed back for Fort Inge. Barrett thought they had killed ten Indians, but three of his own men were killed and one was wounded. The bodies were abandoned. At the fort, Lt. John Bradley deplored the loss of "three such good soldiers" and his inability to go back to recover the bodies because of a shortage of officers and men.[6]

Despite Bradley's lamentations about losing good soldiers, army losses rarely equaled civilian losses. The raiders that Sergeant Barrett chased were in the area at the same time, but were not part of a large war party of Comanches that had swept in all the way to the south of San Antonio. Like Peta Nocona's raid in the fall of 1860, the fall incursion of 1861 was what one contemporary called "one of the most daring and extensive raids ever known" in the area.

About October 16, Comanches appeared unexpectedly far south in Atascosa County on the outskirts of Pleasanton. Eli O'Brien had gone out to hunt stock unarmed and had been warned by a neighbor, William Dillard, to take a weapon. O'Brien replied, "There are no Indians in the country." Two miles from town Comanches rode at him from a copse of blackjack and post oak. O'Brien saw them under the trees and some of them were wearing hats and pants. He thought they were cowmen, and when they charged out yelling, he believed they were playing a trick on him.

"No use boys; you can't scare me," O'Brien shouted. In a few seconds he saw they were Indians and he spurred his horse toward town as fast as it would run. Three arrows hit O'Brien in the back and a warrior caught up alongside. As he readied to apply the *coup de grace*, O'Brien, in desperation, slashed out with his butcher knife. The warrior just caught the thrust with his shield and dropped back. In front of O'Brien was a ten-foot ditch, but he ran his horse directly at it and leapt, clearing it with a few feet to spare. The warriors stopped at the ditch. When O'Brien rode past Dillard's house he was reeling from his wounds, but still riding hard. Dillard saw him go past and called out, "What's your hurry, O'Brien? There are no Indians in the country."

Nearby, Napoleon Tucker and William Herndon were setting out on a cow hunt. Herndon took his pistol and said, as Tucker recalled, "that it had but three loads in it, but he had seen no Indians yet, and supposed he would not this time."

As he mounted his pony his wife called to him that he better load it fully, but Herndon ignored her. In open blackjack country about three miles from town they saw people appearing to be hunting cows in some trees ahead. Tucker wondered who they were, but Herndon said, "Them are Indians, and we have got to run for it." Both men turned and sped off as fast as they could with the Comanches right behind. Tucker, on a splendid horse, could have easily outdistanced the Indians, but Herndon with his little cow pony was doomed. "Go," Herndon called to Tucker, "carry the news to town; it is no use for both of us to be killed." Tucker looked back and saw Herndon fire his three shots before the Indians overwhelmed and killed him.[7]

A number of townspeople hurriedly got their guns and horses to see if they could recover Herndon's body. As they rode out a mile from town they saw what appeared to be two men on horseback racing toward them. The nearest one was Alexander Anderson. A posse member raised his rifle to fire at the second man, but was restrained, for the second rider also appeared to be a white man. Seconds later, the trailer raised his bow and shot an arrow into Anderson's back; he was a Comanche wearing Herndon's clothes. The horse carried Anderson to the posse, who helped him back to town. The arrow, however, was deep in his back, and when a doctor tried to extract it the sinews had already softened enough that the shaft slipped off, leaving the head deeply embedded. Anderson lingered for nearly a year before succumbing to an infection.

The warriors stole more horses, killed one of Marcellus French's black slaves and captured a black child, and then moved south out of the area. On San Miguel Creek in McMullen County the raiders hit W. A. Cavitt's place, stealing two horses. The Comanches then curled upstream and continued their killing spree when they murdered "Mustang" Moore on Black Creek near present-day Moore, Texas, in northeast Frio County.

On the upper San Miguel on October 19, settlers James M. Winters, Thomas Speed, T. L. Ward, James Bishop, James Craig, W. W. Davidson, and N. Kennard, gathered to block the raiders. They found the Indians' trail crossing the divide between Siestedero Creek and San Miguel Creek near the Frio-Medina County lines. They rode hard to the west, crossing the San

Miguel and over the divide to Black Creek. Davidson's horse gave out, leaving six of them, and they were getting strung out. Speed called out that they should stay together. They discovered the Comanches in a blackjack thicket on the banks of Black Creek and it looked like they were outnumbered four to one.

Winters wanted to charge, but the others demurred. When the warriors appeared to run, Winters took the bait and rode after them when they turned and surrounded him. The other posse members could see him firing, get unhorsed, and continue to fight on foot. The Indians took position in some live oaks and the posse saw them stab the black child they had captured. Ward, Winters' brother-in-law, could take it no more and rode out to help. Speed, on a slower mule, finally rode up and saw "our boys in a state of confusion and disorder. Mr. Winters was down on one knee and surrounded by Indians." He called to Ward, "Come to me," and Ward fought his way in to about 30 paces from Winters, only to find him lying motionless on the ground. Ward fired until his bullets were gone and turned to escape, but he received an arrow in the back.

Speed rushed in to help, firing his double-barrel shotgun. A warrior shot his mule and when Speed turned around, he got an arrow in the back. He saw the others fleeing, Craig and Bishop mounted, and Ward and Kennard on foot. Kennard was shot in the shoulder. They got into a clump of trees about 200 yards away and assessed the situation. They had but one shotgun, two rifles, and a pistol, all empty. It looked like they were dead men, but the Comanches didn't press the attack. They gathered what looked to be about 200 horses and rode away. The posse retreated to town and got Ward to a doctor. The arrowhead had lodged under a bone and the doctor pulled so hard he lifted Ward's body off the bed before the iron point pulled loose. Ward survived.[8]

The raiders moved north into Medina County and near Hondo Creek they stole more horses and killed Peter Ketchum. When settlers found his body his nose was cut off, beard skinned, and his face so disfigured that only one man could recognize him. Some of the war party went west to Blanco Creek in Uvalde County, where they killed Sam Long while he was out herding cattle. They also caught his sister as she rode home from a neighbor's house. Warriors grabbed her by the hair and yanked her from the horse, lanced, scalped her, and left her for dead. She recovered, however, and later married William "Seco" Smith.[9]

In other incidents that may have been part of the same raid, John Schreiber (61), who lived near D'Hanis in Medina County, went out to hunt his oxen. Later in the day his mule came back alone with an arrow sticking in it. Searchers went out to look for Schreiber, and soon found his body, lanced and scalped. Mr. Schalkhausen (60), the town's schoolteacher, was asked to hold an inquest. He rode alone to where the settlers had found Schreiber, but never arrived. The settlers then searched for Schalkhausen for six hours, but it seemed that the earth had swallowed him up. It was assumed that he had been killed or carried off by the same Indians who had recently killed Schreiber.[10]

As the raiders swept through the Hondo settlements, more settlers gathered to try to put a stop to them. Residing in the area was legendary frontiersman, Ranger, and stage driver, William A. "Bigfoot" Wallace, said to be a descendent of the Scottish rebel leader William Wallace. At six-feet two inches tall and 240 pounds, Wallace supposedly got his nickname while a prisoner of the Mexicans during the 1842 Mier Expedition when his captors could find no shoes large enough to fit his feet.

A born leader, Wallace quickly rounded up men to pursue the raiders, while Ross Kennedy recruited some from the D'Hanis area. On October 21, the posse moved out. Wallace was elected captain of about 30 men, including Lewis McCombs, Nathan Davis, Fountain Tinsley, John Redus, Monroe Watkins, John Watkins, A. J. Davenport, William Davenport, George Robins, Louis Oge, John Vinton, Malcolm Van Pelt, Frank Hillburn, Jasper Kincheloe, and Chris Kelley. They followed a very large trail up Seco Creek. The Indians knew they were coming and set up an ambush for them on a rock and cedar studded mountain high up the valley.

Wallace found a cross trail and deduced that someone had been chased. He was correct. A short time earlier, John T. McMurray, whose arm was crippled by an accidental shotgun blast, was elected the tax assessor of Bandera County. He was riding west to work in the upper Sabinal settlements and had spent one night on the Seco. The next day he met two men coming from the Frio to the mill in Bandera. They asked him to join them for supper, but he said he was in a hurry. A mile down the road he ran into the Indians. McMurray tried to ride for the men who were eating supper, but the Indians filled him with bullets and arrows, stripped him, and took his pistol. The two men heard the firing and fled. When word reached Bandera, several men found and buried the body in a draw since known as Dead Man Hollow, in the far northwest corner of Medina County.[11]

Just ahead of where Wallace crossed McMurray's trail, the Comanches had tied a horse to a tree in plain view of anyone coming up the creek. Judge A. J. Davenport saw it and called out, "To first sight belongs the property," and rode up after it, while Wallace warned, "Look out, boys; that is a trick of the Indians."

As the company warily approached, the Indians opened fire and William Davenport, the judge's son, was among the first hit, as were Lewis McCombs and Nathan Davis. As they fell back, an Indian popped out and discharged a shotgun at Van Pelt, narrowly missing him. Wallace had them dismount and sent squads around the right and left flanks to work their way up the rocky mountainside. The warriors were near the top, protected by large boulders and cedar trees, and the settlers inched their way up, firing between rocks and around trees in a deadly game of hide and seek. Wallace could get his men no closer than 40 yards from the top, where a series of rocky ledges protected them, but held them back because they could not climb up and over the exposed upper surfaces.

They blasted away at each other for an hour. Lower down, Fountain Tinsley took position behind a cedar tree where he dueled with a warrior wearing the clothing of a slain white man. They took turns shooting at each other at about 200 yards range, but Tinsley figured that his cut-off, old weapon would not carry far enough. He poured two powder charges into it, loaded and capped it, and waited until the warrior next exposed himself to shoot. When he next appeared, Tinsley aimed high on his white shirt and fired, knocking the warrior down, while the breech of Tinsley's rifle exploded and flew backwards.

Similar duels went on up and down the mountain. Van Pelt got one warrior in his sights when Hillburn killed him firing from another direction. George Robins had a shotgun duel with an Indian wearing a hat. Robins blasted him once, but the Indian caught most of the load with his shield, then dropped his gun and ran. Robins went up to get the weapon and found it belonged to "Mustang" Moore, who had been killed earlier in the raid. Kennedy, with a long-range Enfield rifle, fired at an Indian who sat far back on the mountaintop on a black mule. His bullet smacked into the mule, sending the warrior into hiding. One Indian mocked them by waving a U. S. flag, an act guaranteed to anger his adversaries be they Yanks or Rebs.

Eventually the Indians realized they could not defeat the determined white men and as they were likely running out of ammunition, they snaked down the back side of the mountain. Wallace's men warily ascended, finding several dead warriors along with McMurray's pistol. Wallace went back to his horses and circled around, picking up the Indian trail once again. They appeared to be heading northwest, but Wallace decided to cross the divide to the Sabinal and then head up that river to get ahead of them. The weather turned cold, with rain turning to sleet, and most of the men did not have warm clothing. Nevertheless, another day's marching brought them to a place called Ranger Springs, where Wallace set up an ambush for the Indians who moved more slowly while driving so many horses. As the Indians came in view, Frank Hillburn couldn't resist shooting at one of them before they all moved fully into the trap. He wounded his man, but the warriors quickly turned and escaped. The charging settlers rounded up about 140 of the stolen horses. With that, the tired, wet, and freezing men called it quits and scattered back to their homes.[12]

At least ten settlers were killed and eight wounded (one contemporary said 14 were killed) during the "Big Raid" of 1861, but it was not the only one that month. At the same time Comanches were in the south, others were in the Hill Country where they ran into a civilian scouting company on the headwaters of the Lampasas River on the Mills-Hamilton County lines. On October 19, 1861, the day after a full moon, Lt. Robert Carter and ten men, including John Witcher, A. W. Witcher, F. Grundy Morris, John Hurst, Joe Manning, Simpson Lloyd, James Mitchell, and J. R. Townsend, were returning to Hamilton after a ten-day scout. Being out of meat, John Witcher went ahead to the next selected campsite to try to shoot a deer or two to have ready for the company when it pulled in later. Witcher had been out a few hours when Carter reached the campsite, but Witcher was not there. Grundy Morris went out to see if he could find him. He climbed Lookout Mountain, about ten miles northeast of present-day Goldthwaite in Mills County, and he saw Indians chasing a man about two miles from his vantage point. Morris went to Carter and reported, and the scouts hurried forward.

Witcher realized he was not going to outrun the Indians so he jumped off his horse near a heavy thicket, leaving it for the Indians, and he plunged into the tangled growth and scrambled away. He figured he was about 25 miles southwest of Hamilton and if he walked all night he could make it by daylight. After what he thought was 20 miles of walking through brambles and open prairie, he found himself on Cowhouse Creek, but not in the right line of travel. Adjusting course, he set out again, only to hit the creek once more about ten miles downstream. A further adjustment brought Witcher to town, just as the sun was rising. He walked more than 35 miles, but he was safe.

Citizens of Hamilton rode out to see what had become of Carter. Carter's scouts were about a mile behind Witcher when he took to the bush. Minutes later they ran into about 22 Comanches who were probably as surprised as they were. It was almost dark, and whites and Indians clashed in a bloody melee on an individual basis. Somehow the adversaries separated themselves on opposite sides of a draw and Carter ordered a charge, which brought them all together in a hand-to-hand fight. They clashed for a while until complete darkness brought a halt to the battle. The Indians, calling and signaling among themselves in the night, filtered back through the trees, and Carter's party held the ground. Grundy Morris and John Hurst were severely wounded and others had lesser wounds, but where was Carter? A. W. Witcher and Townsend crawled around the battleground in an unsuccessful attempt to find their lieutenant.

The next morning with no better luck, the party continued on to Hamilton, meeting citizens who responded to John Witcher's alarm. The fight was on a

Saturday, but Carter wasn't found until Monday, dead, pierced with a dozen bullets and arrows.[13]

Most of the men in Carter's company, like those in Bigfoot Wallace's company, likely hoped that their efforts and sacrifices would eventually stop the raiding, but realistically they probably knew the Indians would return at the next full moon. They may have thought about their own precarious existence and speculated if someday they would be surprised and killed like scores of their friends and neighbors. Had anyone been keeping track, they might have noted a disturbing trend: the non-combatants were at the forefront of the fighting and more were being killed than the soldiers who were supposed to protect them.[14]

The *New York Times* tried to keep its readers informed of the situation with a history lesson. During the early emigration to California, it stated, emigrants rushed across the country over one or two roads and there were few Indian depredations. "But later, when civilization attempted to make a stand" by settling in Indian country, and many more wagons coursed their "weary way over a variety of routes, the wild Indian commenced his systematic course of plunder and butchery." The *Times* believed that the number of white settlers and emigrants killed by Indians on the frontier averaged 1,000 per year, "a fearful estimate," it acknowledged, but likely accurate. The government was supposed to protect the people on the frontier, yet the *Times* said that the Indian Bureau and War Office constantly report "in language of ease and content," while "congratulating the country on the peculiarly happy manner in which the business in their particular charge is managed, but which, in fact, is so woefully mismanaged as to be a disgrace to a civilized nation, to which the dying shrieks and groans, and the bleaching bones of thousands and thousands of our murdered pioneers can testify."[15]

Chapter 14 notes

1 *WR:* S.1, V.4, 145.
2 Ross Kennedy, Depredation Claim #4233.
3 Webb, *Handbook of Texas I*, 417-18.
4 Frazier, *Blood & Treasure*, 40-41, 43, 61; Ford, *Rip Ford's Texas*, 324; Colton, *Civil War in the Western Territories*, 14-16.
5 Austerman, *Sharps Rifles*, 183, 319-20; *WR:* S.1, V.15, 916; *WR:* S.1, V.4, 26.
6 *WR:* S.1, V.4, 33-34.
7 Sowell, *Early Settlers*, 252-55; Sowell, *Rangers and Pioneers*, 94-95.
8 W. A. Cavitt, Depredation Claim #2765; Sowell, *Early Settlers*, 220, 253, 498-501; San Antonio *Herald*, November 2, 1861.
9 Sowell, *Early Settlers*, 220, 224, 479, 596-97.
10 McConnell, *West Texas Frontier*, 553; Sowell, *Early Settlers*, 275-77. McConnell places this incident in 1866.
11 Sowell, *Early Settlers*, 108-09, 225, 661; Hunter, *Bandera County*, 24-25.
12 Sowell, *Early Settlers*, 108-09, 224-25, 306-07, 660-61; Sowell, *Rangers and Pioneers*, 88-91; Austerman, *Sharps Rifles*, 184.
13 McConnell, *West Texas Frontier*, 363; Wilbarger, *Depredations*, 478-80.
14 About twice as many settlers were killed and wounded in the October 1861 raid than in the famous Elm Creek Raid of October 1864, which has often been called the most destructive raid of the war.
15 *New York Times*, July 3, 1861.

15 "The soldiers did their best, but the Indians generally outwitted them."

After nearly one year of a "vacuum" created by the removal of Federal troops in the West, the predicted inundation of Indian attacks was not borne out. Government officials in the north and south were very concerned. U. S. Interior Department Secretary Caleb Smith decried the removal, divining that it opened the door for Rebels to instigate the Indians to hostility. There was more instability, but the contention that there was more fighting with Indians on the western frontier during the Civil War is in need of a *caveat*. Some histories maintain that there were more Indian raids on civilians and more battles between the army and Indians because the troops were gone. The Indians, so the story goes, were suddenly free of restraints and ran amok.[1]

This idea remains popular, but it is not accurate. Troop strength in the west actually increased during the Civil War. Commanders naturally wanted more troops. Major General Henry W. Halleck encapsulated the situation when he wrote to Brig. Gen. James H. Carleton on September 8, 1863, regarding Carleton's request for help. Said Halleck: "The number of troops now stationed in the frontier departments and Territories is much larger than in time of peace… no extraordinary circumstances are known which require additional troops."[2]

Numbers illustrate the increase. Between the Mexican and Civil War, there were three mounted regiments to patrol the west: the 1st and 2nd Dragoons and the Mounted Rifles. In 1855, the 1st and 2nd U.S. Cavalry were formed. In 1853, the entire Army, counting mounted, infantry, and artillery regiments, totaled only 10,417 men of all ranks. In the decade before the Civil War there may have been only 5,000 effectives available to fight Indians. Contrast that with the numbers available to fight Indians during the Civil War: in the central plains, numbers fluctuated between 2,500 and 3,500; in the northern plains, including Minnesota, numbers ranged from 4,500 to 5,000; in the southwest, numbers were between 2,500 and 4,000; and in the Great Basin to the Pacific Coast, numbers ranged between 5,000 and 6,000. Another source indicates that there were 20,000 volunteers available to fight in the west.[3]

Averaging those numbers, there were between 16,500 to 20,000 men available to fight Indians during the Civil War—three to four times the numbers available in the previous decade. Why then, do we read about the frontier being ravaged by Indians during the Civil War because all the regular troops were withdrawn? First, a story tends to gain credence by repetition. Second, at initial glance it seems reasonable that if troops were withdrawn, the Indians, having fewer restraints, would do more fighting. The logic is reminiscent of a non sequitur attributed to the Yankee sage, Yogi Berra, giving advice not to eat at a certain restaurant because it was so crowded that no one went there anymore. With the soldiers gone, how would the Indians fight with them? Conversely, the very presence of soldiers was tinder for conflict, but not the sole cause.

After the 1861 downturn, the number of battles increased steadily because more volunteer soldiers, some with personal grudges against the Indians, became available to do battle. In 1865 after the war there was another downturn in battles, analogous to 1861, but this time because the volunteers went home and the Regulars had not yet arrived. Fighting then increased again through the end of the decade, when the highest numbers ever recorded were established. During the Civil War there were more troops and there were more battles.[4]

Conditions varied locally. In Texas, the standard story is that there were less troops, the Plains tribes were free of constraints, raids increased, and the frontier line receded as thousands of whites fled.[5] More recent studies belie that interpretation. Using one researcher's numbers, in northwest Texas in 1856 there were 420 Federal troops available to check the Indians. In the next four years from 1857 through 1860, there were, respectively, 378, 546, 420, and 126 soldiers available. During the Civil War, in the years 1861 through 1865, there were 900, 700, 450, 650, and 850 Confederate and state troops to man the border. There were more troops in Texas during the Civil War than before it. The Texas frontier held during the Civil War and the settlement line was not forced back.[6]

It may seem puzzling that in 1860, when the U.S. Army was still on the job, 78 settlers were killed, while in 1861, when the number of fighting men on the borders dropped to new lows, settler deaths went down to 25. What does this mean? It might show that fewer soldiers meant less fighting and it might show that troop numbers were irrelevant. It also might mean that there was little correlation between troop strength and civilian fatalities because the Indians were not reacting solely to troop strength. The Indians had no clue as to how many soldiers opposed them. They raided when numbers were low as well as when they were high.

An argument can be made that in Texas, the Rangers were irrelevant. That might be an outrageous statement to some die-hard Texas Ranger devotees. In reality, however, Rangers were minor irritants at best. The Kiowas, Comanches, and Lipans had their own agendas and they were not contingent on ranger action. Historians have almost universally approached the situation from an angle that assumes the Indians only reacted to white strategies—they simply resisted and retreated before an unstoppable white expansion. On the Southern Plains, however, the Comanches were the expansionist empire dictating terms for a century, from 1750 to 1850, and the Europeans did the reacting, resisting, and retreating. The American arrival in the southwest was facilitated because the Comanches had already weakened their potential adversaries.

Comanches raided Mexico for horses, but in the 1830s, "removed" Indian tribes from the east had an impact on the northern and eastern Comanche borders and they found it more difficult to send large war parties south into Mexico. A treaty signed at Camp Holmes in 1835 allowed trade with the Americans and a peace with the newly arriving tribes, freeing up raiders to head south again. In addition, the power vacuum created by the 1836 Texas Revolution was a magnet for raiders who could now get horses in Texas easier than in Mexico. Texas, however, did not feel full Comanche power because in the late 1830s they were still warring with the Cheyennes and Arapahos in the north. When the Comanches and Kiowas concluded a great peace with the Cheyennes and Arapahos in 1840, it secured their northern border and allowed them to go south in force again. The great Comanche raid all the way to the Texas Gulf coast in 1840 was less the result of anger over the fight at the Council House in San Antonio in March of that year than because of Mexican instigation and a free hand to engage in large raids again.

Texas Governor Sam Houston's peace initiative in 1841 did turn away many of the raiders back into old Mexico, with the blessings of the young Texas Republic, however, the turning was likely as much a result of declining herds in Texas as it was because of peace. The relentless, devastating Comanche raids during decade of the 1840s turned northern Mexico into what one historian called a land of "a thousand deserts." The Texan-Comanche treaty at Tehuacana Creek in 1844 also shifted Comanche attentions to the south. The change in targets because of political and economic considerations had many Texans incorrectly believing that their Rangers had stemmed the tide and that Comanches posed little threat to their settlements.

The comparative ease of the U.S. victory in the Mexican War of 1846-48 was facilitated by the Comanches devastating the northern portion of Mexico. The Comanches were at the peak of their empire, but the great smallpox and cholera epidemics of 1848-1850 began the Comanche collapse. The epidemics arrived about the same time that the tribe had surpassed its limits of ecologically sustained growth, as the 15-year drought beginning in 1845 began to take its toll. Thousands died and the economy collapsed. The Comanches had to kill more bison to trade for agricultural products and the bison declined. The Penetekas nearly disappeared as a recognizable entity in the 1850s. The Comanches signed the 1853 Treaty of Fort Atkinson which contained a stipulation that they cease raiding in Mexico. Unknown to the commissioners they had already seriously curtailed those raids simply because they no longer had the ability. Besides, the U.S. would give them gifts for not raiding, which somewhat made up for the loss. When U.S. gifts stopped during the Civil War, the tribes signed treaties with the Confederates to get them.[7]

The story of the Comanches and Kiowas in Texas in the middle decades of the 19th Century is much more one of the vicissitudes of disease, climate, environment, politics, and economics than of military strategies. Environmental determinism is not the sole explanation, but the impact of such unpredictable events as short-term climate change and its attendant stress-causing societal responses are of utmost importance in explaining Texan-Comanche relations. It made little difference whether the Texas Rangers patrolled from fixed posts or rode on offensive strikes. Texas history was subject to much greater forces than the military could ever hope to muster or influence.

The army only mopped up on the fringes, but in most histories of the Western Indian wars it is the army and Indians who stand in the spotlight. Many boasted that the Rangers were the best fighters; Governor Lubbock, for one, stating that Texas Rangers always "demonstrated their superiority over the United States regulars for frontier service." They are a significant part of the story, but the settlers also deserve a place on the stage. A legitimate focus was provided by Hollywood with its innumerable "B" Westerns in the first half of the 20th Century, where the main adversaries were the "cowboys and Indians." An old cow-puncher, George W. Saunders, commented about the situation at a 1917 reunion of the Old Time Trail Drivers' Association. Saunders said that "The trailers and ranchmen were the most dreaded enemies of the Indians, and Texas Rangers next, most of them being cowboys." According to Saunders the army was the least effective. "The soldiers did their best," he explained, but the Indians "generally outwitted them."[8]

Chapter 15 notes

1 Examples are in Schultz, *Month of the Freezing Moon*, 50-51; Osborn, *Wild Frontier*, 200; Oliva, *Soldiers on the Santa Fe Trail*, 139-40; Nadeau, *Ft. Laramie and the Sioux*, 145; Worcester, *The Apaches*, 80; Hebard, *Bozeman Trail*, 71, 139; Springer, *Soldiering in Sioux Country*, 1; Bender, *March of Empire*, 170; Colton *Civil War in the Western Territories*, 121; Josephy, *Civil War in the American West*, 246; Pace and Frazier, *Frontier Texas*, 94; Moneyhon, *Texas After the Civil War*, 9; Fehrenbach, *Comanches*, 446-47.

2 *WR:* S.1, V.26/1, 720.

3 Urwin, *United States Cavalry*, 92-93; Sawicki, *Cavalry Regiments*, 42, 44; Utley, *Frontiersmen in Blue*, 216.

4 Michno, *Encyclopedia of Indian Wars*, 354.

5 Fehrenbach, *Comanches*, 446-47; Wallace, *Texas in Turmoil*, 243.

6 Smith, *Frontier Defense*, 170-71; Roth, "Frontier Defense Challenges," 37-39, 42.

7 Delay, *War of a Thousand Deserts*, 49, 61, 68, 74, 240-41; Hamalainen, *Comanche Empire*, 1-2, 218, 231, 233, 245, 298, 331 343; Kavanagh, *Comanches, A History*, 385, 483.

8 Lubbock, *Memoirs*, 356; Hunter, *Trail Drivers of Texas I*, 20, 23.

Part 4. 1862

16 They behaved "cowardly and disgracefully."

In Texas in the fall of 1861, Earl Van Dorn was reassigned and Gen. Paul O. Hebert became the new department commander. Talk was that Henry McCulloch's 1st Texas Mounted Rifles would be sent east to counter Union threats near the Texas coast, and since their enlistments were to expire in the spring of 1862, a new regiment was needed. Newly-elected Texas Governor Francis R. Lubbock approved an act on December 21, 1861, to organize "a regiment of Rangers for the protection of the northern and western frontier of the State of Texas," that would consist of ten companies of men who enlisted for one year and were to supply their own horses, arms, and accoutrements. Lubbock said the organization was known afterwards as the "Frontier Regiment." They "were to be stationed outside of the settlements at posts about twenty-five miles apart...on a direct line from a point on Red River, in Montague County, to a point on the Rio Grande, and thence down to its mouth." The act provided that the regiment "shall always be subject to the authorities of the State of Texas for frontier service, and shall not be removed beyond the limits of the State of Texas." It was a fine proclamation, but President Jefferson Davis vetoed it; there was no way the regiment would receive pay from the Confederacy while under sole control of the state. While authorities argued, Lubbock appointed James M. Norris colonel, Alfred J. Obenchain lieutenant colonel, and James E. McCord major.

Lubbock and the legislature also passed a bill to create 33 brigade districts, to be filled with companies of militia to take the field whenever the governor felt that "invasion, insurrection, or rebellion" threatened. By the beginning of 1862, it appeared to the people on the frontier that the government was finally taking action to protect them. How well these new units would perform was yet to be seen.[1]

That the state was organizing and equipping new Texas warriors made not a whit of difference to the Comanche, Kiowa, or Lipan warriors. They began the year of 1862 much as they had ended the old, by stealing stock. Louis Oge raised cattle and horses in Frio County. On the night of January 18, 1862, Indians stole three of his horses that were hobbled 200 yards from his house. The next morning Oge got some neighbors, the Shadliffs, Vintons, and Forests, to go with him after his horses. They trailed west on the Leona, over to the Nueces, and cut across to Fort Clark seeking assistance, but the soldiers refused to help them. The posse gave up and returned home. About the same time, Comanches hit Jesse Montieth's place farther north in Brown County, stealing an undetermined number of cattle and horses. In February

1862, Comanches raided into Young County along Red River and got three horses worth $225 from Robert M. Matthews.[2]

In March 1862, Comanches stole horses along the Colorado River in the vicinity of present-day Regency on the Mills-San Saba County lines. The area was then known as Hanna Valley, for Judge Davis S. Hanna (34), who first settled in the area in 1856. Hanna, Owen F. Lindsey, George Robbins, Andrew J. Jones, Enoch Powell, Pink Moss, Isaac West, and four other civilians formed a posse and trailed the raiders downriver to the mouth of Pecan Bayou, where the tracks turned up that stream. Mid-afternoon on March 9, the 11 whites rode into an equal number of Comanches. Owen Lindsey was out in front and charged ahead, assuming the others were right behind him, but the Comanches turned and quickly killed Lindsey before the others came up.

David Hanna recorded that "a desperate fight came off," with Jones, Robbins, and Powell being wounded. The Texans fell back and built a rock fortification, fighting with weapons that failed to fire on many occasions, until the Comanches broke off the engagement. Hanna's "hors" was killed and he wrote, "we killed one or two Indians and wounded others but our force being inadequet [sic] raw citizens, in the most part of them had never seen an Indian, and were very poorly armed, did no fighting." They did recover some of the stolen horses.[3]

Menard County was on the far frontier in 1862. The Parks family lives near the Little Saline in the county's southeastern corner. On April 2, Felix Hale went to Parks's to return a wash tub and discovered the cabin on fire and mattress feathers blowing about. He found the burned body of Henry Parks (67). His wife, Nancy, was dead by the cow pen, and near the creek was the body of their grandson, Billy (12). All of them had been scalped.

Hale rode to spread the news and John Williams raised a party of civilians to look for the Indians who had killed the Parks family. Several neighbors joined the posse, but when Williams asked one local wag, he refused to join, saying that he hadn't lost any Indians.[4]

In Texas, distance from the frontier did not necessarily equate with less danger. On the same day that the Parks family was massacred, Comanches also raided in Gillespie County. A Mr. Berg, who lived seven miles east of Fredericksburg, was going to town with several bottles of whiskey to sell. Comanches killed him but left the whiskey alone—due to a superstition according to a chronicler. When the Indians left Berg they went northeast to Willow Creek (North Grape Creek) about 12 miles from town. There they found Heinrich Grobe (61), who had brought his large family from Hanover, Germany. Grobe was working on his fences not far from the house when the Indians shot him and stole his stock. No one knew until his sons came looking for him and brought him home, grievously wounded. He died on April 4. Mrs. Grobe was left with eight children.[5]

The 1st Texas Mounted Rifles played no part in apprehending the killers. April 1862 was the transition month and the old unit marched to headquarters at Fort Mason to be mustered out. James "Buck" Barry had taken over as major in February when Major Burleson resigned, and he was leading some companies to Fort Mason when they ran into a war party on the upper San Saba on April 9. Barry charged, but the Indians were caught so unawares that they had no avenue of retreat and stood their ground in a desperate little fight. One of the warriors was wearing a woman's silk dress stolen in a recent raid, and a soldier commented to Barry, "Notice how viciously the d--- squaw shoots her arrows." The "squaw" was a male, who loosed a storm of missiles at them, filling Barry's horse full of arrows, and it crashed to the ground pinning Barry underneath. He believed his "bones would now be decaying on the scene of the battle" had not one of his men, M. L. Webster, rushed up and fought off the Indians until Barry could get out from under the horse. In a few minutes the remaining warriors figured running was their only alternative and got away. Barry's men killed three Indians and wounded one. Four of his men were wounded, including one who was said to have had "his lips pinned together with an arrow." One of the wounded was Corporal Ercanbrack, who survived a hot fight the previous year.[6]

April 9 was not an auspicious day for the Frontier Regiment. While Barry battled Comanches in Mason County, other raiders were 70 miles east of him in Burnet and Lampasas County. James N. Gracey (13) rode from Lampasas to Thomas Dawson's place about 10 miles southwest of town in northern Burnet County to help Dawson hunt for horses. On the morning of April 9, Gracey joined young John H. Stockman, who lived with Dawson, hunting for horses about two miles from the cabin. When Stockman went after some turkeys, Gracey heard a bell and went in the other direction. In minutes he rode into 15 Indians driving about 100 stolen horses. They captured and stripped him, scalped him alive, and told him to run. As Gracey fled, crying, with blood dripping down his face, they followed behind and filled him with arrows.

Stockman watched in horror while hiding behind some trees. He was frozen in terror and figured he would be discovered, when George Baker, his wife, daughter, and his father-in-law, Mr. Austin, came riding up in a buggy. The Indians went after them, but Baker was well-armed and blasted the charging Indians, killing one and forcing the others to fall back temporarily. Baker drove the buggy to some timber. As they tried to construct a little fort, the horses ran away with the buggy, taking Baker's other weapons and ammunition. Mr. Austin had no gun and when Baker was wounded, his wife took the weapon and continued to shoot. An arrow hit the baby, Elga, but as she was wrapped in several folds of a thick Navajo blanket, the point barely penetrated her skin.

Stockman, with the Indians' attention diverted, escaped by slithering and crawling to Thomas Espy's house, about two miles east of Dawson's. The runaway horses and buggy showed up at Dawson's and he knew someone was in dire trouble. Quickly he started to ride to Lampasas for help, but one mile from home he ran into Dempsey Pace, John Greenwood, George Weldy, and Newton Knight, who were out hunting. They agreed to accompany Dawson back to the scene. Upon their arrival, the Indians, no longer liking the odds, retreated. The rescuers took Baker's family to Espy's house, where Baker took several weeks to recover.

The spate of murders—six within a week—led to recriminations. Men of the Frontier Regiment were accused of behaving "cowardly and disgracefully" when they disobeyed orders and fled from a small band of Indians. Accusations followed, with feuds breaking out among the officers and men. When Capt. Jack Cureton had a heated argument with Lieutenant Colonel Obenchain, two of Cureton's men killed Obenchain and fled for protection among the settlers of Palo Pinto County.[7]

New strategies were needed. Cattleman Oliver Loving believed he had a plan to put the newly formed Frontier Regiment to good use. In April 1862, Loving had only been home two months since driving a herd of cattle to the Pike's Peak region and being tossed in a Denver jail for being a southern sympathizer. On his trip he ascertained that the Comanches and Kiowas appeared to have a rendezvous on the Arkansas River where he saw upwards of 5,000 horses he believed were stolen. Loving wrote to Governor Lubbock that the Indians were being fed at Federal posts and paid by the U.S. Army for Texan scalps. He was convinced that Texas would have no peace with the Indians, regardless of treaties that they had made with the Confederacy, "until we go to their general rendezvous and destroy them."

Loving wanted to raise a few companies of Rangers, and with help from Colonel Norris and a few companies of the Frontier Regiment he would go north to wipe out the marauders. He also proposed "to take the U.S. posts in the neighborhood." He believed it could be easily done because most of the Federals were currently down in New Mexico fighting Gen. Henry Sibley. In addition, and no doubt a result of Loving's late unpleasant experience in Colorado Territory, he proposed to take the expedition to Denver "and release some sixty or seventy prisoners now in jail there on account of their Southern principles…."[8]

Loving's proposition was never acted upon, likely because of personal quarrels in the regiment, lack of money, and lack of direction. Instead of taking the regiment en masse to seek and destroy the Indians, the unit was used defensively, occupying scattered lonely outposts along the frontier that were placed about a day's ride apart, and manned by about half a company each. The plan was for each post to patrol up and back between camps, thus covering the entire line on horseback at least every other day. Camp Collier was a typical post. Selected by Colonel Norris and Lieutenant Colonel Obenchain on an inspection tour in February 1862, it was located on Clear Creek in Brown County, about 13 miles southwest of present-day Brownwood. Captain Thomas N. Collier officially established the post on March 23, 1862. It never had permanent structures; the men lived in tents and food was in short supply. Meager rations were often supplemented by hunting, with the men using their own weapons and horses. The volunteers spent their monotonous days patrolling north to Camp Pecan or south to Camp McMillan. Such tactics almost never stopped an Indian raider.[9]

More typically the Indians slipped by the outposts and patrols unnoticed. In April 1862 Comanches hit Joseph Cady's place in Llano County, much as they had in February 1861. This time they stole four yoke of oxen that Cady said were "large well broke, in good condition and ranging from 5 to 8 years old, sound and tough, worth $75 each."[10] Such seemingly insignificant losses were usually devastating to the small ranchers and farmers whose entire livelihood might depend on an ox team.

A more serious incident occurred in May 1862. James Tankersley and James Carmean lived northeast of Camp Collier in Comanche County. Over the winter, Tankersley had cured a few thousand pounds of bacon and figured he could sell it at Camp Collier or in Coleman County at Camp Colorado, an abandoned U.S. Army post then occupied by Texas Rangers. Tankersley, with Carmean assisting him, journeyed to Camp Collier where they sold a load of bacon and prepared to return home with money in their pockets. Lieutenant J. H. Chrisman of Company I cautioned them that they ought to wait for a military ambulance that would soon be leaving on the same route and they could accompany it.

"We will ride on slow and you will soon overtake us," said Tankersley.

The two men got several miles from the camp when a party of about 20 Indian raiders swept through the area with a number of stolen horses. Suddenly, there was no time to wish they had waited for the escort. The Indians cut off the two men, who tried to take shelter in a small copse of trees. Carmean was killed early on, but Tankersley apparently put up a good fight before he was killed, as evidenced by the arrows and bullets that had torn up the trees around them.

Nearby, Pat Gallagher and Isham Large heard firing, and when it stopped they cautiously rode to the scene. They saw the two bodies and a lone Indian farther along the road. Smelling an ambush, the two riders quickly cut across a field and galloped toward Camp Collier. In a short distance they came upon the army ambulance and escort, warned them, and then rode to the post. As was so often the case, the soldiers arrived only in time to bury the bodies. Both men were stripped and scalped; the only clothing that remained was one sock on Carmean's left foot. The Indians removed Tankersley's long red hair and red beard. The two men were buried in an oak grove just north of Camp Collier. Once again, the soldiers had missed the action.[11]

While the Texans tried to figure out how to deal with a multi-front Civil War and guerrilla war, for the Indians, it was business as usual. In mid-June 1862, marauders, probably Lipans, swept down Hondo Creek in Medina County. They attacked homesteads in Hondo Valley—some of the same locales that Comanches hit the previous fall. Jerry Bailey had gone to Rube Smith's place on Live Oak Creek to transact some business early one morning. Smith's wife told Bailey that Rube had gone out to get his horse and would be back shortly. After a long wait, Bailey went out to look for him, but instead, saw another neighbor, Manuel Wydick, running toward him. The Indians had just caught and killed Smith, he breathlessly announced. The two men ran toward where Smith had been last seen. They found fresh horse tracks, footprints, and evidence that a man had been knocked down, tied, and dragged behind a horse. They finally found Smith's body in the bushes, lanced and mutilated. Nearby was the body of a dog belonging to another neighbor, James McCombs.

All the nearby families gathered at Smith's house, while the men prepared to chase the Indians. Nine of them were in the posse: Jerry Bailey, William Mullins, Manuel Wydick, Nathan Davis, West McCombs, Lovis McCombs, Sam McCombs, Monroe Watkins, and John Brown. The trail led south, and on the second day they caught sight of about 40 Indians, but could not catch them. Being outnumbered, Lewis McCombs and John Brown rode off to try to enlist the help of a Ranger company in San Antonio.

The Indians slowed their retreat and the posse caught them about June 20. The seven men decided they would fight, no matter what the odds. The Indians waited in a small grove of timber on Chacon Creek, just above its junction with the San Miguel River. Bailey led the charge, but he was the only one to push ahead to the trees—his men veered off to shoot from a cover of boulders. Bailey blasted away with his shotgun, but the Indians moved in. He called for Wydick to help him, but he wouldn't move. Finally, Nathan Davis got the men to charge across the open ground to Bailey. Several horses were hit, but they reached Bailey unscathed. Both sides blasted away from 60 yards range. An arrow struck Davis in the shoulder and came out his back. Mullins cut the arrowhead and pulled the shaft through. The rest of their horses were hit before Mullins got a good look at an Indian they believed was the chief. A well-aimed shot through the chest dropped the warrior, and the rest seemed to lose their nerve. The settlers charged and the Indians broke and fled, never being able to take their dead chief with them. They scalped the Indian and waved the bloody trophy at the Indians, then placed Rube Smith's hat on a stick so all could see. In searching the timber, they found several more dead warriors, and considered their vengeance taken. It was quite a victory against tough odds, but it was a long walk home.[12]

Chapter 16 notes

1 *WR:* S.1, V.4, 162-63; Lubbock, *Memoirs*, 357; Smith, *Frontier Defense*, 39-45.
2 Depredation Claims: Louis Oge #1665; Jesse Montieth #2902; Robert M. Matthews #4500.
3 McConnell, *West Texas Frontier*, 383; Wilbarger, *Indian Depredations*, 491-93; "Hanna Family History," http://www.perardua.net/gen/dshbook.html. Wilbarger placed the event in 1863, while Hanna said it happened in 1861.
4 Zesch, *The Captured*, 10-11.
5 McConnell, *West Texas Frontier*, 384; Biggers, *German Pioneers in Texas*, 170-71.
6 Greer, ed., *Buck Barry*, 143-44: McConnell, *West Texas Frontier*, 387.
7 McConnell, *West Texas Frontier*, 385; Wilbarger, *Indian Depredations*, 623-24; Smith, *Frontier Defense*, 47-48: Wallace, *Texas in Turmoil*, 238.
8 Winfrey and Day, *Texas Indian Papers IV*, 67-68.
9 Lease, *Texas Forts*, 204-05.
10 Joseph D. Cady, Depredation Claim #650.
11 McConnell, *West Texas Frontier*, in www.forttours.co,/pages/toctank.asp; Deaton, *Indian Fights on the Texas Frontier*, 65-66; Wilbarger, *Indian Depredations*, 488-89. Wilbarger places this incident in May 1861, but Camp Collier was not established until 1862.
12 Sowell, *Rangers and Pioneers*, 81-87.

17 "Kill all the grown Indians and take the children prisoners."

The Texas Confederates tried hard to fight a two-front war in the west and north, against the Federals and the Indians, but they were having a public relations problem caused by over-zealous men. In February 1862, Union Brig. Gen. Samuel R. Curtis, with about 11,000 men, chased the Confederates out of Missouri and into northwestern Arkansas. To meet him, Maj. Gen. Earl Van Dorn assembled about 16,000 soldiers, including Pike's Indian Brigade. On March 7, Van Dorn took half of his force in a flank march behind Pea Ridge to hit Curtis's rear near Elkhorn Tavern, while the other half battled Curtis in front. Curtis was caught between two fires, but the Rebels were also divided and by day's end, Van Dorn was out of ammunition and far from his supply train. On March 8, Curtis sent Brig. Gen. Franz Sigel's divisions against Van Dorn's split force and drove it from the field. Brigadier Generals Benjamin McCulloch and James M. McIntosh were both killed.

What appeared most prominently in many northern newspapers and reports, however, was the scalping and mutilation done by Pike's Indians. Pike sent Col. John Drew and his 500 Cherokees into the battle with the instructions to "join in the fight in their own fashion." Curtis later complained that the Indians did just that: "They shot arrows as well as rifles, and tomahawked and scalped prisoners."[1]

Van Dorn tried to keep silent about the incident and did not mention it in his report until news of the mutilations leaked out. The northern press was naturally incensed. The New York *Tribune* sent most of its barbs to Albert Pike, calling him the leader of "the Aboriginal Corps of Tomahawkers and Scalpers," a man like his violent namesake, "a ferocious fish," and who probably "got himself up in good style, war-paint, nose-ring and all."[2]

This was the very thing that the U. S. Secretary of War Edwin Stanton feared, and why he at first rejected Union Indian regiments. Even the Cherokee National Council condemned the episode, stating its troops serving the Confederacy were "to avoid any such acts toward captured or fallen foes that would be incompatible with such usages."[3]

The Cherokee government did not officially sanction scalping, just as genocide was never a policy of the U.S. or Confederate governments. There were more than enough unscrupulous, unprincipled individuals, however, to fill scores of war parties and regiments.

Ensconced in Mesilla, Confederate Territory of Arizona, John Baylor was feeling the effects of the Apache assault. Indians had killed his men in Texas, and now they were killing them in New Mexico and Arizona. When

Union forces abandoned Fort Stanton in New Mexico Territory, Baylor sent a detachment of Company D, 2nd Texas Mounted Rifles, to garrison the fort. Lieutenant John R. Pulliam sent four men 75 miles north to the Gallinas Mountains to watch for Union forces. On September 2, 1861, Mescaleros attacked and killed three of them. One week later, Apaches attacked the village of Placitas (Lincoln), ten miles southeast of Fort Stanton. Pulliam rode to the rescue and killed five raiders, but Baylor realized he did not have enough soldiers to garrison the fort and he abandoned it.[4]

While Baylor got his toehold in the southwest, Henry H. Sibley was in Richmond, Virginia, marketing his plans of empire. Promoted to brigadier general, Sibley returned to Texas with approval of his plan to conquer New Mexico. Sibley and 3,500 men of the 3rd, 4th, 5th and 7th Texas Mounted Volunteers marched across west Texas. The trek was long and hard, taking from late October to December, and some became disillusioned. Captain John S. Shropshire, 5th Texas, confessed, "I would never have come this way had I imagined the country was so mean. If I had the Yankees at my disposal I would give them this country and force them to live in it."[5]

In January 1862, Sibley absorbed Baylor's men and moved up the Rio Grande, but he had to detach units to garrison the territory behind him and protect his long supply lines. Colonel Edward Canby, with 3,810 men—1,200 Regulars, portions of the 1st, 2nd, and 3rd U.S. Cavalry, and 5th, 7th, and 10th U.S. Infantry, and the rest volunteers and militia—tried to stop Sibley from crossing the Rio Grande just north of Fort Craig at Valverde. The battle on February 21, 1862 was a bungled, but bloody affair, with both sides losing about 200 men. The Rebels won, but not because of anything Sibley did. At the start of the fight he became "ill," placed Col. Tom Green in command, and retired from the field, allegedly stone drunk. Baylor called him an "infamous coward and a disgrace to the Confederate States."[6]

Sibley's force continued north and met the Union forces, including the 1st Colorado Infantry, in the Sangre de Cristo Mountains east of Santa Fe. The Battle of Glorieta Pass, sometimes called the "Gettysburg of the West," was fought in a series of disjointed actions from March 26-28, along a dozen miles of mountain and canyon. After it was over, the Confederates had taken about 210 casualties, and the Union about 170. The Confederates had reached their high water mark in the West. With his supplies and transportation destroyed, Sibley had to retreat. Colonel Canby harassed him all the way, but lack of supplies, thirst, hunger, and the elements were the real armies nipping at Sibley's heels. He arrived at Fort Bliss in May, with his brigade strung out 50 miles behind him. By June, almost all of them were back in Texas. The Confederate version of Manifest Destiny and dreams of empire were over.[7]

John Baylor tried to maintain control in southern New Mexico Territory while Sibley had his debacle. The boys in blue might be his occasional adversaries, but the Indians were still the main challenge. Assaulted from all sides, Baylor took a hard-line unauthorized action much as he had done during the Texas "Reservation War."

While Sibley fought at Valverde, Baylor led a force of 100 men to hunt Apaches. The chase led into Arizona and then south of the border. He cornered an Apache band near Casas Grandes in Chihuahua, where it took refuge in the house of a Mexican mine owner. Regardless, Baylor attacked and slaughtered many of them. Satisfied, and believing he had done the Mexicans a favor, he returned to Mesilla, not realizing the political hornet's nest he had stirred up. The American consul in Mexico predicted that, "The atrocities of Baylor's men...will not be overlooked, but...will serve to revive the hatred of the Chihuahuans to the Texans."[8]

By March 1862, Baylor estimated that the Indians, the "cursed pests," had "already murdered over 100 men in this Territory." He was likely surprised when he learned that the Apache chief, Mangas Coloradas, reportedly requested a peace parley. On March 20, Baylor issued a letter to some Apache-fighting citizens called the Arizona Guards, who were at Pinos Altos under Capt. Tom Helm. Baylor informed Helm that he was not to make any peace with the Indians and told him that the Confederate States had passed a law declaring they should be exterminated. "You will therefore use all means," Baylor wrote, "to persuade the Apaches or any tribe to come in for the purpose of making peace, and when you get them together, kill all the grown Indians and take the children prisoners and sell them to defray the expense of killing the Indians." Baylor's plan was to get them together, give them presents, get them drunk, and then kill them. Secrecy was vital. "Say nothing of your orders until the time arrives," he cautioned.[9]

Baylor then left the territory to hurry back to San Antonio to recruit more men and further his ideas to expand his little empire. His dreams were ended in October 1862, when Confederate President Jefferson Davis finally received word of Baylor's "Extermination Order." Baylor had misrepresented the government, stating that it called for killing all Indians when its official position was actually pacification, conciliation, and cooperation. Davis fired Baylor, removed him from his unit, and revoked his commission.[10]

Individual actions taken by men such as Baylor continue to be misinterpreted by some writers, who represent them as proof of officially sanctioned policies of genocide. Union officers sometimes gave similar orders. For instance, on October 12, 1862, Brig. Gen. James Carleton ordered Col. Christopher "Kit" Carson to chase down the raiding Mescaleros. "All Indian men of that tribe are to be killed whenever and wherever you can find them;" he wrote, "the women and children will not be harmed, but you will take them prisoners and feed them at Fort Stanton until you receive other instructions about them."[11]

Carson was shocked; he took no pleasure in slaughtering Indians and he personally did not comply, although some of his men did. Extermination was not the official policy of the Union or Confederate government, although some of their representatives allowed their personal feelings to overcome better judgment. The innocent suffered more from poor decisions than sanctioned decrees.

After the March 1862, Pea Ridge battle, Albert Pike was trying to salvage his image and the perception of his Indians as barbarians. Despite official doubts about the efficacy of using Indians to fight in "civilized" armies, Pike persisted in coercing the tribes to fight against the North. As early as May 1861, he thought he might get 5,000 warriors to join the South, and constantly asked for weapons and ammunition. In October 1861, Confederate Brig. Gen. Benjamin McCulloch "instructed Col. Stand Watie, with one regiment of Cherokees, to move into the neutral land and Kansas, and destroy everything that might be of service to the enemy."[12]

On May 4, 1862, Pike wrote to the Secretary of War George W. Randolph, that the Comanches, Kiowas, and Reserve Indians "have sent to me to know if they can be allowed to send a strong party and capture any trains on their way from Kansas to New Mexico, to which I have no objection. To go on the war-path somewhere else is the best way to keep them from troubling Texas." Pike also wrote, "I have ordered Lieutenant-Colonel Jumper with his Seminoles to march to and take Fort Larned, on the Pawnee Fork of the Arkansas, where are considerable stores and a little garrison."[13]

On June 9, Pike wrote that Col. David McIntosh's Creek regiment was advancing up the Verdigris to the Santa Fe Road, while the Creek, Seminole, and Chickasaw battalions were "now in motion toward the Salt Plains, to take Fort Larned, the post at Walnut Creek, and perhaps Fort Wise, and intercept trains going to New Mexico."[14]

Later in June, Pike wrote to Maj. Gen. Thomas C. Hindman, commanding the Trans-Mississippi District, that he had sent the Creeks and Seminoles to the Santa Fe Road, "with a view to destroying Ft. Larned and the fort on Walnut Creek." Pike tried to get his Indians to attack these places, but they never did. Nevertheless, he was concerned about what might happen, not wanting to go through the embarrassment of another Pea Ridge. He told Hindman that their treaties stipulated that they were not to be used outside their own territory without their consent, but even if they were, Pike wrote, "it would be both ungenerous and unwise to take them out of it. There are many reasons for saying so, but one is enough—that they cannot be restrained from scalping the dead, if not the living."[15]

Few could restrain white men from scalping Indians either. In fact, at times it was hard enough to restrain white men from killing, hanging, and mutilating other white men.

Chapter 17 notes

1 *WR:* S.1, V.8, 195, 289.
2 New York *Tribune*, March 27, 1862.
3 Abel, *American Indian in the Civil War*, 33.
4 Williams, *Texas' Last Frontier*, 24-28; Frazier, *Blood & Treasure*, 64-65; *WR:* S.1, V.4, 25.
5 Frazier, *Blood & Treasure*, 46-7, 76, 97, 128.
6 Colton, *Civil War in the Western Territories*, 26-36; Josephy, *Civil War in the American West*, 61-73.
7 Edrington and Taylor, *Glorieta Pass*, 53, 94, 103-04.
8 Frazier, *Blood & Treasure*, 190-91.
9 *WR:* S.1, V.50/1, 942.
10 Frazier, *Blood & Treasure*, 294.
11 *WR:* S.1, V.15, 579.
12 *WR:* S.1, V.3, 573, 721.
13 *WR:* S.1, V.4, 74; *WR:* S.1, V.13, 822.
14 *WR:* S.1, V.13, 944.
15 *WR:* S.1, V.13, 948.

18 "In the dark corner of the Confederacy."

The Texas frontier always seemed to be a magnet for Indian raiders, but Indians were not the only problem. During the Civil War in particular, Texas civilians fought amongst each other probably as often as they fought Indians. On a small scale, some say the conflict between the Rebels and Unionists in Texas was inevitable. On a larger scale, historians and politicians have debated the causes of the war for more than a century: slavery, sectionalism, economics, culture, states' rights, industry vs. agrarianism, and a second American Revolution have been proposed as factors which made the war inescapable. On the other hand, blundering, a breakdown of the democratic process, a failure of leadership, Republican fanatics, and irresponsible agitators have been blamed—factors that emphasize the human element involved and the likelihood that it all could have been avoided.[1]

The Civil War exacerbated the social and economic divisions among the settlers. Years earlier, the leaders of the Texas Republic recognized the need for a "buffer colony" south of Red River and in 1841 passed the Colonization Law that awarded a land grant to William S. Peters. Peters recruited families from Kentucky, Tennessee, Arkansas and Missouri, but also a substantial number from Ohio, Illinois, and Indiana. The majority, coming from the North or Upper South, were Scots-Irish "Borderers" and non-slaveholders who grew subsistence crops. A minority came from the Lower South and an economy where slavery and cotton ruled. Lower Southerners were said to have learned to "bend their knee to their betters" while the Upper Southerners had a lack of deference to birth, breeding, and wealth. Although a minority, those lower southerners dominated economically and politically. In Cooke County, for example, less than two percent of the people owned slaves, but they called the shots. Two men, James G. Bourland and William C. Young, held one-quarter of the slaves; the non-slave owners felt excluded and ignored.[2]

As the secession crisis grew in the late 1850s, the majority of inhabitants in many north Texas counties figured they had no cause to fight someone else's war, because for most of the people, the crisis was all about slavery. There was talk of slave rebellions, there was talk of Lincoln and other "Black Republicans" who would abolish slavery at first opportunity, and there were preachers who talked abolitionism, making sense to some and frightening others. On July 8, 1860, a series of fires began almost simultaneously in several north Texas towns. It was later shown that the extreme heat had apparently been enough to combust boxes of new-fangled phosphorous "prairie matches" stored in several buildings, but the immediate explanation was that the fires were set by a conspiratorial band of blacks, abolitionists, and Unionists. On July 17, abolitionist William H. Crawford was lynched in Fort Worth, one of the first victims of the spreading hysteria.[3]

In the spring of 1861, people saw a great comet in the northern skies and considered it to be an omen of bad luck, foretelling the great Civil War. Texas voted to secede, but 18 of its 122 counties voted against disunion, eight of them in north Texas. The popular vote was 39,145 in favor of secession and 13,841 against, showing fully one-third of the people casting ballots did not want to leave the Union. They called it a rich man's war and a poor man's fight, and many would not join a cause that they did not believe in. In Denton County, people complained that the conscription law exempted one white man for every six slaves he owned, meaning the poor had to fight to maintain a way of life for another class of people. A substantial number left in wagon trains, either heading west to California or north to Kansas. Many who stayed joined what was called the Union League, and dedicated themselves to restoring a loyal Union government.[4]

Conditions deteriorated. Those with Rebel leanings joined the army early and went to fight in other theaters. Hundreds of white and black refugees moved in, escaping battlefields or slave masters. When the Confederacy passed the Conscription Act on April 16, 1862, authorizing the draft of all able-bodied men between 18 and 35 years old, the situation worsened.

Another area of local resistance was in the Hill Country, north and west of San Antonio and Austin, a region of geologic transition between the coastal plains and the Edwards Plateau to the west. The dividing Balcones Escarpment, which rose from 300 to 1,000 feet, was a land of hills, trees, and artesian wells, which favored mixed farming and stock raising. Many hill people from Tennessee, Arkansas, and Missouri came into the area in the 1840s, but there was also a large influx of Germans—Hessians and Lower Saxons—who settled along a corridor stretching about 100 miles northwest from San Antonio, to Boerne, Fredericksburg, and Mason.

The Germans in particular were opposed to the draft and the war. Many had left the old country to avoid conscription and they were of no mind to fight for the Confederacy. When General Hebert placed Texas under martial law in May 1862 and ruthlessly prosecuted the draft law, the Germans resisted. The counties of Bexar, Gillespie, Comal, Kerr, Kendall, and Medina were seen as flash points. When citizens sent Governor Lubbock complaints that denounced the draft as a "despotic decree," and formed committees to organize protection companies, those counties were declared to be in open rebellion, and Capt. James Duff went in to enforce conscription. Duff said, "the God damn Dutchmen are Unionists to a man," and proceeded to hang a number of them.[5]

In late July 1862, a group of about 65 men and boys under Fritz Tegener decided they did not want to fight for the North or the South, and headed to Mexico. With them was a Confederate spy who sent word to Duff of their plans. Duff dispatched Lt. C. D. McRae with nearly 100 state troops to pursue them, while the spy left signs along the way for McRae to follow. On August 9, the Unionists reached a fine camping spot on the West Nueces River in Kinney County about 20 miles from present-day Brackettville. Several men went out to hunt and returned at dusk saying that they had seen figures moving in the woods. Most of the men, including Tegener, dismissed it as jitters.

Before dawn the next morning and under a full moon, McRae's cavalry charged in, firing indiscriminately and riding over the prone men. Nineteen Germans were shot and killed, including Tegener, and six were trampled to death. John W. Sansom escaped in the woods, but he was close enough to hear swearing and shouts as McRae rounded up prisoners. Sansom heard the crack of carbines as nine men were lined up and murdered. Later, McRae reported to Duff that "they offered the most determined resistance and fought with desperation, asking no quarter whatever; hence I have no prisoners to report." News of the massacre touched off more protest in San Antonio and towns to the north, which led to more hangings to quash the perceived rebellion.[6]

The Hill Country was not the only area of insurgence. German settlements to the east in Austin County were also giving the authorities a hard time. In November 1862, the Confederate draft enrollment officer in the town of Industry warned that "there is evidently a spirit of insubordination existing among the Germans in this region." Sometimes they met in secret, but there was a public meeting in which nearly 500 people attended, calling for arms, clothing, and protection for their families if they submitted to the draft. The enrolling officer sent for sufficient troops to enforce "the majesty of the law" and to keep them in line.[7]

Another hot spot was in Texas's northern counties along Red River. Unionist-leaning citizens resisted the draft, and deserters sought refuge in the frontier counties, forming roving gangs of "brush men" who hid out in the thickets. It was believed that Unionists sent secret agents to the Indians in the area to "incite them to war on the settlements," which was exactly what many Unionists believed the Rebels were doing to them. Along Red River, Unionists were in the majority and the pro-Confederacy minority thought themselves besieged; they cracked down on dissenters and arrested deserters, who were all the more determined to resist when the Confederacy raised the draft age to 45 in September 1862.

Two of the leaders in the purge were Cooke County's biggest slaveholders: William Young and James Bourland. The latter, selected as provost marshal for the 21st District, was uncompromising and violent. He was called warm and friendly, but also arbitrary and deadly. He was said to be a "good fighter and a good hater," and was despised for being "as great a tyrant as ever reigned since Nero."[8]

Bourland lost no time in trying to infiltrate the Union League to ferret out those he considered traitors. Using informants to get names, Bourland launched his strike against the main League cell in Gainesville on October 1, 1862. Anyone suspected of treason was seized on the most trifling pretenses. Bourland declared martial law and filled the jails, while mobs walked the streets calling for lynchings. A "citizen's court" composed of slaveholders and other Lower Southerners quickly went through the list and arbitrarily condemned men on the flimsiest of evidence. After the first wave of hangings, some people came to their senses and realized they had far overstepped their bounds.

In the midst of all this, the Comanches and Kiowas added to the chaos. In October, a war party crossed Red River, went through Montague County and down into central Wise County. On October 15 they raided Joseph H. Martin's ranch and stole 13 of his horses worth $650. They hit other ranches in the area before taking their booty back across the river. Martin tried to get a posse to chase the Indians, but it seemed that everyone was too involved with the business of catching and hanging Unionists.[9]

Some folks tried to talk sense to the hard-liners, but their efforts came to naught, because on October 16, William Young was bushwhacked and killed by an unseen sniper near Red River. Another wave of hysteria swept the region. Nineteen men who had already been acquitted were re-arrested and hanged, and James Young, the colonel's son, personally supervised the executions. The fear hit other counties too; by the end of the month 42 men were hanged or shot in Gainesville, five were hanged in Decatur, and one was shot in Denton. Upwards of one dozen more were hanged in Hunt and Hopkins counties between 1860 and 1863.[10]

The "Great Gainesville Hangings" were caused in large part by hatred and hysteria, the by-products of guerrilla and civil war. There was irony in the situation, however, for one of the main reasons that Texas seceded from the Union was an alleged failure of the Federal government to protect Texans' lives and property. The state and Confederate governments did a worse job. The frontier was in chaos. Some people fled east to "safer" areas. At the same time, strangely enough, people in the east were fleeing west. The grass was always greener elsewhere.

Kate Stone and family abandoned their home in eastern Louisiana near Vicksburg on the Mississippi River, while Union and Confederate forces battled in the area in the summer of 1863. They moved to what they thought would be a safer place far from the battlefields. As they stopped in Lamar County along Red River, Kate immediately knew they had made a mistake.

She wrote in her diary and to a friend never to come to Texas, "but if forced to come to cover herself with a thin coat of tar to protect herself from the myriad of insects along the road." She had fled the Yankees, but found herself in a place "where Union feeling is rife, and where the principal amusement among the loyal citizens is hanging suspected Jayhawkers." She poured out her complaints. "I am already as disgusted as I expected to be." The place was full of "whiteheaded children and buttermilk," which for some reason she couldn't abide. No one seemed to know what a washtub was for, women in hoopskirts were way out of fashion, shoes were luxuries, and all the locals did was go to meetings—places with "swarms of ugly, rough people, different only in degrees of ugliness. There must be something in the air of Texas fatal to beauty," Kate wailed. "We have not seen a good-looking or educated person since we entered the state." She was in exile, stuck away "in the dark corner of the Confederacy."[11]

What Kate didn't realize was that there were many "dark corners" along the borders, a prime example being eastern Kansas, bled white during the slavery and free soil guerrilla war for nearly a decade beginning in the 1850s and culminating with the burning of Lawrence and the massacre of nearly 200 "Jayhawkers" in August 1863, about the same time Kate was lamenting in her diary.

Was this insanity universal and predestined? Historian Allan Nevins wrote more than seven decades ago, "history is violently personal—stars and molecules have no loves and hates, while men do." Nevins said that for Americans in 1861, "war was easier than wisdom and courage."[12]

The historical discussion as to whether men make history or history makes men continues, but it appears that the standard story of the Indian wars being an inevitable clash of cultures is not the answer. Clash of cultures is a euphemism. One historian recently stated, "Cultures do not clash; cultures do not even act—people do."[13] Explaining the wars as a culture clash leaves out the role of men. The self-interest inherent in amorphous concepts such as Manifest Destiny or Course of Empire is a more viable explanation.

Chapter 18 notes

1 Rozwenc, ed., *Causes of the American Civil War, passim.*
2 Collins, *Cooke County*, 5, 10; Pickering and Falls, *Brush Men & Vigilantes*, 6, 8; McCaslin, *Tainted Breeze*, 15.
3 Collins, *Cooke County*, 10; McCaslin, *Tainted Breeze*, 23-24; Bates, *History of Denton County*, 69.
4 Lubbock, *Memoirs*, 309; Bates, *History of Denton County*, 97, 110, 112; Pickering and Falls, *Brush Men & Vigilantes*, 40; McCaslin, *Tainted Breeze*, 34; Collins, *Cooke County*, 11.
5 Webb, *Handbook of Texas I*, 102; Fehrenbach, *Lone Star*, 295-96, 363.
6 Fehrenbach, *Lone Star*, 363-64; Groneman, *Battlefields of Texas*, 132-33; Ford, *Rip Ford's Texas*, 339-40.
7 *WR*: S.1, V.15, 887.
8 Bates, *History of Denton County*, 163; Pickering and Falls, *Brush Men & Vigilantes*, 15; McCaslin, *Tainted Breeze*, 35, 39, 55.
9 Joseph H. Martin, Depredation Claim #4787.
10 Collins, *Cooke County*, 12-15; Pickering and Falls, *Brush Men & Vigilantes*, 18.
11 Gallaway, *Dark Corner of the Confederacy*, 155-56.
12 Rozwenc, ed., *Causes of the American Civil War*, 217, 226.
13 Elliott, *Custerology*, 138-39.

19 "Friendly and true to the White man for years."

There was much fighting across the west in 1862, and in August in Minnesota occurred a great paroxysm of violence when the Dakotas rose up and began killing white settlers by the hundreds. Fears of similar uprisings spread throughout the other western states and territories, but in Texas, although there was raiding and killing, the amount of fighting between Indians and whites was at a low point of the decade. Perhaps trickster fate had simply given the white Texans a break from Indian raids so that they could direct more attention to persecuting and killing themselves. Then again, the severe drought had dried up rivers and burned out what little grasses grew, leaving nothing for raiders to subsist their ponies on. Also, even though some elements of the tribes did not comply with the treaties they had signed, there were many others who did. For much of 1862, Kiowas and Comanches could, and did, get annuities and supplies from both the North and the South. There was some wisdom in sitting on the sidelines and collecting the goods while the crazy whites killed each other.

Unfortunately, the lull would not last forever. Albert Pike resigned because the government and army could not or would not support him or give him the supplies and money to honor the treaties he made. Personal rivals sought his position and power. The situation degenerated to what it had been after the Pea Ridge battle in March, when various commanders blamed each other for their failures. In July 1862, Pike handed command over to Col. Douglas Cooper, the crooked ex-agent, who now commanded a Choctaw and Chickasaw Regiment. Cooper was not having much luck with the "civilized" tribes fighting for the Confederacy, but he was having less luck keeping the "wild" tribes in control. Regardless of all the affirmations of friendship and brotherhood that had been made between the Indian bands in the Leased District and the commissioners and agents, most of the smiles were a façade and the handshakes only an expedient until either side found their agreements were no longer advantageous.

The incident that would permanently sever the tentative ties of friendship between the Confederacy and the Kiowas and Comanches occurred at the agency in Indian Territory. Matthew Leeper, who had once been agent at the Comanche Brazos Reservation, was testing his skills at the Wichita Agency, but was having a bad time of it.

He could never get Buffalo Hump to settle down, the same problem that Superintendent Neighbors had. Leeper said Neighbors "would load him with presents," only to see him "return to the prairies [to] depredate upon the country until his blankets were worn out," and then return begging for more gifts. By the spring of 1862, Leeper was frustrated. The more he tried to cultivate friendly relations, the more it "produced an opposite result." He said the Comanches, who at times conducted themselves with propriety, "are now unruly and are subject to the most unbridled passions and unheard of improprieties." They had been killing all the poultry owned by the agency's Doctor John Shirley, shooting arrows into his milk cows, and killed some of the cattle belonging to the contractor.

The interpreter, Horace P. Jones, admonished Buffalo Hump and told him to make his warriors stop the outrages, but the chief verbally lashed him. Warriors then attempted to kill some of the agency horses, but Leeper was able to stop them. When the "wild" bands came in, things got worse. They tried to break into the commissary to steal supplies and some of them forced open the door of Mrs. Shirley's bedchamber. The doctor had a scuffle with them and they left. Leeper called the Indians "impudent and insolent."

It was springtime and the peace talks of the fall were conveniently forgotten as the new raiding season began. The non-reserve bands came to the agency and held war and scalp dances, inciting the young men who had never been in a war party. They told brave stories of "taking scalps of white men and Mexicans, and of the rapture with which they are received and amorous embraces of the young damsels on their return," after which, Leeper explained, the young men "are driven mad with excitement…."

Despite Leeper's protests, the Indians formed a war party, ostensibly to raid in Mexico, but Leeper was certain that Texas was their target. Leeper begged for soldiers. He believed the agency was becoming "a place of convenience, to rest, feed and recruit themselves, on their return from a stealing expedition, and to procure provisions and a suitable outfit, the better to enable them to prosecute their fiendish designs." The soldiers he needed, Leeper concluded, ought to be Texans, "for the Indians have an instinctive dread of them." Leeper also had Jones dismiss his Indian police because they were never around when they were needed, and as Jones said, they "proved uncontrollable and utterly useless."[1]

Certainly Leeper realized the irony of the situation, for the new agency had developed the same problems as the old one in Texas, and for which the assumed remedy was removal to Indian Territory. Leeper, however, was becoming more jaded, realizing that the Indians were only playing games with him and with the Confederacy, and had no intention of settling down in peace—at least until they had been thoroughly defeated militarily, and that had not yet happened.

In May 1862, Leeper was on an emotional roller coaster. The previous month he thought that it was useless to provision the Indians, which only facilitated raiding; now he came to believe that giving food and gifts kept at least a few of the bands in check. With the rations contract expiring, unsure if he would keep his job, and seeking funds for the new fiscal year, Leeper left for Fort Smith, Arkansas. He met with Albert Pike and smoothed over their differences, but he still did not get the funds needed. Receiving only $1,500, Leeper had enough only to pay his own salary and some of his employees. Nevertheless, he met with more bands on July 11, 1862, distributed all the gifts and supplies he had, concluded that the Kiowas and Comanches were "well satisfied," and that "perfect peace and quietness may soon be expected to prevail on the Texas frontier."

Still, there were nagging questions. Leeper saw that the Kiowas had many horses that were stolen in Texas. The last treaty required him to confiscate stolen property and one article declared that the Kiowas were to "atone for the murders and robberies" they had committed. Just how Leeper was supposed to do this was not stated, and he knew he could not demand the return of the stolen horses, for it "would at once defeat the Treaty with the wild bands and cause them to recommence their depredations with increased violence and renewed vigor."[2]

What exactly happened next is not known. Albert Pike, upon his resignation, wrote to Leeper on August 19, that he was through acting as superintendent, and "for which crowning mercy, God be thanked."[3] Later that month, Leeper left the agency under mysterious circumstances, heading for Texas and leaving the interpreter Jones in charge. He may have been taking his family to safety. In addition to the unpredictable "wild" bands, Union sympathizers among the Indians had been gaining influence. Reserve Indians who had visited in the north had returned telling stories of tribes planning to seek revenge upon those who had driven them out. It appeared that the only people who still kept strong ties with the Confederacy were the Tonkawas, and they were looked down on as cannibals and Texan minions. Indians warned Jones that Leeper should not return, because they were out to get him. Either Jones didn't transmit the warning or Leeper dismissed it, for he was back in at the agency in October.[4]

It was a mistake. The Indians did not like Leeper, but they hated the Tonkawas. For decades, that tribe had helped the Texans fight other tribes. Chief Placido and his warriors had assisted the Texans against the Cherokees in the 1830s, fought the Comanches at Plum Creek in 1840, guided the Texans to the Comanche camp at Antelope Hills in 1858, and fought with them against Peta Nocona in 1860. In addition, the Tonkawas were said to have practiced cannibalism, but the contention is arguable. One day two Tonkawas reportedly murdered a young Caddo boy out hunting, dismembered his body, and brought it to the village to cook and eat. The Caddos were enraged, and easily enlisted other tribes to seek revenge.[5]

On October 23, 1862, the ties joining the Comanches and elements of the Reserve tribes to the Confederacy were abruptly broken. In early September, 96 Delawares and Shawnees led by the Delaware, Ben Simon, left Kansas for the Leased District. They spent some time spying about the agency and learning who would assist them in their attack and who would oppose them. Simon's party found many willing allies, including a few hundred Kichais, Wichitas, Wacos, and Caddos, the latter in particular with vengeance on their minds. They were joined by a number of Comanches, Kickapoos, Seminoles, and Cherokees. About nine p.m. after the agency closed, the Indians struck. In the first rush, the white defenders killed a Delaware and wounded a Shawnee. The furious attackers then shot and killed five white men: Bickel, Harrison, Outzen, Tureman, and Bunger. They threw the bodies into the agency buildings and burned them to the ground. Matthew Leeper climbed out the rear window in his house, fled into the timber, and eventually escaped to Texas. Horace Jones' dogs barked and he went outside to see what was happening. In the darkness he saw Indians approaching his house and ran away, but one of his companions was killed. The noise and flames from the burning buildings alerted other whites in the area and most of them had time to escape.

The Tonkawas were living along the Washita River near the agency. Hearing the uproar, they quickly grabbed what belongings they could gather and fled east. Before daylight they halted to rest in a valley near present-day Anadarko. It was a fatal stop, for the other Indians surrounded them and struck. Chief Placido and his warriors fought bravely with bows and arrows against rifles, but they stood little chance; men, women, and children were indiscriminately killed. Ben Simon and his war party took 100 ponies, $1,200 in Confederate money, orders and correspondence, a Rebel flag, plus copies of the treaties signed between Pike and the Indians, back to their agent, F. Johnson, in Kansas. Johnson was pleased with the Delawares' initiative. "These Indians," he wrote, "few in numbers, marching upon a point more than five hundred miles distant, furnishing their own transportation, forage and provisions, without cost to the Government, certainly exhibit a great degree of loyalty, daring and hardihood."[6]

About 390 Tonkawas were camped near the agency, but only about 150 of them escaped, most of them running to Fort Arbuckle. If the numbers are right, about 240 Tonkawas perished in the massacre, making this incident perhaps the most devastating for any Indian tribe on the Great Plains, exceeding the carnage at Sand Creek, Washita, Marais, Wounded Knee, and every other fight or "massacre" at the hands of the whites. At the Wichita Agency, Indians killed more Indians in a single fight than white soldiers ever did, exceeding even the notable Indian-on-Indian violence when the Lakotas killed perhaps 150 Pawnees at Massacre Canyon, Nebraska in 1873. There were no white chroniclers present to record Chief Placido and his Tonkawas' last minutes, or this tragedy might have taken its place in the Pantheon of memorialized bloody massacres that have splashed across history's headlines. Then again, given the mindset of the day, perhaps the Indian-on-Indian violence would have been dismissed as conventional, emblematic behavior among "savages."[7]

Texans, oddly enough, who were often accused of Indian-hating, knew the Tonkawas were associates that they should cultivate. Even John Baylor, who considered Placido his friend, wanted to help the Tonkawas get revenge. Because of their past services, the remaining Tonkawas were induced to move back to Texas, finally congregating in the Camp Colorado area in August 1863. In a message to the state legislature in December 1863, new Governor Pendleton Murrah proposed to use the last 50 warriors in service with the Frontier Regiment and asked for $10,000 for food, clothing, and blankets for them. The Tonkawas, Murrah said, "have been friendly and true to the White man for years," and "they entertain the most bitter hostility towards their Comanche foes, and are eager to be employed in war against them."[8]

Befriending the white man, however, proved to be almost as dangerous a proposition as being his enemy, and the mixed loyalties inherent in guerrilla warfare meant that one never knew who was friend or foe. The Tonkawas tried to straddle the line and nearly half their tribe was wiped out. The "civilized" tribes of Indian Territory fought brother against brother in the white man's Civil War, and lost their lives and lands. The "wild" prairie tribes made and broke alliances with both sides, but as yet, hadn't suffered as much as the Indians maintaining a closer relationship with the whites. Their comparative isolation and reluctance to form alliances had kept them relatively safe so far, but their time was coming.

Chapter 19 notes

1 Abel, *American Indian as Slaveholder*, Leeper to Rector, December 12, 1861, 315; Leeper to Pike, April 13, 1862, 348-49; Jones to Pike, May 8, 1862, 350.

2 Ibid., Leeper to Pike, May 7, 1862, 345-49; Leeper to Pike, June 26, 1862, 351-53; Leeper to Pike, July 11, 1862, 354-55.

3 Ibid., Pike to Leeper, August 19, 1862, 356.

4 *WR:* S.1, V.53, 828; Abel, *American Indian in the Civil War*, 182-83.

5 Webb, *Handbook of Texas 2*, 383; Nye, *Carbine & Lance*, 29-30.

6 *New York Times*, February 15, 1863; Adkins-Rochette, *Bourland in North Texas II*, A-372-73; Abel, *American Indian as Slaveholder*, 329; Hoig, *Tribal Wars*, 210-11; Hoig, *White Man's Paper Trail*, 120; Nye, *Carbine & Lance*, 30-31; *WR:* S.1, V.13, 920; *WR:* S.4, V.2, 355. Several contemporary reports incorrectly claimed that Leeper had been killed.

7 Hagan, "Counting Coup," 4-5, and *passim*. Hagan chronicles the extensive inter-tribal warfare on the Great Plains and concludes that it "was never the game of mere touching [counting coup] that modern writers have so often and so erroneously portrayed." Inter-tribal war occurred frequently and "was a brutal, nasty business often conducted without quarter."

8 Adkins-Rochette, *Bourland in North Texas I*, 151-53; Winfrey and Day, *Texas Indian Papers IV*, 78-79; Webb, *Handbook of Texas 2*, 789. In 1884 the Tonkawas were moved to a reservation near present Ponca City, Oklahoma, where they were absorbed by other tribes and their language and culture became virtually extinct.

20 "Stock raisers and herders for the benefit of the Indians."

Despite all the Texan efforts, by the end of 1862 it did not appear that any progress had been made in protecting the frontier from Indian incursions. The German communities in Gillespie, Kerr, and Kendall counties had made several non-aggression agreements with the Comanches—the Germans hoping for some respite from raids and the Comanches probably seeking a safe haven during their raids to south Texas and Mexico. Both parties, however, would only keep the terms when it suited them. In early October, the Comanches were back stealing horses and a company of civilian Rangers out of Camp Verde, south of Kerrville, picked up their trail. Taylor Thompson and 14 others went as far west as Fort Mason, 45 miles northwest of Fredericksburg before giving up the chase. On their return they camped on the upper Medina River about 20 miles above Bandera.

As was so often the case, as the soldiers searched the frontier, the Indians were already within the patrol lines and causing havoc. In October on the Medina, about 30 miles below Bandera, Comanches stole stock from the inhabitants of Castroville. Ten miles from town they attacked the Krawitz cabin. Mrs. Krawitz was assisting a sick neighbor and Mr. Krawitz was home with their three children. The Indians suddenly appeared, seriously wounded the father, and captured Fritz (11), Willie (8), and their sister (6). They rode north along the river and a few nights later, had unknowingly camped within three miles of Thompson's men.

When it got dark, Fritz and Willie saw an opportunity to slip out of camp, but they were unable to get their sister, who was kept separated from them. The boys wandered in the woods until about ten p.m. when they were on the fringe of the ranger's campsite. Thompson was making the rounds when he heard a voice in the dark saying, "Say, Mister, stop." The startled Thompson hesitated when the voice said, "Mister, you're a white man ain't you?" Thompson replied in the affirmative and the two boys stepped into view holding each other's hand. They went back to camp and told their story, estimating the Indian camp was a few miles away and there were about 30 Indians. Thompson and his men decided immediately to try to rescue the little girl.

The boys couldn't find their way, however, and it was pure luck that the Rangers came upon the camp while probably half the warriors were then out searching the woods for the escaped boys. As they approached, they heard the girl crying. They left two men to stay with the boys and with the rest, charged in from two directions. Luck was still with them. They got within 30 steps of the camp before an Indian sentinel gave a holler, but by then the Rangers were inside and shooting. One of the Rangers happened right upon the Krawitz girl and swept her up in his arms. The startled warriors fought for five minutes, but six of them were killed and the rest fled. One of Thompson's men was killed and five were wounded.

They carried everyone out and hurried away to their horses before the other Comanches arrived. Finding a secure place for the rest of the night they waited, but no Indians followed. In the morning they scooped out a hole with hatchets and knives and buried the dead man, packed up, and headed south. Five days later they reached the Krawitz home and returned all three children safely to their parents. It was one of the rare occasions that captives were recovered from their abductors without having to be ransomed months or years later.[1]

A few days later, possibly the same band of Comanches were in northern Llano County looking for vengeance. John Williams, who had fought Indians on several occasions, was at the time living near Cherokee in southern San Saba County. On October 14, 1862, he, Ed King, and Ned, David, and John Truman were driving cattle to sell to the Confederate Army. While crossing Baby Head Gap in northern Llano County, about eight revenge-minded Comanches burst upon them from the rear. On the left they cut off Ed King, who was riding a slow mule, and quickly killed him. John Williams charged back toward the Comanches, hoping to bluff them and give King a chance to get away. The bluff backfired. Incomprehensibly, Williams had no weapon, and the Indians quickly noted that and rode in and shot him down. They scalped him and crushed his head with a rock. The Truman brothers made their escape.[2]

Most of the raiding activity was along a north-south line through the central part of the state, but Indians did not neglect the far western frontier. There were stock raids in the El Paso area too. In late November, Indians, perhaps Mescalero Apaches, raided Gregoria Garcia's spread at San Elizario in El Paso County and took three horses worth $300. Garcia filed a loss claim, as did many of his fellow Hispanics, but it appeared that Mexican losses along the Rio Grande in the west were not as high on the priority list as were the Anglo complaints in central Texas. The trans-Pecos territory was never allocated the troop coverage given the rest of the state.[3]

On December 6, Governor Lubbock wrote to Maj. Gen. John B. Magruder, commanding the District of Texas, New Mexico, and Arizona, stating that despite all their efforts, he believed that Texas was still not secure from wild Indians or Northern invasion. Confederate troops in the state were nearly "destitute of arms," Sibley's men were "not half armed," and Baylor's old command was "without any arms at all." There was little ammunition to go around for the few weapons they had. Lubbock reminded Magruder of the importance of Texas to the Confederacy. "Her wheat fields and her hog and cattle ranches contribute largely to feed the armies; her wool and cotton factories clothe them in part; her sons have not been behind the foremost at the call of duty, and have poured out their blood like water upon the battlefields of liberty. She deserves a better fate at the hands of the authorities than to be left with the old men and boys to defend herself, while denied the means of effectually doing it."[4]

Another player in the drama re-appeared at the end of 1862. John Baylor, deprived of his command in Arizona because of his "extermination" order, summed up the situation in a long, revealing letter to General Magruder. Writing from Houston on December 29, Baylor tried to justify his actions. He said he had lived on the frontier since his childhood, where "I have witnessed repeated outrages and barbarities almost beyond conception committed by the various savage tribes upon the frontier people of this State." One of his greatest vexations was the Indian treatment of captives. "It is equally notorious," he wrote, "that on numerous occasions the women of our State have been taken prisoners, and, after being subjected to every outrage that the brutal passions of the savage could prompt, they were murdered in cold blood, and their scalps used to ornament the shields of the Indian warriors."

Baylor still had a white scalp he had taken from the Comanches in a fight in 1860. "I respectfully request," he asked of Magruder, "that it be sent to His Excellency the President, to enable him to judge whether there is not some cause for the bitter feelings I, in common with the people of our frontier, entertain toward the Indians."

Baylor said that the late U.S. Government tried to "tame and reclaim the savages," but with a false philanthropy and little success. "The Indians lived on the reserves and in the homes provided for them, expended their annuities, devoured the Government provisions, pretended friendship with the whites, played at agriculture and civilization, and in the mean time committed robberies and murders innumerable on the citizens of the frontier."

The Confederate Government follows the same policy, Baylor lamented, and with the same poor result. It needed a new direction. Baylor tried to give it to them as governor in Arizona. "More than 100 of our citizens were murdered by these Indians in the face of a treaty which they had broken without provocation," he declared, and he felt this justified his extermination order. In addition, Baylor said, he had read an article in a Charleston, South Carolina, newspaper that indicated the Confederate Congress had recently declared a war of extermination, and believing "that such a policy was the only one suitable to the hostile and treacherous tribes, I acted on it."

Baylor continued: "If the Confederate Government adopts the policy of making treaties and endeavors to purchase peace and affords no more adequate protection from Indians than the Government of the United States has afforded on the frontier of this State and in Arizona the result will be that the citizens there will be reduced to the condition of stock raisers and herders for the benefit of the Indian tribes alone." He declared that, "extermination of the grown Indians and making slaves of the children is the only remedy."

Like Governor Lubbock, Baylor believed "that heretofore the Government was either unable or unwilling to protect our people," but even "If the Government had the combined wealth of the world it could not purchase peace with the Indians, and in my humble opinion it would be far cheaper to board the savages (were that possible) at first-class hotels than to continue the reservation, feeding, paint, and blanket system longer." One of the major reasons that Texas left the Union "was the hope and belief that our new Government would drop the old 'peace-purchasing' system with the Indians and adopt the extermination policy."

To sum up, Baylor was not sorry he had issued an extermination order, but he was sorry it was made public and "paraded before the country." The order "may not read well in Richmond," he wrote, but its sentiment was applauded in Texas and Arizona.[5]

Viewed as a racist Indian-hater today, John Baylor's views in the 1860s were shared by many frontier people. Magruder forwarded Baylor's correspondence to Secretary of War James A. Seddon. In the meantime, Baylor fought as a private in an artillery unit in battle with the Yankees at Galveston on January 1, 1863, distinguishing himself in action. Magruder commended his bravery and added that his ideas might not be far out of line, because the Indians, "whom I happen to know well" were "not better than wild beasts and totally unworthy of sympathy." Seddon passed Baylor's letter to President Davis, who answered, "This letter requires attention. It is an avowal of an infamous crime and the assertion of what should not be true in relation to troops in Texas, &c."[6]

The controversy once again illustrated the gaping divide between East and West. Those in the midst of a guerrilla war had a far different view of events than the Eastern intellectuals and philanthropists whom they believed viewed Indians through the eyes of American novelist James Fenimore Cooper and his "Leatherstocking Tales" or English poet Alexander Pope in such essays as "Lo, the poor Indian!" In the Trans-Mississippi West, neither the noble or ignoble savage could stand up to 19th century racism. If extermination was not official policy, it was certainly a valid notion in the minds of many frontier people. Likewise, a significant number of Indians, although they lacked the written word to express the thought, believed that extermination was the only way to alleviate the "white" problem.

Chapter 20 notes

1 Hunter, *Bandera County*, 248-52.

2 Wilbarger, *Indian Depredations*, 627-28; McConnell, *West Texas Frontier*, 362. McConnell places the incident in 1861.

3 Gregoria Garcia, Depredation Claim #4231.

4 *WR:* S.1, V.15, 896-97.

5 *WR:* S.1, V.15, 914-18.

6 *WR:* S.1, V.15, 918-19.

Part 5. 1863

21 "No army, no means, no system, no order."

In Minnesota in August of 1862 there occurred the greatest Indian "uprising" in American history. Over the course of about two months, the Dakotas killed more than 600 white settlers. If such a thing could occur in an area where the Indians had made great strides in settling on the reservation, farming, and following the "white man's road," what might occur in places where the Indians were unrestrained? Apprehension spread across the plains.

Texas was far from Minnesota, but the people had their own worries. The Comanches and Kiowas were as formidable a foe as the Lakotas or Cheyennes and the Texans operated under more severe handicaps than in the northern states. In Texas, only one percent of the available capital was involved in industrial production. It had few manufacturing establishments, few railroads, and poor transportation. The government could not arm its soldiers. There was plenty of cotton and cattle, but the armies could get few supplies; its soldiers dressed in rags and they had no shoes. The agricultural base was there, but the nearly non-existent infrastructure meant that little could be produced and transported to those in need. Texas likely had the poorest armed armies in the Confederacy, never having enough weapons for its soldiers.

It was overwhelmingly rural. Its largest town, San Antonio, only had 8,000 people. The state had 420,000 white citizens and 182,000 black slaves. When about 60,000 whites left to join the Southern armies, it left only about two whites for every black slave. They were extremely worried, not only of Indians on the frontier, but of a slave insurrection in the interior.

By the start of 1863, Texans were losing hope. In Clarksville the newspaper editor complained that "In this department there is some error of management, which brings the most splendid preparations to the most lame and impotent conclusions." He said that Confederate forces lose battles, territory, supplies, and their Indian allies, while the enemy knows more about their designs then its own generals. He was certain "there is miserable inefficiency somewhere," and hoped the War Department could fix it.

The new Trans-Mississippi Department Commander, Gen. Edmund Kirby Smith, grumbled of the same problems. "I have a herculanian task before me…no army—no means—an empire in extent, no system, no order, all to be done from the beginning."[1]

Before Smith arrived to try and make some sense out of the disorder, Governor Francis Lubbock was making similar complaints to District Commander General Magruder, saying that they could not arm their people, could not utilize and distribute their livestock and agricultural produce, and were still threatened by Indians on the frontier. How to solve frontier defense problems was a tough issue, with outspoken calls from men like John Baylor to exterminate the Indians, pleas from those who wanted more peace treaties, and tactical questions on how to use the troops most effectively, in defensive patrols or in offensive sweeps to take the war to the Indians.

Expecting he could still get President Davis to take the Frontier Regiment into Confederate service, Lubbock reorganized it into ten companies to serve three years and called it the Mounted Regiment, although it was generally referred to by its original name. Colonel Norris resigned and James E. McCord became the new colonel, with James Barry the lieutenant-colonel. The reorganization made little difference, however, for Davis still rejected the proposal to pay for it without control of it.

With no money coming from Richmond, the Texans could use the regiment as they saw fit. McCord, an experienced, aggressive, frontiersman, figured that passive patrols had not worked in the past and he would begin offensive operations. In the ten months prior to January 1863, Colonel Norris reported that the regiment had killed 21 Indians, followed 52 trails, and recovered 309 stolen horses. The results were mediocre, especially given the often inflated claims of Indian casualties. With the new year and reorganization, there was hope of better results. It has been said that the Frontier Regiment had its days of greatest effectiveness in the summer and fall of 1863,[2] but that assertion does not appear valid. Lt. Col. "Buck" Barry, who is often cited as proof, filled his reminiscences during these months with other concerns. Their guns were inferior, the ammunition was worthless, the powder was unfit, many of their horses had died, the men caught typhoid fever and had other ills, and the widows of slain soldiers were pressing the government for financial help.

The regiment's big spring scout was a "Failure to encounter Indians," and the plans of a campaign into Indian Territory never materialized. Governor Lubbock was afraid to send the regiment away for fear that the Federals might invade along the coast, the citizens were afraid the Indians would side-step the expedition and raid while it was gone, Unionist Indians were said to be making invasion plans, and there was no money available to fund the campaign.[3]

McCord's plans never came to fruition and it likely would have made little difference if they had. As discussed above, the Indians didn't know or care how the Texans patrolled their frontier. Other factors were more important in determining their moves and they did not operate solely as a reaction to Texan initiatives. While "Buck" Barry patrolled the frontier line in the north with six companies, and Maj. W. J. Alexander patrolled the south with four companies, the Indians slipped through at will.

On January 31, 1863, James Billings and his son, John (12), were on horseback hunting stray sheep at the head of Willow Creek, about a dozen miles northeast of Fredericksburg in Gillespie County. About three miles from their home, 15 warriors surrounded them and wounded them each five times. John was either clubbed or hit in the head with a rock, for he was knocked unconscious and played dead while the Indians scalped his father. When the Indians left, John crawled to a neighbor, Wesley Cadwell, who got help and went back to get Mr. Billings. He wasn't at the scene of the attack, but had crawled to Willow Creek to get water, where he died. He was stripped naked except for one sock. John and seven other children were fatherless.[4]

Although the Germans of Fredericksburg had made peace agreements with the Comanches there were always those who would not abide. On February 13, 1863, Henry Arhelger and a companion were scouting six miles from town when Indians attacked. The other man escaped on a fast horse, but Arhelger was on a mule and was soon caught. He dismounted and apparently put up a good fight, for there was evidence of blood indicating he hit some of his assailants, but he was killed nevertheless. The next morning searchers found him; he had 40 wounds in his body and it was said that a nearby tree and the ground surrounding it held 83 arrows.

About this time Conrad and Heinrich Meckel, Fredericksburg merchants, and Yoakum Hench, who lived a few miles north of town, had gone to Mason County on business. As they returned driving some milk cows, Comanches attacked and killed them about two miles northwest of Loyal Valley in Mason County. The mail carrier, Ludorff Meyer, found their bodies that night. They were robbed, but not scalped. Meyer reported the discovery and a number of townsmen returned the bodies to Fredericksburg for burial.

Although the date is uncertain, about this time Indians killed Mathis Pehl while he was out alone and afoot hunting stock near his home about ten miles southeast of Fredericksburg. On February 28, 1863, George W. Kendall wrote from Boerne in Kendall County about the depredations, stating that Jim Little was also killed about this time, his body mutilated and "the flesh being cut from him as if the Indians had cooked it." Kendall said that two Holstein boys had been killed on Beaver Creek in Mason County, and a Mr. Hudson was killed while hunting sheep with his 12-year-old son. The boy was wounded, but escaped.

Kendall complained that none of the militiamen were "supplied with ammunition enough, of good quality, to shoot a rabbit." He also wondered about the draft officers roaming the county, speculating that they had better hurry and "get all their conscripts before the Indians kill them off." Kendall believed it was folly to draft the remaining men because of a "threatened invasion from the abolitionists, and leave their own women and children exposed to a real and positive inroad of murderous savages, who respect neither age nor sex."[5]

The Union Army was far removed in space and thought for most frontier people; they had more pressing issues. On February 19, raiders were in San Saba County where they killed an old man named Black at his house near the mouth of the San Saba River.

On February 20, they were in Burnet County. Jonathan P. Ragle and Lewis Jackson, who lived about 12 miles northeast of Burnet, were taking a wagon load of corn to Morgan's Mill to be ground. Less than two miles from home, Indians ambushed and killed them, cut the corn sacks, and dumped about 15 bushels worth on the ground. They filled the oxen with arrows and rode west. Within six miles of Burnet they ran into three boys, Lorenzo Holland (18), and brothers Marcus (12) and Benton (10) Scaggs (Skagg?). The boys took refuge in a thicket and defended themselves as well as they could, having only one pistol among them. A bullet pierced Holland's head from temple to temple. Marcus Scaggs was wounded in the leg, and little Benton fired the pistol with such determination that the Indians finally left them.

Benton fled to Ragle's cabin for help, stumbling across Ragle's and Jackson's bodies on the way. He told Mrs. Ragle the sad news. The next day, citizens gathered to help, but all they could do was recover the bodies. Marcus Scaggs recovered from his wound.[6]

In February 1863, Mr. and Mrs. Wofford Johnson and three children lived near the Burnet-Williamson County line on Dog Branch, a tributary of the San Gabriel River. They had been making molasses at Mr. Whitehead's and were returning home when Indians struck, killing both parents and their daughter, Mary Jane (8). Georgianna (18 months) was hit and dropped into the brush. Elvira (5) fled down the trail. Just then, Katie Johnson, the Johnsons' niece, rode up and saw her aunt and uncle being killed. Elvira ran up, Katie hoisted her on the horse, and they galloped home where she told her father what had happened. Wofford's brother immediately rode to the scene, but the Indians were already gone. He returned, got some help, and they searched for the missing, finding Mr. Johnson and Mary Jane all shot with arrows. A second search located Mrs. Johnson, lanced in the breast and with nine arrows in her. The next day a boy, Jimmie Gilliland, discovered Georgianna shivering in the branches of a fallen blackjack tree. When he called to her, she ran to him with arms outstretched. An arrow had passed clear through her forearm. The three dead were buried in the Hopewell Cemetery seven miles west of Liberty Hill.[7]

Camp Davis, on the Pedernales River west of Fredericksburg, guarded the line in Gillespie County. In February 1863, Lt. James M. Hunter got word of Indian marauders in the area and led out 11 soldiers to find them. They picked up a trail on the Llano River and traced it up the James River to its source, then east toward the headwaters of the Pedernales west of present-day Harper, Texas. Hunter suddenly came upon an equal number of 11 Comanches, but having only two horses among them.

Hunter charged, but the Comanches stood their ground until about half of them were hit, and when a warrior who appeared to be the leader was killed, the Indians fled. The warriors stopped to fight whenever the soldiers paused to reload. John Benson was hit by an arrow in the hip and the spike curled around the bone like a fishhook. Hunter believed all the Indians would have been killed except for the fact that the Rangers used what Hunter called "Confederate powder," an ersatz substance of poor quality. Even so, Hunter reported killing six Indians.[8]

The raiders may have been the ones who had hit William G. Fuch's farm on February 25. Fuchs lived inside the patrol line in central Burnet County, but that made little difference to the thieves. They took two of his horses that he claimed were worth $175. The two horses may have been the ones Comanches used to escape from Hunter.[9]

In addition to the Frontier Regiment, there were many Texas State troops scattered in military districts along the frontier. None of them seemed to deter the raiders. In the north, the 21st Brigade District under Gen. William Hudson, based in Gainesville, did its best to help protect the region. One company under Capt. Joseph Ward was based at Camp Brunson in Clay County. On February 10 they discovered an Indian trail on Lodge Creek leading into the settlements. They followed it for two days and lost it. Back in camp they picked up another trail only a mile away. Lieutenant Charles Lindsey took ten men and followed the trail 13 miles and found the Indians holed up in some timber. Ward wrote, "The men being keen for a fight, they charged the Indians, but were repulsed, with the loss of one man killed [Thomas G. Birdwell], one man slightly wounded [Beverly Lawrence]," and three horses killed and wounded. The defeat, he said, was "on account of the men not being provided with good gun powder, and plenty of good caps, for they wanted to fight, and could not, for their arms would not fire." The Indians held the field and Ward did not know how many were hit, but he believed one was killed.

Ward got more men and pursued. "They are between us & our homes, and in large numbers, from 50 to 100 in a bunch," he reported. The Indians were indeed inside the defense perimeter. Spencer Moore (or Mueller) and his family lived near Denton Creek in southern Montague County. In mid-February Spencer and his oldest son, Ira, were working splitting rails for Lewis Davis. The job had lasted quite a while and they were nearly finished and looked in anticipation to deliver the rails and get paid. The woods had been ringing with the sound of their axes, but one morning, their neighbor, Cash McDonald, noticed that the sound had ceased. To him, the silence meant trouble. He got some neighbors and they went to the site, discovering the two killed and scalped. From the blood around it looked like Ira had fought his assailants with his ax. Both were buried in their "Sunday shirts" in the Denver Cemetery, about midway between present Sunset and Forestburg.

The morning after the Moores were killed, the Indians came upon John K. Stump and a young man named Bailey, who lived on Clear Creek, seven miles southwest of Head of Elm in Montague County. They were headed to Gainesville to get their grain ground but only made it two miles before the Indians appeared. Stump likely recalled his wife's admonition to take his gun with him, but he preferred to leave it behind for the family's protection. Bailey, who worked for Stump, began to wail that they would be killed. The Indians toyed with them, explaining in broken English that they were good Caddos and would not harm them, but only wanted their clothes. The men stripped down and the Indians began to chase them. They shot and killed Bailey, but Stump ran into the brush where the mounted Indians could not follow as easily. He ran a quarter mile, but was hit by nearly a dozen bullets and arrows as he fled. He made it to Bill Priest's field and collapsed near Priest, who was working with his rifle at hand. He bluffed the Indians away, and carried Stump to the house. Stump could not be moved for nearly a month, but he recovered from his wounds.

Captain Ward wrote that the raiders left a calling card. When they caught their victims, he said, "they scalp them, they cut off their left ear, & take out the left eye, & cut off the left hand, & then leave a piece of red blanket flying by their victims." The marauders also killed stock, cutting out the tongues. Ward concluded, "they are carrying out death and destruction wherever they go…" but promised to "root them out, or fall in the attempt."[10]

Indians raided into Parker County, stole horses, and were heading back out along the Brazos. On the last day of February they met Benjamin F. Baker who lived three miles east of the town of Palo Pinto. Baker had left home that morning to see Dr. G. P. Barber a few more miles to the east. Barber had just killed some hogs and Baker wanted to buy some fresh pork. He made his purchase and was only a quarter mile from Barber's when about eight warriors surprised him. Baker galloped back to Barber's, but took four arrows in his back, arm, and thigh. He reached Barber's gate and dropped dead, but Barber ran out with his weapon and kept the warriors from Baker's body. They took Baker's horse, and one of Barber's, and rode away.

The next day, March 1, William M. Peters (30), who lived in western Palo Pinto County on Ioni Creek, was riding to town on business. His wife asked him to saddle up the best horse, but he said it was too much trouble, and he took his old, slow work horse. The Indian raiders met him five miles west of Palo Pinto. He tried to escape but the horse gave out and Peters dismounted and ran to a deserted cabin built by George Hazelwood. The cabin was of dubious protection, due mainly to the large cracks in the walls. Peters held out as long as he could, but he ran out of ammunition. Finally, a warrior must have gone right up to the cabin and blasted Peters in the face at close range through one of the cracks. He had a fatal wound in his forehead and his face was powder burned. The Indians scalped him and finally vacated the county.[11]

A letter from Mason County dated March 17, 1863, reported that 16 Indians attacked a cabin just north of Fort Mason. They approached with a white flag and asked the unnamed man and woman for food. As they ate, the couple slipped out the back, but the woman was overtaken, "tied and whipped with a lariat, after which she was scalped and turned loose. The man made his escape. The woman died shortly after.[12]

In March, Comanches raided Llano County. For the third time in three years they stole stock from Joseph D. Cady, this time getting away with a six-year-old "cream horse" worth $100 and a seven-year-old bay worth $75.[13]

According to Capt. William C. Twitty, 21st Brigade, Comanches killed eight homesteaders during the first two months of 1863 (it was actually about 22), while stealing hundreds of horses and cattle. He warned that unless they could get more help, "the frontier will be entirely broken up." James Diamond said that the settlers west of Gainesville were "almost ready to flee their homes and sacrifice…their possessions." It was a familiar litany, and the authorities tried their best to respond.

In February 1863, Cooke County residents James J. Diamond and James G. Bourland, the latter who had figured prominently in the Gainesville Hangings, went to Governor Lubbock and got authorization for more companies to protect the border. The unit, never more than 500-men strong, was known as Bourland's Cavalry or Diamond's Cavalry or Bourland's "Border Regiment." Lubbock could barely raise enough money, but although it was being funded by Texas, it was eventually attached to the Confederate Army and spent its service partly in Texas and partly in Indian Territory.[14]

On March 3, Brig, Gen. William Hudson, 21st Brigade District, wrote from Gainesville to headquarters in Austin, that "our troubles…have greatly increased." Indians "have killed 1 woman, 1 white man & one negro, the two latter in this county [Cooke]. There is small bodies, from six to 10 together have been in the edge of our town, stolen horses in 1-½ miles of this place & appear to be all through the country portions of this and Montague counties have given way." Hudson said that he advised the settlers to drive their surplus horses into the interior and get together with other families and fort up.[15]

While Hudson wrote of Indians depredating in Cooke and Montague counties, raiders were in Palo Pinto County again. On April 5, they hit Henry Welty's ranch four miles south of present-day Graford. Welty (45), from

Arkansas and one of the first settlers in the county, saddled up his horse, "Old Blaze," and went out to round up his milk pen calves, which were grazed separate from the cows.

Night fell, Welty had not returned home, and Mrs. Welty and her five children heard Indians howling and hooting on all sides of the house. She had one gun and stood guard all night. In the morning she took the children and walked to the nearest neighbor, George R. Bevers. On the way, the family met Bevers and Dave McClure, who were on their way to Palo Pinto. They got help and searched for Welty, finding him a short time later, shot with several arrows and bullets, stripped, scalped, and with the flesh on his limbs sliced off. They buried him near his house. Mrs. Welty gave birth to another daughter only a few weeks later.[16]

On April 8, Comanches or Kiowas crossed Red River and re-visited the ranch of Joseph H. Martin in Wise County. They had stolen horses from him the previous October, but no one could help him at the time because of the great uproar caused by the trials and hangings that month. There were no such distractions this time, but the border companies still didn't help. The Indians got away with eight horses worth $400.[17]

On April 16, men named Williamson and Hendrickson were attacked in western Coryell County. They lived near the present village of King and had been west in Mills County looking to recover horses stolen in a previous raid. On their return while riding near Cowhouse Creek about eight miles from home, one dozen Indians jumped them. Hendrickson rode rapidly away, but Williamson, an old man who was leading another horse tied to his saddle horn, struggled unsuccessfully with the knot. He decided to fight it out, which no doubt enabled Hendrickson to escape, but cost Williamson his life. Hendrickson found some men to help him, but when they returned, Williamson was dead and scalped. They buried him where he fell.[18]

Chapter 21 notes

1 Kerby, *Kirby Smith's Confederacy*, 1-5, 51, 54, 73, 77, 79; *The Standard* (Clarksville, Texas), January 31, 1863.

2 Roth, "Frontier Defense Challenges," 29-30; Smith, *Frontier Defense*, 52-53; *The Texas Almanac* (Austin), June 4, 1863.

3 Greer, ed., *Buck Barry*, 146-50, 157, 167.

4 McConnell, *West Texas Frontier*, 411; *Semi-Weekly News* (San Antonio), February 12, 1863.

5 Biggers, *German Pioneers in Texas*, 170; McConnell, *West Texas Frontier*, 434, 445; Tiling, *German Element in Texas*, 105; *The Texas Almanac* (Austin), March 7, 1863.

6 McConnell, *West Texas Frontier*, 410; Wilbarger, *Indian Depredations*, 625; *The Texas Almanac* (Austin), February 27, 1863. The Ragle-Jackson story varies slightly. Wilbarger says the boys were with Ragle and Jackson when attacked, and that Holland lived a week before dying.

7 McConnell, *West Texas Frontier*, 457; Wilbarger, *Indian Depredations*, 625; "Mrs. C. C. Proctor," http://www.rootsweb.ancestry.com/~txburnet/ProctorMrsCC.html.

8 Sowell, *Early Settlers*, 561, 564-65; Smith, *Frontier Defense*, 97.

9 William G. Fuchs, Depredation Claim #7155.

10 Adkins-Rochette, *Bourland in North Texas*, I, 158-59; Adkins-Rochette, *Bourland in North Texas*, II, A-262; Potter, *Montague County*, 22-23, 63-65; McConnell, *West Texas Frontier*, in forttours.com/pages/mueller.asp and forttours.com/pages/bailey.asp.

11 McConnell, *West Texas Frontier*, 414, 415; Wilbarger, *Indian Depredations*, 510-11. Coincidentally, George Hazelwood was killed by Indians on March 1, 1868, five years after Peters.

12 *The Texas Almanac* (Austin), April 4, 1863.

13 Joseph D. Cady, Depredation Claim #650.

14 Collins, *Cooke County*, 18-19; Smith, *Frontier Defense*, 64; Adkins-Rochette, *Bourland in North Texas*, I, 162, 175.

15 Adkins-Rochette, *Bourland in North Texas*, II, A-263.

16 McConnell, *West Texas Frontier*, 416; Wilbarger, *Indian Depredations*, 511.

17 Joseph H. Martin, Depredation Claim #4787.

18 McConnell, *West Texas Frontier*, 417; Wilbarger, *Indian Depredations*, 487; *The Texas Almanac* (Austin), May 7, 1863. McConnell gives the date as April 12, but Lt. J. M. Chandler, Company I, Frontier Regiment, reported the incident happening on April 16.

22 "I am afraid to live in this country any longer."

The situation on the frontier seemed to be deteriorating. The German counties north and west of San Antonio were still resisting conscription and seemed on the point of rebellion. In early 1863, Governor Lubbock finally gave up and excused neutral Germans from the draft while permitting them to form their own home defense units, which naturally angered the non-Germans who were not happy with the draft either. In late February in Indian Territory, the Cherokee Nation assembled at Cowskin Prairie and decided to nullify their treaty with the C.S.A. and appoint commissioners to negotiate a new treaty with the U.S.A.[1]

On May 1, Comanches were in Brown County, stealing three horses worth $135 from William Williams. It was the second time he had been robbed. Two days later, about 40 miles to the east, possibly the same raiding party was in the area where Comanche, Hamilton, and Erath counties meet. Samuel Rogers, a native of Tennessee, had settled in the southern tip of Erath County just west of present-day Carlton. He had spent the night at the home of a neighbor, Mr. Secrest, and was on his way home when the Comanches found him. Rogers rode his little sorrel pony as fast as he could. He was almost home when several other warriors, who had been at his house trying to steal horses, were returning to the main war party and they caught Rogers in between. He rode his pony into a deep gully and was trapped. The Indians closed in from above, killed and scalped him. His son, James Rogers, got a posse, and they were soon on the trail which led west to Resley Creek, the Leon River, and up Copperas Creek. The posse caught up and in a running fight, many shots were exchanged, but it did not appear that anyone was hit.[2]

Governor Lubbock searched for a better scheme to counter the Indian raids and the increasing desertions, and in May 1863, he reorganized his defenses. The Third Military District, usually called the Northern Sub-District, was given to Brig. Gen. Smith P. Bankhead and headquartered in Bonham, Fannin County. As Bourland got his force ready and Bankhead familiarized himself with his district, there was guarded optimism in the ranks. On May 17, an officer, writing from Camp Colorado under the pseudonym "Rifle," was concerned that it appeared "little or nothing of our doings has found its way into any of the papers." The regiment was out on the frontier, hoping to do great things, and with proper supplies "we can't fail to do good service." "Rifle" said that the Indians come and go, "Stealing like a shadow through our midst," and "we rarely if ever hear of his presence in the settlements, until his depredations have been committed, and he is gone far beyond our reach…."

The correspondent said that the old tactic of daily patrol between camps was a great drawback on their usefulness, since it "served but to break down our horses and depress the spirits of the men" and proved "but a melancholy farce." He was hopeful that offensive operations would take them "to the homes of the Indians themselves" and achieve great results. Lieutenant Colonel Barry was to take 260 men to the Canadian River, Captain Callahan was to take 85 men to the head of the Brazos, and Captain Hunter was to take 100 men to the Horsehead Crossing of the Pecos. "Rifle" was certain "that they will give a good account of themselves."

Instead, lack of money, supplies, direction, and reluctance to send the regiment away when the Indians and Federals might appear, resulted in few of the great plans ever getting off the ground. The patrols were continued as usual and the Indians came and went as usual.[3]

On May 30, raiders in Parker County stole 40 horses, making, according to the report, 140 taken from that county within three weeks. Thomas Cavness (30), an Arkansas native, lived on Cherokee Creek, three miles west of present Cherokee, San Saba County. While out searching for cattle on June 12, 1863, Indians charged him. After a long chase, they shot an arrow into him and left him to die. Some settlers found him late in the day and buried him nearby.[4]

In early June, raiders made an appearance farther east than they usually went. Nathan Holt, who lived near the Brazos on the Johnson-Hood County line, went out alone one sunny morning to drive in his cattle. He had a cow and her calf nearly home when warriors rode up to him and pierced him with a dozen arrows. His body was found the next day. A Johnson County neighbor, Lucy Dennis, in a letter to her soldier husband, said that Holt was "barbarously murdered and scalped." In addition, she told him that "Tom Hill, your brother soldier, was shot and scalped by the barbarians." She said, "The Indians are very bad here—worse than they have ever been before. I think ere long they will take and kill the last horse in the settlement." She said the Indians were in the area for six weeks, taking all the neighbors' stock and all of her horses, except one. Some of the people were moving farther east of the Brazos. "I am afraid to live in this country any longer," she wrote. "I will go to father's if possible."[5]

About this time in Coryell County, John Sellars (Sellers) (14) and Almond Boyd (13) were searching for horses. Almond, a son of James J. Boyd, lived about four miles south of present, Pancake, in the northern part of the county. The boys had been down around the Leon River and were returning home about sunset when Boyd pointed to the brush and told Sellars to look out for a large panther. The "panther" rose up and turned out to be an Indian, and several others also appeared. Sellars, in front on a good horse, dashed down the hillside, but Boyd, on a blind pony, was quickly caught and shot. The Indians chased Sellars for a time, but gave up and returned to finish off Boyd, cutting his throat and lancing him 11 times. Sellars rode quickly to Boyd's to report to his father and the man got some companions and when the moon rose about nine p.m., rode back to find his son's body in a cedar brake. The raiders rode west of Gatesville and then disappeared.[6]

As often happened, while some raiders were in the settlements, detachments of soldiers were chasing others on the frontier. In June, a squad of men under Sgt. James G. Willett, Company G of the Frontier Regiment, went out on a scout. Willett, with S. M. "Babe" Williams, Hail Woods, Maliki Wood, A. M. Williams, Gordon Bedford, George Dodson, Gilbert Morgan, Granger Dyer, Pete Littlefield, and four others, left the Fort Belknap area and headed west. They picked up an Indian trail and followed it far beyond the settlements into Stonewall County. On June 18, about ten miles northwest of Double Mountain, they found the Indians in a large brushy thicket near the Salt Fork Brazos. The soldiers skirmished with the Comanches as they dashed in and out of the bush. One warrior dueled with "Babe" Williams and then darted between Williams and Willett. Williams followed and saw Willett's horse get shot as the sergeant battled another warrior. Williams shot Willett's adversary and the Comanches soon pulled away. Willett was wounded while the soldiers believed they had killed four warriors.[7]

On July 18, 1863, Lt. James R. Giddens took 26 men of Company D, Frontier Regiment, out from Red River Station "on an Indian hunt." They traveled up and down the Wichita and Little Wichita, up Beaver Creek, and north to Pease River. On July 26, Farrier C. A. Wooldridge and Pvt. John Higgins got separated from the command "through carelessness on our part," said Wooldridge. They rode in vain for three days trying to pick up the trail, but instead found plenty of evidence that a large Indian war party had passed through, heading for the Clay County settlements. On the fourth day, the two decided they had better ride straight for civilization before they starved, "having had nothing to eat since leaving the scout, but one prairie dog and one rabbit." On August 1, sick, faint, and tired, they reached a cabin on the Little Wichita where a settler fed them and gave them a bed. Two days later, Lieutenant Giddens pulled in, having seen none of the war trails.[8]

The raiders were already past them. It didn't appear that passive patrols or active scouts could stop Indian incursions. John Kisor, ranching in the southeast corner of Clay County, was directly in their path. About July 25, Kisor (45), Kisor's son, William P. Hodges, John W. McGee and Levi "Bud" Hill, were rounding up cattle south of Buffalo Springs near the Jack County line on what Kisor called Ten Mile Prairie. Kisor said they found a pool of water, hobbled their horses, let them graze, and sat down to eat dinner. By the time they finished, the horses had wandered about 150 yards away. As Kisor was unhobbling his horse, he said he "ris" up and "seen the Indians coming and there was 18 of them; they charged on us and we were unarmed with the exception of one 6-shooter and we could not find them." Did Kisor mean that five men were on the border during an Indian war with but one pistol among them, or did they each have one but couldn't locate them? In either case it seems to be the height of folly to be so unprepared, yet we have seen the various states' inability to supply weapons for their citizen-soldiers, including a similar dearth of firearms on the Minnesota frontier.

Kisor called to the others to make for a rocky place nearby, but "they made no effort" and he hopped on his horse to get away. The horse, however, threw Kisor to the ground, hurting him badly. He stumbled into some briars and dogwood and hid. Some Comanches expertly corralled the horses while others surrounded the other dismounted whites and calmly shot them down. Kisor watched as they tried to run and hide behind a few scattered trees, but it was hopeless. Kisor "ris" up again to see the warriors blasting the whites at close range, then ducked until all was quiet. "I went out and there lay three dead men;" he said, "two was scalped and one was cut all around for his scalp, but it was not taken off...and one of the other men was badly mutilated." Hodges and Hill were shot full of arrows and McGee was killed with a spear.

Kisor walked toward Red River Station. Two miles from Buffalo Springs he found his son, who had gotten away, but was badly wounded and could go no farther. Kisor got help from Capt. Joseph Ward at Camp Brunson, who sent men with a wagon and team back to pick up Kisor's boy and the three bodies. Hodges, McGee, and Hill were buried at Buffalo Springs.[9]

Raiders were all over Texas in July and August. On July 17, Comanches raided Peter Lang's farm in Llano County near the village of Castell, stealing Lang's sorrel horse and roan mare, worth $110. A witness to the affair was Fritz Hoerster, whose brother, William, had been abducted by Kiowas in almost the same spot on July 19, 1859.[10]

It was bad enough that the Indians stole horses, but many settlers figured it just wasn't right to kill so many. On July 20, near the town of Llano, they captured a number of horses, but killed 20 of them, an act the settlers considered a senseless waste of horseflesh. In Blanco County on July 21, a resident of Round Mountain, "J.T.C.," complained to the newspaper that Indians "stole and killed all the horses they could lay their eyes upon." The writer expressed what so many frontier settlers were apparently thinking: "If the Frontier Regiment keeps on hauling cotton (a reference to the army's impressment of cotton to pay its bills), making dancing parties, visiting their friends and relatives, &c., &c., it may well be disbanded at once." He also said that he recently heard from a man from Uvalde with the same opinion, that the people there "have represented the company stationed in that vicinity as a *nuisance*, and requested its removal by the Governor."[11]

Nothing was going well. After the Confederacy lost Vicksburg and control of the Mississippi River in July 1863, they were effectively cut-off from the rest of the country. Lubbock tried to call out more troops, but they "know they can not be armed. Despondent and disheartened, they have but little hope of the result."[12]

In late-July, Comanches were in Erath County where they shot the widow Rasin near her home on Barton Creek. They then rode into western Hood County (then Johnson County) while Jeremiah Green, Wylie Price, Woodson Bell and two others were riding the range between Paluxy River and Squaw Creek looking for cattle. Under the hot noon sun they went to a creek for water and let their horses graze, when 16 Comanches approached. The five whites had two guns among them and were divided in what course of action to take. One of them made the decision by fleeing, then two more followed, leaving Green and Bell with one gun and no other choice but to run also. At the rear of the line, they were soon overtaken. Bell, with the gun, dismounted, fled into the thick cedars and got away. Green, on the slowest animal, was caught and mortally wounded. The men who fled eventually returned with help and brought Green in, but too late.[13]

In the same area, the Indians killed Rigman Bryant and his dog while he was out alone hunting foxes. They lanced him through his body, scalped him, and stole his horse. Later that day the Indians came upon W. C. Walters, Silar Scarborough, and an old black slave, who were returning from a mill to their home on Squaw Creek. When they rode into a herd of stolen horses, they knew Indians were near. In minutes the warriors appeared and the men fled. The two whites on fleet horses escaped, but the old man riding a mule was caught. The warriors tried to convince him to join them, but he refused and they speared and scalped him, much as they did Bryant. The old man lived about two weeks. The locals said it was one of the few instances when Indians scalped a black man.

A party of settlers encountered the raiders near Squaw Creek about two miles north of the present town of Glen Rose, Somervell County. A short fight followed and Daniel McBride was wounded by an arrow above his eye. They chased the Indians about six miles and recovered a few stolen horses, but they got away, heading north. In northern Hood County and southern Parker County they made up for losses by stealing more horses on Long Creek and Bear Creek, and then turned west to Spring Creek.[14]

Chapter 22 notes

1 Kerby, *Kirby Smith's Confederacy*, 93, 122.

2 William L. Williams, Depredation Claim #4739; McConnell, *West Texas Frontier*, 418; Wilbarger, *Indian Depredations*, 502-03; Deaton, *Indian Fights on the Texas Frontier*, 120-21.

3 Smith, *Frontier Defense*, 66; *The Texas Almanac* (Austin), June 4, 1863.

4 *Galveston Weekly News*, June 24, 1863; McConnell, *West Texas Frontier*, 518; Marcell, "Family Lines," http://freepages.genealogy.rootsweb.ancestry.com/~stumbo/pafg340.htm

5 Wilbarger, *Indian Depredations*, 464; *Galveston Weekly News*, June 24, 1863. Wilbarger places the Holt killing in 1859, but the June 1863 paper is most likely correct.

6 Deaton, *Indian Fights on the Texas Frontier*, 122-24; McConnell, *West Texas Frontier*, in http://www.forttours.com/pages/boydalmond.asp. There was speculation that the boys had been attacked by white renegades disguised as Indians.

7 McConnell, *West Texas Frontier*, 419.

8 *The Standard* (Clarksville, Texas), September 17, 1863.

9 John Kisor, Depredation Claim #4198. Kisor's son recovered and joined the Confederate Army, but died of measles before the war's end.

10 Peter Lang, Depredation Claim #434; Michno, *A Fate Worse Than Death*, 180-81.

11 *Galveston Weekly News*, August 5, 1863.

12 Lubbock, *Memoirs*, 492.

13 McConnell, *West Texas Frontier*, 453; Wilbarger, *Indian Depredations*, 465; *Galveston Weekly News*, August 19, 1863. A family history indicates that Green lived until August 22 and died in Granbury.

14 McConnell, *West Texas Frontier*, 472; Wilbarger, *Indian Depredations*, 466.

23 "If you are a prisoner, don't be afraid."

In Parker County it had been two years since the last large raid and perhaps the settlers had let their guard down. About July 24, 1863, several families living near Mt. Nebo, 12 miles south of Weatherford, gathered together to make sorghum into molasses at Oliver Fulton's new mill on Spring Creek, about one mile northwest of Mt. Nebo. Living with Fulton were his two orphan nieces, Lou and Hannah Akers. Fulton's brother-in-law, Hiram Wilson, lived one mile southwest of Mt. Nebo. It was customary for the youngsters to have a "candy pull" after the molasses making was done. Fulton wanted to borrow Hiram Wilson's ox and sent William Wilson (12) and Hannah Akers (12) back to Wilson's house. Mrs. Richardson, who lived about halfway between the Wilson and Fulton homes, saw the two children go by about ten in the morning.[1]

Only half a mile from Wilson's, seven painted Comanches blocked their path. Bill wanted to run home, but Hannah pleaded with him not to leave her. They both ran, but a warrior knocked Bill down with the butt of his lance, and hauled him up on the horse behind him. Hannah cried and angrily swung her bonnet, but she was also placed on a horse behind a rider.

The Indians rode for Mt. Nebo and from the slopes they looked for pursuers and planned their moves. They could see the settlers busy making sorghum, still unaware that two children had been captured. They also saw a wagon train with plenty of horses go into camp on the east side of the mountain. At nightfall two Comanches stayed behind to guard Bill and Hannah, while the other five crept downhill, rounded up 18 horses, and brought them back to the foot of the mountain. They were "necked" together for travel and the victorious Comanches with their horses and captives rode off to the west, using the moonlight to illuminate their path.

The "candy pull" at Fulton's place ended about nine p.m. Hiram Wilson and Oliver Fulton were not aware that the children were missing. Each assumed the cousins had spent the night at the other's home. It was not until the next day when Wilson visited Fulton to see how the sorghum making was progressing, that they both learned the children were gone. Just then, a rider approached with the news that Indians were seen crossing the Brazos the day before, heading for Mt. Nebo. They finally realized the children had been taken.[2]

The Indians rode all night and crossed the Brazos before they stopped to rest. They next day about noon they stopped to eat at Sunday Creek near the

Erath-Palo Pinto County line. Bill and Hannah discussed their predicament; he wanted to cooperate, but Hannah fought and cried.

The Mt. Nebo settlers organized a search party and followed the trail two days before they lost it and sadly returned home. Another party had more luck. The raiders were seen coming through a pass in the Palo Pinto Mountains in western Palo Pinto County and heading east to the settlements. About 45 frontier scouts under Captain Hughes from Stephenville, currently camped around present-day Ranger, in Eastland County, moved to the pass, hoping to intercept the Indians when they returned. It was a long shot, but on the trail leading to the pass the scouts placed a horse and a mule as bait. Remarkably, the raiders took the same escape route, probably through Metcalf Gap. Two Indians rode in front, with Bill and Hannah next in line, then the horses, and five Indians bringing up the rear. Part way up the pass, the lead Indians spotted the horse and mule in the moonlight. One had a saddle on it, and tied to it was an old white hat with turkey feathers. The puzzled Indians halted, consulted, and then one howled like a wolf, and others hooted like an owl, but there was no answer. The curious warriors rode forward to investigate when the night air was shattered by gunfire.

The lead horses were hit, as was the old roan that Bill and Hannah rode. The children tumbled to the ground and took shelter behind a boulder. Bill was certain that the gunfire came from rescuers at Mt. Nebo and he couldn't understand why they were shooting at him. One of the men was Judge Marvell from Stephenville. He considered himself one of the best shots on the frontier. He fired at Bill six times and couldn't believe he missed him. When most of the horses were killed and the firing slackened, Bill called out for the men to stop. A voice answered, "Just wait till I load my gun and I will be down there."

Another voice asked if they were prisoners. Bill answered in the affirmative and told them to come down and see.

"You come up here," the man called out, "and be sure to hold your hands up. If you are a prisoner, don't be afraid."[3]

Hannah was in tears and afraid to move, but Bill told her to put her hands up and follow him out. When she saw they were white men, she fainted. The children were safe, but the horses fared badly, almost every one being killed or wounded. The Indians were gone. If any were hit, their comrades had carried them off. After the fight, they rode a few miles to the Clayton Ranch and rested. Captain Hughes sent a rider to Mt. Nebo to tell the families that the children were safe. The next day they rode to Stephenville. Hannah was too weak to ride a horse back to Mt. Nebo, so Judge Marvell put her in his buggy, and with Bill Wilson riding a horse along side, they slowly made their way back home.

The children were captives about four days and their only losses were Bill's straw hat and Hannah's bonnet. All things considered, they were extremely lucky. Hiram Wilson and Oliver Fulton, however, were in no mood to tempt fortune. They packed up their families and moved to Dallas County, where, hopefully, they would encounter no more Indians.[4]

As the Indians raided into Parker County, Captain N. B. Loyd (Lloyd) had his Company E of the Frontier Regiment at Camp Colorado in Coleman County, nearly 100 miles southwest of Mt. Nebo. His experience well illustrates the ineffectiveness of positioning the soldiers on such an outer defense cordon, for the Indians slipped right past and the soldiers were too far away to respond to attacks. Loyd took seven of his troopers from camp on July 19 for a 20-day scout. They went to Camp Salmon, up the Clear Fork Brazos for five days, then northeast for a day to Paint Creek in Haskell County. There they found a hobbled Indian pony and signs of a campsite. Loyd decided to set a trap and wait for the Indians to return. He hurried to Camp Cooper to get supplies and picked up seven men of Capt. Robert M. Whitesides' Company H, under Sgt. Lewis Collins.

Back on Paint Creek about July 28, they found a shield attached to a tree which Loyd figured was there as a guide and he was certain that the Indians would soon return. Loyd wanted to lie in ambush, but eventually they decided the Indians might become suspicious and not walk into the trap. He would attack. A look-out saw warriors approaching and Loyd let them get within a quarter mile before dashing out. The Indians, about in equal number to the soldiers, whirled around and fled. Loyd barely got moving when his stirrup strap broke and he slowed to try to fix it, shouting out to his men not to run too far ahead and be trapped themselves. In their enthusiasm, however, the troopers caught and passed some of the rear warriors, and when the lead warriors turned back, they found themselves between two fires.

The warriors, shouting and brandishing their shields, spooked the troopers' horses and some of them became unmanageable. The terrified horses ran back through the others coming up and threw them into a frenzy. With the soldiers in a confused mass, the Indians fired, killing Sergeant Collins and wounding Privates Tankersley, Hester, Howard, and Powers. Private Seymour had emptied his weapons when a warrior with a large knife attacked him in hand-to-hand combat. Seymour, a large man, crashed his empty pistol into the warrior's head, sufficiently deterring him from finishing the duel. Loyd came up, got the men in order, and tried again to charge, but the Indians had pulled out of range. Loyd pursued, but some of his horses were wounded, two dropped dead, and two others were crippled. He had no other choice but to take his casualties back to Camp Cooper. The next morning Loyd got 15 men and went out again. The trail led northwesterly for 25 miles before it disappeared.[5]

The pursuit of Indians on the Texas frontier could be likened to the arcade game where one tries to knock plastic prairie dogs in the head before they dive back in their holes and pop up from a different hole. As Loyd and other companies chased trail dust, other raiders were back in the settlements.

Approximately the same day Loyd was fighting on Paint Creek, Comanches were stealing stock in Stephens County. The raiders may have been the same ones that abandoned William Wilson and Hannah Akers in Metcalf Gap. Their direction of travel ran in a fairly straight line northwest toward Red River, from Mt. Nebo in Parker County, through the pass in the Palo Pinto Mountains, and to northwestern Stephens County. There, on July 28, they hit Samuel Lindsey's ranch near Hubbard Creek. Brothers Joseph H. Schoolcraft and H. Schoolcraft lived about five miles to the east on Gonzales Creek and they rode over to visit Lindsey the morning after the raid. They accompanied Lindsey to his corral where 19 of his 20 horses were stolen, which he estimated were worth $1,235. There were moccasin tracks all around and the trail led northwest to the Clear Fork Brazos. They trailed only a short way before giving up.[6]

Only a few miles from Lindsey on the north bank of the Clear Fork lived Mr. and Mrs. T. E. Jackson. While Mr. Jackson and his cowhands were out with the cattle, the raiders swept through his ranch. While Mrs. Jackson and her other children were inside, little Henry Jackson was at the cow pen playing with a whip, busily trying to get it to "crack" like the men could do. The mounted Comanches burst out of the nearby timber at the river and trampled Henry. While he was semi-conscious, a warrior dismounted, stepped on the back of his neck, made a cut, and popped off his scalp. Then they rode away, just as Mr. Jackson and his men were driving in the cattle. Henry, faint and bleeding, picked up his whip, and staggered to the house. The boy lived a few months; his head never healed completely and an infection finally killed him.[7]

The Comanches left the country with their stolen stock passing close by Camp Cooper, in spite of the soldiers' heightened awareness of Indians in the area, and likely rode near Captain Loyd as he returned to the post.

On August 3, 1863, 15 Indians appeared at the James Boyce ranch a dozen miles northeast of Burnet. A Mr. Cook, who herded sheep for Boyce, was sleeping outside in a shed to protect the sheep from wolves. On a moonlit night the Indians found Cook alone and mortally wounded him. Earlier that morning they shot Noah Taylor through the shoulder and killed his horse right outside of Burnet. The raiders continued southeast as far as Bagdad (present Leander) only 15 miles from Austin, and killed several horses belonging to a Mr. Huddleston. A. T. Nicks took two arrows from Cook's body and brought them to Austin, where they were given to Governor Lubbock, apparently in the hope that he needed more proof of the seriousness of the raids.[8]

Chapter 23 notes

1 Marshall, *A Cry Unheard*, 93.
2 Marshall, *A Cry Unheard*, 94-95; McConnell, *West Texas Frontier*, in forttours.com/pages/tocwilson. Brown, *Indian Wars and Pioneers*, 122, and Grace and Jones, *History of Parker County*, 72, name the girl Diana Fulton and incorrectly date the capture in August 1866.
3 McConnell, *West Texas Frontier*, in forttours.com/pages/tocwilson. Grace and Jones, *History of Parker County*, 72, name the white scouts' leader as Captain Marthell.
4 Marshall, *A Cry Unheard*, 96-98, 196; McConnell, *West Texas Frontier*, in forttours.com/pages/tocwilson.
5 Greer, ed., *Buck Barry*, 151-53; McConnell, *West Texas Frontier*, 422.
6 Samuel Lindsey, Depredation Claim #4532.
7 McConnell, *West Texas Frontier*, 426.
8 McConnell, *West Texas Frontier*, 409; *Galveston Weekly News*, August 12, 1863.

24 "What is one man's family to the whole of the Confederacy?"

On August 12, 1863, about two weeks after Wilson and Akers were captured, Comanches returned to Parker County, making a vicious raid along Patrick Creek, ten miles southwest of Weatherford. The first victims were Stuart and William Hamilton, sons of Reverend John Hamilton, one of the county's first settlers. While the parents were unknowingly engaged at a tan yard near the creek, Indians jumped the brothers in the woods, killing and scalping them both. They also cut off one of Stuart's ears and part of his head.[1]

The raiders moved upstream to the cabins of the Brown, Gatlin, and Welch families. Franklin C. Brown was then in the Confederate Army serving in Gen. Smith P. Bankhead's Northern Sub-District. Harriet Brown was home with her son, Joseph (4), and her seven daughters, Sarah (16), Martha (14), Jane (12), Elizabeth (10), Moie (8), and twins Tennessee and Estell (10 months). The Browns were then walking over to visit the Gatlins, except for little Joe, who was playing with Ike Welch at the creek where Ike's parents were washing wool. The Browns heard shooting downstream toward the Hamiltons and Harriet hurried her children to Gatlin's cabin.

Mrs. Welch heard the shooting and called, "Come on Ike." He ran to his mother and Joe was alone. He walked back to his house when he saw Indians. They chased him and Joe ran back to the creek, scrambled along the bank, and found an overhanging rock. He crawled under. Indians came by and Joe heard them talking, but he stayed hidden until dark.

Harriet Brown was hurrying the children along when she apparently had the thought that she had left someone behind. She ran back to the house, went in for a minute, but emerged empty-handed. She tried to run to the Gatlin's but the Comanches caught her, shot her with nine arrows, and clubbed her to death with the butts of their rifles. The girls reached Gatlin's and helped barricade the place. Fourteen women and children congregated there, but the men were all absent. The Comanches jumped a low rail fence and circled the house, shouting, and occasionally firing at it. Martha Brown had the presence of mind to take an old gun barrel with the stock broken off, and poke it through a small firing loop in the door. Lowering her voice, she called out as gruffly as she could to the nearest warrior, that if he got down off his horse she would "blow his brains out." The man backed up, consulted with the others, and they rode around the house once more, jumped the fence, and were gone. The stress was so great that Martha collapsed in a faint, and it was said it took several days for her to come to her senses.

Somewhere along their escape route, Elizabeth Brown had become separated and perhaps it was she that her mother went back to look for. The Comanches shot Betty with an arrow and captured her momentarily, but either let her go or she escaped. The oldest girl, Sarah, took two arrows in her back while she was carrying Essie. A warrior caught her also, but apparently not wanting to be burdened with a captive, cruelly broke off both shafts at the skin, leaving the arrowheads embedded. Sarah died in two weeks. Essie, with her mother dead, would not take nourishment and also died within two weeks.[2]

When word of the killings reached Franklin Brown he applied to General Bankhead for a furlough to see to his remaining children. Bankhead, however, frustrated and harried, would not grant him leave. The Federals were advancing south through Indian Territory and Confederate Gen. William Steele was falling back. On July 11, he wrote to Bankhead, telling him it was "necessary that we should work together harmoniously for the common good," and asked him to move his force north, because "It will not do to wait in Texas until the State is invaded." Bankhead was not cut out for the task. On August 9, he wrote to his uncle, District Commander Gen. John Bankhead Magruder, "unofficially in the hopes of eliciting some word of censure or of commendation of my course since I have been here in command of this God-forsaken country." He tried his best, Bankhead wrote, but "I am becoming nervous as to the right or wrong of my judgment.... I do not desire the position," he stated. "My labors are so exacting and I receive so little encouragement that I wish myself anywhere but here....You see I write in bad spirits."[3]

Brown's tragedy was not Bankhead's concern, but Brown was not deterred. He reportedly told the general he would go anyway. Brown informed the pickets that he would take a horse and leave that night, and since they were sympathetic to his plight, they conveniently turned their backs as he rode out. Brown returned to Parker County and found his children parceled out among several families. He made arrangements for their care and promptly returned to his unit to face a court-martial. Bankhead reportedly asked him, "What is one man's family to the whole of the Confederacy?" He threatened to have Brown tied up by the thumbs, but sentiment in the camp was overwhelmingly in Brown's favor and Bankhead wisely let the matter drop after placing Brown in the guardhouse for a short term.[4]

The folk history of the affair is somewhat different from Bankhead's own report. On August 16, he wrote to Magruders's adjutant, "that affairs in my district are not going on as satisfactorily as I could desire. On the western frontier the Indians are committing many outrages, and I am overwhelmed with petitions asking relief. Several companies of my command were raised in the border counties, and the families of several have been butchered. A natural result of this has been to render those companies exceedingly restless, and a disposition to desert was becoming so prevalent in one company of Hardeman's regiment that I disarmed the company."

Bankhead claimed he wanted to assist the suffering families of soldiers by moving some of them out of harm's way. He believed that would quiet his men down, and said that it was "my duty to render them and their families any aid in my power." On the other hand, he gave his soldiers "the solemn assurance that if there were any more desertions I would follow them up and shoot down every man I caught."

While Governor Lubbock affirmed that the Frontier Regiment "performed good and efficient service" and "has given the settlers confidence," Bankhead had a different take. He wanted to know why there seemed to be so little help forthcoming from the Frontier Regiment. He asked for its whereabouts, and wrote, "I am informed that that regiment is utterly inefficient, if not disaffected, and that the citizens of the border counties are petitioning for their removal."[5]

The efficiency of the Texas Indian fighters is still debated, with some chroniclers praising their prowess. Ex-Governor Lubbock, writing his memoirs in 1900, said that "the importance of maintaining a barrier between the Indians and the settlements" was of one of his greatest considerations. He was proud that during his term "so few depredations were committed by the savages, and that no formidable raids were made." Apparently his memory was faulty.

Ex-Confederate Colonel O. M. Roberts, writing in 1899, said that the frontier cavalry companies were stationed "at such a distance from each other that soldiers could ride every day from one to the other and thereby get notice of any raid attempted or made by the Indians. That enabled them to combine their forces when necessary to repel any invasion." Roberts was plainly wrong. He also claimed that in 1862 and 1863, "There were no fights of much importance on the frontier during those two years." Contemporary observers who lived on the cutting edge had a completely different take; to them all of the fights, thefts, captures, and murders were very real and tragic.[6]

On August 17, Captain Twitty wrote to Governor Lubbock that "The Indians have lately killed some twenty or more persons…lately carried off two children [Wilson and Akers] that has since been retaken as I am informed."[7]

On August 19, a letter written from a woman in Williamson County was published in the Galveston *News*, which summed up the settlers' mood and commented on the sagacity of the military's tactics. Most of the frontier settlers, she said, had husbands and brothers in the army, leaving them defenseless while "The Indians are thick amongst us, stealing our horses and murdering our people…." She said that the governor "has got a few men stationed a hundred miles west of us, but what good are they doing? They have never stopped the Indians from coming in, for it is a certain fact that there are more Indians in the country at this time, than there has been since the country was settled. I would like to know what kind of people Governor Lubbock thinks we are!" With their protectors gone were they to defend themselves? She concluded, "I say if we are to be given up to our enemies, let us choose which we will go to. If we are to be murdered, for God's sake don't let it be done by the savage Indians."[8]

Chapter 24 notes

1 Marshall, *A Cry Unheard*, 99; Wilbarger, *Indian Depredations*, 524.

2 Taylor, "Indian Massacre of the Brown Family," 18-19.

3 *WR*: S.1, V.22/2, 921-22; *WR*: S.1, V.53, 888-89.

4 Taylor, "Indian Massacre of the Brown Family," 19. The story goes that Brown promised that after the war he would bring Bankhead to account for his lack of compassion. Brown never got satisfaction, however, in March 1867 Bankhead was beaten to death on a street in Memphis, Tennessee, a case which remains the city's oldest unsolved murder.

5 *WR*: S.1, V.53, 890-91; Lubbock, *Memoirs*, 469-70. Some historians writing a century and more after the events have given a more sanguine picture of the effectiveness of Texas' frontier defense. In addition to Roth and Smith cited above, Kerby, *Kirby Smith's Confederacy*, 215, also believed the regiment's "vigorous employment of search and destroy tactics threw the Indians off balance" until they learned to avoid direct confrontations. Actually, the Indians always knew how to avoid confrontations and it was the soldiers who were most often "off balance."

6 Lubbock, *Memoirs*, 474-75; Evans, ed., *Confederate Military History*, Vol.XI, 71.

7 Adkins-Rochette, *Bourland in North Texas*, II, A-265-66.

8 *Galveston News*, cited in Kerby, *Kirby Smith's Confederacy*, 216-17.

25 "We but little dread now of an invasion this winter."

Smith Bankhead finally had enough and resigned. Lieutenant Colonel Samuel Roberts temporarily replaced him as commander of the Northern Sub-District on August 28, until Gen. Henry McCulloch took over in mid-September. Roberts and McCulloch faced the same problems. In August, Spencer O'Neill and George Tackitt (Tackett) were in Company G, Frontier Regiment, under Capt. Newton White, Jr. based at Fort Belknap. They were sent on patrol from Belknap to Camp Salmon, in northern Callahan County, and Fort Picketville (Breckenridge) in Stephens County, bases where Captain Loyd's Company E men shared duties. They reached Camp Salmon with nothing to report and made their return journey. About nine miles north of Fort Picketville they saw five Indians in the valley ahead. O'Neill suggested that they retreat into some timber on their right, but Tackitt said, "We can whip five Indians, so let's fight."

The Indians charged, but as the two held their ground and fired, the warriors circled around at a distance. O'Neill again suggested that they should go to the timber but Tackitt said if they ran, the Indians would kill them. "They will also kill us if we remain," O'Neill said, "so I am going to the brush." The two rode for the timber, when a dozen warriors confronted them and they realized it had been the Indians' intention to force them into the trees. Spencer O'Neill was on a slow mule and the warriors caught him and shot him down. Tackitt raced his horse for all it was worth, galloping about four miles before losing his pursuers in a dogwood thicket. O'Neill was killed about nine in the morning and Tackitt reached Fort Belknap at one in the afternoon. Soldiers returned to the spot and buried O'Neill where he fell.[1]

Indians raided into Wise County. They killed and scalped a man named Long, who was walking alone near the village of Paradise. Nearby they rode past Parson Nehemiah Vernon's place and shot three children playing outside: Andrew Vernon (7) was shot with several arrows and killed; Thomas Vernon (9) was mortally wounded, shot twice and lanced; and Frances Vernon (14) was shot in the back and arm. The raiders then shot two arrows into Buck Reynolds' back while he was near Jesse Kincannon's farm. The Kincannons came out with their weapons and turned the Indians away.[2]

On August 29, 1863, Lt. T. C. (Jack) Wright and 11 men of Company I, Frontier Regiment, were far west in Taylor County when they saw a band of Comanches moving north after stealing horses in Mason County. Wright had ridden to Buffalo Gap, south of present-day Abilene, where he hoped to intercept the raiders as they left the settlements, for once again, the raiders had easily slipped past the outposts. Wright's squad had been waiting for four days and was running short of rations. They had just concluded to head back to Camp Collier when they saw the Indians approaching. As luck would have it, the day was gray and rainy and the ammunition the scouts carried was homemade "Citizen pattern" and "wholly unreliable."

The Rangers with poor powder and the Indians with wet bowstrings made a long range fight almost impossible, so the whites charged right in, uphill and outnumbered. The Indians, determined to keep their stolen horses, fought back stubbornly hand-to-hand. George Gentry, E. Powers, and Billy Ellison were badly wounded. Wright, himself wounded, pulled back while the Indians escaped. A rider went 45 miles back to Camp Colorado to get an ambulance for the wounded men. They reported finding the bodies of nine warriors buried in the rocks.[3]

Early in September a war party hit Thomas W. Bogard's large ranch on Fish Creek north of Gainesville in Cooke County, stealing 150 cattle with an estimated worth of $1,500. It was a slap in the face to the military, happening right on the doorstep of the 21st District headquarters. The thefts of large numbers of cattle were also harbingers of a trend also noticed on the Central Plains: Indians, who almost exclusively stole horses in the past, were now targeting cattle.[4]

They were also targeting whites who got in the way. John Wood, a soldier then on furlough, and Henry Mills, lived on the Paluxy River in the southwest tip of present Hood County, which was then part of Erath County. Mills, the son of Gideon Mills, county tax assessor, and brother-in-law of Wood, decided to join him as they went out hunting hogs. On September 13, while they were on the Sycamore about eight miles west of their homes, Indians stealing horses ran into the unlucky pair. Only Wood had a six-shooter while Mills was unarmed, and they were killed and scalped. A posse found their bodies the next day and chased the raiders north into Palo Pinto County where they claimed to have killed two of them. They recovered 15 horses, plus buffalo robes, blankets, three saddles, and two blood-stained lariats.[5]

McCulloch had no new solutions to the constant problems of Indian raids, desertions, and from men shirking their duty. John S. Chisum, who operated a ranch near Bolivar, Denton County, from 1854 to 1864, and later became a famous cattle baron, may have been included in the latter group. In September, he, James Chisum, Enoch Ottley, and C. Fitzgerald penned a letter to General Hudson in the 21st District. They had been drafted into state service, but they protested that they were in the cattle business, and had furnished the Confederacy with 15,000 beef cattle. If they were drafted, the Confederacy would suffer, and they deemed "that they are of most benefit to the Service in their present position than they would be in the army...."

Colonel Bourland, a distrustful, conspiracy-minded man, always suspected John Chisum's loyalty to the South.[6]

On September 18, the day after McCulloch took over, Governor Lubbock wrote to Col. John S. Ford, the "Commandant of Conscripts," that there were too many men still on the frontier, exempt from the draft because they were needed at home for defense. Lubbock wanted Ford to issue an order that unless those men organized into militia units, they would be subject to conscription in the Confederate Army. Lubbock said that their frontier forces were inadequate, and he told Ford that the Indians in the north, "incited by Jayhawkers, Renegades, and our savage, brutal and vindictive enemy, have become more cruel and bold than at any former period of our history."[7]

As usual, the North blamed the South and the South blamed the North for inciting the Indians to mischief. Although there was some truth to the accusations, neither side seemed to grasp the reality that the tribes had their own agendas and would operate in their own interests regardless of outside persuasions.

As if there weren't enough problems in north Texas, in October 1863, several hundred Rebel guerrillas under William C. Quantrill appeared. They had committed a deadly massacre of more than 150 men and boys in Lawrence, Kansas, on August 21, and fled from Union vengeance to the supposed safety of Texas. McCulloch didn't want them there. On October 22, he wrote that Quantrill's mode of warfare "is but little, if at all, removed from that of the wildest savage." He appreciated his service but said that Christian people could not "sanction a savage, inhuman warfare, in which men are to be shot down like dogs" after surrendering. General Kirby Smith had a different conception, stating that Quantrill's followers were "bold, fearless men, and…are under very fair discipline…in a measure of the very best class of Missourians." McCulloch was not convinced, believing them "but one shade better than highwaymen."[8]

Smith saw a solution in using Quantrill to round up the deserters and "brush men;" highwaymen could fight highwaymen. In August, Smith had issued a pardon for all deserters who would return to their units by the end of September. The results were negligible, and early in November, McCulloch sent Quantrill into the swampy, wooded, badlands in Fannin, Lamar, Hunt, and Hopkins counties, known as Wild Cat, Mustang, Black Cat, and Jernigan's Thickets, to capture or kill the holdouts. Quantrill captured a few, killed several others, but caused more trouble than help. He was shifted from district to district in the hopes that someone could deal with him. McCulloch even sent him to Shreveport, Louisiana, to report to General Smith. When some of his men killed Confederate recruiter Maj. George N. Butts in Grayson County, orders were issued for his arrest, and Quantrill and his men fled Texas.[9]

In October, McCulloch assigned James Bourland to a similar task: finding the deserters and extending pardons to all who came in peacefully, taking the resistors "dead or alive," and letting the others know "that they must go to the army and stay, abandon the country, or be killed." McCulloch's efforts resulted in almost 1,500 men coming in to enlist by the end of the year. One large group of 500 was led by Henry Boren, a deserter from the 10th Texas Cavalry Battalion, and came out of hiding to be placed in the newly formed "Brush Battalion," slated to be led by Colonel Bourland. The men knew Bourland's reputation, however, and figured they'd be tricked and would be "hung or shot." When they were assured that John R. Diamond would command them, they joined up.

There was even more help. In the fall of 1863, John Baylor was back. After losing command early in 1863, Baylor served as a congressman for a time, but was back itching to fight in the summer and organized a company of partisan Rangers. The unit became known as the "Ladies' Rangers," after several fund-raising benefits given by the "young misses" of Houston. McCulloch sent Baylor's company to north Texas, where it took in three companies of the Brush Battalion to aid Bourland in flushing out shirkers. Baylor called the underachieving state troops "flop-eared militia," and "soft shells," who he would deal with severely.[10]

With all the extra troops flooding north Texas in the fall, it would seem that they could have deterred the Indian raiders. About October 10, Comanches raided northern Montague and Cooke counties. The Pendleton Porter family lived on Mountain Creek five miles northeast of Head of Elm (St. Jo) at the western edge of Cooke County. George, Isaac, and Richard Porter were at Red River to butcher a cow when the raiders arrived at the house and began their own butchery. They quickly killed Mr. and Mrs. Porter, a daughter, and their daughter-in-law, Mrs. George Porter. George Porter's baby, named Buck, was wounded in the throat, but their little girl, Missouri Porter, was unharmed.

The Indians were plundering the house when William Porter (16) drove up with a load of rails. The Comanches charged and he ran from the wagon and raced to hide underneath an old mill on a nearby creek, but not before receiving 16 wounds. They left him and went back to set the house aflame. When they rode away, William, although badly wounded, got back to the house in time to pull Missouri and Buck from the flames. He got them to the mill when George Moore came by in an ox-wagon, heading from Head of Elm to his farm two miles east of the Porters. He saw the smoldering cabin and at the mill he found the three children, hurrying them all back to Head of Elm. They survived. William remembered seeing a white man riding with the Comanches.

The raiders rode west and Capt. F. M. Totty of Company E, Bourland's Border Regiment tracked them. Near Red River Station Capt. John T. Rowland's Company D of the Frontier Regiment joined them. They managed to catch about 25 Indians, but in a brief skirmish, one soldier was killed and the Indians escaped.[11]

On October 23, Colonel Bourland optimistically wrote to Governor Lubbock. Although he did mention "the Indians have made several successful raids upon our frontier people," he was certain the future would be better. "We but little dread now of an invasion this winter from our enemies upon Northern Texas. We have cause to be very proud of our success everywhere. Our people in Northern Texas are now better united, and more thoroughly determined than they have ever been."[12]

On October 26, raiders were back. Mann D. Tackitt lived in the southeast corner of Jack County on Boons Creek. That afternoon, Mann took a shotgun and pistol and went north of his cabin to see if he could locate any of his stock, most of which had just been run off by Indians. His son, J. H. Tackitt, went on a similar mission to the southwest. Mann was suddenly surrounded by 15 or more Comanches, and he tried to escape, but the poor horse he had was no match for the quicker Indian ponies. He dismounted half a mile from his cabin and fought from behind a small tree. He was overwhelmed, but not before he got off seven or eight shots, which were heard back at the house. When J. H. returned home he got his brother, Caleb, and the two went to search for their father. He was found stripped and scalped, with many arrows sticking in his body and in the tree. The boys got a posse together and trailed the Indians, but they were gone. They did find one dead warrior, hastily covered with stones and brush. The Indian's body was dragged to Tackitt's cabin and propped against a tree on display.[13]

Lieutenant W. S. Campbell of Company C, Frontier Regiment, was "embarrassed while on a scout," said Lt. Col "Buck" Barry. In mid-November, Campbell took part of the company along the Wichita River, across the Red, and up Beaver Creek in Indian Territory. Just before dawn one day, "They found the Indians, or the Indians found them," said Barry. The Indians "made a furious surprise attack," some on horseback and some on foot. Armed with rifles and pistols, the dismounted warriors engaged the guards while the mounted ones cut through to Campbell's horses. Within five minutes they had run off 24 horses and six pack mules, and seriously wounded one soldier. Campbell had to walk back to Texas, and to top it off, about 30 of the company contracted typhoid fever.[14]

While soldiers were on the outside, raiders were on the inside. In November in San Saba County they easily slipped past the cordon of Camps Colorado, McMillan, and San Saba. Alexander S. "Beardy" Hall (53) and his son, Alex Jr., lived on Richland Springs Creek two miles east of the present town of Richland Springs. Hall was traveling to the town of San Saba when Indians killed him five miles from home, breaking a spear off in his body.

The raiders continued into Burnet County, stole some horses, and were exiting back through San Saba. At some time during their sojourn, either coming or going, they ran into a Mr. Merryman (Merrimond), who lived 23 miles northwest of San Saba. He had spent the night in town on business. The next morning while driving a yoke of steers back home, the Indians killed him only a few miles out of town on Jerry's Branch. His body was not found for a week and he was buried where he lay.

The raiders did not get away unscathed. A posse of settlers, including Alex Hall, followed them west into eastern McCulloch County. Half a dozen miles east of present Brady, they had a running fight. A posse member named Truebridge was wounded, but they killed and scalped one Indian. Alex Hall recovered his father's horse, hat, and wallet. The posse also gave him the Indian scalp, which he displayed on a fence post at his house.[15]

Chapter 25 notes

1 McConnell, *West Texas Frontier*, 429.

2 Cates, *Wise County*, 199; Smith, *Frontier Defense*, 68.

3 McConnell, *West Texas Frontier*, in http://www.forttours.com/pages/enfort.asp; Deaton, *Indian Fights on the Texas Frontier*, 149-51.

4 Smith, *Frontier Defense*, 67; Thomas W. Bogard, Depredation Claim #437.

5 *Galveston Weekly News*, September 23, 1863; McConnell, *West Texas Frontier*, in http://www.forttours.com/pages/wood.asp

6 Adkins-Rochette, *Bourland in North Texas*, II, A-266.

7 Winfrey and Day, *Texas Indian Papers IV*, 77-78.

8 *WR*: S.1, V.26/2, 348; Kerby, *Kirby Smith's Confederacy*, 214.

9 Smith, Frontier Defense, 79; Pickering and Falls, *Brush Men & Vigilantes*, 19; McCaslin, *Tainted Breeze*, 134.

10 McCaslin, *Tainted Breeze*, 130-31; *Houston Tri-Weekly Telegraph*, June 18, 1863, August 20, 1863.

11 *Tri-Weekly Telegraph* (Houston), November 25, 1863; McConnell, *West Texas Frontier*, in www.forttours.com/pages/porter.asp; Adkins-Rochette, *Bourland in North Texas*, I, 176; Smith, *Frontier Defense*, 73.

12 Adkins-Rochette, *Bourland in North Texas*, I, 178. Lubbock was still governor until November 5, 1863. On that date Pendleton Murrah, who beat Thomas J. Chambers in the August election, took office.

13 McConnell, *West Texas Frontier*, in www.forttours.com/pages/tackettmann.asp; Wilbarger, *Indian Depredations*, 522-23. Wilbarger spells the name as Marion Tacket. A family website says the name was actually Mann Darius Tackitt.

14 Greer, ed., *Buck* Barry, 166-67.

15 McConnell, *West Texas Frontier*, 462, 446; Wilbarger, *Indian Depredations*, 628.

26 "Too late to pray now, the Devil has come."

By December 1863, some of the highest numbers of troops assembled in Texas during the Civil War were on the northern frontier along Red River. Men of Captain Rowland's Company D, Frontier Regiment, had been scouting north from Red River Station and picked up rumors of a Comanche raid. Men of Bourland's Border Regiment heard similar news, as did Tonkawa scouts aiding the Confederacy.

Colonel Bourland spread his men obliquely across Red River to intercept the anticipated raid. On the far left were John Baylor's "Ladies' Rangers," Capt. Andrew J. Nicholson's Company C, and Capt. Totty's Company E of Bourland's Regiment, placed along the Wichita River in Wichita and Clay counties. Next, the Confederate "Brush Battalion" was to fit along the lower Little Wichita River and across the Red into Indian Territory. On its right were more of Bourland's units: Capt. Charles L. Roff with Company A and Capt. James Ferrell with two companies of the "Brush Battalion" stretching on a southwest to northeast line across today's Jefferson County and into Carter County, roughly centered at Mud Point. On the far right was Capt. A. B. White's Company D, anchoring on the Washita River. Behind the center of the line was Captain Rowland's company at Red River Station.[1]

It appeared that everything was in order. The only pieces of the puzzle not quite in place were the rest of the "Brush Battalion" and Baylor's men. John R. Diamond was still back in Denton County getting supplies, and the Indians were approaching. Even the troops on line could not seem to prioritize enemies. On the left, John Baylor moved into Weatherford in early December and hanged two men accused of treason, looted a few stores, and moved north to Jack County. In mid-December, he located the camp of bushman Uel D. Fox, who had been hiding from Bourland's dragnet since the Gainesville hangings in 1862. Baylor attacked Fox's camp of draft dodgers and deserters on a midnight raid. Although Fox and several others escaped, Baylor killed eight men in a savage hand-to-hand fight.[2]

Regardless of the prior warning and troop dispositions, the Comanches rode right through Barry and Bourland's lines. Whether they came through the gap in the center where the last of the "Brush Battalion" had not plugged, or slipped between the other companies is uncertain. In any case they arrived, about 250-strong, on the afternoon of December 21, in roughly the center of the line just east of Red River Station. They boldly crossed Red River and headed downstream in the direction of Illinois Bend at the Montague-Cooke

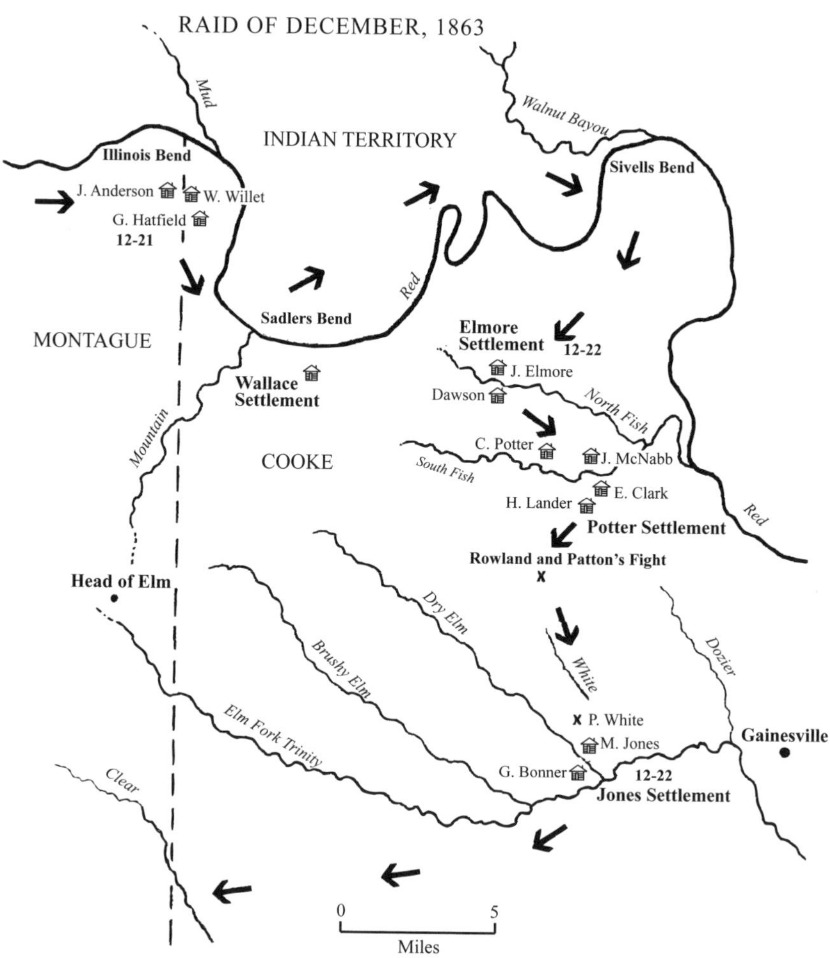
RAID OF DECEMBER, 1863
Mud
INDIAN TERRITORY
Walnut Bayou
Illinois Bend
Sivells Bend
J. Anderson
W. Willet
G. Hatfield
12-21
Red
Sadlers Bend
MONTAGUE
Elmore Settlement
12-22
J. Elmore
Wallace Settlement
Dawson
North Fish
Mountain
C. Potter
J. McNabb
COOKE
South Fish
E. Clark
H. Lander
Red
Potter Settlement
Rowland and Patton's Fight
Head of Elm
Dry Elm
Dozier
Brushy Elm
White
Elm Fork Trinity
P. White
M. Jones
Gainesville
G. Bonner
12-22
Jones Settlement
Clear
0
5
Miles

County border. Rowland soon learned that the Indians had crossed behind him and hastily got his men together to follow.

The Comanches first hit Joseph Anderson's place at Illinois Bend. Finding Mrs. Anderson and her baby, they smashed the infant's head against a tree and killed, scalped, and mutilated the mother, leaving her feet to burn in a fire. Outside Wesley Willet's cabin, warriors shot an arrow right through Willet's temple. They broke inside and murdered Willet's mother while she lay in her sick bed, and then tortured and killed little Amanda Willet. Willet's wife and oldest daughter escaped into a nearby creek bed and hid until the next morning. The warriors plundered the cabin and burned it down. Below Willet's was the home of G. L. Hatfield. Seeing the smoke from Willet's, the Hatfields quickly made their escape. While hiding in the woods they watched the Comanches loot their house and set it aflame.

Done in Illinois Bend, the marauders moved downstream to the next southern loop in Red River known as Sadler's Bend, about ten miles to the southeast, where the Wallace Settlement was situated. For some reason, however, perhaps to throw off their pursuers, the Comanches cut back to the north side of the river before reaching the settlement. In fact, Captain Rowland and some Tonkawas were on their trail, but it is doubtful that their small force could have stopped the raiders. In the evening, Rowland saw their tracks re-crossing the river and likely believed the raiders had called it quits. He went to the Wallace Settlement to rest his horses for the night. The people there were forted up and the news of the raid had spread to the downriver settlements: six miles east to the Elmore Settlement on Fish Creek, four more miles southeast to the Potter Settlement, and by that night, all the way to Gainesville.[3]

Captain William C. Twitty, Bourland's quartermaster, directed Capt. Samuel P. C. Patton, and 25 men of Company G, to go to their assistance. Riding all night, Patton's men reached Wallace Settlement at dawn. Not expecting reinforcements, Rowland nearly fired on them before realizing who they were. The Comanches were active that night also. They had moved downstream on the north bank of Red River and rested. Early in the morning they crossed back to the south side in the vicinity of Sivell's Bend and headed south toward the Elmore Settlement. The same morning, Rowland and Patton headed east, cut the Comanche trail, and realized they had gotten past them. Once more, the soldiers were in a stern chase.

At Elmore Settlement the settlers were prepared, but the huge number of warriors appearing completely unnerved them. Most of them left their fortifications and fled in all directions. Some were killed but most got away. A Mr. Dawson picked up a baby, not his own, and ran. When he reached the timber he tried to rest, but the baby began crying, and Dawson had to run. Every time he tried to stop and hide the baby cried. In despair Dawson laid the baby down in a gully and covered it with leaves, and in a moment it fell asleep. Dawson hid, and when the Indians were gone he retrieved the baby and carried it back to its frantic mother.

The raiders plundered, stole stock, and set the cabins aflame. Years later, John P. Elmore filed a depredation claim and stated that "on this same raid many neighbors lost stock and property of different kinds in Cooke County." If his claim was typical, the peoples' losses were devastating. Elmore said the Indians took a stallion, a mare, a filly, and a mule worth $275. They burned his house, 18 by 18 feet, with a side room 10 by 18 feet, an 18 by 18 porch, weatherboarded, sided and shingled, pine floor, and one and a half stories, worth $1,000. He lost kitchen furniture, utensils, tables, chairs, three beds, feather mattresses, pillows, blankets, clothing and groceries. The total loss came to $2,196.[4]

The people at Potter's Settlement saw the smoke from the burning cabins at Elmore's and had a similar anxiety attack. The majority were women and children; most of the men were in the army. Cincinnatus Potter had moved from Mississippi to Cooke County in 1858. He had served on the Citizens Court during the Gainesville hangings in October 1862 and was currently a captain in the militia. On the 1860 tax rolls, Potter was listed as owning 240 acres of land, six horses, 25 cattle, and 160 sheep, with a taxable property of $1,720. He was a prosperous citizen, but he was not home to defend his property and family.[5]

A number of people forted up at Potter's, but Ephriam Clark and Harrison Lander, who lived about a mile and a half to the south below South Fish Creek, had failed to arrive. The people at Potter's wanted to warn them, but figured it was too late to get them and bring them back, so they concluded to go there. As they left, they were hurried along by James McNabb. He had left Potter's earlier to go to his house and tend to his stock. The Comanches caught him in his yard and nearly trapped him, but McNabb's horse jumped the fence and safely carried him away. His warning that the Indians were on his heels served to nearly panic the people leaving Potter's.

They first fled past Clark's house, gathered his family up and continued to Lander's. Some of the Clark children were pulled from bed and mostly undressed. As they neared Lander's they looked back and saw flames coming from Potter's house. They would have to make a stand at Lander's. His place was set on a knoll near a bluff of Lander's Branch that flowed into South Fish Creek. There were four men, three boys, and a large number of women and children crowded into the dwelling. The men and boys, with a few poor firearms, took position in the yard, behind fences and out buildings.

The Comanches appeared, with their bodies and their horses festooned with stolen clothing, sheets, linens, and gaudy trimmings. The women in the house were frantic, assuming all at Elmore's Settlement were killed, and there were more defenders at Elmore's. They cried, wailed, and prayed. Outside, the defenders watched the Comanches gather; they did not yet make an all out attack, but seemed to be content to circle around the house, firing occasionally, and looking for an opening. When the main body of Comanches moved about 300 yards south of the house, those inside concocted a quick plot to make an escape to the north, where a steep, wooded gully ran alongside a high bluff 150 yards away. The men formed a cordon around the women and children and began to make their run, but the Indians quickly charged to that side and cut them off, driving them back to Lander's.

It looked hopeless when about that time Captains Rowland and Patton rode in from the north. They had easily followed the Indians' path by the trail of burning houses. By the time they had arrived, their horses were exhausted, and several men exchanged horses with the few that the settlers had corralled in Lander's yard. The Comanches, uncertain as to how many soldiers were coming, rode to the south to the divide between South Fish Creek and Dry Elm Creek and waited.

Some of the settlers joined Rowland and Patton and the combined force went after them. Near the high point Rowland had to tear down portions of a rail fence in their path. He tried to get everyone into some semblance of a battle line, but with much difficulty. The Comanches began spreading out east and west to overlap the south-facing whites. As the Indians closed in and fired, the whites decided they had bitten off too much and fled back uphill. James Clark said, "They came down on us like a storm (from all sides) shouting and yelling." The Comanches killed four and wounded several; one of the dead was Pvt. Daniel Green, while Sgt. Isaac D. Pollard was badly wounded with four arrows in his back, and S. B. Potter, a son of Cincinnatus, was hit in the head by an arrow. Captain Rowland finally rallied them, getting most of them to re-form behind the partially dismantled rail fence. It was a marginal physical barrier, but psychologically important.

When the Comanches charged the fence line, Rowland blasted a warrior not 30 yards away with his shotgun. The soldiers and settlers, seeing the Comanche fall and the others pull back, were encouraged enough to hold their position at the fence. This time the Comanches left the field, heading southeast. Rowland tried to get his men to follow but they had enough. There would be no more pursuit of Indians that day. Rowland sent out couriers to spread the alarm and with those he could gather, headed west toward Head of Elm where he figured there still might be some families that had not gotten the word.[6]

The Comanches were not quite finished, however. They rode west of Gainesville, where, about six miles from town they attacked the Jones Settlement on Dry Elm Creek. Miles Jones, a Mr. White, and his step-son, Parker, were riding toward the sound of shooting. Parker, in the Confederate

Army, had been wounded in battle the previous June and was home on sick leave. Jones protested that it was too dangerous and turned back, but White and Parker continued. They ran into the Comanches and White and Parker were mortally wounded, Parker dying ten days later.

The Comanches approached George Bonner's house and a few dashed into his yard and ran off with two of his horses. The angry Bonner grabbed his rifle, got on another horse, and chased after them. When he rode up a hill to get a better view, he suddenly saw about 200 Comanches below him. He wheeled around and galloped back to his house, meeting Mrs. Shannon who was racing her wagon to safety. Indians had already been at her house, wounding her son and nephew with arrows. She got them into the wagon and with her children, nephews, nieces, and grandchildren, sped toward Bonner's.

Inside the cabin, Bonner tried to organize a defense, passing out axes, pitchforks, and hatchets to the older children. His daughter, Martha, put on her father's clothes, tucked her hair under a hat, and took a defiant stance at a window. Tennie Bonner began to cry and suggested that they all pray for deliverance. Martha, who put no faith in such measures, snapped, "too late to pray now, the devil has come." Bonner took a stance on his porch with his rifle. A young warrior approached and taunted him, and Bonner answered with defiant shouts and gestures, but neither man fired. Bonner began shouting orders, as if he was directing imaginary soldiers and the Indians hesitated and backed away.

Luckily, at that moment a company of volunteers approached from Gainesville and the Comanches pulled back and divided, most of them taking the stolen horses toward Red River while about 40 others turned west. Somewhere along the way they ran into a military courier named Sprouse and killed him, leaving him in the road with 11 arrows in his body. A few warriors rode past a young woman named Gouna, who was carrying water from the spring to her cabin. They speared her in several places and cut off part of her hair, but the woman survived her wounds. It was said that at many of the burned houses, the Comanches left blankets, probably what they had received as part of their annuities, stamped "U.S."[7]

The raiders went west to Forestburg in Montague County. By then, Captain Totty, Company E, Bourland's Regiment, had learned of the incursion and pulled back from his position near the Wichita and Red Rivers and headed east. A portion of the company under Lt. Van R. Robbins (24) had pulled into Forestburg. The story goes that they had stopped to hear church services in town, leaving their horses picketed nearby. The Comanches opportunely rode by, saw the horses there for the taking, and began to drive them off. A young man named Alec Frasier saw them and rode out on an unsaddled horse, gun in hand, to try to slow them down. Frasier saved all but two, and when Robbins arrived they went after the Comanches.

When the Indians dismounted to fight in a thick grove of live oaks, Robbins called for his men to dismount and fight on foot. Only Frasier and Robbins dismounted and when the Comanches fired, the rest of the Rangers retreated.

"For heaven's sake, boys," Robbins called, "don't leave us like this," but to no avail. Robbins and Frasier fought alone until their ammunition was gone and they had to make a run for it. Frasier mounted and rode off, but a warrior approached and waved a blanket, spooking Robbins' "high spirited blue roan." Several arrows hit Robbins before he let the horse go and tried to run with nothing but his Bowie knife to fight with. He did not get far before collapsing, and he was scalped alive.

Frasier made it to town and went to Hegler's Store, trying to find some civilians or soldiers to help him, but no one would leave town. When things quieted down, Frasier went back alone and found Robbins' body. Coincidentally, Robbins' family lived nearby, and the retreating Comanches took some shots at the lieutenant's younger brothers as they rode past. In a while, Captain Totty arrived with the rest of the company and informed Mr. Robbins that his son had been killed.[8]

On December 24, a full moon night, Comanches, although probably not of the same large band that attacked Montague and Cooke counties, were in Parker County. There they stole horses from Nancy Ann Burrow and rode away unmolested.

That same day in Gainesville, Colonel Bourland wrote to General McCulloch: "I give you as nearly as I can ascertain at this date the number of citizens killed and wounded in the last raid made by the Indians. They killed 9 citizens, 3 soldiers, and wounded 3 soldiers and 4 citizens; burned 8 or 10 houses, some grain, and caused a number of good citizens to leave their homes…." Major John R. Diamond and Capt. James J. Diamond were in pursuit, but, Bourland wrote, "they were about eight hours behind them; consequently, I judge they will not be able to overtake them." As the soldiers chased, the Indians' trails separated. Bourland wrote that "those breaking off appear to be falling back; consequently we expect but small parties to commit raids upon us."[9]

Recriminations followed. Bourland never had a good opinion of McCord's Regiment, saying that it was useless for fighting Indians and catching deserters. Captain Rowland later wrote that "Bourland has done a great deal against our Regiment…and in fact enough to make us have very hard feelings toward him." In the December raid, it was McCord's men who complained that Patton's company fled, leaving Rowland to fight the Comanches alone, which resulted in a few of his men being killed. In early January 1864, Colonel McCord couldn't resist asking, "I wonder what the immortal Colonel Bourland thinks now of keeping the Indians out?"

One of the reasons the Indians got through was possibly because of overconfidence. With the great number of men he had at his command, Bourland had said that he expected "to make a move against the Indians & Federals" in Indian Territory, a campaign that McCord had not been able to organize all year. Perhaps he could not believe that the Indians would still attack him. In addition, the failure of the rest of the "Brush Battalion" to plug the last gap in the line was also cited as a reason for being surprised. Still, General McCulloch had his doubts. "I am unwilling to censure any one unjustly," he wrote on January 7, "but it seems rather strange to me that the Indians should be in this country in such large numbers before they were discovered. Small straying parties may escape the observation of the vigilant, but certainly such a body of men could have been discovered, if their watch had been any at all."[10]

Nothing had changed. All the Frontier Regiment, Bourland's Regiment, Texas State Troops, Rangers, and civilians could not make the borderlands safe. There was little correlation between troop strength or troop placement, and effectiveness. In fact, during the summer and fall of 1863, there were 1,500 or more soldiers on the northern frontier, and when the "Brush Battalion" came on line, there were 2,000 soldiers, some of the highest numbers ever. Governor Lubbock, in his final speech when he left office, lamented, "I regret to say that for several months past the depredations have been very frequent."[11]

What was happening? The more soldiers the more Indian raids! They could not understand that numbers were not a primary factor. Indians infiltrated whenever they wanted to. Sheer numbers of soldiers mattered little in a guerrilla war—it didn't then and it doesn't now. United States military planners currently increasing troop strength to fight terrorists in the Middle East might learn a lesson from their own nation's frontier experience.

Chapter 26 notes

1 Smith, *Frontier Defense*, 82-83; Adkins-Rochette, *Bourland in North Texas*, I, 192-93.
2 McCaslin, *Tainted Breeze*, 131-32.
3 Brown, *Indian Wars and Pioneers*, 115-16; Collins, *Cooke County*, 19. Willet's first name is rendered as Wesley and John.
4 Brown, *Indian Wars and Pioneers*, 116; Collins, *Cooke County*, 19; John P. Elmore, Depredation Claim #423. Elmore remembered the raid occurring on December 24.
5 McCaslin, *Tainted Breeze*, 219.
6 Brown, *Indian Wars and Pioneers*, 116-18; Collins, *Cooke County*, 20.
7 Brown, *Indian Wars and Pioneers*, 118-19; Collins, *Cooke County*, 19; *Galveston Weekly News*, January 20, 1864.
8 McConnell, *West Texas Frontier*, in www.forttours.com/pages/robbinslt.asp; Potter, *Montague County*, 44-47.
9 Nancy Ann Burrow, Depredation Claim #762; *WR*: S.1, V.26/2, 531-32.
10 McCaslin, *Tainted Breeze*, 136-37; Adkins-Rochette, *Bourland in North Texas*, I, 195, 212; Greer, ed., *Buck Barry*, 171.
11 Smith, *Frontier Defense*, 184; Lubbock, *Memoirs*, 519.

Part 6. 1864.

27 "I saw my sister's ghastly look."

In early 1864 the Frontier Regiment was on its way out. It had been in existence since December 1861, although it had gone through reorganizations and personnel changes. In August 1863, Pendleton Murrah won the election and in November he took over from Lubbock to become the state's last wartime governor. As usual an incoming legislature hoped to fix the old problems. A predominant question was how to ease the financial burden on the treasury. Lubbock had tried to get the Confederate Government to pay for the Frontier Regiment, but he never would consent to having its men removed from the state, and Richmond would not accept that condition. There were also the continuing charges of inefficiency from civilians and from rival organizations such as Bourland's Border Regiment. In December 1863, Governor Murrah agreed to transfer the regiment to Confederate control and it became the 46th Texas Cavalry.

The transfer left a potential hole in the frontier defense line—more of a psychological gap than a real one—and before the regiment moved, new units would have to be created. The new Frontier Organization was the final defense modification during the Civil War years. The law declared that all persons of military age who were residents of 59 frontier counties were to be enrolled in companies of from 25 to 65 men. Murrah divided the counties into three frontier districts. The First was headquartered in Decatur and commanded by William Quayle; the Second was in Gatesville and commanded by George B. Erath; and the Third was located in Fredericksburg and in command of James M. Hunter. Many men seeking alternatives to conscription joined up, and at the time of official transfer of the Frontier Regiment on March 1, 1864, there were nearly 4,000 enlistees. Effectively, each county company averaged about 50 men in strength, so the total was nearer to 3,000. The law required, however, that no more than one-fourth of the men could be in the field at any one time, meaning that about 750 men were available to patrol. Generally, 15-man squads, rode post to post, just as before, or went out on patrols for about ten days at a time. In March, Colonel James McCord and six companies of the Frontier Regiment were removed to the interior. Lieutenant Colonel James Barry with Companies C, D, G, and H remained based at Fort Belknap. In August, he too was ordered to move to the Gulf to counter perceived Union threats.[1]

The Frontier Organization and Bourland's Regiment then constituted about 1,250 men, considerably down from the high numbers achieved in the latter half of 1863. The units spent some of their time fruitlessly searching for Indians, but mostly trying to round up deserters, enforcing conscription, and chasing bandits. Where were the Indians? For the most part of 1864, the Comanches and Kiowas seemed to have disappeared, leading some to conclude that the frontier defenders did a good job. Once more it looked like less soldiers translated into less fighting, but again, cause and effect are not necessarily what they appear to be at first glance. Texas experienced less raiding during the year, not because of what its soldiers did, but because the Indians were raiding elsewhere.

Eighteen sixty-four was the bloodiest year of the Indian Wars, but for a change that blood flowed more beyond than within Texas' borders. Apaches and Navajos battled in Arizona and New Mexico and Cheyennes and Arapahos fought in Colorado and Kansas. General Alfred Sully led one of the largest commands ever into North Dakota to battle the Lakotas at Killdeer Mountain and the Badlands. There was increased fighting with the California Indians, and the Snake War was beginning in Oregon. Cheyennes, Arapahos, and Lakotas killed more than 50 whites in Nebraska during the first week in August. For much of the year, Kiowas and Comanches raided in Colorado, New Mexico, and Kansas, destroying wagon trains, devastating the Santa Fe Trail and Oregon Trails, and nearly closing them down during the summer months.

Texas may have had a slight reprieve for most of 1864, but it was no comfort for those settlers who were attacked. As James Hunter was settling into his Third Frontier District in Fredericksburg, problems with outlaw gangs and bushwhackers seemed to be on the increase. In January 1864, two soldiers, six settlers, and four outlaws were killed during robberies and pursuits.

The Comanches also paid the people a visit. Peter Metzger had emigrated from Nassau, Germany, and settled on the divide above Palo Alto Creek about three miles north of town. One of his daughters, Katy, was employed at the Nimitz Hotel in Fredericksburg, while two others, Emma (14) and Anna (11), helped their mother around the farm. One day in February 1864, Mrs. Metzger sent Anna and Emma to Fredericksburg to deliver a message to Katy. It was cold and snowy and the girls bundled up appropriately.

In town they delivered the message and talked to their friends until the sun was setting. On the way home they passed Charlie Wattenbach, who Anna shyly spoke to before the girls hurried home before dark. Two miles from town they saw riders in the road and thought they were Rangers, but they turned out to be Indians who immediately caught them. A warrior pulled Anna by her hair up on his horse. Emma was stronger and got away. They grabbed her and lost her three times. Anna heard her scream that she would never be taken alive. The last time she broke free she fell to the ground, kneeled down, and began to pray. One warrior, fed up with her resistance, put an arrow through her. "The Indian then scalped her," said Anna, "deprived her of her clothing, mutilated her body in other ways and left her lying upon the cold snow." The Indians rode away with Anna. She remembered Emma's face until the day she died. "I saw my sister's ghastly look as she fell to the ground," she recalled. "It was one of horror mixed with pleading. That look I shall never forget."[2]

That night the Indians camped near Kreuzberg (Cross Mountain), a hill north of Fredericksburg. While the Indians made camp they ordered Anna to carry out tasks, but when she didn't understand, she said, they "took turns in beating me with their quirts. I cried till my eyes were swollen; but the more I wept the more I was beaten." They also pulled her by the hair "so that I thought none of it would remain." That night she nearly froze, because the Indians had taken most of her clothes and she had only "a blanket of snow" for a bed. While she waited in camp, some warriors went out to find horses.

After returning with the stolen horses, the Indians broke camp about midnight and rode west. A posse was formed the next morning, which included young Charlie Wattenbach. They trailed the Indians to Pecan Creek, Town Creek, and to the headwaters of the Pedernales near present-day Harper, after which they lost the tracks. The Indians rode for nine days, crossed Red River and took her to their village. The women were very bad to her, Anna said, "and beat me in a most atrocious and unmerciful manner." They painted her face, teased, and abused her while her captors whooped in hilarity. In the village the children called her "The White Devil," as she understood when she later learned the language. That night they held a scalp dance, and warriors thrust her sister's clothing and bloody scalp in Anna's face. After the ceremony they painted Anna and gave her to a family as a slave. She was held in captivity until being ransomed and returned home in November 1864.[3]

Indians were in Coleman and Callahan counties in February 1864. William Blair and Aaron Hart lived with their families on the upper reaches of Deep Creek in Callahan County. Far out on the frontier they had to ride about 20 miles south to Camp Colorado to get supplies, and sometimes the task fell to the boys. James Hart, about 15 years old, and James Blair (9), made the ride to pick up coffee and other commodities. On February 28, which was Jim Blair's birthday, they were about halfway home when they ran into nine Indians. Young Jim pulled a pistol and shot one of them, but they soon grabbed the gun and jerked him from his horse. Hart rode away, but a warrior shot him through the shoulder with an arrow.

With Blair captured, the warriors chased Hart, who got off his horse and hid in some prickly pears, which they chose not to search. When they moved on, Hart stumbled away, heading toward his house, watching the stars for his guide throughout the night. A panther smelled the blood and tracked him for a few miles. When the boys didn't return that evening, Messrs. Blair and Hart rode out to find them early the next morning. They found the wounded boy five miles from the house, took him home, and pulled the arrow through his body. Hart recovered. Jim Blair was tied up and left behind when the warriors went to look for Hart, but he managed to work himself free, escape, and also found his way home.

In the area where the two boys were attacked was another unlucky group of boys. The Rolland (Rowland) Family lived near the Coleman-Callahan line, near Joe Manley's place a mile from Mudsprings. John, Henry, Thomas, and one other Rolland brother, along with David Crockett, an orphan boy living with the family, all went in a wagon to Mud Springs for water. Indians, likely the same band that had attacked Blair and Hart, caught them unawares. They quickly killed Crockett, and mortally wounded John and Henry Rolland. One of the brothers, wounded slightly with an arrow in the chin, ran home where he told his grandfather, in his shock and confusion, that black men were killing his brothers. Thomas Rolland was captured, but unlike Blair, he did not escape. In 1865 he was later ransomed along with several other captives.[4]

Chapter 27 notes

1 Webb, *Handbook of Texas, I*, 651-52; Smith, *Frontier Defense*, 87-88, 90-94, 99; Greer, ed., *Buck Barry*, 172, 174.

2 Smith, *Frontier Defense*, 157; Passmore, "Captivity of Mrs. Wattenbach," 20; McConnell, *West Texas Frontier*, in www.forttours.com/pages/tocmetzger. McConnell says that Emma was staying in Fredericksburg with her uncle, John Metzger, and Anna was sent to town alone. She accompanied Anna home when the Indians attacked.

3 Passmore, "Captivity of Mrs. Wattenbach," 21-25; Hunter, "Indian Captivity Retold," 194.

4 McConnell, *West Texas Frontier*, 464, and http://www.forttours.com/pages/tocblair.asp.

28 "I have never been in a country where the people were so perfectly worthless."

If Indians weren't overly conspicuous on the Texas frontier there were other pressing problems. The Confederate Congress passed a new draft law on February 17, 1864, opening conscription for all white men aged 17 to 50. The counties in the First and Third Frontier Districts that had so opposed conscription in 1862, now had further cause for complaint. When Confederate Gen. Elkanah Greer, head of the Bureau of Conscription, ruled that men in the frontier counties could organize for defense temporarily, but were still subject to Confederate enrollment, it triggered more unrest because the state law declared that enrollment in the Frontier Organization held priority. When Confederate enrolling officers tried to take men in the First District, Major Quayle protested that "I claim the conscripts in this Frontier District" and said that he would not give them up.

While Texas continued its feud with Richmond, Governor Murrah wrote to President Davis asking that his frontier counties be exempt from national conscription. Davis said that he could not do that, but would enroll them in Confederate service and leave them there to defend the frontier. The men who flocked to the frontier to avoid Confederate conscription could no longer hide. In fact, many of the thieves, deserters, unemployed, and undesirables who had gone to the frontier perpetrated many of the robberies and murders that were often blamed on the Indians. The area was so overrun with troublemakers that in May, Murrah proclaimed that further emigration to the frontier counties was prohibited. Anyone aged between 18 and 45 not a resident before July 1863, could be turned over to Confederate authorities.[1]

The frontier counties were being overrun with people and the territory just beyond the settlement line was also experiencing an influx. On March 15, 1864, McCulloch wrote "that there are a good many persons now on the Concho...with the view of moving their stock and families to California, and that large numbers of deserters are flocking to them.... [They] will concentrate at some point either to go out of Texas in the spring or return to the brush and steal, plunder, rob, and murder." McCulloch figured he might have to prevent people from taking their stock and property beyond the lines because he did not know if they planned to go over to the enemy. "It is a strange thing," he wrote, "to see men moving entirely outside of our lines among the Indians at a time like this."[2]

The standard story is that population in the frontier counties was denuded during the Civil War because of Indian raids. In reality, the frontier counties were being inundated with people fleeing from the east. The threat of dying in the Civil War from Union bullets was apparently a greater fear than dying from Indian arrows.

Through the spring and summer, while the Comanches and Kiowas were devastating Kansas, the authorities in Texas were chasing deserters. General Henry McCulloch commanded the Confederate Northern Sub-District, which overlapped the Texas First Frontier District. He obtained cavalry from Gen. Samuel Bell Maxey's command in Indian Territory, and with companies of Bourland's Regiment, sent them to hunt deserters and bushwhackers. In January they went into Denton County to find a camp of Union supporters. Maxey's men were told to capture as many as possible because they were thought to be deserters from Maxey's units. Bourland, on the other hand, heard they were deserters from the Brush Battalion and vowed to "take or kill" them all. Bourland killed a number of them and only captured 14, angering Maxey. Bourland, however, said that McCulloch told him it would be a "blessing" to remove the Unionists from Texas, but "it would be a much greater one if we could intercept and kill the last one of them."

Maxey was not averse to killing. When about 100 men left Texas to flee to Kansas, Maxey followed them in Indian Territory, captured their leader, a Dr. Penwell, and eight others, and killed seven more. He executed four of them by firing squad on February 18.[3]

The "Brush Battalion," which was formed with high hopes that it would perform useful frontier service, proved to be a failure. It had always been more of a hindrance than a help. The men behaved badly, robbed, fought, and killed. Useless for Indian scouting, McCulloch tried to use it for rounding up deserters, but its commander, Maj. John R. Diamond, could not keep the men "from deserting constantly and going back to the Brush or to the Federals." McCulloch was fed up with them and wrote to General Magruder on January 23, "I have never been in a country where the people were so perfectly worthless and so cowardly as here." The experiment ended on March 21, when the battalion was disbanded.[4]

There was also trouble with William Quantrill and his men, who had been robbing citizens, shooting up towns, and committing an occasional murder. On February 5, McCulloch wrote to Gen. Kirby Smith that he planned to arrest Quantrill and would use Bourland's men as his police force. "I have ordered him and his command arrested; got General Maxey to let Col. Stand Watie help Colonel Bourland do it." The great chaos on the border is illustrated by the irony of employing Indians to arrest Rebel guerrillas who were ostensibly in Texas to help fight Indians.

When one of Quantrill's lieutenants, "Bloody" Bill Anderson, had a falling out with his boss, he agreed to testify against Quantrill for his crimes. Learning of the dragnet after him, Quantrill and a dozen men rode in to Bonham, Texas, about March 28, 1864, for a meeting with General McCulloch. McCulloch told him he was under arrest and Quantrill calmly laid his guns on the table, apparently accepting the situation. When McCulloch left for dinner he invited Quantrill, but the guerrilla leader declined, stating that on his honor, he would remain in the office until McCulloch returned. Incredibly, the general took him at his word. When left alone, Quantrill grabbed his guns, escaped, got his men, rounded up the rest of the band camped near Sherman, and fled the state.[5]

With Quantrill gone and the "Brush Battalion" disbanded, it may have seemed that tensions in north Texas would have eased up, but one crisis followed another. In April, Capt. James M. Luckey rode in to Decatur to see First District commander William Quayle. Luckey knew that Quayle had first opposed secession and asked to talk to him privately. Luckey then unfolded an alarming story, saying that he was a Unionist, and with other conspirators, was trying to overthrow Confederate rule. He wanted Quayle to assign his company to catch deserters in Indian Territory, where it would instead be a cadre to assemble and organize all the Unionists in the area, establish communications with the Federal Army, and facilitate a Union invasion.

Quayle listened as calmly and sympathetically as possible, seeming to accede to Luckey's plans, but when the captain was gone, Quayle notified Bourland and McCulloch. McCulloch told Quayle to play along until he could learn the names of other conspirators. He gave mixed messages, telling Bourland to capture them and send them to Houston, and telling Quayle, "Better kill than capture them." Bourland was not happy with his orders and said to Quayle it was best to "manage this affair in the same way we did in Cooke" County. In other words, Bourland wanted vigilante executions. Bourland sent John R. Diamond with 100 of his most loyal men to make the arrests, set for April 19, 1864, but regardless of their precautions, word of the roundup got out and hundreds of conspirators stampeded. Only a few score men were caught, and those judged most guilty were sent to Fort Worth. Luckey and seven others were sent to Houston in irons.

When Bourland learned that the conspiracy involved some of his own men he ruthlessly rooted them out. Diamond surrounded some of them in Montague County and opened fire. They caught several, tied one man to a tree, and "shot him all to peaces [sic]." There was a propensity for other prisoners to disappear before they arrived at the jails. McCulloch admonished Bourland in July, writing that it was reported that his prisoners have been "killed without trial in cold blood when not trying to make their escape." He said his orders were already "sufficiently barbarous for any Christian land," but he did not intend for any man to be shot "after they throw down their arms and hold up their hands...."

The admonishment had little effect on Bourland. As for Luckey and his co-defendants, incredibly, given the temper of the times, they were released for lack of evidence. Luckey joined his family in Bell County, but authorities in Parker County were outraged that he had escaped "justice." They found some other indiscretions to charge him with and issued a writ for his arrest. On the ride to Weatherford on August 1, a posse overpowered his escort and hanged Luckey from the nearest oak tree.[6]

There were similar problems in the Third District where gangs of deserters and renegades raided out of Mexico and James Hunter's small patrols were no match for them. After a series of robberies and killings, the people of Gillespie and Kendall counties were in an uproar. In late April, Hunter received five men of the Frontier Organization, arrested by the sheriff of Gillespie County, as being implicated in the recent crimes. On May 1, Hunter wrote to Governor Murrah that the Fredericksburg jail was not secure and he wanted to send them to Austin or San Antonio. Hunter was instructed to move the prisoners to Bexar County, but it was too late. In mid-May about 200 men stormed the jail, overcame the guards, and, with no intention of freeing them as Hunter had feared, they shot all five, killing or mortally wounding three.[7]

The late troubles with deserters and Unionists bore similarities to the conspiracies in 1862, yet there were no mass hangings this time. Apparently the zeal for war was fading fast. One historian believes that a number of conditions affected Texans' will to fight, among them impressments, inflation, conscription, dislocation, state's rights, poor communications, poor discipline, poor supplies, incompetence in civil and military matters, and internal violence. By 1864, morale and spirit had broken down, but, with one golden lining—at least it dampened the peoples' ardor for witch-hunting.[8]

There were a few raids in the Second and Third Districts in the spring that were not attributed to white renegades. About the first of April, Amos McKeen and other ranchers were hunting cows along Kickapoo Creek in Concho County. While camping one night, Kickapoos crept in and cut loose a number of the men's horses. McKeen lost four of them worth $270. He claimed that he and others trailed them right to the Kickapoo Reservation, but could get no satisfaction.[9]

A band of Lipans were in Medina County on April 10, where they stole 58 horses from William A. "Big Foot" Wallace. Wallace had a ranch about 12 miles south of Castroville where he owned about 500 horses. He lived in Bexar County at the time, but his ranch hands said that the Indians came down from the north along Hondo Creek, where some of the herd was grazing. The cowboys, joined by Capt. John F. Tom of the Frontier Organization, chased them west over the divide to Seco Creek and had a fight, claiming to have killed two raiders with the loss of one soldier killed. The angry Lipans killed or ran to death 43 of the stolen horses, virtually eliminating the prizes that they had originally come for. Wallace filed for losses of $2,900.[10]

Area citizens who complained about the uselessness of the soldiers also complained when they were gone. After the removal of the few Frontier Regiment companies, the people of Bandera and Medina counties felt abandoned. E. M. Downs wrote to Maj. A. G. Dickinson, Confederate commander in San Antonio, that within the two weeks since the removal of troops from Camp Verde "the Indians have made two visits to this neighborhood, killed two good, loyal citizens, killed and driven off nearly all our horses. We are now not only exposed to the depredations of the Indians, but our worse foe, the renegades and organized members of the Union League."

W. A. Lockhart, who lived near Camp Verde, wrote to Dickinson on May 11, that the troop removal "has left the inhabitants wholly defenseless, being exposed not only to Indian depredations, which are now of frequent occurrence, but to the still more dangerous and destructive depredations of deserters, jayhawkers, and robbers, who already infest the whole country from the Colorado to the Rio Grande." Lockhart also erroneously reported the death of William Wallace by Indians. Downs and Lockhart both asked for the return of Capt. John Lawhorn and Company B, Frontier Regiment, to Camp Verde or "every loyal citizen in that part of the country will be sacrificed or compelled to abandon the country and fall back to San Antonio in less than sixty days."[11]

Because of Hunter's problems handling the Third District, brigadier general of state troops, John D. McAdoo, assumed command on June 23. He made an inspection and reported the population was "under the greatest excitement," since within the past few months about 20 men had been waylaid and shot or hanged. "The Indians," he wrote, "seemed to be the least talked of, the least thought of, and the least dreaded of all the evils…."[12]

Chapter 28 notes

1 Smith, *Frontier Defense*, 99-102.
2 *WR*: S.1, V.34/2, 1045.
3 McCaslin, "Dark Corner," 63-64; Smith, *Frontier Defense*, 107; *WR*: S.1, V.34/2, 942, 945.
4 *WR*: S.1, V.34/2, 909; Smith, *Frontier Defense*, 108-09.
5 WR: S.1, V.34/2, 945; Smith, *Frontier Defense*, 110-11.
6 McCaslin, *Tainted Breeze*, 139-44; Smith, *Frontier Defense*, 112-15.
7 Winfrey and Day, *Texas Indian Papers IV*, 83-84; Smith, *Frontier Defense*, 158-59.
8 Kerby, *Kirby Smith's Confederacy*, 432-33.
9 Amos McKeen, Depredation Claim #742.
10 William A. Wallace, Depredation Claim #676.
11 *WR*: S.1, V.34/3, 817-19.
12 Smith, *Frontier Defense*, 161.

29 "There we found mother's bleached bones."

The dreaded evils varied locally. In the spring of 1864, Brig. Gen. Douglas H. Cooper's concerns were in Indian Territory, where he feared a Union advance. "I think," Cooper wrote on March 21, "we will have the Kansas jayhawkers, the Indians, and negroes down upon us when grass rises." He wanted Colonel Bourland's men moved up to him at Fort Washita while the First District settlers wanted them south of Red River. These triple bogeymen constantly haunted the Texans in the 1860s.

For much of 1864, at least one of the threats, the Comanches and Kiowas, were in the north tearing up the Santa Fe Trail. Some bands, however, were still raiding in Texas. David White had moved from Palo Pinto County to Jack County after Indians raided his place in 1860. The Whites, along with Earl Kemp's family, were living on the old Jack Bailey place on the Keechi, about nine miles southwest of Jacksboro. On June 27, the women had spent most of the day doing laundry and had hung the clothes to dry on the bushes along the creek. Both of the men were away from home. That evening it looked like rain, and Mrs. White and Mrs. Kemp told the children to gather in the laundry. Sarah Kemp (16) and her two younger brothers, and Elonzo "Lon" White (9) went to gather the clothes about 100 yards from the cabin.

Lon went running far ahead when a small band of Comanches sprang out from behind the clothing-draped bushes and surrounded them. Sarah put up a fight, giving her brothers time to run into the brush. A warrior shot a bullet into her right side. She grabbed the gun and wrestled with the warrior, and was shot through the left arm. When she fell, another attacker tried to get a grip on her hair, but got tangled up in the intricate hair net she wore. While the Indians tried to get the net off, the Kemps' bulldog ran up and bit one of them on the leg. When they turned their attention to the dog, Sarah broke free and ran to Mrs. Kemp and Mrs. White, who both had rifles. The Comanches were startled by the two determined women advancing toward them, and headed the other way. When they did, they ran right into Lon White.

Everyone else made it back to the house, shut the doors and windows, and waited for the probable attack when they realized Lon was gone. In a few minutes it was nearly dark, and the returning David White heard crying before he got to the door. When he learned what happened, he ran to the spot Lon was last seen, but it was too dark to find any tracks. The next morning, White and some neighbors got a search party together. They found tracks leading toward the Keechi and saw signs of a struggle on a sandbar in the river. David White was grief-stricken and began planning how he could rescue his boy. He would later join a black man named Brit Johnson, who also lost children to the Comanches, and together they would begin a lengthy quest that would become the basis for the book and film, *The Searchers*.[1]

In the summer of 1864, Richmond "Mack" Boren (39), older brother of Henry Boren, once the nominal leader of 500 deserters who formed the "Brush Battalion," was in Montague County looking for stray horses. Boren lived at Red River Station and was about four miles to the south on Salt Creek when Indians surprised him. Boren jumped his pony down the ten-foot bank to the creek as an arrow pierced his hat. He fled another mile before the warriors caught, killed, and scalped him. When searchers found his body, it was in a sitting position and had swelled up so much that they could not straighten him out. He was buried sitting up.[2]

The long drought had hit Palo Pinto and Jack counties hard and cattle raisers had to take extra measures to keep their stock alive. Charles Goodnight and his brother-in-law, Alfred Lane, had both been in Company G of the Frontier Regiment, but Goodnight's term had expired and Lane had a furlough in the spring of 1864. They drove 1,000 head of their cattle from the range along the Keechi, up the Brazos beyond Fort Belknap to try to find better grass. They stayed near the fort on July 14 and overnight, Lane had a nightmare that Indians had massacred some of his family back on the Keechi. The dream was so strong that he felt he must go home immediately. Goodnight cautioned Lane about riding back alone and said he would accompany him once they got the cattle delivered. Lane, however, told Goodnight "it was not necessary and he would go back that day." Goodnight reluctantly bade him farewell.

Lane was riding a good gray horse, called "Driver," and on the morning of July 15 reached Cement Mountain, about eight miles east of present Graham. As fate would have it, Indians surprised him. Lane was shot and the horse ran a few hundred yards when it passed under some trees. Apparently Lane was knocked off by a low limb and Driver kept going toward home. The Indians chased the horse, not seeing or caring that the rider was missing. Driver reached home that evening and the family began a search the next morning. Word reached Goodnight and he too looked for his brother-in-law. Lane was found on the slopes of Cement Mountain, dead, but otherwise untouched. He was temporarily buried where he fell, but was later moved to a graveyard near the family home, west of present-day Oran.[3]

By July 1864, the people of southwest Palo Pinto County had not seen any Indians in quite a while and may have become complacent. A number of ranchers and cowboys, including W. W. Cockran, his son, Walker (12), Jim Daniels, James Reed, William Cureton, Benjamin Harris, and Boykin Bradley, left the Strawn area to round up cattle. They hunted by Captain Ellis's place near Little Cedar Creek in Stephens County. After a few days it was too much trouble to haul their rifles along and they left them at Ellis' ranch. After the noon rest, the elder Cockran, his son, and Ben Harris, went down to the creek where Indians cut them off from the others. Walker Cockran rode a fast horse and outdistanced the two men, and the Indians sensed that the boy was on a fine horse that they had to capture.

While one warrior almost succeeded in grabbing the reins, Walker pulled away and circled back to join the two men in a live oak thicket. The other cowboys heard shooting and rode to the rescue, joining them in the thicket. Having only pistols, the cowboys fought at closer range than they liked. One warrior rode up and James Reed was surprised to recognize a distinctive horse that he knew was his. Unknown to Reed, these Indians had just raided his place near Strawn and stolen four of his horses. Reed told Ellis, "If that Indian riding my black horse makes another dash at me, I know I am riding the best horse. I am going to run over and kill him."

The warrior charged in again to fire, and Reed rode after him, but when he got close he snapped his pistol several times but it failed to fire. Instead, the warrior shot Reed dead. Jim Daniels' pony took an arrow through the neck and Daniels was pitched to the ground. He hid in the brush until the fight ended. That evening they made it back to Ellis' house. "The next day," said Walker Cockran, "we tied Reed on his horse, and took him home to his wife and three children. That was a sight, when we rode up to the house, with Reed tied to his horse, that I never want to see again."[4]

The Second District under George Erath was somewhat quieter than the First and Third, but there was a notable fight in August. Corporal James L. Head and eight men were on a ten-day scout and on the night of August 8, they camped at McGough Springs, about five miles southeast of present Eastland. The next morning they picked up an Indian trail that led south. One of the men's horses had gone lame and he pulled out. They located about thirty-five Indians west of present Gorman. "There we overhauled them," said T. E. Keith. "We fought them at long range for awhile...when our commander ordered a retreat to the Gilbert Ranch for reinforcements." There they picked up Lt. Singleton Gilbert and five more men, making twelve, which included W. C. McGough, Burton Keith, James Temple, James Ellison, Tom Cadenhead, and Tom and Jasper Gilbert.

They picked up the trail again and rode a dozen miles east to Ellison's Spring where they found the Indians. The 12 men, armed with shotguns and pistols, charged. Many of the Indians were on foot, apparently planning on stealing horses during the raid, and they counter-charged the Rangers. "Captain Gilbert ordered a halt," Keith said. "We fired on them but they kept coming. Our Captain ordered us to fall back. We turned right in their faces, and on that turn is where they got in their deadly work."

Keith said the Indians had shields that would turn their bullets, and their arrows were accurate at such close range. "On that turn our Captain was shot in the neck with an arrow, and died in less than two hours. Burton Keith's horse fell, and they killed him right there. Jim Ellison received a deep arrow wound in the hip, which disabled him for life. Tom Cadenhead was shot through the thigh just below the hip joint and pinned to the saddle, and Tom Gilbert was shot twice through the arms.... Five out of twelve knocked out and not a load left in gun or pistol! Well, there was nothing left for us to do except to outrun them to Ellison's house, which we did in grand shape."

The Indians charged up to within 80 yards of the house before breaking off the attack. A few runners later left for help, but when rescuers arrived, the Indians were long gone. Singleton Gilbert and Burton Keith were taken to Stephenville for burial, and T. E. Keith concluded, "the curtain was dropped on the bloodiest battle with Indians ever fought in Eastland."[5]

The next month raiders were in Young County. A group of ranchers and cowboys were on a roundup in Lost Valley near upper Flint Creek. The men included William R. Peveler, who was a lieutenant in Company G of the Frontier Regiment, Harvey Staten "State" Cox, the sheriff of Young County, George Hunter, Cole Duncan, and Perry Harmonson. On September 15, 1864, several Indians suddenly rode up to them, feigning friendship and repeating, "How de do, how de do." Since there had been little Indian trouble during the year, the five Texans had not anticipated any problems and were poorly armed. Nevertheless, they tied their horses to some mesquite trees and prepared to defend themselves.

Within a minute, nearly fifty warriors appeared and the five knew they were in deep trouble. "Boys, let's get away if we can," Perry Harmonson suggested. Seconds later, the Indians opened fire and George Hunter called out, "Yes, I am wounded, and I am shot in the arm." The men frantically tried to mount up and flee, but State Cox may have failed to untie his horse and when he galloped away, the rope caught and snapped the horse's neck, throwing Cox to the ground. A volley of bullets and arrows blasted them, and Cox shouted, "I am killed, I am shot through the body."

One of the Texans thought that a warrior caught Cox's dragging lariat and jerked him to the ground. Cox either called out, "Go and leave me boys, I am killed," or, "Don't leave me boys." In any case, no one stayed behind to help. Warriors chased Peveler and Duncan in one direction, while Harmonson and Hunter took a different path. Peveler's pony soon tired and Will was hit many times. As he rode down a ravine into Flint Creek, a warrior caught up and grabbed him by the shoulder, but Will pulled his pistol and shot the Indian through the neck. Wounded in sixteen places, with an arrow sticking in his neck, Peveler made it to Flag Springs about six miles away.

The arrow that pierced Peveler's neck had gone through his throat so that he could not swallow. Doctor W. H. Robinson, surgeon at Fort Belknap, was called to Flag Springs, which was the earliest settlement in the county, located about three miles northeast of present Graham. Someone had pulled the arrow out, only to leave the head stuck in the bone. When Robinson arrived, he had no forceps, so he showed a blacksmith how to fashion a pair of rude pincers and the doctor extracted the arrowhead. Peveler, however, was too badly wounded. Blood poisoning set in and he died three weeks later.

Duncan, Harmonson, and Hunter got away. The latter two got to a Ranger camp north of Fort Belknap near sundown. They traveled to the scene and found Cox's body. Harmonson was certain that Peveler was dead, but they later learned that he had made it to Flag Springs. Peveler was buried along the Clear Fork Brazos near Eliasville and Cox was buried at Fort Belknap. Cox Mountain, on the eastern border of Young County, was named for State Cox, who was killed nearby.[6]

The same band of Indians who were in Young County in mid-September may have been in Parker County later in the month. Andrew Berry and his family lived on Sanchez Creek about ten miles southwest of Weatherford. Berry and his two red-haired sons, five and ten years old, took their ox-wagon to the Thomas Hamilton home in the Horseshoe Bend of the Brazos about five miles away. Berry's wife insisted he should take his gun, but he dismissed her worries because Indians had not been seen in the area for quite some time. At Hamilton's they loaded the wagon with pumpkins and corn. Mrs. Hamilton warned them that the Indians were "in" and that they should stay, but Berry chose to ride home.

They had not gotten far when the Indians suddenly fired on them from concealment. Bullets and arrows hit Andrew Berry and the five-year-old boy and killed them instantly. They beat the ten-year-old, scalped him, and left him for dead, but he later crawled away, hid under a haystack, and was rescued. Warriors smashed several pumpkins over Berry's head and rode away unscathed.[7]

While the raiders in the north were likely Comanches or Kiowas, the Lipans were also active in the south. In the fall of 1864 they visited Edwards and Real counties. George Schwandner, his wife, and son, Albert (7), lived where Camp Wood Creek runs into the Nueces River, raising sheep on a frontier with few other whites. Uvalde, about 40 miles to the south, was the nearest town to purchase supplies. Mr. Schwandner was out tending the sheep one sunny day when five Lipans approached his cabin. Mrs. Schwandner saw them coming and called to Albert to run and hide. He tried, but they caught him.

"I saw them take hold of mother and drag her across the creek," Albert said. "She tried to get loose, but they beat her and dragged her on. They tied me to a tree nearby with the suspenders that mother had worn to hold up her skirts." He watched the Indians shoot arrows into his mother, while she continued to scream out for him to run away. When she was dead they plundered the house and took Albert with them when they left.

George Schwandner got home that evening and knew what had happened. All the horses had been stolen so he ran and walked all the way to Uvalde overnight. He formed an 18-man posse including Cook, Melliphant, Robbins, Bowles, Stratton, Davis, and others. They went back up the Nueces and then followed the trail west to the Pecos. The Lipans knew they were being pursued. While camped on the west bank of the river, a rainstorm came up. Although some of the posse argued against it, the others built a big fire for warmth. As the area lit up, the watching Lipans sent a shower of arrows and bullets into the camp, hitting George Schwandner and a Mexican guide. As someone threw a buffalo robe over the fire, enveloping the camp in darkness, a Lipan shouted out in Spanish, that they had killed the woman and they had the boy with them, and if the whites wanted a fight, to hang around until the morning and they would give them a fight.

The Lipans, however, pulled out in the night. As Albert remembered, they went up the Rio Grande as far as El Paso del Norte, and back down to the vicinity of Eagle Pass. Albert was sold for a horse and some whiskey to a Mexican named Pablo Ramos who treated him well. Nearly a year later, a man named John Crawford from Fort Inge, went to Mexico on business and became learned of Albert's presence. Crawford got Mr. Schwandner and both came back to buy Albert from Ramos. Almost exactly one year from the day of his capture, Albert and his father went back to their home where Albert led him directly to the site of the attack. "There we found mother's bleached bones," Albert said, "and we reverently buried her there where she met such a tragic death."[8]

Chapter 29 notes

1 Cox, "Capture of Lon White," 59; Nowak, "Painted Post Crossroads," in forttours.com/pages/ewhite; David White, Depredation Claim #6316; *Galveston Weekly News*, August 8, 1864.

2 McConnell, *West Texas Frontier*, 485; "Descendents of John Boren," http://familytreemaker.genealogy.com/users/b/o/l/nancy-gail-bolding-OK/gene7-0005.html.

3 McConnell, *West Texas Frontier*, 463; Haley, *Charles Goodnight*, 113-14; Wilbarger, *Indian Depredations*, 546.

4 McConnell, *West Texas Frontier*, 465; Robert C. Reed (James Reed), Depredation Claim #6297. Different witnesses in the claim state the incident happened in 1861 or 1866.

5 McConnell, *West Texas Frontier*, 470; Langston, *Eastland County*, 41-44.

6 McConnell, *West Texas Frontier*, in http://www.forttours.com/pages/coxpeveler.asp; Wilbarger, *Indian Depredations*,547-48; Hunter, "A Great Indian Raid," *Frontier Times*, 6; "Officer Down Memorial Page," http://www.odmp.org/officer/3544-sheriff-harvey-staten-cox.

7 McConnell, *West Texas Frontier*, in http://www.forttours.com/pages/berryandrew.asp; Wilbarger, *Indian Depredations*, 524-25; Smythe, *Historical Sketch of Parker County*, 187.

8 Hamilton, "Albert Schwandner," *Frontier Times*, 403-05.

30 "Indians are coming; get in the brush!"

One of the largest raids to hit north Texas during the Civil War occurred in Young County on October 13, 1864. Many Kiowas and Comanches had been in Kansas for much of the year. They raided along the Great Bend of the Arkansas in May, and in July, the Kiowa, Satanta, killed a sentry at Fort Larned and his warriors ran off 172 mules and horses. Throughout July they decimated wagon trains in the Great Bend area before moving southwest in August, where they continued raiding wagon trains near the junctions of the Mountain and Cimarron branches of the Santa Fe Trail. Kiowas Set-maunte and Iseeo later said about these months in Kansas: "We had a lot of fun, but soon got scared, so we went down to the Canadian and camped with the Comanches."[1]

In the Texas Panhandle near the ruins of Bent's old adobe fort, many bands had gathered for the winter. The ongoing drought and shrinking bison herds increasingly forced the proud Comanches and Kiowas, who would rarely have considered eating a cow a decade earlier, into actively seeking cattle as well as horses during their raids. As the Civil War dragged on in Texas and most of the men were in the army, the militia, or hiding out from conscription, the cattle were multiplying. As cowman Charles Goodnight remarked, almost no beef had been driven out for sale during the war, "not a hoof of she-stuff had ever left the Western Cross Timbers," and "Vast herds of wild, unbranded cattle filled the country…." On the Canadian River, Comanche chief, Little Buffalo, organized a raid below Red River, promising a great haul of horses, cattle, and captives. His enthusiastic instigation was successful, and many warriors joined him.[2]

The raiders crossed Red River near present Burkburnett in Wichita County and headed directly south through Archer County and into Young, almost on a direct line toward Fort Belknap. About six miles above the fort they crossed the Brazos at Johnson Bottom just below the mouth of Elm Creek. Some of the settlers remembered seeing what they thought was a smoke signal on Thursday, October 13, about 11 a.m. Shortly after that, the Indians struck. The Elm Creek settlement consisted of about 12 families and 50 or 60 people and stretched from near the mouth of Elm Creek west about four miles.[3]

The first place hit was Peter Harmonson's old ranch, where four years earlier, Indians had killed the slave, Lindy Harmonson. The house was on the east side of the Brazos between the mouths of Elm Creek and California Creek. Peter (63) was outside with his son, Perry (28), who only three weeks earlier had escaped death when Peveler and Cox were killed. The two men rode to

Author's collection

Brit Johnson

the thick timber. Peter Harmonson, who was Young County's first chief justice, was dismounted when his horse was hit and it ran away with his coat and pistol. He held on to his shotgun, however, and Perry had a six-shot rifle. The adversaries exchanged shots for a time and a ball struck Peter's shotgun and plowed through his hand. Perry took aim at the Indian who shot his father, who was wearing an army shirt with brass buttons. The warrior was hit and fell off his horse and the rest of them grabbed him and left, apparently figuring to find easier pickings than these dangerous white men. The Harmonsons mounted the remaining horse and rode up the Brazos about six miles to Fort Murrah. The Indian was found three days later, buried in his army shirt.

While some Indians were fighting with the Harmonsons, others crossed the Brazos and sighted Joel Miers (Myers) (42) in the bottomland east of Elm Creek. Miers lived at Belknap and was out hunting oxen when the Indians killed and scalped him. A short distance west was the Fitzpatrick Ranch, a two-story house once called the Carter Trading Post. When the Indians arrived, Milly Susanna Carter Durkin (21), a mulatto, futilely tried to defend her family with a shotgun, but she was tomahawked, gang-raped, scalped, and killed. Inside the house were Milly's mother, Elizabeth Ann Carter Sprague Fitzpatrick (38); her brother, Elijah Carter (13); Milly's daughters, Charlotte Elizabeth "Lottie" Durkin (5); Milly Jane (2); and Milly's newborn, unnamed son, all of mixed black and white heritage. A black family also lived there. Brit Johnson was the head of household. A free man, Brit had gone with Judge Henry D. Williams to Weatherford for supplies. There were no men at home. Brit's pregnant wife, Mary Johnson (24), was with her daughter (4), and two sons, Jim (7), and a five-year-old.

While Milly Susanna was being raped, Jim Johnson ran from the house, but Indians killed him before he reached the gate. These violent murders caused the others to realize that resistance was useless. Even so, when the Indians found the Durkin baby hidden in a box under the bed, they pulled him out and smashed him against a wall. The Indians plundered the houses and the remaining seven captives were tied on ponies. When the Kiowa Satanta blew a bugle, the raiders took them away.

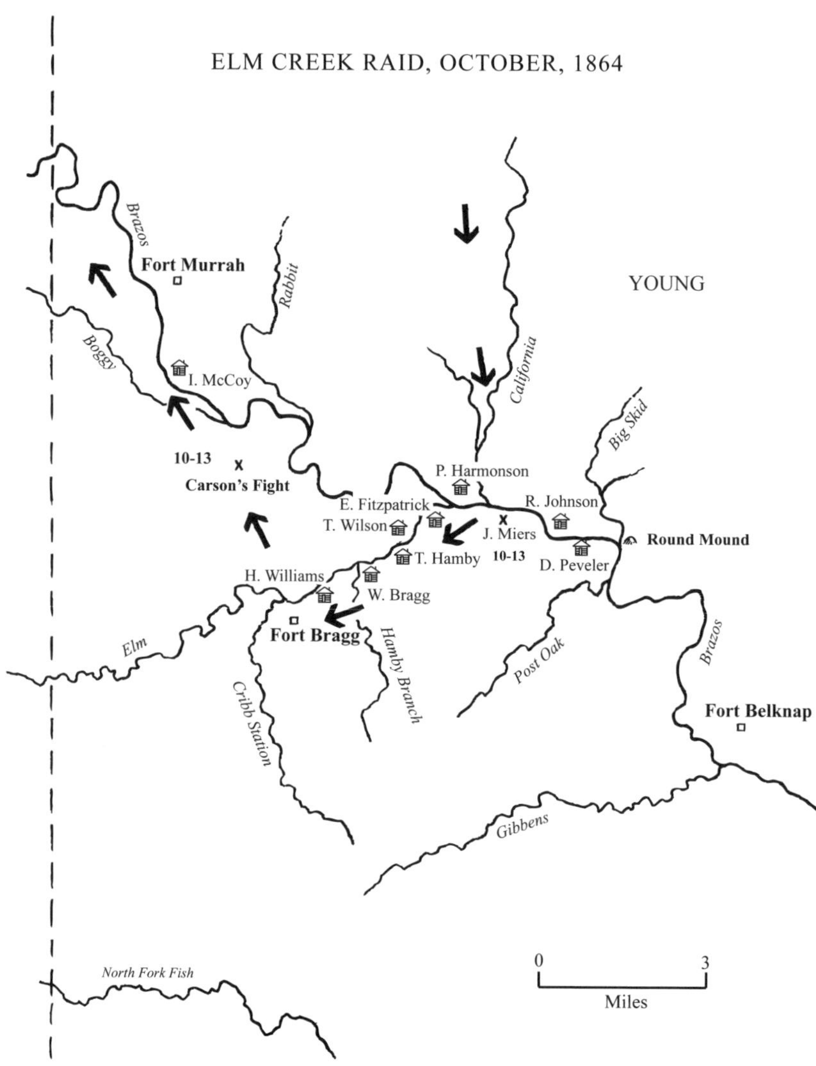
ELM CREEK RAID, OCTOBER, 1864
Brazos
Fort Murrah
Rabbit
YOUNG
Boggy
I. McCoy
California
Big Skid
10-13
Carson's Fight
P. Harmonson
E. Fitzpatrick
R. Johnson
T. Wilson
J. Miers
Round Mound
T. Hamby
10-13
D. Peveler
H. Williams
W. Bragg
Fort Bragg
Elm
Hamby Branch
Post Oak
Brazos
Cribb Station
Fort Belknap
Gibbens
0
3
Miles
North Fork Fish

They rode northwest for almost two days and nights before stopping on Saturday morning near Pease River. Elijah Carter was sick, probably from drinking gypsum water, and he was too ill to travel. The Indians built a fire in a brush heap and threw the boy in it. They forced Elizabeth Fitzpatrick to watch her grandson burn to death. From there the Indians headed into the north Texas Panhandle.

In the bottoms south of Elm Creek, Henry W. G. Wooten (34) saw the Indians coming. A volunteer in Lt. Charles Newhouse's (Neuhaus) Company B in Quayle's First District, Wooten grabbed his shotgun, got on his horse, and rode hard for Fort Belknap to spread the alarm. Warriors chased him and shot his horse, but Wooten hopped to the ground and kept running. Two warriors chased him, as if toying with him before coming in for the kill. When Wooten stopped and pointed his shotgun at them, one of them called to him in English, "Don't shoot me Wooten! Don't shoot! You run." This went on a couple of times. It was almost as if they wanted him to get away. The warrior once called out, "You know me Wooten. I know you long time 'go. You fed me on beef, Camp Cooper. Me know you, Wooten. You run."

He complied, running more than three miles through brambles and over rocks, across the Brazos and through a thicket. When he emerged at the fort, he'd lost everything but his tattered shirt and drawers. The ordeal left Wooten coughing and spitting blood, but he later believed that the Indians must have been some of those he fed when he butchered beef for them on the old Brazos Reservation years ago, and must have been trying to save his life by driving him away from the other Indians who would have killed him.

While some raiders were plundering the Fitzpatricks, Durkins, and Johnsons, others moved up Elm Creek. The next cabins were those of Thomas Hamby (49), his wife Viney, and five children, including son Thornton K. Hamby (23), who was home on leave from the Confederate Army, and Thomas K. "Doc" Wilson (39), wife Rowena (28), and three children. Tom Hamby already had one son, James, killed by Indians in 1860 while working for Thomas Lambshead. Hamby, Thornton, and Wilson were out branding cattle east of the cabins when they saw the commotion at Fitzpatrick's. They immediately understood what was happening and rushed to get their families to safety. Hamby took his family about 250 yards southwest to a cave along the bank of Elm Creek. Wilson got his family into a large cistern and placed a large, flat rock over the top of it. With that done, Thornton Hamby took over and told Wilson to ride up creek to warn the rest of the settlers. He and his father would try to make a rear guard action to distract the oncoming Indians. The two men rode along from timber to thicket, firing, advancing, retreating, and generally being enough of a nuisance that the Indians had to slow down to deal with them.

Wilson made it to the William Bragg ranch and gave the warning. William (52) was away in Weatherford, and his wife Mary (46), and four children who still lived at home escaped to the riverbank. Son Jesse (21) was serving in the Confederate Army. Mary led the children under a large shelving rock that made a little cave. They stayed there all day and could hear the Indians walking above them. The family dog, said Mary, "seemed to sense the danger and lay quietly." When they crept out at night and went back to the cabin, everything was stolen, including the wool suit that Mary had just made for Jesse.

Wilson next rode to the house of Henry D. Williams, who was gone with Brit Johnson to Weatherford. Henry C. Williams, just short of his seventh birthday, saw Wilson ride up and heard him shout, "Indians are coming; get in the brush!" Henry could hear the shooting downriver from where the Hamby's were fighting. A young man named Joe Cullen was visiting. He hopped on a horse and rode away.

"Doc" Wilson took charge and herded everyone to the creek, crossing and re-crossing twice to throw off their tracks. There were Sally Jane Williams and five of her children; a nephew, David Allen (5); a visiting boy named Reuben Johnson (17); Mrs. Martha Bragg Causey (18) and family; Mrs. Amelia Stanley, whose husband was away in the army, and two babies; and two neighbor women who were sisters. Rube Johnson and Sam Williams (14) both had guns. They crawled into the thickest briars and brush they could find and huddled down. On the way in, Amelia's long braided hair got tangled in a tree branch as she slid down the riverbank and she was securely hung up. Mrs. Williams kept a knife in her skirt pocket and sliced off the braids. Said Henry Williams, "The Indians robbed our house and tore up everything in it, and destroyed all of the provisions, bedding, and clothing, but failed to find these helpless women and children." They remained hidden all day. "Not a child whimpered," said Mrs. Williams.

Tom Wilson returned to the house just in time to meet the Hambys, who were being hard pressed and falling back. Young Henry Williams could not resist crawling to the creek bank and peering out to watch the three men fighting the Indians. Just before they were surrounded, they broke out and galloped west, heading for George Bragg's. Called "Fort Bragg" by the locals, George's place consisted of three houses and a slave cabin and was fortified with picket walls. Several families converged there: George Bragg (49), his wife Mary, and four children from four to 12 years old; George's son, Martin Bragg (25), and his wife Martha; George's married sister, Elizabeth Bragg Foster (26), and her four children; Mrs. William Vine and family; Nathan Bragg's family; Sallie Johnson (17), a child of Brit Johnson by his first marriage; and Eliza and Sol Bragg, who may have been George Bragg's slaves. Living in the vicinity were four of George Bragg's brothers and their families: William, Joseph, Benjamin, and A. C. Bragg. Some of them may also have congregated at Fort Bragg.

It was noon when the Hambys and "Doc" Wilson reached the fort with the Comanches at their heels, but for Wilson it was a few seconds too late. They hopped off their horses and got to the door, just when an arrow ripped into Wilson's heart. He yanked it out, said, "Bragg, I am a dead man," and expired. They barred the door as most of the women and children crawled under beds or tables, while a few stayed out to reload the guns. The men took position at windows or fired from between chinks in the logs. They estimated there were 200 Indians surrounding them and in a short time, George Bragg caught an arrow in the chest and Tom Hamby was shot twice in the same shoulder.

As the fight continued, the defenders' ammunition dwindled and Thornton Hamby and Sol Bragg were the only two adult males effectively resisting. Even so, the attackers were getting frustrated that they could not take the picketed post. Finally, one of them, said to possibly have been Little Buffalo, broke into the fort and ran to the main house. Using a pick, he tried to separate the boards on a back wall to get inside. Tom Hamby lay wounded on the bed but clutched his pistol. The Indian was working on the wall only a few feet from Hamby's head, and Hamby waited until he breached a slight opening before putting the pistol in the warrior's face and blasting him. As was often the case when a prominent warrior was killed, it seemed to take the heart out of the others. They got in to recover the body, but soon broke off the fight. When they left, the people in Fort Bragg could hear more firing in the distance. As they contemplated staying or making a run for it, they also considered leaving behind a large quantity of sugar and lacing it with two bottles of strychnine, hoping the Indians would later steal the sugar. For either "humane or economic reasons," however, they did not carry out their plan.

One reason the Indians may have left was because a short distance away, a squad of soldiers stumbled into the fighting. Lieutenant Nathan F. Carson (51) and about 20 men of Company D, Border Regiment, were camped about 13 miles northwest of Fort Belknap, near the Brazos about four miles northwest of Fort Bragg. Carson was returning from a scout up on Pease River when two of his men discovered a few warriors driving horses. Leaving six men in camp, Carson and 14 men rode after them to what he called "Elm Flats" when he "discovered a large body of some 300, formed in a semicircle and most concealed within fifty yards of me."

The Indians attacked and drove him back along the south bank of the Brazos. "While I was forming my men in line," Carson wrote, "the Indians were advancing and firing on me. I ordered my men to fall back some 100 yards to gain a better position, in slow order, to save the men that were on weak horses, fighting them from one position to another until 5 of my brave men were killed. I received two flesh wounds. We killed some 7 or 8 Indians from the saddles and sign, and seeing a number fall." The five men killed were Sgt. Sim Jones and Pvts. Erastus Blue, Robert M. Neatherly, Isaac H. Snodgrass, and James G. Walker. Pvt. William Fields was shot in the thigh.

Carson retreated past the Isaac McCoy house where they gathered up Mrs. McCoy and her niece, Betty Morris, doubling them up on horses, got the remaining men out of his camp, and crossed the Brazos to Fort Murrah, about one and a half miles from McCoy's. The Comanches were right on their heels. They plundered and destroyed McCoy's house, stole or destroyed all the tents, blankets, and clothing in Carson's camp, and caught and killed Isaac McCoy and his son, Miles (17).

Fort Murrah, sometimes written as Fort Murray, was on the north bank of the Brazos about six miles above California Creek. About ten or 12 families had congregated there in February 1864 and built pickets around the cabins, similar to Fort Bragg. David Peveler had moved his family to the area in 1858, building one of the first houses about four miles above Fort Belknap. He and his sons supplied the fort with beef. Francis M. "Franz" Peveler said that at the time, "We were right on the frontier—nothing north of us but the North Star." Other settlers included the Harmonsons in their new cabin, Bill and Cole Duncan, Bill Powell, Bob Matthews, Bill Mullins, and Champ and Will Farris, some of whom had been in the fight near Cox Mountain in mid-September. The Harmonsons, after their skirmish with the Indians, fled there and were among the first to arrive.

Earlier that morning, Franz Peveler (21) and a black slave named Seth had been at Fort Belknap getting wagons to take back to Fort Murrah so the community could pool their grain for a trip to the mill. They left Belknap and were passing Harmonson's old ranch when they saw what they thought was signal smoke. They hurried on to Fort Murrah and learned that the Harmonsons had been attacked, but there was little as yet to indicate that a large raid was in progress. After eating lunch they heard a commotion to the south and Lieutenant Carson and his survivors came streaming into the fort. He reported that he had five or six men killed and "the country was alive with Indians."

Franz Peveler and Perry Harmonson climbed on a rooftop and with a spyglass surveyed the country to the south, confirming Carson's report. Peering through the glass, Peveler told Harmonson, "They are killing old man McCoy and his son right now." Perry cautioned him, "Don't say anything about it for Mrs. McCoy will be mightily distressed." Peveler counted 375 Indians. "As I watched," he said, their pack horses came in so fast that I could not count them. They even had their dogs along."

Auther's photo

Marker at the Elm Creek Raid site, not far from Fort Bragg.

The people of Fort Murrah quickly emptied out their milk cans and filled them with water from the spring to prepare for a siege, but the Indians did not assault the place as they did at Fort Bragg. They surrounded the place for a time and there was some shooting, but they seemed content to steal cattle and horses and plunder the abandoned homes. That night, Franz Peveler said someone had to go to Fort Belknap for help, but of Carson's men, only the wounded Fields would go with him. Riding out in the darkness, they stuck to the low ground so their silhouettes would not "sky-light" on the horizon. They passed Harmonson's old cabin, crossed the Brazos, and stumbled across something white on the ground: the dead and stripped body of Joel Miers. They approached Roland Johnson's cabin and "hollered 'hello,' but no answer."

Those at Fort Belknap were already aware of the raid, but there were only 25 soldiers available and nothing more could be done. A young man named Chester Tackett volunteered to ride 75 miles to Veale's Station in Parker County, hoping to find some Rangers. He rode all night, using up six horses, but there was no one available there to help. Word finally reached Major Quayle at Decatur in Wise County, and he quickly dispatched 280 men to ride to the rescue. The soldiers were too late; the Indians were already gone. On the night of October 13, the Indians set hundreds of bonfires in the hills to suggest there were many of them still camped in the area, but they had already ridden away with their stolen horses, plunder, and captives. They rode nearly non-stop for three days and nights back to the Canadian River in Indian Territory.

The day after the Indians left, the settlers came out of their fortifications and holes to assess the damages. Sam Williams, who had spent the night in a cave along Elm Creek was walking near the ruins of his house when he spotted something shiny in the grass. It was a medal that had been in the possession of one of the Indians who had just helped burn down his house. It was about three inches in diameter and on one side was an engraving, titled, "James Monroe, President of the United States." On the other side was stamped a tomahawk and a pipe in the form of a cross, the date, "1817," and the word, "Peace." The medal was kept in the possession of the Williams family ever since, an ironic symbol of the harmony that existed between the Texan settlers and the Indians of the Plains.[4]

Chapter 30 notes

1 Nye, *Bad Medicine & Good*, xiv.

2 Nye, *Bad Medicine & Good*, xiv; Haley, *Charles Goodnight*, 100.

3 The story of the Elm Creek raid was compiled from a number of sources, cited in the footnote at the end of the section.

4 McConnell, *West Texas Frontier*, 475; Bedford, *Texas Indian Troubles*, 95-98; Williams, "Indian Raid in Young County," in http://www.rootsweb.ancestry.com/txbaylor/1elmcree.html; "The Children of John C. Carson," in http://www.carsonsofbrazos county.com/children_of_john_c.html; Ledbetter, *Fort Belknap*, 109-21; Mayhall, *Indian Wars of Texas*, 124-45; Adkins-Rochette, *Bourland in North Texas I*, 273-82; Greer, ed., *Buck Barry*, 175-79; *WR*: S.1, V.41/1, 886. Peter Harmonson died of his wound on January 9, 1865, and was buried in Tarrant County.

31 "I am astonished at the number of fools in Texas."

The Elm Creek raid has become the most celebrated raid of the Civil War years in Texas. It was called "the classic frontier Texas Comanche raid," "the largest, most destructive raid of the war," "one of the largest ever made in West Texas," "the wartime era's most destructive Indian raid," and paradoxically, "the first sizeable Indian raid of the Civil War," as well as "the last big warring onslaught of the Comanches and Kiowas in Texas."[1]

In fact, none of the above assertions are fully accurate. Much of the tale persists because it has been repeated enough times to make it "true" by volume alone. When we make comparisons with other raids, the Elm Creek affair comes out not as the most destructive, but one among many. Lieutenant Carson likely started the ball rolling by erroneously reporting that 11 citizens were killed, when in fact, seven settlers were killed during the raid and one more was killed on the trail several days after being captured. Of other notable attacks, nine were killed in the raid of February 1860, nine were killed in the November 1860 raid, ten were killed in October 1861, seven were killed in February 1863, and seven died in the December 1863 raid. There would be many more, such as the 12 civilians killed in the raid of January 1868. In numbers of settlers killed, Elm Creek was like a dozen others.

How "large" was the raid? In terms of numbers of Indians engaged, estimates vary widely, from 250, up to an incredible thousand. Peveler counted 375, Carson estimated 350 to 400, and young Henry Williams, who couldn't have seen much from his cave, said there were 600. It seems that such a great number of Indians would have caused much more destruction than occurred. About 11 houses were robbed or burned; a large number of cattle and horses were stolen, but numbers are unknown. Time- and mileage-wise, the raid was very short. The Indians crossed Red River, attacked Young County for one day, and were gone. It was over quickly and it did not penetrate deep into Texas as so many other raids had done. Lieutenant Colonel "Buck" Barry likely gave the most accurate assessment: "The Indians had had, on the whole, rather poor luck in killing and capturing families."[2]

That was little comfort to the prisoners. The Elm Creek captives were whisked northwest to the Canadian River in the Texas Panhandle where the Comanches and Kiowas, no doubt, hoped to spend the winter in comparative peace. It was not to be. The Union Army was also on the hunt for Indians who had been raiding across the Central Plains throughout the summer of 1864. Governor John Evans of Colorado Territory, and Col. John M. Chivington organized an operation against the warring Cheyennes and Arapahos in their winter quarters along Sand Creek in southeast Colorado. On November 29, 1864, the Colorado troopers hit Black Kettle's Cheyennes, a village of about 500 people, including many warriors who had taken direct part in the raiding. The Coloradans killed perhaps 130 Indians, many of them non-combatants. The 1st and 3rd Colorado Cavalry, however, suffered 24 killed and 52 wounded, putting that battle as the seventh highest in terms of soldier casualties out of more than 1,400 battles in the Indian Wars from 1850 to 1890. Tragically, some soldiers committed atrocities, which forever tarnished the incident as a massacre. Scores of innocent Indian women and children were killed—just as scores of innocent white women and children had been killed. As usual, the non-combatants suffered the most.[3]

In the Department of New Mexico, Gen. James H. Carleton had the same idea of punishing the raiders while in their winter quarters. Through the entire summer of 1864 the Indians had "held high carnival on our western plains," according to Lt. George K. Pettis, 1st California Infantry, and it was payback time. In November, Col. Christopher "Kit" Carson left Fort Bascom, New Mexico Territory, with about 335 soldiers from the 1st New Mexico Cavalry and Infantry, 1st California Cavalry and Infantry, plus 72 Ute and Jicarilla scouts, searching for the Kiowas and Comanches who had been raiding along the Santa Fe Trail.

The Federals cared little that the Indians had just returned from a raid in Texas. In fact, they would have encouraged such raids. On November 25, Carson first hit the 150-lodge village of Little Mountain's Kiowas on the Canadian River. They fled downstream and Carson followed, coming upon more Indians as he went. When he approached Stumbling Bear's 350 lodges, about 1,000 Kiowa and Comanche warriors confronted him. Satanta was present, blowing his bugle, and now it was Carson's turn to fall back. Kiowas had reoccupied the first village, and Carson's soldiers had to fight their way in again. Only the howitzers kept the charging warriors at bay. Carson wisely vacated the area, but he torched the lodges and supplies before he left—a severe blow to the Indians at the onset of winter. Lieutenant Pettis said that in the village they found "white women's clothing, as well as articles of children's clothing, and several photographs; also a cavalry sergeant's hat...." Three soldiers and a scout were killed, and 29 soldiers and scouts were wounded, while the Indians lost about 60 killed and wounded.

Some of the captive whites were indirect casualties of the attack. A few years later, Pettis learned from some Comancheros who were then trading in the village that Carson retreated from, that "there were seven white women and several white children, prisoners." They were removed when the soldiers approached. One of them, Milly Jane Durkin, had been hidden in the bushes when Carson approached Stumbling Bear's village, and she was whisked away when the Indians counter-attacked. When the soldiers were gone, the angry Indians rode off for help from their kinsmen on the Cimarron River. The months of December 1864 and January 1865 were cold and harsh, and the Indians and their captives suffered greatly. People of all ages perished due to disease, starvation, and exposure. Milly Jane was one of them, dying during what the Kiowas called the "Muddy Traveling Winter." The Indians blamed the "Great Father" for all of their deaths.

The five remaining captives spent the winter and spring in various Comanche and Kiowa camps between the Cimarron and Arkansas Rivers. Few inquiries were made concerning their fate, possibly because they were illiterate, they had few relatives in Texas, and Young County had a very small population and an inefficient government, barely able to manage its own affairs, let alone to organize any rescue attempts. Apparently the only male relative able and willing to try to rescue the captives was Mary's husband, Brit Johnson, and he made a few trips into Indian Territory looking for his wife, children, and the Fitzpatricks and Durkins, for a time joining David White in the search for his son, Elonzo.[4]

In Texas there were more destructive raids before Elm Creek and there would be more after, and Young County was not the only place attacked in October 1864. A raid that penetrated much deeper than Little Buffalo's, hit San Saba County. Many horses were stolen along the San Saba River and in the southwestern part of the county, Indians attacked Chancy Couch's and William Hayes's ranches. Couch had been in the area since 1858 and his daughter married William Hayes and lived nearby. On October 7, Couch went out with a wagon and saws to cut timber. His son was to join him in the afternoon, but when the young man arrived, he saw the wagon and oxen, but his father was gone. Searching around, he noticed buzzards circling in the distance and hurried to find his father's body, "pierced with arrows and so mutilated as to be almost beyond recognition." The raiders also stole one large black stallion from Hayes and disappeared.[5]

Although there were other raids, the Elm Creek incident was the most talked about at the time and resulted in recriminations just as had followed the raid of December 1863. Major Quayle had resigned for health reasons and because he was heartily sick of dealing with Colonel Bourland. Governor Murrah appointed James W. Throckmorton as his replacement in the First Frontier District, but he had not yet arrived. General McCulloch had taken a leave of absence from the Northern Sub-District, and Col. George Sweet was to be his temporary replacement. The raid came in while there was no one in clear overall command. In addition, "Buck" Barry's four companies of the Frontier Regiment were on assignment near the coast and Colonel Bourland had to spread his Border Regiment across the gap created by Barry's departure. It was a very inopportune time for the Indians to have made a raid.

On the other hand, Gen. Douglas Cooper had been sending in reports from Indian Territory of large columns of Indian warriors moving down toward Texas. Major Quayle knew of the reports and anticipated an attack, writing a warning to Murrah six days before the raid. When it was over, Bourland was still much in the dark as to what happened. On October 20, he wrote to Colonel Sweet that he had received no more news from Fort Belknap "in regard to the Indian invasion." He got secondhand reports from one of his lieutenants "in relation to the number and depredations being committed by the Indians," and "was disposed to believe he has been wrongfully informed, or I would have gotten other news before this. If anything should turn up indicative of a heavy raid, I will notify you immediately."[6]

Bourland was under attack for not protecting the frontier and it wore on him as it did on every other commander. On December 1, he wrote of his troubles to Col. L. M. Martin in Indian Territory. "My Dear Col. & friend," he began in a personal letter, asking Martin to "disabuse the minds of the ignorant or designing who are eternally assaulting me for not protecting the frontier." He said, "I am astonished at the number of fools in Texas" who assailed him, both politicians and newspapermen. "I done all I could," he said. Did the complainants all "suppose that I have millions at my command, when I have not a dollar. I really some times think it would matter little if the Indians could get hold of such and let their fool tongues be stopped. I have already done more and gone further to stop Indian depredations than any man that has ever held this office."[7]

Bourland was caught in the same vise as the many men who were charged with frontier protection: there was never enough money, manpower, ammunition, and supplies, they were strapped with the same ineffectual tactical and strategic options, and they had too many critics. Few of them ever realized that it mattered little what they did, for the Indians operated on their own schedules and could penetrate any barriers the Texans erected.

When General Throckmorton assumed command of the First District in December 1864, his first order was that all families should "fort-up;" it would not stop raids, but it would certainly help in defending against them. The Elm Creek raid caused another flurry of responses, once more illustrating that it was the Texans who generally reacted to Indian initiatives, and not vice-versa. The responses were nothing new, however. The tactic they believed necessary to stop raids was a pre-emptive strike against the Indian villages, the very same response that had been used on several occasions in the past with little or no positive results. The second solution was another reorganization, which also occurred about every year with equally lackluster results. Throckmorton wanted to completely revamp his available forces into a permanent unit of 500 to 600 men for continuous service in the field. The men would donate three-quarters of their state pay to the government and the

Confederacy would be charged with providing arms and provisions while being allowed to direct the unit in joint operations against the enemy.

The consolidation never got formal approval, but Throckmorton made the changes and cooperated with Bourland and McCulloch for the upcoming operation. These modifications were the last organizational changes to be made before the Confederacy's collapse. How well the "new" strategies would work remained to be seen.[8]

The Texans had put forth a great effort to find a solution to the Indian raiding, including increasing troop strength, shifting their locations, reorganizing, employing soldiers, Rangers, and militia, and changing tactics from passive patrols to search and destroy missions. The frontier still experienced quiet periods as well as active raiding periods, and there rarely appeared to be any correlation between troop strength, organization, and tactics. What influenced the ebb and flow of raids?

The frontier settlers would experience one of the reasons in 1865, although few of them would comprehend it. Successful frontier defense was always thought to be a factor of numbers and tactics, but there was something more important: climate. A change in the climate from a dry to a wet cycle was about to cause more suffering. In 1865, the 15-year drought was coming to an end, a change that was certainly seen as auspicious by the farmers and ranchers. Unfortunately, better crops meant better grass for the Indian ponies. There was an adage, for many years believed by men of learning as well as by land promoters, that rainfall followed the plow. It was finally and dramatically proven in the Dust Bowl of the 1930s that rainfall did not follow the plow. What did appear to be true, however, was that raiders followed the rainfall.

Chapter 31 notes

1 Fehrenbach, *Comanches*, 456; Roth, "Frontier Defense Challenges," 33; McConnell, *West Texas Frontier*, 475; Smith, *Frontier Defense*, 130; Anderson, *Conquest of Texas*, 339; Ledbetter, *Fort Belknap*, 111.

2 Greer, ed, *Buck Barry*, 179.

3 Michno, *Encyclopedia of Indian Wars*, 157-59, 355; Michno, *Battle at Sand Creek*, 304.

4 Ledbetter, *Fort Belknap*, 6-7, 12n36, 145-46; Michno, *Encyclopedia of Indian Wars*, 156-57; Pettis, *Kit Carson's Fight*, 5-44; Mooney, *Calendar History of the Kiowa*, 314-15; Nye, *Carbine & Lance*, 37.

5 William L. Hayes, Depredation Claim #1667; Wilbarger, *Indian Depredations*, 627. Wilbarger incorrectly places Couch's death in 1860.

6 Smith, *Frontier Defense*, 131, 134; *WR*: S.1, V.41/1, 885.

7 Adkins-Rochette, *Bourland in North Texas I*, 282, 287.

8 Smith, *Frontier Defense*, 135, 138-39.

Part 7. 1865

32 "He recognized no friendly Indians on the Texas Frontier."

The largest fight that Texas soldiers participated in against the Indians in Texas during the Civil War was not with their traditional enemies, the Comanches, Kiowas, or Apaches, and it should not have happened. More than 600 men, women, and children of the Kickapoo tribe were fleeing war-torn Kansas and Indian Territory to find refuge with the rest of the tribe in Mexico. The tragedy began as Capt. Nicholas W. Gillentine and men from Erath's Second District found their abandoned campsite 30 miles west of old Fort Phantom Hill on the Clear Fork Brazos. It was ironic that Gillentine was beyond his district boundary and it would have been better had he not picked up the trail, for he discovered a peaceful band that was trying to avoid the Texans and heading away from the settlements, while so many hostile war parties went by undiscovered.

Gillentine reported his find on December 9, 1864, and the news went to Lt. Col. Barry, who had returned to the frontier with four companies of the Frontier Regiment, and to the First and Second District headquarters. In Decatur, General Throckmorton had reports that a band of Kickapoos had left Kansas with the intention of depredating in Texas and enthusiastically lent his men to intercept them. In Gatesville, Major Erath was absent, and Capt. Silas Totten readied his district's soldiers. In the last days of December they assembled at Fort Chadbourne: Capt. John Fossett with about 50 men from Co. A, Frontier Regiment; about 60 men under lieutenants James R. Giddens, Co. D, James A. Brooks, Co. H., and J. R. Carpenter, Co. G. The force was augmented with a force under Capt. Jack Cureton of the First Frontier District and the advance companies of nearly 500 men being forwarded by Captain Totten.[1]

It was a large force, but coordinating it was a problem. As the Indian trail led south, Captain Fossett took his men in advance and followed it. Captain Totten decided not to go to Chadbourne, but to angle southwest to save miles. On January 7, 1865, Fossett's eager Texans located the Indian camp on Dove Creek about 20 miles southwest of present San Angelo on the Tom Green-Irion County line. Totten's men were still 30 miles behind, but the commanders made plans to attack the next morning. Totten pushed ahead with 220 men, "A forced march all night," said Pvt. Dave Cunningham, "facing the coldest south wind that mortal man ever experienced." Even when the tired soldiers arrived about eight in the morning, there would only be about 380 men total, and they still didn't know who the Indians were, how many there were, or the layout of the camp.

Brigadier General John D. McAdoo, the commander of the state militia who took over the Third Frontier District in June 1864, reported in a later investigation, "The evidences seemed abundant to all whom I have conversed, that they were civilized Indians, and there was nothing discovered that led to the belief that they were unfriendly, further than the simple fact that they were Indians traveling upon the soil of Texas...." Fossett and Totten met for a few minutes, and, said McAdoo, "without any council of war, without any distribution of orders, without any formation of a line of battle, without any preparation, without any inspection of the camp, without any communication with the Indians or inquiry as to what tribe or party they belonged to, without any knowledge of their strength or position, the command "forward" was given, and a pell-mell charge was made for three miles."[2]

Some of the same recipe ingredients were involved which preceded Lt. Col. George Custer's attack at the Little Big Horn in 1876, and Dove Creek nearly degenerated into a similar disaster. Actually Totten and Fossett did have a brief meeting and Fossett planned to circle around and hit the village from upstream, cutting off the Indian horses and retreat route, while Totten attacked from downstream. There were mixed reports as to the village's preparedness. It was aptly situated for defense, running about three-quarters of a mile long on the south side of Dove Creek, inside dense thickets of brush and oak, astride two dry creek beds, and backed by a high bluff.

Totten's horses were exhausted and he dismounted his men and initiated the battle, pushing along the few twisting paths toward the village. Said McAdoo: "No fire was made by the Indians until after they were fired upon and some of them killed. They showed no disposition to fight. The women were screaming about the camp, some of them in plain English declaring they were friendly." The Kickapoos did not seek battle, but they fought back from good defensive positions behind trees, creek beds, and ravines. Some of the Indians used bows and arrows, but many had Enfield Rifles and they blasted the oncoming Texans who tried to take cover, but the fire was deadly.

"We had to dismount and leave our horses on the ridge and wade Dove Creek," said E. L Deaton of Comanche County, "which was over knee-deep, to get at the Indians. This we did several times, and in consequence suffered great loss, as we were laboring under great disadvantage."

Lieutenant James Cunningham in Totten's command, Captain Gillentine of the Texas State Troops, and Pvt. John Anderson in Cunningham's company, took shelter behind a riverbank. As they loaded their guns, Gillentine said he was going to the top of the bank to get a shot at the Indians. Cunningham warned him to stay low, but the captain stood up, fired once, and turned around, handing his gun to Anderson, who asked what was the matter.

"John, I am a dead man," Gillentine said, as he stumbled down the bank. Anderson helped him to the rear, but there was not much of a rear, for it seemed the Indians were firing from almost everywhere. They shifted positions but could gain no advantage. Anderson said the Texans would have taken more casualties except that the Indians "had long range guns and overshot us was all that saved us." The men pled with Lieutenant Cunningham to get them out of there, but he said that "Totten will rally the men, I never will." Ike Richardson and John Anderson decided to get out, besides, they were thirsty, and as they moved toward the river the two men looked into the thicket, which was crawling with Indians. They looked at each other and had the same thought. "Ha! Ha!" Richardson said, "I don't want any water either."[3]

On the upriver side of the village, Captain Fossett, Lieutenant Giddens, and some militia under Captain Cureton and Lieutenant Morton, along with the Tonkawa scouts, charged down to try to cut out the horse herd. The charge was successful at first, and they caught more than 600 ponies, but the Kickapoos would not allow such a coup to stand. They counterattacked with a fury that resulted in a score of Texan casualties, including seven men killed and the mortal wounding of Lieutenant Giddens. Fossett fell back to a hilltop, but was soon nearly surrounded. After a stubborn fight, he had to retreat and the Kickapoos recaptured their horses.

With Fossett completely cut off but still fighting, Totten tried to extricate himself, falling back downriver. "While we were retreating," said Dave Cunningham, "the Indians flanked us on both sides and came up in the rear. They used long range guns and killed several of our men on the retreat." The beaten Texans rallied on a hilltop a few miles northeast near Spring Creek. Fossett extricated his command, circled around, and found his way to the camp. Said E. L. Deaton, "Fossett came into our camp between sundown and dark, with his men terribly cut up. They had fought like demons all day." The Kickapoos did not follow far, but were more concerned with gathering their families and property and getting away.

It snowed that night, reportedly nearly three feet, and completely immobilized the Texans and cut them off from their pack train which was still about 30 miles behind them. They ate their dead horses. A few days later, when the rest of the force and supplies had gathered, they went back to the battlefield and found much abandoned property still lying about. Both Indian and Texan dead littered the area where they fell. None of the whites were scalped or mutilated.[4]

A tragic incident came to light later when participants compared notes. Lt. James Mulkey, said to have been born and raised in the Cherokee Nation, rode with Captain Fossett and informed him and others that he believed these were friendly Kickapoos and they ought to talk to them and learn their intentions before attacking. Fossett, however, said that "he recognized no friendly Indians on the Texas frontier." Men said "that flags of truce raised by the Indians had been disregarded and their bearers shot down in cold blood."

Compounding this, after Fossett had first charged and captured many horses, a man and two children approached him, and, "with his hands raised, told Captain Fossett that they were friendly Indians and that if he would see their principal chief all things would be made satisfactory. Fossett told the Indian he recognized no friendly Indians in Texas. The Indian then told him he was his prisoner. Fossett's reply was, 'We take no prisoners here,' and thereupon ordered him shot, which was done." He showed Fossett a pass from "W. M. Ross, Agent of the Pottawatomies," authorizing the bearer to be off the reservation to hunt until February 4, 1865, but it did not matter. Fossett then reportedly ordered the children shot, but wanting no part in such infamy, his men refused. The children were taken prisoner but escaped when the Texans abandoned the field.

As the reports arrived, General McAdoo became convinced of the Indians' innocence. "My own opinion is," he wrote on February 20, "from the route these Indians were traveling, their having their families and apparently their entire property with them, that they were a moving party, probably going to Mexico to escape the turmoil of the present war. They were outside of our settlements and still diverging in their course from them. There were no evidences showing that any parties were being sent in the direction of the settlements…and I consider the attack upon them without a parley as extremely unfortunate, if not culpable."

In February, citizens in Eagle Pass talked with these same Kickapoos who had finished their journey, crossing into Mexico at Piedras Negras. The Indians confirmed McAdoo's belief that they were simply moving to Mexico to avoid the war, they were friendly, their white flag was fired upon, and prisoners were killed. They were going farther into Mexico to avoid the crazy Texans. They were certain "that the men who attacked them were lawless men, desirous of plunder, and not authorized by the Government."

"What shall be done?" McAdoo asked. If the government did not send a peace commissioner to them to explain what had happened and offer restitution, "it is greatly to be feared that they will return to avenge their losses in the attack." The Texans had made a new enemy.[5]

The Battle of Dove Creek was the largest and deadliest fight that the Texans had with the Indians in Texas during the Civil War. The Texans lost, according to participant E. L. Deaton, "twenty-six left on the field, several dying afterward," plus about 60 wounded and 65 horses killed. "Buck" Barry reported 23 killed and 60 wounded. Some Texans believed they had killed or wounded 75 Indians, but the Kickapoos in Piedras Negras said that they lost 11 killed and seven wounded. In March, a burial party returned to Dove Creek and took several bodies home for burial, but laid most of them to rest on the battlefield. "On this ground lie the remains of twenty of our noble brave," said Deaton. "In a wash their friends placed them, there to await the call of the Master at the Resurrection."[6]

Compared with Civil War battles, the casualties seem minor, but compared to other Western Indian battles, the 86 Texan casualties rank number five on the list of more than 1,400 fights that took place between 1850 and 1890. Only at the Little Big Horn (1876), Badlands (1864), Pyramid Lake (1860), and Birch Coulee (1862), did the white forces take more losses. The Texas soldiers finally had their big battle, but even so, the settlers still suffered more.

Chapter 32 notes

1 Smith, *Frontier Defense*, 151-52; Greer, ed., *Buck Barry*, 182-87.

2 Straley, ed., *Pioneer Sketches Nebraska and Texas*, 32; *WR*: S.1, V.48/1, 26-27.

3 Smith, *Frontier Defense*, 153; *WR*: S.1, V.48/1, 27; Deaton, *Indian Fights on the Texas Frontier*, 43; Straley, ed., *Pioneer Sketches Nebraska and Texas*, 29.

4 Greer, ed., Buck Barry, 191-92; Straley, ed., *Pioneer Sketches Nebraska and Texas*, 32-23; Deaton, *Indian Fights on the Texas Frontier*, 44-45.

5 *WR*: S.1, V.48/1, 28-30.

6 *WR*: S.1, V.48/1, 29; Deaton, *Indian Fights on the Texas Frontier*, 46-47. McConnell, *West Texas Frontier*, 496, compiled a nearly complete list of the dead: Capt. N. W. Gillentine, Capt. William H. Culver, Capt. Sam Barnes, Lt. James R. Giddens, Jake Dyer, Don Cox, Tom Parker, Joe Byers, James Gibson, Nelson Maroney, William Parsons, Noah Bible, John Gillentine, James Mabry, Albert Everett, Noah Gibbs, John Stein, William Etts, and Latham, Land, and Harris.

33 "Don't let them carry me away!"

By 1865 the latest dry cycle was ending. The Palmer Drought Severity Index (PDSI) using tree ring analysis from 1698 to 1980 showed that Texas was subject to 15-year extreme drought cycles in the north and 10-year cycles in the south. The cycles had always come and gone. Phin W. Reynolds moved to Stephens County as a child and some of his earliest recollections were of a severe drought in 1862 to 1864. He and his brother walked half a mile along the bed of the Clear Fork Brazos without finding any water. Much of the area north and west of present-day Abilene, all the way to the Llano Estacado, was covered with what the settlers called the Dead Mesquite Forest, a huge area of dried, rotten mesquite that had been there since before the settlers arrived. Reynolds later talked to an old Tonkawa, who could only tell him that they died in a drought that occurred "way back."[1]

Texas was always subject to climate fluctuations. In 1865, the shift to wetter conditions was beginning, although it was not readily apparent at first. Had anyone been taking notes, he would have seen that for the past five years about 60 percent of the raids and killings occurred during the winter months, from October through March, perhaps due to the severe conditions that burnt the summer grasses and dried up watercourses. Overall, battles with the Indians in the West from 1850 to 1890 followed an opposite pattern, with fights occurring in the summer, April through September, about 60 percent of the time. With more rain, the grass became more abundant, the rivers ran, and the decline in the numbers of bison was temporarily checked. In Texas this resulted in increased raids and a shift to a more "normal" pattern of summer raids.[2]

Such patterns were irrelevant to the settlers on the receiving end, when no time of the year was good to be attacked. The first month of 1865 proved to be the worst January of the decade in terms of civilian and soldier deaths. Several branches of the McDonald and Taylor families lived on the Gillespie and Kimble County border along the far edge of the settlement line. In order to avoid Confederate service, Lafe McDonald had gone to Mexico and his wife, Alwinda, was staying with her parents, Mr. and Mrs. Wylie Joy, about 15 miles west of Harper, in Kimble County. She was very concerned about Lafe's safety, so when she learned letters from him were at Tom McDonald's place on Spring Creek eight miles east of Harper, she was anxious to get them.

About the first of January, Alwinda and Mrs. Joy took a horse and buggy and made the trip. They retrieved the letters, spent the night, and started home the next morning. Near the head of the Pedernales River near Harper, they crossed a little ravine overgrown with thick brush when Indians attacked them. They seized the horse and clambered into the buggy. The warriors may have believed someone was approaching, for they did not bother to capture the women, rob them, or steal the horse. The women were quickly killed and left in the buggy; Mrs. Joy's throat was cut from ear to ear and Alwinda McDonald was attacked so savagely that her head was sliced completely off. After a time, the horse continued its journey and reached Joy's late in the day. Wylie, horrified, found his wife and daughter dead, soaked in blood, and his daughter's head rolled under the seat.

The Indians continued their raid into Kerr and Kendall counties stealing a number of horses. Part of the folklore of the episode indicates that Wylie Joy, swearing to get revenge, followed the Indians' trail and caught three of them sleeping one night. He charged in with his six-shooter and shot two of them in the head before they could rise from their blankets. The third ran, but was slowed enough in a bramble thicket that Joy caught up with him and put a bullet through him. Vengeance sated, Joy went home and then moved east into Kerr County, somewhat farther removed from the frontier.[3]

In what may have been part of the same raid, Indians also visited Mason County. On the border between the Second and Third Frontier Districts, and with Fort Mason abandoned, the area was a good target. George Todd, a Virginian, helped organize Mason County in 1858. He was the first county clerk, postmaster, and became a lawyer and businessman. George, his wife, Dizenia, and their 13-year-old daughter Alice, lived four miles south of the town. Dizenia's father, Joshua Peters, lived near them on a large plantation and owned several slaves. George had been one of the most vocal settlers, often writing to the newspapers about the lack of protection in his area.[4]

Alice had been home from the San Saba Female Seminary for Christmas vacation and was due to return to school soon, but on January 7, 1865, the family went to town to see Dizenia's newborn nephew. Alice and her father rode on one horse, and Dizenia and a black female servant on another. Their dogs ran alongside. While crossing a small pass just west of a low mountain, they noticed some men on horseback and assumed they were ranchers, but when they neared, they discovered they were Indians. The warriors attacked in an instant; the black servant was killed first, and Dizenia was hit by an arrow and fell from the horse. The Indians even killed the dogs. George's horse reared up and Alice slid off.

"Don't let them carry me away!" she shouted to her father, but he sped off, later explaining that he could not stop the frightened animal.[5]

Author's photo

Todd Mountain, near Mason, Texas, was the site of the attack on the Todd family in January 1863.

In town, George Todd gathered up some men and rode back to the attack site. His wife lingered for five days before dying. Dizenia and the servant woman were buried near the foot of the mountain where they were attacked, an eminence that became known as Todd Mountain. The searchers followed tracks to the east, until they found some travelers who said they saw Indians go by, but insisted that they did not have a white girl with them. The pursuers doubled back, found another trail heading west, and followed it. The weather turned cold and snowy. In Kimble County, a family awoke one morning to find an Indian campsite nearby, with a snowy circle of small footprints around a tree, as if a young person had been tethered to the trunk. The rescuers traveled into Menard County and then west to the Concho River. When the trail divided into three branches, the cold, exhausted pursuers gave up.

George Todd sent word of the abduction to Alice's stepbrother, James H. Smith (19), then serving in the Confederate Army in Arkansas. Smith obtained a furlough to look for his stepsister, which continued after the war ended in the spring. He attended the Little Arkansas Treaty in Kansas in October 1865, but could not find news of Alice's whereabouts. The Indians said that Alice Todd had been killed shortly after her capture. Smith and Todd were not convinced. George Todd searched for her for several years, writing to U. S. officials, state officials, the military, and the press. Todd rued the day he moved to Texas. He pleaded for the government not to give the Indians guns and ammunition, "for they come right down here and use them on us."

He wanted to get away, he said, "but I am too poor." He had been on the frontier since 1853, he said, "and I now curse the day when I commenced it."

Todd was destined never to learn what became of his daughter. Perhaps it was his destiny to remain tormented and guilt-ridden for the rest of his life, for it was he who had first fled and abandoned her.[6]

About 250 miles to the north of Mason County, Comanches were in Montague County. On January 6, 1865, they attacked a detachment of Lt. Jasper F. Hagler's Company F, Bourland's Regiment, on Simon Creek in Indian Territory north of Sivell's Bend, wounding one man and stealing six horses. The next day, Lt. Jasper S. O'Neal and a 15-man detachment of Company E, Bourland's Regiment, scouting near the Montague-Clay County line caught 24 Indians eating dinner. They got within close rifle range before they were discovered and charged before the Indians could put up a defense. Three warriors were killed and a few wounded before the rest scattered. Sgt. A. Gooding and Pvt. J. W. Wilson were wounded. The whites captured eight horses and saddles, blankets, bridles, bows and arrows, at an estimated worth of $4,500. One of the soldiers, D. A. Say, got himself an Indian scalp as a souvenir.

A few days later, on the night of January 10, Lieutenant Hagler caught six Indians, this time on Salt Creek south of Red River Station. They recaptured the six horses stolen from them plus all the saddles, equipage, and two pistols. These skirmishes were some of the few "successful" fights of the Border Regiment.[7]

The continued raids further emphasized the need for action. In January, Generals Throckmorton and McCulloch, Colonel Bourland, and Lieutenant Colonel Barry met in Decatur "to discuss how to better protect the frontier," and agreed that the best tactic would be to take the fight to the enemy. It was sound in theory, but never seemed to work in practice. Major Charles Roff, Bourland's Regiment, was to take command of 400 men from the various forces and attack the Indians. They left on February 1, heading for where they believed the Indians were in winter quarters in the Wichita Mountains in Indian Territory. Coordination was a problem and not all the units reached the jump-off point, then, within a few days, severe weather hit, driving rain, sleet, and snow into their faces. There were cattle and bison to kill and eat, but little forage for the horses.

The men tried to keep up their spirits, with some of the younger men playing tricks on the older fellows whose heart was not into chasing Indians in the winter. In camp, some of them crept out, fired their guns and began yelling. The old men who were not in on the joke went off running, "minus clothing but taking their rifles with them." They splashed through a shallow, icy lake, until reaching some timber on the far side. When they discovered it was a hoax they were very angry, plus, some of them had lost their weapons in the lake. The pranksters played the same trick again a few nights later, and by this time, few people were amused.

On February 7, Roff wrote to Bourland of his troubles. He had sent patrols into the Wichita Mountains, but they found nothing but abandoned camps. Already he was sending men with broken down horses back home. The grass they could find was brown or covered with crusts of sleet. If he ever found the Indians, Roff said he would barely have 200 effectives to fight them. His horses were so poor that half of them "cannot go any place." He unloaded his pack mules and sent them back. Stragglers dropped out and Roff said the men "are very much out of heart." They found not one Indian and after ten days, Roff ordered those who were still left, to return to Texas. They began straggling in on February 12, "afoot driving their horses before them," and "Lt. Hagler came in very sick with pnuamony [pneumonia]."

Throckmorton tried to remain positive, writing on February 22, that the campaign "will teach the Indians that even in mid winter, we intend to hunt them in their retreats. The expedition has prevented any raids of consequence during the present light moon."[8]

It was a Pollyanna declaration. The expedition failed to stop anything and the Indians might not have even known it was in the field. The "light moon" of February fell on the 10th, the same day that Roff ended his expedition, and Indians were raiding in Texas.

The Graham family lived in Coryell County about 12 miles south of Gatesville near Sugar Loaf Mountain. The town was the headquarters of George Erath's Second Frontier District, but that mattered little to the raiders. They swept by in mid-February, stealing horses and killing anyone who got in the way. Gideon Graham had several sons in the Confederate Army and was carrying clothes to one of them stationed nearby. While away, he left his youngest, Samuel Graham (13), at home to help his mother. While Sam searched for stock about two miles from the cabin, the raiders came by and snatched him off his pony, adding it to their herd and moving out.

The Indians went into Lampasas County, stopping few times to eat. Although they had buffalo meat, they only offered Sam some poor horseflesh and indicated he must drink water from a dead horse's stomach, which he could not do, and was whipped for his refusal. A short while later, the posse caught up with them. Sam was riding behind a warrior and tried to jump off, but the man grabbed his arm and thrust a lance through his body, throwing him into the brush. The posse claimed to have killed one of the Indians while the rest got away. They carried Sam Graham home but he died two days later.[9]

About the same time, raiders visited southwest Parker County. Lemuel C. Barton (26), his wife, Margaret Maybury Barton (20), and their sons, Columbus (4), and one younger child, lived in the Littlefield Bend of the

Brazos near the Parker-Palo Pinto line. Margaret and the two children were eating dinner when she saw horseman running stock behind Sam Littlefield's house nearby. At first she thought it was her husband and other cowhands, but when she realized they were Indians, she grabbed the children and ran toward Tack Barton's house, 200 yards to the east.

Carrie Ried Barton and her daughter, Vashti (15), saw what was happening, quickly put on men's hats and coats, grabbed rifles, and went out to help. The Indians caught Margaret by the hair and shot an arrow into her breast and she fell to the ground still trying to clutch her children. They whipped Columbus in the face with a lasso until the skin ripped off his nose. The Indians left them in the field and plundered the house until Carrie, Vashti, and a younger son approached, threatening them with their rifles. When the Indians cleared out, the three of them dragged Margaret to their cabin, but she died about two hours later.[10]

From the first days of the war to the last, Texans were still out on the frontier hunting Indians while those Indians were raiding inside their protective barrier.

Chapter 33 notes

1 Stahle and Cleaveland, "Texas Drought History," 65; Galloway, *Dark Corner of the Confederacy*, 169-70.

2 Michno, *Encyclopedia of Indian Wars*, 358.

3 Wilbarger, *Indian Depredations*, 196-97; McConnell, *West Texas Frontier*, in http://www.forttours.com/pages/joy.asp; *Galveston Weekly News*, January 4, 1865.

4 Zesch, "Alice Todd," 3-4.

5 Zesch, "Alice Todd," 4-5.

6 Zesch, "Alice Todd," 11-15.

7 Adkins-Rochette, *Bourland in North Texas I*, 288-89, 298; *Galveston Weekly News*, February 1, 1865.

8 Smith, *Frontier Defense*, 136-37; Adkins-Rochette, *Bourland in North Texas I*, 288, 292.

9 McConnell, West Texas Frontier, 461; Wilbarger, Indian Depredations, 487-88. A genealogy website states Sam was born in 1851 and died in February 1865.

10 McConnell, *West Texas Frontier*, 611; "Parker County Texas," http://www.rootsweb.ancestry.com/~txparker/history/indianraids2.html.

34 "The Booger-Man did it."

Indians were in the settlements, but the various military organizations often seemed to be occupied elsewhere. With the failure of the Indian Territory offensive and the Confederacy collapsing around them, Bourland, McCulloch, and Throckmorton were going after deserters again. In late March 1865, a large number of deserters left east Texas and were thought to be crossing Wise County. Captain George B. Pickett took his First District men out of Decatur, to hunt them, joining an expedition under Lieutenant Colonel Diamond with skeleton companies of the Border Regiment. The drought and harsh winter having destroyed the wheat crop in north Texas, Bourland had furloughed many of his troops to get an early start to plant corn, and only a handful were available for the chase. McCulloch lent some of his troops too, but even so, the motley force consisted of only about 140 men.

The deserters, about 100-strong, crossed into Clay County and camped near the Little Wichita. Diamond unknowingly stopped on the opposite side of a ridge separating the camps. At dawn on April 3, Diamond's men discovered the deserters, but being of approximate equal numbers, Diamond was unsure of what to do when Captains Pickett and S. Shannon stepped forward and volunteered to take 30 men each, circle around and drive off the deserters' horses. It worked. The deserters had superior arms and mounts, but with their horses gone, they put up the white flag. They would surrender if they were given a guarantee that they would not be turned over to Colonel Bourland. Diamond promised their safety, and escorted them to Gainesville where McCulloch had them moved to Galveston. The operation mattered little. They just had been confined when the war ended. One of the latest schemes to help make the troops self-sustaining was to let the soldiers confiscate enemy property and divide it up, which would be deducted from their pay. Throckmorton's and Bourland's men spent the last days of the war arguing over who should get the spoils of the captured property and horses.[1]

When General Lee surrendered his Army of Northern Virginia to General Grant at Appomattox, Virginia, on April 9, 1865, it effectively ended the war east of the Mississippi. In Kirby Smith's Confederacy in the west they still tried to struggle on, but the harvest of 1864 was bad, and prospects did not look good for rain in early 1865; the few railroads they had were barely in operation; horse raids had depleted the stock so badly that there were no horses to re-supply the cavalry; by the last month in 1864, the Confederacy was converting cavalry to infantry; the drought had killed so many cattle that there were few to be sent east to the meat-packing plants; and the situation was so bad in March 1865, that the Confederacy even began arming its slaves.[2]

In the spring of 1865 the Third Frontier District initiated an Indian-hunting operation comparable to the First District. Brigadier General McAdoo, with about 1,400 men enrolled, was proud that Indian raids were down in his bailiwick. He said that "scouts are regularly on duty; and the Indians seen scarcely into the settlements anywhere without being immediately discovered and pursued." Cooperation between the various commands, however, was lacking. Confederate Gen. James Slaughter of the Western Sub-District, McCulloch's counterpart, tried to usurp McAdoo's authority, seeking to take over command of some of McAdoo's counties. Slaughter claimed that his informants said, incredibly, that there had been no Indians in that region for seven years and the Frontier Organization was not needed. Governor Murrah and others thought differently.

In January 1865, Major Hunter resigned and John Henry Brown took over as second in command in the Third District. He and McAdoo made plans for a spring offensive. On April 10, Major Brown reached Camp Verde where hopefully 400 men of the District, one-quarter of its strength, would assemble. As usual, not even half had the horses and equipment to participate; some counties sent only one or two men. Nevertheless, Brown led out 183 men in four columns, proposing to sweep the upper San Saba and Concho Rivers. Traveling through rough country and with the men's hearts not in it, by the time they reached Fort McKavett on April 21, 22 men had already deserted. On Kickapoo Creek they finally saw action, but not with Indians. They caught about 15 "Jayhawkers" and chased them until nightfall. The next day, searching for their quarry, Brown caught another band, this time 23 deserters from the Frontier Regiment. Three days later, back near Fort McKavett, Brown found five of the "Jayhawker" band, arresting two who were known horse thieves.

Gathering a few more deserters, Brown paroled them and continued his expedition, but only found more deserters and bushwhackers. His men killed two and arrested seven and then headed for home, reaching Fredericksburg on May 4. The results of the expedition were poor; like Roff's in the north, not an Indian was seen. In addition, waiting for them in Fredericksburg was the news that General Lee had surrendered and the war, at least in the East, was over.[3]

Amid the chaos there were still the ever-present raids. While the military chased deserters in north and central Texas, raiders hit Uvalde County in the south, stealing horses and cattle from Robert Kincheloe. They were in Hood County on April 12, where E. B. "Dick" Dennis was on furlough from the army and planning to return soon. He and his wife were riding not far from home when Indians approached them. They thought the riders were cowmen at first, but when they dashed toward them it was too late. A warrior shot an arrow into Dick's spine and then speared him, and another knocked Mrs. Dennis off her horse. "I felt that I was killed and that my wife would be, in a few minutes, and both of us scalped," said Dick. "I resolved, however, to sell our lives for as many Indian lives as possible."

Mr. Dennis got his pistol from its scabbard and just as two Indians approached his wife, he blasted the closest one with a bullet. The others yelled, ran back to their horses, mounted, and rode away, but not after taking the Dennis's two horses. Mrs. Dennis helped her husband back to their cabin and a doctor extracted the arrow from his spine with a pocket knife and a bullet mould. He survived.[4]

On May 1, raiders hit Hamilton County, stealing 28 horses worth $700 from Solomon Barron. The theft nearly wiped him out, but he persevered, until they hit him again the next year.[5]

With no end of the Indian conflict in sight and not knowing how long the western Confederacy could survive, authorities tried to forge another treaty to stem the raids. There were rumors that the Plains Indians wanted peace, possibly because of the Union offensives that struck them during the fall of 1864. In March 1865, General Smith appointed James Throckmorton as Texas commissioner to treat with the Comanches and Kiowas. Throckmorton was reluctant to take the job but Smith insisted that peace with the Indians was essential for the survival of the Confederacy. Throckmorton wrote to Bourland for advice on dealing with the Indians. "You know our condition," he wrote, and "You are familiar with the Indian habits…." He also added that "We know the Indian character too well to trust to their promises."[6]

General Smith wanted a three-part treaty to bind together all the Plains tribes hostile to the North, the five Civilized Tribes, and the Confederate government. In May they were ready. Colonel W. P. Reagan joined Throckmorton as co-commissioner, and with wagons of supplies and gifts, plus nearly 500 mounted troops, rode to Cottonwood Grove, or Camp Napoleon, on the Washita River (now Verden, Oklahoma). The Indians slowly gathered throughout the month, and by May 24, there were an estimated 5,000 to 7,000 Indians representing 20 different tribes.

If the Confederates believed they could get a tripartite agreement and patch up decades of hatred, they were mistaken. Throckmorton and Reagan proved to be minor players, for as historian Anne Abel put it, "The Indians had it all their own way for once." They knew the Confederacy's fight was not going well, and they used the time to meet with all the tribes to arrange a united front to approach the United States and get the best deal they could. They finally realized that they had little to gain and much to lose by an attachment with the South. "It was a pity," said Abel, "that they had not thought of it sooner."[7] On May 26, the Indians, which included the five Civilized tribes, Osages, Caddos, Comanches, Kiowas, Arapahos, Lipans, and others, agreed to perpetual friendship, stating "The tomahawk shall be forever buried," and forming "an Indian confederacy or band of brothers, having for its object the peace, the happiness, and the protection of all alike, and the preservation of our race." There was little that benefitted the Confederacy, and the Indians would not agree to stop crossing below Red River. Throckmorton passed out his gifts, the Indians took them, and nothing much had changed.[8]

There were, however, some positive results. In the spirit of goodwill, albeit temporary, several white captives were recovered. David White and Brit Johnson had been searching for their families since Elonzo White was captured in June 1864, and the Johnsons and Durkins were taken in October 1864. The two men went to Throckmorton for help and he informed them that a meeting would take place in Indian Territory in May 1865. Some of the captives were being held in Peneteka Chief Tosawi's (Silver Brooch) camp. The Peneteka Asa Havey (Milky Way), who was considered a peacemaker, assisted them. White and Johnson accompanied Throckmorton up the Washita to bargain for the captives, paying out a number of horses, goods, and a $20 gold piece. White got his son back for a horse, a blanket, and some trinkets. After nearly a year with the Comanches, Lon White thought he was being tricked when he was told to enter a tipi and go to his father. He hesitated, as if unsure of what awaited him, but once he saw his father, the boy ran to his arms. Lon asked in broken English, "Did the Indians kill Mama and the other children?" David White was shocked at his son's appearance. The Indians had stained his skin with a pecan shell dye, and he was as dark as any Comanche.

Brit Johnson got back his wife, Mary, her son, and an additional daughter, an infant born to Mrs. Johnson during her captivity, and Lottie Durkin. Brit Johnson gave seven ponies for the return of his family. The Indians had tattooed Lottie, inking a dime-sized blue moon on her forehead, marking her for life. Johnson and White also secured the release of an orphan boy being raised by George Light prior to his capture, and Thomas Rolland, taken in Texas in February 1864. After bargaining, White and Johnson had no horses to make the journey home so Asa Havey gave them four ponies out of his own herd. The freed captives were sent to Decatur, Texas. By mid-summer of 1865, they all went to Veale's Station in Parker County, where Brit Johnson had relocated after the Elm Creek attack.[9]

While the Texans made "peace" with the tribes in Indian Territory, war parties were below Red River conducting their own diplomatic relations with the settlers. Isaac Brisco had lived in Jack County since before the Civil War, but that conflict convinced him it would be safer to move down into Parker County. Staying behind in southeast Jack County was his daughter,

Cynthia, who had married James McKinney on April 12, 1858—theirs said to be the first marriage license issued in Jack County. In the spring of 1865, the McKinneys, with their three children, Mary Alice (6), Joe (3), and a baby, took a wagon to Springtown in northeast Parker County to mill their grain. Jim McKinney was short of money and hocked his pistol for provisions. Business in Springtown done, they decided to visit Cynthia's parents before returning home.

Isaac Brisco did not move to a safer place. His new home was three-fourths of a mile northwest of present-day Agnes, and about 15 miles north of Weatherford. The McKinneys filled their kegs at a spring known as Jenkins Water and then traveled two miles farther west until they were about two miles east of Brisco's. Warriors swooped down out of the wooded hills and attacked, quickly slaughtering and scalping Jim and Cynthia. They killed the baby, lanced little Joe, and carried away Mary Alice. They rode north about 15 miles near present Bridgeport in Wise County and for whatever reason, decided not to take her north of Red River. They murdered her and left her body on the trail. Joe McKinney was not dead; he managed to walk away and hide in the brush.

The next day, two settlers hunting for stray cattle found a place where there looked to have been a struggle, and followed a child's footprints a little ways until they heard a voice crying, "Papa! Papa!" When Joe saw it was not his father he tried to run, but the men quickly caught the naked, wounded boy, who was punctured and scratched with thorns. When they asked him what happened, little Joe could only say, "The booger-man did it." They took him home and the wives washed and dressed him and removed the thorns. Searchers returned to the site the next day and followed tracks 400 yards to the place of the massacre, discovering a wagon, an ox with an arrow in it, and the bodies of James, Cynthia and the baby. When Mary Alice was later found, the bodies of all four were buried in a single grave in Goshen Cemetery, west of Springtown.[10]

Isaac Brisco and his wife grieved over the loss of their daughter, son-in-law, and grandchildren, but they carried on, unknowing that they, too, had only about one year to live.

Chapter 34 notes

1 Smith, *Frontier Defense*, 139, 141-42; Howell, *James Throckmorton*, 92; "McCaslin, "Dark Corner," 67-68.

2 Kerby, *Kirby Smith's Confederacy*, 382, 384, 385, 396.

3 Smith, *Frontier Defense*, 161-67.

4 Robert Kincheloe, Depredation Claim #2764; McConnell, *West Texas Frontier*, 498.

5 Solomon Barron, Depredation Claim #5255.

6 *WR*: S.1, V.48/1, 1440; Smith, *Frontier Defense*, 142; Adkins-Rochette, *Bourland in North Texas I*, 304.

7 Abel, *American Indian and the End of the Confederacy*, 139.

8 *WR*: S.1, V.48/2, 1102-03.

9 Michno, *A Fate Worse Than Death*, 263, 266; Ledbetter, *Fort Belknap*, 135-36, 157n11, 12.

10 Marshall, *A Cry Unheard*, 135-37; Huckabay, *Jack County*, 23, 94-95; McConnell, *West Texas Frontier*, in www.forttours.com/pages/tocmckinn and www.forttours.com/pages/toc/brisco.

35 "The wounds caused by scalping gave off such an offensive odor."

On June 2, 1865, Gen. Edmund Kirby Smith surrendered at Galveston, officially bringing the Civil War in the trans-Mississippi west to a close. In Texas there were still men able to fight, but almost all of them had lost their will. They seemed to realize the futility of fighting earlier than did the civilian leaders. Many of them, who had just weeks earlier been chasing deserters, adopted the same course and went home. Looting was widespread and many civilians were anxious for Union troops to arrive and stabilize the situation. Naturally, the collapse of the Confederacy left most Texans with feelings of anxiety and foreboding. Would the predictions of disaster if ever the Lincoln-led black Republicans took over now come true? President Andrew Johnson began the process on June 17 when he appointed Andrew J. Hamilton, an old Texan and Unionist, as the new provisional governor of Texas. Hamilton was instructed to restore civil authority and ensure a loyal Republican government, assemble a convention to renounce secession, repudiate the state's Confederate war debt, provide for elections, and ratify the 13th Amendment ending slavery. On June 19, Gen. Gordon Granger brought in the first Union soldiers to keep order, and in his General Orders No. 3, he declared all slaves in Texas to be free.

Texas had just fought in a terrible war, but unlike many of the other states, it had not been ravaged by Union armies and economic and social conditions remained relatively stable. Disenfranchising Confederate officials and high-ranking military men and insisting that future relationships of former masters and slaves would now be on an employer and hired laborer basis was a system shock for many. The "problem" of how to treat with the freedmen would haunt Texans for years to come.[1]

On the frontier, however, most of the farmers, ranchers, and laborers had never owned any slaves, and the problems of the cotton-growing coastal regions were not directly theirs. On the frontier, little had changed. One of the reasons Texans voted to secede from the Union was because the army seemed unable to protect them. The protection offered by the Confederacy and the state was little or no improvement. Now, they assumed the Federals would take over their old job again. There was, however, a coverage gap, similar to what had happened in 1861when the Federals left and before the state and Confederate troops could fill the void. This time the Confederate and state forces were disbanded, and the Federals had not yet filled in the holes on the frontier. The settlers feared the worst, and rightfully so, but their concerns were likely focused in the wrong direction. As has been illustrated, the

Comanches and Kiowas cared little for their adversaries' political affiliations, and troop strength was only a minor part of the equation.

The main problem was that the rain was back, and with it came the raiders. In 1865 the eastern half of Texas was back into normal and above normal rainfall range on the Palmer Drought Severity Index; the first time it was into the "green" since 1858, which was also a year of much fighting and raiding.

In June, Kiowas were in Llano County stealing horses from George Hardin, A. Davis, and T. H. Shugart, and they killed Shugart in the process. Farther south in Frio County, Martin's Settlement was an isolated community of scattered ranches on Todos Santos Creek near its junction with the Leona River, about a dozen miles northwest of present-day Dilley, Texas. Settlers in the vicinity included the Martin, Bennett, Hays, Parks, English, Burleson, Williams, and Berry families.

On the morning of July 4, Ed Burleson Jr. was herding horses when two Indians chased him, nearly capturing him before he reached his ranch. Neighbors had already gathered there, preparing to celebrate Independence Day. Instead, 11 men got their weapons and horses and formed a posse: Levi English, Bud English, L. A. Franks, G. W. Daugherty, W. C. Bell, Frank Williams, Dan Williams, Dean Oden, John Berry, Ed Burleson, Jr., and Mr. Aikens. Levi English was named captain.

They trailed the Indians down the Leona River and crossed the stream near Bennet's Ranch, about four miles from Burleson's place. Ten miles farther on, near Martin's Ranch, and just above the junction of the Leona and the Frio, the settlers saw the Indians about two miles off. They rode out of sight in a valley, and when they emerged they were only 200 yards away from 36 Comanches, mounted two to a horse. The warriors galloped away and the impetuous settlers dashed after them, firing their weapons without any effect. After a mile, the Indians stopped, correctly figuring their pursuers had fired all their ammunition. One rider dismounted from every horse and charged directly at the settlers, while the remaining mounted Indians circled to the left and right.

Captain English tried to pull his boys back out of the deadly circle, but within a minute the settlers were nearly surrounded and frantically reloading their guns. The warriors charged in, shooting Dan Williams from his horse. English mounted a counter-charge to rescue him, but in doing so they fired their last loads. The Indians counter-charged. Frank Williams tried to get his brother on a horse, but Dan gave him his pistol and told him to get away. "Take this and do the best you can. I am killed—cannot live ten minutes. Save yourself."[2]

Dean Oden was hit and pitched off his horse. He tried to remount, but was hit six more times and the Indians were on him. Bud English went down with a bullet in the chest. His father tried to stay with him, but the last of his men were retreating, and he had to leave his boy behind. As the settlers raced off, the Indians were among them in a moving fight. An arrow struck Levi English in his side, another struck Daugherty in the leg, and yet another hit Burleson in the leg. Bell took an arrow in his side and Aikens was hit in the chest. They finally made it back to Burleson's Ranch and the warriors gave up the chase.

The women and children, once ready to celebrate the Fourth, instead took up a mournful wailing and crying. The next day, after more settlers arrived, they returned to recover the three mutilated bodies. Oden and Williams were brothers-in-law and were buried in the same coffin. Later in the fall, Levi English moved his family to Carrizo Springs in Dimmit County.[3]

Raiders were everywhere. About 350 to the north in Montague County on July 6, they crossed Red River in the vicinity of the now abandoned Red River Station and stole two steers worth $100 from William R. Sullivan. Later in July, Comanches were in the central Hill Country. They swept within 300 yards of Isaac Newton Jackson's ranch in Llano County and stole a good sorrel saddle horse worth $150.[4]

On July 25, raiders were in Hamilton County. County Judge John S. White later reported that "About the 25th of July 1865 they killed an old man and a boy about six miles from here [Hamilton] the old man was name Cox the boy was name Hollis I do not know their given names they did not live in this County."[5]

Henry and Johanna Kensing and their family lived on upper Beaver Creek near the Gillespie-Mason County border. On July 26, Henry (40) drove a light wagon to his brother's place on Squaw Creek where Johanna (38) was helping her sister-in-law. It was already getting late and H. Bierschwale, a teacher at the Beaver Creek school, advised him not to go because it would be dark before he could get home. Kensing said he had good horses and they would get back in time. Bierschwale noted that he did not even take his revolver.

Kensing reached his brother's and got Johanna. They turned down an invitation to spend the night and drove home, but within a mile, six mounted Comanches attacked them. Kensing tried to turn and drive the wagon back to his brother's, but they cut him off. He turned toward Beaver Creek and they chased him a mile before they caught up and pulled the horses to a halt. They pulled the Kensings out of the wagon and tied a rope around Johanna's neck. Henry tried to fight back but they shot an arrow into his chest. He ran, but a warrior chased him into the brush and lanced him through the back. Johanna fought all she could, but she was dragged into the bushes, punched, stripped, and raped by all of them. One of the Indians tried to gouge her eyes out. They scalped her, stabbed her several times, sliced open her abdomen, and left her with nothing but her stockings on. Incredibly, she was still alive.

Next morning the mail carrier rode by, saw signs of the struggle, and hurried on to report the news at Squaw Creek. The Lehmann, Buchmeier, Crenwelge, and Welge, families, along with several others of German descent, lived in the area. Mr. Lehmann may have been an uncle of Herman Lehmann (5), who was living with the Buchmeiers after his father died and his mother married Philip Buchmeier in 1863. Herman would be captured by Lipans in the same area five years later.

Mr. Lehmann rode to the scene and found Johanna Kensing. He wrapped her in a blanket and went for more help, returning with Peter Crenwelge, Henry Welge, and a few others. They also found Henry's body and placed it in another wagon, not telling Johanna that he was dead. The mortally wounded woman lived another two days, relating the story of what had happened. The women who attended her said that "The wounds caused by the scalping gave off such an offensive odor" that they could not bear to serve her. Johanna gave birth to a premature son just before she died. They were all buried next to each other near Squaw Creek. They left seven children, from two years to 16 years in age. Mr. Bierschwale was named their guardian and raised them to maturity.[6]

The raid was not over. The Comanches moved southeast into Gillespie County. For the past 14 years Gottlieb and Sophie Fischer worked a 110-acre farm six miles southwest of Fredericksburg on the north bank of the Pedernales River. On July 29, Gottlieb sent his oldest son, Rudolph (13), a strong boy with curly black hair and dark eyes, who spoke only German, to look for stray cattle. The Comanches spotted the lone barefooted boy, wearing buckskin pants and a striped shirt, and they easily swept him up on one of their horses. Rudolph knew enough not to resist and maybe they would let him live.

A scouting party unsuccessfully tried to follow the Indians, who got far away to the Texas Panhandle. In December 1865, citizens of Gillespie County, including Gottlieb Fischer, wrote to Texas Governor Andrew J. Hamilton, decrying the Indian raids and asking for help in rescuing captives. Gottlieb even wrote to President Andrew Johnson, giving him a description of Rudolph and asking him for help in locating him, but by the spring of 1866, Gottlieb Fischer came to believe his son was dead.[7]

Rudolph was alive, and given the name Gray Blanket. He later took a wife and became, in effect, a Comanche. When the tribe surrendered in 1875, Rudolph came in to Fort Sill and was reunited with his father in 1877. He was not happy back in white society and less than a year later, Rudolph returned to Indian Territory to be with his Indian family. Rudolph Fischer died in 1941, having lived with the Indians longer than any other captive taken in post-Civil War Texas.[8]

The raiders were apparently finding the Mason-Gillespie-Kimble County area ripe for the pickings because they hung around for weeks. In early August they were in the settlement along the Little Saline Creek, which ran into the Llano in the extreme northeast corner of Kimble County. Fred Conaway (34), who had a wife and four children, left his home to go to Adolph Reichenau's place to borrow a yoke of oxen. Reichenau was the last to see him alive. He lent him the oxen and Conaway drove home. He was waylaid on the way and fought a number of Indians in a little cave along the Llano. Being wounded and thirsty, Fred crawled out to get a drink when the warriors finished him off.

Several days later, Reichenau rode to Conaway's, found his wife who was five months pregnant, and asked her where Fred was. "God, I don't know," she said. She thought he had stayed at Reichenau's. Adolph and some neighbors went to search for Fred and only located his body by seeing circling buzzards. He was face down on the riverbank with his hand dangling in the water, so decomposed that they couldn't carry him, but buried the remains beneath a tree.[9]

After Conaway's death, people on the Little Saline began to question if they should move back east. When Kiowas hit the Taylor and McDonald place on August 8, it convinced them. Pioneer preacher Matthew Taylor and his wife, Hannah Axley, had come to the head of the Pedernales River in 1863, at the western edge of Gillespie County. They had ten children, and three of their adult children and their families moved with them. The extended clan included son James Taylor, married to "Gilly" Taylor; daughter Cola Caroline Taylor (26), married to Elijah McDonald; and their daughters Mahala (4), and Rebecca Jane (1). Son Zedrick Taylor had married Margaret A. Halliburton. They had two children, Alice Almeda and James (7). When Margaret died, Zedrick married Angelina Dorcas Hays and had one daughter, Dorcas Angelina (3). When Zedrick died, the three children lived with their grandparents. Matthew and James Taylor were away in Kimble County when the Indians struck.[10]

Gilly Taylor had just gone to the spring to get water when about 20 Kiowas sprang out from behind the trees. One shot her in the breast with an arrow and she ran to the cabins shouting, "Indians!" Another arrow hit her and she fell to the ground so hard that the arrow was driven through her body. Eli McDonald grabbed his gun, but Cola Caroline and Hannah pleaded for him not to shoot, for it would only enrage the Indians. Nevertheless, he fired and drove the Indians back. They then waved a white flag in front of the cabins to signal a parley. Grandmother Hannah Taylor slipped out the back and hid in a small cave along the creek.

Eli McDonald stepped outside to talk, but warriors rushed him from around the cabin, shot him full of arrows, and burst inside. One of them

Author's photo

Site of the Taylor-McDonald cabin, Harper, Texas.

pushed Mahala McDonald into the fireplace and her hand was burned so badly that the fingers were charred and permanently deformed. Warriors took their clothing, ripped open the feather beds, and stole what they wanted before destroying much of the rest. While they were busy plundering, Cola Caroline tried to usher the children away, but when Mahala went outside and saw her father and Aunt Gilly lying dead, stripped, and scalped, she screamed. Warriors quickly rounded them up and put a close watch on them. The Indians set the cabins aflame, grabbed Cola Caroline by the hair and threw her and the five children on ponies and rode off.

Grandma Hannah watched the cabins burning from her hiding place. That night she started walking and by daybreak she reached the Doss Ranch about seven miles to the north. The Kiowas captured some horses near Fredericksburg and then headed north and crossed Red River. Mrs. McDonald was treated brutally. She was about two months pregnant when captured, and often sick and feverish. She and the children were given so little water that their tongues blackened and swelled. In Indian Territory they were stripped and they blistered and burned in the hot sun. One of Mrs. McDonald's worst memories of her captivity was her forced nudity in front of her children, nieces, and nephew. Cola Caroline lost track of time, forgetting when she was captured or how long she was with the Indians. Mahala and Alice were separated and given to different bands.[11]

Chapter 35 notes

1 Clampitt, "The Breakup," 505, 518, 530-31; Moneyhon, *Texas After the Civil War*, 6-8.
2 Winfrey and Day, *Texas Indian Papers, IV*, 253; Sowell, *Early Settlers*, 268-69.
3 Sowell, *Early Settlers*, 269-70, 567; "Martin, Texas," Texas Online Handbook, www.tsha.utexas.edu/handbook/online/articles/view/MM/hrmbb.html.
4 Depredation Claims: William R. Sullivan #5680; Isaac N. Jackson #2644.
5 Winfrey and Day, *Texan Indian Papers IV*, 164.
6 Zesch, *The Captured*, 15; *Fredericksburg Standard*, "Woman's Death Recalls Frontier Tragedy," 532-33; McConnell, *West Texas Frontier*, 440.
7 Ledbetter, *Fort Belknap*, 151-52; Winfrey and Day, *Texas Indian Papers 4*, 88-89; Zesch, *The Captured*, 39-40.
8 Fischer's story is told in Zesch, *The Captured*, and Michno, *A Fate Worse Than Death*, 278-83.
9 Zesch, *The Captured*, 15-16.
10 McConnell, *West Texas Frontier*, in forttours.com/pages/toc/tayhome; Ledbetter, *Fort Belknap*, 150, 160n74, n75, n76.
11 Wilbarger, *Depredations*, 646-47; Ledbetter, *Fort Belknap*, 146, 150-51, 178.

36 "There must be a frontier somewhere."

The summer dragged on with more of the same news on the frontier. Raiders swept north to south through Lampasas and Burnet counties. About the first of August they hit M. Etheridge's place outside of Lampasas, stealing 15 horses worth $1,000. A week later they were in Burnet County. The Binnions, who had come to Texas from Alabama back in 1838, were in the process of moving from Burnet County down to Uvalde County. Their son, Samuel, had gone back to round up their stock. The Indians caught him about five miles north of Burnet. He ran toward a thicket but they roped him around the neck and threw him down like a calf. They stripped him, tied his hands behind him, dragged him awhile, and then lanced him to death. With her son killed and her husband dying later, Mrs. Minerva A. Binnion filed a depredation claim for stolen cattle, horses, and mules worth more than $1,000.[1]

While some Indians were killing Sam, others saw J.T. (or A. D.) Hamlin in a nearby thicket, but he picked up a long, charred stick and sighted along it as if it was a rifle. They backed off and played hide-and-seek with him through the woods. Hamlin bluffed his way like this until he reached home. Shortly after, when he went out into his plowed field, an Indian approached him and Hamlin again sprinted for the cabin. When he reached the fence, he was so exhausted he could not climb over and the Indian had him. He turned to face his adversary and discovered a Tonkawa who was playing a joke on him. Laughing, he approached and said, "Me good Indian; me no hurt." Hamlin would have choked him to death if he had the strength.

From north of Burnet the raiders moved to Hoovers Valley about ten miles southwest of town. They rode in and grabbed young Lum Tedford while he was plowing his father's field only 150 yards from his house. They threw him on a horse and sped away, as neighbors James and Tom Cooper, Bill McGill, and a few others pursued them. After a four mile ride, Lum broke free and jumped from the horse. The warriors circled him as Lum picked up some rocks and threw them. The posse approached and saw the minuet, with Lum firing rocks left and right and the warriors toying with him, appearing pleased with the game and admiring the boy's courage. They would have certainly soon roped him and continued riding, but the posse arrived. Tom Cooper wanted to shoot, but James cautioned that they might hit Lum and said they had to charge. The Indians saw them galloping in, quickly ended their game, left Lum behind, and rode away. The posse managed only to wound one Indian's horse.

The raiders next moved to Backbone Valley about 12 miles southwest of Burnet. A Mr. Benson and his son, James (9), were walking in the woods gathering timber. When the Indians surprised them, Mr. Benson tried to defend them with his ax, swinging and dodging from tree to tree, but they shot him down and scalped him. They took James Benson captive and headed west up the Llano River into Llano County. They made one last stop at William E. Jennings's place, taking a horse and mule worth $375. With a good haul of stock and a captive boy, they moved north of Red River.[2]

The *Galveston Weekly News* on August 19, 1865, decried the usual lack of protection. "The frontier, which during the reign of the Confederacy was in a terrible condition, owing to the murders and depredations of the Indians and lawless white men, is at present in a worse condition than ever before." The frontier, it said, "having no armed and organized protection, is being… driven in along the entire line, from the Red River to the Rio Grande." Commanding part of the occupation forces, Brig. Gen. Wesley Merritt sent out a detachment of 100 troopers under Lt. Col. Nelson F. Craigue, 4th Wisconsin, to ride southwest toward Eagle Pass to address the complaints of settlers and ranchers in that area.

"But what good are a hundred men west," asked the *News*, "except they are acting merely as a spy company and for but little else?" They didn't only need the army traipsing along the Rio Grande, but "at least three thousand well mounted and well armed cavalry" patrolling the whole frontier line. The paper lamented the bad rap the frontier settlers always got, as being too ignorant to remove themselves from jeopardy, but "There must be a frontier somewhere, and some must be on the outside—suffering the privations of a life removed from civilization, and in hourly danger of their lives from roving bands of the wild Indians of the Plains." If the settlers were not on the cutting edge, then the edge would be in the towns to the east, which would then become the frontier and be in the same predicament. The settlers were "a simple-hearted, industrious people, and by no means the desperadoes the great majority of our citizens imagine them to be." The sooner and better they were protected, the better for the whole state.[3]

While the paper grumbled about the sad state of affairs, raiders crossed Red River and came down into southern Wise and northern Tarrant counties. In mid-August they hit James L. King's place in Wise County, stealing 12 horses worth $1,250. A day later they were in Tarrant County and stole eight horses worth $775 from Lawrence Banister. On August 22, they hit James Wheeler's place in Wise County, getting nine of his horses valued at $1,300.[4]

Protection from anyone was hard to come by that summer and the folks in Shackelford County were generally far beyond any "safe" zone. In 1862, William H. Ledbetter settled on the Salt Prong Hubbard Creek about nine miles southwest of present Albany. There was a salt springs there; it was bitter, but it could be raked up or boiled in kettles to a bright white crystal. Several settlers made use of the springs, and Ledbetter set up a business there supplying the Confederacy. The problem was the Comanches and Kiowas also used the salt springs. The Ledbetters fought an inconclusive gun battle with the Comanches in 1862, but little else happened until 1865.

In August, Phil Runnels, a single man working for Ledbetter, took a yoke of oxen and wagon to gather wood to be used at the salt works. Wood was scarce and he drove about ten miles before finding a good source. While Runnels had the wagon down in a gully by the creek, Indians shot him before he could pick up his gun. The oxen ran about 300 yards before the wagon struck a tree stump and threw Runnels out. When he failed to return, a search party tracked him to the area, found the oxen near Hubbard Creek and Runnels' body about a mile away. The creek near where he was killed was called Runnels (now Reynolds) Creek.[5]

In what might have been part of the same raid, Indians were also in Erath and Palo Pinto counties in late August. Cowmen on the frontier had a rough time during the war, with many of them serving in the army or Rangers, said Charles Goodnight, "virtually no one was left to take care of the cattle." Unscrupulous men gravitated in to gather and brand the thousands of cattle that had not been marked. War widows were hit hard. With no men to look after the stock, the thieves took what they wanted. The "mavericking" became so widespread, Goodnight said, "You could count the honest ones on your fingers and still have one hand left." When the surviving men got home from the war, "the stay-at-home fellows had the cattle, and we poor devils had the experience."

Goodnight said that some of the most famous cattlemen like John Chisum and C. C. Slaughter were guilty of theft. He apparently excluded himself, but at least one of his neighbors in Wise County, Theodore Babb, had a different assessment: "There wasn't a crookeder man in the world than old Charles Goodnight. He stole horses and traded with the Indians."[6]

Goodnight ranched in the Keechi Valley of Palo Pinto County, where scores of men either worked lawfully or came in looking for unbranded cattle. Some who apparently had legitimate business there were Ben and John Carruthers, Lim Vaughn, and several others who were hunting cattle in the lower Keechi Valley when they ran into ten Comanches. The cowboys, armed with six-shooters, chased the Indians until they turned to make a stand. Suddenly, the pursuers halted, unsure of what to do. The Comanches loosed several arrows. One man ducked behind his horse's neck while the arrow whizzed by and struck Ben Carruthers (19). The cowboys retreated, taking the mortally wounded Carruthers with them. He lived only a short time and was buried on the Keechi about three miles northeast of present Graford.

Lim Vaughn was involved in another incident, this time on the Erath-Palo Pinto County line. John B. Robinson and son William, who lived in Tarrant County near Fort Worth, were said to have owned a number of cattle that were running free in Earth County. John Robinson and Bolden C. Reynolds were rounding up the cattle on Barton Creek on August 28. Nearby grazed a remuda of about 25 stock horses, branded with "88" on their shoulders. Reynolds was napping about two in the afternoon when suddenly he awoke to the sound of about 18 Indians running off the horses he was supposedly watching. He got John Robinson and rode after them. A man named Durkee from Parker County was in the area doing a little mavericking, but the Indians took "his" cattle too. They followed the Indians down Barton Creek toward the Palo Pinto but could not catch them. The red raiders, stealing from white raiders, reportedly shot an old lady during their escape, and put a bullet into Lim Vaughn, who got in the way while doing a little mavericking of his own. The Indians got away with 22 head of Robinson's horses worth $550. What the cowmen got were three split-eared Indian ponies, abandoned by them on the trail.

Fed up with all the thieving, Charles Goodnight moved his stock that summer far out into Throckmorton County on the banks of Elm Creek. He was more distant from the white thieves, but closer to the Indians. Early in September 1865, Indians hit his spread and ran off almost everything he had. Fourteen of his men trailed the Indians, later joined by Goodnight and his friend, "One-armed" Bill Wilson. They rode north for 25 miles to the Brazos River where Goodnight, looking at the large number of Indian pony tracks, figured it was useless to pursue them farther. With his beef herd gone and winter approaching, Goodnight could only plan to get more cattle and try something new the next spring.[7]

Another Robinson family was having similar troubles down in Uvalde County. It was not the first time they had been visited by Indians; warriors killed Henry Robinson and wounded his son, George, in March 1861. The widowed Mrs. Robinson and her children moved east to the Frio River, but her luck did not change. In September 1865, Lipans were on the south rim of the Edwards Plateau. They stole a $200 horse from Samuel L. Gibson in Medina County, and a dozen raiders stole horses on the Sabinal near Waresville, on the Uvalde-Bandera line. A posse that included Captain J. C. Ware, J. C. Findley and Demp Findley, three Kelley brothers, Jim and Alfred Watson, and Jim and George Robinson picked up the trail two miles south of town. It headed west over the hills to the Frio in the vicinity of Concan.

Posse member George Robinson, now 20 years old, may have had increasing concerns as the trail headed downriver toward his mother's new home. At the cabin, brothers Andrew Henry (14) and William Henry Robinson (6) had gone down the creek to collect wood. The Indians were already surrounding the farm and taking down the fence rails to steal the horses. They surprised the boys 150 yards from the cabin and shot Andrew through the left breast. William darted between the trees and just as he ducked behind a hackberry, an arrow struck the trunk inches from his head. He succeeded in getting home, but the Indians took the horses and left another Robinson dead.

Captain Ware arrived too late, but doggedly followed the Indians' trail, which headed west to the Nueces, then far upstream beyond the headwaters and across to the upper Llano in Edwards County. Ware finally overtook the Lipans while they were eating and charged in, killing one warrior and possibly wounding another. They saw one "Indian" with red hair—a man of the same description was associated with the raid in 1861 that took the life of Henry Robinson.[8]

Farther north in Burnet County, Comanches hit Louis C. Kincheloe's ranch seven miles east of the county seat on the Russell Fork San Gabriel River and stole 30 head of stock horses worth $750. He remembered it was during the "light moon," which would have been about September 5. Kincheloe, from Alabama, did not know the guilty tribe for sure: "I can't tell one Indian from another," he said, but they did trail them and found one of his horses shot dead on the trail, and the posse judged the arrows to be Comanche.[9]

In early September, raiders crossed Red River and into Montague and Wise counties, heading down the West Fork Trinity. Alonzo Dill lived at Old Prairie Point (now Rhome) but was beyond the West Fork looking for his father's horses. About 15 Indians chased him, but Alonzo jumped his horse into the river, swam it across, and rode east. The warriors did not give up the chase and as they rode, they sent scores of arrows flying about Dill. As he approached the homestead, Mr. Dill saw him coming and stood at his fence waiting with his Winchester. The Indians also saw him taking aim, and they pulled back, circling and daring him to shoot, but Dill only bluffed them back until his son could get safely in. The Indians left for an easier target. Later, six arrows were found in a tree where Alonzo had climbed with his horse up the bank of the river, two arrows were in his saddle, and one had pierced his hat, but he was untouched.

That night, the raiders hit Joshua G. King's ranch at Prairie Point and ran off 13 head of horses worth $1,230. Next morning, he and some of his men followed a great, confusing trail, some of which went south down the Trinity, and part, with many shod horse tracks went northwest upriver. They followed the horses and the trail got larger, for the Indians had hit Sam Woody's place, Wick Fain's, and Joe Mitchell's. They had hundreds of head before they quit the country.

Some of the raiding party crossed east into Denton County and stole five horses worth $375 from Henderson Murphy. Others went down the Trinity and there the raid turned bloody. Jake Moffett (44), called "Parson" by some of the locals, lived east of present Newark, right near the Wise-Tarrant county line. On September 4, he was traveling to the Trinity and apparently trying to cross in the vicinity of the mouth of Indian Creek when the Indians caught and killed him. Searchers, including the free black man, Sang Kearby (21), found his body next to the river, shot with two bullets and two arrows. He and Frank Holden rode north to King's range, discovering the thefts there and riding with King in search of his stock.

Still in Tarrant County a short distance beyond where they killed Moffett, about five miles northeast of Azle, the Indians found men named Wright and Smith. The two lived at Pilot Knob, southwest of Denton, and were returning from attending a horse race in Parker County. Wright was on a racehorse but was unarmed, and Smith rode a mule but had a pistol and shotgun. When the Indians caught them, Wright's racehorse was little help, for the Indians chased him down and put 36 arrows into him before he died. Smith plodded along on his mule, but kept the warriors back with his weapons. He was only hit once, said to be in the face, cheek, or nose, depending on the report. The warrior who supposedly clipped his nose off, laughed so loudly that the infuriated Smith blasted him with his shotgun when he got too close. The Indians left the dangerous man alone and he made it home. The wound, thought to be trifling at first, was either caused by a poisoned arrow, or was not cleansed properly and became infected, for Smith later died of blood poisoning.[10]

In the same area, now the ghost town of Dido, the raiders caught Nathan M. Davis and ran off three of his horses valued at $380. Crossing the Brazos, the Indians entered Parker County and hit Anderson Greene's place, stealing two horses worth $250. Rounding up additional stock as they went, the raiders curved northwest into the Western Cross Timbers and headed back toward Red River.[11]

Later in September raiders were near Decatur. The Ball families had moved to Wise County from Kentucky about 1852. James S. Ball Jr. married Nancy Green and they had seven children: three girls and four boys. His brother, Moses P. Ball, married Levina Jane Jones and they had nine children: six girls and three boys. They lived about 10 miles northwest of Decatur. To complete some work he was engaged in, Moses Ball sent his son, James "Bud" Ball (7), over to neighbor Preston W. Walker's house to borrow a hand saw. On the way, he stopped at Uncle James's house to ask his cousin, William "Willie" Ball (7), to accompany him. This probably occurred about September 20, 1865.[12]

The boys made it to Walker's place about one mile away and got the saw, but never made it home. Kiowas had just stolen two horses from James Ball and were heading to the next ranch when they captured the two cousins as they strolled down the road. Moses Ball wondered what was taking Bud so long and he went to Press Walkers, only to learn that Bud and Willie had left hours ago. Moses' son, Carlo, joined him, and they followed the boys' tracks back down the road. The dropped saw lay in the dirt, and the boys' bare footprints disappeared amidst numerous pony tracks. Moses and Carlo followed the tracks. They found hand and knee prints at a waterhole where they boys were let down to drink. They followed the trail west to the Jack County line, but lost it when night fell. The Kiowas rode hard for three days, blindfolded and separated the cousins, and then divided and took them in opposite directions.[13]

A week later, other Indians were in Coryell County. They stole two horses that B. F. Gholson had hobbled just south of the present town of Evant in the extreme northwest corner of the county. Continuing southeast along Cowhouse Creek, they next stole horses from the little community of King. Further on they reached the headwaters of Brown Creek on today's Fort Hood Military Reservation. On September 26, Brothers John and Jack Smith were peacefully riding their mules and munching on grapes when the Indians appeared. John rode into a thicket, but Jack decided to try to race for Jeff Everett's cabin which was a mile to the northeast. John saw his brother ride over a hill with the Indians ready to lasso him from behind.

John hid in the brush until a short time later when he heard other horses approaching and men talking in English—settlers from the King settlement out searching for their stolen stock. Smith joined them and they went in the direction that his brother had disappeared. They found him dead, scalped, and stripped. Jack Smith had survived the Civil War and had just made it home two months earlier, but he couldn't survive the guerrilla war on the home front.[14]

While the Indians raided in September 1865, General Philip Sheridan made an inspection trip in Texas, traveling from Galveston to San Antonio, to Fort Duncan, and back through Austin. On September 21 he wrote to General Grant: "I find the condition of affairs in Texas very good," although there were "Some depredations by small bands of the Kickapoo Indians in Western Texas." He decided not to establish any permanent posts with volunteer troops because of the expense and because of their dissatisfaction. Besides, he wrote, "The Indian difficulties are trifling, and I can control them by sending small cavalry expeditions from San Antonio out west as far as the Rio Grande, to stay out fifteen or twenty days, their return alternating with other detachments or regiments. Northern Texas will be controlled in the same way from Austin City."

The military dismissed the Indian threat in Texas, while elsewhere the Bureau of Indian Affairs appeared unaware that Texas existed and was concerned only with the roads crossing the Central Plains. Commissioner

Dennis N. Cooley wrote in his 1865 report that his Kiowa and Comanche agent, Colonel Jesse Leavenworth, "has for a long time possessed their confidence, and by his influence over them they have, for the most part, if not entirely, abstained from all hostilities or interference with travel over the Santa Fe road."

Leavenworth was about as out of touch with actual events as were most of his cohorts. On May 10, 1865, he wrote to then Commissioner William Dole, that "I did not wish a war with the Comanche, as I much feared they would join the Texans, and raid upon the commerce of the road." He was certain that "The Comanches…have not, it is believed, committed any depredations as a tribe…."

The military and agents appeared to be living in a parallel universe, while Texas seemed to be out of sight, out of mind.[15]

Chapter 36 notes

1 Depredation Claims: M. Etheridge #2634; Minerva A. Binnion #1669; Sowell, *Early Settlers*, 337.

2 Wilbarger, *Indian Depredations*, 625-26; McConnell, *West Texas Frontier*, 514, 515; Ledbetter, *Fort Belknap*, 143; William E. Jennings, Depredation Claim #2222.

3 *Galveston Weekly News*, August 19, 1865.

4 Depredation Claims: James L. King #3533; Lawrence Banister #2859; James R. Wheeler #2852.

5 Michno, *A Fate Worse Than Death*, 430; McConnell, *West Texas Frontier*, 509.

6 Haley, *Charles Goodnight*, 100-02; Kenner, "Guardians in Blue," 48.

7 McConnell, *West Texas Frontier*, 508; William Robinson, Depredation Claim #5198; Haley, *Charles Goodnight*, 120.

8 Samuel L. Gibson, Depredation Claim #5724; McConnell, *West Texas Frontier*, 520; Peterson, *Patriot Ancestor Album*, 236.

9 Louis C. Kincheloe, Depredation Claim #2479.

10 Cates, *Wise County*, 166-68; McConnell, *West Texas Frontier*, *http://www.forttours.com/pages/rhome.asp*; Depredation Claims: Joshua G. King #2291; Henderson Murphy #1273.

11 Depredation Claims; Nathan M. Davis #5533; Anderson Greene #4408.

12 Ledbetter, *Fort Belknap*, 161n85; James Ball, Depredation Claim #10172. Sources list the capture in different years. Cates, *Wise County*, 188, has it in 1866; Hunter, "Battle at Ball's Ranch," 31, says it was in 1868, and the capture was three years earlier; Sowell, *Rangers and Pioneers*, 287, says 1869; and Ledbetter, *Fort Belknap*, 146, dates it 1865. In Winfrey and Day, *Texas Indian Papers IV*, 314, the district clerk in Decatur dates it September 20, 1865.

13 Cates, *Wise County*, 188-89; Hunter, "Battle at Ball's Ranch," 31; James Ball, Depredation Claim #10172.

14 McConnell, *West Texas Frontier*, 521.

15 *WR*: S.1, V.48/2, 1235-36; *Commissioner of Indian Affairs 1865*, 46, 390.

37 "They died of too large views."

The Confederates made a last unsuccessful attempt to make a peace treaty with the tribes in Indian Territory in May 1865, and now it was the Union's turn. Thoroughly tired of war, wanting to disband the swollen Federal and volunteer armies, and with a debt of three billion dollars in connection with administering the tribes in the west, the government figured any peace, however tentative, would be better than the constant fighting. How little some understood the tribes they dealt with is illustrated by the comments of U.S. agent Jesse H. Leavenworth, when in May 1865, he wrote to Commissioner Dole that the Comanches had not "committed any depredations as a tribe." Perhaps that was true for the last several months in Kansas, his bailiwick, but not elsewhere. Leavenworth also wished for peace, because "I did not wish a war with the Comanche Indians, as I much feared they would join with the Texans, and raid upon the commerce of the road." As John Wayne said in the movie, *The Searchers*, "That'll be the day."

But peace it would be. Senator James R. Doolittle headed a commission and on June 15, was directed by Secretary of War Edwin M. Stanton: "It is the anxious desire of the President and of this department to avoid Indian hostilities...." The President empowered him "to make such treaties and arrangements...as in your judgment may suspend hostilities and establish peace with the Indians...."[1]

In March 1865, Secretary of the Interior John P. Usher was replaced by Senator James Harlan who was a critic of former Indian policy. In July, Commissioner of Indian Affairs William Dole resigned, to be replaced by Dennis N. Cooley. The two men, with Gen. John Pope as "Indian expert," hoped to wipe the slate clean and start anew, however, their ideas of gathering the Indians on reservations and making white men out of them was nothing new at all.

With the frenzied efforts to get a treaty signed, agents and commissioners gathered a number of headmen from the Comanche, Kiowa, Cheyenne, and Arapaho tribes on the Little Arkansas in Kansas, and on August 15, they agreed to gather all their people together to establish "a perpetual peace" when they met officially the coming October.[2]

When the big day arrived near the mouth of the Little Arkansas at present-day Wichita, Kansas, thousands of Indians were present. Among the prominent Comanches were Buffalo Hump, Rising Sun, Milky Way, Horseback, Over the Buttes, Iron Mountain, Eagle Drinking, and Ten Bears; among the Kiowas were Iron Shirt, Silver Brooch, Lone Wolf, Big

Bow, Kicking Eagle, Little Mountain, Sitting Bear (Satank), and White Bear (Satanta). The white commissioners included John Sanborn, William Harney, James Steele, Jesse Leavenworth, William Bent, "Kit" Carson, and Superintendent Thomas Murphy. The usual speeches were made and gifts were given and the treaty sounded like all the previous ones. The Indians will remain at perpetual peace with the whites and with each other, the Indians shall not depredate, but, just in case, "depredations shall not be redressed by a resort to arms."

They were given a large reservation that included much of western Indian Territory, most of the Texas and Oklahoma Panhandles, and part of west Texas—something that the Texans obviously had no say in. The Indians agreed to go to their reservation and not leave it without permission. They could still hunt south of the Arkansas River with permission, but must stay away from main roads and towns. The U.S. could build roads and forts in the reservation. The Indians who were on the reservation would get an amount of annuities worth $15 per capita, to be paid one-third during the spring and two-thirds during the autumn of each year.[3]

The chiefs put their marks on the paper on October 18, 1865, the day after the Cheyennes and Arapahos had signed a similar document. With hindsight it is incredible to think that the Indians would seriously consider keeping the agreement for such a paltry sum, or that the white man would pay it. Treaties were for convenience and conscience; the Indians signed to get gifts and appease the whites, and the whites signed to temporarily stop raiding and to have a legal paper to point to when the Indians eventually broke the agreement. It was all a game, but bankrupt policies and ineffective statesmen condemned the parties to forever play the role of Sisyphus, with unending labors always coming to naught. A contemporary assessment of the proceedings was made by Samuel A. Kingman, a one-time associate justice on the Kansas Supreme Court, who accompanied Thomas Murphy to the Little Arkansas. Kingman was not sure the government's representatives were down to earth and sensible, writing, "Their fate as commissioners will be that they died of too large views."[4]

For several families of Texans, however, the Little Arkansas conference was fruitful. Commissioner Sanborn told the chiefs that he knew they held white prisoners and there would be no treaty until they were returned, and if returned, "compensation will be given you for them." Little Mountain admitted having four captives and Eagle Drinking said he had three white boys. Thomas Murphy cautioned the chiefs that, "when the treaty is made and concluded, and all the prisoners in your hands given up, then the presents will be given to you, and not before."[5]

It was profitable dealing with the Americans who were easily duped. The Indians could capture white women and children, sell them back to the authorities, and go right out and capture more. On October 24, the chiefs brought five captives to the council grounds, stating that the others were not in the immediate vicinity, but would be delivered to Agent Leavenworth as soon as possible. The commissioners paid the Indians and thanked them for their cooperation. The five captives were Cola Caroline McDonald, Rebecca J. McDonald, James Taylor, Dorcas Taylor, and James Ball.[6]

Jesse Leavenworth was busy rounding up any other captives he could locate. With the help of mixed-blood Cherokee Jesse Chisholm and a soldier escort, he rode to Fort Zarah on the Arkansas River, and on Walnut Creek on November 2, 1865, he found a white woman and a small white girl working like slaves in a Kiowa camp. The girl was Alice Taylor and the woman was Elizabeth Ann Fitzpatrick. Elizabeth knew immediately the soldiers were going to rescue them, although she "thought they must be beings from another world," because "their white faces and blue uniforms looked so beautiful."

Elizabeth had been captive just over one year. She had been starved, beaten, and raped, and her pregnant belly was a constant reminder of her treatment. Leavenworth took them in his care and moved on to a nearby Comanche camp where he collected another captured Texan, James Benson. They joined the other five at the Kaw Agency at Council Grove. Elizabeth learned that her granddaughter, Lottie Durkin, had been recovered the previous May. She also learned that Milly Jane Durkin died the previous winter, but she refused to believe it.

At Council Grove, "Grandma" Elizabeth Ann Fitzpatrick, although only 39-years-old, resumed caring for her new family, the seven other ex-captive women and children. In December, she delivered a still-born child. They were stuck in Council Grove with no money, no family, few friends, and no word as to when they might be sent home to Texas.[7]

The U.S. commissioners may have thought they had gathered most of the troublesome Indians together on the Little Arkansas, but although thousands had participated in the treaty-making, there were plenty of others who had not gotten the word, or refused to attend. One Comanche band that never signed any treaty with the white men was the Quahadi, and living with them was Quanah, the 20-year-old son of Cynthia Ann Parker and Peta Nocona. It was about this time that Quanah began to lead his own war parties. It may have been Quahadis who arrived in Comanche County on October 8, dealing John J. Keith a devastating loss, stealing 420 cattle and 14 horses valued at $6,790. Part of this band may have been in Burnet County on October 10, where they ran off eight horses worth $430 from W. C. Franklin. Franklin's little spread was in Pleasant Valley, north of the Colorado River about four miles east of present Marble Falls. Franklin, Frank M. Lacey and several others trailed the thieves north toward Burnet, finding a few of the horses shot with arrows. Just outside of Burnet, the raiders grabbed a black girl from the plowed field of a Mr. Shugart. They carried her a few miles before killing her and dropping her on the trail. The posse could not catch up to the raiders.[8]

More raiders rode down the Western Cross Timbers and into Jack County. In October 1865, they were on the West Fork Trinity about ten miles east of Jacksboro and hit George Vanderberg's ranch. Mrs. Vanderberg counted about 25 Indians, who easily drove off seven of their horses worth $350.

The raiders headed south into Palo Pinto County where they visited the Weltys again. They had killed Henry Welty in 1863, and this time struck his widow on the ranch south of Graford. They got three horses worth $235 and rode on. On October 31, about 20 Indians devised their version of trick-or-treat when they rode nearly into the town of Palo Pinto. William Metcalf (26) had been a captain in the Confederate Army, had returned from the war in June, and was trying to get back to his business as a stock raiser. His horses were not far north of the court house, but the bold raiders swept off seven of them. Being so close to town, many were unguarded, and they also got stock from Bill Hittson and Joe Mathis before heading southeast.

They next appeared in the Littlefield Bend area. A. B. Gilbert (26), a farmer and stock raiser, lived in Gilbert Valley on the eastern Palo Pinto County line just west of the Littlefield Bend of the Brazos. Gilbert was in the bend rounding up horses when the Indians came through, cutting off Gilbert and two of Littlefield's sons. They successfully escaped through a hail of arrows and made it to the house. The raiders stole Littlefield's stock, the second time he had been hit that year, and crossed the Brazos heading east. Later, Metcalf and a few men arrived and talked to Gilbert and the Littlefields, but they made no further pursuit.[9]

The raiders may have decided to get out without casualties and with all their horses. They turned north along Grindstone Creek in western Parker County, stealing more horses. Settlers Andrew Jackson Gorman, Henry Blue, G. W. Light, Charlie Rivers and a few others followed their trail, which turned west toward present Bennett. The posse believed there were three or four Indians, but when they caught up they discovered considerably more. The warriors turned on them and the posse ran, but on the retreat, Jack Gorman was shot off his horse, killed and scalped. His friends kept running. Gorman's body was recovered later and buried in Soda Springs Cemetery in Littlefield Bend.

The raiders turned north along Rock Creek and then went between Rippy Branch and Dry Creek. About November 2, they ran into more targets of opportunity about a dozen miles northwest of Weatherford in the Bethesda community. Mrs. William Lowe and her two children had been visiting a neighbor half a mile away and were returning home when they discovered numerous horse tracks across the road. When they looked into the field they saw many riders engaged in some mischief. Indians! Mrs. Lowe grabbed her children and they ran the rest of the way home. What they had seen was the murder of two black women, Rose Moore (40) and daughter, Hannah (25). The two had gone to a recently vacated house to look for ash hops and other ingredients to make soap. Articles secured they were on their way home when the Indians caught them. The Indians scalped the mulatto Hannah, but left Rose's hair on her head. William Fondren lived nearby and his family also saw the killings. Finished with the Moores, they rode to Fondren's field and stole his horses. Fondren's dogs ran out and attacked them, but the raiders filled them "so full of arrows they resembled porcupines." The raiders got clean away.[10]

Down in Medina County in November, Lipans attacked Phillip Haas's place near Castroville and stole 18 horses worth $570. The same month, settlers saw raiders in Comanche County driving about 50 head of horses and word of it prompted the locals to form a posse to track them down. They rode west from Comanche, gathering men as they went, with the party eventually including E. L. Deaton, S. H. Powers, Jim Millican, Jack and Tom Wright, Bill Carver, Baz and Malicia Cox, and two others. One of the other Cox brothers, Don, had been killed the previous January in the Dove Creek fight. They left Cox's at night and rode through a rainstorm which forced them to hole up still in their saddles waiting for daylight. They were lucky to find the Indians' tracks in the mud.

About 30 miles from home they discovered the Indians riding slowly and wrapped in blankets because of the cold rain. The posse galloped up close before being discovered and the surprised Indians abandoned their stolen horses and rode for the thick timber. Jack Wright was closest, and he shot a warrior in the back. He fell and Wright's dogs went after him. The warrior threw his blanket over the dogs and stumbled away. Deaton came up and snapped his pistol several times, but it would not fire. When the Indians realized that the whites' powder was poor, they rallied and fought back. Deaton said they charged to within 30 yards, "but our ammunition was so wet that it was only once in a while we were enabled to get in a good shot."

Jack Wright saw a warrior take aim at Jim Millican and he yelled to warn him, when the warrior shifted aim to Wright. He turned and ducked, but the arrow caught him under the shoulder blade with the tip coming out below his collar bone. Wright, sickened, slid off his horse. Deaton ran over, cut the arrowhead off and pulled the shaft back out. A shower of arrows struck the trees around them. Then a warrior ran up and Deaton pulled the trigger, hoping this time his pistol would fire. It did, "the ball striking him in the stomach just above the belt," Deaton said. "I saw the blood spout out the size of the ball." Other warriors ran up, dragged him away, and put him on a horse.

With most of the whites frustrated by snapping their guns with little result, the Indians used the lull to get away. Even with such a poor weapon performance, the whites were certain that they had wounded every Indian but one. With a wounded man and in possession of about 50 horses, the posse turned for home, as "wet as a day and night's rain could make us, nothing to eat, and hungry as wolves." They rode all night until they reached shelter at Cox's ranch. It was, said Deaton, just "one of the many fights we had with the redskins."[11]

The frontier line, if there was any such thing, was an amorphous and fluid border. Folks who lived just west of Austin may have considered themselves on the frontier, but by the end of the Civil War there were already hardy people who were living more than 150 miles to the west. Richard F. Tankersley had shifted his horse and cattle operation far out on the South Concho in Tom Green County back in November 1864, setting up a ranch near present Christoval. Tankersley had come to Texas from Mississippi in 1852, and moved to Williamson, San Saba, and Brown counties before settling on the South Concho. At each stop he increased his herds, and by the time he reached Tom Green County he had about 1,500 cattle and 200 horses. Somehow he had escaped all of the depredations until November 1865. Beginning then, Apaches, Kickapoos, Comanches, and Kiowas found a goldmine along the South Concho, stealing over the next year, 175 horses worth $10,260. There seemed to be nothing Tankersley could do, for the range was too large, there were too many animals, and not enough hired men to guard them. "They made so many different steals that I can't fix the dates," he said.

Thefts were increasing all along the border, but not all the counties kept records. One that did was Blanco County, which was just west of Austin and had not been hit as hard as some of the others. Even so, in 1865, owners W. H. Bishop, G. Daniell, G. F. Daniell, Brit Felps, Jacob Felps, R. B. Hudson, H. McKellar, J. W. Nichols, and Neill Robison, reported stock losses worth nearly $2,500.[12]

With the latest treaties signed, the Interior and War Departments and the Bureau of Indian Affairs may have had a more sanguine hope for the future, but on the Texas frontier it seemed to be the same old story. The military had its big fight with the Indians at Dove Creek, having 26 killed, but throughout the year more settlers lost their lives. And it would get worse.

Chapter 37 notes

1 *Commissioner of Indian Affairs 1865*, 390, 392

2 Kvasnicka and Viola, *Commissioners of Indian Affairs*, 99-101; *Commissioner of Indian Affairs 1865*, 394-95.

3 Kappler, *Indian Treaties*, 892-95.

4 Kingman, "Diary of Samuel Kingman," *Kansas Historical Quarterly*, 450.

5 *Commissioner of Indian Affairs 1865*, 528, 530-32.

6 Ledbetter, *Fort Belknap*, 137, 139-40, 146; *Commissioner of Indian Affairs 1865*, 534-35. James Ball's name was recorded as James Burrow.

7 Ledbetter, *Fort Belknap*, 141, 143, 145-49, 151; Winfrey and Day, *Texas Indian Papers IV*, 165.

8 Depredation Claims: John J. Keith #5258; W. C. Franklin #5726.

9 Depredation Claims: Mary E. Vanderberg #7487; Henry Welty #2853; William Metcalf #5702.

10 McConnell, *West Texas Frontier*, 510; Winfrey and Day, *Texas Indian Papers IV*, 223; Marshall, *A Cry Unheard*, 108.

11 Phillip Haas, Depredation Claim #3348; Deaton, *Indian Fights on the Texas Frontier*, 36-40.

12 Richard F. Tankersley, Depredation Claim #6501; Winfrey and Day, *Texas Indian Papers IV*, 82-83.

Part 8. 1866

38 "The last time I saw my father, he was running for the creek."

An argument has been made that depredations and deaths multiplied on the Texas frontier after the Civil War because the government delayed sending U.S. Army soldiers to afford protection, the Indians discovered the soldiers were gone, and increased attacks.[1] There is some merit to the case, but it comes with *caveats*. Texas was swamped with Union soldiers after the war. General Gordon Granger and his XIII Corps moved to Marshall, Texas, in the northeast, and to Galveston, Houston, and Brownsville along the coast in June 1865. General David S. Stanley's IV Corps moved in from Indianola to Victoria. Elements of Gen. Godfrey Weitzel's XXV Corps landed at Corpus Christi, while other units went up the Rio Grande beyond Ringgold Barracks. Following the infantry was Gen. Wesley Merritt's 5,500-man cavalry division, riding from Louisiana to San Antonio, and then Gen. George Custer's slightly smaller division marching to Houston, Hempstead, and Austin. As early as August 5, 1865, Gen. Philip Sheridan reported that when all the troops arrived and others mustered out, there would still be 45,000 U.S. soldiers in Texas.

It was, according to General Stanley, enough troops "to smear all over the country, the only difficulty being the question of transportation." There was also another problem: few soldiers wanted to be there. The war was over and the volunteers wanted to go home. Stanley said, "In truth our men felt so wronged in having been sent to Texas at all that it was a wonder we could hold them in hand."[2]

Of course, Texas Provisional Governor Andrew J. Hamilton wanted the troops to stay as long as possible to control the Texans who were not too happy with losing the war, being overrun with an occupying army, and told how they should treat their "Negroes." Hamilton fought to keep the soldiers, and although many were mustered out, by the end of 1865, the 4th Cavalry had arrived to replace Merritt and the 6th Cavalry came to replace Custer. In March 1866, the 17th Infantry, a large regiment with 24 companies in three battalions under Gen. Samuel P. Heintzelman, arrived to further add to the army's presence.

The Texans did not see the great number of soldiers as being very helpful. They wanted them away from the coast and out of the largest cities and moved to the frontier. It was the same complaint that they had as a republic, in the Union, and under the Confederacy: they always figured their Indian problems would be solved if only there were enough troops on the frontier.

It was true that most of the soldiers were not close enough to the frontier to afford protection, but when high numbers of troops were there in the past, it made little difference either. Texans always had to protect themselves, and cherished traditions notwithstanding, they were never very good at it.

The southern counties experienced some of the first raids of 1866. Kickapoos were in Bexar County in January, stealing "20 head of gentle saddle horses" from Jose A. Torres.

At the same time, Lipans were in Bandera County. The Buckelew family had moved to Texas from Louisiana in 1852 to get some "elbow room." When both parents died, their seven children went to live with their uncle, L. B. C. "Berry" Buckelew, on the Sabinal River near present-day Vanderpool in Bandera County. It was a beautiful location, near where the stream issues from a canyon, but it was also in the crossing area of several Indian warpaths. The settlers took turns to go to San Antonio for supplies, and Berry Buckelew was nearly back from the several-day journey when he stopped to see his friend Crossgrave on Seco Creek, only half a dozen miles from his home. It was late on a Friday evening, January 26, 1866, and Crossgrave told Buckelew to spend the night, but he wanted to hurry home. While taking a short cut, Indians ambushed and shot him, then crushed his head with a rock. Crossgrave rode to Buckelew's place on Sunday, but the children told him their uncle was not yet home. A search party went out and discovered his remains. Berry's dog, Cuff, was still keeping vigil over his master's body.[3]

No one was certain who the Indians were. Lipans, who at one time were comparatively friendly with the Texans and assisted them fighting Comanches, were raiding more often after an informal truce with the German settlements northwest of San Antonio broke down. They often crossed the Rio Grande to make life hell for the southern and central counties. In addition, after the Texans attacked the Kickapoos at Dove Creek in January 1865, they also warred with the Texans, crossing the Rio Grande from their safe haven in Coahuila, Mexico.

The party that had attacked Buckelew moved southeast into northwest Medina County where they found more targets. Augustus Rothe (19), George Jacob Miller (17), and Herbert Weinand (13) were on upper Hondo Creek hunting stray cattle. Jacob Sauter had been with them, but found his cattle and returned home. The three boys discovered an old man, Ludwig Mumme, who was traveling south from Bandera County and had lost his way. They fed him some of their provisions and insisted he stay with them, but Mumme, now getting his bearings, went on with his journey. The boys continued their search and while Rothe was away from camp he heard shots. Hurrying back, he discovered that Miller had taken Rothe's gun and emptied it into a tree for target practice. The angry Rothe said, "George, you should not have done

Author's photo

The Hondo River, near the site of the attack on Rothe, Miller and Weinand in January 1866.

that. I have no more loads, and now suppose the Indians should come upon us."

The irony of the situation became apparent next morning, January 27. Rothe and Weinand went out to get their horses, which had strayed from camp. In a few minutes Miller came running up to them, saying that he had seen Indians approaching. He had barely spoken when eight warriors surrounded them. The boys ran, with Weinand taking a different track from the other two. Rothe managed to bluff the Indians back with his empty pistol. They ran for all they were worth, but Miller dropped back and a warrior beat him over the head with the butt of his lance.

Rothe looked back into the valley and saw warriors holding Weinand up by the hair of his head, and then lost sight as he crested the divide. The warriors killed Miller and took Weinand captive. Rothe made it to the nearest ranch and got help. The next day searchers found Miller's shoes sitting neatly in camp, but his body was under a bluff, stripped except for one sock on his left foot. His hands were tied so tightly that the flesh was cut to the bone. He had been lanced in the side and his throat was sliced open. He was said to have been "murdered after having suffered nameless tortures."

The Indians killed some cattle, stole horses, and circled back across the Hondo. Weinand was probably still young enough to be assimilated into the tribe, but was swallowed up in the vastness of Mexico. His father, of the same name, lived in D'Hanis. He searched and wrote letters for a year, and in February 1867, he learned that either Kickapoos or Lipans held a boy of Herbert's description in Mexico, about 30 miles from Eagle Pass. Mr. Weinand tried to recover his boy many times over the next six years, but apparently without any luck. After 1871, references to the recovery of Herbert Weinand are silent. It may be that young Weinand was finally united with his father. It may be that he lived out the remainder of his life with the Indians.[4]

About two weeks later, Comanches hit the same area. James W. M. Johnson (30) moved from Illinois to Texas in 1857 and was engaged in freighting in 1866. He, his brother John, and a dozen employees were hauling nine wagons of goods, along with cattle and mules, from Robertson County to Eagle Pass. In mid-February they camped for the night on the Bandera-Uvalde County line at the edge of a hollow surrounded about 200 yards away with a rim of prickly pear and chaparral. It seemed like a safe spot and they set the stock to graze at the edge of the brush, but as they cooked supper, Comanches "attacked the camp on horseback, on a dead run." One of the men, Jasper Tatum, was certain that the Indian who appeared to be the leader was a Comanche he knew from years ago.

The Indians did not make a sound until they had cut out nearly the entire herd, and only whooped when they drove it out of the hollow toward the southwest. Before the freighters could react, the raiders were nearly out of firing range. They took some long range shots, but hit no one. While some of them sought out other ranchers to purchase more stock to continue the trip, several followed the trail the next morning, but they only went five miles. "We thought that perhaps we could get somebody after the Indians," employee J. M. Chapman said, "but concluded that we couldn't, so just gave it up." Johnson lost 40 work oxen, 21 mules, and 11 horses, valued at $3,915.[5]

In February there were scattered raids all across the frontier. Jerome B. Edwards had come from Kentucky and had a ranch two miles south of Strawn in Palo Pinto County. Comanches struck from the east, filled several of his cattle with arrows, stole two good saddle horses, and were gone toward the west. No one even bothered to chase them.

Indians stole a fine iron gray horse worth $160 from William Moorehead on Henson Creek south of Gatesville in Coryell County. On February 20, raiders hit Adolph Kappelmann's place in Comal County, stealing a mule and a mare. At first, Kappelmann did not believe it could be Indians, as he was located far within the settlement line between San Antonio and Austin, but after he got a few neighbors and trailed them north, he discovered others with stock stolen and found several horses killed with arrows. On February 25, raiders got a horse from Edward Ebeling in Blanco County west of Austin. It had been a while since the Indians had been so bold as to come down so near those two towns—and with the 4th and 6th Cavalry there it seemed like a slap in the face.[6]

The spring of 1866 was a harbinger of coming events. While elsewhere across the West there was a downturn in the fighting, Texas experienced what may have been the worst year for raids in its history.

On the first of March, Comanches were in Mason County right near old Fort Mason where they stole two horses worth $200 from William S. Hinds.[7]

Also about the first of March, Indians were in Hamilton County, stealing horses all along Bennett Creek, hitting Charlie Teuton, Joe Curtis, brothers John, William, and David Morris, and a Mr. Stiles. Since the county lines were redrawn, the creek today is in southeast Mills County. Teuton first noticed his horses missing and rode to the Morris' ranch asking for help. It was then that John Morris saw his stock was gone too. The Morris brothers rode with Charlie Teuton on the Indians' trail about three miles to a gap in the hills. Believing there were more Indians than they could handle, they went to get Joe Curtis and a few more men. Back on the trail they discovered the body of a man who proved to be Fayette Bond, who was on his way to Bennett Creek when the Indians killed him. He was scalped, and Dave Morris said the "moccasin tracks all around showed they had had some time in killing him. He was so torn up we had to bury him there, couldn't carry him away." The posse gave up and rode home.[8]

March 2 was the 30th anniversary since Texas had declared its independence from Mexico, and Comanches were raiding the frontier more than in 1836. Amesley Parsons lived a few miles southwest of Weatherford in Parker County, farming and stock-raising. That morning he was out in his field when a band of Indians boldly rode up to his horses. Parsons had a rifle with one load, and he tried to bluff them by pointing the weapon, but they shot at him and took four horses anyway. Parsons got the one remaining horse and rode to a neighbor, got him, and headed northwest in the direction the Indians went.

The next ranch was near Sanchez Creek about two miles away and was owned by Bolen Savage (33). Less than two miles beyond him lived James Savage (40). The brothers were Civil War veterans who probably hoped to leave that turmoil behind and live out the rest of their lives in peace. Marion Savage (11), James Savage (6), and Sam Savage (5), left their cabin about ten in the morning to help their father, Bolen, as he plowed his field 300 yards from the house. Just then, nine Comanches rode across the field, shot arrows into Mr. Savage—one missile going through his neck—and scalped him in front of the children's eyes. Sam Savage said, "The last time I saw my father, he was running for the creek, and I heard a gun directly.... I think that we stood still and watched them awhile, and then we got scared. Then the

Indians came along and took my brother and I up behind them...." A bullet hit Marion in the shoulder, but he got away and hid in the brush by the creek.

Mrs. Elizabeth Savage heard one of her boys yelling and she went out of the cabin to the fence line. She saw the Indians and recognized Parson's horses. It was a raid. Instead of running, Mrs. Savage began "hollowing for my husband and children." A warrior rode up within ten yards and nocked an arrow, but Elizabeth defiantly "stood right in the way" and continued shouting. Oddly enough, the warrior left the white woman in the road and went after the others. "I saw the Indians take my two youngest children and carry them off," Mrs. Savage said. Young Cassie Savage watched the affair. "I was scared so bad," she said, seeing the frightening apparitions of Indians "painted in black and with long hair flying." The Indians also got three of Savage's horses and continued west.[9]

Amesley Parsons, a Mr. Brown, a Mr. Kincaid, and a few others arrived, talked briefly to Elizabeth Savage, and rode after the Indians, but they were too late. They had already reached James Savage's farm on Patrick Creek. James was also plowing his field. He did not feel well that morning and skipped breakfast. His daughter, Arrena (11), fixed him a snack, and with Jennie Belle (5), and Jim (2), walked across the field to take it to him. James's wife, Caroline, and their daughter, Sarah Jane (22), were hanging laundry near the cabin. Sarah saw about 14 Indians approaching and ran to get a gun.

James fought like a wild man, severely injuring one of the warriors before they overwhelmed and killed him. Mounted Comanches pulled Jennie and Jim up on their ponies. Arrena tried to pull Jim down, but a warrior thrust a lance through her arm and into her side. When he tried to pull the lance free the shaft broke, leaving the point pinning her arm to her ribs. The Indians saw Sarah coming with a gun. They circled back to the cabin, stole two horses, and rode away.

The posse arrived, assessed the situation, and followed in the Indians' wake. As the Indians traveled west, they picked up numbers from the consolidation of other parties once scattered throughout the county. At Bolen Savage's there were nine, at James Savage's there were 14, and as they went by the Newberry farm on Grindstone Creek, Mrs. Newberry counted 20 Indians. At Fuller Millsap's near Rock Creek there were 30. They tried to steal Millsap's horses, but a brave freed black woman took a shotgun and held them off. The Indians abandoned little Jim Savage along the trail.

James T. Pollard, who had chased Peta Nocona during his raid in October 1860, was driving a wagonload of bacon to Weatherford. West of Millsap's he saw a band of men whom he took to be Rangers at first, but he cautiously parked the wagon and rode his horse to investigate. As he approached he saw the posse riding in and joined them. They caught the Indians west of Rock Creek on the Parker-Palo Pinto border and exchanged shots. Pollard said that one man cautioned them that there were two children with them and "to be careful how we shot."

Just east of present Mineral Wells the Indians stopped to rest. There, a warrior decided to ride one of Bolen Savage's horses. He tied a rope to the animal and wrapped the excess length around his waist, but the horse bolted and dragged him over rocks and cactus. The rope slipped up over the Indian's neck, strangled him to death, and nearly pulled his head off. The horse ran free and found its way back to Savage's farm. Other warriors severed the head of the dead Comanche, most likely to prevent it from being scalped by the pursuing posse. They gave the head to an Indian woman who carried both it and little Sam Savage on her horse. The raiders got away and the brothers were held in captivity until that fall.[10]

On Sunday, March 4, 1866, Parson Nehemiah Vernon, who had two sons killed by Indians in August 1863, was conducting services at the house of Anderson Smith in the communities of Terrapin Neck and Opal, which were then about three and four miles northeast of Springtown, just north of the Parker-Wise County line. Vernon was preaching for some time when the door burst open and in came Sug Brown, breathlessly telling that the Indians had chased him nearly to the door. The service was over; James Sanders, John and Polk Matthews, James Kearby, Jack and Andy Gore, Elmer Blackwell, and a few others rushed out to get horses and guns to go after the Indians.

Seeing the whites swarming after them, the Indians turned back to the north. It was the same old trick of drawing the pursuers into a trap. The whites chased until the Indians suddenly stopped and more of them appeared on both flanks. The whites pulled up, seeing they had been fooled. Now the Indians charged and the whites fired, which threw them back for a time. A confused chase, retreat, and counter-chase developed, but the whites took the worst of it. Jim Sanders was shot off his horse and killed. John Matthews got two arrows in his shoulder. Polk Matthew' and Jack Gore's horses violently collided, knocking Matthews to the ground. As he dazedly got to his feet, an arrow without a metal point sliced under the skin of his scalp. With things going badly, the whites retreated back to Smith's house. The Indians seemed to have tired of the fun also, and headed north in the direction they had come.

Passing through Montague County on the way back to Indian Territory, the raiders hit the Gibbons' ranch. Nancy Gibbons filed a claim stating that about the middle of March, Comanches had stolen 16 horses from her and her husband, worth $1,100.[11]

As usual, while Kiowas or Comanches were in the Cross Timbers, Lipans were on the Edwards Plateau, paying visits to the families in Bandera and Uvalde counties. It had only been about six weeks since Berry Buckelew had been killed. His widow, Maryanna Buckelew, could not run the ranch herself, nor could she take care of her nieces and nephew. She moved to a "safer" location, and once again the Buckelew children were shuffled to another home, this time to James Davenport's ranch farther up the Sabinal.

The youngest of the Buckelew children, Francis Marion "Frank," (13), was watching the cattle, which he did with a companion, Morris, the son of a freed slave. One day, Morris failed to fasten the bell to the lead steer and it fell off. Mr. Davenport told Morris he had better find the bell or he would "beat him to death." Morris begged Frank to help him, and the next morning, March 11, they started out. Frank took an old shotgun that Davenport had given him, but on the way out of the house, Mrs. Davenport told him to leave it behind, for there were no Indians about, and he was more likely to kill Morris or himself than any Indians. The two boys hunted through the thickets, but Frank tired of the search and decided to pick flowers for his sister. Morris reminded him of his promise to help find the bell. Frank went only a few steps when he saw an Indian watching him from the thicket. He called a warning to Morris, and, Frank said, "with a yell of terror fled from me like the wind." Frank ran too, but the Lipan was on him in an instant. He stopped in his tracks. The Indian looked at the fleeing Morris, laughed, and then knocked Frank in the head, pointed in the other direction, and said, "Vamos."[12]

When they got to a glade and met the other warriors, they stripped off Frank's clothes and whipped his back with a thorny catclaw branch. They moved at a trot across the rugged terrain, with one warrior in the rear continually whipping Frank to keep him moving. They climbed out of the Sabinal Valley and over the divide to the Frio. On top they met a fourth Lipan. He extended his hand to Frank and said, "Howdy! How old you be? You be Englishman or you be Dutchman? You be Englishman me killie you; you be Dutchman me no killie you?"

Frank had heard that Indians would kill boys more than 10 or 12 years old, so, although he was nearly 14, he said he was ten. To the second question he told the truth, regardless of the consequences. He was an Englishman and not a Dutchman (German). It turned out that the Lipans were killing all Germans for what they considered treachery in breaking an informal peace treaty between them. The truthful answer saved young Buckelew, although the Lipan, a chief named Custaleta, eyed him warily.

"Heap big ten-year-old boy," he said.

Custaleta pondered Frank's fate for a moment, but decided to adopt him into the tribe. They moved to their camp on the Pecos for several months, and then crossed the Rio Grande to Mexico. After several failed attempts to ransom him, Frank, with the help of a Mexican, escaped in January 1867.[13]

In March, Comanches were in Stephens County visiting the Browning ranches, where they had killed Josephus Browning back in 1860. Benjamin F. Browning and his wife, Susanna Schoolcraft Browning, lived on Gonzales

Creek near its junction with the Clear Fork Brazos. This time the Indians were simply on a stock raid; they crept in and out, stealing horses without anyone being aware of it. Said Mrs. Browning: "We knowed they were missing and there was the Indian signs and the horses gone and we never seed them anymore." That was how it worked most of the time.

The Schoolcraft family lived on the same ranch. Some of the brothers joined the Brownings and trailed after the thieves. All they could find was the usual Comanche calling cards. Said J. H. Schoolcraft, "they dropped a split-eared sore-backed rode-down pony, and moccasin tracks where they had turned him loose," and that was all. They followed the trail which crossed the Clear Fork and headed upstream, and then gave up.[14]

In March, Johnson Miller, an expert carpenter from Michigan, Bob Sensibaugh, and a Mr. Browder, were working on the West Fork Trinity in Wise County cutting timber to build wagons. Miller was called to Decatur to build a fancy coffin for a Mrs. Hardwick, who had recently died. With his task completed, he went back to the Trinity, riding Sensibaugh's best horse. It was said that Miller was frequently warned about carrying a weapon, but he always dismissed the advice. On March 25, Miller was only a mile from the wood camp when Indians killed him, stripped him, and hung his clothing in a tree…and Sensibaugh never saw his horse again.[15]

Chapter 38 notes

1 Smith, *Frontier Defense*, 170; Roth,"Frontier Defense Challenges," 40; Richardson, *Frontier of Northwest Texas*, 269.
2 Richter, *Army in Texas During Reconstruction*, 14-18; *WR*: S.1, V.48/2, 1171; Stanley, *An American General*, 188.
3 Jose A. Torres, Depredation Claim #3344; Banta, *Buckelew*, 7-13.
4 Winfrey and Day, *Texas Indian Papers IV*, 134, 136, 178-79, 228, 262-63, 306; McConnell, *West Texas Frontier*, 497.
5 James Johnson, Depredation Claim #6170.
6 Depredation Claims: Jerome B. Edwards #5703; Martha Wilson (for William Moorehead) #2686; Adolph Kappelmann #8323; Edward Ebeling #2083.
7 William S. Hinds, Depredation Claim #8316.
8 Laura Ogle (John Morris), Depredation Claim #4342.
9 Marshall, *A Cry Unheard*, 119; Grace and Jones, *History of Parker County*, 72; Winfrey and Day, *Texas Indian Papers* 4, 219, 223; Amesley Parsons, Depredation Claim #6213; Bolen Savage (Elizabeth Woods), Depredation Claim #5221.
10 Marshall, *A Cry Unheard*, 120-21; Winfrey and Day, *Texas Indian Papers* 4, 219; Depredation Claims: Amesley Parsons #6213; Bolen Savage (Elizabeth Woods) #5221.
11 Cates, *Wise County*, 202-03; McConnell, *West Texas Frontier*, 546; Bates, *Denton County*, 397; Nancy Gibbons, Depredation Claim #3896.
12 Banta, *Buckelew*, 16-22; Winfrey and Day, *Texas Indian Papers* 4, 202, 226.
13 Banta, *Buckelew*, 23-26.
14 Benjamin F. Browning, Depredation Claim #4608.
15 Cates, *Wise County*, 189-90; McConnell, *West Texas Frontier*, 528.

39 "They do not yell like white people."

In September 1865, there were more than 45,000 Union troops in Texas, but most of them were on the Mexican border demonstrating U.S. opposition to French intervention. Since then, numbers had been drastically reduced when the situation stabilized in Mexico and the volunteers were sent home. By February 1866, there were about 5,000 soldiers left, with "most of them," according to historian Carl Moneyhon, "assigned to the frontier."[1] Five thousand soldiers doubled the peak numbers during the antebellum and Civil War years, but most of them were not actually on the frontier. The provisional government under A. J. Hamilton, the Freedmen's Bureau, and the Unionists wanted troops in the interior to safeguard blacks and Republicans; the coastal planters wanted the troops on the frontier to enable them to continue to manage black labor and keep them subjugated; those on the frontier wanted the troops to protect them from Indians; and unreconstructed secessionists wanted the troops gone, period.

The Indians were unaware of the turmoil. It was simply a good time for raiding and that's what they would do, soldiers or no soldiers. There were so many raids that some settlers were hit multiple times. Minerva Binnion had lost her son in August 1865, when Indians attacked them as they moved from Burnet to Uvalde County. A new home made little difference. Indians hit them on April 10, running off about $1,300 worth of stock. Raiders hit William Moorehead again in Coryell County, stealing more horses. Also in April, they hit William Metcalf, who had been raided in October 1865. This time they got a "blue roan gelding" and "three bay gelding saddle horses," taken a quarter mile from his home in Palo Pinto.[2]

During the war, C. C. Carter had been a private in the Lampasas County militia and lived near the head of Bee Cave Creek, east of present Lometa. On April 22, he was going to see his daughter and son-in-law, A. J. Ivey, who lived about four miles away. Carter was unarmed and had made it three miles before he was surprised by five warriors, who chased and shot him three or four times. Carter's horse carried him into Ivey's yard, where the mortally wounded man called for a gun, but it was too late. He slid dying from his horse and was carried inside. Several settlers fired at the warriors but they easily got away. Carter was buried on his own land northeast of Lometa. In the vicinity during this raid, the Indians also caught and killed Joseph Bond.[3]

Not many settlers were in Kinney County in 1866. The San Antonio–El Paso Road went through the area, the little town of Brackett (later Brackettville) was on Las Moras Creek and Fort Clark was established nearby.

The Cox, Bingham, Beckett, Cantrell, and Mouser families had migrated west together, through Virginia, Kentucky, and Missouri, and reached Fannin County, Texas, in 1837. By 1866 with the war over, they decided to move on, and pulled in to an area on the West Nueces in the northeast part of the county. Their camp was not far from the 1862 massacre site of the German settlers fleeing to Mexico.

William Cox, Jr. (50) had several generations of family with him. He had been married three times already, and his third wife, Sara Jane Yates had died in March, at only 32 years of age. Some of his adult children from his second wife, Letty Larrison, were there, including Henry Clay Cox (26), Martha Jane Cox Beckett (22), and Serilda Jane Cox (14). Henry Cox was married to Julia Lewis Cox and they had two children, Tilitha (6) and Tabitha (3). Martha Jane had married Thomas B. Beckett (24) and they had three children, ages one, two, and four.

The families still lived in tents, for they had not even had the time or means to construct cabins. In late April, Tom and Martha Beckett and their children decided to make a trip to Brackett to get supplies. On the way, they stopped at the cabin of one of their few neighbors and were invited to supper. In the evening they heard a rooster crowing after going to roost for the evening. The hosts warned them that it was a bad omen and they should not continue the journey. The Beckett's dismissed the admonition as superstition. The next morning, April 28, they had only gone a few miles when the inevitable happened: Indian ambush. No one knows exactly what occurred, but people who found them later said it appeared that Tom put up a good fight, as evidenced by the battered condition of several camp utensils, including skillet and stool legs. All five of the Becketts died.

About this time the Indians also found the tent camp of the other families. Henry Cox was at his father's tent that morning, about 50 yards from his own. John Bingham's was on the other side, also about 50 yards away. Mrs. Bingham was the first to see the Indians enter the valley, about 25 of them and all on foot.

"Lord, God! Look at the Indians!" she cried out. William Cox grabbed his old rifle and went outside when he realized he had shot at a turkey that morning and had not reloaded. As he hastily tried to ram a ball down the barrel, an arrow hit him in the knee. He pulled it but the shaft snapped, leaving the point in the bone. Henry came to his assistance, but his gun was in his tent. When William reloaded, he and Henry "charged" the Indians. William fired and wounded one warrior, who limped away much in the same manner as William.

The other families made a dash to get to the William Cox tent. Mr. and Mrs. Bingham had no weapons; they ran together, and were both shot and wounded in the legs. Julia Cox only had time to grab Tilitha and run for the tent. Tabitha crawled to hide under a wagon. A warrior wrenched Tilitha from her mother and pulled her away with him. The Indians ran to Henry Cox's tent and rummaged through it, finding his gun. At William Cox's tent, it was William, with one rifle, versus two dozen Indians with bows and arrows and several firearms. Even so, William's sharpshooting kept them back; he hit at least a few warriors and dropped one who was coming out of Henry's tent with his arms full of plunder.

While the firing was going on, Henry saw Tabitha sitting under the wagon and crawled and ran out to rescue her, successfully getting her back with the others. One of the warriors, apparently the leader, blew a whistle to direct his men. William had been following his movements, and vowed to get him. When the man rose up to blow a signal, old Mr. Cox's rifle cracked and the warrior dropped. His men crawled up to drag him out of range, as usually happened when a leader was hit and the "medicine" was broken and the Indians pulled away. His death may have sealed the fate of Tilitha. The settlers later followed the Indians' trail, located a waterhole in the timber, and found the dead leader's body partly hidden underwater. They pulled him out and scalped him. On the way back they found Tilitha's body; she had been lanced to death.

With all the horses and cattle stolen, the settlers could only yoke together two remaining oxen, packed whatever they could fit into one wagon, and slowly made their way to Fort Clark. Six more settlers were dead in their pursuit to make a life for themselves on a few acres of free land.[4]

A major reason that the Indians were raiding in such numbers was because creeks were running and there was lush grass for the horses. Where drought had once been a major concern for the settlers, now rain was increasingly in the news. They had prayed for it, but the weather gods sometimes gave them too much. One great rainstorm hit Denton County on May 10, 1866. The morning began beautiful and clear, but before noon the sky turned black with great thunderclouds. Torrents of rain fell from ten in the morning to four in the afternoon, enough, the *Denton Chronicle* reported, to produce "the greatest flood known in the history of Texas." All the creeks were far out of their banks and the town of Denton was underwater. The forks of the Trinity River were one vast lake. From Denton into Dallas "the country was from five to twelve feet deep in water, and the damage done was enormous." Only one death was recorded, when Billy Bain drowned trying to swim his horse across Hickory Creek.[5]

Rainfall increased dramatically. Officially measured at the Deaf and Dumb Asylum in Austin, rainfall in April in 1863, 1864, 1865 and 1866, went from 1.9 inches, to 3, to 2.4, and to 6 inches respectively. In May during those same years it changed from 2.5, to 1, to less than 1, to 6. In July it went from 1.3, to 1, to less than 1, to 7.5. In September 1860, rainfall was 1.3 inches, and in 1865 it was 8.6 inches. In March 1860, rain was less than an inch and in 1865, it was 6.5 inches.[6]

Although few settlers realized it, the rainfall that promised them bumper crops also brought a plague of marauders. In May there were at least ten raids in nine different counties. On the first of the month, Indians hit Wiley A. Montgomery in Comanche County, stealing four horses worth $340. In mid-May, Comanches revisited Young County in the Elm Creek area that they had devastated in October 1864. William W. Anderson, unperturbed by the event, moved near the junction of Elm Creek and the Brazos shortly after, and paid the price. The raiders cleaned him out, stealing 250 cattle valued at $2,000, and 18 horses worth $900. In Jack County, the Indians hit Moses Dameron's place and got 15 horses worth $1,500.[7]

In what might have been part of the same raid, Comanches were along the Parker-Wise County lines late in May, revisiting the Springtown-Terrapin Neck area where they had raided in March. One of the main informants was Sang Kearby (22), son of a white Irishman and a mulatto, but called "a colored man" in his deposition. In Texas in the late 1860s, Kearby would never have been allowed to depose in court in a case with white plaintiffs or defendants. When he gave his testimony nearly 40 years later, things had improved somewhat. Kearby was once owned by James Kearby, and the two were involved in the March 1866 raid when James Sanders was killed. Sang had also found the body of Jake Moffett.

Kearby lived at Springtown, Parker County, and was then employed as a wagon driver for Daniel Waggoner. Kearby said that late in May, Comanches hit John P. Hart's ranch near Springtown, while the folks "were all gone to meeting" and they got a paint mare and a bay mare. Kearby lived at McCracken's place less than 200 yards away. The raiders took McCracken's horses, and before Kearby could get outside, they ran off his horse too, and then got stock from a man named Mayfield before heading west. Kearby and others got a posse and trailed them, but another group of whites had the misfortune to run into them first.[8]

Captain John McMahon, Andrew J. "Jack" Culwell, Sam Leonard, J. W. Miller, Frank Smith, C. G. Cogbourne and a few others were out scouting for Indians, while, as usual, the Indians had infiltrated past them. Jack Culwell had survived the Civil War with his brothers, Jonathan and Thomas. Jack got a furlough for illness and never returned to the army, and Confederate records listed him as a deserter, but he remained on the frontier joining Ranger groups to fight Indians.

McMahon's company was on upper Salt Creek on the Parker-Wise County line on May 30, 1866, when they collided with the raiders leaving the Springtown area. The civilians charged and a running chase developed. Soon the whites' guns were empty and it was the Indians' turn. Culwell got separated and after a mile chase he was run down and killed. Sam Leonard was hit in the neck and knocked from his horse. Paralyzed, he could see and hear, but could not move or talk. Miller dismounted to stay with him, but McMahon thought he was nearly dead and wanted to leave. A few others were determined to remain anyway, and when they pulled together to make a stand, the Indians backed off. They all got away, taking Leonard, but leaving Culwell. Leonard recovered, and said that he wanted so much to speak and tell them not to leave him behind, but he could not say a word. Culwell's body was later recovered and buried near Goshen, Parker County.[9]

While some Comanches were in Parker and Wise counties, others were in Brown County. Kentucky-born Edmund B. McReynolds (50) lived near the junction of Jim Ned Creek and the Colorado River along the present Brown-Coleman County line. On May 18, he had gone to old Camp Colorado for supplies and was on his way home, unarmed, and riding a slow pony. Six miles east of Camp Colorado, Indians easily caught, killed, and scalped him.[10]

On May 10, in Llano County, Indians swept through Jack Hinton's range and drove off 380 head of cattle worth $3,800. They moved south into Gillespie County and raided along Grape Creek northeast of Fredericksburg, stealing stock from Rube Miller and taking 150 cattle valued at $1,500, from William Banta. Banta owned about 500 cattle. At the time he was captain of a "ranger" company riding in search of Indians but could not recover any of his own stock.[11]

The Indians moved south and west. In western Gillespie, now Kimble County, they raided Elbert M. Walker and stole four horses worth $300. In Kendall County, George Nichols had a ranch on the Guadalupe near the German community of Comfort. Raiders arrived on "the light moon in May," which was the 28th. Nichols was sleeping when he heard noises, and his horses "seemed terribly frightened." He said, "I jumped up and jerked on my pants and slipped on my shoes and run out after them," but the Indians already had them 300 yards away. Nichols's son came out but they lost each other in the darkness, gave up and went home. Nichols sat up all night and worried, "having a big crop and nothing to plow with and nothing to go on with, I was in a terrible fix."

In the morning he and his son followed the trail, found one of his mules dead, and a little farther found "blood on the bushes." In a thicket was his best mare, dying. "Every time she would take a breath," Nichols said, "the blood would gush out at her side."

They followed the trail a few more miles, which was very easy to see because it went through wet, tall grass. Nichols owned 1,107 acres, a third of a league, and they were now crossing into the range of J. S. Goss, who lived in Kerr County, 20 miles up the Guadalupe. Goss's stock often came downriver and used Nichols' salt lick. Goss, a young man, sometimes came to Nichols' to court one of his daughters, but it didn't work out. Said Nichols, "I reckon everybody ain't alike; sometimes a young man will love a young girl and the girl won't love him." Goss was apparently unlucky in love, and unlucky in keeping his stock away from the Indians. This time he lost about 16 horses worth $400, and it would not be the last time raiders visited him.[12]

Down in Frio County, Peter F. Tumlinson knew the Indians. He had ridden with Ranger companies and had been in a few skirmishes. In May 1866, he lived on the south side of the Leona River about a dozen miles upriver from Martin's Settlement, which was attacked in July 1865. Comanches came in the night and ran off 19 of Tumlinson's horses and mules in the same method they always did. When they arrived, he said, "they usually came in quietly but when they went out they made 'a right smart fuss' sometimes, and this time they were hollowing at the horses."

Jose Maria Lopez, one of Tumlinson's hired men, knew they were Comanches, "for he heard them hollow and could tell their yell from that of American's or Mexican's." Sarah Tumlinson, Peter's wife, also said, "They did not yell like white people."

The Comanches had an easier time than usual because the Tumlinsons were not in their cabin by the river with the stock. With all the rain that been causing problems from Denton County to the Rio Grande, the Leona had overflowed its banks and driven them from the house. They were camped in tents and wagons on the bluff when the Indians cleaned them out. The next morning, Peter, his brother, J.M.W. Tumlinson, Lopez, and a few others, trailed the Indians upriver a few miles to a fording place. The mud showed many moccasin tracks and prints of hundreds of horses. Peter found a Comanche arrow and he commented, "The Kickapoos hardly ever used arrows, they used guns." The men scratched their heads, amazed that the Indians could get the stock across the raging river. They did not even attempt it. After a few days the water receded and they went farther upstream to cross, found the trail again, but gave up after another day. It was the same old story.[13]

Chapter 39 notes

1 Moneyhon, *Texas After the Civil War*, 37.
2 Depredation Claims: Minerva Binnion #1669; Martha Wilson (William Moorehead) #2686; William Metcalf #5702.
3 Wilbarger, *Indian Depredations*, 628-29; McConnell, *West Texas Frontier*, 398; Winfrey and Day, *Texas Indian Papers, IV*, 162. McConnell places this incident in 1862, but Carter's headstone has a death date of April 22, 1866.
4 Sowell, *Early Settlers*, 602-04; "William Cox of Fannin County," http://freepages.family.rootsweb.ancestry.com/~texascantrells/williamcox.html. Sowell places some of these events in 1865, but the family history indicates 1866.
5 *Denton Chronicle*, May 12, 1894.
6 *The Texas Almanac 1867*, 194.
7 Depredation Claims: Wiley A. Montgomery #6197; William W. Anderson #5295; Moses Dameron #352.
8 John P. Hart, Depredation Claim #4557.
9 Grace and Jones, *History of Parker County*, 100-01; McConnell, *West Texas Frontier*, 590; "Parker County," http://familytreemaker.geneaology.com/users/r/e/i/lorene-h-reid/gene1-0005.html.
10 McConnell, *West Texas Frontier*, 541; "Thomas Jefferson McReynolds," http://genforum.geneaology.com/mcreynolds/messages/573.html.
11 Jack Hinton, Depredation Claim #5298; William Banta, Depredation Claim #2640.
12 Depredation Claims: Elbert M. Walker #4419; J. S. Goss #1810.
13 P. F. Tumlinson, Depredation Claim #10644.

40 "I never sent anyone in search."

By June 1866, Texas had a new governing regime. There had been a continuous battle among the Radicals, Unionists, Conservatives, and Secessionists ever since A. J. Hamilton was appointed provisional governor in 1865. Many conventions and caucuses later, the Radicals nominated Hamilton for governor, but he was burned out and declined to run. They next picked Elisha M. Pease as their candidate. The Conservatives settled on James W. Throckmorton, ex-general and peace commissioner. Throckmorton came from a conservative Whig background with traditional Protestant values and supported economic development and tough frontier protection for his north Texas constituency. He was against the planter class dominating the government and believed it had gotten Texas into a war it did not need. Hand-in-hand with Throckmorton's dislike of the rich slaveholders was his dislike of the slaves, who he saw as competition for the small-time farmers. Throckmorton, like so many other Texans, was in the dichotomous position of supporting states' rights, but wanting a central government to protect them. One of the reasons they seceded from the Union was because the Union Army could not defend their borders. In return, they got the Confederate government, which, ironically, asserted that Confederate law was superior to state law and it still could not protect the borders. With the Federals back in control, Texans were back to square one, wanting army protection but despising army control and all that went with it, like shielding the recently freed blacks.

The election on June 4, 1866, was not close; Throckmorton defeated Pease by about 49,000 to 12,000 votes. The bitter Pease said they had just gone back to "Secession rule," with no reconstruction at all and the last year's provisional government being a complete failure. Unionists hoped President Johnson might refuse to accept the election results, but Johnson was not as strict on the ex-Confederate states as Congress wanted him to be. After a month of deliberating, Johnson backed the results and Throckmorton and the conservatives were back in power.[1]

While this was transpiring, the Indians were running rampant. In Palo Pinto County, Tipton Seay, who had been in the Confederate Army during the war, had recently married and had a nine-day old baby. He and his young wife, however, had not the means to strike out on their own and purchase some land in a safer place. They all huddled together, forted-up on Palo Pinto Creek a mile north of present Santo. The make-shift citizen's fort was mockingly called, "White's Town, and Burnet's Street, Stubblefield's Fort, and Nothing to Eat."

Several of the men had gone to the mill in Weatherford and taken all the guns. Tip Seay, weaponless, took a black horse he was breaking for another man, on a trip to Erath County to try to purchase another horse. It was not far and he left on June 1, saying he would be back by Sunday, June 3. On Saturday night, word reached the family that Seay never reached his destination. A search party went out and only about seven miles from home, near the Palo Pinto-Earth County line, they found Seay's body. Indians likely killed him only a few hours after he left the "fort." He was temporarily buried in a shallow grave dug with sticks, until he was later removed to a graveyard in Parker County.[2]

The Indians who killed Seay may have been the same ones who stole stock in Erath County. In mid-June they made a big haul at David A. Martin's place, stealing 34 horses and 250 cattle, valued at $4,050. The same month, Indians were in San Saba County. They hit Samuel E. Holland's spread in the southwest corner of the county near the McCulloch and Mason County lines. It was another devastating strike, with Holland losing 175 cows, 50 calves, 38 heifers, and 172 steers, worth $3,950.[3]

Cattle were increasingly becoming targets. About June 15, Kiowas and Comanches rode to Elm Creek in Young County and hit several of the ranches that they had devastated in October 1864. The Bragg families had taken much of the brunt of the raid, but they refused to leave. George W. Whittmore had come to the area in 1857 and had been building up his cattle herd ever since. Although the Indians missed him in 1864, they made up for it this time. Whittmore said that "The Braggs and I were loose herding something like 5,000 head of cattle" when the Indians arrived. Whittmore, Nathan and Martin Bragg, and Christopher Painter, were a quarter-mile away and watched helplessly as the raiders ran off everything within reach. The Braggs lost hundreds of cattle and Whittmore lost 170 cattle plus 12 horses, valued at $4,300.

The next day they trailed the Indians northwest for 50 miles, finding dead cattle scattered along the way. Apparently they never thought about what they would do if they caught up. Five days later they got within 300 yards of the Indians, but couldn't do a thing. They "made no effort to recover the property," Whittmore said, "because there was not enough of us for the Indians."[4]

In Clay County the Comanches and Kiowas made one of their biggest hauls of cattle ever. Clay County was a cinch for them, literally a quick splash across Red River and back into Indian Territory before anyone could react. A cattle cornucopia was waiting for them between the Little Wichita River and the Red where half a dozen ranchers set their stock free to fatten up on the grasses that were more luxuriant than any of them had seen in years. George B. Pickett, E. P. Earhart, William P. Russell, J. W. Hale, Daniel Waggoner, and Sylvanus Reed, who had his own stock plus that of the recently deceased William H. Hunt, had moved their cattle out of Cooke, Montague, and Wise counties in April 1866. In mutual agreement, they called it Waggoner's Ranch because he owned the largest portion, and they figured if they banded together, they could more easily protect their investment. They didn't even know how many cattle they had, somewhere between 12,000 and 15,000 head. The trouble was, on June 21, they only had five herders on guard: George Halsell, Peter Harding, William H. Graham, Henry Buchanan, and a Mr. Cook.

Forty mounted warriors slashed into them almost without warning. The herders fired a few shots and rode for their lives, clear back into Montague County, all except for George Halsell, who was caught, murdered, and scalped. Cook may have been caught and killed too, for as W. H. Graham testified in 1891, "he has never been heard from that time to this."

Dan Waggoner knew it was a dangerous place to run cattle and he and the other owners argued about the efficacy of hiring herdsmen. They might protect the stock and they might not—and they might get killed in the process. Most of the time, Waggoner said, cattlemen "could not guard and protect" their cattle. When they went out to the range and camped, they always waited until after dark and moved their horses about one mile away to keep them hidden in case of a raid. Waggoner didn't say what might happen if they were raided and found themselves without mounts. "Indians were all over the country," he said. "They were killing every man, woman, and child, or taking captive the women and children wherever they could be found." One might wonder, then, why they sent the five herders in harm's way. When Waggoner learned of the raid, he didn't appear too concerned, even though Halsell was his brother-in-law. "I never sent anyone in search of these cattle after the depredation," he said. No one even buried Halsell until ten days later. The fact that Indians would take Waggoner's cattle apparently surprised him. "These were the only cattle I ever knew of them stealing," he said. It surprised owner Bill Russell too. He said he had chased Indians on raids from 1865 through 1867 and "I never at any time saw or found Indians rounding up or driving away cattle."

In fact, Indians had been stealing cattle for years. Although they preferred horses, cattle thefts increased since about 1863. While the North and South battled over Indian Territory, the "Civilized" tribes felt the devastation and loss of their herds and made up for the damages by stealing Texas cattle. Not all the thieves were Comanches and Kiowas. Waggoner and Russell were likely rationalizing the death of Halsell and disappearance of Cook by saying they had never known Indians to take cattle and therefore, figured the herders were not likely to be molested. When several of these men filed depredation claims for their losses, the government, always looking to save a dollar, picked up on those statements and found other witnesses who claimed Indians didn't steal cattle. They got five men from nearby counties to testify that in the summer of 1866 many cattle were dying of some mysterious disease and that "Indians were never known to drive away herds of cattle…from Clay or any of the other border counties in the year 1866 or 1867 or at any other time." The affirmation was nonsense, but the government denied the claims on the basis of such statements.[5]

Author's collection

James W. Throckmorton was Governor of Texas from August 9, 1866 to August 8, 1867.

About 6,000 cattle were gone, but perhaps the score evened out. The white ranchers probably acquired most of the stock running free on the open range or "mavericked" them from others. The Indians reclaimed them in partial payment for their stolen land. The court system got to adjudicate thousands of claims and gave hundreds of people jobs.

While raiders were cleaning the cattle out of Clay County, another band was in Shackelford and Throckmorton counties stealing horses. They hit John G. Irwin's place in northern Shackelford and took six horses worth $445. In Throckmorton County, Barber W. Reynolds had moved his outfit to the Old Stone Ranch, built by the army during a temporary move of Camp Cooper and about four miles to the west of the old post. Reynolds survived a Civil War wound and in 1865, began to build up a cattle business. In June of 1866, he brought his wife, his seven children, and 100 cattle and looked forward to a prosperous future. Unfortunately, the Indians now targeted cattle as much as horses. Reynolds lost almost everything.

The raid turned deadly half a dozen miles to the northeast. Brothers John N. Hittson and William Hittson ran a large cattle ranch based at old Camp Cooper on the Clear Fork Brazos. William had served in the Confederate Army for a time, but "resigned" because he refused to leave his family alone on the frontier. He and John, along with James Dulin, moved west to the Cooper area to begin building a little empire, branding ownerless cattle and selling them in Mexico. By 1865, "Cattle Jack" Hittson was said to be the richest man in the area.

On June 30, 1866, John and William Hittson, John's son, Jess, Press McCarty, and Freeman Ward, a freed slave, were out hunting cattle on Tecumseh Creek about three miles north of the ranch. A large band of Comanches appeared out of nowhere and the first reaction of the surprised whites was to run. McCarty, on the fleetest horse, quickly outdistanced the rest and sped back to the ranch, reporting everyone else had been killed.

Actually, Freeman Ward began to ride away but lost his hat and, incredibly, stopped to pick it up. The Comanches were on him in a second. He ran his horse into the rocks where it stumbled and fell. The warriors jumped Ward and slaughtered him. Jess Hittson's pony was young and hard to manage, so John got him up behind him on his own horse, and they and William rode about a mile down Tecumseh Creek with arrows flying; John caught one in the thigh and William one in the hip. They rode to a rocky bluff on the right bank of the creek, jumped off the horses, and took shelter in a cave barely large enough to hold the three. The warriors soon had them surrounded, killed the horses and peppered the opening with missiles. One bullet clipped the gunsight off Hittson's rifle.

The Comanches kept them pinned down until nightfall when they gave up the siege. The three crept out and made their way two miles back to the ranch, where wives and children had already been grieving over the death of their husbands and fathers. Freeman Ward was buried where he fell, and today, Hittson Bluff still appears on topographical maps.[6]

In late June, Kiowas were back in Parker and Wise counties for the third time in four months, again visiting the Terrapin Neck-Springtown area. A raiding party of nearly 20 warriors came down the Cross Timbers in central Wise County and struck first near Terrapin Neck. On June 26, along the Dry Branch they stole several horses and moved on. Mrs. Frank Holden, Mrs. Mary Kearby, and Sang Kearby's mother were out doing the washing and watched the raiders go by heading west. A number of locals quickly formed a posse to chase them, including Alvin Clark, John Hill, Tom Howard, Jim Keasly, Frank Holden, and Sang Kearby. They headed toward the community of Goshen where they were joined by Bob Thompson, Jack and Andy Gore, Louis Hutchinson, Lige Keeling, and a few others. The posse was seemingly of sufficient number to punish the raiders, but it was not to be.

In the Goshen area they caught the Kiowas, or the Kiowas let themselves be caught in a good defensive position in a blackjack grove. The posse abruptly halted but got its signals crossed. Some men apparently heard a call to dismount. Alvin A. Clark (20) had enlisted in a Parker County militia company in April—formed temporarily by the besieged frontier counties even though organized "ranger" companies had been banned by the occupying Federals. Clark and John Hill hopped off their horses to attack, but as they moved forward, the others saw what they believed were too many

Indians advancing from the grove. The posse beat it. Hill saw them going and managed to remount and join them. Clark, however, was too late. By the time he could mount, the warriors were all around him. He fled down a fence row, cut off from his comrades, while warriors shot him from all sides. When he dropped dead from his horse, he was hit by four arrows and three bullets. They quickly scalped him and headed off to the northwest.[7]

Right in their path was the Isaac Brisco cabin. It had been a little over a year since the McKinney family—Isaac Brisco's daughter, son-in-law, and two grandchildren—were killed only two miles to the east. Brisco had moved from Jack County in 1865, but his new house was built near a break in a line of hills along the Wise-Parker County border that was a favorite route for Indian raiders approaching or leaving the lower settlements. Brisco and his wife grieved over their losses, but carried on, probably being too poor to relocate again. Isaac was a carpenter. He owned a lathe and may have been working in the shade of a grapevine arbor near the house when Kiowas struck. They killed and scalped Mr. and Mrs. Brisco, then mutilated their bodies in the presence of the children. The warriors plundered the house and carried away Eliza (10), Isaac (3), and a younger sister.

Jim Mayo, who lived one mile east, discovered the Brisco corpses and hurried to spread the alarm. The Indians moved on to Sam Stack's ranch and were stealing his horses when the Tackitt Brothers, who had ridden with the Rangers, ran into them and shot at them, but were outnumbered and retreated. The Kiowas went to W. H. Allen's home, but Mrs. Allen and her five children hid in a nearby creek. The Indians destroyed the house and went to the Caldwell place, where Mrs. Caldwell and her children hid in a cornfield. Next, the raiders hit J. T. Gilliland and Jack Wynn's ranch. The men tried to protect their horses, but the Indians drove them into the house. They stole the horses and rode north and out of the settlements. The bodies of the Briscos, like their daughter Cynthia and her family, were buried in a single grave in the Goshen Cemetery, which was rapidly filling up.[8]

Peter B. Emory had a ranch in Concho County. In late June he and a few companions rode east to Stephensville to buy provisions. On July 2, he camped at Mercer Creek west of the town of Comanche. The next morning as he was preparing to leave, Comanches raided the area and added Emory to their list, shooting and killing his black servant, stealing two horses and two mules, and destroying the harnesses and bridles.[9]

There was not a lot to celebrate on Independence Day 1866. The Confederacy had surrendered more than a year before, and Texas was still occupied by United States forces that seemed to be doing nothing but protecting the freed blacks in the interior instead of the whites on the frontier. At least the Indians hadn't raided much in Johnson County. Pleasant H. "Pleas" Boyd (38) had come to Texas from Missouri in 1854, and he and his wife, Serepta, had six children. "Pleas" was riding in the far northwestern part of the county in the vicinity of today's Lipan, which in 1867 would become part of Hood County. Boyd was likely not too concerned with Indians as he herded his cattle. He did carry a six-shooter, but four chambers would not admit a round and his pony was slow. When Indians arrived, Boyd had little chance. He tried to run but was caught, killed, and scalped. Two cowboys going to a roundup discovered his body. Boyd was buried on a hill above Crockery Creek that later became Evergreen Cemetery northeast of Lipan.[10]

In July, Indians raided Eastland County and stole two of George W. Gilbert's horses, worth $150. During that same raid, the Indians probably killed Thomas Eubank, whose fate was unknown for years. John A. Eubank had moved to Hubbard Creek in Shackelford County during the Civil War. About July 16, 1866, he sent his 17-year-old son to attend a cattle roundup to be held down between Pecan Bayou and the head of Jim Ned Creek in Callahan County. Nine days later, when the business was concluded, John Eubank learned that his son had never even arrived. John and his brothers and friends formed a search party and headed along Tom's probable route. In the southeast corner of Shackelford County they talked to a man who had heard shots in the area, and searching a little more, they found an Indian grave. Buried with him were two shields, silver plates, moccasins, and Tom's belt, scabbard, and powder horn!

They searched the area for days, but could not find any more clues. John Eubank could not believe his son was dead, but figured he had been captured, which would have been highly unlikely for a boy of his age. In November, the old man wrote a letter to Governor Throckmorton saying he was going to the agencies to look for news and, if he found his son, he wanted to ransom him. "But Sir," he wrote, "I am a poor man and can't raise the means to pay what they ask for prisoners. Can you assist me?" John Eubank went to the reservations and other white boys were shown to him, but not his son. It was about three years later that cowboys accidentally found a skull, bones, a shoe, and a stirrup in a creek bed a couple of miles south of present-day Moran and half a mile from where the dead Indian was found. The items were identified as belonging to Thomas Eubank. Old John's boy was not captured, but apparently he put up a good fight before he was killed.[11]

A large band of marauders was in Lampasas County from about July 7 to July 15. James Throckmorton had been elected, but had not even taken office when the citizens began sending him letters. On July 7, Thomas Adams wrote that Indians took 92 of his horses and some from a Dr. Derryberry's. They needed "pretison" (protection), Adams said, for depredations "are being comited by them dayley."

On July 15, 59 citizens of the county wrote to Throckmorton "that for more than one year past the frontier has received no protection from the

General Government," and that Indian raids "have encreased in number boldness and violence…."[12]

Barely two weeks after the big raid in Clay County, Indians were back. Jesse McGee and James L. McGee, Thompson Stansell, Aaron Anderson, and Culvin Smith were running cattle west of Waggoner's group, at Culvin Smith's ranch where Smith Creek meets the Little Wichita. On July 5, from 50 to 60 Comanches or Kiowas charged in and the herders were too few to do anything about it. They drove off 500 head of the McGees' cattle, worth $6,075; 505 cattle and a "blue mule" from Stansell, worth $7,570; 1,250 cattle from Anderson, worth $16,140; and 495 head from Smith, valued at $6,035. Years later, in their depredation claims, attorneys cut their claims of losses by one-third.

About July 15, Morris Gilbert and Levi Bennett were looking over their cattle in the triangle formed between the Red and Wichita. To their surprise, a number of men rode into view and calmly began driving the cattle toward Red River. They rode closer and saw they were a half dozen Indians, who apparently didn't care that white men were eyeing them. Gilbert and Bennett stopped under some trees and watched the procession incredulously, but felt powerless to interfere. The Indians drove the stock along and combined with another group, and all of them pushed the huge herd of cattle across the river as if it was just another day's work. Gilbert estimated that he had lost 250 cattle and five horses, valued at $3,250.

The two rode to Red River Station and got Richard Boren, John Friend, Harrison Forsythe, Jim and Jett Davis, Joe Carter, and a few others to go back with them. They went to the crossing and followed the trail into Indian Territory. They found a few cattle killed on the trail, plus the usual split-eared ponies indicating Comanche ownership. After several miles, the posse realized there was nothing much else they could do and went home.[13]

On July 18, 216 citizens of the northern counties sent a petition to Governor-elect Throckmorton, asking for help, stating that Indians were coming into the heart of their counties, "with a boldness never known before, committing murders and stealing horses and driving off cattle in large numbers and herds." The petitioners said that the U. S. forces were unable to protect them and they wished Throckmorton to authorize raising more citizen forces.

Late in July, more raiders crossed Red River and stole cattle from Clay and Montague counties. On July 26, they were in the Spanish Fort Bend and took 35 horses. S. F. Mains, from Montague, met J. M. Stephens, who brought word that two of his acquaintances, upon returning on business from the Chickasaw Nation, met up with 17 Creeks who were driving 750 head of cattle north from Red River, all branded with the marks of owners in the northern tier of Texas counties. The "wild" tribes of the plains were not the only ones getting some of the action.[14]

The action wasn't all along the northern border. In Gillespie County, raiders hit Stephen G. Raines' place and stole three horses worth $150. They rode south into Kendall County and were stealing more horses when they ran into Henry Meier and his son, Henry Jr. The Meiers lived on the Gillespie-Kendall county line and were driving a wagon to Henry Heiligmann's place on the Guadalupe about 15 miles northeast of Boerne. Heiligmann, Meier's son-in-law, needed help in cutting timber. The Meiers drove within two miles of Heiligmann's house and camped near the place they were to begin cutting. In the morning of July 20, Henry Jr. went to Heiligmann's to tell him they were ready, but he had only gone 500 yards when he heard his father scream. He ran back in time to see his father being killed and stripped by Indians. Henry Jr. ran to Heiligmann's and only later did they venture out to recover the body.

About this time, possibly the same raiders were in eastern Kendall County where they killed Theodore Gotthardt (50) and a free black man on Curry Creek.

In July, Mary E. Cochran of Lampasas County, wrote to Throckmorton complaining that Indians had recently taken 171 horses from the area. She also said they had killed a man named Mr. O'Neal in Erath County, captured a child from Dublin in Stephens County, and killed a herder. "I have stated the facts," she wrote. What was the governor going to do about it?[15]

Chapter 40 notes

1 Richter, *Army in Texas During Reconstruction*, 50-51; Howell, *James Throckmorton*, 3-5, 33, 42, 45, 65, 73, 76, 88, 112-13.

2 McConnell, *West Texas Frontier*, 538.

3 Depredation Claims: David A. Martin #354; Samuel E. Holland #2292.

4 George W. Whittmore, Depredation Claim #349.

5 Belle Hunt Shortridge (for William Hunt), Depredation Claim #5734.

6 Johnson, *History of Texas and Texans*, 1120; John G. Irwin, Depredation Claim #3895; McConnell, *West Texas Frontier*, 533; "Chasing our Tales," http://www.rafandsioux.com/chasingourtales/hittson.html.

7 Cates, *Wise County*, 203-04; McConnell, *West Texas Frontier*, 537; "Officer Down," http://www.odmap.org/officer/19708-private-alvin-a.-clark.

8 Marshall, *A Cry Unheard*, 137-38; McConnell, *West Texas Frontier*, in www.forttours.com/pages/toc/brisco.

9 Peter B. Emory, Depredation Claim #4492.

10 McConnell, *West Texas Frontier*, 540; Sears, "Pleasant Boyd," http://lipantexashistory.com/pleasant_press_boyd.html.

11 McConnell, *West Texas Frontier*, 500; Wilbarger, *Indian Depredations*, 504-05; Winfrey and Day, *Texas Indian Papers IV*, 122; Hesekiah B. Eubank, Depredation Claim #5901. Eubank's name has been also spelled Ewbank.

12 Winfrey and Day, *Texas Indian Papers IV*, 95-96.

13 Depredation Claims: Jesse McGee #4778; Thompson Stansell #3544; Aaron Anderson #10258; Culvin Smith #1681; Morris Gilbert #674.

14 Winfrey and Day, *Texas Indian Papers IV*, 97-100.

15 Stephen G. Raines, Depredation Claim #3543; McConnell, *West Texas Frontier*, 549; Winfrey and Day, *Texas Indian Papers IV*, 101, 173, 380.

41 "They are Indians—we are gone."

James W. Throckmorton was inaugurated as the governor on August 9, 1866, in a month in which may have seen the largest number of Indian raids in all of Texas history, one of the biggest single raids ever, and one of the most infamous captivities of the Indian Wars. Once again, increased raids coincided with a new troop presence. On July 5, Capt. George C. Cram and Company I, 6th Cavalry, arrived in Jacksboro. More companies should have been sent, if for no other reason than Jack County was one of ten Texas counties that voted against secession and the people welcomed Federal troops. Once again, the Indians knew not, and cared not. Grass and water were good and cattle were plentiful.

On the first day of the month, Kiowas crossed Red River into Clay County and stole 500 cattle worth $8,712 from Elijah Emerson. Astonishingly, Kiowas were back in Springtown in Parker County early in August, where they once again stole horses from John P. Hart, Sang Kearby, and Joshua Culwell. Kearby, Hart, Jack Gore, Jesse Franklin and a few others trailed the raiders to Salt Creek in Wise County and then gave up. Some of this same party may have been down farther into Parker County where they stole four horses worth $500 from Ann A. Murphy.[1]

Menard County was usually spared the big raids, but not so in August 1866. The locals knew that Indians came through the area, but conventional wisdom, as expressed by rancher Zachariah Kemp, was that the Comanches raided "generally in every light of the moon." That may have caused people to let down their guard, for he also cautioned, "They sometimes came in the dark of the moon." That was the situation on August 6 with the last sliver of a waning moon when about 250 to 300 Comanches crossed the western county line just a few miles north of Fort McKavett. They thundered down Rocky Creek, Clear Creek, and Dry Creek and struck the ranches on the San Saba stretching from Fort McKavett to 30 miles downstream near the mouth of Elm Creek. Thomas Hillyard, who lived at the head of Clear Creek, was one of the first men hit.

Shortly thereafter the Indians attacked the ranches of Jasper Norfleet and W. C. Shaw, which were lower down Clear Creek, a small stream that joined the San Saba between the other creeks. The two lost a total of 1,013 cattle. The raiders went down the San Saba and crossed to the south bank near the mouth of Fields Creek and in the area, took nearly 800 cattle from Patrick Fields. On the south side of the San Saba, the raiders went up and down Las Moras Creek, stealing cattle from George Coon, Sam Philips, Curt

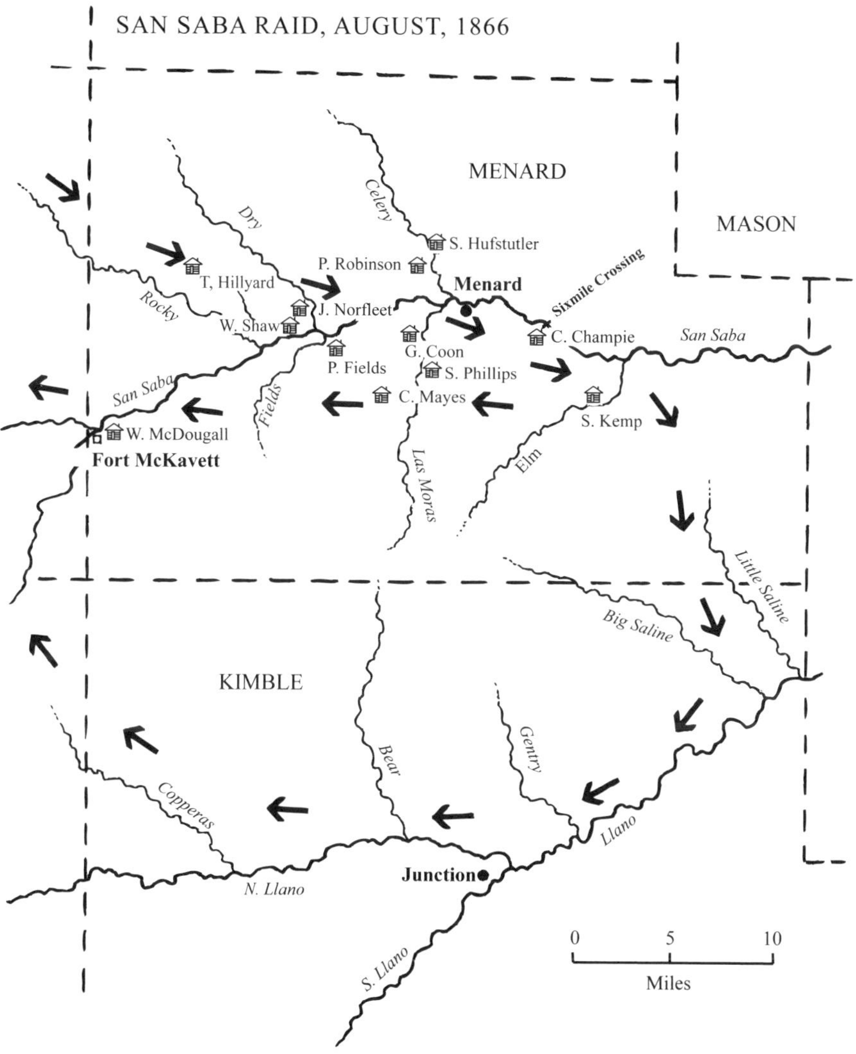
SAN SABA RAID, AUGUST, 1866
MENARD
MASON
KIMBLE
Celery
Dry
Rocky
S. Hufstutler
P. Robinson
T, Hillyard
Menard
Sixmile Crossing
J. Norfleet
W. Shaw
G. Coon
C. Champie
San Saba
P. Fields
S. Phillips
San Saba
Fields
C. Mayes
S. Kemp
W. McDougall
Fort McKavett
Las Moras
Elm
Little Saline
Big Saline
Bear
Gentry
Copperas
Llano
Junction
N. Llano
S. Llano
0
5
10
Miles

Mayes, William Vaughn, and Mr. Wickoff. Las Moras entered the San Saba from the south and Celery Creek from the north, where the town of Menard is today, but said stock buyer James M. Hunter, "only a few people lived there, it could not be called a town at that time." Up Celery Creek, raiders stole Peter Robinson's and Sanford Hufstutler's stock. Charles Champie lost about 400 head at Sixmile Crossing about six miles east of the mouth of Las Moras. Farther east and up Elm Creek they got 200 cattle from Simeon and Zachariah Kemp.

This part of the San Saba River was considered by many to be some of the best grazing lands in all of Texas, which was shown by the great number of ranchers in the area, including absentee owners who hired cowboys to ride herd over their stock. Still, the raiders did not limit their thefts to the San Saba.

Near the mouth of the Elm, half of the Indians turned back upstream on the San Saba, sending out smaller bands to go up and down the converging side creeks to round up any cattle missed on the first sweep. The other half continued south over the divide to the Big and Little Saline Creeks, stealing cattle until they hit the Llano, and then headed up the Llano for a ways before cutting across country to converge back in the Fort McKavett area.

Surprisingly enough, there were only two white casualties that day. William McDougall had his ranch less than two miles east of Fort McKavett. McDougall had married the widow of old Mr. Schellenbarger. Three men who ranched in the area had married Schellenbarger's daughters: Robert Casey, Charles Champie, and Oscar Splitgarber. After a long day's rounding up cattle on August 5, McDougall went home and got a late start the next morning. He first missed the raid that had entered the San Saba Valley just east of his cabin, but later in the morning on August 6, he was riding east when he ran into the Comanches. McDougall spurred his horse one mile and crossed the river, but the Indians caught and killed him. Shortly thereafter they arrived at the ranch. Clara Schellenbarger, McDougall's step-daughter, was returning from the garden with her arms full of cantaloupes and believed the approaching riders were cowboys. She was almost home when she realized the "cowmen" were Indians. She dropped the cantaloupes and ran for the fence as widow Schellenbarger came outside.

"O mother, they will get me," she cried.

A mounted warrior lanced her as she scrambled over the fence and she fell into the yard. The woman, not knowing McDougall was already dead, shouted out as if she was calling to him and several other men in the house. The warriors hesitated and pulled back, giving her time to pull Clara inside. The girl survived the wound.

As the Comanches rode back up the San Saba, they stole stock from many others, including Pat Coghlan, John Sloan, Peter Robertson, Decatur Martin,

Lafayette Helms, Adam Bradford, Rance Moore, Clara Mergenthaler, Fayette Taylor, Robert F. Casey, William P. Black, Guilford R. Chapman, James Hendricks, and Nathan and Ham Cavin.

In the Indians' wake, about 52 settlers and ranchers gathered and began following the trail which grew larger as it went west of Fort McKavett. When the trail from the cattle stolen on the Llano converged, the trail was massive. Tom Hillyard said, "Lots of places it was half a mile wide. It was the biggest cow trail I have ever been on." George Kemp said it was a mile wide in places. They counted about 1,000 cattle shot with arrows or lanced; a needless and tragic slaughter according to the cowmen. George Kemp said they followed the trail 75 miles out to the head of Devils River, but never caught up with the Indians.

The Comanches drove the cattle west toward the Pecos, which was the southernmost route of the Comanchero trade, or northwest to Muchaque (present Gail, Texas), where the trail across the Staked Plains went up to Canyon de Rescate, to Yellow House Draw (Lubbock), and across to New Mexico.

Cattleman John Hittson later found much of these cattle at New Mexican ranches, no doubt traded to the Comancheros for ammunition, weapons, and other supplies. The cattle "trade" was a burgeoning business opportunity for the whites, Hispanics, and Indians.

Although it is virtually forgotten today, in the late 19th century, the San Saba Raid was called "the most noted and widely-known raid ever committed by Indians in the State of Texas." Many of those involved figured the Comanches drove out 15,000 to 20,000 head of cattle, but in counting up individual claims we find there were 59 cases filed for a total of about 31,000 cattle lost, with a value of $300,000. There were 42 judgments ruling in favor of the claimants, with 17 still pending or dismissed as late as 1916. Even with some individuals no doubt exaggerating their losses (which the government always tried to trim down), there were many who never even bothered filing. Some, like Peter Robinson, who lost several hundred cattle, didn't file a claim "because Texas had been in the rebellion and he did not think the government would ever pay anything."[2]

After the San Saba Raid and other losses during the summer of 1866, the settlers and ranchers finally realized that there had been a marked shift in targets from horses to cattle. Some reasons were that there were much greater numbers of cattle to steal, Indians were more often substituting cattle for buffalo as a food source, and the Comancheros were finding markets in New Mexico. Horses, however, were still on the list. In August, raiders hit Louis C. Kincheloe in Burnet County again, getting ten horses worth $250. In Mason County they stole two horses worth $145 from George W. Holden. At Center Mills in what was then Johnson County, Indians got three horses worth $200 from Malachi Gregory. They hit Solomon Barron's place in Hamilton County a second time, stealing 25 horses worth $625.

On Simms Creek in northwest Lampasas County, Indians attacked Mark B. Hatley's ranch not far from where they killed Pleasant Boyd the previous month. Hatley didn't know marauders were nearby until he woke up one morning and found his stock stolen or killed, valued at $1,100. His hogs were slaughtered and seven horses were gone, including an expensive stallion. Hatley met up with George Carter, whose father, C. C. Carter, had been killed nearby in April, and Thomas Jones, all with similar stories of theft. They got a few other men and trailed the thieves; Hatley found one of his mares and a colt lanced to death, but the Indians got away.[3]

In mid-August, Comanches or Kiowas were in Wise County visiting Moses Fallowill's place along the West Fork Trinity River and stealing five horses worth $700. Nearby, Thomas Harvey lived on the West Fork Trinity about ten miles south of Decatur. Raiders attacked his farm on August 12. Harvey was away in Jacksboro and his wife was surprised when her children came running into the house, terrified, saying that the Indians were after them. They ran out the back door and hid in the creek bed before going to a neighbor, Martha Ann Armstrong. The Indians ransacked the cabin, destroying four featherbeds, blankets, stove, furniture, and clothing, valued at $1,430. Nearby the warriors caught, killed, and scalped another boy coming home from school, Logan B. Higgins (17).

Martha Armstrong saw about one dozen Indians plundering Harvey's house and leaving with his horses and property, but they did not come over to her cabin. Sarah Higgins waited until dark, but her boy did not come home. The next morning she went out to look for him. He was lying 300 yards from Harvey's house, she said, "and the arrows were sticking in his head when they found him."[4]

Tennessean Lewis T. Cofer came to Texas and married Amanda E. Henshaw in 1856 in Smith County. In 1863 they joined the Temple and Cadenhead families and moved to Eastland County. Lewis served in Capt. Nicholas Gillentine's Company, Texas State Troops, and in 1864, reenlisted in Capt. E. B. Pugh's Company. They all lived near Mansker's Lake and the Leon River in the southeastern corner of the county.

There hadn't been any killings in their section since the fight at Ellison's Springs two years earlier when Gilbert and Keith were shot. Lewis Cofer (33), Amanda (26), and their four children lived in a house on J. L. Duffer's ranch, where Lewis was employed as a ranch hand and laborer. Lewis had been sick with a fever for a few weeks and his brother-in-law, Jim Temple, came over to see him with his wife and their four-year-old daughter, as well as Frank Cadenhead, Temple's brother-in-law.

With Lewis incapacitated, all the chores fell on Amanda, and she welcomed visitors, who could sometimes help with the work. On the evening of August 20, however, she left the others in the house, strapped on a Navy Colt revolver, and walked 400 yards down to the stream to check on a filly she had staked out where the grass was good. Back in the house they heard five rapid shots. Temple and Cadenhead went running, but all they found was Amanda's bonnet. They continued and heard screams. Running as fast as they could, they reached a clearing in time to see Amanda struggling with an Indian as he tried to secure her on his horse. The warrior decided the woman was too much trouble and he shot her in the head with the last bullet in her revolver.

When Temple and Cadenhead appeared, the Indians quickly rode away. Lewis Cofer had reached them by this time on horseback and they placed Amanda across it and walked home. Temple's daughter always remembered her aunt draped over the horse, "and seeing her brains running out of her head." They fashioned a coffin out of an old wagon bed and on August 24, buried her on a knoll near the house, which was the first burial in what became the Alameda Cemetery. Lewis Cofer moved his remaining family to Bell County a short time later, and the Temples followed him soon after. More families were starting to pull out now than had during the Civil War.[5]

On August 28 in Tom Green County, George B. Brown had 25 cattle stolen, worth $625. Ludwig H. G. Mumme, who had been saved and fed by the boys, Rothe, Miller, and Weinand back in January when he became lost on a trip from Bandera to Medina County, had successfully moved his residence to Medina County, setting up in the area of New Fountain near Hondo Creek. He did not, however, escape from the Indians, for in August 1866, they stole 11 horses from him, valued at $660.

Elbert M. Walker had moved from western Gillespie County to Llano County, but on the last day of the month the Indians found him at his new place. During the night they quietly took down the fences and walked off with three horses and a mule.[6]

One of the most infamous murders and captivities occurred in Cooke County. It is not often that we know the leader of the raiding party, but in this one, the Kiowa, Satanta, was the chief. Early on August 25, a full moon, his war party crossed Red River in the Sivell's Bend area heading south. Reaching Elm Fork of the Trinity west of Gainesville, they turned west and began stealing stock.

Brothers James B. Davenport (33) and John W. Davenport lived on the Elm Fork about ten miles west of town and their stock roamed all the way up the Elm Fork to near the county line. The Kiowas got 135 horses, colts, and mules, valued at $6,175. Simon and Louis Woody, free black men once owned by the Davenports, tended their horses. Simon said that many people were reluctant to search for the Indians after the raid. "Fraid they would kill us," he said.

Thomas P. Gossett had a ranch four miles north of Davenport and lost several head of horses.

About one mile beyond Gossett's was James T. and Emma Coursey's ranch. The Kiowas swept off 14 of their horses and continued to the west. Emma's father, George W. Grant, lived nearby and the Kiowas got 11 of his horses. George's sons, Charles R. and William Grant, John Loring, and Zeke Huffman were riding up a hill about four miles southeast of Head of Elm (now St. Jo) and heard gunfire ahead of them. When they crested the hill there was a commotion about a quarter mile in front. There were about 20 Indians riding around a lone wagon. The unarmed men could only watch. In a few minutes the Indians were gone, plundering the wagon, stealing the man's horse, and carrying away what looked to be five women and children.

The white riders cautiously approached. The dead man was James Box. Charlie Grant said he was "lying on his back, he was scalped, had a couple of arrows in his back, shot through the temple and under the arm...." John Loring said Box had three arrows sticking in him "and was cut from the pit of his stomach to below his navel someplace." In addition, "the top of his head was gone; the scalp was off with it." They rode back to George Grant's house to get more men and weapons. Later, several other curious neighbors arrived at the scene, "looking to see what mischief was done," said Josiah G. Moss. He said, "I saw a man with his head skinned, I had had never seen anything like that before."[7]

James Box and Mary Matthews Box had been in Texas since the early 1830s. They had lived in Titus and Hopkins counties, where all of their children were born except the baby, Laura. Box was a Union man, and when the Civil War began, he moved his family to Montague County to avoid being conscripted. They survived the war and hoped to live in peace, but it was not to be. In June 1866, two of James' brothers were ill or injured, and the Boxes hurried to Hopkins County to help them out. They remained about five weeks, until about August 20, when they started back to Montague County. It rained for much of the five-day journey, and during the melancholy trip, James Box declared to the family that he had a premonition that he would never get home. On August 25, only about three miles from their cabin near Head of Elm, which consisted of a blacksmith shop, a store, a few homes, and a stockade, James spotted someone moving along a hill and assumed it was a neighbor.

"I wish that man would come down to us," James told Mary, "so that I could borrow his horse for our jaded one, and then we could get home faster."

When Mary looked in the direction he pointed, she said, "Why, there are three or four of them."

"They are Indians—" James realized, and said, "we are gone." Turning to his 17-year-old daughter, he said, "Margaret—get my six-shooter, quick!"

Author's collection

The Kiowa Satanta participated in many raids. He led the infamous Box Raid in 1866.

Before she could get the pistol, Satanta and 20 Kiowas were on them. One of them shot an arrow into James' chest and he fell backwards into the wagon. He sat up, yanked the arrow free, took the pistol and fired. Another arrow hit him in the head, this time knocking him out of the wagon. Somehow, James Box rose again and stumbled to the far side of the wagon before he fell dead. The warriors scalped him and cut open his jaw. A Kiowa grabbed Mrs. Box (42) by the hair and pulled her out of the wagon. The screaming girls, Josephine (13), Ida (7), and infant Laura, were quickly grabbed and tied to ponies. Margaret broke free and ran to her dead father, holding tight to him until the Indians pulled her away and rode off at a gallop.[8]

After Charlie Grant, Bill Grant, John Loring, and Zeke Huffman made a quick inspection, they high-tailed back to George Grant's. Years later at a depredation claim hearing, an attorney asked Charlie Grant why he didn't go to the rescue. He made no excuses. "Well, I was afraid to go," he answered.

The next day a larger posse gathered, including Jim Coursey, Dan Brunson, Harrell Cherry, John A. Hendricks, and Jack Loring, John Loring's freed slave. Cherry was worried sick about his family. His ranch was a few miles beyond where Box was killed. When the posse finally reached his place, he thankfully found his family safe, but about 500 head of his stock were gone. The Kiowas also robbed the Williams and Langford families. The cowboys followed the trail where it crossed into Indian Territory just below Red River Station and continued on for 75 miles.[9]

The Kiowas traveled north night and day for two weeks. Margaret ripped off pieces of her dress, hoping that pursuers would spot them. Instead, the warriors saw what she was doing and tore the remaining clothing from her body. Mary and Margaret were raped. On the eleventh day, Mary Box dropped Laura as they rode and she was badly injured. The crying irritated the warriors and one of them threw Laura against a tree and left her behind. They would not allow Mrs. Box to drink, and her tongue swelled. One of her daughters took off her slipper as they crossed a stream and filled it with water for her mother, but a warrior knocked it from her hands and then they beat the girl. After reaching the main village near the Arkansas River, the spoils and prisoners were divided up. Mary was separated from her children and taken to another camp about six miles away where she worked from dawn to dusk.

"I had to pack wood and water," Mary said. "When I delayed they would hit and beat me and even the squaws would knock me down. I was very sick while with the Indians, notwithstanding they would beat me. It was a terrible life…."

Margaret, described as "a beautiful girl just ripening into womanhood," fell into the hands of a chief who forced her "to become the victim of his brutal lust," and then bartered her to another Indian for two horses. This Indian used her until he tired of her, and traded her to a third Indian, who used her and passed her on. Ida, too young to be sexually abused, nevertheless spent much of the time alone and crying. When the bands camped near each other she tried to run to her mother, and for punishment, her captors stuck her bare feet into a campfire "until every portion of the cuticle was burned therefrom." With charred feet she could not run.[10]

After a few weeks the Kiowas realized that they had more to gain by selling their prisoners. They had been taking captives for decades, and the white men always gave money or supplies to get them back. The Indians had returned a dozen captives at the Little Arkansas Treaty the year before, and they were rewarded with many presents. Eager to turn a profit, Satanta rode to Fort Larned on September 9, to talk to Maj. Cuvier Grover, 3rd U. S. Infantry. Satanta told Grover that they had gone to Texas "to make peace with the whites there, but had been received in a hostile manner, and, in consequence, had taken the captives." As a peace gesture, Satanta was ready to give them up.

Grover asked Agent I. C. Taylor for advice and Taylor met with Satanta, who proposed to sell the captives if he was paid "liberally." Instead, Taylor angrily told Satanta "that he knew perfectly well that it was in violation of the treaty." Taylor said he "would not pay him one dollar for them" but that he must bring them all to the fort and deliver them to Grover. Satanta asked Taylor for ten days to talk it over and Taylor agreed.[11]

Instead, Satanta rode to Fort Dodge, met Capt. Andrew Sheridan, 3rd U. S. Infantry, and made a similar offer. Sheridan sent Lt. Gustave A. Hesselberger, an interpreter, and two soldiers, Lee Herron and John McLaurie, to the Indian camp to negotiate for the prisoners. They agreed on a combination of money and supplies worth about $2,800. That evening, the lieutenant paid cash to the two Indians who owned Margaret and Josephine to prevent "a repetition of indignities to which…they had been continually subjected." A few days later, Indians brought Mary and Ida in, and they were given additional blankets and provisions. Gen. William T. Sherman, on an inspection tour, arrived at Fort Dodge shortly after the affair, and angrily instructed Captain Sheridan not to purchase any other captives. The Boxes had been rescued just in time.[12]

That summer of 1866, several other captives were recovered and returned home. Cola Caroline McDonald, who gave birth to a baby in March, was ready to go whenever her daughter was found. In June, Agent Leavenworth found Willie Ball, and delivered him to Council Grove. In July, Leavenworth and Elizabeth Fitzpatrick found out where Mahala McDonald (5) was being held and were able to negotiate her release. By then, the women were frantic to get home but it took time to arrange transportation. They left in a wagon train for Texas on August 27.

The trip was long and arduous, and not without dangers. The women were afraid that they might be attacked and recaptured. It was good that they did not know that they were riding through the very area where a few weeks earlier, Satanta had captured the Box family. The wagon train, however, came through unmolested and went south to Decatur, where the passengers were split up into several parties to continue on to their various homes. Elizabeth Fitzpatrick reached Parker County in October, where she met the Johnsons and her granddaughter, Lottie Durkin.

Back in Kansas, when Agent Taylor learned of Satanta's duplicity, he wrote to Commissioner of Indian Affairs Dennis N. Cooley on September 30. He "urgently" called the attention of the department "to the fact that every prisoner purchased from the Indians amounts to the same as granting them a license to go and commit the same overt act. They boastfully say that stealing white women is more of a lucrative business than stealing horses." Taylor added that he believed it was time that "the strong arm of the government" brought the Indians to their senses.[13]

In November 1866, Lieutenant Hesselberger escorted the four Box women to Fort Leavenworth. They stopped at Fort Riley, where they met Lt. Col. George A. Custer and his wife, Elizabeth. Both of them commented on the Boxes' horrible condition. Mary Box told them that many Indians raped and abused her and the oldest girls, and burned Ida's feet. Said Libbie: "I could not find any language to repeat what the poor mother and eldest daughter told me of their horrible sufferings during…their captivity." After talking to Margaret, Libbie came to believe that Indian captivity truly "was worse than death."

The Boxes' ordeal made a lasting impression on the Custers, and it was one of the reasons that Custer later ordered his trusted officers that they should shoot Libbie dead if she was about to be captured. Keeping the last bullet for yourself became ever more entrenched in the American frontier psyche. The Box killings and captures were significant incidents that led to Gen. Winfield S. Hancock's Kansas expedition in 1867, and later to Custer's Washita expedition in 1868—campaigns that only served to increase hostilities and contributed to more of the depredations that they sought to curb.

With few relatives in Texas having money to arrange for their return, the Boxes stayed at Leavenworth for a time before reaching Texas by way of St. Louis. Ida, perhaps because of her burned and infected feet, died shortly thereafter. Josephine reportedly married a man named Crowe, while Margaret married Dan Brunson, a childhood sweetheart and one of her would-be rescuers.[14]

Three years after the Box raid, several cowboys from Cooke County went up to Fort Sill in Indian Territory. Wallace Ligon, a freed black man who lost two of his own horses during the raid, rode with Messrs. Metcalf, Fletcher, Stone, Grayson, and John Rowland, once a captain in the Frontier Regiment, driving cattle to sell to the government to feed the Indians. At the fort they noticed many of Davenport's horses, with the "M.D" brand. "We supposed we would get them;" Ligon said, "but the colonel, agent, or whoever he was, said, 'We got these Indians here on the reservation, and we don't propose for you men to bother them.'"

The Davenports and the others never recovered their property because it was considered inexpedient at the time. Decades later they filed depredation claims, but even so, the government argued that the length of time between occurrence and filing "suggest moral presumptions against the claims." Besides, one attorney declared, "there is no proof as to who took the property, all the testimony on this point being hearsay."[15]

Certainly there were fraudulent claims, but the infamous Box Raid was well-known and documented. There were too many victims who received nothing from a system that was constructed to remunerate them for these very acts.

Chapter 41 notes

1 Hamilton, *Sentinel of the Southern Plains*, 1, 16; Depredation Claims: Elijah Emerson #1544; John P. Hart #4557; Ann A. Murphy #1666.
2 McConnell, *West Texas Frontier*, 556; Depredation Claims: Patrick Field #8448; Felix Eaker #3537; Jasper Norfleet #5537; Simeon Kemp #4777; Thomas Hillyard #5109; Sanford Hufstutler #4352; Robert F. Casey #9522; Guilford R. Chapman #1548; James Hendricks #5311; Richard S. Coon #10834; Curtis F. Mayes #2171; William J. Vaughn #4988.
3 Depredation Claims: Louis C. Kincheloe #2479; George Holden #4782; Malachi Gregory #5538; Solomon Barron #5255; Mark B. Hatley #4234.
4 Depredation Claims: Moses Fallowill #431; Thomas Harvey #348.
5 Langston, *Eastland County*, 49-52; Clark, "Eyewitness Account of Amanda Cofer's Murder," http://www.rootsweb.ancestry.com/~txeastla/story/amandacofersmurder.html.
6 Depredation Claims: George B. Brown #4781; Ludwig Mumme #7820; Elbert M. Walker #4419.
7 Depredation Claims: James B. Davenport #5372; James T. Coursey #3876.
8 White, "White Women Captives," 332-33; Winfrey and Day, *Texas Indian Papers, IV*, 107; Herron, "Box Rescue."
9 Depredation Claims: James T. Coursey #3876; Harrell Cherry #4415.
10 White, "White Women Captives," 330, 333; Herron, "Box Rescue"; Potter, *Montague County*, 25-27; Custer, *Life on the Plains*, 60, 62; Custer, *Following the Guidon*, 223.
11 Winfrey and Day, *Texas Indian Papers, IV*, 114; *Commissioner of Indian Affairs 1866*, 280-81.
12 White, "White Women Captives," 330-33; Herron, "Box Rescue."
13 Ledbetter, *Fort Belknap*, 163-176; Foreman, "Jesse Leavenworth," 21; *Commissioner of Indian Affairs 1866*, 281.
14 Michno, "The Box Family & the Last Bullet," 6-7.
15 James B. Davenport, Depredation Claim #5732.

42 "Go with him and be a good boy."

On August 20, one week after Governor Throckmorton took office, President Johnson proclaimed that the rebellion in Texas was officially over. Although General Sheridan, in charge of the Fifth Military District, still had supervision of Throckmorton's actions, the governor took his election as a mandate that the civil government had precedence over the military. Throckmorton tried to be conciliatory, addressing the legislature that laws should be passed to safeguard "Negroes" rights, and, most importantly, that Federal troops should be moved from the interior to the frontier. In August there were 24 companies of cavalry and infantry based in Austin and San Antonio, while 100 more were spread across the coast and lower Rio Grande. Only a few token cavalry companies had been sent to the frontier. Throckmorton wrote to Gen. Horatio G. Wright, in command of the District of Texas, asking for a troop shift. Wright was willing, but his boss, Sheridan, did not feel that Texans in the interior were yet civil enough to treat the freedmen fairly. The frontiers still suffered, and Throckmorton continued to be hit with calls for help.[1]

On August 3, T. W. Thomas wrote to Throckmorton that he had been to see Captain Cram of the 6th Cavalry in Jacksboro and recommended an additional 500 Rangers to protect the area. Cram, he said, met his suggestion with "hearty approval." George Pickett, ex-captain in the Texas State Troops, told him "there never has been as many Indians in the west part of Wise and Jack County before…." Thomas conceded that with the recent raids there was not "much left in the way of property to protect…but Hughmanity demands" every man to do his part, for it was in "the Intrust of all to keep the frontier as far out as possible…."

Citizens of Lampasas County wrote on August 15, about what was becoming increasingly apparent: "It will be observed that these depredations are now extended to Cattle, and not confined, mostly, as heretofore to horses." A citizen of Wise County informed Throckmorton of the death of James Box and the capture of his family, and said he felt assured that "the earliest relief there can be given us will be given by you…."[2]

Throckmorton, however, could not do much until Sheridan realized that the governor's and the citizens' complaints were not just tricks to get the army out. In the meantime, the raiders kept coming in. The cattlemen paid dearly for moving their stock out into Clay County. Wilburn "Tip" Mooney had a ranch on the East Fork Little Wichita where he ran about 2,300 cattle. On September 1, Indians crossed Red River and plowed into Mooney's stock, stealing 2,150 head, worth about $30,500, plus some of Dick Boren's stock which were mixed in. They battled with some of the cowboys just northwest of present Henrietta.

J. M. Koger (33) and Thomas Norris had a running fight of half a mile. Koger was hit in the arm and when Norris was hit in the back he stopped and wanted to surrender. Koger thought that was crazy, but since the Indians had them surrounded and a warrior walked up to them with his hand extended, he conceded. When the warrior took his hand, however, another one shot Koger in the back.

"I jerked loose and went back to my rifle," Koger said. "They run away from there, and got behind trees, and shot a fatal shot at my comrade. They killed and scalped him right there. I went off and left him." Koger didn't know how many warriors they fought. "I was too busy engaged to count Indians," he said. The wounded Koger made it to Red River Station and a posse went out after the Indians, but, as usual, the Indians were gone and all they found were some abandoned split-eared ponies. They buried Norris. He was scalped and his hands were holding his head, as if he had been scalped alive and tried to stop the flow of blood before he died.[3]

The number of stock stolen from Clay and Montague counties in September was astonishing. Perhaps 40 cowmen were running cattle between Red River Station and the Wichita River. Woodford Bennett lost 300 cattle worth $3,540, from near the mouth of the Little Wichita. Levi Bennett, Woodford's brother, lost 500 cattle worth $6,075 from his place on Beaver Creek. Mabel Gilbert claimed to have lost 1,190 cattle and horses worth $14,862 from the range above the Little Wichita. Indians were said to have taken 585 cattle from Frank S. Brown in Clay County, worth $7,530. William B. Martin and David S. Hagler were partners in a cattle ranch west of Red River Station, and the Indians stole one-quarter of their stock, about 590 head, worth $7,542. Government attorneys routinely allowed only about one-third of the numbers claimed. Sometimes they argued that many of the cattle "lost," really just strayed across Red River on their own.[4]

The cowmen would have scoffed at the idea of tens of thousands of cattle migrating north like bison. Although cattle theft was up, the Comanches and Kiowas had not lost their taste for horses. They stole 15 horses worth $1,500 from Nancy Jefferson in Montague County, and got six horses worth $600 from Hiram Williams. Down in Uvalde County near Fort Clark on September 8, Indians killed D. J. Davis while stealing horses.[5]

On September 2, old ranger Jack Cureton wrote to Governor Throckmorton to inform him of the complaints he had been hearing "in all parts of the country." Citizens asked him what he believed the governor would do to help them, and Cureton answered, "Throckmorton will do all in his power to protect us," because he was "a friend on whom we can depend." Cureton said that the people wanted to be able to organize as they had always done, because "there are no men in the world so capable of doing justice to the service as those who have lived and battled with the enemy for the last eight years."[6]

Although the citizens may have believed they had been effective Indian fighters, the record speaks to the contrary. Indians had been, and still were, raiding with near impunity. While the latest forays targeted livestock, sometimes a war party crossed Red River with murder on its mind. A large war party of 60 or more Comanches rode boldly down the Western Cross Timbers and passed close by Jacksboro, not knowing or caring that the U.S. Cavalry was now on the job.

On the night of September 12, about 30 of them camped just east of the town. The next morning they attacked a Mr. Hynson's (or Henson) cabin, but were driven off by a determined defense. They went east on the Decatur road to Beans Creek about one dozen miles east of Jacksboro where they ran into four men. Enoch M. Jones (52) and his son, Richard, both of Sherman, Texas, and two freedmen were on their way to Jacksboro to cut hay for the troops. The Indians killed them and left their bodies by the roadside.

The party split up around the Jack-Wise county lines. They plundered Armstrong's place on Willow Creek in Wise County, while Mrs. Armstrong and her children were at her brother's, Westley Higgins, about two miles away. The Indians came to Higgins', but the defenders reported killing and scalping one warrior. The raiders stole their horses and left. They came next to the Pearce Woodward place. There they caught Lona Buchanan 100 yards from the house as she was drawing water from the well. She ran to the house but was lanced before her brothers came out and bluffed them back. They stole three horses. Lona survived.

The Comanches stole one pony from J. B. Floyd, almost capturing his little boy as he ran to the cabin from the corn crib. They met Lee Dean and Asa Henson at the Big Sandy Creek crossing of the West Fork Trinity, as they left Decatur to travel to Jacksboro. The Indians charged, but the two men, on good horses, galloped two miles back toward Decatur before losing their pursuers.[7]

Near the old bridge that spanned the West Fork Trinity near today's Bridgeport, the Indians ran into three cowmen, Ben Blanton, Lansing Hunt, and Glenn Halsell. They retreated to the old Thorn house where Richard Couch was residing and where they knew a number of cowboys were nearby in Thorn Prairie branding cattle. All the men forted up at Couch's and when the warriors emerged from a patch of timber and began driving off the horses, the whites let them have several well-aimed volleys. Dick Couch shot a couple at long range with his buffalo gun and they pulled back out of range. During the lull, Ben Blanton got on his horse and rode hard for Decatur.

In a few hours, Blanton returned with several more men, including Dan Waggoner and Sheriff Robert Cates. The posse took the trail, which headed north along Dry Creek to the house of John Babb, where they found a scene of destruction. The Nokoni Comanche, Persummy, led this division of the war party, and he was likely not too pleased about the losses they had sustained. John Babb, who had moved to Texas from Wisconsin, and Hernando C. Babb, his oldest son, were gone to buy cattle and horses in Arkansas when the Indians struck. At home were Isabel Babb and her children, Theodore "Dot" (14), Bianca (10), an infant daughter, and Sarah Renfrow Luster (25), a widow whose husband had been killed fighting for the Confederacy.

The children were playing outside about three in the afternoon on September 14, when they saw riders approaching their cabin. Isabel Babb called to Dot and asked him to see if they were cowboys.

"No," Dot answered, "they are Indians!" They ran inside and Isabel and Sarah slammed the door. Sarah hid in the loft. Dot got out an old gun, but the Comanches burst in, grabbed the gun and beat him. Isabel tried to ease the situation by shaking hands with them, but to no avail. They grabbed Isabel but she resisted. Walking Face drew out a big knife and stabbed her four times. Dot ran to his mother and pulled her to the bed, trying to patch her wounds. When they stabbed Mrs. Babb, Sarah Luster screamed, and the Indians crawled into the loft, hauled her out, and tied her on a horse.

Warriors dragged Bianca outside, but she grabbed hold of a fencepost and would not let go. The warrior "jerked me so hard that the rough bark on the post tore the flesh from the inside of my hands until the blood ran freely from the wounds." But, she said, "I did not cry."

Inside, Mrs. Babb was still alive, clinging to her daughter. Walking Face shot an arrow into her left lung. Dot pulled the arrow out. The Indian pointed another arrow at Dot, motioning for him to leave. Isabel Babb told him, "Go with him and be a good boy." Soon, all three prisoners were tied on horses. The baby, Margie, was left crying beside her dying mother.[8]

The Indians took six of Babb's horses worth $300 and continued on, heading rapidly northwest to get away from any pursuing settlers. Ironically, John Babb and about 220 settlers in Wise and surrounding counties had recently signed a petition to Governor Throckmorton, complaining of murders and horse theft and asking for protection. When the posse reached Babb's, the feathers from the slashed-open beds covered the ground and looked like snow. Bob Cates said that Mrs. Babb "was breathing her last when I went in, a little child was in the bed with her alive," but completely soaked in her blood. The posse did not get on the Comanches' trail until the next morning. Dan Waggoner found a family Bible on the trail that belonged to the Armstrongs, whose house was robbed the previous day. They chased the Comanches all the way to the Little Wichita before their jaded horses gave out.[9]

The Indians moved rapidly for three days and nights until they believed they had lost their pursuers. The captives had almost nothing to eat. Sarah Luster, described by Dot as "a shapely vivacious brunette," was "made to suffer an excruciating penalty for her captivating personal charm and beauty." After being raped, Sarah vowed to escape. One night she slipped away in the darkness and rode away. She got to Red River, but was caught again, this time by Kiowas. After a month with them, she pulled the same trick, but this time rode northeast. In late November 1866, after four days and nights she reached the Running Turkey Ranch east of Fort Dodge, Kansas. Luster had unknowingly ridden through an area occupied by Satanta and his Kiowas, who had just been at Fort Dodge to sell the Box captives. The ranch owner took Sarah in, contacted Jesse Leavenworth, and the agent had her taken to Council Grove.

Within 12 months, Sarah Luster had married a Mr. Van Noy, and they made a home in Galena, Kansas. Dot Babb wrote a fitting tribute to her. She spent the rest of her life, he said, not with bitter, brooding memories, but "in a spirit of serene repose, reciprocal happiness and affection." Pioneer women like Sarah and Isabel were special, Dot said, and their trials were typical "illustrations of the sacrifices and perils of the pioneer women…." Dot believed that their unwavering fortitude defined them more than any contrived eloquence from a novelist's pen.[10]

Sarah Luster reported the Babbs' capture to Leavenworth and he chastised the chiefs, but they apparently ignored him. In January 1867, John Babb asked for $800 from his relatives in Wisconsin to help pay for their ransom and traveled to Indian Territory to look for them. At Fort Arbuckle, post interpreter Horace Jones, and Jacob J. Sturm and his Caddo wife agreed to help.

In April 1867, Sturm found Bianca, paid the Nokonis $333, and took her back to Fort Arbuckle. She stayed overnight with Horace Jones and the next morning he took her to her father. "Of course," she said, "I was tickled to death to get back to him."[11]

Dot was located on the Canadian River in Chief Horseback's band through the efforts of Chief Asa Havey, who had been instrumental in gaining the release of several other captives. Horseback, the uncle of Walking Face, who had killed Mrs. Babb, was sure that the white boy would stay with them, but, Dot said, "in this they were in great error, as my decision was instant and unalterable to return as quickly as possible to my father and kindred." Asa Havey still had to bargain for two weeks before Horseback sold him for several horses, saddles, bridles, blankets, and other gifts. Asa Havey took him to Fort Arbuckle. John Babb embraced him, saying, "This is my long lost darling boy."[12]

Some researchers have claimed that Dot and Bianca loved being with their Indian families, but bottom line, when they had the chance to go home, they had no doubts. The ransoms were paid against the wishes of Gen. William T. Sherman, who saw the payments as incentives. Nevertheless, grieving families would often do anything they could to get their children back. The army knew it and the Indians knew it. There would be many more captives taken.[13]

When word of the raid reached Captain Cram in Jacksboro, he detailed Lt. William A. Rafferty with 25 men of Company I, 6th Cavalry, plus the newly arrived Company A, to punish the Indians. Rafferty went north to the Little Wichita hoping to intercept the raiders, but with no trail or idea where they might be, the scout was a failure. The U.S. Cavalry was back, but it wouldn't make any difference.[14]

September's full moon fell on the 24th, and it should have been no surprise that marauders were in Texas—they were there almost every day of the month. On September 16, Kickapoos were in Medina County. Jacob Bendele (36) had emigrated from France to Texas in 1847. He farmed and ran a store near San Francisco Perez Creek about seven miles west of Castroville. Jacob and his son George (11) were returning with a wagon load of dry goods they had bought in San Antonio. A few miles west of Castroville, about eight Lipans attacked them. Jacob saw them waving a bloody shirt taken from a man they had just killed a few miles to the north.

Jacob and George knew what they were after, and quickly abandoned the wagon and fled. Jacob said the warriors got within 15 steps of him "and they shot me." He had a pistol and fired as he ran. George outdistanced him: "I got away as fast as I could..." he said, "because they would have killed me." The Lipans took the two horses, harnesses, bridles, rope, and some of the dry goods, to the tune of $945. Another man had a close encounter with the Lipans about the same time; he made it to town to give warning, plus show off the bullet hole through his hat attesting to his close call. About five townsfolk mounted up and gave chase, passing the Bendeles as they came in. They caught the Lipans less than two miles from the wagon as they broke into the boxes and sacks. The two parties exchanged some shots, but the whites never pressed the fight and the Lipans rode off to the northeast.[15]

On September 20, raiders were in Palo Pinto County, where John A. Eubank had moved some of his horses only two months after they had killed his son, Thomas. This time they got three horses worth $225.[16]

Other raiders crossed from Indian Territory in the vicinity of Red River Station and moved to Head of Elm in eastern Montague County. Since the Box raid, a number of settlers had forted up there, and some cowboys passing through at the time were also there when the raiders arrived. There was a brief skirmish, but the Indians would not assault a position so well-defended. They moved down the Brushy Elm and about four miles east in Cooke County they found and killed James Harris, who was out alone hunting stray horses about two miles south of his cabin. A Confederate veteran, Harris was buried in a private cemetery just outside Head of Elm.

The Indians went down the Brushy Elm to its mouth where they attacked the Newton Gilbert and James Coursey families while they moved to Gainesville for safety. The families ran to an abandoned homestead and took a defensive stance. The Indians detoured and headed southwest toward Forestburg in Montague County. About seven miles northwest of town they ran into Andrew Powers and Winfield Williams. Williams was riding a fast horse and escaped, but Powers, on a slow mule, was caught and killed.

The raiders crossed Clear Creek where another party that had stolen several hundred horses in Denton County joined them. The large band, now with more than 60 warriors, headed northwest. As they had swept through the area stealing horses and killing, settlers and cowboys from several locations were tracking them, and in the Forestburg area, about 20 men had gathered, including Charlie Grant, Joseph Field, and Alec Frasier. They tracked the raiders where they had passed just east of Montague. The first posse met up with a second, with Joe Bryant, John McFarland, John Hall, J. M. Grayson and about 20 others. As they rode northwest into Clay County, another posse from Red River Station had picked up the trail ahead of them. Knowing there were other posses coming, they left a note in a forked stick on the trail: "Come on, boys; they have passed this way."

The Red River Station posse found the Indians first, on the banks of the Wichita River. About 25 whites battled the 60 warriors from the tall grass and timber along the banks. It was like a shooting gallery as adversaries would duck down, pop up and shoot, and duck down to crawl to a new location. The fight lasted until nightfall. No white casualties were reported and they thought they had killed several Indians, so as the sun set and they were low on ammunition, they re-crossed the Wichita and retreated. Back on the trail they left another note: "Turn back, boys; they have given us a warm reception." When the other posses rode up and read the message they followed the advice.[17]

After repulsing the whites, the raiders had a more leisurely time to round up all the cattle they wanted between the Little Wichita and Wichita Rivers. On September 29, they took about 1,000 head from Allen H. Friend, valued at $15,357. Friend, his brother, John Friend, and Caswell Carter rode over from Red River Station to look after the stock north of the Little Wichita. The Indians came out of the south and boldly moved the cattle north, right in front of the whites, who watched helplessly. "They were out of our sight in about fifteen minutes," Allen Friend said.

They waited until it was clear, and then rode east where they saw more Indians driving cattle to Red River from Joe Carter's and Edwin Morris' ranches. Morris had brought in his herd in April, selecting a site at the mouth of the Little Wichita for a ranch. Soon after, he wondered if that had been a good idea. Morris and other ranchers at first hired herders to keep track of the cattle, but after a few months it was hard to find any who would work. "The Indians got so bad," Morris said, "the line riders had to move out, for the Indians were scalping and killing all around there, and the line riders were afraid to stay there."

With no one to guard the stock, Morris lost about 1,000 cattle. During one of the raids, two cowboys named White and Purcell were killed. One of Morris's men, Arrington Gray, said that was the last straw. He quit. When asked why, he answered, "Well, the Indians got too hot for me.... I thought too much of my topknot."

About the last day of September the Indians also took 1,545 head, valued at $19,025, off the Beaver Creek range on the Clay-Montague line, from Lemuel J. Edwards. This time it was Edwin Morris who saw them. He estimated there were 500 or more Comanches involved. Morris had actually gathered 12 cowboys with him, which he thought would be enough. The great number of Indians was shocking. "They did not have enough men to resist them," Morris said. He and his men powerlessly watched the Indians drive them across the Red. Nevertheless, as the Indians left, the cowboys felt compelled to follow. Morris knew they were Comanches and Kiowas from the way they dressed and the abandoned horses: "The Comanches split their horses' ears and the Kiowas brand with three marks across the thigh." Morris believed that the last raids in September removed 25,000 cattle from Clay and Montague counties.[18]

The October 6, 1866 edition of the *Dallas Herald* printed a letter from J. G. Stevens, who had recently been in north Texas and reported on the devastation. "There is not to be seen, at this time," he said, "one single cow located on the Wichita prairies, north of Belknap and Jacksboro, where twelve months since, you could see thousands of them in one day's ride. They are all gone. The Indians have driven them off."

Chapter 42 notes

1 Richter, *Army in Texas During Reconstruction*, 54-55.
2 Winfrey and Day, *Texas Indian Papers, IV*, 102-03, 107.
3 Tip Mooney, Depredation Claim #9650.
4 Depredation Claims: Woodford Bennett #1545; Levi Bennett #3525; Mabel Gilbert #5695; Frank S. Brown #6163; William B. Martin #5718.
5 Depredation Claims: Nancy Jefferson #1550; Hiram Williams #6174; Winfrey and Day, *Texas Indian Papers, IV*, 202.
6 Howell, *James Throckmorton*, 123.
7 Winfrey and Day, *Texas Indian Papers, IV*, 109, 115; Cates, *Wise County*, 175; "Capt. Enoch Madison Jones," http://www.earljones.net/pafn18.html; *Dallas Herald*, October 6, 1866. Various sources report this raid occurring on September 12, 13, and 14.
8 Cates, *Wise County*, 175-76; Babb, *Bosom of the Comanches*, 20-24; White, "White Women Captives," 328; Gelo and Zesch, "Holiday," 49-50; Bianca Babb, untitled manuscript.
9 Babb, *Bosom of the Comanches*, 24; Winfrey and Day, *Texas Indian Papers, IV*, 97-99. Cates, *Wise County*, 176; Hernando C. Babb, Depredation Claim #4606. Hernando Babb asked for $10,000 for the death of his mother, but the government did not pay for deaths, only property.
10 White, "White Women Captives," 329; Winfrey and Day, *Texas Indian Papers, IV*, 128-29; Babb, *Bosom of the Comanches*, 36-38.
11 White, "White Women Captives," 330; Gelo and Zesch, "Holiday," 44, 65-66.
12 Babb, *Bosom of the Comanches*, 56-60.
13 Bianca Babb Bell died in Denton, Texas, on April 13, 1950, the last of Texas' Indian captives.
14 Hamilton, *Sentinel of the Southern Plains*, 18.
15 Jacob Bendele, Depredation Claim #3347.
16 Hesekiah B. Eubank, Depredation Claim #5901.
17 McConnell, *West Texas Frontier*, 559; Potter, *Montague County*, 27-28.
18 Depredation Claims: Allen H. Friend #6172; Edwin T. Morris #5730; Lemuel J. Edwards #3542.

43 "Someone has killed a maverick here."

On September 25, 1866, Governor Throckmorton wrote to the District of Texas commander, then in a transition from General Wright to Gen. George W. Getty, and asked for a post to be built at the mouth of the Wichita River. Figuring his pleas would be ignored, Throckmorton then telegraphed details of the attacks to President Johnson. General Sheridan was not pleased with Throckmorton's by-passing him, but continued complaints led him to shift the 4th Cavalry from San Antonio to Camp Verde and Fort Martin Scott near Fredericksburg. Throckmorton said the main problem at that time was in the north, but Sheridan still maintained that the governor was exaggerating. General Grant, in command of the army, finally told Sheridan to move troops to the frontier. In addition, the recently recruited black 9th Cavalry was coming, and Sheridan hoped to use it on the frontier, one reason being that there would be less friction with white civilians in more populated areas.

On September 29, Throckmorton asked for authorization to raise 1,000 men for frontier defense, but Sheridan would not approve it. Former officer and ranger, Buck Barry, put it diplomatically, stating that "armed forces of ex-Confederates were frowned upon by the Congress...." General Grant believed that there were enough regulars in Texas to handle the job. In late October, General Heintzelman replaced Getty as Fifth District commander and Throckmorton started again. He told Heintzelman that he would not raise state troops if the army would send more troops west immediately. An angry Sheridan absolutely refused. While they argued, the raids continued.[1]

On October 1, Indians were in Comanche County at Andrew Miller's ranch about 20 miles southeast of the town of Comanche. They took 11 horses worth $1,350 that Miller had staked in his front yard. Miller ran out to the gate to find nine Comanches, and when they shot at him, he ran back to the house. He and neighbor Thomas N. Shockley rode after the raiders and found one of his mares killed with arrows. Farther down on Cowhouse Creek the Indians chased, but could not catch, cowboys Jack Parker and John Albin.[2]

Lipans were causing havoc in the south. They stole horses from William J. Slaughter, Robert B. Witter, and a Mr. Waugh in La Salle County and headed northwest, up Cibolo Creek through Frio and Zavala counties. Local ranchers trailed them but lost them in the hills of the Edwards Plateau.

The Lipans went up the Sabinal River and about three miles east of present Utopia in northeast Medina County they came upon the cabin of Robert H. Kincheloe. Living in a hut 100 yards away was F. M. Bolin (Bowlin), his wife, Cynthia (32), and two daughters. Kincheloe and Bolin had gone to work threshing wheat at James Davenport's, and the women and children were all at Kincheloe's with a hired Mexican sheepherder. On the night of October 10, three Lipans came to the house. Four of the family dogs kept them away, and they continued to bark all night, keeping everyone on edge.

In the morning the Indians came back, riding stolen horses from Wilson O'Bryant and Minerva Binnion, and roped a large black horse tied near the house. Sarah Kincheloe looked to the hired man for help, but he had disappeared. When no one came out to challenge them and the dogs proved to be more bark than bite, the Lipans boldly approached the cabin and tried to get inside. Sarah had her husband's seven-shot Spencer and fired through the large cracks between the log walls, but when the repeater was empty she did not know how to reload. The Indians returned fire through the cracks, hitting Sarah with several arrows. She handed the gun to Cynthia Bolin, who tried to bluff the Indians with it, but to no avail.

They burst in both doors, and seeing Bolin with the gun, blasted her with bullets and arrows. They lanced Sarah several more times and left her for dead on the dirt floor. Sarah, semi-conscious, watched them plunder the cabin. Somehow during the fracas, Jo Ellen Bolin (16) escaped, jumped from a bluff, and hid in the brush. Georgeann Bolin (14) crawled under the bed with the other children, John, Charles, Buddy, and Eliza Kincheloe. It seems impossible that the Lipans did not notice the children under the bed, or perhaps they were too busy stealing, but they soon left and the children all got away and ran to Snow's cabin on the Sabinal two miles away.

After some of his horses were stolen, Wilson O'Bryant rode to Kincheloe's and found two women on the floor covered in blood. He raced back to John C. Ware's, who was Cynthia Bolin's brother, and breathlessly announced that both were dead. There was a preacher at Ware's that day, and several neighbors were there to hear him. A number of them got their horses and rode back to Kincheloe's, and, incredibly, they found Sarah still alive; witnesses said she had from 13 to 16 stab or arrow wounds. While some doctored Sarah, others followed the trail to a hilltop where the Indians had stopped and sorted out the plunder, leaving behind a dress and some other articles. By the footprints it looked like there were half a dozen Indians. The trail went off in the direction of Bandera.[3]

David Cryer and a Mr. Foster, who lived along Hondo Creek, went to Bandera in a two-horse wagon to purchase supplies. They had traversed the narrow Tarpley Pass and were nearly home, when below Sugar Loaf Mountain between Thomas and Commissioners Creeks, the Lipans jumped them. Foster saw them as they popped up out of the brush only 30 feet away and he whipped the horses into a run, but not fast enough to prevent one arrow slamming into the small of Cryer's back. He arched backward and fell into the wagon bed. Foster whipped the horses while trying to pick up a gun and shoot at the pursuers. On the wild run, a wheel hit a rock and bounced the bed off its mooring and onto a wheel, dragging the vehicle to a stop. Foster sprang out and aimed his gun back down the road, but the Indians had already given up. He shoved the bed back into position and hurried the last two miles home. O. B. Miles, who had been a hospital steward, extracted the arrow only with great exertion. He bandaged Cryer up, but he had lost too much blood and died three days later.[4]

The Lipans were still out to kill. From the Hondo they went north to the Medina River and hunted along the road between Medina and Bandera. On October 12, Thomas B. Click left Bandera to ride to Medina to see a man named Huffman, who was moving out of the area. Click was unarmed and riding a mule borrowed from Andy Mansfield. Three miles outside of Bandera the Indians surprised him. Click tried to run the 300 yards to the Medina River, but a warrior cut him off and he turned back to the road, only to be caught by the others and lanced to death. They dragged him into the brush and stripped him of his fine buckskin breeches. The next morning, Marcellus C. Click, Tom's brother, and David A. Weaver were riding to Medina and passed the ambush site.

"Someone has killed a maverick here," Click said, seeing the dried blood in the road. Just then he noticed the shiny blade of a small butcher knife. He examined it and immediately knew it was his brother's. A short distance away they found the body in the bushes. Click was buried in Bandera. The Lipans got his mule and cleared out of the county.[5]

Early in October, Comanches were in Hamilton County where they stole six horses from Thomas Malone, worth $450. Raiding south along Cowhouse Creek they moved north into Coryell County and about October 15, they cleaned out J. M. Lanham, taking 92 horses valued at $5,475. The Indians were likely very pleased with their haul and might have become too complacent as they pulled out to the northwest.[6]

Heading south were three men and two wagons going for winter supplies from Comanche to San Saba. Larkin Stone, Frank Brown, and another driver, stopped at a water hole about 16 miles south of Comanche to give their mules a rest. As they ate lunch, John Roach, an acquaintance from Comanche, rode up to them as he was heading to Comanche from San Saba. The four passed the news when suddenly about 30 Comanches driving their stolen horses charged in, shooting and whooping. The whites did not panic, but took careful aim and blasted the leading warriors, knocking three of them from their horses. The Indians came up close and the whites shot another one, but before they broke, they wounded Brown in the face and hit Roach three times.

With the Indians pulling back, the whites did not plan to try their luck again; they all got on horses or mules and it was every man for himself. When they ran, the Indians chased. They all got away but Roach. On a slower mule, they soon caught up, shot the animal, and filled Roach with arrows.

The three others made it to James Cunningham's place, about four miles away. Cunningham, an ex-officer in the Texas State Troops, and his son, David, who had both survived the Battle of Dove Creek, were ready for a fight. The ex-lieutenant quickly summoned his hired men and called out the neighbors. They went back to the scene and found Roach still alive, the wagons destroyed, and the stock gone.

The trail went northwest into Brown County. Within three miles they found a fresh grave and dug it up, finding the body of one of the warriors. They took his leather shield with a bullet hole through the center of it. By now, nearly 40 settlers and cowboys had gathered and hit the trail with renewed vigor. Trying to anticipate the Indians' path, they split up, with James Cunningham taking half the posse and Dave Cunningham the other. Riding through the night, Dave Cunningham's company came by Salt Mountain and he sent out two scouts to see if the Indians might be in a pass in the hills ahead. The scouts found 25 Indians camped with about 200 horses along what might have been Gap Creek northeast of present Brownwood.

Cunningham moved his men in to be ready to attack at daybreak, and with the first rays of the sun they charged in yelling and shooting. Four or five Indians were killed within the first few minutes and then a confused fight began among the trees and rocks for another hour. Larkin Stone took a scalp, and William Cunningham, another of James' sons, got two. Freeman Clark (18) rode up to a fleeing warrior and took aim, but the cap snapped and the gun failed to fire. The warrior turned and point blank shot Clark in the chest. Others rushed up and dispatched the warrior. The Indians finally got away, but the Texans didn't pursue. They had killed seven and wounded several more, and left with one of their own dead, and one wounded. James Cunningham's company heard the shooting and rode up just as it was over. The Cedar Gap fight was locally thought to be one of the best managed fights on the frontier. Certainly it was one of the few contests the settlers won.[7]

Another raid came through the central Hill Country in mid-October. Marauders struck William Wood in San Saba County on October 10, stealing seven horses worth $725. A day or two later they were in Llano County where they hit William R. Jackson's ranch, destroying buildings, stealing property and running off stock, for a whopping $17,750 in damages. On October 15, the raiders were in Blanco County. They attacked Crocket Harbert's ranch located at what is now Johnson City, chasing herder Andrew Maddox to the ranch house. The defenders grabbed weapons and took positions at the windows, but the Indians just ran off the stock and headed north.

They came to Alexander Roberts' ranch three miles south of Round Mountain. William Roberts (21) saw them coming and told his father, brother, and neighbor, Cicero R. Perry. The men made a stand near a fence line where their horses were tied. When the Indians drew near they fired, believing they had seriously wounded one warrior. The raiders fell back and took some other stock farther from the house and not so well guarded. Later in the day the whites tracked them north to Round Mountain, finding five or six dead horses needlessly slaughtered, perhaps in retaliation for the wounding of one of the Indians. Roberts lost 17 horses, colts, and mares worth $815.[8]

The raid, culminating in Blanco County, was like a slap in the face to the army, who had ten infantry companies in Austin and ten companies of the 4th Cavalry shifting to Fort Mason. The raiders had ridden between them while driving stolen stock, went within 35 miles of Austin, and rode back out again while the army stood by unaware and General Sheridan dismissed reports of raids as nonsense.

In the northern counties it was business as usual. George Whittmore had lost stock in a June raid near Elm Creek, and on October 11, nearly the same thing happened. About 40 or 50 Kiowas or Comanches rode into the valley while Whittmore and a few cowboys watched helplessly. They drove off 130 cattle and ten horses, valued at $3,350. The next day, with a few more men, Whittmore trailed after the thieves for 30 miles, but found nothing but dead cattle for their efforts.

Over in Montague County, Kendall Lofton was on his way to Spanish Fort on Red River. About five miles from his destination, Indians jumped him. He was hit a few times but rode to Red Branch on Farmers Creek where he found a little cave to hole up in. Lofton held the Indians back for a time, but soon succumbed to his wounds. Locals found and buried him where he died.

Comanches were in Parker County in mid-October. They had come south in the Western Cross Timbers like they did so often, passing a gap in the hills near the Brisco farm that they had devastated in June. On the Campbell Prairie five miles north of Weatherford they visited John A. Long's farm while the family was out making sorghum molasses. The Indians rode in shooting and Long ran with his family into the house. The Indians got his horses and rode two miles south to John Mitchell's where they got seven of his horses.

The raiders had come close to Weatherford, and now turned back north. About 12 miles north of town they came across John Leeper (Leaper) (70) in his field throwing corn in a wagon. He saw the Indians coming and ran towards the house but they easily caught him. They shot him twice and he fell so close to the cabin that those inside could hear him calling, "O don't shoot me anymore." A warrior dispatched him with a bullet in the head.

The next day, John Mitchell, John Long, Benjamin F. Hemphill, and a few others rode north. They found a split-eared Comanche pony and one with three marks on its hip—a Kiowa pony. Mitchell found several of his horses lanced or shot with arrows. They followed the trail beyond Leeper's cabin to Slipdown Mountain, southwest of present Poolville, went to Bill Stowe's place, and then to Thomas Sullivan's.[9]

Thomas Sullivan and Upton O. Blackwell had cabins close together southeast of Slipdown Mountain. That morning, Margaret Sullivan went to visit a sick friend, and she and her sister, Charlotte Blackwell, cautioned their children to be on guard for Indians.

The four boys were in the garden picking peas where they were surprised by five Comanches who had been spying on them from the mountain. Robert Harvey Sullivan (13) grabbed his brother's hand, Thomas Jefferson Sullivan (6), while their cousins, Joe Blackwell (10) and John Charles Fremont Blackwell (7), also took off running. As the Indians gained on the boys, the older Robert and Joe realized that none of them would escape if they dragged their little brothers behind. They made a decision that haunted them the rest of their lives. They let Fremont and Tommy go and ran for their lives. An arrow hit Robert in the shoulder and a rifle ball clipped Joe's hip, but they dove safely into a cane thicket. When they peered out they saw the Comanches taking Fremont and Tommy up on their horses.[10]

The two cousins stayed in the cane until they heard their fathers calling. Back at the house, the fathers quickly dressed their wounds and were organizing a rescue party when Long, Mitchell, Hemphill, and James S. Stinnett rode up. The homesteaders found the trail and discovered a small cowbell that was Tommy's favorite toy. About 20 miles north of Weatherford, the horses shied at the smell of blood. There was little Tommy's body, "bruised and mangled almost beyond recognition." Crows had even pecked out his eyes. He was killed because he would not stop crying. They buried him right there and took his clothes home. Most of the searchers were so sickened by the sight that they could not continue the pursuit. The remaining few continued on the trail all the way to Red River before calling it quits.[11]

The Comanches took Fremont to the Big Bend of the Arkansas River in Kansas. After a rough breaking-in period, he learned the Comanche language, how to shoot a bow and arrow, and became thoroughly "Indianized." In the spring of 1867, trader Charles Whitaker saw him and notified authorities. Word got to Agent Leavenworth and he arranged for his release. On June 9, 1867, Parker County Judge A. J. Hunter learned of Fremont's rescue and wrote, "The Blackwell child has bin bought at Fort Dodge Kansas but not yet got home I have not bin in formed as to what it cost." Fremont could not remember his name, but he did tell Whitaker that his father's name was Upton and he lived near Weatherford, Texas. Whitaker inquired in Parker

County and eventually Mr. Blackwell met the boy when he was sent to his grandmother's in Collin County. Fremont was sick with scurvy, but a diet of vegetables soon cured him. Not so easy to remedy was his habit of playing "Indian" and shooting his brothers and sisters with blunt-tipped arrows until they were "blue all over."[12]

Chapter 43 notes

1 Greer, ed., *Buck Barry*, 203; Richter, *Army in Texas During Reconstruction*, 66-67, 69-70.

2 Andrew Miller, Depredation Claim #5013.

3 McConnell, *West Texas Frontier*, 560; Robert H. Kincheloe, Depredation Claim # 2764.

4 Sowell, *Early Settlers*, 508-09; Hunter, *Bandera County*, 134-35.

5 Sowell, *Early Settlers*, 510; Hunter, *Bandera County*, 175; Winfrey and Day, *Texas Indian Papers, IV*, 228.

6 Depredation Claims: Thomas Malone #5681; J. M. Lanham #647.

7 Wilbarger, *Indian Depredations*, 493-98.

8 Depredation Claims: William R. Wood #7052; William R. Jackson #1270; Alexander Roberts #3929.

9 Depredation Claims: George Whittmore #349; John R. Mitchell (Benjamin F. Hemphill) #5682; Grace and Jones, *History of Parker County*, 102-03; McConnell, *West Texas Frontier*, http://www.forttours.com/pages/leaper.asp. Several dates are given for the Leeper killing.

10 Marshall, *A Cry Unhead*, 141-42; Grace and Jones, *History of Parker County*, 100.

11 Marshall, *A Cry Unhead*, 142-43; John R. Mitchell (Benjamin F. Hemphill), Depredation Claim #5682. Marshall says that Tommy's body was found 20 miles south of Weatherford, but the pursuers cited in Mitchell's claim said they were riding north.

12 Marshall, *A Cry Unheard*, 143-45, 147; Winfrey and Day, *Texas Indian Papers, IV*, 223.

44 "The Indian can be taught that Texas is part of the U.S."

By mid-October, Sheridan, tired of the complaints, authorized the entire 4th and 6th Cavalry, nearly 2,000 men, to be moved to the frontier, but he still did not believe all the reports of depredations. He ordered Maj. George A. Forsythe to travel to the northern frontier and investigate. In early November, Forsythe hadn't even reached Waco when, with no evidence, he wrote, "I am convinced that many of the people who are moving in from the frontier are doing it to better their economic condition, and not from any fear they may have of Indians." Forsythe went to Weatherford and made more inquiries. Captain Cram of the 6th Cavalry said the settlers were very afraid and rarely ventured out to report attacks. He said with too few men, poor horses, and late reports of raids, he could never catch raiders who were long gone before he could respond. Forsythe told Sheridan that he found a few instances of depredations and the newspapers highly exaggerated them. Besides, the primary goal of the Indians seemed to be stealing stock, not killing whites. Forsythe did change his mind about the fear factor, however. It was not that there were so many raids, he wrote, but that the frontier people were not the stout, brave settlers of legend, rather, they had let themselves be swept up in a general fear. In modern terms it would likely be called mass hysteria.[1]

As Forsythe investigated, the Indians raided and killed. On November 1, Comanches attacked Peter B. Emory's ranch in Concho County, stealing 40 saddle horses worth $3,000.

On November 3, they were back in Wise and Parker counties, seemingly drawn to the settlements at Springtown, Opal, and Terrapin Neck. John B. Thomas of Opal was threshing wheat when he saw Indians pull down his fence and go after his horses. The men working there, including Brice Mann, John and Bill Mathews, Jack and Andy Gore, and John Thomas and his son, Soney, got to their horses, grabbed guns, and went after the Indians.

The raiders had already driven the stock through the gap in the fence and were chasing them, but the horses were making straight to Thomas' house, about three-quarters of a mile away. The pursuing whites were coming from behind, but the Indians broke off their horse chase and circled behind the whites. Within a few minutes the pursuing whites could see no Indians and they ran up on old John Montgomery (75), who was riding to Thomas' to see the threshing. Just then the Indians charged them from behind. The others urged Montgomery to put spurs to his horse, but the old man, either oblivious or unconcerned, refused to hurry. While the others sped away, the Indians easily caught Montgomery and shot him through the back. His horse carried him to the house where he fell off dead.[2]

About this time, Indians, perhaps of the same party, attacked Joshua King's place at Prairie Point for the second time, getting 12 horses worth $955. As usual, Sang Kearby joined the posse, which included Moses Fallowill, who brought news of more raiding up the West Fork Trinity. They rode west, past present Boyd, to Mr. Lolly's place on present Lola Creek. They saw three Indians on a hilltop and pursued them. The Indians ran, and the posse soon came upon the body of an unknown youth, about 17 years-old, three-quarters of a mile from Lolly's. They continued west to the junction of the Cottonwood and Salt Creek and met about 20 warriors. "We had a little fight with them," Kearby said, "and about 40 or 50 shots were fired on each side. Then we ran down in a little mott of timber and fired a few shots at them down there. Then the Indians made a circle and drove the horses off." The posse recovered a few head, but none of King's.[3]

In late November, raiders revisited W. C. Franklin in Pleasant Valley in Burnet County, stealing three of his horses, along with stock from a rancher named Davis. They also hit Albert Gieseke's place and stole a few horses and mules worth $320. Down in Uvalde, Lipans were back stealing horses from Robert H. Kincheloe, although he only had a couple left to take. Joel D. Fenley was severely wounded and lost two big gray horses during the raid, and John C. Ware lost two horses stolen right from in front of his cabin.[4]

On November 25, Indians were in Young County right at Fort Belknap. Christopher C. Mills lived at the post, which was not then occupied by the army, but was one of the civilian forts that had sprung up all over the frontier. Mills hobbled his five horses at the edge of a thicket near his cabin on the evening on November 25. Thornton Hamby, the hero of the Elm Creek raid, had stayed overnight with Mills. When the two went out to check the horses in the morning they were gone. There was a fire circle nearby where Indians had leisurely stopped, killed a calf, cooked a meal, ate, stole his horses, and rode away. Neither the army nor the armed civilians were deterrents.[5]

When Governor Throckmorton learned of Forsythe's report, he was very dissatisfied and he wrote to all county judges for a complete account of all depredations in their districts. On November 6, he wrote to Col. James Oakes, commander of the 6th Cavalry, and asked why the troops had not all gone to the frontier. Actually, that same day Sheridan had ordered General Heintzelman to send all of the 4th and 6th Cavalry out to the frontier posts as well as shift the 2nd Battalion, 17th Infantry, to Austin.

The public still bombarded the governor with complaints, and Throckmorton had authorized the organization, arming, and equipping of a new regiment of citizens despite orders to the contrary. On November 20, ex-captain in the Frontier Regiment, John T. Rowland, wrote to the governor from Cooke County, saying that on November 18 about 20 Indians came in and took "all the horses in that section of the country," and he was "listening to hear of some cruel act every day...." He told Throckmorton that he could put 65 men in the field at any time if only he could get subsistence and horses for them. "Pleas instruct me what to do at the earliest date possably," Rowland wrote.

Throckmorton wanted to do something but he was hamstrung. On November 21, he wrote to Buck Barry, offering him a commission as major, but with a caveat. Since Sheridan approved moving troops to the borders, Barry should incur no expenses to be charged to the state, yet, Throckmorton said, "I would be gratified if your company was organized in order that its services might be made available in any sudden emergency, arising from Indian invasion or depredation." He believed his state troops could help the army, "Our own people being much better qualified to follow trails, etc."

The next day, Throckmorton wrote a private letter to Barry, stating, "I will say that if the Indians continue to depredate and the government does not effectually stop them, in the Spring I contemplate a campaign even if it has to be done secretly." Throckmorton also mentioned wanting the government to send commissioners to the tribes to sign a new peace treaty "so that the Indians can be taught to know that Texas is a part of the U. S. If this treaty can be got up we may succeed in getting back our children and women who are prisoners."[6]

The idea that the Indians believed Texas was not part of the U.S. held sway with a number of government officials. Commissioner Cooley in his annual report for 1866 wrote that the majority of Kiowas and Comanches "had been peaceably disposed toward the whites." On the other hand, he wrote that some bands appeared to be making raids into Texas. "It is true... that in the case of some of these raids, they have been induced...by a dim notion that they were really performing a friendly act for the government by attacks upon its enemies. Their agent has labored...to remove this idea from the minds of the tribe...." Cooley, however, cited the Box incident as proof that Indians who actually signed a non-aggression treaty with the whites had the temerity to kill, take captives, and then demand ransoms. His faith in Indian promises was beginning to crumble.

Cooley needed to take an eyewitness trip to the Texas frontier, but then again, the Central Agency superintendent never visited it either. Thomas Murphy wrote to Cooley that he called on most of his charges, but not the Kiowas or Comanches, "which I failed to visit, owing to the remoteness to this office...." Somehow he still concluded that everyone was behaving splendidly, with the exception of some Kiowas, "who have made a raid into Texas, stealing horses and capturing some women and children."[7]

The Bureau probably knew ten percent of what happened, but fall was here and once again the raiding slackened as the various bands, well-stocked with stolen cattle and horses, began to settle in for the winter. There were still those warriors, however, who could not resist the war path and the full moon. Kiowas or Comanches had crossed Red River and ridden down through the Western Cross Timbers. Near Big Sandy Creek near the Wise-Montague line they attacked a settlement which consisted of Archie McDonald, James Green, Chesley Marlett, C. B. Ball, and Moses Ball, whose son, James, and nephew, Willie, had been captured in Wise County the previous year.

The Indians struck two different families this time. On Sunday, December 23, Daniel B. Green and William Bailey, both about 18 years old, went out to hunt a strayed pony. Less than a mile from Green's cabin, 11 Indians suddenly appeared. The boys were on foot and both ran toward the bed of Sandy Creek. They wounded Bailey before he got to the creek and he stumbled along for about 50 yards before they caught him. They threw him to the ground and played with him for awhile, clubbing and cutting him. A warrior thrust a lance completely through his arm. He was found later, dead and scalped, with 19 wounds. Green made it to the creek, but to no avail. He splashed through the water and just reached the south bank when three arrows hit him, one in the back, and two more in the breast as he spun around. He was later found with his head in the creek, pockets turned inside out, but he was not scalped.

Archie McDonald passed through the area later in the day and found a small looking glass, red paint, and some squirrel skins, and knew that the Indians were in. He hurried to C. B. Ball's and reported. Ball and Marlett were sure the boys had been overtaken and they hurried to where McDonald had found the items. Sure enough, after a short search they found the bodies, and then realized that the Indians might still be in the woods watching them that moment. It was getting dark and they hurried home. The next morning, a larger party went out to bring the boys back home to the heartbroken parents. Bailey and Green were both put in a makeshift coffin made out of spare planks and wagon beds. They were buried together in the Selma Graveyard a few miles from Bowie in Montague County.[8]

It was a sad Christmas Eve for the Bailey and Green families, as it was for the Willis family in Hamilton County. William Willis lived about 20 miles southwest of Hamilton down near the county line. He planned to attend the Christmas dance and began his journey on an old mule. B. F. Gholson offered to lend him a fast horse for his own safety, but Willis turned him down. As could be expected, about one dozen Indians surprised him just two miles south of Hamilton. Willis ran his mule as fast as it could go, but the animal gave out a mile short of town. Willis got off and ran, reaching a pair of giant old oak trees, since celebrated as the Twin Oaks. He had a rifle and tried to defend himself, but the warriors put one arrow deep into his back. Willis managed to shoot a few times, and the warriors, so close to town, decided not to continue the attack.

Judge James M. Rice lived close by and his children were playing in the yard watching the affair. They ran for help, and soon, people arrived to help the wounded Willis to W. S. Walker's house. The arrow was removed, but Willis did not recover. He died three weeks later.[9]

The late-December raids notwithstanding, perhaps Throckmorton and the U.S. Army looked to 1867 with a bit of hope. With nearly 2,000 regular cavalrymen on duty, the frontier was protected better than ever.

Chapter 44 notes

1 Richter, *Army in Texas During Reconstruction*, 70-71.

2 Peter B. Emory, Depredation Claim #4492; Cates, *Wise County*, 205-06

3 Joshua G. King, Depredation Claim #2291.

4 Depredation Claims: W. C. Franklin #5726; Albert Gieseke #429; Robert H. Kincheloe #2764.

5 Christopher C. Mills, Depredation Claim #5679.

6 Howell, *James Throckmorton*, 126-27; Winfrey and Day, *Texas Indian Papers, IV*, 126-27; Greer, ed., *Buck Barry*, 205-06.

7 *Commissioner of Indian Affairs 1866*, 3, 54, 244, 246.

8 Potter, *Montague County*, 30-32; McConnell, *West Texas Frontier*, 561.

9 McConnell, *West Texas Frontier*, 544; "Twin Oaks," http://www.mygeoinfo.com/2010/03/12/twin-oaks/.

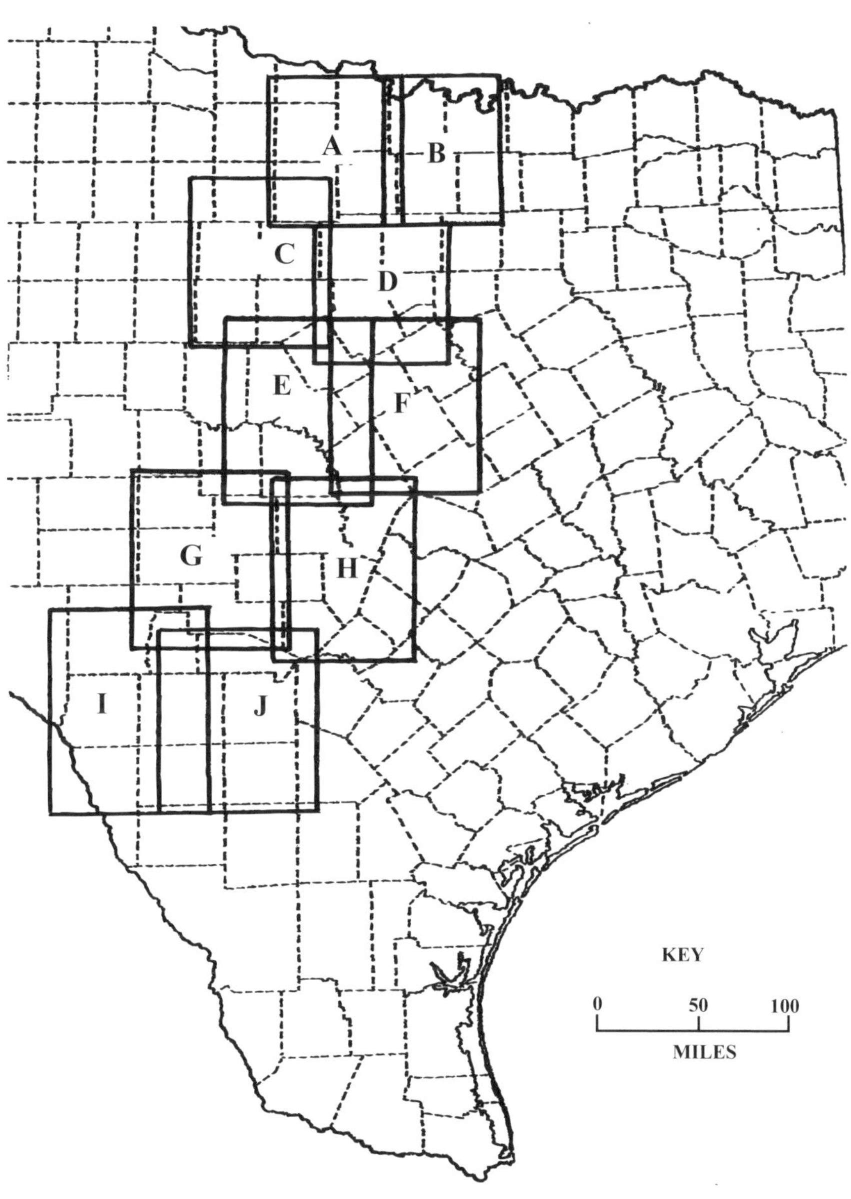
A
B
C
D
E
F
G
H
I
J
KEY
0
50
100
MILES

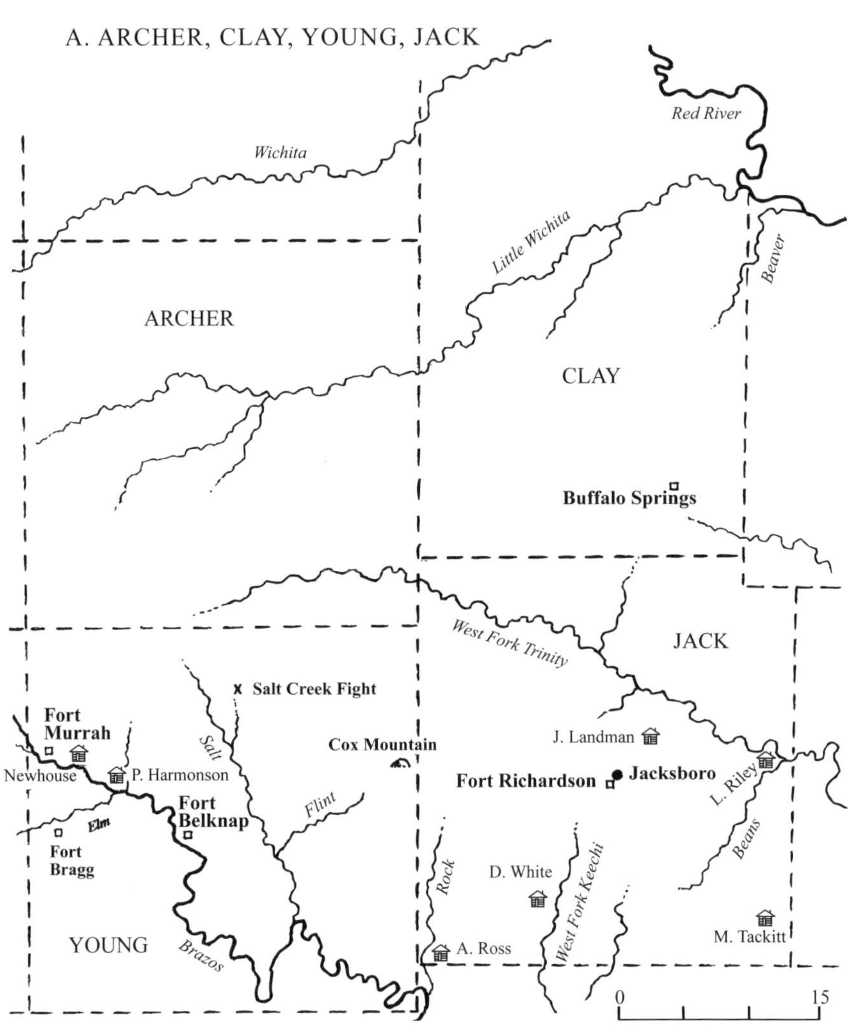
A. ARCHER, CLAY, YOUNG, JACK
Wichita
Red River
Little Wichita
Beaver
ARCHER
CLAY
Buffalo Springs
West Fork Trinity
JACK
Salt Creek Fight
Fort Murrah
Salt
Cox Mountain
J. Landman
. Newhouse
P. Harmonson
Fort Richardson
Jacksboro
L. Riley
Fort Belknap
Flint
Elm
Fort Bragg
Beans
Rock
D. White
West Fork Keechi
YOUNG
Brazos
A. Ross
M. Tackitt
0
15

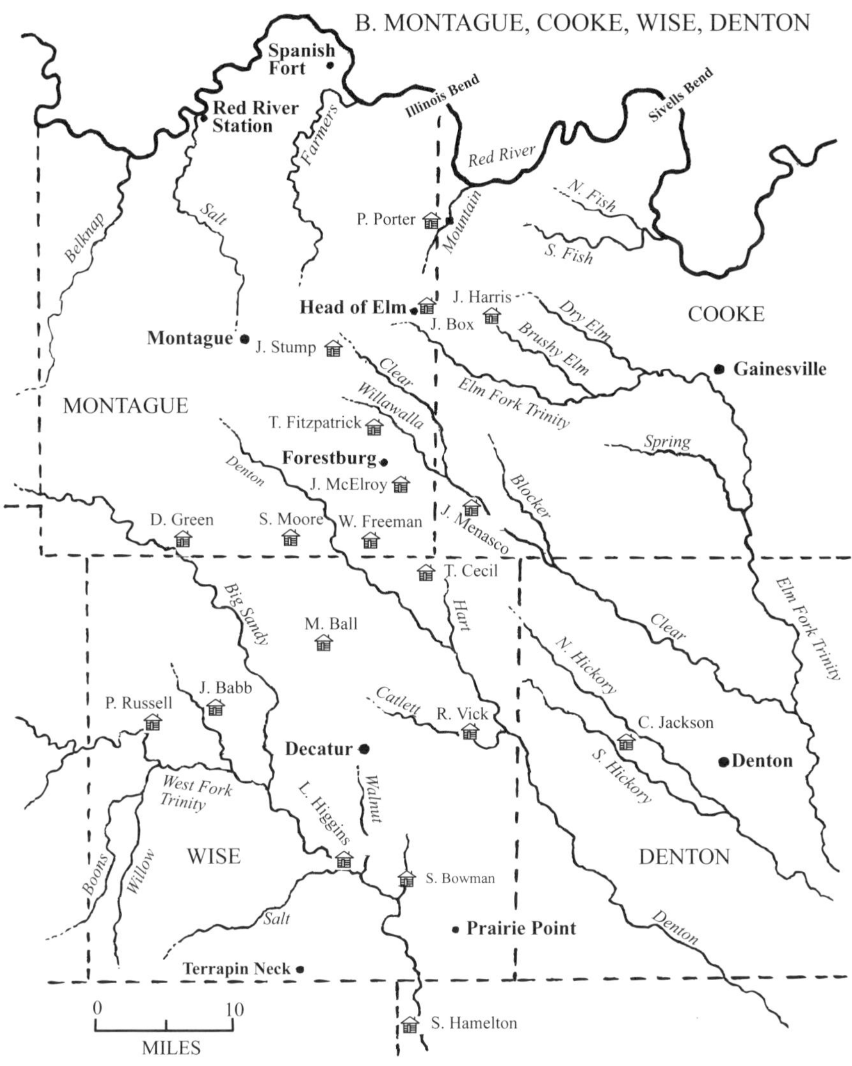
B. MONTAGUE, COOKE, WISE, DENTON
Spanish Fort
Red River Station
Illinois Bend
Sivells Bend
Farmers
Red River
Belknap
Salt
P. Porter
Mountain
N. Fish
S. Fish
Head of Elm
J. Harris
J. Box
Dry Elm
Brushy Elm
COOKE
Montague
J. Stump
Clear
Gainesville
MONTAGUE
Willawalla
Elm Fork Trinity
T. Fitzpatrick
Spring
Forestburg
Denton
J. McElroy
Blocker
D. Green
S. Moore
W. Freeman
J. Menasco
T. Cecil
Big Sandy
Hart
M. Ball
Clear
Elm Fork Trinity
N. Hickory
J. Babb
P. Russell
Catlett
R. Vick
C. Jackson
Decatur
Denton
S. Hickory
West Fork Trinity
L. Higgins
Walnut
WISE
DENTON
Boons
Willow
S. Bowman
Salt
Prairie Point
Denton
Terrapin Neck
0
10
MILES
S. Hamelton

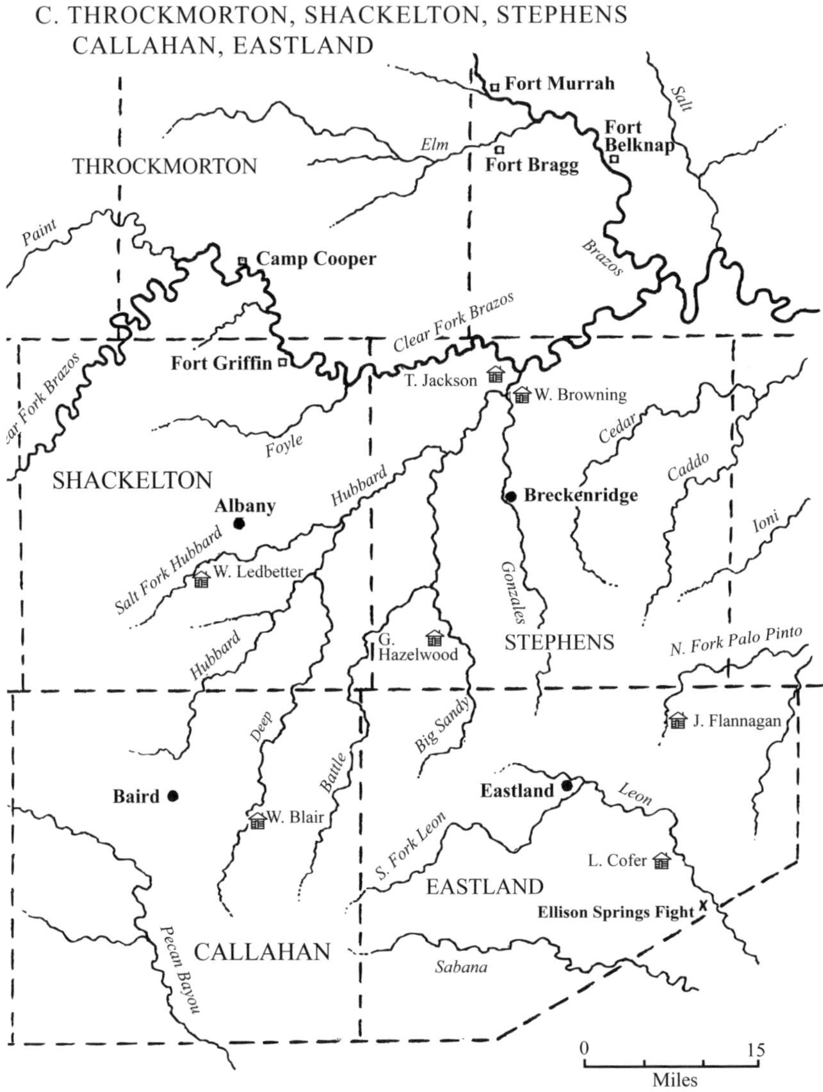
C. THROCKMORTON, SHACKELTON, STEPHENS
CALLAHAN, EASTLAND
Fort Murrah
Salt
Fort Belknap
Elm
Fort Bragg
THROCKMORTON
Paint
Camp Cooper
Brazos
Clear Fork Brazos
Fort Griffin
T. Jackson
W. Browning
Clear Fork Brazos
Cedar
Foyle
Caddo
SHACKELTON
Hubbard
Breckenridge
Albany
Ioni
Salt Fork Hubbard
W. Ledbetter
Gonzales
G. Hazelwood
STEPHENS
N. Fork Palo Pinto
Hubbard
Deep
Big Sandy
J. Flannagan
Battle
Baird
Eastland
Leon
W. Blair
S. Fork Leon
L. Cofer
EASTLAND
Ellison Springs Fight
Pecan Bayou
CALLAHAN
Sabana
0
15
Miles

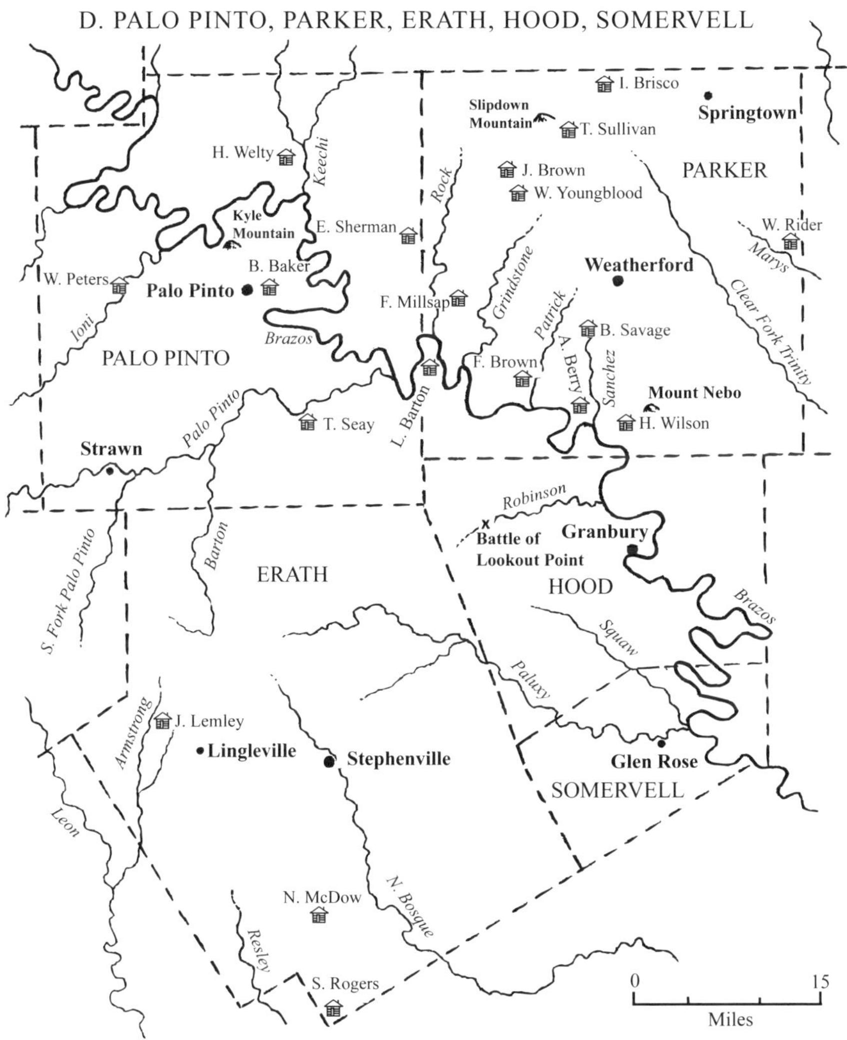
D. PALO PINTO, PARKER, ERATH, HOOD, SOMERVELL
I. Brisco
Slipdown Mountain
T. Sullivan
Springtown
H. Welty
Keechi
Rock
J. Brown
W. Youngblood
PARKER
Kyle Mountain
E. Sherman
W. Rider
Marys
B. Baker
Weatherford
W. Peters
Palo Pinto
F. Millsap
Grindstone
Clear Fork Trinity
Patrick
B. Savage
Ioni
Brazos
PALO PINTO
F. Brown
A. Berry
Sanchez
Mount Nebo
L. Barton
T. Seay
H. Wilson
Palo Pinto
Strawn
Robinson
Battle of Lookout Point
Granbury
S. Fork Palo Pinto
Barton
ERATH
HOOD
Brazos
Squaw
Paluxy
Armstrong
J. Lemley
Lingleville
Stephenville
Glen Rose
SOMERVELL
Leon
N. McDow
N. Bosque
Resley
S. Rogers
0
15
Miles

E. BROWN, COMANCHE, SAN SABA, MILLS

F. HAMILTON, BOSQUE, LAMPASAS, CORYELL

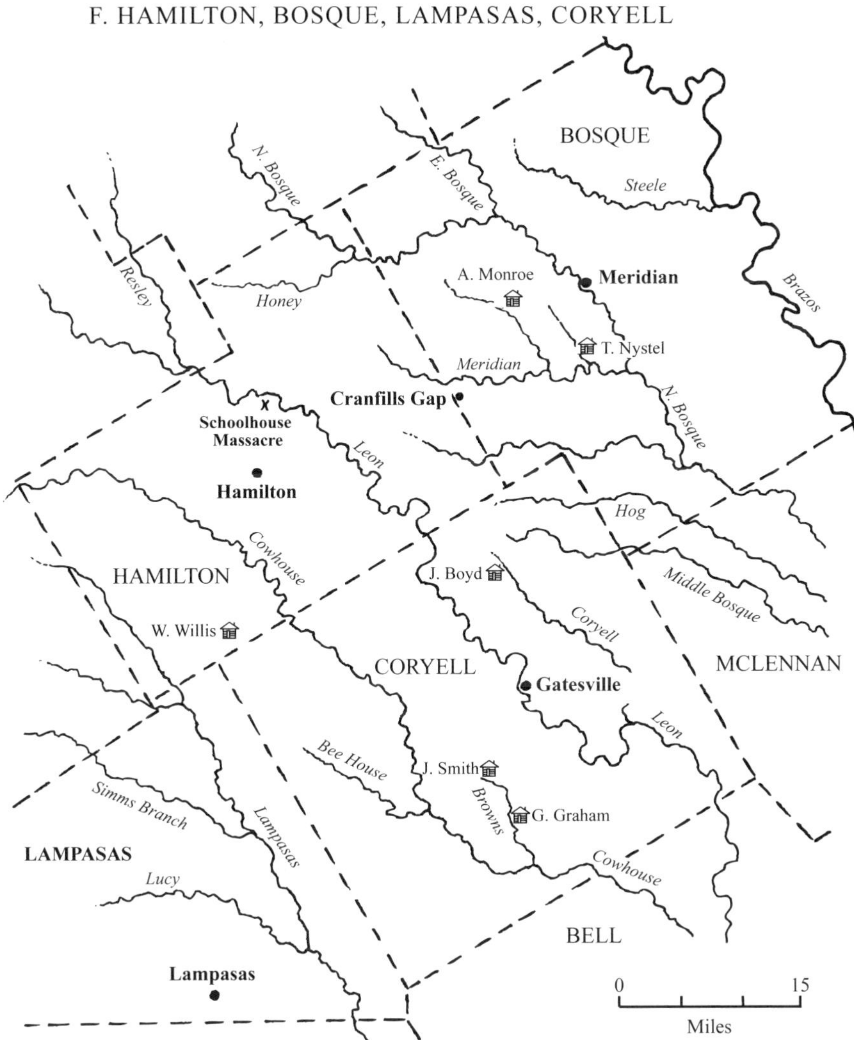

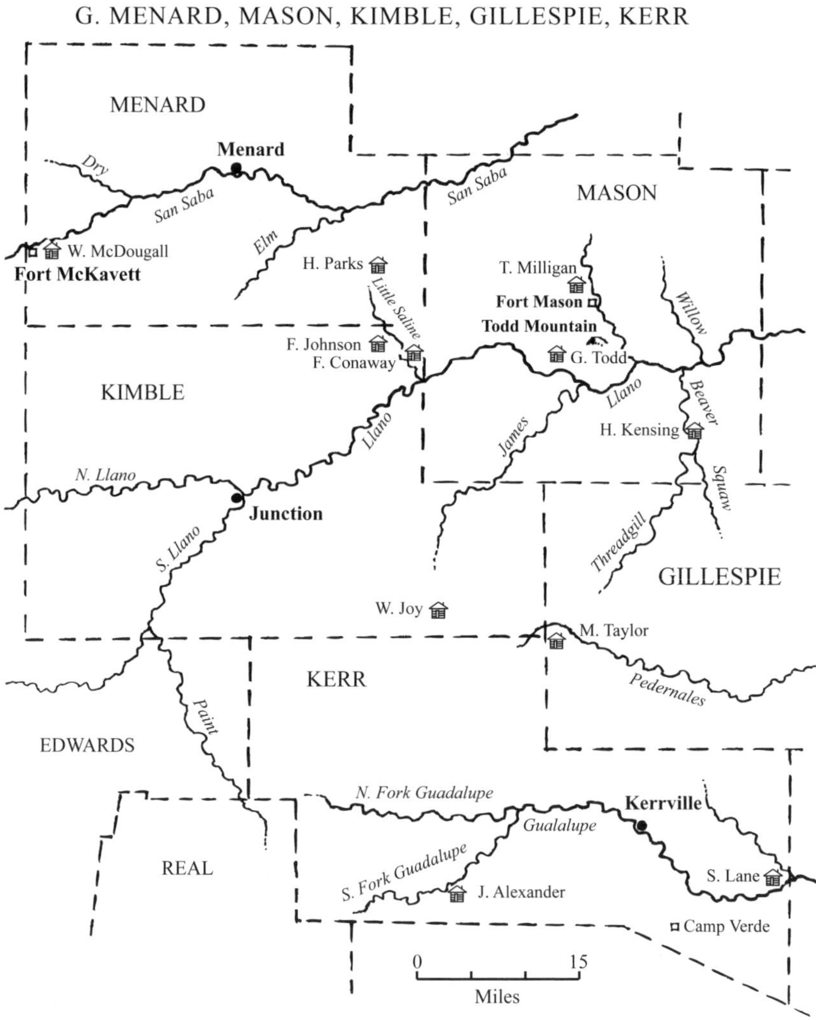
G. MENARD, MASON, KIMBLE, GILLESPIE, KERR
MENARD
Menard
Dry
San Saba
San Saba
MASON
Elm
W. McDougall
Fort McKavett
H. Parks
Little Saline
T. Milligan
Fort Mason
Willow
Todd Mountain
F. Johnson
F. Conaway
G. Todd
KIMBLE
Llano
Beaver
James
H. Kensing
Llano
N. Llano
Squaw
Junction
S. Llano
Threadgill
GILLESPIE
W. Joy
M. Taylor
KERR
Pedernales
Paint
EDWARDS
N. Fork Guadalupe
Kerrville
Gualalupe
REAL
S. Fork Guadalupe
S. Lane
J. Alexander
Camp Verde
0
15
Miles

H. LLANO, BURNET, GILLESPIE, BLANCO, KENDALL

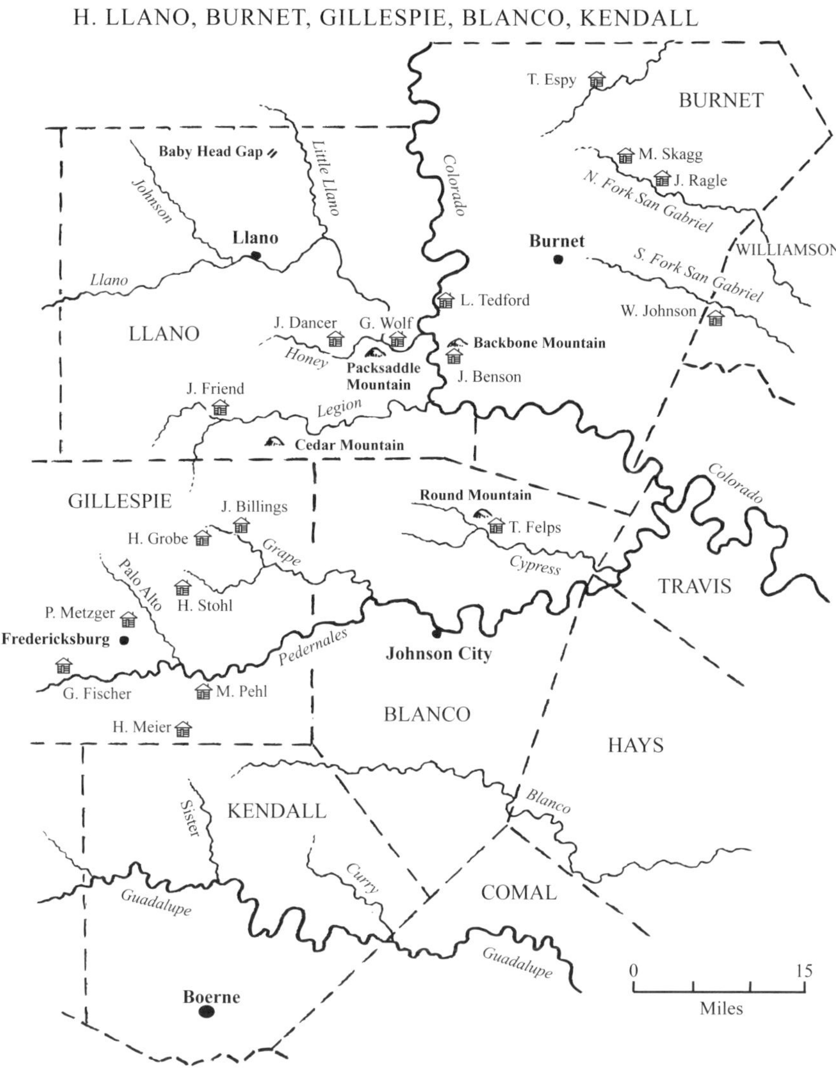

I. REAL, KINNEY, UVALDE, MAVERICK, ZAVALA

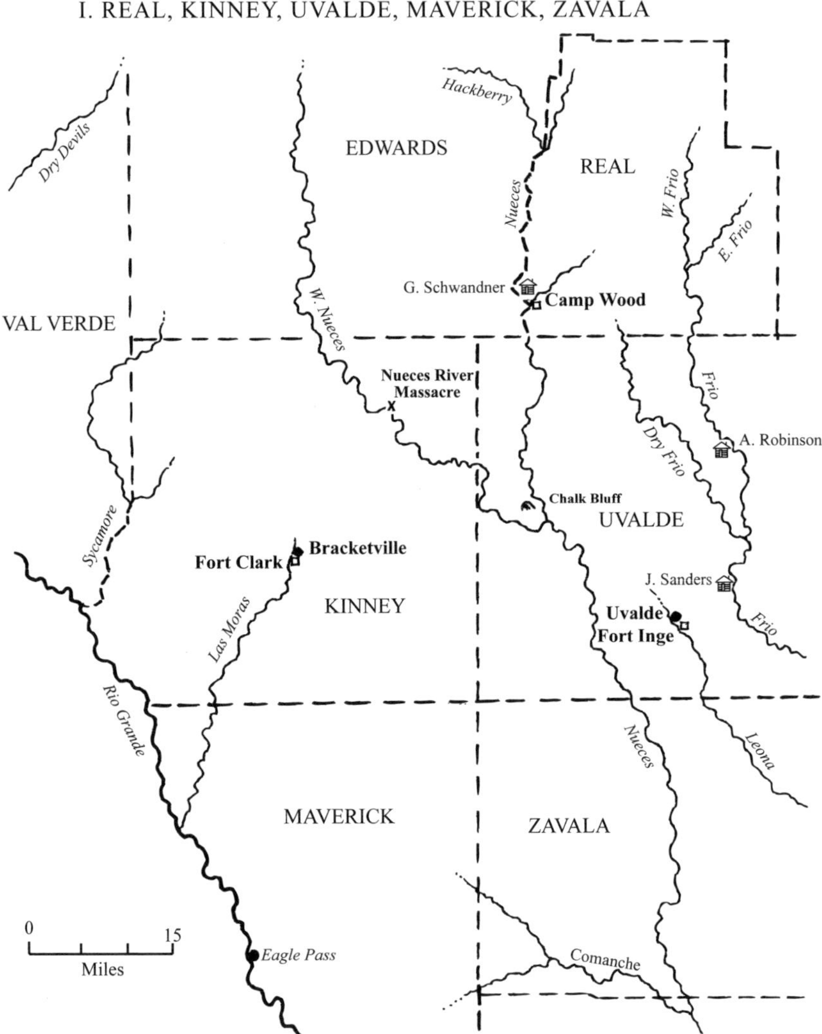

J. BANDERA, UVALDE, MEDINA, FRIO

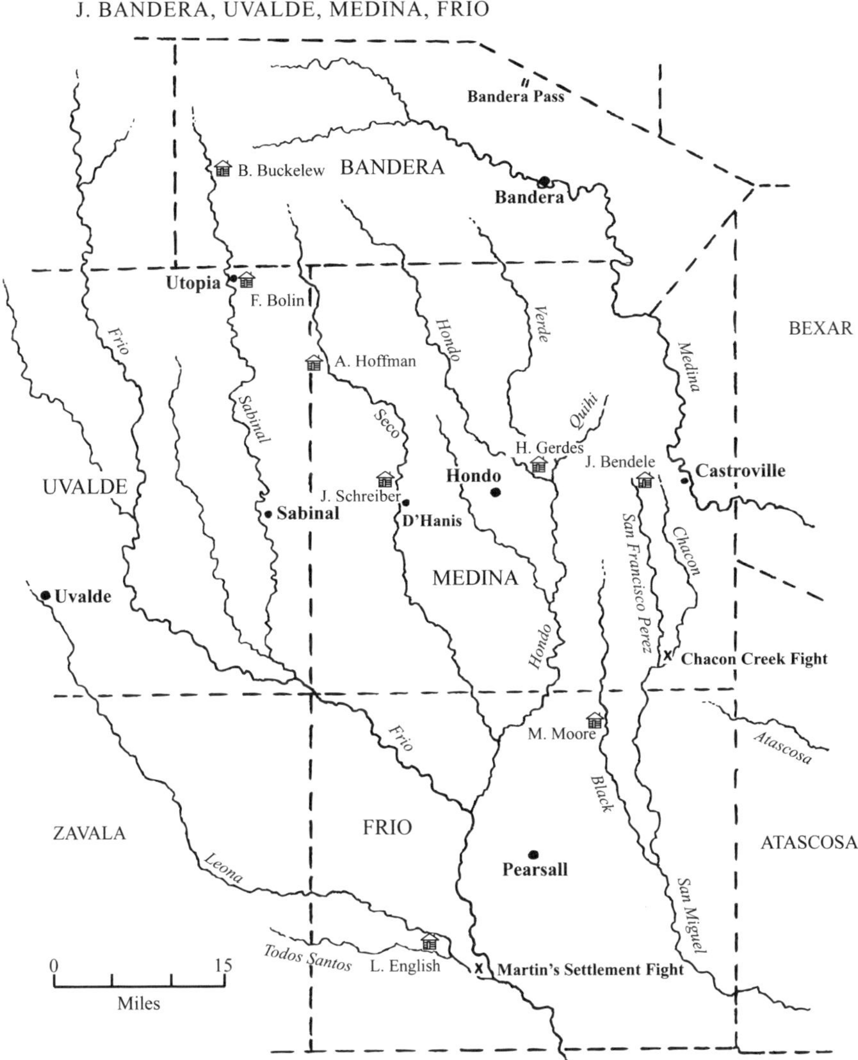

Part 9. 1867

45 "When the soldiers got there the Indians got mean."

The U. S. Cavalry was coming to the rescue a few troops at a time. In December, seven companies of the 6th Cavalry were at Jacksboro, and on January 14, 1867, 125 new recruits arrived, bringing the total to 465 officers and men and 325 horses. One of them, Sgt. H. H. McConnell, called the village a "sorry and forlorn" place. On the march in he noticed that almost all the locals were "packing," that is, carrying guns. "Every man and boy," he said, "old and young, rich or poor, at home or abroad, in church, at court, the wedding or the funeral… inevitably carried" a double-barreled shotgun or a dragoon pistol. He thought the habit was "an unmixed evil," but realized that the lawless condition on the frontier necessitated it. The men were often down and dirty, but he came to believe that "an honest, a brave and noble heart was beating beneath the rough exterior." McConnell said his first impression was wrong. "I did not at the time appreciate the rough characters I saw, simply because I did not know their *worth*."[1]

Everyone McConnell saw might have been "packing," but there were still many who went about unarmed. As usually happened, the army sat at frontier posts but the Indians passed them unmolested and came into the settlements. On January 23, 1867, about 90 miles south of Jacksboro, near present Alexander in Erath County, Nathan McDow and his son, Francis, were splitting post oaks into rails along Green Creek. When the wagon was full, Joe Grady McDow, Nathan's brother, drove it to the cabin. He had just gotten out of sight when eight Comanches rode in and caught the father and son taking a rest. With nothing but axes for defense they were easily overcome, and Comanches quickly killed and scalped them. Joe McDow heard the shooting and rode back, but only in time to see the Indians leaving after finishing their bloody deed.[2]

Alexander Roberts, who had lost stock in Blanco County in 1866, had moved to Llano County shortly thereafter. On January 15, he discovered that a change in location made little difference. Indians hit his new place near Packsaddle Mountain and stole 25 horses worth $500. They also stole horses from E. M. Walker, Jack Martin, and J. C. Crownover. Roberts, Walker, Crownover, Amos Harden, Eli Shelly, and a few others trailed the thieves, finding several lanced animals on the way. Three miles beyond Packsaddle Mountain, they caught the raiders and had a short fight. The Indians rode away with most of the stolen stock, but the settlers recovered seven horses belonging to Jack Martin.[3]

In January, Throckmorton's requests for county depredation reports began arriving. One of the first was from Llano, which covered from July of 1865 through the end of 1866, and listed 25 owners reporting either horses, mules, or cattle stolen. Medina County reported 81 instances of theft of stock valued at $12,340. Webb County listed 25 thefts and seven killings between August 1866 and January 1867, but with no details of the circumstances. The men killed were H. P. Darling, Pablo Pastor, Charley Freidman, Jose Maria Cantu, Juan Bela, and Messrs. Smith and Cason.

In February, Judge William Fanning wrote to Throckmorton from Montague County and said he had been on the frontier 14 years and the raids "have been frequently made for ten years past…." He believed the only difference was that before the Indians took horses and now they were taking more cattle. He said that there were fewer citizens in the county in 1867 than there were in 1860. Fanning listed 30 owners losing more than 20,000 cattle valued at more than $124,000.

Erath County's report came in mid-February listing 28 people losing horses and mules worth $5,350. Kerr County listed 23 people who had lost horses or mules. Lampasas County listed two people killed (Carter and Bond) and 13 people losing 409 horses and 400 cattle worth $26,765. Hamilton County recorded more than 50 people losing stock worth $19,425.[4]

While the reports arrived, so did the Indians. The full moon fell on February 18, and it foretold the death of more settlers. Alfred T. Ross (49), his wife, Emily Terry Ross, and their children, Isaac, Emeline, and Amanda, lived in a double log cabin separated by a "dog run" from Slade Hightower, Mr. Ross' son-in-law. The cabins were two miles north of old Finis, on Rock Creek in the southwest corner of Jack County. Emily Ross was washing clothes under the "dog run" while Alfred, Isaac, and Slade were working in the field. The Indians seemingly came out of nowhere, cutting between the houses and the men in the field. Mrs. Ross grabbed her other children and ran in the cabin.

The warriors formed a line across the yard but Alf Ross made a dash to get through them to his family. They shot him dead. Ike and Slade ran toward Rock Creek but the warriors caught and killed them too. While they were being chased, Mrs. Ross took her children and ran to the creek on the other side of the cabin where they hid until nightfall. Emily crept back to the cabin to look around and found her husband's scalp lying on a rock. She got some dried beef and took it to the children still in hiding. They ate and hid in a little cave by the creek. About midnight, Mrs. Ross crawled out of the cave and saw an Indian standing on the bank above, his silhouette plain in the silver moonlight. She ducked back inside until morning.

With daylight, Mrs. Ross tried to return to the cabin but saw two warriors still rummaging around the property. She went back to the cave and they remained until nightfall, when they left their shelter and made their way to Emily's mother's place a few miles away. Emily's brother, Mose Terry, hurried to John Lemley's place nearby and spread the news. John Lemley was involved in the 1860 raid in which his daughter Liddie was killed, and had moved to Jack County for "safety." Terry and Lemley could hear guns firing from the direction of the Carter ranch, where the Indians were apparently attacking. The next day, Mose Terry, John and Jeff Lemley, and John Van Houser located the three bodies and buried them together near the Ross cabin in an unmarked grave.

The next month, Buck Barry wrote to Governor Throckmorton and mentioned their deaths, saying that 200 horses were stolen in the area during the same raid. Many of the horses were taken from the Big Keechi, 75 of them from John W. Sheek's place at Black Springs (near present Oran) in Palo Pinto County, and from his neighbor, Oliver Loving. The raiders were also near Palo Pinto, where a dozen civilians battled Comanches in the breaks along the Brazos River southeast of town. Barry said that the murders were becoming "so frequent that they are only noticed by their friends and acquainted as they would notice ones dying a natural death." He suggested that more posts be established farther out, such as at old Fort Phantom Hill, Camp Cooper, and at the salt works on Hubbard Creek in Shackelford County, from where he believed the cavalry "would cover this section of the country."[5]

The army wasn't having much luck covering anything, one reason being the epidemic that broke out in February among the cavalry horses in Jacksboro. According to Sergeant McConnell, the culprit was the "musty corn" and the "poor quality of hay" that had "about as much nourishment in it as a match." They hauled out dead horses every morning.[6]

Even with healthy animals, however, it would have made little difference. The cavalry was not catching or stopping any Indians. In February they were south of Jacksboro and in March they were north of it. William E. Fisher had moved to northern Montague County after the Civil War, joining scores of other ranchers coming in to take advantage of the wetter conditions, better grass, and thousands of unbranded cattle. His range was near Red River Station, close to Messrs. Quillen and Roberts, who had moved there during the war. Only a handful of Comanches were enough to drive off about 100 of Fishers' cattle and about an equal number from Quillen and Roberts. Levi Bennett, Louis Quillen, and Henry Vincent, the latter two being freedmen, were loose herding them when the Indians cut out the cattle and drove them to Red River. Quillen noticed the Indians were riding some of Morris Gilbert's horses. The cowboys followed and found a few cattle shot with arrows. They hurried to catch up, but that proved to be a mistake when the Comanches turned and killed Vincent. Quillen and Bennett got away.

Years later, in 1891, Quillen testified in Fisher's depredation claim. Robert Spearman, the counsel for the government, did all he could to deny the claim, first by insisting that white men stole the cattle. "No," Quillin said, "if they were, they were painted."

Spearman asked Quillen if he had heard the accusations that Morris Gilbert and Allen Friend were cattle thieves. "No sir, I never heard anything about it," he said.

The attorney then tried to blame the weather for the losses, asking Quillen if it was true that the winter of 1866-67 was "the severest winter that ever was known."

"No, it was not particularly cold," he answered.

Spearman continued, stating that Quillen must have known that the weather was horrible in February and March of 1867, "and that nearly all of the range cattle died."

"There were very few died in that country," Quillen countered.

Spearman tried to impugn Quillen's testimony, asking how well he knew Fisher and if they had talked previously about the case. "Did he tell you what he wanted you to swear?" Spearman asked.

"No sir," Quillen answered.

"You and he are pretty good friends, aren't you?" the attorney probed.

"Pretty good friends," Quillen said, "I haven't saw him for twenty years."

And so it went. The government counsels did all they could to deny settlers' and ranchers' rightful claims. It was true, unfortunately, that there were white thieves in the same business as the Indians, and legitimate claims were thus complicated and occasionally rejected.

Louis Quillen's testimony also reinforced a theme that has surfaced several times during this narrative: more troops meant more problems. Attorney Spearman persistently tried to discount Quillen as a witness, one time asking, "Don't all Indians look just alike to you?"

"Pretty near," he replied, "some are larger than others, and some have their hair put up and cut in a different a shape."

"You never saw any Indians in Montague County…except when you or the Indians would be running at a great distance," Spearman stated.

Not true, said Quillen. When he first came to the county "they would come to your house and ask for something to eat and would not bother you at all." Spearman asked when the Indians became unfriendly. It was only "when the soldiers got there," Quillen said, "when they got mean and wanted to kill you or take your horses."[7]

The presence of soldiers facilitated a self-fulfilling prophecy. It was not unlike in the movie, *Field of Dreams*, where if you build the field, the people will come. Perhaps a better analogy is in a quote from Chicago Mayor Richard J. Daley: "The police are not here to create disorder, they're here to preserve disorder." Unfortunately, soldiers often inadvertently served the same purpose.

The 6th Cavalry in the north had little luck finding Indians, but the 4th Cavalry in the south did make contact, although not with the best results. Captain John Wilcox and a detachment of Company C were camped on Live Oak Creek near abandoned Fort Lancaster. They picked up a trail and followed it for four days, twisting downstream along the lower Pecos. On March 12, they located an Indian camp, burned it, and recovered a Mexican captive. The Indians returned and attacked, drove the cavalrymen out of the camp and chased them for 15 miles. Wilcox claimed to have killed between 25 and 40 Indians, but given the circumstances of his retreat, the number was likely highly exaggerated. The guide, Severino Patino, was killed, four soldiers were missing, and five were wounded.[8]

Even when the soldiers found and fought the Indians, there were repercussions. H. I. Richards, a sheep rancher and judge in Medina County, wrote to Throckmorton on March 19: "As everybody anticipated, the Indians have taken advantage of the absence of the troops from Fort Inge and Fort Clark being on scout to the Devil's River and Pecos River. They have crossed the Rio Grande in three different parties, each consisting of twenty warriors and more, and are at present ravaging this part right down to Bexar County…."

On March 14, Lipans were in Medina County where few had been seen since the previous fall. A large number of Germans had settled near the junctions of the Hondo, Verde, and Quihi Creeks at Quihi and New Fountain. Many of them had left the old country to escape war and conscription and wanted to be left alone. Harms Gerdes, his wife, Eite Ehmen, and five children, immigrated to America in 1851, and in 1854, they purchased lots near all three above mentioned creeks. By 1867, Harms was 60 years old and all of his children were grown and had families. On March 14, Harms went out to look for his horses, which he believed had gotten loose and wandered off during the night. Harms found his horses, but they were in the possession of Indians. They chased and easily caught him. The day was frigid, with some of the creeks frozen and icicles hanging from the tree branches. As a joke, the Indians forced Harms to strip and they marched him three miles until his feet and legs were so frozen he could no longer walk. Judge Richards wrote that the Indians "made him undress himself and when naked priked him with their lanses taking care not to wound him mortally…." He had been pierced 50 times before they finished him off with a spear through the heart. A neighbor, Mimke M. Saathoff, found and buried the body less than three miles southeast of Quihi.

The raiders also went into Bexar County and stole horses on Medio Creek only 15 miles from San Antonio where six infantry companies ineffectively sat. On the San Geronimo about 18 miles northwest of San Antonio, Judge John Rosenheimer reported that Indians killed Mr. G. Pendleton only 300 yards from his house, "mutilated shockingly and as normal in such cases scalped." Lipans also stole horses from around Castroville and killed sheep at Judge Richards' ranch on the upper Verde. The army was damned if they acted either on offense or defense.[9]

About the same time, Comanches were up in Bosque County where one of the few Norwegian communities was located. Terje Nystel moved to Texas in 1850 and the next year he married Signe Knudsen and they had three children. Ole Tergerson Nystel was born in 1853, followed by his sisters, Tone and Anna Marie. When Signe Nystel died in 1861, Terje married Gunnar Grann in 1865, and the family moved to Bosque County to start a farm.

Ole helped his father farm in an idyllic setting along Bee Creek, but on March 20, 1867, their peaceful world was shattered. Ole was cutting timber with neighbor Carl Questad right next to a camp of six Comanches. Two warriors rushed Ole and he ran for Questad's wagon, only 50 steps away, but an arrow pierced his right leg. Another warrior caught Ole, placed a gun in his face, and took him prisoner. Questad ran, leaping over a 20-foot bluff above Bee Creek and didn't stop for four miles. He got back to Nystel's, cut, bleeding, and down to his underwear after his desperate dash through the brambles, no doubt trying to figure out how he would break the news to Mr. Nystel. A search party went out, but they never could catch the Indians. Later, Ole looked back on the incident as a "plain case of God's providence," he rationalized, because if they caught the adult male Questad they would have killed him, while he, being only 14 years old, was likely to be spared.[10]

Just before sundown the Indians came upon James Hasty, a black freedman hauling corn. He begged for his life but they speared him through the heart. They left him unscalped and made signs that they would rather have Ole's fine locks. Before leaving the settlements, the Comanches killed Clint McLennan, another black freedman. On the way west the warriors abused Ole badly. "They would kick and knock me about just for pastime it seemed, whip my bare back until it was perfectly bloody, with frequent repetitions fire their pistols held so close to my head that the caps and powder would fly in my face, producing powder burns and bruises, until I was very much disfigured." Ole said, "my head was a solid sore, and the scab had risen above my hair. Oh! horrible condition. The Lord deliver any of my countrymen… from ever being brought into it as I was."[11]

In the village in Indian Territory, Ole acted crazy at times, which may have worked in his favor. After a few months they decided they would be better off selling him. In June 1867, near the Big Bend of the Arkansas River in Kansas, they took Nystel to a trading post where Eli Bewell bought the boy for some brown paper, blankets, sugar, flour, and tobacco in the amount of

$250. Bewell grew to like Ole so much that he did not want to give him up, but eventually Agent Leavenworth found them and convinced Bewell to part with him, paying him the $250 he spent to ransom the boy.

They took Nystel to the mouth of the Little Arkansas River where Ole met some of the same Comanches who had captured him. Ole had learned their language and they talked. They wanted him to return with them, but Ole refused, saying he was going back to Texas. The Comanches were astonished. They could not understand why anyone would want to go there. They could understand if he stayed in Kansas, but were certain that the Texans were "bad" and would kill him. Ole's understanding was, "Here were these Indians receiving at the hands of the government in Kansas and other points their supplies—*tame Indians you know*—and...going off along the frontier of Texas, committing their acts of atrocity, killing, plundering, stealing, etc."

Ole's family was in Texas, and it is there he would return, riding in government wagon trains and hitching rides with freighters. He reached home six months after his capture.[12]

Chapter 45 notes

1 Hamilton, *Sentinel of the Southern Plains*, 18-19; McConnell, *Five Years a Cavalryman*, 44-45, 48.

2 McConnell, *West Texas Frontier*, 564; Winfrey and Day, *Texas Indian Papers, IV*, 145-46; "Erath County Kin," http://wc.rootsweb.ancestry.com/cgi-bin/igm.cgi?op=get&db=93stealth&id=I30335

3 Alexander Roberts, Depredation Claim #3929.

4 Winfrey and Day, *Texas Indian Papers, IV*, 132-37, 141-42, 148-52, 154-58, 160-62, 165-66.

5 McConnell, *West Texas Frontier*, 513, 580; John W. Sheek, Depredation Claim #5312; Winfrey and Day, *Texas Indian Papers*, IV, 177.

6 McConnell, *Five Years a Cavalryman*, 55.

7 William E. Fisher, Depredation Claim #5714.

8 Williams, *Texas' Last Frontier*, 69.

9 Winfrey and Day, *Texas Indian Papers, IV*, 178, 186; McConnell, West Texas Frontier, 522; "Ancestors," http://familytreemaker.genealogy.com/users/l/o/t/donna-loth-tx/gene1-0009.html.

10 Nystel, *Lost and Found*, vii, 3-6.

11 Winfrey and Day, *Texas Indian Papers, IV*, 186; Nystel, *Lost and Found*, 7-8.

12 Nystel, *Lost and Found*, 14-17, 27.

46 "Well, I would call them unfriendly."

James Throckmorton was sincere in his beliefs that the Texas frontier was being inundated and he never stopped badgering the various district commanders for more help. From December of 1866 through the spring of 1867, Throckmorton wrote letters to Gen. Charles Griffin, the latest man in charge of the District of Texas, stating he needed more troops and additional posts. Similar pleas to Sheridan and Washington brought Sheridan's response that if the governor would be patient, he would supplement each fort with smaller posts placed about 20 miles apart and connect them all with a series of roving patrols. It was the same old solution. If any of them had studied the attempts at frontier defense over the past decade, they might have realized that this tactic had never worked.

Perhaps going through the motions of doing something, whatever it might be, would assuage the situation. In April, the army abandoned Jacksboro and moved about 28 miles north to set up a new post at Buffalo Springs in southern Clay County, believing it had more timber, better water, and would be easier to stop incursions across Red River. Part of the 6th Cavalry went there and part to old Fort Belknap. General Grant authorized $250,000 extra for defense, but Sheridan objected, still believing the Indian problem was mythical and only designed to remove troops from the interior. Sheridan wrote to Throckmorton and said "there are more casualties occurring from outrages perpetrated upon Union men and freedmen in the interior of the state than occurs from Indian depredations on the frontier."[1]

Sheridan's assertion may or may not have been true, depending on who did the counting, but neither locale wanted to be shortchanged. As they debated, the Indians enjoyed the rain, grass, and good raiding weather. In Llano County in April, Indians stole nine horses worth $865 from Otto Lange, along with two mules from William O. Phillips. In Coryell County about April 15, they got three horses worth $275 from Ambrose S. Latham.

Thomas J. Shannon and his son Robert, ran about 5,000 cattle in Grayson County, but in 1862 they moved about half of them to Montague County, building a house, lots, and pens about three miles below Red River Station. Their cattle sometimes mixed with William Fisher's, whose range was nearby. The Shannons lost some cattle in 1866, but because of the nearly continuous raiding, by the spring of 1867, virtually all of it was gone. They filed a claim for 2,848 cattle worth $34,356.[2]

The depredation reports kept coming in. Kendall County's list named 45 people who had lost horses or mules worth $6,890. Bosque County and Hood

County each listed nine people losing horses. Uvalde County reported 35 people losing stock for a total of $30,235. The tabulation included three men killed in addition to those mentioned above: Messrs. Shulkhouser, Barnes, and an unnamed Mexican. Comanche County informed Throckmorton that 30 people lost horses worth $4,940, and one unnamed freedman was killed. Parker County reported on June 9, listing 165 people claiming horses killed or stolen, valued at $36,905.[3]

One historian said that depredations declined in 1867 because the frontier finally had enough soldiers,[4] but there were other factors involved. If depredations were down, the change was marginal and due to other considerations. One of them might have been the weather. Where there once was drought, the weather had turned exceptionally wet. Sergeant McConnell, who was stuck at Jacksboro doing administrative work, could not join the unit at Buffalo Springs because in June, the rains had flooded the area, with the West Fork Trinity bottomlands completely inundated and most of the country "was still under water." Most importantly, much of the stock along the northern tier of counties bordering Red River had been taken. There was not much left to steal.[5]

If it was true that there were slightly less raids than in 1866, it was no comfort to those who were attacked. If cattle were not as readily available, there were other targets. In April, Satank, Satanta and 60 Kiowas crossed Red River by Doan's Store, passed by Fort Belknap, traveled down the Brazos, cut east across Parker County, and went all the way to the Tarrant County line. There they ran into some unfortunate settlers. James Myres, his wife, and six children came from Missouri to Texas in 1860, and settled in the northwestern corner of Tarrant County. Life was hard and Mr. Myres died in 1861, leaving Sally to care for William (16), Mahala Emilene (15), Eliza (13), Sarina (11), Samuel (9), and John (7). A year later Sally married William Hamleton and settled in the same area, a few miles north of present-day Azle. By the spring of 1867, Sally had two more children: Mary (5), and Gus (1).[6]

In 1867, the area even so close to Fort Worth and Dallas was not safe. As the Kiowas neared the Hamleton cabin, they saw a number of adults and children working in a cotton field and attacked. The Myres children ran home and the warriors tried to beat them there before whoever was inside could bar the door. William Hamleton was away at the mill and William Myres was rounding up cattle. Sally Hamleton was inside weaving cloth on a handloom, while Sarina Myres, Mary Hamleton, and little Gus played inside.

Kiowas burst in the door before Sally, who the Indians called, "a great big fat woman," could get a gun. "The woman tried to defend herself," a warrior explained, "so we killed her." They grabbed the three children and quickly rode off. Next morning the Kiowas spied a cloud of dust in the distance and believed the Texans were chasing them. Sait-aim-pay-toy left Mary

Hamleton behind, thinking she would slow him down. After riding a few minutes they discovered that the dust cloud was coming from stampeding cattle and Sait-aim-pay-toy told the others that he had left a child behind. Hah-bay-te went back after Mary because his daughter had no children of her own and he knew she would want one. Sarina Myres recalled that Mary was crying a lot and the Indians were angry with her. When Sarina did not see her on the second day after their capture, she assumed the Indians had killed her, which is what she later reported.[7]

Satanta, who had no intention to stop taking captives, went north to Indian Territory. Sarina, believing Mary was killed, resolved to "endure without murmur the indignities and hardships incident to her condition...." The Kiowas held Sarina about six months before selling her at Fort Arbuckle. Sarina's brother, William, came to take her home.

Satank's eldest son, An-pay-kau-te, saw Mary Hamleton in the village and said she had "fair hair and light blue eyes" and "ran around the camp in a lively way." She was given to Tope-kau-da and brought up "in a good Kiowa family." Tope-kau-da always hid Mary Hamleton from prying white eyes. "We all told the army officers that she was dead," said An-pay-kau-te. Mary spent the rest of her life with the Kiowas while her Texas relatives believed she had been killed in the April 1867 raid.[8]

Raiders swept across Texas in the spring and summer of 1867. In May, Indians were in Erath County stealing 60 horses valued at $3,200 from Thomas M. Leath. William and Amanda Jackson had a ranch in northern Montague County near Spanish Fort. So far they had been spared, but on the last of May, 1867, raiders crossed Red River and easily drove off 500 horses, leaving them with only a few that they had corralled near the house.

From about May 7-9, raiders swept along the length of Battle Creek in eastern Callahan County and out along Pecan Bayou, stealing stock from several families, including Sevier McDonald, Thomas Pollard, James Hart, Tony Clayton, William Hittson, and Messrs. Rossbrook, Gathern, and Heslop. Several cowboys met at Hittson's to hunt and buy cattle. After making arrangements, they bedded down for the night, only to wake before sunrise to the calls of the men on guard, to find most of their horses and much of the cattle gone. "We all run out afoot," said James Hart, to the edge of Battle Creek, where they saw the Indians "a roping and catching the horses." They quickly decided to charge in and shoot. When they did, the Indians "let in to hollowing and running" and drove off almost everything on four feet. The cowboys had no choice but to go back to Hittson's and wait for daylight. They scrounged up a few horses and followed the raiders 80 miles but never could catch them.

On May 15, raiders hit Leroy Lee's place in Backbone Valley, Burnet County. A neighbor came to Lee's door and told him the Indians were in the country and it looked like they had gotten some of his horses. Lee, his son, G. W. Lee, and a few neighbors followed the trail, but when they got too close, the raiders began killing the stolen stock. They found numerous animals dead on the trail. Lee lost six horses, all killed, a filly, a sorrel mare, and four colts, shot with arrows or speared. The senseless slaughter sickened the settlers. When a hard rainstorm blew in, they gave up and went home, saddened and angry at their helplessness and the seeming impunity with which the raiders attacked them.[9]

In June, raiders visited Kendall County and took three horses from Henry Dietert, right near the town of Boerne. In neighboring Kerr County, Indians weren't done with the Metzger family. In 1864 they killed Emma Metzger and captured Anna. On June 15, 1867, they hit Frederick Metzger's farm, stealing 31 horses and four cows, and destroying his cornfield and other property for damages of $2,600. The same month at Pilot Point in Denton County, raiders stole 78 horses worth $3,900 from William A. Bragg's ranch.[10]

There were some changes in raiding patterns beginning in the spring of 1867. As the cattlemen found new markets for their longhorns in New Mexico, Colorado, Kansas, and even California, the Indians also found new avenues of opportunity. Before they always had to go to Texas to steal, but now the Texans were coming to them. Andy M. Adams had contracted with the army at Fort Sumner, New Mexico, to deliver beef cattle at $18 a head. He visited cowmen in Llano, San Saba, and McCulloch counties to buy cattle, making arrangements with John Oatman, James S. Bourland, Joel D. Hoy, Seth Mabry, Paul Deats, and a few others to take their cattle and sell them. Oatman sold Adams 500 cattle, Bourland sold him 200, and the others sold similar numbers. Adams left with about 1,500 head, but several of the sellers came along to keep an eye on the stock. Oatman's son, Orville, had charge of part of the herd; Joel Hoy oversaw his portion, and others, such as Jim and Charlie Moss, Ham Cavin, Allen Roberts, and Mort Holton, looked after the rest.

On May 27, they rested on Dove Creek and then hit the waterless 80-mile stretch to the Pecos. In a few days they pushed the thirsty cattle to Horsehead Crossing where the Comanches were waiting for them. No one could have driven the thirsty cattle away from the water, so about 50 warriors patiently waited while the cattle drank their fill. When the cowboys got them watered and rounded up into a good bunch, the Indians rode in shooting and whooping. They got nearly the entire herd and drove it northeast toward the Llano Estacado. About half of the warriors stayed behind and attacked the herders, wounding two of them and chasing them to a sanctuary in the rocks where they holed up for two days. When the Comanches left, the destitute owners and herders could do nothing but make the long trip back home.[11]

Some cowmen never got far from their home counties before Indians relieved them of their stock. In June, Robert H. Taylor was driving cattle to Fort Garland in Colorado Territory when Comanches took 105 cattle and some horses, worth $5,012. John Sheek, a partner of Charles Goodnight, had driven a few herds to New Orleans before the war. Now he headed for New Mexico, but up the Brazos River only 80 miles from his Palo Pinto County ranch, the Indians ran off 308 head.

Later, government attorneys tried to discount Sheek's claim. They asked him if the Comanches were friendly in 1867, because if they were considered unfriendly, or, not in amity, the claim could be denied. Sheek said, "Well, I would call them unfriendly."

"What unfriendly acts did they do?" counsel asked.

"Well, they would kill you and steal horses," Sheek answered.

"Wasn't there a constant state of war existing," asked counsel, "between the Texans and the Comanche Indians in the year 1867?"

"We either had to fight or run, one of the two to save ourselves," said Sheek.[12]

By such admissions, the settlers and ranchers disqualified themselves from any monetary compensation. The government would not pay claims if the parties were in a state of warfare, only if they were at peace...but if they were at peace there wouldn't be any raiding. Catch-22.

Chapter 46 notes

1 Richter, *Army in Texas During Reconstruction*, 87-88; Howell, *James Throckmorton*, 144.
2 Depredation Claims: Otto Lange #3539; Ambrose S. Latham #2770; Robert E. Shannon #5721.
3 Winfrey and Day, *Texas Indian Papers, IV*, 173-74, 187, 199-200, 203-06, 218-22.
4 Howell, *James Throckmorton*, 127.
5 McConnell, *Five Years a Cavalryman*, 84.
6 Brown, *Indian Wars and Pioneers*, 118-19; McConnell, *West Texas Frontier*, in www.forttours.com/pages/tochamil.
7 Marshall, *A Cry Unheard*, 160-61; Nye, *Bad Medicine*, 136-38.
8 Brown, *Indian Wars and Pioneers*, 119; Marshall, *A Cry Unheard*, 161; McConnell, *West Texas Frontier*, in www.forttours.com/pages/tochamil; Nye, *Bad Medicine*, 138-42.
9 Depredation Claims: Thomas M. Leath #3888; Amanda Jackson #7754; Elizabeth J. McDonald #350; Leroy Lee #351.
10 Depredation Claims: Henry Dietert #10270; Frederick Metzger #10628; William A. Bragg #5291.
11 Depredation Claims: John Oatman #1187; James S. Bourland #3893.
12 Depredation Claims: Delilah Taylor #3528; John W. Sheek #5312.

47 "I regret having to be laid away in a foreign country."

Had the citizens of Texas been aware of what was happening on the plains of Kansas during the spring and summer of 1867, they would have likely howled in protest. General William T. Sherman, touring his Division of the Missouri in the summer of 1866, found it in comparative peace. "As usual," he wrote, I find the size of Indian stampedes and stories diminishes as I approach their location." In October, while passing through Fort Dodge in Kansas, Sherman learned of the Box killings and captures and forbade paying further ransoms. The Box story circulated and raised the tension level, affecting army officers and their wives, along with settlers and politicians. Kansas Governor Samuel J. Crawford stirred emotions as much as possible by trumpeting Indian depredations. Through 1866 and into 1867 he regaled the army with tales of "the wild beasts and savage barbarians" veritably burning down every cabin and killing, raping, or carrying off every settler. While Governor Throckmorton constantly badgered the army with similar pleas and alarms, the Texas governor was truly reporting a very real situation; in comparison, Crawford's state was enjoying an idyllic picnic.

One of the most advertised incidents, the Box captures, did not even happen in Kansas. Agent Edward Wynkoop reported the Cheyennes were peaceful. In January 1867, Gen. Winfield S. Hancock wrote to General Grant that the major troubles were the killing of a Mexican at Fort Zarah, theft of livestock at Fort Wallace, and an attack at Chalk Bluff Station—enough, according to Hancock, to punish the Cheyenne tribe. The generals purposely tried to provoke a war. Hancock told Sherman he would demand that the Cheyennes give up the murderer of the Mexican and deliver two chiefs as hostages. He assured Sherman that this action would certainly "lead to war." Hancock said, "I think it would be to our advantage to have these Indians refuse the demands I intend to make, a war with the Cheyennes would answer our purposes, as some punishment seems to be necessary."[1]

On that shaky premise, General Hancock led 1,600 cavalry, infantry, and artillery to western Kansas to punish the Cheyennes. The expedition, later derisively termed "Hancock's War," turned out to be a fiasco, causing more problems than existed in the first place. Regardless of its outcome, the Texans could rightfully have asked, "Why?" Why did the army send a punitive expedition to Kansas when Texas was in much more dire straits and was begging for help for years? The answer may lie in the simple fact that General Sheridan stuck to his belief that the depredation reports were false, and besides, who wanted to help a passel of unreconstructed ex-Rebels fight Indians? Let them suffer for awhile.

Then again, the Texans didn't need any "help" in the form that Hancock provided. Hancock and his mounted arm, the 7th Cavalry under Lt. Col. George Custer, spent April through July chasing Indians through Kansas, Nebraska, and Colorado for virtually no results. Indeed, Custer might have had more casualties (5) through his own actions, by either shooting deserters or abandoning his men, than the number of Indians he killed. In Texas there were already 2,000 cavalrymen who could produce the same results.

On July 2, the 4th Cavalry, with several companies based not far away at Fort Mason, was nowhere to be found when they were needed. Just across the line in McCulloch County, a couple of outfits were rounding up cattle on the San Saba River. The cowboys had driven a large number into a pen about a mile west of old Camp San Saba and the Indians were watching. As they looked for an opportunity to steal the cattle, Ben Smith and Mr. Ruff took their horses across the river. As they came up the bank, they inadvertently rode into the Indians' hiding place and the warriors blasted them with a volley. Smith was killed instantly, but Ruff rode a few miles before disappearing. He was never seen again, but several years later a skeleton was found with a rusty pistol by its side, likely the remains of Ruff.[2]

On the "Glorious Fourth," while the 7th Cavalry marched across Colorado Territory fruitlessly searching for Cheyennes, and the 4th Cavalry, according to Sergeant McConnell at Buffalo Springs, spent the day celebrating by "horse-racing, foot-racing, etc., serving to pass the day pleasantly," the Indians had not taken the day off. In Hood County they attacked Jesse Caraway's ranch on the Paluxy River and stole 33 horses worth $1,320. They were also in Denton County on Spring Creek, where they stole 109 cattle valued at $5,450, from Reuben Wright.

In Throckmorton County at the Old Stone Ranch, Comanches hit Barber Reynolds again, taking nearly 500 head of steers, cows, and calves. Young Phineas W. Reynolds learned of the attack when he saw a neighbor, Mr. Gilbert, and a discharged soldier named Samuel Blue, come running to the house pursued by four Indians. They scrambled inside as the warriors, joined by four more, circled around firing into the cabin. While they kept the occupants pinned down, others ran off the stock. The raiders had come from the west and left heading over a ridge to the west. "This was the last we saw of them," said Phin. When asked later by a government attorney, "How did you know these were Indians?" Phin answered, "I had seen a good many Indians before that, and these looked like Indians. I was raised on the Texas frontier."[3]

Plenty of youngsters were raised on the frontier, and for some, it was a traumatic experience. In Hamilton County, a score of families living along the Leon River sent their children to a new school on the right bank, five miles northeast of Hamilton. The one-room schoolhouse was constructed of unfinished logs with a crawl space underneath, a door on one side and a window on the other, and wide chinks between the logs let in the summer breeze. The schoolteacher was Miss Ann Whitney. Among her pupils were Olivia Barbee, Jane and John Kuykendall, William Badgett, Mary Jane and Louis V. Manning, Gabriella and Alex Power, John H. Cole, and some children from the Dean, Gann, and Massengill families.

In the afternoon of July 11, Olivia Barbee looked out the door for her father, John Barbee, a stockman who was rounding up cattle, to come and pick her up. Gabriella Power also looked out the door and said she saw Indians. Miss Whitney dismissed her concerns and told her to take her seat, saying that it was either Mr. Barbee or some other ranchers. Gabriella looked again and cried out, "They are Indians."[4]

Gabriella grabbed her brother and they crawled out the window on the north side and ran to the brush along the river. Ann Whitney finally went to the door and saw Indians untying her horse, Mary. She loved the horse, and had often said, "If the Indians ever take Mary, I want them to take me too." When faced with that option, however, she slammed the door and ushered the children out the window. Most of them escaped, but Mary Jane Manning clung to her teacher. Olivia and Louis Manning lifted a floorboard and crawled underneath. Jane Kuykendall hid behind a desk in the corner.

While some Indians stole the horses, four of them came to the cabin. One of them, who had reddish hair and appeared to be a white man, looked between the logs and in fair English, said to Ann Whitney, "Damn you, we have got you now." Ann answered that they could kill her if that would satisfy them, but pleaded for them to leave the children alone. Her plea was answered by a shower of arrows that flew between the logs. Ann was hit several times, but continued to shield the remaining children. As she tried to push Jane Kuykendall out the window, an arrow hit the little girl in the back, inflicting a severe wound. The Indians then burst through the door and finished off Miss Whitney.

The English-speaking Indian asked John Kuykendall and John Cole if they wanted to go with them. Kuykendall (8), with auburn hair and a freckled face, said "yes." Cole said, "no." Strangely enough, the Indian said, "Damn you, sit there," to Cole, and took Kuykendall outside. At the back of the schoolhouse, a warrior saw children emerging from underneath and caught Olivia Barbee. He tried to throw her on his horse while she screamed and kicked. Just then, horses and riders were approaching and they dropped Olivia.

The Indians chased the riders, who were two women, Amanda Howard and her brother's wife, Sarah Howard. The women galloped away. Sarah leapt a rail fence and made it to a neighbor's house. Amanda (17) continued riding and spread the alarm. The Indians gave up and turned west, but before they left the area, they attacked a family riding in a wagon, killing Mr. Standley and wounded his wife, a daughter, and their baby. Olivia Barbee ran screaming from the schoolhouse and was not found until the next day. The Indians also ran into J. E. Pinkerton, a farmer who was traveling from Hamilton to Carlton in northern Hamilton County. They killed him as his horse was bogged down while trying to cross a muddy creek. He was buried in the Carlton Cemetery.

Since there were no soldiers anywhere around, a posse went after the raiders. Aided by hunting dogs, they rode 25 miles to the head of Cowhouse Creek until the dogs' feet were cut and bleeding and they could go no farther. The pursuers called it off after 100 miles. Kuykendall saw the posse about sundown the first day, but the Indians outdistanced them. The boy was a prisoner for about two years until an unnamed Samaritan in Kansas defied orders and purchased him. Isaac Kuykendall, John's older brother, traveled to Kansas and took him back to Texas.[5]

After the Civil War, the R. L. Lane family in Arkansas was left with a destroyed farm and all their stock gone, so with a few neighboring families they decided to move to Texas to start anew. They had relatives in Springtown in Parker County, and headed there. Their horses and wagons broke down and they had a tough time ferrying the swollen West Fork Trinity on a makeshift raft, but they got fresh animals from their kin. On July 15, when camping at the Matthews home in Wise County a few miles north of Springtown, Comanches made another one of their many visits to the area, stealing stock and shooting anyone who got in the way. The Lanes' kinsmen, J. H. Matthews and Polk Matthews, were both wounded and the Lanes once again had lost their horses and mules. That was enough. The Lane, Matthews, and Hudson families called it quits and pulled out, re-settling in Argyle in Denton County. "After our experience with the Indians," said R. L. Lane, "we were sure that place was as far west as we cared to go."[6]

On July 17, 1867, Comanches were back at Elm Creek in Young County. John W. Proffitt had taken 150 cattle and moved to the area in 1863, settling near the Brazos between Forts Bragg and Murrah, but somehow his place was spared in the October 1864 raid. The story was different this time. John's brother, Patrick E. Proffitt, Rice Carrollton, and Reuben Johnson, who had survived the 1864 attack at Fort Bragg, were branding cattle near the old Fitzpatrick place that been devastated in 1864. About ten in the morning, 75 Comanches appeared and charged after the young men, all about 19 years of age. They ran, but within the span of a mile, all three were caught and killed.

The Comanches also went to the Hamby ranch, but Tom Hamby, Roland Johnson, and John Cochran, all veterans of the first raid, were quite a different story from the three young men. The men began blasting away and the Comanches beat a hasty retreat. Johnson's family went to the creek and hid in the same cave they had used three years earlier. The Indians got some horses and rode away to the north.[7]

While the Indians were raiding on all sides of the 6th Cavalry post at Buffalo Springs, they decided to test the soldiers' mettle also. A detail with a sergeant, corporal, 12 men, and some mule teams driven by civilians had gone 18 miles south of the post to the West Fork Trinity to cut timber. While they prepared supper on July 19, nearly 300 Comanches swept into the campsite and stampeded all the mules, lancing and killing one teamster as they rode through. All 24 mules were gone. The detail quickly buried the dead man and marched north through the night, reaching the post next afternoon.

Captain Benjamin T. Hutchins took 70 cavalrymen and went in pursuit, leaving 45 soldiers and 60 civilian employees behind under command of Lt. Francis Matheny. There were only 27 rifles among them. On the 21st, the Comanches appeared, driving hundreds of stolen stock with them. The garrison manned the corral and unfinished buildings they had been constructing. The Indians leisurely placed a half-circle around the post at 400 yards range. Without orders, two soldiers crawled out to get a closer shot, fired, and knocked a warrior off his pony. The Indians responded with a great whoop and fired from all around the circle, but most of their shots fell short. They were getting ready to charge when the 60 civilians, who had gone to their own camp about half a mile to the north, came running back in. The warriors, believing they were armed reinforcements, fell back temporarily and the civilians entered the post grounds.

With the odds no longer so favorable, the Comanches pulled back half a mile and made their own camps. They sat in their relative positions for two days, apparently hoping to wait for the soldiers to turn out their animals to forage or to get thirsty enough to make a move. On the third day, Captain Hutchins belatedly appeared, causing the Comanches to pull out. The story was told that when Hutchins went south to the West Fork, instead of heading to the settlements, he turned west to Fort Belknap and spent two days playing poker with the officers."[8]

Apparently the Army's heart was not fully committed to defending Texans in their settlements, and cowmen making cattle drives were completely on their own, at least for another year. In July, John H. Yancey, Joel W. Curtis, and John D. Parish were driving herds from Texas to New Mexico. Yancey and Curtis had about 1,600 head being driven together, and Parish was slightly behind with a smaller bunch. On July 15, about 15 miles southwest of old Fort Phantom Hill, Kiowas and Comanches attacked them, numbering between 36 and 80 depending on the witness. They cut out 900 head from Curtis and 280 cattle and horses from Yancey. Parish got off easy, losing only

15 cattle. They continued on to Fort Sumner, but their losses meant that they did not break even on the sale.[9]

Raiders were also in Wise and Jack counties in July. On July 24, only two miles south of Decatur, Indians stole ten horses from Robert Sensibaugh, and from James White they got 14 horses worth $720. The next day in Jack County they got John Luttrell's prize stallion, valued at $500.[10]

Author's collection

Texas cattleman Oliver Loving co-pioneered the Goodnight-Loving Cattle Trail. He was killed on that trail in 1867.

One of the most famous attacks on a cattle drive occurred on the Pecos River in late July 1867, and became the central episode in Larry McMurtry's novel and television western of the same name, *Lonesome Dove.* Charles Goodnight and Oliver Loving had teamed up to drive cattle to New Mexico and Colorado in 1866. After a few successful ventures, they set out for what they hoped would be a profitable drive. Joining them with his own herd was William J. Wilson, known as "One Arm." Wilson never seemed to have much luck. He farmed, worked cattle, and ran a saloon. In Jacksboro after the Civil War he was robbed and the "Yankee Carpetbag" courts would do nothing for him. Wilson and another fellow found the thief one night, called him out of his house, and shot him dead. Wilson was caught and taken to the post at Jacksboro. Goodnight found out and got money to Wilson to buy whiskey to get the guards drunk while they escorted him to Decatur for trial. They willingly drank and when tipsy enough, Wilson spurred his horse into the trees along the Trinity bottoms. The guards shot up the woods, but could not catch him. Wilson disappeared for awhile and became a "resident" of Trinidad, Colorado.

In the summer of 1867, Wilson was back, claimed to have purchased 800 cattle in Young County, and joined Goodnight and Loving on their drive. Whether these were really Wilson's cattle or not was later questioned in his depredation claim; they may have been Loving's, but arrangements may have been made to allow Wilson to cash in after Loving's death.[11]

The drive successfully crossed the waterless stretch from the Concho to the Pecos, but after it headed up the Pecos about 60 miles, the Comanches struck. At midnight on July 15, Goodnight woke Wilson for his night shift, and he joined John F. Kutch, James Schultz, and a few others to ride guard. Goodnight said he felt that Indians were around, but the vigilant men could do nothing. The Indians stampeded the cattle and ran them to the east toward the Staked Plains. In the morning, Wilson and six others followed 25 miles east, 25 miles south, and then west back to the Pecos, coming upon 100 Indians with the cattle. As so often occurred, the cowboys were too few to do anything but creep away. They rode 50 miles upriver to meet the rest of the outfit.

There was nothing else to do but continue with what was left. It was late July, and as contracts were to be given in August for next year's drive, Loving was getting impatient. He decided to leave the main herd and move ahead on his own. Goodnight cautioned against it, but Loving insisted, and he wanted "One Arm" Wilson to ride with him.[12]

They rode during the nights, passing Pope's Crossing near the Texas-New Mexico state line. Loving detested night riding, and since they had seen no sign of Indians, he talked Wilson into riding by day. Moving across the open plain north of Black River on July 25, they spotted a large band of Indians riding fast toward them from the Guadalupe Mountains to the west. The two cowmen broke into a four-mile run for the breaks of the Pecos River to the east, reaching the sandy banks and digging in. Wilson had Goodnight's revolving six-shooter rifle as well as his own six-shooter and Loving had side-arms and a Henry Rifle. The Indians poured over the bluffs, crossed the river, and surrounded them. Wilson thought there were several hundred of them. The only opening in the circle of dunes was toward the river, but Loving shot the first Indian who tried to get a bead on them from that angle.

Late in the evening someone called to them from the bluffs in Spanish, proposing surrender terms. The cowmen suspected treachery, but Wilson wanted to try to talk if Loving would cover him. He stepped up on the dune with Loving carrying the Henry behind him. Indians already moved in behind them, and as they climbed the dune, a bullet ripped through Loving's wrist and into his side. They jumped into the ditch and drove the Indians back.

The warriors showered them with arrows, but none hit. That evening, Loving was feverish, and Wilson slipped to the river to get a boot full of water for him. Loving felt sure he would die, and urged Wilson to get away. He said he would keep a six-gun and kill as many Indians as he could before putting the last bullet into his own head. If the Indians left, Loving said he would get into the water and move one mile downriver to hide and wait for help. Wilson should be able to move downriver and run into Goodnight and the rest of the cowboys who were a few days behind them.

Wilson took the Henry, for the metallic cartridges would be unaffected by the water. He removed all of his clothing but his hat, drawers, and undershirt, and slid into the stream. In the moonless night, he slipped past a Comanche watering his horse in midstream, but when in deep water he realized he could not swim with one arm and still hold the rifle. He jammed the barrel deep into the sand below the surface and swam off weaponless. Downstream, Wilson climbed out, and by daybreak, was well on his way. Unfortunately, Goodnight was moving slowly and was still 50 miles away. Wilson walked shoeless for three days across the cactus and rocks.[13]

Ahead of the herd, Charles Goodnight thought he saw someone near the riverbank. The person looked red, but Goodnight spurred his horse ahead to take a look. Said Goodnight: "The river water was red with sediment, and his underclothes were as red as the river itself. But when he beckoned to me, I knew positively that it was Wilson…." He could barely talk, his eyes were bloodshot, his feet were swollen, and he left bloody steps in the sand. Goodnight put him on his horse and hurried back to the outfit, where they wrapped his feet in damp blankets, cleaned him, and fed him. When he related the story, Goodnight took six men and raced ahead to find Loving.

The rescuers rode all night, but when they got to the site of the siege, no one was there. Goodnight said, "I knew they had not got him, as there was ample evidence that they had been hunting for him everywhere." They searched downriver but could not find Loving. When Wilson left, Loving fought off his attackers for two more days and on the third night he slipped into the river, but went upstream, hoping to reach the trail that neared the river about six miles north, and perhaps be found by some passer-by. Eventually he gained the trail and passed out.

Several Mexicans traveling to Texas found him. They gave him water and fed him and he came to his senses. Loving offered them $250 to take him to Fort Sumner and they swung the wagon around and headed north. They met up with other cowmen on the trail, under Jim Burleson, who carried the news to Fort Sumner. An ambulance took Loving to the fort and Burleson hurried downriver to find Goodnight. When he met him, he related the story.

"Loving was killed by Indians, way below on the Pecos," Goodnight said.

"Loving is at Fort Sumner," Burleson replied. Whereupon, Goodnight saddled up his best mule, Jenny, who could canter all day long, and rode 110 miles to the fort in one day and night. Loving's side had healed up, but the shattered wrist was infected and gangrene set in. He did not want the amputation, and the doctor seemed reluctant to perform it because he thought that Loving would not be able to survive the shock. Goodnight told the doctor in no uncertain terms that he must operate. The amputation was performed, but the artery could not be successfully tied off; it kept breaking open and bleeding. Loving slowly faded.

"I regret to have to be laid away in a foreign country," Loving told Goodnight before he died.

Goodnight promised to take his remains back in Texas. Loving died September 25, 1867, and was buried temporarily at Sumner. When Goodnight finished transacting their business, he set about fulfilling his promise the next winter. His cowboys fashioned a tin casket for the body. They placed the wooden casket inside it, packed it with powdered charcoal, sealed it, and placed it in a wagon. They left Sumner on February 8, 1868, six big mules pulling the funeral wagon with Texas cowmen riding front and rear. The cavalcade took the Goodnight-Loving Trail all the way back to Loving's place at Weatherford, where he was buried by the Masonic Lodge with fraternal honors.[14]

Chapter 47 notes

1 Chalfant, *Hancock's War*, 65-66, 68-69; Crawford, *Kansas in the Sixties*, 231-33, 250-51.
2 McConnell, *West Texas Frontier*, 586.
3 McConnell, *Five Years a Cavalryman*, 91; Depredation Claims: Jesse Caraway #4199; Reuben Wright #10632; Ann M. Reynolds #6502.
4 Wilbarger, *Depredations*, 472-73; McConnell, *West Texas Frontier*, in www.forttours.com/pages/tocwhitne.
5 Wilbarger, *Depredations*, 473-78; Winfrey and Day, *Texas Indian Papers, IV*, 231; Marshall, *A Cry Unheard*, 86; "Carlton Cemetery," http://www.cemeteries-of-tx.com/wtx/hamilton/cemetery/carlton.html.
6 Bates, *Denton County*, 396-97.
7 McConnell, *West Texas Frontier*, 587; http://historictempletonmccanlessdistrict.com.
8 McConnell, *Five Years a Cavalryman*, 93-100; Hamilton, Sentinel of the Southern Plains, 23-24.
9 Depredation Claims: John H. Yancey #5822; John D. Parish #6212.
10 Depredation Claims: Robert Sensibaugh #2857; James White #2851; John Luttrell #3494.
11 Haley, *Charles Goodnight*, 123-25; William J. Wilson, Depredation Claim #4315.
12 William J. Wilson, Depredation Claim #4315. In the TV version of *Lonesome Dove*, Charles Goodnight was Woodrow Call, played by Tommy Lee Jones; Oliver Loving was Gus McCrae, played by Robert Duvall; Bill Wilson was Pea Eye Parker, played by Timothy Scott.
13 William J. Wilson, Depredation Claim #4315; Michno, *Forgotten Fights*, 253-54. Wilson claimed losses of two horses, two saddles and bridles, three revolvers, one rifle, 300 head of cattle, plus wages, food, horses, and supplies for five hired hands, amounting to $8,292.
14 Haley, *Charles Goodnight*, 169-84.

48 "The Children cried for milk."

As of August 8, 1867, James Throckmorton was no longer governor of Texas. His constant supplications for more soldiers on the frontier were aggravating to Generals Sheridan and Griffin, who believed he had more than enough. Both men, who had fine military abilities, were lacking in civil administration aptitude. They expected men to follow their orders to the letter and Throckmorton was too independent. The governor was a champion of civil law taking precedent over military, which went against the grain of reconstruction. Throckmorton was thought to be too lenient on citizens who committed crimes against soldiers and freedmen, and he angered Griffin when he refused to give wholesale pardons to 229 freedman serving sentences in the Huntsville penitentiary. The crime rate was going up. Sheridan was told that between 1865 and 1867, homicides had increased from 77 to 331 and the country was infested with bandits. Griffin saw Throckmorton as a façade, espousing moderate principles, but secretly being a hard line conservative. The governor may have followed the letter of the law, but not the spirit, and Griffin said if he didn't "do right," he would remove him from office.

In July 1867, when Congress passed a Third Reconstruction Act, which authorized military commanders to remove civil officers who obstructed reconstruction, Sheridan and Griffin had their ticket. On July 30, Sheridan decreed that Throckmorton "is an impediment to the reconstruction of the State" and removed him from office. Sheridan appointed Elisha M. Pease as governor, effective August 8.

President Johnson, in his ongoing battle with Congress, was angered at Sheridan's action and decided to get rid of two of his adversaries. In early August he removed Secretary of War Edwin Stanton from office and on August 19, Sheridan was gone. The president believed his rule was "one of absolute tyranny" and that personally he was arrogant and "exceedingly obnoxious." Johnson appointed Gen. George Thomas as his replacement, but Thomas did not want the job. Johnson then appointed General Hancock as Fifth Military District commander. Fresh from mucking up his assignment to chastise the Cheyennes on the Central Plains, Hancock needed to be put someplace where he would not have to lead troops in the field against Indians. Commanding the district from New Orleans would be just the place, and besides Hancock was a Democrat and had a more lenient attitude toward ex-Rebels than did Sheridan.

There was more. General Griffin died of Yellow Fever in September, and Gen. Joseph J. Reynolds took over as District of Texas commander. With strong Republican leanings and a mind for political intrigue, he and Hancock would now be at odds.[1]

Before Throckmorton left office he compiled a report from all the counties that had been tallying depredations for him. The August 5 report to Secretary Stanton was not complete, since only 35 counties had responded. Since the summer of 1865 to the summer of 1867, 162 people had been killed, 24 wounded, and 43 taken captive, of which, 29 had been recovered. Stolen were 30,838 cattle, 3,781 horses, and 2,430 sheep and goats. Fighting for his constituents to the end, he recommended more posts spaced closer together, and even extending across Red River north to the Canadian River. But Throckmorton was gone, Governor Pease was not the same staunch settler advocate, and the army generals still did not believe the truth of the reports.[2]

Throckmorton's suggestion for posts in Indian Territory was a reaction to Indian initiatives, but, as usual, before raiding patterns could be discerned and acted upon, the Indians shifted tactics. Raids still came from north of Red River, but increasingly they came out of the west from the Llano Estacado. The Indians who robbed the cattlemen on their drives seemed to be taking the stock to the Staked Plains. In the central counties, more raiders entered and exited from the west, the great San Saba raid being a prime example.

The Quahadi Comanches inhabiting the Llano Estacado, who for years had stayed away from whites and never signed any treaties, were becoming more active in raiding. As the bison disappeared, cattle became the new beef on the hoof. The Indians were becoming pastoralists; where they once were hunters relying on bison, they were now relying on horses, mules, and cattle for sustenance, tending their herds, using some animals for food and others for trade. After their basic needs were satisfied, excess stock went to the Comancheros for guns, ammunition, and manufactured goods.

A government agent who visited the Comanchero "town" of Quitaque in 1867 reported the Comanches were herding 15,000 horses, 300 or more mules, and cattle "without number," while 18 war parties were out at one time raiding the settlements. New Mexicans, who long felt that they had suffered at the hands of land-hungry, acquisitive Texans, were getting their revenge by proxy.

The Comanche and Kiowa revival in the latter half of the 1860s was not due to troop strengths or dispositions, but rather to an increase in rainfall, a shift to pastoralism, diversification of the old bison-centered economy, and increased receipt of U. S. annuities.[3] Soldiers could scout and skirmish with Indians all they wanted, but until they changed to tactics that would disrupt the Comanche and Kiowa economic system, they only would be spinning their wheels.

Raids in August 1867 were far less than the previous August, but it was just a temporary lull. Indians took 14 horses worth $1,400 from Tenville Cecil of Wise County. In Stephens County they got three horses from Ben Browning on Gonzales Creek, and several horses from Mr. Byrd's ranch nearby. Other raiders were deep in Comal County. Charles Power wrote to Governor Pease about the theft of his horses, and those of his neighbors, Parish and Martin. Powers thought the thieves were Tonkawas and he asked if the governor could send him ten Spencer Rifles.[4]

On August 23, Company A, 4th Cavalry, had a skirmish with Indians on the Middle Concho, losing one man killed. On the 30th, Lt. Gustavus Schreyer, Company F, 6th Cavalry, fought with Comanches near Fort Belknap and lost two men killed.[5]

On September 2, raiders were in Hood County stealing horses from Eliza Shipman and later they hit Montague County, stealing six horses worth $950 from Levi Blankenship. In Burnet County Indians got a gelding and a mare from Samuel Holland. William Banta, who had been hit in 1866, was struck again at his Gillespie County ranch in September 1867. He had 200 cows and steers left after the first raid, but none after the second. His daughter, Eliza McGown, said the Indians "took everything he had; he had nothing left." When a government counsel later questioned her as to how she knew there were no cattle left, she answered, "The children cried for milk, and we had no cows to give them milk."[6]

In the south, the 4th Cavalry was becoming more active. On September 10, Lt. Neil J. McCafferty skirmished with Lipans on Live Oak Creek in Kinney County, reportedly killing one. Six days later he fought near Fort Inge and one enlisted man was killed.

In September, Indians captured Frank Gebhard (10) in Medina County. On September 17, 42 Kickapoos wrecked Charles Callahan's sheep ranch in Webb County between the Nueces River and Laredo. They "smashed up everything I had," Callahan said. Gathering a posse, he trailed toward the Rio Grande finding destruction and death. The Indians killed five shepherds and wounded one who worked for Juan Ortiz. The dead were Atanacia Garza, Amador Besa, Jose Luis Ramirez, Luz Luna, and Silberio Baez. They also killed an old man named Alegia, his wife and child, and captured Bernave Landin. Twenty-one people lost horses, sheep, and other property worth $10,700. "The people around here are badly at loss," said Callahan.

He sent a letter to Thomas Dwyer in San Antonio, who had received several letters from Webb County. Dwyer wrote to Governor Pease, saying that the Indians "are committing the most dreadful destruction of life and property" and argued that the situation "shows the need of cavalry protection."

The cavalry protection was there, but it didn't matter. On September 20, Lt. David A. Irwin had a fight near Devil's River and killed one Indian. Occasional harassment of raiders did not stop them at all.[7]

By the fall of 1867, the 9th Cavalry, mostly based in west Texas, was getting into the action. On October 1, Kickapoos killed Cpl. Emanuel Wright and Pvt. E. T. Wright of Company D at Howard's Well as they escorted the mail stage from Fort Clark to Fort Stockton.[8]

In Kimball County it had been more than a year since the big San Saba raid and perhaps the settlers let down their guard. Frank Johnson (55), well-known in the area for his grandfatherly long white beard, lived on the Little Saline in the northeast corner of the county. He went out looking for cattle armed with nothing but a knife and on October 12, Indians caught and killed him near Leon Creek on the Mason County line. When he failed to come home, a search party found his scalped and mutilated body.[9]

In Jack County the post at Buffalo Springs was not working out. The springs, once thought to be a permanent supply of water, had almost dried up, and Captain Hutchins recommended a return to Jacksboro where there was a better water supply. Construction of a permanent post, to be called Fort Richardson, was begun. Before that, the 6th Cavalry had been seeking other areas to locate posts. In 1866, a detachment went to Maxwell's Ranch on the Clear Fork of the Brazos, where they set up a post called Camp Wilson, which later became Fort Griffin.

On October 13, 1867, Sgt. W. A. T. Ahrberg led a scout out of Camp Wilson, composed of 45 enlisted men of Companies F, I, K, and L, and 22 Indian scouts. They rode east through Shackleford, Stephens, and Palo Pinto counties, and circled back on a southern loop. On the way they found and buried the bodies of five murdered civilians. In southeast Shackleford County along Deep Creek near present-day Moran, they ran into some Comanches. Ahrberg's men killed three, captured a woman, 19 horses, a mule, and two revolvers. They rode back to Camp Wilson on October 19, after traveling 160 miles. There were few victories to cheer about, so in November, Col. Joseph J. Reynolds, commanding the District of Texas, decreed that the commander "takes pleasure in commending the energy and courage displayed by Sergeant W. A. T. Ahrberg, Troop 'L,' 6th U. S. Cavalry, and the detachment under his command, in their recent encounter with a party of Comanche Indians."[10]

While the 6th Cavalry was chasing marauders in Shackelford County, the Indians were within the settlements of Montague County. William Freeman built a cabin about six miles south of Forestburg at New Harp, and after the Civil War he became a stock raiser. His son, Dick Freeman, became an expert horseman and his father placed him in charge of a herd of cattle when he was only 12 years old. Staying with the Freemans was Thomas Bailey (12), whose parents, John and Easter Ball Bailey, lived with Easter's parents

Authoor's photo

Fort Richardson, nears Jacksboro, Texas, was in operation from 1867 to 1878.

on the James Ball Ranch about six miles south of the Freemans in northern Wise County.

On October 11, the two boys were herding cattle east of the Freeman home, when suddenly a band of Comanches surprised and captured them. Tom Bailey was riding a splendid, large red sorrel, and had he a warning he could have easily outraced the Indians. As it was, they captured a fine horse along with the two boys. Since they believed the Indians punished any show of emotions, they tried to wear stoic faces. They gave up without a struggle and as the Indians took them north they passed by the Freeman home. They stuffed a gag into Dick's mouth so he couldn't make a sound.

The Indians moved north and came to Levi Perryman's place. They tied the two boys to a tree and searched Perryman's fields for his horses and cattle. Neither the Indians nor the Perrymans were aware of each other's presence; Levi and his wife were both asleep in the cabin. Tom Williams, who lived about one mile south of Perryman, saw the Indians and trailed them to his house. He watched them steal his stock, then crept away and came back the next day, telling Levi about his close call.[11]

The Indians stopped half a mile from Montague while a few warriors crept right into town to steal horses. When done, they continued on and crossed into Indian Territory. When the boys failed to return home, William Freeman organized a search party, but when they located Dick's discarded saddle, he figured his son had been killed. About this time, these raiders or another party captured Alexander Holt (12) in Montague County. He was recovered by Agent Leavenworth in 1868.

Nearly a year passed before traders discovered Freeman and Bailey in Comanche camps on the upper Washita. They were only able to purchase Tom Bailey, but word got to Mr. Freeman and he rode to the Washita in August 1868. There, to his great joy, he found Dick still alive, but to all appearances he was a young Indian, with long hair, painted face, and bracelets. Dick recognized his father at once and begged him to take him home. Dick said he was often beaten, and at times choked to unconsciousness when he failed to understand an order. Dick's first owner, who he called Miattiby, sold him to Myopi, who sold him to Mow-way. Mow-way very reluctantly sold him to his father for a high price: the fine iron-gray horse Mr. Freeman was riding, valued at $150, two pistols worth about $60, and $250 in gold.

Although Mow-way sold the boy back, he told Mr. Freeman that he never wanted to see them again, and if he did, he would scalp them both. The two hurried out of the camp. In William Freeman's depredation claim he asked for $550 for money and property he had to pay for his son's ransom. In addition, Richard Freeman stated, "I further believe that I am entitled to the consideration of $5,000 for the abuse of person which I endured for near one year…by these brutal savages," but the government did not pay a dime for captivities.[12]

After the latest Montague raid, 42 citizens petitioned Governor Pease, saying that the Indians raided them three times within the last six weeks, boldly coming right into the town of Montague in the daylight. They said the military at the Buffalo Springs post "is inadequate," and wanted to raise a company of Rangers to act in conjunction with the army.[13] The military, however, was still not ready to arm ex-Rebels.

In the meantime the Indians were still running all over the state. In October in Medina County they stole $600 worth of horses from Joseph Campbell. In Wise County, Indians got horses from Nick Dawson at his place near Prairie Point, and stole $5,000 worth of horses and mules from Mary T. Bishop. In Cooke County near the junction of Fish Creek and Red River, Comanches stole several of John Scanland's horses, moved a mile downstream and got ten horses worth $625 from John Hobbs. The two men, with Ed Perry, John Cooper, and Thomas Bogard followed ten Indians, but gave up when the trail went across Red River.

On October 22, James Burleson had a roundup on his ranch on Blanket Creek in Brown County. Indians rushed in shouting and shooting, scattering the cowboys, killing a hired man named Devine, and cutting out with 400 cattle and 25 horses.[14]

Some raiding parties didn't have very far to go to get their cattle, especially when the whites brought the stock to them. In the 1865 Little Arkansas Treaty, the Comanches and Kiowas were "given" much of western Indian Territory as a reservation, and part of the deal was to supply them with beef cattle.

Cowmen from north Texas contracted to sell the government stock to supply the tribes. In one instance, John E. Gilliam, who had a ranch on Fish Creek in Cooke County, pooled herds with William Cloud, and moved 640 head north. The cowboys in charge of the herd, including trail boss Tom Sullivan, George Russeau, Alex Simeral, William Davenport, and R. W. Cossett were on their way to Wichita Agency in mid-October. They got the cattle 80 miles north of Cooke County and beyond old Fort Arbuckle when the Indians relieved them of their burden. The cowboys informed the owners and a few weeks later they all rode up to the agency to make a complaint and get the cattle back, or get their money.

They found the cattle, Gilliam's with a "J.G." branded on the left hip, and identified them to the officer in charge. He "ordered us to leave and not bother the Indians," said Cossett.

Years later when Gilliam filed a claim for $4,500 in losses, the government argued that William Cloud actually had the contract, and since Gilliam delivered them in the charge of Cloud, Gilliam did not own them. Cloud, however, died in 1868 and never filed for compensation. The men and their families got nothing.[15]

Chapter 48 notes

1 Richter, Army in Texas During Reconstruction, 104, 111-15; Howell, *James Throckmorton*, 154-55; Wallace, *Texas in Turmoil*,193-96.

2 Winfrey and Day, *Texas Indian Papers, IV*, 235-36.

3 Wallace, *Texas in Turmoil*, 244; Hamalainen, *Comanche Empire*, 315-20.

4 Depredation Claims: Cecil Tenville #2296; Benjamin Browning #4608; Winfrey and Day, *Texas Indian Papers, IV*, 241-42.

5 Adjutant General's Office, 29; Carter, Yorktown to Santiago, 138.

6 Depredation Claims: Eliza Shipman #2228; Levi Blankenship #649; Samuel Holland #2292; William Banta #2640.

7 *Adjutant General's Office*, 29; Winfrey and Day, *Texas Indian Papers*, IV, 243-45, 307.

8 Michno, *Encyclopedia of Indian Wars*, 211.

9 Zesch, *The Captured*, 16; McConnell, *West Texas Frontier*, 608.

10 Hamilton, *Sentinel of the Southern Plains*, 24-25; Carter, *Yorktown to Santiago*, 137-38; *Secretary of War 1868*, 712.

11 Perryman, *Thrilling Indian Raids*, 6; Potter, *Montague County*, 54-56; William M Freeman, Depredation Claim #839. Most accounts place the attack in September, but Dick Freeman said it happened on October 11, 1867.

12 McConnell, *West Texas Frontier*, in www.forttours.com/pages/tocfreeman; Potter, *Montague County*, 57-58; Michno, *Fate Worse Than Death*, 339; William M Freeman, Depredation Claim #839.

13 Winfrey and Day, *Texas Indian Papers, IV*, 246-47.

14 Depredation Claims: Joseph Campbell #2769; Nick Dawson #9960; Mary T. Bishop #6173; John Hobbs #3891; Ellen Burleson #6302.

15 John E. Gilliam, Depredation Claim #6171.

49 "The Indians of my agency have remained perfectly quite and peaceable."

Because treaties were rarely kept by either side, by the fall of 1867 the United States was ready to try again. Apparently the ongoing war on the Texas frontier did not concern federal authorities as much as did the increased fighting in Kansas, brought on by the ill-conceived and poorly conducted operations of Hancock and Custer. When Kansans cried out for help, it brought a response. The peace council at Medicine Lodge in southern Kansas was meant primarily to assuage the Cheyennes, but the Kiowas and Comanches could benefit too.

On October 20, Satanta, although he had never stopped killing and taking captives in Texas, got deferential treatment as a great orator and chief. Standing with his general's coat and bugle dangling at his side, he insisted that he and his people wanted to remain free to roam the prairie and act and live as they had always done. He wanted no houses built because Kiowas always sickened when living inside them. Ten Bears, Silver Brooch, and Satank made similar speeches about not wanting houses, farms, or hospitals. Silver Brooch said the white man promised much, but delivered little. He said that Comanches believed if a person called upon the Great Spirit and lied, he would be destroyed. If the same belief existed among the whites, he said, "I think a good many of their big chiefs would have died long ago."

Thus it went. The Indians accused the whites of perfidy when they were usually just as guilty. Nevertheless, after all the speeches, they signed the document to get the gifts and to get the whites out of their hair for another round. The stipulations were much as in every other treaty: all war would cease; bad white men on the reservation would be arrested; bad Indians would be delivered for white man's justice; buildings to be used for agents, carpenters, millers, blacksmiths, and physicians would be constructed; the Indians would settle down and learn to farm; the Indians' children would go to school; everyone would get clothing; the tribes would get $25,000 annually for 30 years; the tribes would occupy much of the southwest portion of Indian Territory; the tribes would withdraw any opposition to military posts or railroad construction; the tribes agreed "They will never kill nor scalp white men," they "will not attack any persons at home, nor travelling," and "will never capture or carry off from the settlements white women or children."

There were several whites at the proceedings, reporters and officers, who claimed that the stipulations were never read or interpreted to the Indians and they had no idea what they were signing. Correspondent Henry M. Stanley wrote that the treaty was "a very farce, which had the people seen upon the stage, they would have laughed their very eyes out."[1]

As usual, employees of the Bureau of Indian Affairs wrote optimistic reports, in part because they wanted to paint a rosy picture of themselves doing a good job, yet there was tarnish on the buoyant reports of the preceding years. Acting Commissioner Charles E. Mix was coming to believe that "many of the charges of outrages" against the Kiowas and Comanches were true. Still, he couldn't shake the belief that "They do not seem to have fully comprehended that the annexation of Texas made its people citizens of the United States, whom they were bound to respect…." Mix mentioned a number of accusations of depredations, attacks, murders, and captures, but, incredibly, he concluded, "The charges do not appear to have been sustained, except that of the [Box] raid into Texas in 1866…."

Superintendent Thomas Murphy seemed as oblivious. He wrote that assertions were made that his Kiowas were depredating, but "a careful examination of the facts satisfies me that as a nation or as a band they have had nothing whatever to do with the late war." The Kiowas, he said, as well as the Comanches, "have opposed the war from the beginning." The only exception was "an occasional raid into Texas," but in general they have remained faithful to their treaty pledges.

The denials continued down the line. Agent Leavenworth wrote to Mix on September 2, 1867: "I do not wish you to think there are any hostile Indians south of the Arkansas except a very few Cheyennes of 'Black Kettle's' band." He insisted that reports of depredations were false and as proof, he cited one cattle drive that had just brought beef from Texas to feed the Indians at the Wichita Agency. The herders, he said, "report the seeing of a very few Indians, and those very friendly." He dismissed reports "from those seated at military posts and merely writing letters," and challenged them to get out in Indian country and see for themselves. If they did, Leavenworth stated, they would know "The Indians of my agency have remained perfectly quiet and peaceable…." True, there may have been some raids in Texas, he said, but "other Indians, besides the Kiowas and Comanches, have been doing much of this wrong."[2]

While bureaucrats looked through their rose colored glasses, and while the Medicine Lodge Treaty may have been a joke to some, for those settlers who perhaps had gotten some hope that they might live in peace, it was not a laughing matter.

With winter's approach, the raids slowed, but there were occasional incursions. George W. Kendall, for whom Kendall County was named, lived about four miles east of Boerne and ran a large ranch with an estimated 15,000 sheep. Few were expecting a raid, and his herders were caught completely unaware. After the Indians swept through, six men were dead, including two named Baptiste and Schlosser. None were left to provide details.

In Gillespie County, Herman Stohl lived about eight miles northeast of Fredericksburg, and he was out hunting oxen one fall morning. As the story goes, an old freedman asked him if he wasn't afraid to be out alone with no weapon. Stohl reportedly pulled out his pocket Bible and told him as long as he carried the Book, he would not be harmed. History thrives on irony, and just as preachers Griffith and White held up their Bibles as protection from the Indians during the first big raid of 1860, so did Mr. Stohl. And, as happened with the preachers, Stohl ended up just as dead.[3]

Simeon Kemp, who had lost stock in the big San Saba raid in 1866, was at his ranch in Mason County when Indians came right up near his house on November 15, and stole some roan saddle horses, along with 13 horses from a neighbor.

In November, raiders were in southeast Wise County again. Joshua King, who had been hit twice previously, left his home and moved farther east. A man named Van Meter moved into his abandoned cabin. King returned to gather the last of his belongings and stock, but was a little too late. He got there in time to see "9 or 10 bareheaded Indians sporting and cutting up." As it was nightfall, he stayed in his old cabin with Van Meter. In the morning, five of Van Meter's mares were missing, as well as 11 of King's horses. Marcus T. Oates, who also lived at Prairie Point, rode over for help, claiming Indians had just stolen his stock also. Then a man named Sweet arrived with the same story. Sang Kearby and a Mr. Smith joined them and trailed the thieves west to Terrapin Neck where they had a short skirmish. Oates said, "There was a big bunch of Indians and seven or eight of us. When Smith got shot that stopped the fight. We took him to the house and never overtook the Indians again that night."[4]

By the end of the year, more of the information that Throckmorton had requested was coming in. Menard County reported that in 1867 alone, 25 people had stock stolen. In Llano County there were 21 raids resulting in losses.[5]

Near Eagle Springs in west Texas on December 5, about 100 Mescaleros attacked the stage eastbound from El Paso and killed an escort, Pvt. Nathan Johnson, 9th Cavalry. With four horses wounded, the stage barely made it into Eagle Springs Station where Capt. Henry Carroll and Company F, drove the Mescaleros away.[6]

One of the largest fights the Army participated in on the Texas frontier occurred at old Fort Lancaster on December 26, 1867. Captain William T. Frohock and Company K of the 9th Cavalry were guarding horses near the old fort on Live Oak Creek when perhaps 900 Lipans, Kickapoos, Mexicans, and white renegades attacked them, looking for an easy haul of horses. About

Author's photo

The ruins of Fort Lancaster, built in 1855 and abandoned 1861. The fort was occasionally occupied by Union troops after the Civil War.

200 mounted raiders came in from the north, overwhelming a detachment moving the herd to water. At the same time, 400 mounted men attacked the main camp from the west. The troopers formed a defensive circle and tried to corral the remaining horses, but to no avail.

While the raiders were busy gathering the running horses, Frohock got his company secured in the fort ruins and drove off several charges. Frohock figured that the stampeding horses occupied enough of the raiders that they didn't mount a full attack on him, which would have certainly overwhelmed his company. After a time, the captain sent men out on foot to drive the raiders back, but continued threats from all sides limited his options. The raiders, apparently content with getting almost every horse, pulled back at nightfall. Frohock mounted a few men on the last horses and searched, but came back empty-handed. Colonel Edward Hatch, 9th Cavalry, later came from Fort Stockton, inspected the fort, and concluded that his troopers had killed 20 attackers, and among the debris they found an old Confederate uniform. Surprisingly, only three soldiers were killed, all herd guards who were roped and dragged away to their deaths.[7]

Three cavalry regiments were now on the Texas frontier: the 6th was in the north, the 4th in the south, and the 9th in the south and west. Fort Stockton was re-occupied by the 9th Cavalry in July 1867, and Fort Concho was established by the 4th Cavalry in December 1867. The 6th Cavalry established Camp Wilson in July 1867, which became Fort Griffin, and was building Fort Richardson in November 1867. There were nearly 3,000 soldiers on the frontier, but they were largely ineffective. From July 1 to December 31, 1867, the three cavalry regiments sent out 26 Indian hunting "expeditions," averaging 33 men, eight days, and 186 miles for each scout. The result was that they all reported "No Indians seen," or, "abundant signs but no Indians seen."[8]

One is reminded of the story of the man who lost his wallet at the end of a dark alley, but searched for it at the other end under the streetlight because that was where the light was. It seemed as if the army would fight, at least when the Indians came to them. Finding the Indians first and stopping them from entering the settlements was a different matter. Still, frontier troop numbers were the highest they had ever been. Those who had argued that high troop strength resulted in less raiding and killing would see if they were right.

Chapter 49 notes

1 Hoig, *White Man's Paper Trail,* 147-48; Kappler, Indian Treaties, 977-81; Jones, Medicine Lodge, 200.

2 *Commissioner of Indian Affairs 1867*, 18, 292, 314-15.

3 McConnell, *West Texas Frontier*, 595, 600; Sowell, *Early Settlers*, 753.

4 Depredation Claims: Simeon Kemp #4777; Joshua G. King #2291.

5 Winfrey and Day, *Texas Indian Papers, IV*, 251-54.

6 Leckie, *Buffalo Soldiers*, 85.

7 Burton, *Black, Buckskin, and Blue*, 152-53.

8 Aston, "Federal Military Reoccupation," 129.

Part 10. 1868

50 "He was scalped and frozen when we found him."

It did not take long to discover three regiments of cavalry on the Texas frontier didn't make a difference. There were a number of "big raids" remembered by the pioneers of the 1860s, but arguably, perhaps the biggest, at least in terms of white casualties, was known as Big Tree's Raid. In early January 1868, under a three-quarters waxing moon, the Kiowa, Big Tree, led about 300 Kiowa and Comanche warriors across Red River into Montague and Cooke counties on what was primarily a murder raid.

If any of the settlers had faith in the recent Treaty of Medicine Lodge, their hopes were soon dashed. The Comanche and Kiowa pledge that they would no longer kill whites or carry off women and children meant nothing. After the presents were distributed most of the Indians went down to their assigned reservation around Fort Cobb, but within a month, they were complaining about insufficient rations. The Senate had not yet ratified the treaty, and Agent Jesse Leavenworth had not made adequate preparations to feed them during the oncoming winter. Some warriors went west to attack Navajos, while others went east to attack the more peaceably disposed Wichitas, Caddos, and Chickasaws. In January 1868, the marauders stole about 4,000 horses and cattle from the Chickasaws and killed a number of them. Cyrus Harris, governor of the Chickasaw Nation, wrote for help, and said, "The wolf will respect a treaty as much as Mr. Wild Indian."[1]

If the Comanches and Kiowas were truly hungry, then buffalo, cattle, and horses could have supplied their needs. Given the tens of thousands of cattle stolen in Texas over the past two years, there were probably one dozen cattle for each living Comanche and Kiowa in Indian Territory. Hunger was not a reason for their murder spree into north Texas.

On Sunday, January 5, one of the first places the Kiowas hit was Robert F. Clark's farm in the upper Willawalla Valley about 13 miles southeast of Montague. Clark and his wife, who was pregnant with her first child, were not home. They barely eked out an existence through the soil and had nothing but a mule to help with the plowing. Martha Clark (14), Robert's sister, was home when she saw the Indians approaching and she ran out into the brush and hid. Not finding much worth stealing, the Kiowas destroyed the property, including feather beds, quilts, linens, clothing, dishes, hides, tobacco, a barrel of sorghum and a spinning wheel, worth $506.[2]

The Kiowas traveled downstream near the homes of Allen H. Newberry and W. D. Anderson. Mr. and Mrs. Newberry had gone to church and told their sons to stay at home, but when they left, Henry Newberry and Duke

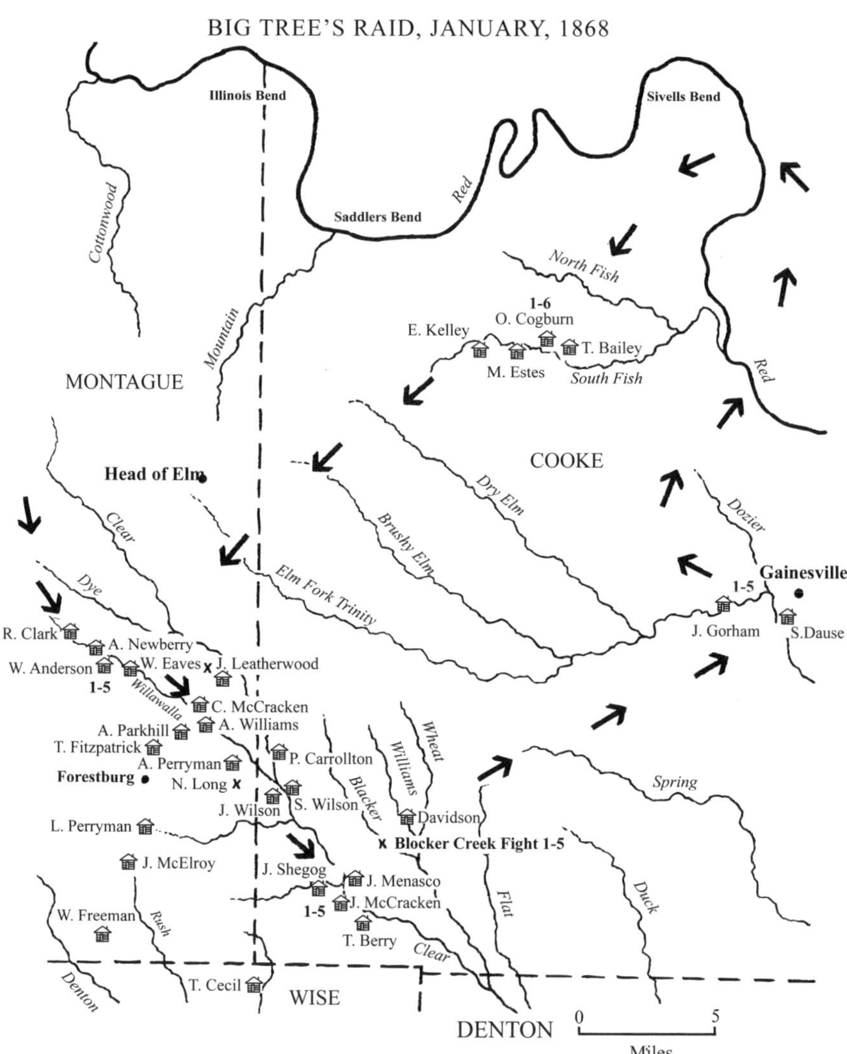
BIG TREE'S RAID, JANUARY, 1868
Illinois Bend
Sivells Bend
Saddlers Bend
Red
Cottonwood
Mountain
North Fish
1-6
O. Cogburn
E. Kelley
T. Bailey
M. Estes
South Fish
Red
MONTAGUE
COOKE
Head of Elm
Dry Elm
Brushy Elm
Clear
Dozier
Dye
Elm Fork Trinity
Gainesville
1-5
J. Gorham
S.Dause
R. Clark
A. Newberry
W. Anderson
W. Eaves
J. Leatherwood
1-5
Willawalla
C. McCracken
A. Williams
A. Parkhill
T. Fitzpatrick
A. Perryman
P. Carrollton
Wheat
Williams
Forestburg
N. Long
Blacker
S. Wilson
J. Wilson
Davidson
Spring
L. Perryman
Blocker Creek Fight 1-5
J. McElroy
J. Shegog
J. Menasco
J. McCracken
1-5
Duck
Flat
W. Freeman
Rush
T. Berry
Clear
Denton
T. Cecil
WISE
DENTON
0
5
Miles

Anderson decided to gather pecans. Butler Newberry warned, "Your mother said for you not to leave the place in her absence." Henry replied, "We will get back before papa and mama return from church."

About 400 yards from the house they saw riders they thought were cowboys, but on closer look they turned out to be Indians. Henry and Duke ducked down into the Willawalla creek bed and snaked upstream almost a mile. They hid until late in the evening before creeping back home, after the parents got home and went on a frantic search for them. They were all lucky, however, for the Kiowas apparently missed the Newberry home, while the Andersons saw the Indians approaching, barred the doors, and pointed their weapons. The Indians, seeking easier prey, moved on.

Riding nearby, W. A. "Bud" Morris and D. S. Hagler saw the Indians and spurred their horses downstream to warn the other settlers. They reached the home of William R. Eaves, and they all galloped on, three Paul Revere's spreading the alarm. The Kiowas split into several smaller parties and ranged up and down hill and valley. The white riders rode up to Charles McCracken's home, but too late; it had already been burned to the ground. The McCrackens, however, were already hiding in the woods since a fourth Paul Revere, George Masoner, had gotten there first to give the alarm.

After burning McCracken's cabin, some Kiowas went up the divide toward Clear Creek and found brothers John and Daniel S. Leatherwood (23) riding their horses. They galloped away, but only Daniel escaped. Warriors shot and killed John Leatherwood and stole the sorrel mare he was riding. A few days later, David P. McCracken (22) and a few other men found the lanced body. "He was in a pretty bad condition," said McCracken. "It turned cold, and he had no clothes on. He was scalped and frozen when we found him."[3]

John Leatherwood was one mile from Millis Joel C. McCracken's place when the Indians attacked. The McCrackens were from North Carolina, but had lived in Texas since 1860. Charles McCracken and his wife had a cabin and their sons, Millis McCracken and David P. McCracken had another cabin nearby. When Dan Leatherwood rode up to Millis' with the news that Indians had killed his brother, David and Millis McCracken joined him. Dave McCracken said, "we went down there to fight them. We were going to meeting that day, and we heard the Indians were down there. We did not know that there was any more than five Indians at the time, and we thought that we would go down there and give them a little fight, but...there was too many for us, and we had to go into the brush." While thus engaged, other warriors went to McCracken's, stole horses and destroyed the place. The whites watched from a hillside while the house went up in flames.[4]

Tennessean Alfred Williams, his wife, Amanda, and sons Thomas and Nathaniel, lived just downstream from the McCrackens, sharing a cabin with his brother George W. Williams and family. After seeing his house burning, Dave McCracken rode downstream to warn the Williamses, but found they had already been warned by George Masoner. He saw them as they were just about to disappear into the brush and he followed them. George Williams and his family had gone to church and were not in the area. After Masoner left, Amanda Williams saw the Indians approaching about a quarter mile away. As they hurried to hide, McCracken arrived. A few warriors saw them going into the timber, but McCracken bluffed them back with his shotgun. They decided not to press the determined man and went back to the house.

Amanda was not all that thrilled at first, believing McCracken led the Indians right to them. "The Indians followed Mr. McCracken," she said. "I saw them after him."

The Indians didn't follow into the trees, but they plundered the cabin, stealing gold watches and rings, money, clothing and blankets, and destroying beds, linens, shoes, and dishes, losses amounting to $750. When the Indians left, they went close by the hiding place where a warrior dropped Alfred Williams's hat, which he was able to retrieve.[5]

When Morris, Hagler, and Eaves reached the home of Alfred Williams, they found they were losing the race; the Indians had already been there. They rode to Morris' house where his family and mother-in-law, Mrs. Dennis, lived. Morris learned that they had just returned from church and had gone home with W. H. Perryman and family. The riders, now joined by Millis McCracken and Sam Dennis, rode to warn the Perrymans.

One band of warriors crossed over a ridge to the Carrollton home on Clear Creek. George Masoner had warned them already, but they could not get out fast enough. The Indians killed Mrs. Carrollton and captured her daughter, Paula (15). Her brother, Rice Carrollton, had been killed with Proffitt and Johnson the year before.

The Indians reached the Perryman home, but the fast-riding Masoner had already warned them. Mrs. Perryman put on a hat and some of Austin's clothing, and joined her husband at the window, with rifles pointing out. The Indians, again seeing a potential fight on their hands, swerved around the cabin and kept going. Nathan Long was in their path. He tried to hide in the timber, but they found and killed him. Masoner warned Mrs. Long and her children, who lived at Joe Wilson's place four miles east of Forestburg, and they had time to hide in the woods before the Indians arrived.

Next in line was Savil Wilson's cabin. His wife was dead and he was not home, but George Masoner rounded up his children and took them into the woods. The Indians found the place vacant, robbed it, and burned it down. They had just ridden away when Morris, Hagler, Eaves, McCracken, and Dennis arrived, followed a minute later by Savil Wilson. He saw his house aflame, did not know Masoner had already gotten his children out, and went crazy with grief, believing they had been captured or burned to death. Shortly after, they came out of the woods, as did Mrs. Long and her children. There were now six men there to protect them. Mrs. Long, however, recognized a saddle that the Indians left behind as belonging to her husband, and knew that he had been killed.[6]

Some Kiowas crossed the line into northeast corner of Wise County and came to Tenville Cecil's place. Cecil had lost horses to Indians before. This time they got 18 head. He and a few neighbors followed the tracks five miles to Clear Creek in Cooke County where they arrived at Daniel Menasco's place. The Indians had just been there.[7]

Daniel G. Menasco and his wife, Sophia Brown (32), built their cabin on Clear Creek near Cooke County's southern border in 1859. In 1861, Menasco's father, Joseph, along with his wife and two remaining children arrived from Arkansas and moved in with him. James and Louisa Shegog lived a mile west of the Menascos with their five children: Anna (24), R.E. (21), Louis (19), W.E. (17), and Jennie (15). An adult son, Edward (called Captain Shegog), had a cabin nearby. He was married to Elizabeth Menasco Shegog. Daniel Menasco, his brother, and some of the Shegog boys served with the Confederacy during the Civil War. Old Joseph Menasco looked after the families while they were away.[8]

About three in the afternoon a rider brought word of an Indian raid and Joe Menasco, knowing that Edward was away, decided to hurry to the Shegogs and bring back his daughter and two of his grandchildren who were there visiting their Aunt Elizabeth. He placed them in a wagon, but only made it 200 yards from the house when the Indians struck. The old man was shot and scalped. The Indians captured Elizabeth Shegog, her infant child (18 months), her nieces, Lizzie Menasco (8) and May Menasco (6), and a black child who stayed with the Shegogs.[9]

Sophia Menasco heard shots and recognized the screams of her sister-in-law. Daniel was about 200 yards from the house when the Indians appeared and he ducked into the woods. Sophia saw about 15 Indians. They had her sister-in-law and her child, two of her own little girls, and a black child. "I gathered my two little girls that were with me and put them in a room and gave them some play-things," Sophia said, and then "returned to the hall of my house, took my husband's gun and went back to the room where my children were." The Indians came within 20 yards of the window, but saw a person holding a rifle and did not come closer. They went to a back lot, stole four horses, and rode off. Within three miles, Elizabeth Shegog's baby began to cry and a warrior smashed it against a tree. When either Lizzie or May Menasco began to cry they killed her too.

When the Kiowas left, Daniel Menasco got his wife and two daughters, and went to Julius McCracken's house for help. He left them there and convinced another neighbor, Thomas Berry, to go with him to where his father was killed. In a short time about 20 settlers were ready to follow the Indians' trail. One of them was Tenville Cecil, who was tracking Indians from Wise County. He said "we found where they had killed a man by the name of Menasco, I saw his dead body." He joined others and trailed the Indians north.[10]

The sun went down early in January, and a storm was brewing. Nevertheless, the pursuing settlers caught up to one band of Indians on Blocker Creek and had a short, sharp fight. In the confusion, Paula Carrollton slipped from her horse and hid in a thicket. In the gathering darkness and pressed by the settlers, the Indians had no time to search for her. They rode away, veering northeast toward Gainesville. Paula wandered in the dark for a time before hearing dogs barking. She followed the sound and came upon the home of Dr. Davidson on Williams Creek. Thinking Indians may have captured the house, she took shelter in a ravine and covered herself with brush. About one in the morning, January 6, a strong blizzard blew in from the northwest, covering Paula under a carpet of snow and dropping the temperature to only a few degrees above zero. She waited until morning when she saw white men at the house. Davidson took her in and gave her warm fluids to thaw her out.

After the Blocker Creek skirmish, the Kiowas went within six miles east of Gainesville. The storm was bad and they may have lost their way. They backtracked around the town before stopping to camp about a mile southwest of the unsuspecting residents. One band actually rode into Gainesville before realizing their mistake and quickly exited. An Indian's horse was found next morning standing near the door of the hotel. That night the captives began to freeze, but the warriors gave them no blankets. To the contrary, Elizabeth Shegog was stripped nearly naked, and one warrior found the time to take his knife and hack off her long hair down to the skin. She went numb and fell off her horse and the warriors left her in the deepening snow. She fainted and when she regained consciousness she could barely move, but she saw a lightening sky to the east and heard a rooster crow. Elizabeth dragged herself toward the sound. Eventually she crawled to the door of Sam Dause (Doss), who lived about one mile southwest of Gainesville. He took her in, warmed and fed her. Her limbs were badly frostbitten and she was unable to move for several days, but was said to have "partly recovered from her experience."[11]

Before the storm fully hit on the night of January 5, Kiowa bands were stealing stock. Thomas W. Gahagan and his wife, Manda, lived in Gainesville but ran stock on Clear Creek near the Shegog's. When the Indians came in, they easily ran off 50 of their horses and mules, worth $2,825. With their investment gone, said Mrs. Gahagan, "her husband was broken up in business, and had to go out to work at anything he could do."

A few miles west of town they visited Joshua Gorham's ranch and took 19 horses Gorham had recently brought from Wisconsin that he valued at $1,385.

James Davenport, who ran his stock from west of Gainesville up toward Head of Elm, was right in the Kiowas' path. He lost horses and mules in the Box raid and was in the wrong place again. The freedmen Simon and Louis Woody were tending Davenport's horses as they did in 1866, and they had just as bad luck the second time. The Indians took 36 horses worth $1,495. The Woodys trailed a little ways, but were afraid to get too close, instead going after one horse that the Indians shot and abandoned. They chased the horse "to get the arrow out of it, but we couldn't catch it, or nothing;" said Louis, "it was scared to death."[12]

Author's collection

Kiowa Big Tree led a devastating raid into north Texas in January 1868.

The Kiowas headed west up Elm Fork and then cut north and crossed Red River. Behind them they left the black child and the other Menasco girl, either Lizzie or May. They shot them with arrows and threw their bodies in the snow; if they weren't dead, the storm soon killed them. It wasn't until several days after Joshua Gorham discovered his horses missing that he, Ward Bland, and Sinclair Jones followed the trail. Instead of finding horses or Indians, they discovered a recently abandoned camp. There was a rifle that belonged to one of Gorham's neighbors that the Indians apparently had dropped. There was a wounded mule with Davenport's "M. D." brand. There was also the body of a dead white girl about six years old with three arrows sticking in her body.[13]

On January 6, the settlers assumed the raiders were gone and began to assess the damages and look for the bodies. Big Tree, however, with the storm waning and perhaps angry that he had once had six captives and now had none, or not satisfied with the number of whites killed or horses stolen, circled back and re-crossed Red River in the Sivell's Bend vicinity. In northern Cooke County they did not even know a raid had occurred. Big Tree struck early Monday morning. One of the first places attacked was Dr. Thomas Bailey's on South Fish Creek. After stealing 12 of his horses, the Kiowas went up the creek one mile and stole stock from O. A. Cogburn, and then from M. W. Estes, E. M. Kelley, and a Mr. Palmer. The men got together and followed the Indians west toward Head of Elm. "We run them all day," Cogburn succinctly explained. "We missed them. They dodged us. The ground was frozen. We never got in sight of them. That is all I know." The losses hurt because with the constant thefts, horseflesh was getting scarce. "Horses were very high then," said Cogburn. "Most any kind of horse was worth from $50 to $75." From Head of Elm, the Kiowas turned southwest back down to the middle of the Willawalla Valley in Montague County.[14]

Arthur Parkhill, who lived one mile from "Bud" Morris, one of the horseback criers of the previous day, didn't know anything about the raid until Morris rode over to see him. Now concerned, Parkhill hurried to his brother's place and convinced him to come to his cabin because it was better fortified. Parkhill then rode one mile to Thomas J. Fitzpatrick's place two miles north of Forestburg and convinced them to come to his cabin. Fitzpatrick got his wife, their two daughters, Susan (6) and Alice (8), and their son (2), and hurried to Parkhill's. Just then the Kiowas arrived, killed Parkhill and Fitzpatrick, scooped up Mrs. Fitzpatrick and the three children, and were gone.

Once more the settlers tried to follow, but it began snowing again and they gave up. The next day, settlers found Mrs. Fitzpatrick's body frozen in the snow. She had been raped, and her skirt was pulled up and tied around her head. "Bud" Morris found the body of the Fitzpatrick boy, half eaten by animals. Susan and Alice were gone. Cooke County Judge J. E. Wheeler wrote to Governor Pease on February 15 that the people were moving out, and almost hourly their wagons were passing through the streets of Gainesville. The settlers were frustrated and in despair, and increasingly blamed the Reconstruction government for protecting freedmen, persecuting former Confederates, and not guarding the frontier. It seemed as if Texas and the United States had forsaken them.[15]

Daniel Menasco and Edward Shegog were among those leaving, pulling back to Pilot Point in Denton County. Menasco was not convinced his girls were dead—either the bodies had not been found or identified as yet. He wrote to Agent Leavenworth: "Colonel, I would give the world if I had it for my dear children back again. Their broken-hearted mother is grieving herself to death for them. It is a hard trial; it looks like it is more than we can bear, but we have no way to help ourselves."[16]

The raid finally convinced Jesse Leavenworth to resign. Before the winter of 1868, he had been a champion of the peace policy, but since then he was telling his superiors that the Indians were uncontrollable. "They have all," he wrote, "without an exception, as bands, been engaged in acts of violence and outrages in Texas, and should be dealt with severely." Leavenworth spent the spring trying to buy captives, but it seemed that the more he rescued, the more were taken prisoner. In May 1868, he located Susan and Alice

Fitzpatrick and purchased them, but then he walked off his job and left Indian country for good. No one claimed the Fitzpatrick girls and they ended up in the Protestant Orphan Asylum in Washington, D. C. Their names were changed to Helen and Heloise Lincoln.[17]

The 12 settlers killed in Big Tree's raid made it the decade's costliest in terms of civilians killed. It occurred during a time when there were more mounted troops on the frontier than ever before, and was more proof that numbers were not the primary factor in curtailing aggression.

Chapter 50 notes

1 Nye, *Plains Indian Raiders*, 111-113.
2 Robert F. Clark, Depredation Claim #507.
3 Perryman, *Thrilling Indian Raids*, 8-9; Daniel S. Leatherwood, Depredation Claim #2079.
4 David P. McCracken, Depredation Claim #7159.
5 Amanda Benns (Williams), Depredation Claim #3875.
6 McConnell, *West Texas Frontier*, in *www.forttours.com/ page/tsocbigtre*; Potter, *Montague County*, 32-34. Brown, *Indian Wars*, 119.
7 Tenville Cecil, Depredation Claim #2296.
8 McConnell, *West Texas Frontier*, in www.forttours.com/pages/tocbigtre; Wilbarger, *Depredations*, 586-87; Winfrey and Day, *Texas Indian Papers, IV*, 56-62; Louis Shegog, Depredation Claim #4360.
9 Wilbarger, *Depredations*, 587; Louis Shegog Depredation Claim #4360; Daniel Menasco Depredation Claim #4211.
10 Depredation Claims: Daniel Menasco #4211; Tenville Cecil #2296.
11 Daniel Menasco Depredation Claim #4211; McConnell, *West Texas Frontier*, in www.forttours.com/ pages/tocbigtre; Wilbarger, *Depredations*, 588; Brown, *Indian Wars*, 119-20; Potter, *Montague County*, 37.
12 Depredation Claims: Manda A. Gahagan #5257; Joshua Gorham #424; James B. Davenport #5732.
13 Joshua Gorham, Depredation Claim #424.
14 Thomas Bailey, Depredation Claim #4346.
15 McConnell, *West Texas Frontier*, in *www.forttours.com/pages/tocbigtre*; Winfrey and Day, *Texas Indian Papers IV*, 257-58; Brown, *Indian Wars*, 120; Potter, *Montague County*, 29.
16 Rister, *Border Captives*, 143. Menasco may have learned that the Indians had two white girls (the Fitzpatricks) and hoped they were his daughters.
17 Richardson, *Comanche Barrier*, 160; Hoig, *Kicking Bird*, 124; Foreman, "Jesse Leavenworth," 27; McConnell, *West Texas Frontier*, in www.forttours.com/pages/tocbigtre. More on this story can be found in Michno, *Fate Worse Than Death*, 379-86.

51 "This is my poor child's hair."

The winter of 1868 was one of the worst seasons of raiding in Texas history. About the last day of January or first of February, Indians were back in Stephens County stealing seven horses from Ben Browning, but there was one they could never get. He was a fine specimen that had been captured before, but broke loose and made his way back home. This time the Brownings found the other horses gone, but this one was still in the pen, with a snapped lariat around his neck, nearly choked to death. There were "six arrows sticking in him." If the Indians couldn't capture him, they tried to kill him.

Other Indians were in Cooke County again, only weeks after Big Tree's raid. This time they only got five horses worth $650 from Elijah C. Perry. Down in Bexar County, Kickapoos came close in to San Antonio and stole three horses from Thebolt Monier.[1]

In Kerr County, John J. Alexander, his wife Mary, and their daughter, Nancy, who married W. C. Wachter, shared a cabin on the South Fork Guadalupe about 18 miles upriver from present Kerrville. They made shingles out of cypress wood that grew along the river and on February 2, Messrs. Alexander and Wachter were gone to Fredericksburg to sell their product. A son of Alexander and a freedman were about half a mile from the cabin cutting more shingles and the mother and daughter were by themselves.

When the dogs began barking, Nancy Wachter looked out to see Indians coming to the door. She grabbed an iron and when a warrior burst in, she clubbed him with it, knocking him down. The two women ran in different directions but Mary Alexander didn't get far; she was shot down just off the porch. Nancy ran toward where her brother was working but an arrow struck her in the shoulder. She fell and crawled behind a log while the Indians went in to plunder the house. When Nancy reached her brother, he sent her to a neighbor's and he returned to his house, but looking from a ridge he saw the place engulfed in flames.

They all took refuge at Fritz Tegener's cabin. Word went out and surrounding settlers converged there, but when they got to the Alexander cabin there was nothing but ashes. They found Mary Alexander's body partly consumed by the flames. Samuel Fessenden, an ex-ranger, helped bury her. Her clothing was burned off, he said, and they had to handle the remains carefully to keep the arms and legs from coming off. The men tried following the Indians but a snowstorm blew in and they gave up.[2]

In February there occurred the bloodiest tragedy ever in Llano County. John S. Friend arrived at picturesque Sandy Creek in Legion Valley, about 15 miles south of Llano in 1856. Friend was a stock raiser and farmer with a daughter, Florence, and a younger son, Lee Temple, who was born in 1860. When his wife died, John Friend stayed in the area, married Matilda Jane Dancer, and moved to what he called the "Dancer Ranche" in March 1867.[3]

There were few households in Legion Valley; the Bradfords and Johnsons lived nearby and members of the families were related. On the morning of February 5, John Friend was at the mill in Fredericksburg. Brothers Asa G. "Boy" Johnson and Thomas "Babe" Johnson were both away on business, and several people congregated at Friend's place: the pregnant Samantha Johnson Johnson and her child, Fielty (1); Rebecca Stribling Johnson and her child, Nancy (3); Amanda Townsend (18); Malinda Ann "Minnie" Caudle (8); Lee Temple Friend (8); and the pregnant Matilda Friend (20). Florence Friend was not home. The previous night Becky Johnson had a nightmare and told her Aunt Betsy Johnson that Indians killed her and wild animals ate her remains. The dream was horrible. Aunt Betsy laughed at her foolishness. The stage was set for more memorable historical irony.[4]

It was sundown when Lee and Minnie ran to the house, exclaiming that someone was taking their pony, "Button." The women went out, saw it was an Indian, and hurried inside to bar the door. A few minutes later 15 Comanches surrounded the house and tried to force their way in. Matilda gave a shotgun to one of the Johnson women and told her to shoot if they broke in, but the Johnsons wanted to surrender. Meanwhile, the warriors easily broke through the thin, picketed walls. Matilda grabbed a Spencer rifle, but a warrior wrested it away. She grabbed a smoothing iron and struck one of them, while another shot her in the side with an arrow. The projectile hit a rib, glanced around her breastbone, and came out the other side. Matilda collapsed on the bed, feigning death.

The others gave up and were led outside and tied. The Comanches plundered the cabin, taking clothing, food, a double-barreled shotgun, the Spencer, a Navy pistol, a sidesaddle, four horses, and $287 in currency. Matilda was silent, face to the floor. A warrior bent down and severely slashed her left hand three times, cutting the nerves. He twisted the arrow in her side to make sure she was dead, and then cut a two- by four-inch "scalp" from the front right side of her head, and a two- by three-inch patch from the back of her head. The pain was intense, but Matilda played dead. When the Indians left she forced herself up, wrapped a cloth around her head, and half-crawled to the Bradfords, a mile to the southeast, reaching there at eight p.m. The family was shocked at her appearance and Mrs. Bradford insisted upon fleeing immediately. Mr. Bradford helped pull the arrow from her side, but did not stay to dress her wounds. They built a fire, left her with a bucket of water, and fled.[5]

Matilda Friend sat in a chair all night. At eight the next morning, two neighbor women came to her rescue. The cloth had dried to her head, and they removed it with hot water. Her body was so swollen that it was very difficult to remove her clothes. During the day her husband came and a doctor finally arrived that night.

The Comanches probably had no intention of letting all of their prisoners live. Only a mile and a half from the Friend cabin a warrior choked Fielty Johnson. Samantha tried to take the baby away, but the angry Indian smashed its head. A posse of about one dozen men from Llano, including Messrs. Luce, Miller, Oatman, Holden, and Amanda's father, Spence Townsend, picked up the Indian trail about 36 hours later. Mr. Luce said they found "Mrs. Johnson's babe, with its brains knocked out." In another mile, the Indians murdered Nancy Johnson (3). Minnie Caudle watched the warriors cut the girl's throat and hold her in front of Rebecca's eyes, "up by the feet with its head down right before her, as if to see the blood flow. Mrs. Johnson screamed and fainted, at which they laughed as if it were great sport." They scalped the girl, leaving one small tuft of hair near her neck.

The Comanches camped the first night near the top of Cedar Mountain, several miles east of the attack site. They built a fire, roasted some meat, and raped the women. Minnie Caudle watched the warriors draw their knives, "but just then," she said, "my squaw threw a blanket over my head." Minnie couldn't see, but she knew what was going on. "They cried and prayed all the time and they knew they were going to be murdered," Minnie said. In the morning, Samantha Johnson either refused to move, or could not go any farther. The posse found her in a sitting position, with a lance entering her right shoulder blade and coming out above her left hip. Her throat was slashed and she was scalped. It looked like Becky Johnson had run before she was murdered. The posse found her "stripped of nearly all her clothing, and the body nearly eaten up by the hogs." Her nightmare had come true.

The trail led four miles down Cedar Mountain to Cut Off Gap. There, the posse found Amanda Townsend's body. Said Mr. Luce: "She had been tied down upon the cold ground, which was covered with snow, and from all appearances, had been outraged in the most brutal manner. She was then killed, and her body mutilated almost beyond recognition." Spence Townsend picked up a piece of flesh with a lock of yellow hair attached and screamed, "This is my poor child's hair!" He was so distraught that he began to have chest pains and the other men made him go back home. The posse moved on, but a new layer of snow made trailing difficult. They rode for five days until giving up at the headwaters of Devils River.[6]

Over the following months, John Friend spent $1,000 "doctoring his wife." He and his father, Leonard S. Friend, spent much time and money trying to rescue the children. Back in October 1866, the Texas Legislature passed a law that appropriated $2,500 to be used at the governor's discretion to aid in rescuing captives. In July 1868, Governor Pease appointed Leonard Friend as an agent with use of the funds to buy back captives, but before Friend went to Kansas, Agent Edward Wynkoop discovered Malinda Caudle in a Comanche camp near Fort Larned and compelled them to give her up.

John and Leonard Friend were not so lucky. In September they moved to Butler County, Kansas, and continued their hunt for Lee Temple. During the next few years, Leonard traveled more than 15,000 miles in Texas, New Mexico Territory, Indian Territory, and Kansas. He made three trips to Washington to personally talk to officials who he hoped could help him get back his grandson. The years passed. Not until November 1872 did the Comanches turn in Lee Temple Friend to Agent Lawrie Tatum at Fort Sill.

Having been in captivity nearly five years, Temple could hardly remember a word of English, but he remembered his father's name was John, that he had an older sister, and that he believed his mother and aunt were killed. Temple, now 13, rode in a buggy with his grandfather to his new home in Kansas. Although he appeared healthy, he had contracted some unnamed malady. Temple died suddenly on June 2, 1876, at only 16 years of age.

John and Matilda Friend tried to get compensation for their losses from the Bureau of Indian Affairs. John had spent $1,000 on medical bills for his wife, but she was never able to use her left hand again, plus the wound on the right side of her head never healed properly. John claimed $3,000 for her injuries and $2,500 more for money spent searching for his son. The proverbial red tape and delays went on for two decades. In 1894, government attorney Charles B. Howry concluded that while the attack was terrible, "the sympathy it awakens and the sentiments it inspires have no place in this Court." He submitted, "that the petition should be dismissed." Court of Claims Judge Charles J. Richardson was not that cold. Although he ruled, incredibly, that it could not be proven that the Indians were liable for the injuries, he would allow the property claim. The Friends received $897.[7]

Chapter 51 notes

1 Depredation Claims: Benjamin Browning #4608; Elijah C. Perry #5717; Thebolt Monier #7488.

2 Sowell, *Early Settlers*, 739; McConnell, *West Texas Frontier*, 605.

3 Wilbarger, *Depredations*, 630-31, 633; John S. Friend Depredation Claim #3379.

4 John S. Friend Depredation Claim #3379; Winfrey and Day, *Texas Indian Papers* 4, 269, 310; Zesch, *The Captured* 69-70; McConnell, *West Texas Frontier*, in www.forttours.com /pages/toclegion; Wilbarger, *Depredations*, 633.

5 John S. Friend, Depredation Claim #3379; McConnell, *West Texas Frontier*, in www.forttours.com /pages/toclegion; Wilbarger, *Depredations*, 634-35.

6 McConnell, *West Texas Frontier*, in www.forttours.com /pages/toclegion; Wilbarger, *Depredations*, 636; Hunter, "Tragedy in Legion Valley," 22; Reeves, "Scalping of Matilda Friend," 51; Zesch, *The Captured*, 76-78.

7 John S. Friend Depredation Claim #3379; Michno, *Fate Worse Than Death*, 391-95.

52 "The savings of all our youthful days was gone."

By March 1868, troop levels on the Texas frontier reached new heights. General Hancock, a Democrat and more sympathetic to the Texans than previous commanders, had moved all the troops out of the interior that he could spare. Forts Concho, Griffin, and Richardson were under construction and smaller posts were established at old Forts Belknap, Phantom Hill, and Chadbourne. Hancock recommended telegraph lines connect all the posts. The 26th Infantry went to the Rio Grande and the 17th and 41st moved to the frontier. About 42 companies were on the frontier and all the cavalry was in the west. One historian observed that more than 3,000 soldiers was the largest number ever stationed on the frontier until 1873, when the final campaigns to subjugate the Comanches and Kiowas went into high gear. Another made an exact count of 3,226.[1]

The Indians probably never noticed. The rain was still falling, the weather was good for raiding, and there were still cattle and horses to steal. G. F. and Mary J. Bowman lived on Deep Creek in southeast Wise County, where Bowman farmed, raised horses, and practiced as a physician. So far they had escaped the numerous raids that came into that portion of the country, but that changed on March 2. Their daughter, Sallie Bowman (18), said to be a beautiful and courageous young woman, often rode herd on her father's horses. Riding a fine, fast horse, she was unconcerned about Indians, but as she was watering her horse in Deep Creek, about two miles from the house, Indians surprised her. She made a grand run, jumping the horse over ditches and fallen trees. The warriors cut her off from her home and she headed toward a neighbor named Jones. She almost reached safety when two Indians finally sped up close behind her and shot her twice in the back. Sallie flipped off the horse and dropped dead almost in Joneses' yard. The Indians got her horse and the bunch she was guarding. Sallie was one of the first to be buried in the Deep Creek Cemetery.[2]

George Hazelwood had moved from Palo Pinto County in 1860 and started a new ranch on the Big Sandy in southwest Stephens County. Late in February the ranchers organized a cattle roundup and built pens on Hazelwood's and James Walker's ranches. On March 1, Hazelwood told his men to begin branding at the pens while he rode out to look for any strays they might have missed. A strong wind blew in and the dirt and sand in the air made it difficult to see. During the branding a cowboy from Walker's place rode in and told them to be on the lookout, for he had seen Indians in the area.

Hazelwood's men went out to find him, but the blowing sand covered any trail. They did run into the Indians, however, and a short running fight ensued before the Indians got away. The men continued their search for Hazelwood and it was some time before they found him less than two miles from the camp, lying dead in a gully. Hazelwood's rifle, pistol, horse, saddle, and bridle were gone, but he was not scalped. He was said to have had either a Spencer repeater or a .50 caliber Sharps and several blood spots nearby led the men to believe he had shot some of his attackers. Scattered around were several curious-looking black arrows.[3]

The Comanches moved into Shackelford County and next appeared at William Ledbetter's salt works on Hubbard Creek. They were setting up an ambush when a young man named Thornton, who worked for Ledbetter, left the house very early to go to the creek. He saw an Indian, pulled his pistol and fired. The shot woke everyone in the house and Ledbetter came to the door with his gun. The ambush spoiled, and with Thornton and Ledbetter blasting away at any Indian who came out from cover, the Comanches rode off to the southeast.

After the attack at the salt works, William Ledbetter rode up to Fort Griffin, prompting Capt. Adna R. Chaffee to take detachments of Companies F and I, 6th Cavalry, to hunt down the raiders. Aided by Tonkawa scouts, Chaffee left on March 5, marched to Ledbetter's and picked up the trail heading northwest. They crossed the Clear Fork Brazos north of Fort Phantom Hill and followed the trail, which was easy to see because the Indians were dragging litters, perhaps carrying wounded warriors. On the morning of March 6, the soldiers and Tonkawas found the Comanche camp on Paint Creek south of present Haskell.

The dawn attack was devastating, with the Tonkawas brandishing knives and clubs and taking vengeance on their hated enemies. The battle report stated that they killed five Comanches "one Mexican and one Mulatto (both of whom were leaders)…." A few wounded Comanches were captured and questioned, and Chaffee learned what the black arrows were for. They were made in honor of their "chief," a black man said to be named Cato, who sometimes resided near Fort Concho and split his time living with the whites and Indians. Cato was likely the "Mulatto" killed in the fight. When Chaffee learned what he could, he set loose the Tonkawas to dispatch the remaining Comanches. They got seven scalps that day—partial revenge for the massacre of their people back in 1862.[4]

On March 1, four days before Chaffee left Fort Griffin, Comanches were in San Saba stealing mules from Jack Hinton. The day Chaffee left Fort Griffin heading west, Comanches were east of him in southwest Jack County along Rock Creek where they stole three horses from John C. Vanhooser, robbed his house, and killed all his chickens. The day Chaffee battled the

Comanches on Paint Creek, another raiding party was south of him on Hords Creek in Coleman County where it stole five horses from Jefferson W. Brannon. On March 17, Comanches were far south in Bandera County and stole "three large black mules" and one horse from Ezra A. Chipman. Some 4th Cavalrymen got on the trail and followed the Comanches north for two days before losing them.[5]

As usual, the troopers chased to and fro while the Indians were usually behind them in the settlements. Raids throughout the succeeding months were repetitions of a never-ending story. Indians raided Phillip Haas in Medina County for the second time and took four stock horses and one "buggy mare," all valued at $220. In Montague County, Indians crept around Samuel McDonald's house on Denton Creek at midnight on April 15. His stock was secured in a picketed corral, but the thieves wiggled the posts loose and pulled them out of the ground. They proceeded to quietly walk the animals through the gap. Sam went "to see what the horse was snorting about," but when he stepped outside in the darkness a rifle flashed, fired, and a ball slammed into the wall near his head. "It like to of scared me to death when they shot at the old man," said Sarah D. McDonald. Sam stepped inside, got his rifle and stepped back out. He took one shot in the dark toward where sounds were coming from; one shot came back in return, and Sam called it off. He wouldn't go back out until morning, but by then, all his animals were gone except the snorting horse, which refused to leave the corral.[6]

On April 15, Comanches were in Coleman County stealing along the course of Jim Ned Creek. They stole 75 cattle and five horses worth $1,050 from David McDonald, and also got stock from Sevier McDonald and Lat Edmonson.

James B. McGough and his brother, William C., had a beautiful site for a ranch at the springs that were named after them along the Leon River in Eastland County. On May 1, they had ten horses hobbled and guarded within 100 yards of the house. When the guard went to the springs only 60 yards away, Indians cut loose and stole the horses. They also stole horses from J. C. Tolliver the same day. It wasn't the first or last time that the McGough's lost stock. James was sick of it. He had lived there for years and said, "The Indians made a raid about once a month." After several raids, the McGough's losses came to $4,425.[7]

On May 1, Indians were at Flat Rock Springs in Jack County, stealing or destroying $1,000 worth of property and cash from M. D. Bullion. In Wise County, Indians got seven horses worth $475 from Nancy A. Armstrong. On May 1, Indians got four horses from Jack Hinton in San Saba County, and on May 6, they cleaned him out, taking 3,000 cattle from his range on the San Saba River. At ten dollars a head, he said his losses were $33,000. In May, Indians were in Palo Pinto County where they stole horses from Jerome B.

Edwards near Strawn. The same month they stole four horses worth $300 from Elbert M. Walker in Llano County.

Peter B. Emory had been raided twice and moved his ranch from Concho County east into Coleman County, but his stock was not safe there either. In mid-March, Indians got 30 of his saddle horses and on May 15 they were back again to get the last 25 of his horses. Losses in the two raids totaled $3,575 and cleaned him out. On May 27, Indians took 500 cattle worth $3,000 from William E. Costley in Coleman County. On June 1, Comanches got three more horses from John A. Eubank from his range in Palo Pinto County.[8]

At the Wichita Agency near Fort Cobb, Agent Leavenworth was ready to quit. He had always believed that with kind and fair treatment, he could keep his charges in line and turn them into law-abiding farmers. It seemed, however, that no matter what he did, he could not change them from their old ways; if anything, they were getting harder to control. Leavenworth began fearing for his life and numerous times he called on the 6th Infantry officers at Fort Arbuckle to send soldiers to the agency for protection. In May, while some Comanches were in north Texas, others were causing havoc at the agency, stealing agency horses and cattle and robbing Leavenworth and the trader's store. They set fire to the buildings and told the whites that they wanted no more houses and no more timber cut. Many of the whites got out, some going to Fort Arbuckle and some to Texas, although that was not a much safer proposition. At the end of May, Leavenworth walked off his job.

Reinforcements arrived in the form of Col. Benjamin H. Grierson and the 10th Cavalry. They marched from Fort Gibson to Fort Arbuckle, and in early June headed to the Wichita Mountains to scout out a location for a new post. It rained on them for two weeks, but the miserable journey was rewarded when they located a fine site at the junction of Cache and Medicine Bluff Creeks; the post would later be called Fort Sill. They met Comanches who seemed to be friendly, dined, and talked. They rode to the Wichita Agency and all was peaceful, and they rode back to Fort Arbuckle where the expedition was disbanded. Leavenworth must have been crazy; there were no hostile Indians.[9]

By June, the Kiowas and Yamparika Comanches headed north to Fort Larned to get the annuities promised at Medicine Lodge. Other bands apparently celebrated the coming annuity distribution by going to Texas to conduct business. On the last of June, a band came into Wise County. Thomas J. Davis had a small ranch in Collin County but decided to expand his range west where he believed the grass and water were better. By the spring of 1868, Davis had more than 400 horses on upper Denton Creek. Davis' men were guarding the horses, and had marked just about all of them with his "O.K." brand when about 15 Indians appeared and in a flash, had gotten between the cowboys and the horses. The Indians had been watching for an opportune moment. "We were afoot;" said cowboy James. W. Ogle, "our horses were staked out and the Indians run in yelling and were gone with the horses. We did not have a chance to do anything, and in fact, we did not want to tackle them, there were so many of them and few of us."

Later, a government attorney wanted to know why Davis "just let them" drive off the horses without a fight. Davis answered like Ogle: "I was pretty glad to get away myself." About 405 horses were gone, valued at $13,325.[10]

In Stephens County, Indians hit Ben Browning again, stealing ten horses. In Tom Green County, Richard Tankersley was making a cattle drive from his ranch to New Mexico and on the Pecos River, Indians stole five saddle horses. In northern Lampasas County near the junction of Bennett Creek and the Lampasas River, F. G. Morris, Seaborn Sneed, and a Mr. Townsend herded their horses. Comanches found them on June 30, stealing seven from Morris, 40 from Sneed, and several from Townsend. They trailed the raiders north, but found only several slaughtered animals.

Also on June 30, Indians were as far into the settlements as Bulverde on Cibolo Creek in southwest Comal County where they stole two horses from Johann Rittimann. A neighbor, Henry Theis, saw some riders he thought were cowmen and he rode up to them. Suddenly the "cowmen" chased after him shooting arrows. "After the Indians run me" for a ways, Theis said, he ducked into a thick brush and the Indians got his horse too.

Marauders were on the Big and Little Saline Creeks in northeast Kimble County. Families had been leaving the area since the big San Saba raid. Indians struck Adolph Reichenau's place and stole nine horses, but he stayed. After two more raids, in December, and in March 1869, he finally pulled back to Mason County.[11]

Where some frontier counties increased population during the Civil War, Kimble and others were losing population during "peacetime." The state almanac for 1867 said "The people of Kimble have suffered terribly from Indian depredations for the last twelve months. Very few residents are living upon their own lands. No lands are selling in that county."

The almanac promoted boosterism, but many counties could not avoid some unpleasant facts. The Frio County report read, "This county would have been organized and settled up but for the insecurity to life and property from Indian raids." Gillespie: "The county has been subject to occasional Indian depredations, and considerable property, chiefly horses, has been carried off." Coryell: "Life and property are secure, except from Indian depredations." Cooke: "Life and property would be perfectly safe, were it not for the occasional raids of Indians through the county, when they steal and drive off all the horses and cattle they can collect." Comanche: "The depredations committed by Indians have discouraged those owning horse ranches, and many have given them up...." Clay: "Stock-raisers commenced moving in about 1858, but have mostly left on account of the Indians." Llano: The county's "salubrity, minerals, and stock-raising advantages would, however, cause it to be settled rapidly, but for the Indians." Mason: The people here "are very much disheartened at present by the great insecurity of life and property...." Medina: "Life and property are secure, except in case of Indian raids." Menard: Only 100 families still reside in the county. There are two schools and 200 children, "besides what the Indians carried off in the last raid." Palo Pinto: "Indians keep the inhabitants in continual alarm." Parker: "Our population is at a stand-still...subject to frequent depredations of the hostile Indians." San Saba: "Life and property would be secure in this county, but...we are exposed to Indian depredations." Wise: "The grass is better now than for several years." The problem is that "Indian raids are of frequent occurrence, in which citizens are often murdered, and children carried into a hopeless captivity, a thousand times worse than death."[12]

Wise County acknowledged the problem but Montague was silent. In June 1868, both were hit again, by Satanta and his Kiowas, and by Nokoni and Kotsoteka Comanches. It was the same area struck by Big Tree in January. John R. McElroy, his wife, and five children lived three miles from Forestburg. When the Indians struck on June 7, John was not home. His wife, two youngest children, and Mrs. Mary Fannon were at the cabin, while their children, Nathaniel J. (9), W. D. (6), and Martha Ellen (12), and Robert H. Lackey (18), an adopted son of Mrs. McElroy's sister, were in the field picking berries.[13]

The children saw the Indians coming and ran for the cabin, about 150 yards away, which had a strong picket around it. The Indians caught Martha Ellen first, thrusting a lance into her back and knee and knocking her down. W. D., a boy who was nicknamed "Dora," was gashed across the breast, back, and knee. Nathaniel stopped running and was not shot or stabbed. Bob Lackey almost reached the picketed gate when a warrior with a Spencer shot him through the heart. The warriors came up to the gate when Mrs. McElroy and Mrs. Fannon came out. They tried to scalp Lackey but Mrs. McElroy had a gun and kept them back. "I would aim the gun at them," she said, "and they would hold my children between myself and them." The women had "good well-loaded rifles" and kept the Indians out of the stockade.

The three "were crying 'Mama,'" she said, "and I dare not fire for fear of killing my own children." The warriors backed away, holding the children as shields. Mrs. McElroy heard W. D. screaming until they got out of range. His crying and fighting only angered the warriors. "He cried a great deal for his mother," said Nathaniel, "and they whipped and abused him and scarred him with a knife." Nathaniel quickly learned to shut up and be still.

Author's photo

Upper Willawalla Valley, Montague County, Texas.

Nearby, Levi Perryman was in his oat field when his dogs began barking and he heard shooting, and a black child ran up to him and said the Indians were attacking. Perryman ran back to his cabin and met his wife.

"The Indians are killing Mr. McElroy's folks," she exclaimed. "Can't you hear them screaming?"

He could. Perryman got his horse and rode to the McElroys'. He saw Lackey's body and Mrs. McElroy cried out, "Oh, the Indians have stolen my children; my little children are gone, and we will never see them again."

Perryman followed the trail and Jim White joined him. Topping a rise, they saw the Indians half a mile away. The children saw riders following them and thought they would be rescued, but it was not to be. Badly outnumbered, Jim White went for more help, while Perryman tried to keep on their trail. The delay was costly, however, for the Indians went north, and Perryman took a trail they had made earlier which headed east toward Clear Creek. He went to the cabins of George W. Williams and Allen Newberry. When they got up a search party, they realized they were on the wrong trail and darkness ended the day. Perryman went back to the Willawalla Valley to warn the settlers.

The Indians took the children to the agency near Fort Cobb, arriving on June 10, and holding a scalp dance and celebration about the time Colonel Grierson and the 10th Cavalry were on their way from Fort Arbuckle to the Wichita Mountains. The McElroys immediately contacted authorities in Indian Territory and within two months the children were located and purchased. Instrumental in their release was an Indian woman called Cheyenne Jennie, the wife of Fort Cobb trader William Griffenstein, who was a go-between with Agent S. T. Walkley and the Indians. John McElroy came to pick up the children about the same time William Freeman was there to get his son, Dick. Bill Griffenstein told McElroy he had to pay $1,800 in horses, money, and supplies to buy them. Now, heavily indebted to Griffenstein, John McElroy went back to Texas and took virtually all of his 100 cattle to the agency to pay him back. The ransom ruined them. Said Mrs. McElroy "the savings of all our youthful days was gone, the toil of many years, and we were left in poverty."

W. D. was crippled for life and Martha Ellen's back wound never healed. She suffered 11 more years with a suppurating wound until she died in 1879. The U. S. Government, in all its wisdom, declared that the family was not damaged of "any valuable consideration" by Lackey's death, nor was there evidence "that the wounds of Martha Ellen or W. D. McElroy were of a nature to permanently disable them." In addition, it claimed that the evidence did not prove that McElroy ever paid Griffenstein 100 cattle "for the redemption of the children."[14]

Such were the tribulations of the frontier settlers.

Chapter 52 notes

1 Richter, *Army in Texas During Reconstruction*, 133-36; Shook, "Federal Military in Texas," 48.
2 Cates, *Wise County*, 165-66; McConnell, *West Texas Frontier*, 609.
3 McConnell, *West Texas Frontier*, http://www.forttours.com/pages/hazlewood.asp; Biggers, *Shackelford County Sketches*, 53-54.
4 Carter, *Yorktown to Santiago*, 138-40; Cashion, *A Texas Frontier*, 106-07.
5 Depredation Claims: Jack Hinton #5298; John C. Vanhooser #6301; Jefferson W. Brannon #5259; Ezra A. Chipman #167.
6 Depredation Claims: Phillip Haas #3348; Samuel McDonald #343.
7 Depredation Claims: David McDonald #4537; James B. McGough #10616.
8 Depredation Claims: M. D. Bullion #3522; Jack Hinton #5298; Jerome B. Edwards #5703; Elbert M. Walker #4419; Peter B. Emory #4492; William E. Costley #2224; Hesekiah B. Eubank #5901.
9 Nye, *Carbine and Lance*, 48-51.
10 Thomas J. Davis, Depredation Claim #8007.
11 Depredation Claims: Benjamin Browning #4608; Richard Tankersley #6501; F. G. Morris #1188; Johann Rittimann #7258; Zesch, *The Captured*, 16-17.
12 *Texas Almanac 1867*, 91, 95-6, 109-10, 128, 132, 136, 138, 143, 146, 155, 174.
13 Mayhall, *The Kiowas*, 244; John R. McElroy, Depredation Claim #10037. Most sources place the raid in May, but McElroy said it was on June 7.
14 Potter, *Montague County*, 39-41; McConnell, *West Texas Frontier*, in www.forttours.com/pages.toclackey.asp; Perryman, *Thrilling Indian Raids*, 6-7; Hyde, *George Bent*, 279, 282; John R. McElroy, Depredation Claim #10037.

53 "The troops delight is seeing the savages commit their murderius deeds."

Reconstruction in Texas was not going well. General Hancock did not last long as Fifth Military District commander. Seen by congressional Republicans as an unenthusiastic supporter of official policies and too sympathetic to ex-Rebels, they looked for an excuse to remove him. When Hancock interfered with a city council election in New Orleans, General Grant reversed his decision and Hancock, feeling compromised, resigned on March 14. General Robert C. Buchanan took over. Buchanan only lasted until July. When Louisiana was re-admitted to the Union, he took over another district, and Gen. Joseph Reynolds was now commander of the Fifth District and the District of Texas.

The more lenient Presidential reconstruction was giving way to a harsher Congressional reconstruction with tougher military control and pressure to make the Texans ratify the 14th and 15th Amendments.[1] Texan moderates, conservatives, and radicals fought for control. In January 1868, conservatives met at Houston and concluded to vote against a convention, stating that they preferred military rule to letting the radicals win. In the February election most conservatives did not vote and the radicals won, 44,689 to 11,440.

The convention met at Austin on June 1, 1868, and did not adjourn until February 1869. They argued over who would be in control, making a more powerful centralized government, constitutional issues, and special interests. Few were willing to compromise. It wasn't a case of Nero fiddling while Rome burned—the capital was safe, but the frontier was aflame.[2]

Those flames came from settlers' cabins, certainly not from army posts. The army seemed to face less danger from Indian attacks than from accidents. An example came during the heavy rains in the summer of 1868 near Fort Richardson. While riding to Fort Worth, Lt. James F. Hill and a private in the 6th Cavalry, drowned while crossing the rain-swollen Clear Fork Trinity. Very few soldiers in Texas died in battle with the Indians.[3]

The army's ineffectiveness was shown by a Comanche raid deep into Blanco and Comal counties where there hadn't been an attack for a few years. Tennessean William Riley Huckobey settled near Lockhart, in Caldwell County, where he married and had at least two sons and two daughters. When his wife died he married a widow named Tanner who already had several children of her own, including Isaac, James, and Sam Tanner. The Tanners lived near Blanco in Blanco County. Huckobey apparently maintained two households with both families and this was the situation prior to the beginning of the Civil War.

About the first of July, a small party set out from Huckobey's, consisting of William Irvin Shepherd (23), his wife, Elizabeth (18), who was William Huckobey's daughter, their child Joel (1), and Huckobey's son, Thomas, who may have been about 14, but was small in stature. Remaining behind was Mary Caroline Huckobey (16), and at least one brother. She watched her brother Tommy ride away on a mule. It was the last time she ever saw him. Irvin Shepherd was employed by William Huckobey and they were all supposed to round up cattle as they rode to a camp that Huckobey had set up near the Tanner place three miles from Blanco.

The four rode at a leisurely pace. On the morning of July 3, Comanches surprised them. They shot a bullet and nearly ten arrows into Mr. Shepherd and put at least seven arrows into Mrs. Shepherd's back, one of them coming clear through to her breast. They cut Joel's head off and threw it some distance from the body. All were stripped and scalped. They took Thomas Huckobey captive.

When they did not arrive at Tanner's or the cow camp, William Huckobey became worried and rode back down the trail. Four miles away and seven miles from the Blanco County courthouse he found the bodies. William Huckobey rushed back with the news. Sam Tanner rode all the way to Lockhart to tell the other Huckobey children what happened. Huckobey went back to the massacre scene with his stepson, Isaac Tanner, neighbor, John R. Palmer, and a few others and tried to follow the trail.

In addition to Huckobey's two horses and the mule that they took from Shepherd, the Comanches stole about 45 horses from Bill Jonas, worth $1,800, and several more from Ben Shropshire and the Trainer Brothers, who lived only half a mile from the Tanners. They hit John Kneupper, Fritz Fisher, and Andreas Wagenfuhr and got perhaps 50 horses. They also crossed the line into northern Comal County and stole three horses from Adolph Kappelmann and a dozen from Frederick H. Faigaux. John Kneupper and his neighbors pursued the thieves, and two miles from his home near Twin Sisters, they stumbled across the massacre site, finding the bodies with many arrows sticking in them. The trail went west toward Fredericksburg. The pursuers traveled more than 100 miles, said Palmer, "to see if we could not get back the boy." They finally gave up and rode home. "We never saw or heard of him afterwards," said Isaac Tanner.[4]

On the Fourth of July, 1868, under a full moon, another Comanche band was in the settlements. In western Tarrant County they stole horses from Nancy J. Moore and others, but settlers drove them across the line into Parker County.[5]

The same day in the western part of the county, Indians were raiding on Rock and Grindstone Creeks. Jesse Hales and Mary Cathey Hales lived near Palo Pinto, but their son, John Jackson Hales (9), and his cousin, Armstead

Martin Cathey (18), were taking a wagon to Weatherford for a minstrel show and Fourth of July celebration. About noon, the boys were between the creeks northeast of present Millsap when several Indians charged the wagon. The boys had a sheet over the wagon bed, where John crawled under to get out of the sun and take a nap. Without warning the Indians were on them. They killed John in the wagon bed and scalped him, but no one was sure what happened to Martin.

There were many people on the road that day traveling to Weatherford, and in a wagon right behind the boys were Judge William Veale with two sons and a nephew. They reached Fuller Millsap's place just past Rock Creek to have lunch when two riders came up and said that two boys were dead in the road ahead. Veale and the others hurried to the spot and Veale, who had taught school in Palo Pinto, quickly identified both of them as his former students. Some reports said that the boys were both shot and scalped, but another claimed that there wasn't a mark on Martin, and it was surmised that he had been frightened to death. The holiday turned into a funeral procession as Veale and the others put the bodies in his wagon and drove back to Palo Pinto. The funeral and burials one day later were indelibly impressed on young Fannie Veale, the service preached by rancher and missionary George W. Slaughter and the agonizing wailing of the families. She tried to bury her face in her mother's skirt but was unable to block out the crying. The emotional stress of living in constant danger on the frontier remained with her for years.

The William Light family lived near Grindstone Creek and had spent the Fourth at a neighbor's celebrating the holiday. Two dozen Indians jumped them on the way home, mortally wounding Bill Light and killing Mary Light and her infant daughter, Dora. Emma Light (9) and William Lee Light (4) were wounded, but Sarah Ann (12) jumped over a fence and hid in a cane field. Both parents were scalped.[6]

Raiders were all over the country. On July 4, they also stole horses from George Burton in Presidio County. During the first week of the month they got 11 horses from Christopher C. Mills in Young County. On July 15, they got three horses from Charles Dinger in Kendall County. In late July, Indians hit William M. Allen's place in Eastland County for the third time, getting seven horses. He had them hobbled right near his house, but in the morning all that was left were cut pieces of rope. Allen's father-in-law, J. P. Davidson, also had his stock stolen.

On August 1, Indians crossed Red River at Illinois Bend and attacked ranches and farms along North and South Fish Creeks in Cooke County. Thomas Bailey lost stock again, this time ten work horses worth $450. Raiders also took four horses worth $510 from W. W. Bland. In August, raiders were in Parker County, stealing horses from Hezekiah B. Davis and

W. C. Brashear. The men heard Indians were in the county and tried to do a pre-emptive strike. They gathered up some men and looked for the raiders, but while they were out, the Indians got their horses anyway. On the trail, Davis later found one of his horses killed and it affected him. She was a fine red roan, he said. "Nice mare.... It was always a wonder to me why they killed that mare because she was so gentle."[7]

On August 27, Comanches were in Denton County stealing stock from Giles Chisum, Zerrill J. Harmonson, Anderson Lewis, and L. S. Forester. The men got up a posse and chased the raiders, but were outmatched. In a running skirmish, "Sol" Forester was killed and Jeff Chisum and Alf McDaniels were wounded.[8]

Most of the raids during the remainder of 1868 were concentrated just below Red River. The Russell family built their cabin in northwest Wise County on Martin's Prairie about four miles southwest of the present Chico. When Polly Russell's husband died, she considered moving out, but decided to hold on to the farm. She lived there with her four children: Bean (22), Martha "Lucy" (18), Harvey (16), and James (11).

During June 1868, one dozen buffalo hunters stopped to camp near the Russell place. One of them, John O. Allen, went to the house to see if he could buy some milk and was immediately smitten by the sight of Martha. Mrs. Russell saw the attraction and she invited the young hunter to return after supper. When it was time for him to leave, Martha requested that he talk to her oldest brother Bean, about how dangerous it was where they lived, and tell him he should move the family back into the settlements. He promised that he would. That night, John Allen thought of nothing but the girl he had just met. "Lucy was a perfect brunette," he said, "and the finest specimen of womanhood that I had ever beheld." The next morning Allen hurried back to the cabin to talk to Bean, but he had not returned from the mill and his promise went unfulfilled.

Before he left, Allen asked Martha if she would wait for him and she said she would." I took her face in my hands and sealed our troth with a kiss," Allen said. He had to go, but he would come back next year.[9]

The Russells did not have that much time. About August 26, Comanches were hiding near the Russell cabin in a dense cane patch, planning their move. Bean Russell was working at the mill and the warriors saw only women and children. They attacked, but did not count on Harvey Russell. He opened fire with a Winchester rifle, but to no avail, for the warriors killed James in the yard and Polly in the doorway. Harvey fell back into the house, firing until he ran out of ammunition. He tried to crawl under the bed, but the Indians caught him and killed him in the corner against a wall. They kept the beautiful Martha for themselves.

The warriors plundered the house and rode off with Martha tied to a horse. When Bean Russell got home that evening, he was shocked. James was dead and mangled in the yard and his mother was on the doorstep, lying in a pool of blood, but he did not see Harvey or Martha. He ran back to the mill. The next day, Bean returned with a search party. They found Harvey part way under the bed, and gathered the three bodies for interment. Among the burial party was Theodore "Dot" Babb, who had been captured nearby two years earlier.

When the Indians left the Russell cabin they headed east. Martha Russell probably fought her captors. Had she meekly submitted she would likely have been raped, but kept alive as excellent ransom material. As it was, the warriors stopped, threw Martha to the ground, raped, scalped, mutilated, and killed her. The Indians then rode to Dick Couch's place and almost captured young Dick Couch. The Couches later told Bean Russell that they had seen the entire band go by, and Martha was not with them, which led him to believe that she was killed somewhere between the Russell and Couch cabins. Bean Russell was a nervous wreck for ten days after the attack, with the premonition that his sister was lying on the prairie being devoured by wolves. Searchers finally found Martha only three miles from her cabin. All that remained were scattered bones and a disjointed frame from which wild animals had torn the last bits of flesh. Beside the remains lay Martha's sunbonnet.[10]

After leaving Couch's, the Indians went to J. D. White's on upper Catlett Creek just north of Decatur and destroyed much of his corn and melon crop. On August 27, they stole 49 horses worth $2,080 from Asenatha McDaniel in eastern Wise County, crossed into Denton County and took three horses from Harriet Lee, and headed north. In another day they were safely across Red River.[11]

There was the usual outcry from angry, frustrated residents. Some 6th Cavalry companies were engaged in hunting down outlaws and recalcitrant ex-Rebels who had joined secret white societies such as the Ku Klux Klan and were terrorizing and killing freedmen. Northeast Texas was a haven for these white terrorists and some of the 6th Cavalry's attention was shifted to that section. Many locals, however, thought the army behaved as badly as the outlaws they were hunting. A citizen of Denton County wrote on August 30, that, contrary to their usual behavior, the soldiers in Dallas appeared to be "really nice and genteel fellows…especially since we have so many that were not." He said they were getting along fine with the citizens. "About the only place I know where they are."

Other news was not so good. The correspondent noted that last week there was another attack. "The way these raiding Indians manage to escape is truly wonderful," he wrote. It appeared that "the troops that are stationed on our frontier are vastly injurious to the lives and property of our people. They give no protection themselves and will allow no organization of the citizens for that purpose. It has been openly stated…that there is such antipathy against Texas existing among the officers of these troops that they even delight in seeing the savages commit their murderous deeds upon her people."[12]

Perhaps the citizen's perception was harsh, yet there did seem to be something in the fact that the army was preparing another expedition in Kansas to drive out the Cheyennes and Arapahos. Although depredations had increased in Kansas since Hancock's campaign in 1867, the state never experienced the constant ravages on the levels seen in Texas, but it seemed to get much more of the army's attention and resources.

Chapter 53 notes

1 Richter, *Army in Texas During Reconstruction*, 136-38. The 14th Amendment stated that all people born or naturalized in the United States were citizens and the 15th Amendment stated that the rights of a citizen could not be denied because of race or color.

2 Webb, *Handbook of Texas I*, 446-47.

3 McConnell, *Five Years a Cavalryman*, 172.

4 Winfrey and Day, *Texas Indian Papers, IV*, 265, 326-29; Depredation Claims: William R. Huckobey #3474; William Jonas #6164; John Kneupper #8319; Andreas Wagenfuhr #7273; Adolph Kappelmann #8323. Huckobey claimed the attack was in 1867, but contemporary documents indicate it was most likely in 1868.

5 Nancy J. Moore, Depredation Claim #1816.

6 Marshall, *A Cry Unheard*, 189-90; McConnell, *West Texas Frontier*, 615. A family genealogy clarifies the names, ages, and relationships of Hales and Cathey. Marshall says these events happened in 1869 and McConnell places them in 1868. The three Lights were buried in Porter Cemetery in Parker County, and the death dates on their graves are July 4, 1868.

7 Depredation Claims: George Burton #6006; Christopher C. Mills #5679; Charles Dinger #1812; William M. Allen #4605; Thomas Bailey #4346; W. W. Bland #4413; Hezekiah B. Davis #6774.

8 Giles Chisum, Depredation Claim #5016.

9 McConnell, *West Texas Frontier*, in www.forttours.com/ pages/tocruss; Cates, *Wise County*, 168; Hunter, "Trail of Blood, 14.

10 McConnell, *West Texas Frontier*, in www.forttours.com/ pages/tocruss; Hunter, "Trail of Blood," 15; Winfrey and Day, *Texas Indian Papers, IV*, 316; Cates, *Wise County*, 169-70; Babb, *Bosom of the Comanches*, 121-22.

11 Depredation Claims: Asenatha McDaniel #1197; Harriet Lee #5687.

12 Bates, *Denton County*, 375-76.

54 "Father, you will never come back."

Generals Sherman and Sheridan were of one mind when it came to the Cheyennes and Arapahos. "These Indians require to be soundly whipped," Sherman wrote on September 26, "and the ringleaders in the present trouble hung, their ponies killed, and such destruction of their property as will make them very poor." They would unleash Custer and his 7th Cavalry to press a winter campaign against the offending villages in Indian Territory and crush them once and for all. The Comanches and Kiowas were still seen to be neutral and would not be attacked; certainly they raided in Texas, but somehow that did not seem to count.[1]

During the summer of 1868, Kansas settlements experienced raids, the likes of which they had never felt before, and not unlike what Texas had been experiencing for a decade. The army made no expedition to punish the Kiowas and Comanches, but they would go after the Cheyennes, who were the primary perpetrators in Kansas. Sheridan finagled the release of George Custer from his one year's suspension and the 7th Cavalry struck the Cheyennes on the Washita River in Indian Territory on November 27, 1868, killing Black Kettle and 103 Indians, and capturing 53, although the Cheyennes claimed only half that number were killed. The army lost 21 killed and 16 wounded. It was far more soldier deaths in battle than the three cavalry regiments in Texas suffered in the three years since the Civil War ended. With a follow-up campaign in the spring of 1869, many bands were ready to sue for peace and come in to the reservations.

The campaign showed that an expedition to take the war to the Indians' home villages could be very effective. Few had been done, however. The 1858 attacks at Antelope Hills and Rush Springs and the 1864 attacks at Sand Creek and Adobe Walls were examples, but they did not always have the intended results. It would take years before the army realized that the only way to put an end to the constant raids was not by a single strike, but rather to constantly attack the Indians' families in their villages at all seasons and with no let up.

That was in the future. In late 1868, what the Texans saw was another army expedition to chastise Indians threatening the Kansans while they cried out for similar relief and were continuously ignored. The army in Texas seemed to be sitting on its hands. Indians were all around Forts Richardson and Griffin as if they didn't exist. In September they hit John Irwin's place in Shackelford County again, this time getting a mule and three horses worth $250. The same month they took 50 cattle and three horses from Morris

Gilbert in Clay County, for losses of $800. In Palo Pinto County, Indians got 12 horses worth $850 from William Metcalf. George W. Ross lost 11 horses worth $1,025 from his ranch in Denton County.

On September 5, Comanches were in northeast Coleman County along Pecan Bayou where they took stock from David McDonald, William Pollard, Robert Stephens, and Barry Meadows. On September 10, Indians were right near Fort Richardson where they stole five horses from William H. Gatlin. On September 23, they were down in Erath County getting four horses worth $500 from William S. Keith. In Burnet County, Indians raided Louis Kincheloe for the fourth time, getting 31 stock horses worth $775.[2]

There were several "big raids" during the decade, and one of them was in October 1868, despite all the forts and the cavalry. Perhaps the superstitious could have predicted it. October 31 was Halloween and a "blue moon," the second full moon in the month. The raid may have been in revenge for a disastrous encounter the Kiowas had with the Utes in July 1868, the season which was remembered in the Kiowa calendar history as "Sun dance when the Ute killed us." In a fight on the upper South Canadian in New Mexico Territory, the Utes got the best of a Kiowa war party, not only killing Heap of Bears and seven other warriors, but capturing the *taime*, a stone human figure in a white feathered robe and sacred in the sun dance ceremony. The catastrophe called for vengeance, and the targets did not have to be Utes.[3]

In Texas, October had been comparatively quiet. On the first, the first full moon, Indians hit Jesse Caraway's ranch on Paluxy Creek in Hood County and got 28 horses worth $1,120. Near Castroville in Medina County, Lipans visited Phillip Haas for the third time and stole seven horses worth $240. There was little more activity until late in the month.

The Kiowas and Comanches arrived in Montague County about October 27, crossing Red River in the Spanish Fort area and going south through the center of the county to the headwaters of Clear and Willawalla Creeks. Either the settlers were on guard or there was little left to steal, for the Indians left those valleys and continued to Denton Creek where the first recorded attack was at Sam McDonald's place. They had raided his place in April and there was not much left. Sarah McDonald said, "I saw a whole lot of the Indians, about 200 of them. They was shooting." The Indians drove off the only horse, and seemingly in frustration, they shot or lanced five cows, one steer, and two hogs, everything the family owned. Later, a government attorney asked Mrs. McDonald if the Indians were on the war path. "They shot at my brother as he run into the house," she answered, "it looked like they was on the war path."

The Indians went to Sam McDonald's father-in-law's cabin. He and his son saw them coming while they were at their well. They raced home and just barely beat the Indians to the door. The raiders shot at the cabin a few times, killed their dog, shot down the cattle, burned an oat stack, and rode on.[4]

In northern Wise County, the raiders came to the Ball families' cabins. Kiowas had captured James and Willie Ball there in 1865. The boys had been home about two years and they were not about to be taken again. A story, sometimes said to be apocryphal, was that a warrior named Red Feather had once owned Willie Ball and wanted him back. Kiowas surrounded and besieged Moses Ball's ranch. Willie and John Bailey, the husband of James Ball's daughter, Easter Melvina, had gone to the field that morning to gather corn. While they worked, Mr. Shira, a neighbor, dropped over to visit. Just then, Indians appeared all along the fence and wood lines and peppered the place with gunfire and arrows. John Bailey had two six-shooters and held them off. Two passers-by, John W. Hunter and a man named Holford, chanced to blunder into the fight and rode to the house. Bailey ordered Willie to crawl under the wagon while he fired until his pistols were empty, when he was gunned down. Easter Bailey fainted in the yard. Indians crawled closer to the wagon trying to get Willie while gunfire from the house made it hot for them.

"Shoot all around the boy! Don't hit the boy," Moses Ball told Hunter and Holford. When Willie ran from the wagon, a warrior named Tan-guadal, whose name translates as "Red-feather-head-dress," darted out and grabbed him. Mrs. Ball screamed and the defenders hit the warrior with two or three bullets, dropping him to the ground. Willie reached the house as the Indians dragged the warrior away. With that, the fight ended. The men buried Bailey, and a few days later they discovered another grave in the timber about 150 yards away. They dug it up and discovered the dead Indian, complete with a "scarlet feathered cap," various army accoutrements, and a deed to a settler's ranch in Kansas.[5]

From the Balls', the raiders turned east and southeast. In northeast Wise County, they hit Tenville Cecil for the third time, this time getting 30 mares, 16 colts, and one stallion, valued at $2,460.

East of Decatur on Catlett Creek, J. D. White had ridden from his home and was gathering grapes from a vine when he saw a few Indians running a calf. He quickly rode to a hilltop and saw about 200 Indians "in regular cavalry double line," a quarter mile away. White thought of a ruse. Making sure he could be seen, he waved his hat as if he was hurrying forward troops who were on the opposite side of the hill, and then boldly advanced a short distance down toward the Indians, who halted as if they were unsure of what to do. The Indians changed direction to the west. White was pleased at his stratagem, but it did not turn out well at the Vick farm. Warriors went there next, found Mrs. Rebecca Vick, and shot her in the back as she was stooped over her washtub. Given the respite, White rode home, got his family and that of Granger Salmon's, and hid along Catlett Creek.

The Indians soon continued their southeast course, coming to Jackson Connelly's cabin. Connelly got his wife and daughters dressed in his clothing, put hats on them, and positioned them at the windows. Incredibly he had only one gun with one load of ammunition. The others held broom handles and sticks as if they were weapons. The Indians got close enough to see the potential danger, milled around awhile, and left.

Warning had reached Decatur where many of the men were gone on cattle drives and the few remaining men, along with the women and children, were panicking. Word was that 200 "savages" were murdering people just four miles north of town. Almost everyone congregated at the courthouse, which was fortified and supplied with food and water for a siege. Others "fortified" themselves at Bishop's Tavern, where, besides giving themselves a shot of courage, they likely reduced their fighting abilities. Most of them stayed awake in terror through the night, but at dawn, the Indians were gone. They had moved on into Denton County.[6]

Near the county line they caught Randolph Vesey, who had been a servant and voluntary aide to Confederate Gen. William L. Cabell. Normally they would have killed an adult male, but perhaps because Vesey was black they took him along. Later, he briefly testified, "I was captured by the Indians. They took me out to Madison Bluff (Medicine Bluff in Indian Territory)…. After I was with them 10 or 12 days they turned me loose."[7]

In Denton County the raiders got into some territory that hadn't been cleaned out. On October 29 they were heading east toward the town of Denton and hit several ranches from Denton Creek to South and North Hickory Creeks and then north to Clear Creek. William T. Clark lost 25 horses worth $1,250. Jesse McGee lost nine horses worth $420. Cotsworth H. Jackson lost eight horses worth $320 from his ranch on North Hickory Creek. On Clear Creek about nine miles north of Denton, the raiders stole 35 horses from John W. Gober, which he valued at $2,190.[8]

Frank Coonis had been at his father-in-law's home on Harts Creek in northeast Wise County when the Indians came through on October 28 and ran off some of his horses. The next day a neighbor told them that some stolen horses had been recovered and were being held on the Hickory Prairie in Denton County. Frank Coonis rode over to look. He got there just in time to meet the Indians who were still actively raiding in that area. Coonis ran for it, taking shelter in the abandoned Keep ranch house in western Denton County. Warriors surrounded him and blasted the ramshackle cabin with bullets. When he did not return, neighbors went to look for him and eventually saw buzzards circling over the cabin. Inside was Coonis, shot dead through the neck. Two of his pistols were on the floor, with every chamber empty except one.[9]

After dark on October 29, the raiders were right in Denton. Sarah Jane Edwards had 50 horses in her pasture on the west edge of town, never believing the Indians would come that close. The horses, valued at $3,750, were gone in the morning, as were those of C. Daugherty, which shared the same pasture. Sisters Nannie McCormick and Elizabeth Elms had recently inherited 75 horses worth $5,700 from their deceased father, Isaac Hembree. That same night or early on October 30, the raiders relieved them of their inheritance.[10]

With daylight on October 30 and the raiders so close to Denton, it was time to pull out. After losing horses the previous night, Cotsworth Jackson gathered about ten of his neighbors and assembled between North and South Hickory Creeks when the Indians went by driving their stolen stock in a grand procession, estimated at between 600 to 1,000 head. William McCormick counted 325 Indians, coming, going, and driving horses in from all directions. The settlers would need a lot more men.

The Indians headed northwest, but before leaving Denton County they cleaned out all the stock in their path. B. T. Parr lost seven horses worth $425. William R. Eaves, who was one of the criers bringing warning during Big Tree's raid, had been herding his horses down Clear Creek. This time the Indians got his four "all American bred large, sound, good condition" horses, and Eaves was angry. He got his pistol and went after the thieves.

As the Indians were driving an immense herd, their progress was slow, giving the angry whites time to catch up. Crow Wright led a party of about 40 men and they caught up to about 125 of the Indians on upper Whites Creek, in the northeast corner of Wise County. Tenville Cecil lived about five miles from there. He gathered half a dozen men and met them on Whites Creek about the same time.

The whites came in shooting, and the Indians replied. Living nearby was Ambrose H. Sevier Fortenberry (50) and his family. Fortenberry counted 18 shots and climbed his roof for a better look. Coming down he told his wife, "Jane, I must go," picked up his squirrel rifle, mounted a horse, and left. In a minute he returned to grab something he had forgotten and his daughter, Lucy (13), ran to him and said, "Father, you will never come back."

"You don't know, child," he told her, and rode off for the fight. Abe Fortenberry joined Cecil's party and charged in, but Cecil, Wright, and others quickly learned that they were outnumbered and outgunned. In a few minutes the whites were retreating. Several were wounded, including William Eaves, who was shot "in the lumbar region near the hip bone" which left him partly crippled, and he said "he has suffered severe torture" ever since. Abe Fortenberry did not return. Indians caught him, scalped him alive, piled dry grass on his body and burned him to death.[11]

The raiders headed out through central Montague County, half-heartedly pursued by some Montague citizens. In a few more days they were safely back at the Wichita Agency celebrating their successful foray with scalp dances and stories of bravery.

If the people of those counties breathed a sigh of relief, it was too soon. On Sunday, November 1, about 25 Indians crossed Red River north of Gainesville in Cooke County. Judge J. E. Wheeler wrote to Governor Pease, *sans* punctuation, about what happened. The Indians "collected a lot of horses five men pursued them and the Indians charged them and killed a Mr. Pace broke the arm of another and shot him in the hip he will probably recover speared a third man above the eye and slightly wounded the fourth in the thigh and killed the horse under him…." The judge added, "Gainesville is now the frontier people are every day leaving the country and gloom broods over us all…." He complained that 15 men went after the Indians, but for organizing without authorization, they were reported to Maj. Samuel H. Starr, 6th Cavalry, at Fort Richardson. Now they faced censure, fines, or jail time. It was 75 miles from Gainesville to Fort Richardson, Judge Wheeler said, and before any dispatch could be sent to Major Starr and assistance rendered, "we are all scalped the horses are already taken out of the country…."[12]

When the big raid ended, it finally quieted down in the counties bordering Red River. It was late fall and most of the raiders were settling into winter camps, but some remained active. Around the first of November, they entered Kendall County and got 12 horses worth $890 from Sophie Amman. Out in Tom Green County, the ranches along Spring Creek and the branches of the Concho were subject to attacks from Kickapoos and Mescaleros, as well as Comanches and Kiowas. Richard Tankersley had already been raided three times, but there was little he could do. He lost horses and cattle, as did his fellow ranchers, James and Aaron Burleson, Sam and Dave Delong, and Felix McKitrick. In late October or early November 1868, Indians made a daylight raid on Tankersley's pens along Spring Creek. His cowboys tried to stop them, but Jim Cummings and a man named Compton were killed. The raiders got away with 18 saddle horses worth $1,080. Tankersley later filed a claim, but the government decreed that in the fall of 1868, the Comanches (if they were Comanches) were not in amity with the United States and therefore Tankersley was not eligible for compensation.[13]

Earlier in the year, John and William Morris raised stock near present Evant, in northwest Coryell County. They sold their small herds to Jim Burleson out in Tom Green County and joined him and Tankersley on a cattle drive to sell the beef at Fort Sumner in New Mexico Territory. Using the Goodnight-Loving Trail was generally a dangerous proposition, but this time, the drive went off without a hitch. The beef was sold, the men got their pay, and they returned without incident. The Morris Brothers, with three horses and a wagon, returned as far as present Mills County where they camped on Mullins Creek. They hoped to be home with one long day's drive. The next morning they traveled about seven miles to a point a few miles north of present Goldthwaite.

Will Morris saw a deer in the thicket and went off to shoot it while John drove the wagon. As soon as they separated, Indians charged after the wagon. John whipped the horses and Will soon joined him, shooting whenever the Indians got close. They tried to battle their way to John Williams' ranch nearby, but John only got as far as Browns Creek. He was wounded five times and could go no farther. Dying, he told his brother to get away. Will managed to reach the ranch. When he got some cowboys to return with him to the creek, all they found was John's mangled body. They buried him on William's' ranch.[14]

On December 31, marauders were in Kerr County. J. S. Goss was described by his neighbor, George Nichols, as "a clever man and an honest man and a good man too," but he could not win the hand of Nichols' daughter no matter how hard he tried. She married another. Goss lost his sweetheart, and on New Year's Eve he lost all the rest of his horses. The Indians concluded the year of 1868 just as they had begun it.[15]

Inexplicably, the Bureau of Indian Affairs, like the army, seemed to be oblivious to Texas' plight. In the nearly 400-page report for 1868, hardly a word was devoted to the Kiowas and Comanches, some of this was no doubt due to Agent Leavenworth's departure. The latest commissioner, Nathaniel G. Taylor, wrote that the Kiowas and Comanches were being "troublesome," raiding into the Chickasaw Nation, and some of them raiding into Texas. What he was more worried about was if they decided to join the Cheyennes and Arapahos and raid in Kansas. The Wichita Agent, Henry Shanklin, was most concerned about the Kiowas and Comanches, who he called "the very worst of the Plains Indians," hanging around at his agency. They threatened to kill the agency physician, burned down an agency building, and destroyed the Wichitas' corn crop. Shanklin said, "Their conduct was insolent and humiliating to the last degree…."[16]

There was ample evidence of the tribes' disregard of the treaties they had signed and their continued attacks, killings, and thefts in Texas. While other tribes had been punished more for doing less, the Kiowas and Comanches seemed to hold a perpetual "get out of jail free" card.

If there would be no large punitive expedition, there was at least one positive response. The raid of October 1868 may have been the catalyst to finally convince District of Texas Commander General Reynolds to allow citizens to form local companies for their own protection. On November 2, settlers on the northern frontier got their wish. Major Samuel H. Starr, 6th Cavalry, was allowed to send notice to the citizens of Wise and adjoining counties that they "are authorized to embody a sufficient number of their people to protect themselves from depredating Indians." A Mr. Shoemaker was elected captain of the Wise County militia, R. H. Hopkins was the Denton County captain, and Levi Perryman was elected in Montague.

A Denton County history later claimed that when the Indians learned that "citizen soldiers" were now on their trail "it was time for them to move farther northwest." The history claimed that it was to the militia that "we are indebted largely for the settlement of the Indian question…."[17]

The Indians never vacated the area when the "citizen soldiers" were on their trail for the first seven years of the decade and they didn't in 1868. The contention is wishful thinking steeped in sentiment and hallowed by myths that are plainly incorrect. Sergeant H. H. McConnell of the 6th Cavalry at Fort Richardson summed up the regiment's success in 1868. Plenty of money was disbursed by the government into civilian hands, and the fort helped settle the country, but "we didn't actually kill many Indians…."[18]

The soldiers were largely ineffective and the civilians didn't do any better. Texans like to believe their Rangers and gun-toting pioneers were the sole defenders of their homesteads and families, an immovable barrier as well as an irresistible force that would defeat the Indians and tame the West. In reality, militia, Rangers, state troops, and U. S. troops could not settle the "Indian question," not while using the same tired tactics and strategies that had always failed. As usual, there were more important factors than numbers of armed men, no matter what they called themselves.

Chapter 54 notes

1 Utley, *Frontier Regulars*, 149-50, 154.

2 Depredation Claims: John G. Irwin #3895; Morris Gilbert #674; William Metcalf #5702; George W. Ross #5719; David McDonald #4537; William H. Gatlin #5684; William S. Keith #4738; Louis Kincheloe #2479.

3 Mooney, *Calendar History of the Kiowa*, 322-25.

4 Depredation Claims: Jesse Caraway #4199; Phillip Haas #3348; Samuel McDonald #343.

5 Hunter, "Battle at Ball's Ranch," 22-34; Sowell, *Rangers and Pioneers*, 287-94; James Ball, Depredation Claim #10172; Mooney, *Calendar History of the Kiowa*, 325,424. More details of this incident are in Michno, *Fate Worse Than Death*, 287-91. In the Kiowa calendar the winter of 1868-69 was called "Winter that Tan-guadal was killed," which happened during "an encounter with a white man and a boy."

6 Tenville Cecil, Depredation Claim #2296; McConnell, *West Texas Frontier*, http://www.forttours.com/pages/popups/sttrirai.htm; Cates, *Wise County*, 171-74.

7 Tenville Cecil, Depredation Claim #2296. Vesey was not ransomed by Brit Johnson as is written on a marker in the Oaklawn Cemetery in Decatur.

8 Depredation Claims: William T. Clark #4553; Jesse McGee #5819; Cotsworth H. Jackson #5254; John W. Gober #4551.

9 Cates, *Wise County*, 190; McConnell, *West Texas Frontier*, 567.

10 Depredation Claims: Sarah Jane Edwards #5253; Nannie McCormick #5416.

11 Bates, *Denton County*, 164-65, 327-29; Depredation Claims: B. T. Parr #1602; William R. Eaves #421; Tenville Cecil #2296.

12 Winfrey and Day, *Texas Indian Papers, IV*, 290-91.

13 Depredation Claims: Sophie Amman #651; Richard Tankersley #6501.

14 McConnell, *West Texas Frontier*, 636.

15 J. S. Goss, Depredation Claim #1810.

16 *Commissioner of Indian Affairs 1868*, 3, 21, 287-88.

17 Bates, *Denton County*, 165-66.

18 McConnell, *Five Years a Cavalryman*, 161.

Part 11. 1869

55 "What sort of tale will we tell when we get home?"

At the beginning of 1869, Texas politics were still a muddy mix of conservatives, moderates, and radicals fighting for supremacy, with the conservatives slowly falling behind. The radical Republicans supported blacks' rights, restrictions on Confederates, and cautious economic development. In the proposed constitution, the moderates included provisions restoring the franchise to former Confederates. Because of this, the radicals opposed a vote to ratify the proposed constitution. In November 1868, Ulysses Grant won the national election, and when it became clear that he approved an election to fill state offices and ratify a new constitution, both parties looked for candidates and prepared for the upcoming election, which would not be held, however, until the following December.

The day after Grant's election, President Johnson, sick of his inability to get Texas re-admitted to the Union and blaming General Reynolds for complicating matters, removed him from office. He appointed Gen. Edward R. S. Canby as commander of the Fifth Military District in his place. Canby was charged with ensuring the Texas convention come together and vote on a constitution, a charge that he could not fulfill either. On March 5, the day after Grant's inauguration, he removed Canby and re-assigned Reynolds.[1]

On the frontier, nothing had changed. The weather was still good and there were still horses and cows to steal. In 1867 there had been 2,479 soldiers on the frontier and in 1868 the number had gone up to 3,226.[2] The *Galveston News* editorialized back in August 1865 that if there were only 3,000 cavalrymen on the frontier, the settlers would be sufficiently protected. There were more than that in 1868 and the results were increases in raids and settler deaths. If 1869 followed the general trends of the previous nine years, there would be another direct proportion in the making: more troops meant more deaths; fewer troops meant fewer deaths.

As a New Years' greeting, Lipans celebrated in Medina County, stealing horses from David W. Fly, G. W. Harper, and S. Wantz near the western county line. The men trailed the thieves into Uvalde County, going up the Sabinal River and west to Frio Canyon. They found one dead mare and came to a recently abandoned Indian camp with a fire still burning and meat half cooked, along with lariats, blankets, sacks, and a cow paunch filled with water. The harried Indians dropped 19 horses on the trail, and the posse was content to pick them up and go home.

On February 10, 1869, Indians stole five horses from Peter Gousalans in Jack County. On February 15, they took four horses from Jack Hinton from his ranch on the San Saba River in San Saba County. The same month Kickapoos were in Bexar County not far from San Antonio and stole 85 saddle and stock horses worth $1,425 from Jose A. Torres. On March 10, Kiowas stole 11 horses worth $715 from Haden M. Hill in Parker County, eight miles north of Weatherford.[3]

Kickapoos seemed to be unaware or unafraid of the three companies of cavalry and infantry in San Antonio, for on March 29, they were back near the city, getting horses from several ranchers, including a Mr. Marnoch and Joseph Huebner. Huebner lost 117 head of horses and mules worth $2,865. The stolen stock, said to have numbered more than 400, were taken west past Castroville, where a force of "Rangers" failed to stop them. When people later filed claims for this and similar raids, the government counsels, as defendants, questioned the veracity of the claimants. They simply did not believe that raiders could get so far into the settled portions of the country, and said that "the court should not award judgment in cases coming from this section," and besides, they argued, there was no proof that the "Indians" were not really Mexicans in disguise.[4] Indians, Mexicans, or alien invaders, the settlers still suffered.

In April, Comanches visited Mark B. Hatley again near his ranch in Lampasas County, taking three horses at Simms Creek. They also got stock from his neighbors, John Patterson and a Mr. Jennings. Hatley said, "they were so far gone there was no use in trying to overtake them."

The same raiders went out through Mason County, and on April 15, stole 17 mules and horses worth $800 from Joseph D. Bridges. Later in the month, Indians were at Reuben Vaughn's in Palo Pinto County, taking five horses that were hobbled only 200 yards from his cabin. They took the horses up to Fort Sill where several months later a neighbor saw them with Vaughn's brand, but the soldiers were not willing to do anything about it.

The boldness of the Indians was shown during that raid when they came right to the outskirts of Jacksboro. Hernando Babb, older brother of the Babb children who were captured in 1866, was in town on business. He said he had "three head of horses which were hobbled on the open range about one fourth of a mile south of the government post at Jacksboro." The Indians came in the night and took them. Babb followed the trail about two miles the next morning but gave up.

On April 23, raiders were in Parker County. John B. Tompkins had a farm six miles northwest of Weatherford and owned about 80 horses. He was away from home on business that day, but Sarah Tompkins and her children were in the yard about nine in the morning when 25 Indians rode in. It was raining and the Indians were all wrapped in red blankets. Only 200 yards from the house the Indians cut out 32 horses worth $2,825, and calmly drove them away. Mrs. Tompkins and the children could do nothing but watch. The

Author's photo

Reconstructed cabins at Fort Griffin, occupied from 1867 to 1881.

next day the raiders moved west and took four horses worth $300 from John Long.[5]

There was a springtime cattle roundup in western Parker County and the cowmen gathered at Poe Prairie near present Millsap. Sam Newberry and Tom Cox drifted into Milt and Bose Ikard's camp and shared dinner. After eating, they rode out to help the others hunt for cattle when they cut a large Indian trail heading west. Newberry and Cox joined Elbert T. and John Doss, Bill Gray, and Milt and Bose Ikard to follow the trail which led into Palo Pinto County. On April 24, they discovered the Indians in the breaks along the Brazos about six miles west of present Mineral Wells. Four warriors stayed on their horses, but a dozen of them took position under the bluff. Sam Newberry dueled with a warrior who fired an Enfield Rifle. After several minutes of dodging among the trees and circling for better position, John Doss was wounded, but when a fatal bullet knocked Elbert Doss to the ground, the cowboys figured they had enough. They had already captured some of the Indians' horses and supplies and they picked up the Doss brothers and carried them back to Parker County. Elbert Doss was buried in Porter Cemetery near the Light family, killed the previous year.[6]

The army occasionally had some successes, and one of the first in a long time was, surprisingly, not by the cavalry, but the infantry. In March 1869, Congress reduced the size of the army to 25 infantry regiments, which resulted in a series of troop movements across Texas. The 17th Infantry was moved to the Atlantic coast and to replace it, the 15th and 35th Infantry shifted to Texas, although they would soon be combined into one, the 15th. While the 35th was on the frontier, Capt. George W. Smith got a squad of Tonkawas and found mounts for a detachment of Companies E and F and left Fort Griffin on a scout. On May 7, they discovered about 25 Comanches camped on the headwaters of Paint Creek in present Haskell County. With no losses of his own, Smith reported killing 14 Comanches. They captured 14 Indian horses and gave them to the Tonkawas.[7]

Much more typical were the constant raids that slipped by the patrols and got into the settlements. About a week after the Paint Creek fight, Comanches were in Jack County, where they stole horses from William Hensley on Keechi Creek about ten miles south of Jacksboro. Hensley and Mortimer Stephens were going fishing in the Keechi and Stephens got there early in the morning, but Hensley was hours late. He had a good reason. When he met Stephens, he said, "Steve, my horses are all stolen." Stephens asked if the Indians got them. "Yes sir," Hensley answered, "they was in last night, and they got the last horse I had."

"Well, that knocks the fishing in the head," Stephens replied.

The men went to Stephens' pasture to round up some horses, but discovered they were gone too. All they found was "an old sore-backed Indian pony…its ear was split…rode plumb down."[8]

The Indians went southeast and into the northeast corner of Parker County where they had raided dozens of times before. On May 18, they were on the west bank of the West Fork Trinity in the areas of present Reno and Azle. They stole horses from James M. Clifton, Robert A. Parker, Ira Slover, and William Nix. The Davis' lived a quarter mile from Clifton. After the Comanches drove off the stock, they turned abruptly northwest and ran into William H. Davis (12), who was right near his cabin. The warriors swept the boy up on a horse and continued, barely slowing their stride.

Davis said the Indians rode hard, breaking down their horses without a care. Whenever a horse slowed, they killed it or left it behind. A posse followed the raiders for 30 miles before giving up, finding a few of the tell-tale split-eared ponies by the roadside. Once the Indians got out of the settlements they slowed down. Davis said it took ten days to get to Fort Sill, where the new post and agency were being constructed. Davis' captivity ended abruptly at the fort. He was there "about three hours," he said, before the military demanded his release.

Down in San Saba County, raiders attacked Jack Hinton's ranch about May 15. It was the seventh time he had been hit. This time they only got four horses worth $400, but he was nearly ruined. Since 1866 they had stolen $39,065 worth of his cattle, horses, and mules.[9]

One of the most desperate fights between the settlers and Indians occurred on May 16, 1869, on the Salt Creek Prairie in Young County. Eleven ranchers, Ira Graves, William Crow, Perry Harmonson, John and George Lemley, Shapley Carter, Jesse McClain, W. C. Kutch, J. W. Gray, Rube Secrist, and Joe Woody had gathered about 500 head and realized that such a large herd would surely attract Indians. On a cold morning with a strong wind and intermittent rains and snow showers, they began moving the herd south. Near Salt Creek about 15 miles northeast of Fort Belknap, the Indians found them.

Kutch and Carter were driving some strays in when about 60 Indians rode in and cut them off from the rest of the cowboys. They were half a mile away from a copse of trees where the others had taken refuge and faced a decision.

"We can get away without any trouble," Kutch said.

"What sort of a tale will we tell when we get home?" Carter responded.

There was nothing more to be said. The two men charged toward their friends and a few cowmen came out to meet them. One of the Lemleys yelled to them that they should run for the timber to the west, but Kutch said it was too far across "bald prairie." All of them decided to head for some better cover in a thicket under a bluff about 300 yards away. The Comanches anticipated the move and had already taken over the spot. When the cowboys drew near, they blasted them from the cover they sought. The cowboys had to veer into the open prairie and take cover in a buffalo wallow.

They took a chance by abandoning their horses, hoping the Indians would be satisfied with them, but their ploy failed; the Indians pinned them down and peppered them with rifle bullets and arrows. The defenders had no rifles, only cap-and-ball pistols. Will Crow was the first killed; Jesse McClain and Ira Graves were wounded; George and John Lemley, Jim Gray, Shap Carter, and Rube Secrist were hit twice; Kutch was hit three times. Since they were trying to lie flat and had to raise their heads to shoot, most of their wounds were in the head or shoulders. Only Harmonson, Woody, and the cook, called "Negro Dick," were not hit.

The fight went from about ten in the morning to five in the afternoon. When the Comanches pulled back to a small hill as if to discuss what to do, Ira Graves had the cowboys stand up, with the wounded propped up by their companions and they waved and cheered and dared the Indians to attack them again. The demonstration seemed to work, for the Comanches left. They gathered 31 horses, more than 200 cattle, and drove them away to the north. It was very fortunate, for the cowboys were down to their last few bullets.

The unwounded Harmonson traveled south to his ranch near the Brazos to get help. John Lemley died that night. When rescuers arrived the next morning, they took the men to Harmonson's and made pallets on the floor for all of the wounded. Kutch, with three arrows in him, pulled one out of his leg, but talked a man named Whitten into digging one out of his shoulder. The arrow had gone into the top of his shoulder and down into his shoulder blade. Whitten said he couldn't get it out, but Kutch knew he had once dug an arrow out of Will Peveler. Whitten found a bullet mold, dug a hole, and twisted the arrowhead out. Kutch survived, but Shap Carter died before a doctor could be found. McClain lived two more years, but died from complications of his wound.[10]

Chapter 55 notes

1 Richter, *Army in Texas During Reconstruction*, 157-58;

2 Shook, "Federal Military in Texas," 46, 48.

3 Depredation Claims: David W. Fly #2690; Peter Gousalans #5217; Jack Hinton #5298; Jose A. Torres #3344; Haden M. Hill #5296.

4 Joseph Huebner, Depredation Claim #7821.

5 Depredation Claims: Mark B. Hatley #4234; Joseph D. Bridges #432; Reuben Vaughn #6300; Hernando Babb #4606; John B. Tompkins #4175; John Long #5688.

6 McConnell, *West Texas Frontier*, 644.

7 Richter, *Army in Texas During Reconstruction*, 180; Williams, *Texas' Last Frontier*, 112; *Adjutant General's Office*, 40.

8 William Hensley, Depredation Claim #7484.

9 Depredation Claims: James M. Clifton #5260; Ira S. Slover #5012; Jack Hinton #5298.

10 McConnell, *West Texas Frontier*, in http://www.forttours.com/pages/tocscprairie.asp; Horton, *History of Jack County*, in *www.forttours.com/pages/saltck.asp*; Wilbarger, *Indian Depredations*, 549-51; George W. Lemley, Depredation Claim #4200.

56 "If the Indians are going to kill us, we need not let them get the watermelons."

John Allen, the buffalo hunter who had been smitten by Martha Russell in 1868, had only received two letters from her and then the letters stopped. He anxiously waited all winter until he could get back to north Texas, when he would go on a hunt again in June 1869. When he returned to the Russell cabin in Wise County, he found the place wrecked and abandoned. He made inquiries and learned of the massacre and that only Bean Russell survived. The heartbroken John Allen continued west to the buffalo range. While hunting, they had a sharp skirmish with Indians. One hunter was wounded, but they thought they killed three Indians. John Allen walked over the skirmish area and found a warrior's buffalo hide shield that was decorated with a beaded scalp. Allen examined the scalp closely and his heart skipped; in color, length, and texture it was very familiar.

"The minute I found this scalp on the shield," Allen said, "it flashed through my mind that it was Lucy Russell's scalp." Its age, color, and length, "convinced me at once." He choked back his feelings, hid the scalp in his saddlebag, and said nothing.[1]

June 1869 was a repetition of the preceding months. Indians stole horses along Battle Creek in Callahan County from Sevier McDonald, James Hart, William Hittson, Joseph Lawson, and Messrs. Lynch, McNaulty, and Greer. Up in Montague County, marauders stole three horses from John McClure. In Comal County, Kickapoos were blamed for robbing Gustav Vogel of three horses. Kickapoos also hit Val Verde County hard that month. John J. Inselman was a freighter running wagons between Texas and Mexico. They attacked his ranch near present Del Rio, stealing 50 oxen, 25 horses, and 25 mules, plus damaging his house and stealing other property, for losses of $15,750.[2]

To the northwest, the 4th Cavalry managed to make contact with the Kickapoos. Ranald S. Mackenzie, colonel of the black 41st Infantry, rode out of Fort McKavett with 42 men from Companies G, L, and M, 9th Cavalry. On June 7, on the Pecos River about 50 miles up from the Rio Grande, they attacked an Indian camp. The Indians fled south but the broken down cavalry horses could not follow. It was reported that one enlisted man and two Indians were killed in the skirmish.[3]

In the north, a large raid entered Young, Throckmorton, and Shackelford counties in June. More than 30 Indians rode once again to the Fort Murrah, Elm Creek, and California Creek area. John C. Duncan, Zerrill J. Harmonson, Robert M. Matthews, and George T. Hunter were all running their cattle

Author's photo

The ruins of Fort McKavett. The fort was occupied off and on my Union and Confederate troops until it was abandoned in 1883.

together, about 4,000 head, on California Creek north of the Brazos. Despite the cowboys they employed, no one was aware of the raid until, less than three-fourths of a mile from the herders' camp, Indians cut in and began driving the cattle up the creek to the north. The ranchers got together and easily followed the trail of torn up prairie up to 100 yards wide. They found the usual dead horses and broken down, split-eared ponies along the way, and also typically, they could do nothing because they didn't have enough men to challenge the raiders. Duncan's losses were 250 head worth $2,200. In total, about 3,000 cattle were lost, with a value of about $30,000.[4]

In June, some of the raiders came down as far as Belknap where they stole five horses from Christopher C. Mills. From there they swung northeast and ran into Frank Taylor, who was carrying the mail between Belknap and Jacksboro in an old buggy. Indians easily caught him about ten miles east of Belknap. They killed him, scalped him, cut off half of his mustache and one of his thumbs. They sliced open the mail sacks and scattered the letters to the wind. Some men in a cow outfit saw the commotion and reported to Belknap. Civilians found Taylor's body a few hundred yards from the road and threw brush on him to cover him up, but were apparently too frightened to stay and bury him. Soldiers from Fort Richardson later came and buried the remains. At least they were useful in some respects.

Sergeant McConnell at Fort Richardson commented that killing mail carriers was a frequent occurrence. He recalled a man named Mason who used to stop at the post almost nightly on his rounds. "Poor Mason!" he said, "soon after was killed by Indians when in the line of his duty." McConnell said that eight silent graves of earth and rocks marked where stage drivers and mail carriers lay scattered along the roadside in the 35-mile stretch between Jacksboro and Belknap.[5]

The raiders also stole stock in Throckmorton County and swung into northern Shackelford County to the gates of Fort Griffin. The post sat on a bluff above the Clear Fork Brazos and down in the flat grew the rough and tumble town of Fort Griffin, with its merchants, saloons, cowboys, rustlers, buffalo hunters, and ladies of the evening. In 1869, however, the flats were still comparatively empty, and some of the earliest structures were right near the post on the bluff, called Government Hill. Freed slaves Samuel and Amelia Jannett lived on the hill where Samuel worked as a cook for the army officers. They had saved for a long time and were able to purchase two white and two brown mules and one mare, which they kept hobbled and close to their cabin.

The raiders apparently were as much deterred by soldiers at Fort Griffin as at Fort Richardson. About June 15, they crept right up to the post and cut loose Jannett's mules and mare. Amelia had seen them safe and sound about 11 p.m. and in the morning they were gone. A Mr. Glisk who ran the stage station nearby lost all of his mules. Mr. Bell and his wife had an unfinished cabin and slept in a wagon with their mules tied barely ten yards from their heads. Bell heard something just before sunup and arose to find the ropes cut and his mules gone. He thought he saw someone leading them away and fired into the shadows. The shot woke the Jannetts and others, who discovered almost all of them had lost their animals.

Amelia Jannett went to the fort to give the alarm and met a detail of soldiers who were aroused by the shooting. They weren't too enthusiastic about chasing Indians. "This first detail having not gone any further than my house," said Amelia, she sent her son by a previous marriage, Clark Barber, to the fort to demand that men be sent after the raiders. Apparently no one was very concerned. "It was at least nine o'clock the next day, however," said Amelia, "before the second detail of soldiers took the trail. They followed them until about four o'clock that afternoon and returned to the post."[6]

If the army was so unconcerned about depredations in its own backyard, little help could be expected in the settlements. George Washington Wolfe, a Methodist preacher from Mississippi, had settled at Wolfe Crossing between the junction of the Llano and Colorado River in Llano County at present Kingsland. He had three sons, Hiram (17), Washington (13), and W. B. (6). On June 22, 1869, the two oldest brothers were hunting hogs near the confluence of the two rivers, both armed with Colt pistols. When they saw Indians closing in, they ran to the wooded bank of the Llano and took cover, firing several shots at them. One warrior jumped off the bank, got behind a pecan tree, and had a clear shot from behind them. His rifle snapped and Hiram fell dead. The others charged in and grabbed Washington. George Wolfe later found Hiram's body lying half in the water.

The Indians took the boys' horses and headed west passing near the village of Llano, generally following the course of the river. About six miles southwest of Mason, Jim Bidy saw them coming. He hid in the bush and took a shot at them as they passed, wounding an Indian woman. The warriors did not know where the shot came from and didn't know how many enemies were near. They hurriedly split up, leaving two men with the wounded woman. Bidy also saw what appeared to be a white boy with them.

Bidy hurried to Mason and spread the alarm. A search party quickly gathered, including William Gammer, James Johnson, Boy Johnson, and a half dozen others. The men caught up to them 15 miles west near Little Saline Creek in Kimball County. The slow-moving Indians with the wounded woman dropped Washington Wolfe and ran off, probably hoping that the whites would be satisfied with recovering the boy, which they were. Wolfe had only been captive three days, but his face was painted and he was already learning to eat jerked meat and prickly pears.[7]

About July 2, 1869, Indians were back again in Jack County contemptuously raiding just east of Fort Richardson. Hernando Babb was on a roundup near Beans Creek about ten miles from Jacksboro when the Indians stole two horses from him and more from other ranchers, including W. M. Carroll. Babb said there were about 35 Indians, but the cowboys went after them. In less than a mile, the Indians turned and gave battle. Suddenly, Jim Harding "hallowed that he was 'shot out,'" said Babb, and "we retreated into the brush." The cowboys rallied and counter-charged. This time the Indians retreated. They chased them about two miles, Babb said, "but we did not recover any of our horses."

The raiders moved into southern Wise County and stole two horses from Wesley McMahon. On the afternoon of July 4, they traveled south along the Tarrant and Parker County lines until nearly sundown when they approached Marys Creek, just a mile and a half inside Parker County. Eleven Indians appeared on a hill under a rainbow just after a heavy rainstorm, but the folks at William R. Rider's house did not have time to ponder the picturesque scene. Mr. Rider was not home, and after Annie Rider (11) counted the Indians, she and her mother, Melissa, crawled into the loft and hoped the Indians would leave them alone. As the Indians corralled the horses, the family dog, trained to assist in rounding up stock, "tried to help them," Annie said, "and the Indians speared the dog." Annie was not frightened. Later, she said "I was raised on the frontier and Indian raids were common, we understood the situation…and being used to the Indian raids I knew what to expect and took it as nothing more than what might fall to my lot any time."[8]

The raiders got the horses and moved on to Clinton B. Rider's place half a mile away, where they stole more stock. Half a mile south of the house they overtook teamster William Tinnell, mortally wounded and scalped him, and took his two horses. He was carried to John Kauffman's house where he died a week later.

Citizens were coming to Weatherford for the Fourth of July celebration from all over the county, and the raiders had aroused several parties who were crossing the territory hunting for them. The raiders camped for the night two miles west of Clinton Rider's cabin and the next morning they moved to Campbell's Prairie five miles north of Weatherford, where they chased John Murphy and Joe Henson who were on their way to town. The men got away, changed horses in Weatherford, and recruited a party to go after the Indians. In the meantime the Indians rode north and killed a local settler, John Lopp. For some reason, the Indians were particularly vicious as they shot him more than 60 times, flattened his head with blows from clubs or gun butts, and hung the body in a live oak tree.

The Indians attacked a few other places, getting five horses worth $425 from James J. Barker, and 18 horses worth $1,800 from James T. Roberts. They would not steal much more, however, because a posse was catching up. Riley and Fine Earnest, John Robinson, Henry and John Gilliland, and several others, tracked the raiders to Slipdown Mountain where they had holed up in a cave. The settlers set fire to the brush at the entrance and smoked them out, and they shot one warrior near the entrance. Earnest tried to throw a lasso around the Indian to drag him away, but caught an arrow in his wrist for the effort. The rest of the Indians escaped. The settlers scalped the one, took his tomahawk, shield, and accoutrements, and cut off a finger to get his ring. They felt pretty good that they had exacted an ounce of flesh in vengeance, but the scales never approached a balance.[9]

On July 10, Indians raided Lucy E. Lindsey in Stephens County, taking $550 worth of horses. Down in Medina County they hit Phillip Haas for the fourth time, getting seven horses worth $230.[10]

During the nearly full moon of July 21, Thomas C. and Elizabeth V. Felps were the targets. Unlike so many instances when the victims were traveling or stock hunting, this time they were innocently fishing on Cypress Creek in northern Blanco County less than a mile from their home. A black child had seen Indians in the area and ran to tell Felps, but he dismissed the warning. The boy ran to hide in a cornfield and the Indians found and killed Thomas and Elizabeth. They stripped them and scalped Elizabeth, but not Thomas. Her arms and face were broken with a club and she was lanced in the breast. As they rode away they happened to pass near Elizabeth's parent's cabin and waved the clothing stuck high on their lances as if they were bloody flags. Her parents cared for the couple's orphaned children, Thomas and Caroline. Thomas and Elizabeth Felps were buried in Miller Creek Cemetery southeast of Johnson City.[11]

About July 23, Barber W. Reynolds, his wife, Ann, their son Phineas, Samuel Newcomb and his wife, Silas H. Huff, and Rice Derrett were on the road from Weatherford to Fort Griffin. They had seen Indian sign and were wary, but they couldn't find a suitable place to camp. Finally near dark they rolled their two wagons to a stop in a mesquite flat near the junction of Keechi Creek and the Brazos in Palo Pinto County. They bedded down under the wagons and hobbled the horses nearby. Silas Huff and Rice Derrett slept out near the horses. Huff was on watch and about 11 p.m., under a full moon, he heard a noise and believed he could see the forms of Indians sneaking nearby. "He came running to where we were and waked us up," said Ann Reynolds. Ann woke Phineas and told him what was happening. With the thought processes of a little boy, Phineas cut to the chase.

"If the Indians are going to kill us we need not let them get the watermelons," he said, "but had better eat them."

They spent a sleepless night on guard, but to no avail. Somehow the Indians had still crept in, cut loose five of their horses, and slipped away. They had a few unbroken horses the Indians did not get and managed to hitch them to the wagons for a rough ride home.[12]

Chapter 56 notes

1 McConnell, *West Texas Frontier*, in www.forttours.com/ pages/tocruss.
2 Depredation Claims: Elizabeth J. McDonald #350; John McClure #3890; Gustav Vogel #7495; John J. Inselman #7494.
3 Michno, *Encyclopedia of Indian Wars*, 232.
4 John C. Duncan, Depredation Claim #7349.
5 Christopher C. Mills, Depredation Claim #5679; McConnell, *West Texas Frontier*, 650; McConnell, *Five Years a Cavalryman*, 170-71.
6 Samuel Jannett, Depredation Claim #4417.
7 McConnell, *West Texas Frontier*, in http://www.forttours.com/pages/tochiram; Winfrey and Day, *Texas Indian Papers, IV*, 310; George W. Wolfe, Depredation Claim #10315.
8 Depredation Claims: Hernando Babb #4606; Wesley McMahon #4786; William Rider #4340.
9 Marshall, *A Cry Unheard*, 177-80; McConnell, *West Texas Frontier*, 632; Smythe, *Historical Sketch of Parker County*, 121-24; Depredation Claims: James J. Barker #4555; James T. Roberts #5290.
10 Depredation Claims: Lucy E. Lindsey #1813; Phillip Haas #3348.
11 McConnell, *West Texas Frontier*, 634; Wilbarger, *Indian Depredations*, 643; Winfrey and Day, *Texas Indians Papers, IV*, 326.
12 Ann M. Reynolds, Depredation Claim #6502.

57 "If you can make Quakers out of the Indians it will take the fight out of them."

In the summer of 1869, Texans were graced with a new United States Indian policy. For years there had been a debate as to whether the Bureau of Indian Affairs should be placed under the U.S. Army or the Department of the Interior. After 1789, Indian affairs were handled by the War Department. In 1824 the Bureau was created, but it was not transferred to the Department of the Interior until 1849. The seeming inability to "civilize" the Indian and the constant wars led many in the army to believe that they could do a better job. Unfortunately, incidents such as the Sand Creek "massacre" led to an investigation of Indian treatment by Senator James R. Doolittle, whose report argued that military supervision was not the answer. Corruption, graft, and dishonest agents were also an ongoing problem in the Bureau. The move to shift the Bureau to the War Department was defeated in December 1868.

While President-elect Ulysses Grant waited to take office, he was visited by the Society of Friends, the Quakers, who suggested that religious men be appointed as Indian agents. After listening to their arguments, Grant replied, "Gentlemen, your advice is good.... If you can make Quakers out of the Indians it will take the fight out of them. Let us have peace." When Grant took office in March 1869, one of his first acts was to clean out the corrupt agents. Catholics and Protestant sects were given various tribes to oversee. In the Central Superintendency the Kiowas, Comanches, and Wichitas were given to the Quakers. Men of war apparently could not tame the Indians; perhaps men of religion could. It was called "Grant's peace policy."[1]

It didn't work.

Iowa farmer Lawrie Tatum knew nothing about Indians and was surprised by the appointment. When he learned he drew the Kiowas and Comanches, who he said "were probably the worst Indians east of the Rocky Mountains," he had his doubts. Colonel William B. Hazen escorted Tatum to the agency where he took over on July 1, 1869. Very quickly Tatum learned what he was up against. He would be fair, honest, and kind, and he would preach love, peace, and brotherhood, but his charges had different ideas. A "prominent chief" told Tatum that they had just been raiding in Texas, "and they seemed very sanguine that they could not be restrained." The chief said that if Washington (the president) "did not want his young men to raid in Texas, then Washington must move Texas far away, where his young men could not find it." The chief said that they had plenty of motivation to keep raiding. "They told me a number of times," said Tatum, "that the only way that they could get a large supply of annuity goods was to go out onto the warpath, kill some people, steal a good many horses, get the soldiers to chase them awhile, without permitting them to do much harm, and then the Government would give them a large amount of blankets, calico, muslin, etc., to get them to quit!"

Satanta told a committee of Friends who visited the agency essentially the same thing. "The good Indian, he that listens to the white man, got nothing. The independent Indian was the only one that was rewarded."[2]

Those independent Indians were all over northern Texas in August. On the first of the month they hit Gip Smith in Lampasas County, stealing $5,540 worth of horses. In Parker County on August 6, they were at John Tompkins' ranch half a dozen miles northwest of Weatherford. It was their third visit. This time they took 40 horses worth $3,000. Some neighbors went after the raiders but found only one mare and one colt killed with arrows. Also near Weatherford, the raiders took three horses worth $200 from Alphonso Freeman. In Llano County, Elbert M. Walker was hit for the fourth time, the Indians getting two mares and a colt worth $175. The Kickapoos were back in Medina County in late August, stealing 30 horses and one mule from Louis Heath, valued at $2,350.[3]

Perhaps one reason for the ease at which Indians slipped into the settlements was because the army was sending some of its companies to guard cattle being driven to outside markets. Often thought of as independent, rugged individualists, the Texas cattlemen (actually called "cowmen" at the time), placed much dependence on the military. It was the military market that initiated one facet of the post-Civil War expansion of the cattle industry and almost every settlement wanted an army post nearby to stimulate the economy.[4]

Men had always rustled and branded calves that they didn't own. It was illegal, and if the law didn't punish the wrongdoers, vigilante justice often saw to it that rustlers were found swinging from a tree branch. When it got too dangerous to rustle and brand, men began to kill mavericks for their hides. Hide prices were going up and it was easier to haul in tons of hides than drive beef on the hoof with the chances of being caught without a bill of sale.

The army tried to curtail the practice. During General Canby's brief stay as commander of the Fifth Military District, he issued an order dividing up Texas into 29 district "posts," charging their commanders with suppressing the illicit hide trade as one of the goals. The region west and northwest of San Antonio was where the hide trade was most rampant and in the sub-district of the Pecos, Col. Ranald S. Mackenzie, in command of the 41st Infantry at the time, was in charge. In addition to scouting for Indians and trying to keep order, he had to now be on the lookout for hide rustlers. The soldiers occasionally teamed up with ranchers and vigilantes to suppress rustling. When, in February 1869, Canby issued an order extending all Texas stock-marketing statutes to cover hides, it seemed to put a damper on the trade. Hide dealers now had to file a list of their hides, giving color, marks, brands, and names and addresses of sellers. Within a few months, hide rustling was declining.

There was still a problem with driving stolen cattle out of the state—the Indians not being the only ones in the business. On June 7, 1869, General Reynolds, back in command of the Fifth District, issued an inspection order that all cattle driven out of the state must also have bills of sale, descriptions, brands, and names and addresses of the sellers. This made much more work for the soldiers at western and northern posts such as Forts McKavett, Concho, Stockton, Griffin, and Richardson. In addition to hunting rustlers and outlaws, chasing Indians, and now inspecting cattle, the soldiers were also expected to escort cattle drives.

Since 1867, when five herds being driven to New Mexico were attacked, cavalry were increasingly being used to escort herds to the Pecos River, to New Mexico, and across the Llano Estacado. The escorts were generally effective at keeping the Indians away, and one researcher concluded that the army played a much greater role in policing, protecting, and expanding the post-war cattle industry than is believed or admitted. One reason for the "amnesia" was that many of the protectors were the often maligned black cavalrymen, and many cowmen who needed and accepted their protection would rarely acknowledge their indebtedness.[5]

With the cavalry protecting cattle drives, it meant there were additional holes in an already porous frontier. William A. Kemp lived in Hamilton County about six miles north of the county seat and near the schoolhouse where Ann Whitney was killed in 1867. During the full moon on August 21, he had purposely brought all his stock in close to the cabin to keep an eye on them, but it didn't help. During the night, Comanches came in, pulled out some of the pickets in the corral, and led out 14 horses. Kemp saw the fence down in the morning and found moccasin tracks all across his plowed field, plus a part of a buffalo robe caught on one of the fence pickets. He and some neighbors trailed the Indians but found only a pony "jaded down with his ears split."[6]

Thomas H. Malone had come all the way from California to Uvalde County to talk business with Ben Briggs, who was getting a herd of cattle to drive to California. Malone stopped at the home of William Shores on the upper Frio, and the next day he planned to continue over to Briggs' place on the Sabinal about three miles south of present Utopia. Shores told Malone that it was unsafe to travel the mountains alone and with no weapons, but he claimed he had come all the way from California without seeing an Indian and he need not bother with a pistol or rifle now. Malone left on August 21, but never made it. Somewhere between the rivers, Indians ambushed and killed him. Malone's body was not found until 16 days later. Eventually, his remains were buried in Waco where he had family.[7]

Indians never again raided the San Saba River in Menard County in such force as they did in August 1866, but they had visited the region in smaller bands many times. On the last day of August 1869, they were back again, stealing horses and cattle from Isaac Chrisman, Frank M. Alexander, James J. Callan, Charles Brock, Hans Williams and several others. Most of the ranches centered on Fort McKavett, but the Indians cared not a whit about the soldiers. The troops made their token pursuit, but found only a few split-eared ponies that the civilians who accompanied the scout collected on their way home.[8]

One of the last raids into Hood County was in September 1869, and it was apparently done by Caddo Indians. They had come through Parker County and into northern Hood about September 10, stealing horses and working their way down Squaw Creek. They had taken some clothes off the line at Robert West's cabin and John Aston's family had seen them pass by. Aston spread the word and soon there were several neighbors who gathered and decided to set up an ambush for them, believing they would return north along the divide between the heads of Squaw and Robinson Creeks where points of timber grew in an area of otherwise open prairie.

The Indians continued into the settlements and stole horses from several people, including nine horses worth $1,350 from D. C. McDonald. They had nearly 200 head by the time they pulled out. Settlers from Star Creek, Strouds Creek, and Thorp Springs arrived. They waited in concealment all night and by dawn they figured the Indians had eluded them. But just then, a lookout in a tree spotted the Indians heading north. The Indians were not about to be caught so easily and they spotted the whites and changed course. A running fight of several miles developed. Near Star Hollow, the settlers shot several of the Indians' horses and during the chase they lost all of their stolen stock. Finally they were all dismounted, but kept together, fleeing on foot into a ravine emptying into Robinson Creek. Near its head was a hole formed by the fall of water over rocks as it descended a steep slope. The Indians took shelter in the tree and brush covered gully and a stalemate ensued.

During the day of September 11, more whites arrived and soon the force was up near 80 men, but they could not get in at the Indians because as soon as they tried to poke their heads up over the bank to get a shot, the Indians would have an easy silhouetted target. Edward P. Ware got too high on the brow of the hill and took a fatal arrow in the chest, dying on September 29. J. D. McKenzie was mortally wounded by a bullet. The whites could not get at the Indians, but the Indians could not get out. The impasse was ended late in the afternoon when a violent thunderstorm rolled in and the dry ravine became a flooded torrent. With their bowstrings and ammunition soaked and useless, the Indians simply floated up higher and higher until they exposed their heads or drowned. Now, a hail of bullets greeted them and very soon it was all over. When the rain ended and the water receded, the whites pulled out seven dead Indians, one of whom was a woman. They scalped all of them. They first assumed the Indians were Comanches, but Joe Arrington rolled one over and was positive that he was a chief known as "Caddo Jim," whom Arrington knew.

The fight, called the Battle of Lookout Point and the Point of Timbers Fight, was said to be the last Indian fight in Hood County.[9]

There was another battle a few days later, but this time the army was involved. After Kiowas and Comanches made their late August raid along the San Saba in Menard County and the first half-hearted soldier pursuit was over, Capts. Henry Carroll and Edward M. Heyl were determined to try again. They gathered about 95 men of Companies B, E, F, and M, 9th Cavalry, and left Fort McKavett on September 2. They lost the trail for a while and went to Fort Concho to re-supply. North of Concho they found another trail that led to the headwaters of the Salt Fork Brazos. There on September 16, Carroll found a large village of nearly 200 lodges, but the buffalo soldiers boldly charged in and set the Indians to flight. The chase went on for eight miles before the exhausted troopers called it off. Carroll reported killing or wounding 20 warriors, at a loss of three soldiers wounded. They destroyed the camp and wearily marched home.[10]

The 9th Cavalry success was commendable, but as was often the case, while they were beyond the frontier line scouting for Indians, the Indians were in the settlements. Ebenezer R. Freeman and his family lived in Kendall County near Comfort. "The Indians had not been in for a year or so," he said, "and he was not expecting them." Of course, that was just the time Indians would be in the area. About mid-September they came to Freeman's corral about 200 yards from the house, cut the hobbles, cut the bell off the mare, and walked out with a stallion, three mares, a saddle horse, and a colt, all valued at $900. The raiders went to Mr. Coffey's and took his horses, got some of Phil Wilson's stock and then split up, some going southeast and others north.

In the morning Freeman discovered his horses gone, and neighbors came over with similar stories. They went after the Indians, and Freeman said he "would have gone with them, but he had nothing to ride." One band of raiders went to a Doctor Nolan's ranch where he had his horses corralled and guarded by Frank Cesar and Charley Wilmouse. When the Indians crept in at night the guards were ready. When Cesar shot one through the head, the others ran off. Doc Nolan came out, frustrated and angry, and took "a grubbing hoe and socked it into the dead Indian's head." Nevertheless, most of the raiders got away as they almost always did.[11]

The same raiding party may have continued north into Gillespie County. On September 12, on the road seven miles from Fredericksburg, they ran across a black woman, Eliza McGill, shot one arrow through her arm and lanced her five times. They left her for dead but she survived.[12]

The 4th and 9th Cavalry had a few fights with the Indians, but it seemed that the 6th Cavalry either had no luck finding Indians or wasn't trying very hard. Sergeant McConnell later bewailed the lack of respect given them. At his lonely post, where his 6th Cavalrymen "have been for four years, doing more scouting, more escort, more fighting, more arduous service than any other troops in the army, no credit is given, no one knows of their great services…." McConnell, however, could not back up those assertions; two skirmishes in two years did not bear out his contentions.[13]

The Indians slipped right past Fort Richardson again in September 1869, and went into Parker County as they had done hundreds of times. Harrison P. Sullivant lived 12 miles northeast of Weatherford near the Clear Fork Trinity. He was away on business about September 15 when 15 raiders approached her back door at sunrise. Sarah Ann Sullivant saw them coming. "I had just got up," she said, "and I was scared almost to death." Nevertheless, she had the presence of mind to grab her two little boys, slip out the front door, and circle around into the cornfield.

Finding no one home, the Indians destroyed $200 worth of furniture, dishes, and bedding, stole three horses, and rode off just before some mounted settlers arrived, including the county deputy sheriff, Jim Bevett, Newt Montgomery, John and Jim Robinson, and Sarah's brother-in-law, John Sullivant, who found her in the field. On the way out of the county, Sarah said, "They killed a child close to Newt Montgomery's and Jim Stannett found the child…."[14] The raiders went back out near Jacksboro. To the neighboring settlers it may have seemed as if the soldiers were avoiding the Indians.

In Burnet County, preacher Meshac Skagg had been dead for more than nine years, killed in one of the early raids in 1860, but his family still persevered. By September 1869, the Indians had hit them several times, and in the latest raid, their losses exceeded $1,100. In Eastland County, Indians attacked William Allen's place for the fifth time. He was also hit in the 1860 raid that killed Skagg. This time the Indians took four horses worth $300. Nearly an entire decade had passed and little had changed.[15]

Chapter 57 notes

1 Tatum, *Our Red Brothers*, 17-18.
2 Tatum, *Our Red Brothers*, 27-30.
3 Depredation Claims: Gip Smith #2637; John B. Tompkins #4175; Alphonso Freeman #433; Elbert M. Walker #4419; Louis Heath #2237.
4 McConnell, *Five Years a Cavalryman*, 116; Kenner, "Guardians in Blue," 46.
5 Kenner, "Guardians in Blue," 48-53.
6 William A. Kemp, Depredation Claim #4232.
7 McConnell, *West Texas Frontier*, 662.
8 Isaac Chrisman, Depredation Claim #4168.
9 Wilbarger, *Indian Depredations*, 466-68; McConnell, *West Texas Frontier*, 658; "Last Indian Raid to Hood County," http://www.rootsweb.ancestry.com/~txhood/hoodcountyhistory/ewell41.htm.
10 Leckie, *Buffalo Soldiers*, 88-89
11 Ebenezer R. Freeman, Depredation Claim #4421.
12 Winfrey and Day, *Texas Indian Papers, IV*, 310.
13 McConnell, *Five Years a Cavalryman*, 214.
14 Harrison P. Sullivant, Depredation Claim #9632.
15 Depredation Claims: Meshac Skagg #2227; William M. Allen #4605.

58 "They still feel aggrieved."

Texas politics continued with the same unresolved disputations throughout the summer and fall of 1869. General Reynolds continued shaping state politics. Of the 300 orders issued by the army between January 1869 and January 1870, 196 of them concerned removals and appointments to offices. Reynolds filled nearly 2,000 political slots with alleged Radicals. His seeming abuse of federal patronage was finally too much for Governor Pease. Unwilling to be associated with an administration that he viewed as delaying a moderate, sensible reconstruction, Pease resigned on September 30. Instead of appointing a new governor from any of the factions, Reynolds took over as director of the Freedman's Bureau, the Fifth District, the District of Texas, and as governor.[1]

Reynolds' three cavalry regiments were still on the frontier for the most part, although some companies were shifted east to police white lawlessness. With consolidations and cutting, the effective frontier strength went down to 2,257 men,[2] but it appeared the soldiers were being used more aggressively.

Colonel Edward Hatch of the 9th Cavalry was pleased with Captain Carroll's success in September, but overall was disappointed with his inability to halt raiding. At Fort Concho he organized a large expedition to drive the Indians out of the region. Companies B, C, G, F, L, and M, 9th Cavalry, detachments of Companies D and M, 4th Cavalry, a detachment of 24th Infantry, and 20 Tonkawa scouts met at Fort Phantom Hill. On October 5, under the command of Capt. John M. Bacon, nearly 200 men headed out to hunt Indians. They scouted the headwaters of the Colorado and Brazos for three weeks with no results.

The buffalo soldiers were getting a little too close for comfort, however, for as they ascended the Freshwater Fork Brazos (White River), they neared an Indian village. To give their families a chance to get away, nearly 500 Comanches and Kiowas attacked at sunrise on October 28. The warriors discovered that they had stirred up the proverbial hornet's nest, for the black cavalrymen fought with bravery and determination. At times the struggle was hand-to-hand, but the troops did not break. Instead, they rallied and counterattacked and soon the Indians were falling back. Bacon knew he must be close to a village, and the next day he pressed upriver and caught the fleeing encampment. Another charge and the people scattered in all directions. The two-day fight cost Bacon only eight men wounded and he reported killing 40 warriors and capturing seven women and 51 horses.[3]

In the settlements the raiding continued, although the frequency was dropping. On October 18, about 16 Indians were in the Littlefield Bend area in southwest Parker County stealing horses, one of them taken from A. B. Gilbert, who had been raided three times. The Indians crossed the Brazos, and headed north between Rock and Grindstone Creeks as they had done many times before. Eight settlers chased them. As the settlers gained, the Indians set loose the stolen horses. Two of them riding double on one horse fell behind and the settlers shot them both. Monroe Littlefield was in front of the rest. Near Fuller Millsap's place the Indians split up and Littlefield took off after one party, only to find them dividing and circling back on him. When Littlefield's pistol was empty, a warrior closed in and shot Littlefield in the shoulder blade, but he pulled free and the following settlers carried him to Millsap's.

It took six weeks before Littlefield recovered enough to go home. The settlers scalped the two dead Indians and got plenty of souvenirs of bows, arrows, shields, blankets, lances, and lariats that the Indians dropped in their flight. A few tied the bodies to their horses and dragged them to Millsap's cabin for viewing. When the bodies became too foul, they were not buried, but thrown to some famished hogs to be devoured.[4]

Lipans were in Kimble County in November, where, by chance, Capt. Edward M. Heyl was on a scout with 20 men from Companies F and M, 9th Cavalry, out of Fort McKavett. On the South Fork Llano on November 24, they ran into each other. The troopers killed one Indian and captured (or stole, if we value consistency) seven horses and mules. Captain Heyl was seriously wounded.[5]

As Heyl scouted in Kimble County, the raiders were in San Saba County. On November 15, they got two horses from Samuel E. Lee. In Burnet County they hit Louis Kincheloe for the fifth time, this time taking 22 stock horses worth $550.

The September 11 fight at Lookout Point was said to be the last fight in Hood County, but it was not the last raid. In November, raiders were near present Glen Rose, now in Somervell County, but then part of Hood, stealing horses from David McCoy, Jesse Kimble, and Lem Ward, among others. Rachel McCoy and her daughter, Nancy, were out in the yard keeping an eye on several children who were herding their goats, because, Rachel said, the "wolves were so bad around there" that they had to guard the goats and the children. When a cloud of dust rose in the distance, Rachel quickly gathered everyone and rushed to the house. The dust was from half a dozen Indians driving about 30 horses. The McCoys watched from a window as the Indians added their three horses to the collection.

The settlers could do little as usual. Lem Ward, like hundreds of others, was resigned to the fact that the Indians "were in there every moon." They usually went after horses and cattle, he said, but "pretty often" they would take people "if they caught them in the right place."[6]

Lorenzo Riley (21) lived on Beans Creek in Jack County only a dozen or so miles east of Fort Richardson. Proximity to a fort did not matter, however, for the 6th Cavalry was not much of a deterrent. In November, Indians on a horse-stealing expedition found young Riley was away from his house, alone, and in the way. They shot him dead and left him in the road.

The great majority of settler deaths occurred while they were tending to their daily affairs, but some went out looking for trouble. On November 17, 1868, Marion and Columbus Smith, Jim and William Strains, Tom Cates, A. H. Edwards, and a few others were hunting Indians in Burnet County. While many settlers' and soldiers' attitudes were, "I didn't lose any Indians," these scouts had a different idea, and unfortunately, they found them. About six miles north of the town of Burnet, the adversaries ran into each other. The scouts reported killing two or three Indians, but Marion Smith was shot down and killed. The chastened white hunters hurriedly went back home.[7]

David McDonald had lived several places in Callahan and Coleman counties, but in December 1869, he was in northwest Brown County along Pecan Bayou, staying at McReynolds' ranch. Edmund McReynolds had been killed in the area in 1866 and his family continued operating the ranch. Earlier in the month McDonald, W. N. Blair, James Blair, and Lat Edmonson went to Waco for supplies. They returned December 23, fed their horses and tied them up in a little valley. During the night their dogs began to bark and the men went out, but it was too cloudy and dark to distinguish anything. All they could do was wait for sunrise when they discovered all the horses were gone.

With the only three ponies left on the ranch, they followed the trail west across Pecan Bayou and over to William Pollard's and Bob Stephens' ranches. There the story was the same: the horses were gone and the ranchers could do nothing about it.[8]

Kickapoos or Lipans appear to have made one of the last raids of the year, and the decade. In December they once again defied the soldiers stationed in San Antonio, coming in close to the city and running off 41 horses worth $1,900 from Charles Muller.

Shortly thereafter, they went out through Medina County, but not before stopping and relieving a few more settlers of their stock around Castroville. They took four mares, two ponies, and a stallion from Jacob Bendele from his place on San Francisco Perez Creek. It was the third time he was robbed. He knew what was happening when he heard noises at midnight. "I heard them running and yelling;" he said, "they made all kinds of noises; Indians made different noises from white people."

Oliver Hodge lived a few miles away. "They took three [horses] from me that night," he said, "and they took some from nearly everyone in the neighborhood; we counted up the horses the next day and we found 52 or 53 missing." They followed the trail over rough country and kept to it only because of the dead animals along the way: Bendele's stallion, one yearling, and a colt owned by a Mr. Huetzel, all shot with arrows.

In Frio County it had been three years since Indians had stolen stock from Peter Tumlinson, and he may have thought that was the last he had seen of the raiders. In December they were back, taking five saddle horses from his place on the Leona River, and heading across the river going north. No one saw the Indians except for their moccasin tracks. Tumlinson followed but found only one of his bay horses shot dead with arrows. It appeared he and his family would not be safe and he was sickened by the danger and constant worry. Before the year was over, he had packed up and moved east. "I sold out and was not in that country in the year 1870," he said.[9]

As part of Grant's "peace policy" in April 1869, authorization was given to form a Board of Indian Commissioners, a group of unpaid philanthropists who were to assist the secretary of the interior in Indian affairs. There was also a new commissioner, Grant's friend and a Seneca Indian, Ely S. Parker. Parker and the Board did their homework throughout the year and made their assessments of the state of affairs. Parker argued that the entire treaty system ought to be discontinued, because the Indian tribes "are not sovereign nations," but rather "wards of the government." Parker was concerned that "something be done to put a stop to the raiding in Texas by Kickapoo and other Indians residing in the republic of Mexico," but offered no solutions.

As for the Kiowas and Comanches, he seemed to have a similar disconnect with reality as did a number of army officers. He believed the majority of them were settled on their reservation, "and have, with the exception of a few depredations in Texas, conducted themselves quite peaceably." Parker said that those tribes are permitted to hunt buffalo on their reservation, "with a promise by them that they would not leave their own country, and it is believed that they have been faithful to their word."

Agent Tatum had hope for his charges, believing he could make farmers out of many. However, he said some Kiowas "are very much dissatisfied here," and appeared "to have no higher wish than to roam unmolested on the plains, and occasionally make a raid into Texas…." As for the Comanches, Tatum said that they once tried farming on their reservation in Texas, "but were driven out without receiving any compensation for their land. They still feel aggrieved, and I think it is the principal cause of their continuing to make raids into Texas to steal horses and mules."[10]

Some might have recalled Governor Hardin Runnels' warning back in 1859: "With the forcible breaking up of these reserves, your troubles and difficulties will not cease…. They will have only begun; for, with such an additional number of savages thrown upon the frontier, who will be enraged and exasperated by a sense of wrong, who can doubt the result?"

Colonel William B. Hazen, 6th Infantry, who was military agent of the tribes after Leavenworth left and before Tatum took over, had a different assessment from the more sanguine Parker and Tatum. Hazen said that the depredations in Texas have been "the most unsatisfactory portion of our work. The Comanches claim truly that they never ceded away Texas, which was their original country, and that they therefore have a right to make war there." Since the Medicine Lodge Treaty in 1867, Hazen believed that they had raided Texas 40 times (an estimate far too low). Whereas many in the army or interior department focused on the Cheyenne and Sioux raiding on the Central Plains, Hazen thought the Texans had it worst: "But few can know what this poor unfortunate people have suffered from the Indians we are now feeding and clothing during the past ten years, and, in fact, are suffering now." Hazen had argued that the stolen stock be returned to their owners, but it was thought best by the military commanders "to do nothing in the matter." Hazen said that the army ought to follow the raiders to Texas to stop them, and punish them if they persisted, but, he said, "I have only to see my warnings laughed at." Until "this Texas business is corrected," said Hazen, "we are almost parties to the outrages."[11]

It is what the settlers had been saying for a decade.

A fourth opinion of the situation was expressed by the Board of Commissioners. Three committees went out to investigate; the southern one dealt with the tribes of the Central and Southern Plains and was chaired by Felix R. Brunot. It reported on November 23, 1869, in the most derogatory and accusatory terms. Indian rights have constantly "been assailed by the rapacity of the white man." All government connections with the Indians have been "a shameful record of broken treaties and unfulfilled promises." The history of "the border white man's connection with the Indians is a sickening record of murder, outrage, robbery, and wrongs," and when Indians retaliated it was "the exception."

The commissioners generously acknowledged that there was "a class of hardy men on the frontier" who have been "the innocent sufferers from the Indians' revenge," but they were victims because of the evil deeds of other whites. The commissioners stated that in our Indian wars, "almost without exception, the first aggressions have been made by the white man." There were also many "robbers and outlaws" who sought to start Indian wars "for the sake of profit to be realized from the presence of troops and the expenditure of government funds…."

In addition, the report stated that "Every crime committed by a white man against an Indian is concealed or palliated; every offense committed by an Indian against a white man is borne on the wings of the post or the telegraph to the remotest corner of the land...." Proportionally, Indian outrages "do not amount to a tithe of the number of crimes committed by white men in the border settlements and towns." It is the white man, the commissioners claimed, who have made the Indians "suspicious, revengeful, and cruel in their retaliation." The worst Indian "is but the imitator of bad white men on the border."[12]

With such a stinging indictment it is surprising that the board would even admit that there were some innocent white sufferers, while surely the settlers would have viewed the board's findings as hogwash coming from Easterners who had probably never seen an Indian. Frontier settlers generally viewed Indians as devils from Hades, while a cohort of investigating committees from the East concluded that the white settlers were fiends of a similar pedigree. The Indians likely had the same opinion of most whites. After ten years there appeared to be no end to the constant fighting, but a change was coming.

As the 1860s ended, the settlers on the Texas frontier certainly realized that they had gone through a hell of a decade, but they probably did not realize that they had undergone what was likely the most sustained and destructive assault that Native Americans ever made on a pioneer population. They had tried to defend themselves, as did the state troops, the Rangers, and the U.S. Army. None succeeded. The settlers fought it out mostly on their own, and it was a conflict of "cowboys and Indians" more than the cavalry to the rescue. Many more non-combatants died than soldiers. The 1860s was a settlers' war. The 1870s would become a soldiers' war. Finally, the soldiers and not the non-combatants would start to absorb the casualties. There were trends pointing to the future and there were possibly some lessons to be learned.

Chapter 58 notes

1 Richter, *Army in Texas During Reconstruction*, 174-75.
2 Shook, "Federal Military in Texas," 50.
3 Leckie, *Buffalo Soldiers*, 89-90; *Adjutant General's Office*, 43.
4 Marshall, *A Cry Unheard*, 181-83.
5 Williams, *Texas' Last Frontier,* 120.
6 Depredation Claims: Samuel E. Lee #5686; Louis Kincheloe #2479; David McCoy #2685.
7 McConnell, *West Texas Frontier*, 641, 663; *Galveston Daily Civilian*, November 29, 1869.
8 David McDonald, Depredation Claim #4537.
9 Depredation Claims: Charles Muller #7496; Jacob Bendele #3347; Peter Tumlinson #10644.
10 *Commissioner of Indian Affairs 1869*, 6, 8, 35-36, 384-85.
11 Ibid., 393.
12 Prucha, *Documents of Indian Policy*, 131-33.

Postscript

One of the reasons for the decrease in Indian raiding after the 1860s was simply that the number of warriors had decreased to the extent that it was nearly impossible to sustain constant warfare. In the 1780s the Comanches were said to have numbered about 40,000 people. After the smallpox epidemics in 1781, 1800, and 1816, and cholera and smallpox ravages in the 1830s and 1840s, the population dramatically declined. In 1849 alone, a cholera epidemic killed 300. By the late 1840s there were perhaps 20,000 Comanches, and by the mid-1850s there were only about 12,000.

In 1869 there remained only 1,928 Kiowas and 2,538 Comanches, a total of 4,466. If about one in every six was an adult male capable of taking the warpath there would be about 745 potential raiders. They could not be all gone at the same time leaving no one to protect the villages. If it was possible for 500 warriors to be raiding in Texas at one time, they would still be outnumbered by the cavalry on the frontier by a five to one margin. It was enough to send in small raiding parties, but the possibility of losing even one warrior in exchange for stealing a cow was not worth the risk.[1]

Disease and starvation had beaten the Plains Indians, not the soldiers.

Troop strength and tactics are often correlated to determine the frequency of Indian raiding patterns. If we can glean anything out of the above discussion, we will see that there was little or no relationship among them and we may have been asking the wrong questions. Bear in mind that the numbers of settler deaths cited in the below charts and appendix are only those which have been detailed in the above narrative. There were many more, most of which had too few details to pinpoint in place and time to weave chronologically into the story. In 1860 with the 2nd Cavalry on the frontier as well as other militia units, troop strength varied from 1,000 to 1,500. During that year there were seventy-eight killings, a high number that may have had much to do with the recent forced removal of the Indians from Texas and retaliations against the attacks on their home villages the previous years.

In 1861 and 1862, contrary to popular conceptions supplied by a number of historians, the coming of the Civil War did not cause increased fighting and casualties. Troop strength went down to between 500 and 1,000 and the corresponding settler deaths decreased to twenty-five and twelve respectively. 1862 had the lowest number of civilian deaths in the entire decade. The Kiowas and Comanches signed treaties with the Texans and at least some of the tribesmen kept their word. There was less fighting during the Civil War years than in the post-war years. The severe drought that lasted to 1865 also limited raiding.

In 1863, concerned with frontier protection, Texas and the Confederacy increased frontier strength from 1,000 to 2,000; the result was that casualties climbed to 66. In 1864, incorrectly said to be the worst year for raiding in the Civil War, troop strength went down from 2,000 to about 1,200 and leveled off at 1,500. Numbers of settlers killed by Indians also went down to 23. The year 1864 had the second lowest number of civilian deaths during the decade.

By mid-1865, all organized Confederate and state forces were disbanded, but from 5,000 to 45,000 Union soldiers arrived, although they were not placed on the frontier. In 1865, a decade-long drought ended. With good grass and plenty of water, the Indians swept into Texas on an unprecedented scale. It is apparent that a substantial number of the Indians had been honoring the treaties with the Confederate States, because with such restrictions gone after 1865, the killings increased to 34.

For most of 1866, it was the same story: thousands of troops, but few protecting the frontier. 1866 was generally a year of peace on most of the Great Plains, but not in Texas. The Comanches and Kiowas no longer had a treaty with Texas, they were not at war with the United States, and generally they were at peace with surrounding tribes. As a result, they could turn their attentions solely to Texas. In addition, the principal Kiowa chief who could control the whole tribe, Little Mountain, died in early 1866, leaving sub-chiefs like Satanta and Lone Wolf to raid as they saw fit. Probably the greatest number of raids on Texas soil occurred in 1866. Killings went up to 65, but considering there were virtually no soldiers on the frontier, deaths were still lower than in 1860 and 1863, when there were 1,000 to 2,000 soldiers on duty.

By late 1866, U.S. Cavalry regiments were finally arriving on the frontier in force. In 1867 there were 2,479 soldiers and there were 37 settler deaths. In 1868 troop strength reached new highs, with 3,226 soldiers, and killings went up to 42. In 1869, units were consolidated and soldiers shipped out. Troop strength went down to 2,257, while casualties went down to 17. Some of the lowest numbers of settlers' deaths occurred while the lowest numbers of troops were on the frontier, and with the exception of 1860, some of the highest numbers of deaths occurred while troop levels were at their peaks.

It is evident that high troop numbers did not translate into more protection in the form of less raids and less killings, and as detailed in the above narrative, tactics that shifted from active scouting to defensive line patrols did not make any difference either. Rainfall was more of a factor in shaping raiding patterns than Rangers. The Indians operated with their own agendas and were not reacting to white initiatives; if anything, the whites were constantly responding to the Indians' moves. What is striking in the above numbers is that in most of the years we find that more troops meant more killing and less troops meant less killing. Throwing more soldiers in harm's way was a self-fulfilling prophesy in one respect, although it was generally not the soldiers who did the dying.

Political, economic, social, and climatic conditions dictated how often, where, and when Indians would raid, not soldiers. One recent writer has argued that the "old" Rangers of the 1840s under John Coffee Hays knew how to fight Indians, but after Hays moved to California in 1849, "It was as though the Rangers had never happened," because the succeeding ranger companies and U.S. Army somehow forgot how to fight Indians.[2] Perception, however, is not necessarily reality. Texans have always believed that their Rangers were the best Indian fighters of all, but Hays' few successes came against the Penetekas in the 1840s, when that tribe was shattered by diseases and was a shadow of its former self. The variola virus and the vibrio cholera bacteria beat the Penetekas, not the Rangers. It is time we realize that pure military force will not always prove decisive, or perhaps, be even marginally effective, especially in a guerrilla war.

There was a downturn in raiding and killing in 1869 that ended the bloodiest decade in the Western Indian Wars, but the "war" was not over. The downturn began because the Indians were numerically too exhausted from attrition by bacteria and virus, and the army was finally ensconced in Indian Territory inside the Kiowa and Comanche Reservation and could keep better rein on them. Raiding still went on in the early 1870s, but the event that would seal the tribes' final demise occurred in 1871. On May 18, in Young County along Flint Creek, Kiowas attacked a wagon train and killed seven teamsters. Two survivors stumbled into Fort Richardson that night to relate what had happened. Nothing out of the ordinary would likely have been done were it not for the fact that Gen. William T. Sherman had just passed the point of attack shortly before the wagon train was destroyed. But for a supposed vision by the Kiowa prophet, Mamanti, Sherman and his escort would have been the victims, and the General of the Army may have ended up dead and roasted on a wagon wheel over a fire instead of wagonmaster Nathan Long.

In that one instant, the army brass finally became aware of the Indian problem in Texas. Now it was personal. Now Sherman finally gave the go ahead for the regiments to take the offensive, to chase down and attack the raiders, to follow them right onto the reservations and arrest or kill them, to attack their villages summer and winter, and finally, by 1875, to kill or drive all the recalcitrant Kiowas and Comanches to the reservation. The constant harassment went hand-in-hand with the destruction of the bison, the collapse of trade networks, and the social, economic, and political fabric, leaving the tribes shattered physically and spiritually. In addition, another mini-drought began in 1870, making raids more difficult. By 1874, rainfall was down to 1864 levels and raiding in Texas had also nearly dried up. Most of the fighting was with the soldiers in the Panhandle, and very few raids penetrated the settlements as they had done in the 1860s.

The end of the 1860s ended the most sustained attacks on any frontier population in American history. The Dakota Uprising in Minnesota in 1862 may have resulted in more settler deaths, but it was virtually over in a month's time, and the settlers who fled soon returned to a landscape cleared of Sioux. They never had to endure the constant, palpable fear that engulfed the Texas settlers for decades. As one historian has written, "it was not the damage actually done but the condition of panic which was created that made the raids a matter of such serious consequences. No physical condition of modern times can be compared with the terror produced by Indian raids."[3]

By the end of the decade, frontier Texans probably did not realize that their long nightmare was coming to a close. They had hoped to live out their lives in search of their dreams, unknowing or uncaring that to fulfill their dreams they had to shatter the hopes and dreams of others. They looked to the U.S. Army, to the state forces, to the Rangers, and to themselves for protection, but that protection was never satisfactory. Short of saturating every square yard of territory with an armed soldier, the number of troops protecting them did not make a significant difference, and troop increases—surges—were many times self-defeating.

It may be wrong to draw the analogy too far, but there are similarities in the situation in Texas in the 1860s and in other guerrilla-type wars such as occurred or are occurring in Viet Nam, Iraq, and Afghanistan. In Texas there was a home population in need, and generally in support of the troops, and the Indians came in from across the Rio Grande and Red River or beyond the frontier line from the Llano Estacado. They attacked, robbed, killed, and ran off. Troop numbers waxed and waned; they reacted, chased, but accomplished little. Soldiers and settlers, mostly settlers, died in attritional skirmishes. Settlers wrote to the politicians for relief, but there were usually political or logistical considerations that prevented effective solutions. The same bankrupt military solutions were tried over and over again.

In 21st Century Afghanistan the home population is in need of protection and security, but not all are in support of foreign troops meddling in their affairs. Taliban or Al-Qaida (Indians) come across the borders to raid and kill and sometimes run back across the borders or stay hidden in mountainous recesses beyond the "frontier" line. Troop numbers ebb and flow, there are surges, they chase the raiders and occasionally go on search and destroy missions (scouts), but they accomplish little. Soldiers and civilians die, mostly civilians, in attritional skirmishes. Civilians complain, but there are political or logistical considerations that prevent effective solutions. The same bankrupt military solutions are tried over and over again.

One might argue that a troop surge was effective in Iraq. The surge, however, was not just a numbers increase. What we heard little about was that the extra numbers freed up special units who played one side against another, infiltrated, assassinated, and played the guerrilla game much as the "enemy" had been playing. A change of tactics was somewhat successful, not simply increased numbers.

There is another variation to this theme. We might view Afghanistan as Indian Territory, and the American soldiers are the raiders, an enemy coming in from across the borders where their presence only exacerbates a bad situation. The troops are the Indians, and the more that arrive, the more deaths that result. They are the bad guys and the bad guys are not wanted and won't go away. Bankrupt military and political policies are so thoroughly entrenched that there is no one who can view the situation, divorced from pride, and lifted from a perspective more than an inch above the rim of the foxhole. William Faulkner once said, "The past is not dead. It is not even past." It might be that our Indian Wars mentality is still with us. Perhaps there is a lesson we can learn from the situation on the American frontier during the Indian Wars of the 19th Century: numbers of soldiers don't make any significant difference in a guerrilla war, especially so among a hostile population where the soldiers are not even wanted.

On the American Western frontier and in Afghanistan, basically, the civilians were and are on their own. Eventually, all the soldiers will be gone while the civilians will still be there to pick up the pieces and try to find a way to survive. When all is said and done, in all times and places when people do battle, it is always a settlers' war.

Postscript notes

1 Anderson, *Conquest of Texas*, 22, 233; Hamalainen, Comanche Empire, 178-79, 303; *Commissioner of Indian Affairs 1869*, 384-85.

2 Gwynne, *Empire of the Summer Moon*, 159-61.

3 Richardson, *Comanche Barrier*, 124.

Appendices

APPENDIX A

Selected List of Civilians Killed by Indians, Year, Month, and County.

1860

February

Mr. Morris, Tom Green
Lucinda Wood, Erath
Liddie Lemley, Erath
Angus Monroe, Bosque
Colin Monroe
James Knight, Hamilton
Jesse Griffith, Coryell
Benjamin Van Hook, Burnet
Meshac Skagg, Burnet
Mr. Hardy, Burnet
Thomas Milligan, Mason
W. D. Wood, San Saba

March

Kenneth McKenzie, Comanche
Gid Foreman, Comanche
Joe Baggett, Comanche
William Cross, Erath
Richard Robbins, San Saba
Mr. Proctor, Bosque
Vincent Bilhartz, Atascosa
John Youngman, Atascosa
Mr. Schroon, Medina
Mr. Anisette, Medina
Sebastian Wolf, Uvalde
Alexander Hoffman, Uvalde
Mr. Freeman, Bosque
Raggett (boy), Bosque
J. J. Keener, Titus
Jess Clemens, Wise

April

William Jenkins, Mills
Nicholas Lee, Erath
Shadrach Styer, Taylor
William Lambshead, Taylor
James Hamby, Taylor

May

Conrad Newhouse, Young
Mr. Martinez, Young
Jonas Dancer, Llano
Francisco Zapeda, Webb
Ignacio Chavis, Zapata
Masadonia Lindon, Zapata
Silvester Santos, Starr

June

Josephus Browning, Stephens

July

Mr. Chapman, Jack
Mr. Cooley, Jack
Mr. Shepherd, Tom Green

August

B. F. Watkins, Uvalde
J. H. Richardson, Uvalde

September

John Bolt, Tom Green
Sostines Alagrid, Zapata

October

Samuel Lane, Kerr
John Bultoff, Jack
Lindy Harmonson, Young

November

Mrs. Landman, Jack
Jane Masterson, Jack
Katy Sanders, Jack
Polly Gage, Jack
John Brown, Parker
Mr. White, Parker
John Branen, Parker

Martha Sherman, Palo Pinto
Hiram Fowler, Foard

December

Gols Flannagan, Eastland

1861

February

William Youngblood, Parker

March

Leonard Eastwood, Frio
Mr. McFarland, Frio
Mr. McElemon, Medina
Julius Sanders, Uvalde
Henry Robinson, Uvalde
Henry Adams, Uvalde

May

Mr. Phillips, Parker
Thomas Killen, Parker
Allen Goans, San Saba

August

Samuel Kuykendall, Hamilton

October

William Herndon, Atascosa
Alexander Anderson, Atascosa
Mr. French's slave, Atascosa
Mr. Moore, Frio
Peter Ketchum, Medina
James Winters, Medina
John Schreiber, Medina
Mr. Schalkhausen, Medina
Sam Long, Uvalde
John McMurray, Bandera
Robert Carter, Mills

1862

March

Owen Lindsey, Mills

April

Henry Parks, Menard
Nancy Parks, Menard
Billy Parks, Menard
Mr. Berg, Gillespie
Heinrich Grobe, Gillespie
James Gracey, Burnet

May

James Tankersley, Brown
James Carmean, Brown

June

Rube Smith, Medina

October

John Williams, Llano
Edward King, Llano

1863

January

James Billings, Gillespie

February

Henry Arhelger, Gillespie
Mathis Pehl, Gillespie
Jim Little, Gillespie
Conrad Meckel, Mason
Heinrich Meckel, Mason
Yoakum Hench, Mason
two Holstein boys, Mason
Mr. Hudson, Mason
Mr. Black, San Saba
Lorenzo Holland, Burnet
Jonathan Ragle, Burnet
Lewis Jackson, Burnet
Wofford Johnson, Williamson
Mrs. Johnson, Williamson
Mary Johnson, Williamson
Spencer Moore, Montague
Ira Moore, Montague
John Stump, Montague
Mr. Bailey, Montague
Benjamin Baker, Palo Pinto

March

William Peters, Palo Pinto

April

Henry Welty, Palo Pinto
Mr. Williamson, Coryell

May
Samuel Rogers, Erath
June
Thomas Cavness, San Saba
Nathan Holt, Johnson
Tom Hill, Johnson
Almond Boyd, Coryell
July
William Hodges, Clay
John McGee, Clay
Levi Hill, Clay
Mrs. Rasin, Erath
Jeremiah Green, Hood
Rigman Bryant, Hood
Henry Jackson, Stephens
August
Mr. Cook, Burnet
Stuart Hamilton, Parker
William Hamilton, Parker
Harriet Brown, Parker
Sarah Brown, Parker
Estell Brown, Parker
Mr. Long, Wise
Andrew Vernon, Wise
Thomas Vernon, Wise
September
John Wood, Erath
Henry Mills, Erath
October
Pendleton Porter, Cooke
Mrs. Porter, Cooke
Porter (daughter), Cooke
Mrs. George Porter, Cooke
Mann Tackitt, Jack
November
Alexander Hall, San Saba
Mr. Merryman, San Saba
December
Mrs. Anderson, Montague
Anderson (baby), Montague
Wesley Willet, Montague
Willet (mother), Montague
Amanda Willet, Montague
Mr. White, Cooke
Parker White, Cooke

1864

February
Emma Metzger, Gillespie
John Rolland, Callahan
Henry Rolland, Callahan
David Crockett, Callahan
July
Richmond Boren, Montague
Alfred Lane, Young
James Reed, Stephens
August
Singleton Gilbert, Eastland
Burton Keith, Eastland
September
William Peveler, Young
Harvey Cox, Young
Andrew Berry, Parker
Berry (son), Parker
October
Mrs. George Schwandner, Real
Joel Miers, Young
Milly Durkin, Young
Durkin (baby), Young
Jim Johnson, Young
Elijah Carter, Young
Thomas Wilson, Young
Isaac McCoy, Young
Miles McCoy, Young
Chancy Couch, San Saba

1865

January
Alwinda McDonald, Gillespie
Mrs. Wylie Joy, Gillespie
Dizenia Todd, Mason
Todd (servant), Mason

February
Samuel Graham, Coryell
Margaret Barton, Parker

May
James McKinney, Parker
Cynthia McKinney, Parker
Mary Alice McKinney, Parker
McKinney (baby), Parker

July
Dan Williams, Frio
Bud English, Frio
Dean Oden, Frio
Mr. Cox, Hamilton
Hollis (boy), Hamilton
Henry Kensing, Mason
Johanna Kensing, Mason

August
Fred Conaway, Mason
Gilly Taylor, Gillespie
Elijah McDonald, Gillespie
Samuel Binnion, Burnet
Mr. Benson
Phil Runnels, Shackelford
Ben Carruthers, Palo Pinto

September
Andrew Robinson, Uvalde
Jake Moffett, Tarrant
Mr. Wright, Tarrant
Mr. Smith, Tarrant
Jack Smith, Coryell

November
Jack Gorman, Parker
Rose Moore, Parker
Hannah Moore, Parker

1866

January
Berry Buckelew, Bandera
George Miller, Medina

March
Fayette Bond, Hamilton
Bolen Savage, Parker
James Savage, Parker
James Sanders, Wise
Johnson Miller, Wise

April
C. C. Carter, Lampasas
Joseph Bond, Lampasas
Thomas Beckett, Kinney
Martha Beckett, Kinney
Beckett (three children), Kinney
Tilitha Cox, Kinney

May
Andrew Culwell, Parker
Edmund McReynolds, Brown

June
Tipton Seay, Palo Pinto
George Halsell, Clay
Mr. Cook, Clay
Freeman Ward, Throckmorton
Alvin Clark, Parker
Isaac Brisco, Parker
Mrs. Brisco, Parker

July
Pleasant Boyd, Hood
Thomas Eubank – Shackelford
Henry Meier, Kendall
Theodore Gotthardt, Kendall
Mrs. O'Neal, Erath, Kendall

August
William McDougall, Menard
Logan Higgins, Wise
Amanda Cofer, Eastland
James Box, Cooke

September
Thomas Norris, Clay
Mr. White, Clay
Mr. Purcell, Clay
D. J. Davis, Uvalde
Enoch Jones, Jack
Richard Jones, Jack
Isabel Babb, Wise
James Harris, Cooke

Andrew Powers, Montague

October

Cynthia Bolin, Medina
Davis Cryer, Bandera
Thomas Click, Bandera
Freeman Clark, Brown
Kendall Lofton, Montague
John Leeper, Parker
Thomas Sullivan, Parker

November

John Montgomery, Wise

December

Daniel Green, Montague
William Bailey, Montague
William Willis, Hamilton

1867

January

Nathan McDow, Erath
Francis McDow, Erath

February

Alfred Ross, Jack
Isaac Ross, Jack
Slade Hightower, Jack

March

Henry Vincent, Montague
Harms Gerdes, Medina
G. Pendleton, Bexar
James Hasty, Bosque
Clint McClennan, Bosque

April

Sally Myres, Tarrant

July

Ben Smith, McCulloch
Mr. Ruff, McCulloch
Ann Whitney, Hamilton
Mr. Standley, Hamilton
J. E. Pinkerton, Hamilton
Patrick Proffitt, Young
Reuben Johnson, Young
Rice Carrollton, Young

September

Atanacia Garza, Webb
Amador Besa, Webb
Jose Ramirez, Webb
Luz Luna, Webb
Silberio Baez, Webb
Mr. Alegia, Webb
Mrs. Alegia, Webb
Alegia (child), Webb

October

Frank Johnson, Kimball
Mr. Devine, Brown

November

Herman Stohl, Gillespie

1868

January

John Leatherwood, Montague
Mrs. Carrollton, Montague
Nathan Long, Montague
Arthur Parkhill, Montague
Thomas Fitzpatrick, Montague
Mrs. Fitzpatrick, Montague
Fitzpatrick (boy), Montague
Joseph Menasco, Cooke
Lizzie Menasco, Cooke
May Menasco, Cooke
Shegog (child), Cooke
black child, Cooke

February

Mary Alexander, Kerr
Fielty Johnson, Llano
Nancy Johnson, Llano
Rebecca Johnson, Llano
Samantha Johnson, Llano
Amanda Townsend, Llano

March

Sallie Bowman, Wise
George Hazelwood, Stephens

June

Robert Lackey, Montague

July
William Shepherd, Blanco
Elizabeth Shepherd, Blanco
Joel Shepherd, Blanco
John Hales, Parker
Martin Cathey, Parker
William Light, Parker
Mary Light, Parker
Dora Light, Parker
August
Sol Forester, Denton
Polly Russell, Wise
Martha Russell, Wise
Harvey Russell, Wise
James Russell, Wise
October
John Bailey, Wise
Rebecca Vick, Wise
Ambrose Fortenberry, Wise
Frank Coonis, Denton
November
Mr. Pace, Cooke
Jim Cummings, Tom Green
Mr. Compton, Tom Green
John Morris, Mills

1869

April
Elbert Doss, Palo Pinto
May
William Crow, Young
John Lemley, Young
Shapley Carter, Young
Jesse McClain, Young
June
Frank Taylor, Young
Hiram Wolfe, Llano
July
William Tinnell, Parker
John Lopp, Parker
Thomas Felps, Blanco
Elizabeth Felps, Blanco
August
Thomas Malone, Uvalde
September
J. D. McKenzie, Hood
Edward Ware, Hood
November
Lorenzo Riley, Jack
Marion Smith, Burnet

APPENDIX B. TROOP STRENGTHS AND CIVILIAN DEATHS

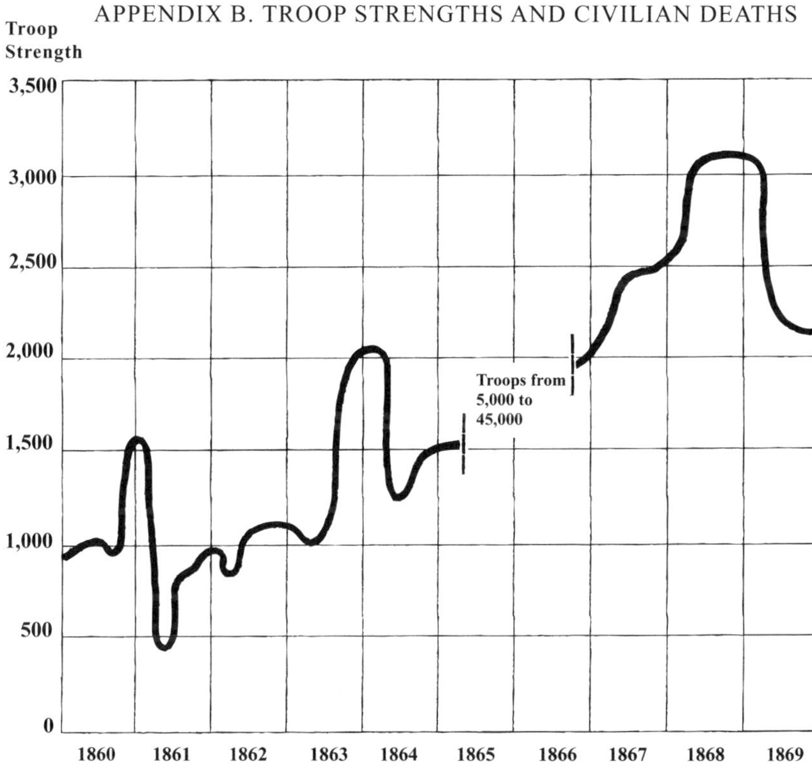

Appendix C, Rainfall in Texas, 1860-65

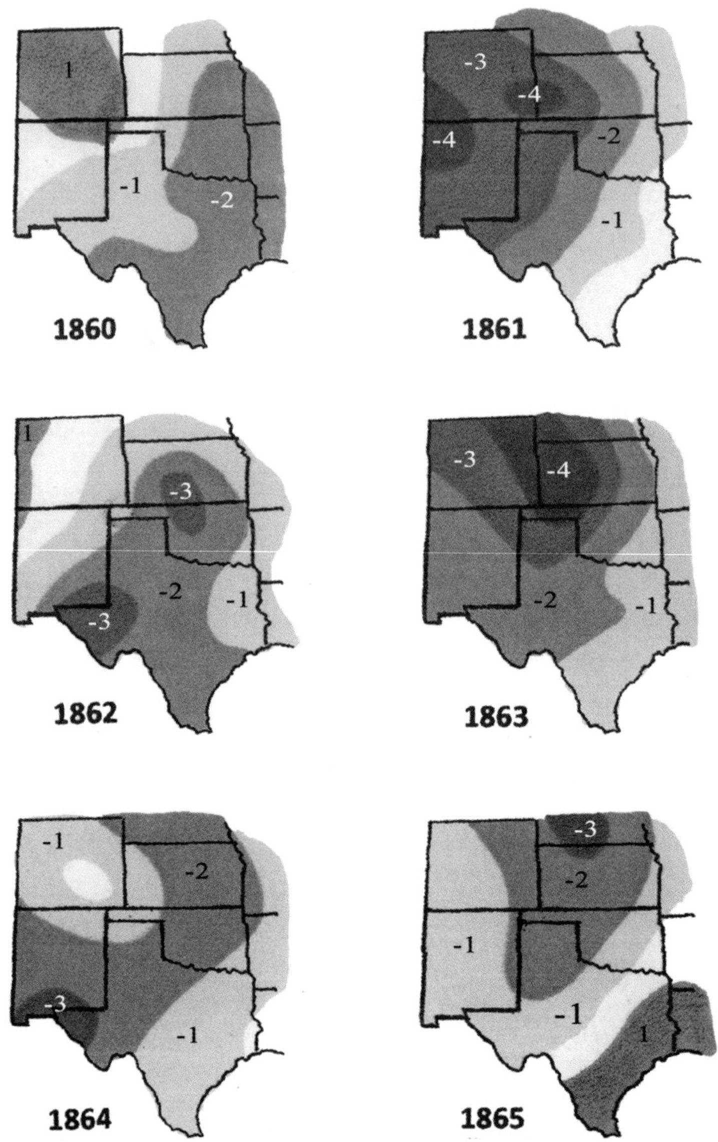

Appendix C, Rainfall in Texas, 1860-65

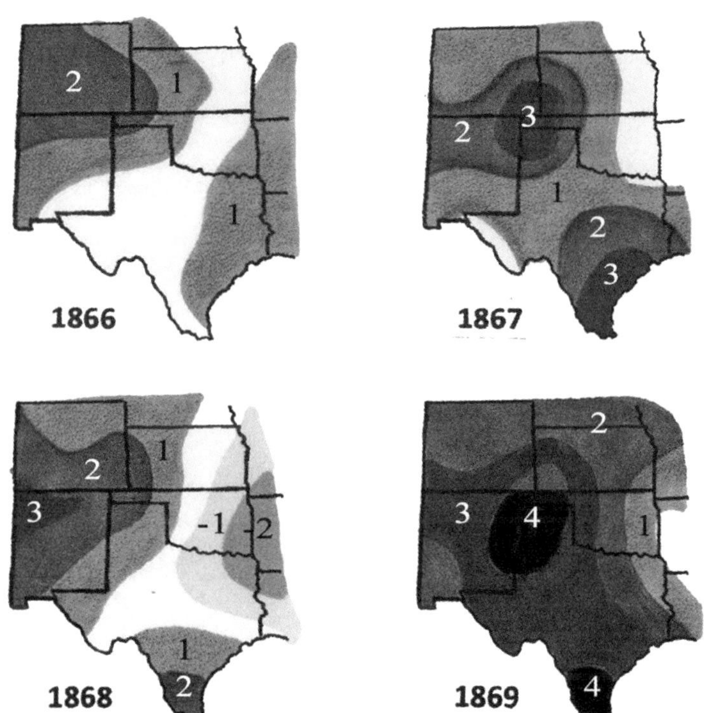

Bibliography

Abel, Annie Heloise. *The American Indian as Slaveholder and Secessionist.* Cleveland, Ohio: Arthur H. Clark Company, 1915. Reprint. Introduction by Theda Perdue and Michael D. Green. Lincoln, Nebraska: University of Nebraska Press, 1992.

_______. *The American Indian in the Civil War, 1862-1865.* Cleveland, Ohio: Arthur H. Clark Company, 1919. Reprint. Introduction by Theda Perdue and Michael D. Green. Lincoln, NE: University of Nebraska Press, 1992.

_______. *The American Indian and the End of the Confederacy, 1863-1866.* Reprint. Introduction by Theda Perdue and Michael D. Green. Lincoln, Nebraska: University of Nebraska Press, 1993.

Adkins-Rochette, Patricia. *Bourland in North Texas and Indian Territory During the Civil War. Fort Cobb, Fort Arbuckle & the Wichita Mountains.* 2 Vols. Broken Arrow, Oklahoma: Privately printed, 2005.

Adjutant General's Office. *Chronological List of Actions &c., with the Indians from January 15, 1837 to January, 1891.* Washington: GPO, 1891.

Anderson, Gary Clayton. *The Conquest of Texas Ethnic Cleansing in the Promised Land, 1820-1875.* Norman, Oklahoma: University of Oklahoma Press, 2005.

Aston, B. W. "Federal Military Reoccupation of the Texas Southwestern Frontier, 1865-1871." *Texas Military History* 8, no. 3 (1970): 123-34.

Austerman, Wayne R. *Sharps Rifles and Spanish Mules: The San Antonio-El Paso Mail, 1851-1881.* College Station, Texas: Texas A&M University Press, 1985.

Babb, Bianca (Mrs. J. D. Bell). "A True Story of My Captivity and Life With the Indians." TMs. Decatur, Texas: Wise County Heritage Museum, nd.

Babb, Bianca. Untitled Manuscript. Decatur, Texas: Wise County Heritage Museum, nd.

Babb, T. A. *In the Bosom of the Comanches.* Amarillo, Texas: T. A. Babb, 1912. Reprint, Azle, Texas: Bois d'Arc Press, 1990.

Barney, Libeus. *Letters of the Pike's Peak Gold Rush.* San Jose, California: The Talisman Press, 1959.

Barry, Louise. *The Beginning of the West: Annals of the Kansas Gateway to the American West 1540-1854.* Topeka, Kansas: Kansas State Historical Society, 1972.

_______. "With the First U.S. Cavalry in Indian Country, 1859-1861." *Kansas Historical Quarterly* 24, no. 3 (Autumn 1958): 257-84.

_______. "With the First U.S. Cavalry in Indian Country, 1859-1861--Concluded." *Kansas Historical Quarterly* 24, no. 4 (Winter 1958): 395-425.

Bates, Ed. F. *History and Reminiscences of Denton County.* Denton, Texas: McNitzky Printing Company, 1918.

Bedford, Hilory G. *Texas Indian Troubles.* Benjamin, Texas: Hargreaves Printing Co., Inc., 1905.

Belich, James. *Replenishing the Earth The Settler Revolution and the Rise of the Anglo-World, 1783-1939.* New York: Oxford University Press, 2009.

Bender, Averam B. *The March of Empire Frontier Defense in the Southwest 1848-1860.* New York: Greenwood Press, 1968.

Berthrong, Donald J. *The Southern Cheyennes.* Norman, Oklahoma: University of Oklahoma Press, 1963.

Bierschwale, Margaret. "Mason County, Texas, 1845-1870." *Southwestern Historical Quarterly* LII, no. 4 (April 1949): 383-95.

Biggers, Don H. *German Pioneers in Texas.* Fredericksburg, Texas: Press of the Fredericksburg Publishing Co., 1925.

Bibliography

_______. *Shackelford County Sketches*. Albany, Texas: The Clear Fork Press, 1974.

Britten, Thomas A. *The Lipan Apaches People of Wind and Lightning*. Albuquerque, New Mexico: University Of New Mexico Press, 2009.

Brooks, James F. *Captives & Cousins: Slavery, Kinship, and Community in the Southwest Borderlands*. Chapel Hill, North Carolina: University of North Carolina Press, 2002.

Brown, John Henry. *Indian Wars and Pioneers of Texas*. Austin, Texas: L. E. Daniell, 1880. Reprint, Greenville, SC: Southern Historical Press, 1978.

Brumwell, Stephen. *White Devil A True Story of War, Savagery, and Vengeance in Colonial America*. Cambridge, Massachusetts: Da Capo Press, 2004.

Burton, Art T. *Black, Buckskin, and Blue: African-American Scouts and Soldiers on the Western Frontier*. Austin, Texas: Eakin Press, 1999.

Carter, Lieutenant-Colonel W.H. *From Yorktown to Santiago with the Sixth Cavalry*. Baltimore, Maryland: Lord Baltimore Press, 1900. Reprint, Austin, Texas: State House Press, 1989.

Cashion, Ty. *A Texas Frontier The Clear Fork Country and Fort Griffin, 1849-1887*. Norman, Oklahoma: University of Oklahoma Press, 1996.

Cates, Cliff D. *Pioneer History of Wise County From Red Men to Railroads—Twenty Years of Intrepid History*. Decatur, Texas: Wise County Old Settlers' Association, 1907. Reprint, Decatur, Texas: Wise County Historical Commission, 1975.

Chalfant, William Y. *Cheyennes and Horse Soldiers*. With a foreword by Robert M. Utley. Norman, Oklahoma: University of Oklahoma Press, 1989.

_______. *Hancock's War Conflict on the Southern Plains*. Foreword by Jerome A. Greene. Norman, Oklahoma: The Arthur H. Clark Company, 2010.

Clampitt, Brad R. "The Breakup: The Collapse of the Confederate Trans-Mississippi Army in Texas, 1865." *Southwestern Historical Quarterly* CVIII, no. 4. (April 2005):499-534.

Clayton, Lawrence and John Halford Farmer, eds. *Tracks Along the Clear Fork Stories from Shackelford and Throckmorton Counties*. Abilene, Texas: McWhiney Foundation Press, 2000.

Collins, Michael. *Cooke County, Texas: Where the South and West Meet*. Gainesville, Texas: Cooke County Heritage Society, 1981.

Colton, Ray C. *The Civil War in the Western Territories: Arizona, Colorado, New Mexico, and Utah*. Norman, Oklahoma: University of Oklahoma Press, 1959.

Coward, John M. *The Newspaper Indian Native American Identity in the Press*, 1820-90. Urbana, Illinois: University of Illinois Press, 1999.

Cox, J. C. "The Capture and Rescue of Lon White." *Frontier Times* 6, no.2 (November 1928): 59-61.

Crawford, Samuel J. *Kansas in the Sixties*. Ottawa, Kansas: Kansas Heritage Press, 1994.

Custer, Elizabeth B. *Following the Guidon*. New York: Harper & Brothers, 1890. Reprint. Introduction by Shirley A. Leckie. Lincoln, Nebraska: University of Nebraska Press, 1994.

Custer, George Armstrong. *My Life on the Plains*. Introduction by Edgar I. Stewart. Norman, Oklahoma: University of Oklahoma Press, 1962.

Danziger, Edmund Jefferson, Jr. *Indians and Bureaucrats: Administering Reservation Policy During the Civil War*. Urbana, Illinois: University of Illinois Press, 1974.

Deaton, E. L. *Indian Fights on the Texas Frontier*. Fort Worth, Texas: Pioneer Publishing Co., 1927.

DeLay, Brian. *War of A Thousand Deserts Indian Raids and the U.S. — Mexican War*. New Haven, Connecticut: Yale University Press, 2008.

DeShields, James T. *Border Wars of Texas*. 1912. Reprint, Austin, Texas: State House Press, 1993.

Dick, Everett. *Conquering the Great American Desert: Nebraska*. Lincoln: Nebraska State Historical Society, 1975.

Dyer, Frederick H. *A Compendium of the War of the Rebellion*. Des Moines, Iowa: Dyer Publishing Company, 1908.

Evans, Clement A., ed. *Confederate Military History.* Vol. XI. Atlanta, Georgia: Confederate Publishing Company, 1899.

Exley, Jo Ella Powell. *Frontier Blood: The Saga of the Parker Family*. College Station, Texas: Texas A&M University Press, 2001.

Fehrenbach, T. R. *Comanches: The Destruction of a People*. New York: Da Capo Press, 1994.

_______. *Lone Star A History of Texas and the Texans*. New York: Collier Books, 1968.

Foner, Eric. *Reconstruction America's Unfinished Revolution 1863-1877*. New York: Harper & Row, 1988.

Foote, Shelby. *The Civil War A Narrative Fort Sumter to Perryville*. New York: Random House, 1958.

Ford, John Salmon. *Rip Ford's Texas*. Edited by Stephen B. Oates. Austin, Texas: University of Texas Press, 1963.

Foreman, Carolyn Thomas. "Col. Jesse Henry Leavenworth." *Chronicles of Oklahoma* 13, no. 1 (March 1935): 14-29.

Frazer, Robert W. *Forts of the West: Military Forts and Presidios and Posts Commonly Called Forts West of the Mississippi River to 1898*. Norman: University of Oklahoma Press, 1965.

Frazier, Donald S. *Blood & Treasure: Confederate Empire in the Southwest*. College Station, Texas: Texas A&M Press, 1995.

Frederick, J.V. *Ben Holladay the Stagecoach King: A Chapter in the Development of Transcontinental Transportation*. Glendale, CA: Arthur H. Clark Co., 1940. Reprint, Lincoln: University of Nebraska Press, 1989.

Fredericksburg Standard. "Woman's Death Recalls Frontier Tragedy." *Frontier Times* 14, no. 12 (September 1937): 532-33.

Gallaway, B.P., ed. *Texas the Dark Corner of the Confederacy*. Lincoln: University of Nebraska Press, 1994.

Gambone, Joseph G. "Economic Relief in Territorial Kansas, 1860-61." *Kansas Historical Quarterly* 36, no. 3 (Summer 1970): 149-174.

Gard, Wayne. *The Chisholm Trail*. Norman: University of Oklahoma Press, 1954.

Gelo, Daniel J., and Scott Zesch, eds. "'Every Day Seemed to be a Holiday:' The Captivity of Bianca Babb." *Southwestern Historical Quarterly* CVII, No. 1 (July 2003): 35-67.

Goodrich, Thomas. *Black Flag: Guerrilla Warfare on the Western Border, 1861-1865*. Bloomington, Indiana: Indiana University Press, 1995.

Grace, John S., and R. B. Jones. *A New History of Parker County*. Weatherford, Texas: *Weatherford Democrat*, 1906. Reprint, Weatherford, Texas: Parker County Historical Association, 1987.

Graves, John. *Goodbye to a River*. Houston, Texas: Gulf Publishing Company, 1959.

Greene, A. C. *900 Miles on the Butterfield Trail*. Denton, Texas: University of North Texas Press, 1994.

Greever, William S. *The Bonanza West: The Story of the Western Mining Rushes 1848-1900*. Norman, Oklahoma: University of Oklahoma Press, 1963.

Grinnell, George B. *The Cheyenne Indians*. Lincoln: University of Nebraska Press, 1972.

_______. *The Fighting Cheyennes*. Norman: University of Oklahoma Press, 1966.

Groneman, Bill. *Battlefields of Texas*. Plano, Texas: Republic of Texas Press, 1998.

Hafen, Leroy R. *Broken Hand The Life of Thomas Fitzpatrick: Mountain Man, Guide and Indian Agent*. Norman: University of Oklahoma Press, 1981.

_______. *Relations with the Indians of the Plains, 1857-1861*. Glendale, California: Arthur H. Clark Company, 1959.

Hagan, Dennis E. "Counting Coup: the nature of intertribal warfare on the Great Plains considered." *The Denver Westerners Roundup*, LX, no. 6 (November-December 2004): 3-20.

Bibliography

Haley, J. Evetts. *Charles Goodnight Cowman and Plainsman*. Norman, Oklahoma: University of Oklahoma Press, 1949.

Hamalainen, Pekka. *The Comanche Empire*. New Haven, Connecticut: Yale University Press, 2008.

Hamilton, Allen Lee. *Sentinel of the Southern Plains Fort Richardson and the Northwest Texas Frontier, 1866-1878*. Fort Worth, Texas: Texas Christian University Press, 1988.

Hamilton, Byrde Pearce. "Albert Schwandner, a Captive of the Lipans." *Frontier Times* 14, no. 9 (June 1937): 403-405.

Harris, Benjamin Butler. *The Gila Trail: The Texas Argonauts and the California Gold Rush*. Norman, Oklahoma : University of Oklahoma Press, 1960.

Heitman, Francis B. *Historical Register and Dictionary of the United States Army*. Washington: GPO, 1903.

Herron, Lee. "Story of the Box Rescue." St. Paul, Nebraska: n.d. Denver Public Library, M349.

Hine, Robert V. and John Mack Faragher. *The American West A New Interpretive History*. New Haven, Connecticut: Yale University Press, 2000.

Hoig, Stan. *Tribal Wars of the Southern Plains*. Norman: University of Oklahoma Press, 1993.

_______. *White Man's Paper Trail: Grand Councils and Treaty-Making on the Central Plains*. Boulder, Colorado: University Press of Colorado, 2006.

Holder, Frances Mayhew. *Lambshead Before Interwoven: A Texas Range Chronicle, 1848-1878*. College Station, Texas: Texas A&M University, 1982.

Horsman, Reginald. *Race and Manifest Destiny The Origins of American Racial Anglo-Saxonism*. Cambridge, Massachusetts: Harvard University Press, 1981.

Huckabay, Ida Lasater. *Ninety-Four Years in Jack County 1854-1948*. Waco, Texas: By the author, 1949.

Hughes, Michael A. "Nations Asunder: Western American Indians During the American Civil War, 1861-1865." *Journal of the Indian Wars* 1, no. 3: 69-114.

Hunter, J. Marvin. *Pioneer History of Bandera County*. Bandera, Texas: Hunter's Printing House, 1922.

_______. *The Trail Drivers of Texas Part One*. San Antonio, Texas: Old Time Trail Drivers' Association, 1920.

Hunter, John Warren. "The Battle at Ball's Ranch." *Frontier Times* 4, no. 12 (September 1927): 22-34.

_______. "A Great Raid in Young County." *Frontier Times* 2, no. 12 (September 1925): 1-8.

_______. "The Tragedy of Legion Valley." *Frontier Times* 1, no. 4 (January 1924): 20-22.

Hyde, George E. *Life of George Bent Written From His Letters*. Edited by Savoie Lottinville. Norman, Oklahoma: University of Oklahoma Press, 1968.

Hyslop, Stephen G. *Bound for Santa Fe The Road to New Mexico and the American Conquest, 1806-1848*. Norman, Oklahoma: University of Oklahoma Press, 2002.

Jackson, W. Turrentine. *Wagon Roads West: A Study of Federal Road Surveys and Construction in the Trans-Mississippi West, 1846-1869*. New Haven, Connecticut: Yale University Press, 1965.

Johnson, Frank W. *A History of Texas and Texans*, Vol III. Chicago, Illinois: The American Historical Society, 1914.

Jones, Douglas C. *The Treaty of Medicine Lodge*. Norman, Oklahoma: University of Oklahoma Press, 1966.

Josephy, Alvin M. *The Civil War in the American West*. New York: Alfred A. Knopf, 1991.

Kappler, Charles J., ed. *Indian Treaties 1778-1883*. Mattituck, New York: Amereon House, 1972.

Kavanagh, Thomas W. *The Comanches A History 1706-1875*. Lincoln, Nebraska: University of Nebraska Press, 1996.

Keleher, William A. *Turmoil in New Mexico 1848-1868*. Santa Fe, New Mexico: Rydal Press, 1952.

Kenner, Charles L. *The Comanchero Frontier: A History of New Mexican-Plains Indian Relations*. Norman, Oklahoma: University of Oklahoma Press, 1994.

_______. "Guardians in Blue: The United States Cavalry and the Growth of the Texas Range Cattle Industry." *Journal of the West* XXXIV, no. 1 (January 1995): 46-54.

Kerby, Robert L. *Kirby Smith's Confederacy The Trans-Mississippi South, 1863-1865*. Tuscaloosa, Alabama: University of Alabama Press, 1972.

Kessell, John L. *Spain in the Southwest A Narrative History of Colonial New Mexico, Arizona, Texas, and California*. Norman, Oklahoma: University of Oklahoma Press, 2002.

Kingman, Samuel A. "Diary of Samuel A. Kingman at Indian Treaty in 1865." *Kansas Historical Quarterly* 1, no. 5 (November 1932): 442-450.

Kirwan, John S. "Patrolling the Santa Fe Trail: Reminiscences of John S. Kirwan." *Kansas Historical Quarterly* 21, no. 8 (Winter 1955): 569-87.

Kroeker, Marvin E. *Great Plains Command William B. Hazen in the Frontier West*. Norman, Oklahoma: University of Oklahoma Press, 1976.

Kvasnicka, Robert M. and Herman J. Viola, eds. *The Commissioners of Indian Affairs, 1824-1977*. Foreword by Philleo Nash. Lincoln, Nebraska: University of Nebraska Press, 1979.

Lamar, Howard Roberts. *The Far Southwest 1846-1912: A Territorial History*. Albuquerque, New Mexico: University of New Mexico Press, 2000.

Langston, Mrs. George (Caroline Lavinia). *History of Eastland County*. Dallas, Texas: A.D. Aldridge & Co., 1904.

Lavender, David. *Bent's Fort*. Lincoln: University of Nebraska Press, 1972.

La Vere, David. *The Texas Indians*. College Station, Texas: Texas A&M University Press, 2004.

Lease, Wayne. *Texas Forts*. Garland, Texas: Texas Forts Distributors, LLC., 2001.

Leckie, William H. *The Buffalo Soldiers: A Narrative of the Negro Cavalry in the West*. Norman, Oklahoma: University of Oklahoma Press, 1967.

Ledbetter, Barbara A. Neal. *Fort Belknap Frontier Saga: Indians, Negroes and Anglo-Americans on the Texas Frontier*. NL Ranch Headquarters, Texas: Lavender Books, 1982.

Limerick, Patricia Nelson. *The Legacy of Conquest: The Unbroken Past of the American West*. New York: W.W. Norton & Company, 1987.

_______. *Something in the Soil: Legacies and Reckonings in the New West*. New York: W.W. Norton & Company, 2000.

Lubbock, Francis Richard. *Six Decades in Texas or Memoirs of Francis Richard Lubbock, Governor of Texas in War-Time, 1861-63*. Austin, Texas: Ben C. Jones & Co., 1900.

McCaslin, Richard B. "Dark Corner of the Confederacy: James G. Bourland and the Border Regiment. *Military History of the West* 24, no. 1 (Spring 1994): 57-70.

_______. *Tainted Breeze The Great Hanging at Gainsville, Texas 1862*. Baton Rouge, Louisiana: Louisiana State University, 1994.

McConnell, H. H. *Five Years a Cavalryman; or, Sketches of Regular Army Life on the Texas Frontier 1866-1871*. Foreword by William Leckie. Norman, Oklahoma: University of Oklahoma Press, 1996.

McConnell, Joseph Carroll. *The West Texas Frontier, or a Descriptive History of Early Times in Western Texas*. 2 Vols. Jacksboro, Texas: Gazette Print, 1933.

Malin, James C. "Dust Storms Part One, 1850-1860." *Kansas Historical Quarterly* 14, no. 2 (May 1946): 129-144.

Marshall, Doyle. *A Cry Unheard: The Story of Indian Attacks in and Around Parker County, Texas 1858-1872*. Annetta Valley Farm Press, 1990.

Mayhall, Mildred P. *Indian Wars of Texas*. Waco, Texas: Texian Press, 1965.

_______. *The Kiowas*. Norman, Oklahoma: University of Oklahoma Press, 1962.

Merrick, Morgan Wolfe. *From Desert to Bayou: The Civil War Journal and Sketches of Morgan Wolfe Merrick*. El Paso, Texas: University of Texas El Paso, 1991.

Michno, Gregory F. *Encyclopedia of Indian Wars Western Battles and Skirmishes, 1850-1890*. Missoula, Montana: Mountain Press, 2003.

Michno, Gregory F. and Susan J. Michno. *Circle the Wagons! Attacks on Wagon Trains in History and Hollywood Films*. Jefferson, North Carolina: McFarland & Company, Inc, 2009.

_______. *A Fate Worse Than Death Indian Captivities in the West, 1830-1885*. Caldwell, Idaho: Caxton Press, 2007.

_______. *Forgotten Fights: Little-Known Raids and Skirmishes on the Frontier, 1823 to 1890*. Missoula, Montana: Mountain Press, 2008.

Michno, Susan J. "The Box Family, the Custers, & the Last Bullet." *Research Review* 20, no. 1. (Winter 2006): 2-7, 31.

Moneyhon, Carl H. *Texas after the Civil War The Struggle of Reconstruction*. College Station, Texas: Texas A&M University Press, 2004.

Moody, Ralph. *Stagecoach West*. Lincoln, Nebraska: University of Nebraska Press, 1998.

Mooney, James. *Calendar History of the Kiowa Indians*. Washington, D.C.: Smithsonian Institution Press, 1979.

Morris, John Miller. *El Llano Estacado Exploration and Imagination on the High Plains of Texas and New Mexico, 1536-1860*. Austin, Texas: Texas State Historical Association, 1997.

Neal, Charles M. Jr. *Valor Across the Lone Star The Congressional Medal of Honor in Frontier Texas*. Austin, Texas: Texas State Historical Association, 2002.

Nichols, David A. *Lincoln and the Indians: Civil War Policy & Politics*. Urbana, Iillinois: University of Illinois Press, 2000.

Nye, Wilbur Sturtevant. *Bad Medicine & Good Tales of the Kiowas*. Norman, Oklahoma: University of Oklahoma Press, 1962.

_______. *Plains Indian Raiders: The Final Phases of Warfare from the Arkansas to the Red River*. Norman: University of Oklahoma Press, 1968.

Nye, Col. W. S. *Carbine and Lance: The Story of Old Fort Sill*. Norman: University of Oklahoma Press, 1969.

Oliva, Leo E. *Fort Union and the Frontier Army in the Southwest*. Southwest Cultural Resources Center Professional Papers No. 41. Santa Fe, New Mexico: NPS, 1993.

_______. *Soldiers on the Santa Fe Trail*. Norman: University of Oklahoma Press, 1967.

Ormsby, Waterman L. *The Butterfield Overland Mail*. San Marino, California: The Huntington Library, 1942.

Paul, R. Eli. *Blue Water Creek and the First Sioux War, 1854-1856*. Norman, Oklahoma: University of Oklahoma Press, 2004.

Perryman, Levi. *Thrilling Raids into Cooke and Montague Counties*. Forestburg, Texas: Levi Perryman, 1919.

Peters, Joseph P. *Indian Battles and Skirmishes on the American Frontier 1790-1898*. Ann Arbor, Michigan: University Microfilms, Inc., 1966.

Peterson, Dorothy Burns. *Daughters of the Republic of Texas, Vol. 1. Patriot Ancestor Album*. Paducah, Kentucky: Turner Publishing Company, 1995.

Pickering, David, and Judy Falls. *Brush Men & Vigilantes Civil War Dissent in Texas*. Foreword by Richard B. McCaslin. College Station, Texas: Texas A&M University Press, 2000.

Potter, Mrs. W. R. *History of Montague County, Texas*. Reprint. Salem, Massachusetts: Higginson Book Company, 1957.

Prucha, Francis Paul, ed. *Documents of United States Indian Policy*. Lincoln, Nebraska: University of Nebraska Press, 1990.

Rampp, Larry C. and Donald L. Rampp. "The Civil War in the Indian Territory: The Confederate Advantage, 1861-1862." *Military History of Texas and the Southwest* X, no. 1 (1972): 29-41.

Bibliography

Ramsay, Jack C. Jr. *The Story of Cynthia Ann Parker Sunshine on the Prairie*. Austin, Texas: Eakin Press, 1990.

Rath, Ida Ellen. *The Rath Trail*. Wichita, Kansas: McCormick–Armstrong, Co., Inc., 1961.

Reeves, George. "The Scalping of Matilda Friend." *Frontier Times* 5, no. 2 (November 1927): 49-52.

Remini, Robert V. *Andrew Jackson and his Indian Wars*. New York: Viking, 2001.

Richardson, Rupert N. *The Comanche Barrier to South Plains Settlement*. Austin, Texas: Eakin Press, 1996.

_______. *The Frontier of Northwest Texas 1846 to 1876 Advance and Defense by the Pioneer Settlers of the Cross Timbers and Prairies*. Glendale, California: Arthur H. Clark Co., 1963.

Richter, William L. *The Army in Texas During Reconstruction 1865-1870*. College Station, Texas: Texas A&M University Press, 1987.

Riddle, Kenyon. *Records and Maps of the Old Santa Fe Trail*. Stuart, Florida: Southeastern Printing Co., Inc., 1963.

Rister, Carl Coke. *Border Captives: The Traffic in Prisoners by Southern Plains Indians, 1835-1875*. Norman, Oklahoma: University of Oklahoma Press, 1940.

Robbins, Roy M. *Our Landed Heritage The Public Domain 1776-1936*. New York: Peter Smith, 1950.

Roberts, Virginia Culin. W*ith Their Own Blood: A Saga of Southwestern Pioneers*. Ft. Worth, Texas: Texas Christian University Press, 1992.

Robinson, Charles M. III. *The Men Who Wear the Star: The Story of the Texas Rangers*. New York: Random House, 2000.

_______. *Satanta: The Life and Death of a War Chief.* Austin, Texas: State House Press, 1997.

Rodenbough, Theophilus R. *From Everglade to Canyon with the Second United States Cavalry*. New York: D. Van Nostrand, 1875. Reprint, Norman: University of Oklahoma Press, 2000.

Roth, Jeffrey M. "Civil War Frontier Defense Challenges in Northwest Texas." *Military History of the West* 30, no. 1 (Spring 2000): 21-44.

Rozwenc, Edwin C., ed. *The Causes of the American Civil War*. Boston, Massachusetts: D. C. Heath and Company, 1961.

Secoy, Frank Raymond. *Changing Military Patterns of the Great Plains Indians*. Lincoln: University of Nebraska Press, 1992.

Shook, Robert W. "The Federal Military in Texas, 1865-1870." *Texas Military History* VI, no. 1 (Spring 1967): 3-53.

Silver, Peter. *Our Savage Neighbors How Indian War Transformed Early America*. New York: W.W. Norton & Co., 2008.

Skogen, Larry C. *Indian Depredation Claims, 1796-1920*. Norman, Oklahoma: University of Oklahoma Press, 1996.

Smith, David Paul. *Frontier Defense in the Civil War Texas' Rangers and Rebels*. College Station, Texas: Texas A&M University Press, 1992.

Smith, Ralph Adam. *Borderlander The Life of James Kirker 1793-1852*. Norman, Oklahoma: University of Oklahoma Press, 1999.

Smith, Thomas T. The *Old Army in Texas: A Research Guide to the U.S. Army in Nineteenth-Century Texas*. Austin: Texas State Historical Association, 2000.

Smythe, Henry. *Historical Sketch of Parker County and Weatherford, Texas*. St. Louis, Missouri: Louis C. Lavat, 1877.

Sonnichsen, C.L. *The Mescalero Apaches*. Norman, Oklahoma: University of Oklahoma Press, 1958.

Sowell, A. J. *Early Settlers and Indian Fighters of Southwest Texas*. Austin, Texas: Benjamin C. Jones & Co., 1900. Reprint, Austin, Texas: State House Press, 1986.

_______. *Rangers and Pioneers of Texas*. 1884. Reprint, Austin, Texas: State House Press, 1991.

Stahle, David W., and Malcolm K. Cleaveland. "Texas Drought History Reconstructed and Analyzed from 1698 to 1980." *Journal of Climate* 1 (January 1988): 59-74.

Stanley, David Sloan. *An American general The Memoirs of David Sloan Stanley*. Santa Barbara, California: The Narrative Press, 2003.

Stephens, A. Ray and William M. Holmes. *Historical Atlas of Texas*. Norman, Oklahoma: University of Oklahoma Press, 1989.

Straley, W., ed. *Pioneer Sketches Nebraska and Texas*. Hico, Texas: Hico Printing Co., 1915.

Tatum, Lawrie. *Our Red Brothers and the Peace Policy of President Ulysses S. Grant*. With a foreword by Richard N. Ellis. Lincoln: University of Nebraska Press, 1970.

Taylor, Morris F. *First Mail West: Stagecoach Lines on the Santa Fe Trail*. Foreword by Mark L. Gardner. Albuquerque, NM: University of New Mexico Press, 1971.

Taylor, T. U. "Indian Massacre of the Brown Family." *Frontier Times*. Vol. 1 (September 1924): 18-19.

The Texas Almanac for 1867. Galveston, Texas: W. Richardson & Co., 1866.

Thompson, Jerry. *Confederate General of the West Henry Hopkins Sibley*. Foreword by Frank E. Vandiver. College Station, Texas: Texas A&M University Press, 1996.

Thrapp, Dan L. *Encyclopedia of Frontier Biography in Three Volumes*. Lincoln: University of Nebraska Press, 1991.

Tiling, Moritz. *History of the German Element in Texas from 1820-1850 and Historical Sketches of the German Texas Signers' League and Houston Turnverein from 1853-1913*. Houston, Texas: Moritz Tiling, 1913.

Turner, Frederick Jackson. *Frontier and Section: Selected Essays of Frederick Jackson Turner*. Introduction by Ray Allen Billington. Englewood Cliffs, New Jersey: Prentice-Hall, 1961.

Unrau, William E. "The Role of the Indian Agent in the Settlement of the South-Central Plains, 1861-1868." Ph.D. diss, University of Colorado, 1963.

Unruh, John D., Jr. *The Plains Across: The Overland Emigrants and the Trans-Mississippi West, 1840-60*. Urbana, Illinois: University of Illinois Press, 1993.

U.S. Congress, House of Representatives. *Report of the Secretary of War*. 40th Cong., 3rd sess., 1868. House Exec. Doc. 1.

U.S. Congress, Senate. "Letter from the Secretary of War." In response to Senate resolution of June 11, 1888, report relative to the raising of volunteer troops to guard overland and other mails from 1861 to 1866. Exec. Doc. 70. 50th Congress, 2nd Session. Washington: GPO, 1889.

U.S. Department of the Interior. Bureau of Indian Affairs. *Reports of the Commissioner of Indian Affairs. 1861-1869*. Washington: GPO.

U.S. War Department. *The War of the Rebellion: A Compilation of the Official Records of the Union and Confederate Armies*. Washington: GPO, 1880-1901.

Utley, Robert M. *Frontiersmen in Blue: The United States Army and the Indian 1848-1865*. New York: Macmillan Company, 1967.

_______. *Frontier Regulars: The U.S. Army and the Indian 1866-1891*. New York: Macmillan Publishing Co. Inc., 1973.

_______. *Lone Star Justice The First Century of the Texas Rangers*. New York: Oxford University Press, 2002.

Vincent, Francis, ed. *Vincent's Semi-Annual United States Register: Events Transpiring Between the 1st of January and 1st of July 1860*. Philadelphia, Pennsylvania: Francis Vincent, 1860.

Viola, Herman J. *Diplomats in Buckskin A History of Indian Delegations in Washington City*. Foreword by Senator Ben Nighthorse Campbell. Bluffton, SC: Rivilo Books, 1995.

Waldman, Carl. *Atlas of the North American Indian*. New York: Checkmark Books, 2000.

Wallace, Ernest. *Texas in Turmoil The Saga of Texas, 1849-1875*. Austin, Texas: Steck-Vaughn Company, 1965.

Watts, John S. *Indian Depredations in New Mexico*. Washington, D. C.: Gideon, 1859. Reprint. Tucson, Arizona: Territorial Press, 1964.

Webb, George W. *Chronological List of Engagements Between the Regular Army of the United States and Various Tribes of Hostile Indians*. St. Joseph, Missouri: Wing Print. and Pub. Co., 1939.

Webb, Walter Prescott. *The Texas Rangers: A Century of Frontier Defense*. Austin, Texas: University of Texas Press, 1965.

Webb, Walter Prescott, and H. Bailey Carroll, eds. *The Handbook of Texas*. Two Volumes. Austin, Texas: Texas State Historical Association, 1952.

Wellman Paul I. *Glory, God and Gold A Narrative History*. Garden City, New York: Doubleday & Company, Inc., 1954.

West, Elliot. *The Contested Plains: Indians, Goldseekers, and the Rush to Colorado*. Lawrence, Kansas: University Press of Kansas, 1998.

_______. *The Way to the West: Essays on the Central Plains*. Albuquerque: University of New Mexico Press, 1995.

White, Lonnie J. "White Woman Captives of Southern Plains Indians, 1866-1875." *Journal of the West* VIII, no. 8 (July 1969): 327-354.

White, Richard. *"It's Your Misfortune and None of My Own" A New History of the American West*. Norman: University of Oklahoma Press, 1991.

Whitford, William C. *Colorado Volunteers in the Civil War: The New Mexico Campaign in 1862*. Denver, CO: State Historical Society, 1906. Reprint, Glorieta, New Mexico: The Rio Grande Press, Inc., 1994.

Wilbarger, J. W. *Indian Depredations in Texas*. Austin, Texas: Hutchings Printing House, 1889. Reprint, Austin, Texas: Eakin Press, 1985.

Williams, Clayton W. *Texas' Last Frontier: Fort Stockton and the Trans-Pecos, 1861-1895*. College Station, Texas: Texas A&M Press, 1982.

Winfrey, Dornum H., and James M. Day, eds. *The Indian Papers of Texas and the Southwest 1825-1916*. 5 Vols. Austin, TX: Pemberton Press, 1966. Reprint, Introduction by Michael L. Tate. Austin, Texas: Texas State Historical Association, 1995.

Wilson, John P. *When the Texans Came Missing Records from the Civil War in the Southwest, 1861-1862*. Albuquerque, New Mexico: University of New Mexico Press, 2001.

Wooster, Robert. *The Military & United States Indian Policy 1865-1903*. Lincoln, University of Nebraska Press, 1995.

Zesch, Scott. *The Captured: A True Story of Abduction by the Indians on the Texas Frontier*. New York: St. Martin's Press, 2004.

_______. "The Search for Alice Todd." TMs (photocopy).

National Archives and Records Administration, Washington, D.C. Indian Depredation Claims. All claims are from Record Group 123 unless indicated otherwise.

Allen, William M. #4605.
Amman, Sophie. #651.
Anderson, Aaron #10258.
Anderson, William W. #5295.
Autobees, Charles. #825.
Babb, Hernando C. #4606.
Bailey, Thomas. #4346.
Ball, James S. #10172.
Banister, Lawrence. #2859.
Banta, William. #2640.
Barcroft, Elisha H. #5292.
Barker, James J. #4555.
Barron, Solomon. #5255.
Bendele, Jacob. #3347.
Bennett, Levi. #3525.
Bennett, Woodford. #1545.
Benns (Williams), Amanda. #3875.
Binnion, Minerva A. #1669.
Bishop, Mary T. #6173.
Bland, W. W. #4413.
Blankenship, Levi. #649.
Bogard, Thomas W. #437.
Bourland, James S. #3893.
Bragg, William A. #5291.

Bibliography

Brannon, Jefferson W. #5259.
Bridges, Joseph D. #432.
Brown, Frank S. #6163.
Brown, George. #4781.
Browning, Benjamin F. #4608.
Brunson, Margaret. #7232.
Bullion, M. D. #3522.
Bunch, Mary Catherine. #833.
Burleson, Ellen. #6302.
Burrow, Nancy Ann. #762.
Burton, George. #6006.
Cady, Joseph D. #650.
Campbell, Joseph. #2769.
Caraway, Jesse. #4199.
Casey, Robert F. #9522.
Cavitt, W. A. #2765.
Chapman, Guilford R. #1548.
Cherry, Harrell. #4415.
Chick, James H. #5019.
Chipman, Ezra A. #167.
Chisum, Giles. #5016.
Chrisman, Isaac. #4168.
Clark, Robert F. #507.
Clark, William T. #4553.
Clifton, James M. #5260.
Coon, Richard S. #10834.
Costley, William E. #2224.
Coursey, James T. #3876.
Dameron, Moses. #352.
Davenport, James B. #5732.
Davis, Hezekiah B. #6774.
Davis, Nathan M. #5533.
Davis, Thomas J. #8007.
Dawson, Nick. #9960.
Dietert, Henry. #10270.
Dinger, Charles #1812.
Duncan, John C. #7349.
Eaker, Felix. #3537.
Eaves, William R. #421.
Ebeling, Edward. #2083.
Edwards, Jerome B. #5703.
Edwards, Lemuel J. #3542.
Edwards, Sarah Jane. #5253
Elmore, John P. #423.
Emerson, Elijah. #1544.
Emory, Peter B. #4492.
Espy, Thomas H. #4410.
Etheridge, M. #2634.
Eubank, Hesekiah B. #5901.
Fallowill, Moses. #431.
Field, Patrick. #8448.
Fisher, William E. #5714.
Fly, David W. #2690.
Franklin, W. C. #5726.
Freeman, Alphonso. #433.
Freeman, Ebenezer R. #4421.
Freeman, William M. #839, RG 75.
Friend, Allen H. #6172.
Fuchs, William G. #7155.
Gahagan, Manda A. #5257.
Garcia, Gregoria. #4231.
Gatlin, William H. #5684.
Gibbons, Nancy. #3896.
Gibson, Samuel L. #5724.
Gieseke, Albert. #429.
Gilbert, Mabel. #5695.
Gilbert, Morris. #674.
Gilliam, John E. #6171.
Gober, John W. #4551.
Gorham, Joshua. #424.
Goss, J. S. #1810.
Gousalans, Peter. #5217.
Greene, Anderson #4408.
Greenwood, Joseph J. #2759.
Gregory, Malachi. #5538.
Haas, Phillip. #3348.
Harkey, Polly. #5251.
Hart, John P. #4557.
Harvey, Thomas. #348.
Hatley, Mark B. #4234.
Haven, Henderson B. #1879.
Hayes, William L. #1667.
Haynes, Louisa. #5310.
Hendricks, James. #5311.
Hensley, William. #7484.
Hill, Haden M. #5296.
Hillyard, Thomas. #5109.
Hinds, William S. #8316.
Hinton, Jack. #5298.
Hobbs, John. #3891.
Holden, George W. #4782.
Holland, Samuel E. #2292.
Huckobey, William R. #3474.
Huebner, Joseph. #7821.
Hufstutler, Sanford. #4352.
Inselman, John J. #7494.
Irwin, John G. #3895.
Jackson, Amanda. #7754.
Jackson, Cotsworth H. #5254.
Jackson, Isaac N. #2644.
Jackson, William R. #1270.
Jannett, Samuel. #4417.
Jefferson, Nancy. #1550.
Jenkins (McKenzie), Mary A. #10571.

Jennings, William E. #2222.
Johnson, James W. M. #6170.
Jonas, William. #6164.
Kappelmann, Adolph. #8323.
Keith, John J. #5258.
Keith, William S. #4738.
Kemp, Simeon. #4777.
Kemp, William A. #4232.
Kennedy, Ross. #4233.
Kincheloe, Louis C. #2479.
Kincheloe, Robert H. #2764.
King, James L. #3533.
King, Joshua G. #2291.
Kisor, John. #4198.
Kneupper, John. #8319.
Lang, Peter. #434.
Lange, Otto. #3539.
Lanham, J. M. #647.
Latham, Ambrose S. #2770.
Leath, Thomas M. #3888.
Leatherwood, Daniel S. #2079.
Lee, Harriet. #5687.
Lee, Leroy. #351.
Lee, Samuel E. #5686.
Lemley, George W. #4200.
Lindsey, Lucy E. #1813.
Lindsey, Samuel. #4532.
Long, John. #5688.
Luttrell, John #3494.
McClure, John. #3890.
McCormick, Nannie. #5416.
McCoy, David. #2685.
McCracken, David P. #7159.
McDaniel, Asenatha. #1197.
McDonald, David. #4537.
McDonald, Elizabeth J. #350.
McElroy, John R. #10037.
McGee, Jesse. #4778.
McGee, Jesse. #5819.
McGough, James B. #10616.
McKee, Joel. #829.
McMahon, Wesley. #4786.
Malone, Thomas. #5681.
Martin, David A. #354.
Martin, Joseph H. #4787.
Martin, William B. #5718.
Matthews, Robert M. #4500.
Matthews, Thomas. #347.
Metcalf, William. #5702.
Metzger, Frederick. #10628.
Miller, Andrew. #5013.
Mills, Christopher C. #5679.
Mitchell, John R. (Benjamin F. Hemphill). #5682.
Monier, Thebolt. #7488.
Montgomery, Wiley A. #6197.
Montieth, Jesse. #2902.
Mooney, Tip. #9650.
Morris, Edwin T. #5730.
Morris, F. G. #1188.
Muller, Charles. #7496.
Mumme, Ludwig H. G. #7820.
Murphy, Ann A. #1666.
Murphy, Henderson. #1273.
Norfleet, Jasper. #5537.
Oatman, John. #1187.
Oge, Louis. #1665.
Ogle, Laura (John Morris). #4342.
Owens, Solomon B. #170.
Parish, John D. #6212.
Parr, B. T. #1602.
Parsons, Amesley. #6213.
Perry, Elijah C. #5717.
Piatt, Richard F., Henry T. Sadorus, James Bryden. #358.
Pollard, John B. #6320.
Raines, Stephen G. #3543.
Reed, Robert C. (James Reed). #6297.
Reynolds, Ann M. #6502.
Rider, William. #4340.
Rittimann, Johann. #7258.
Roberts, Alexander. #3929.
Roberts, James T. #5290.
Robinson, William. #5198.
Ross, George W. #5719.
Sanders, Elick. #1894.
Savage, Bolen (Elizabeth Woods). #5221.
Skagg, Meshac. #2227.
Sensibaugh, Robert. #2857.
Shannon, Robert E. #5721.
Sheek, John W. #5312.
Shipman, Eliza. #2228.
Shortridge, Belle Hunt (William H. Hunt). #5734.
Slover, Ira S. #5012.
Smith, Culvin. #1681.
Smith, Gip. #2637.
Stansell, Thompson. #3544.
Sullivan, William R. #5680.
Sullivant, Harrison P. #9632.
Tankersley, Richard F. #6501.
Taylor, Delilah. #3528.
Thompson, William H. #2756.
Tompkins, John B. #4175.

Torres, Jose A. #3344.
Tumlinson, P. F. #10644.
Vanderberg, Mary E. #7487.
Vanhooser, John C. #6301.
Vaughn, Reuben. #6300.
Vogel, Gustav. #7495.
Wagenfuhr, Andreas #7273.
Walker, Elbert M. #4419.
Welty, Henry. #2853.
Wheeler, James R. #2852.
White, David. #6316.
White, James. #2851.
Whittmore, George W. #349.
Williams, Hiram. #6174.
Williams, William L. #4739.
Wilson, Martha (William Moorehead). #2686.
Wilson, William J. #4315.
Witter, Robert B. #648.
Wolfe, George W. #10315.
Wood, William R. #7052.
Wright, Reuben. #10632.
Yancey, John H. #5822.

Newspapers

The Adams Sentinel (Gettysburg, Pennsylvania)
The Daily Ledger and Texan (San Antonio)
Daily Times (Leavenworth, Kansas)
Dallas Herald (Texas)
Denton Chronicle (Texas)
The Galveston Weekly News (Texas)
Houston *Tri-Weekly Telegraph* (Texas)
Marysville Tribune (Marysville, Ohio)
Milwaukee, Daily Sentinel (Milwaukee, Wisconsin)
New York Times
New York Tribune
Santa Fe Weekly Gazette
Semi-Weekly News (San Antonio, Texas)
The Standard (Clarksville, Texas)
State Gazette (Austin, Texas)
The Texas Almanac (Austin)
The White Man (Weatherford, Texas)

Internet

"Ancestors of Alfred Henry George Schulte, Jr." http://familytreemaker.genealogy.com/users/l/o/t/donna-loth-tx/gene1-0009.html.
"Capt. Enoch Madison Jones." http://www.earljones.net/pafn18.html.
"Carlton Cemetery." http://www.cemeteries-of-tx.com/wtx/hamilton/cemetery/carlton.html.
"Chasing our Tales-John Hittson, Palo Pinto County's First Sheriff, and his Brother, James." http://www.rafandsioux.com/chasingourtales/hittson.html.
Clark, Jeff. "Eyewitness Account of Amanda Cofer's Murder by Comanches Surfaces." http://www.rootsweb.ancestry.com/~txeastla/story/amandacofersmurder.html.

Bibliography

"The Children of John C. Carson." http://www.carsonsofbrazos county.com/children_of_john_c.html.

"Death Records." http://surnamearchive.com/records/records054.html.

"Descendents of John Boren," http://familytreemaker.genealogy.com/users/b/o/l/nancy-gail-bolding-OK/gene7-0005.html.

"Duncans in Young County." http://homepages.rootsweb.ancestry.com/~dobson/tx/txyoung.htm.

"Erath County Kin." http://wc.rootsweb.ancestry.com/cgi-bin/igm.cgi?op=get&db=93stealth&id=I30335

"First Pioneers from Hamilton County." http://hamiltongazeteer.wordpress.com/2008/10/09/first-pioneers-from-hamilton-county/

Horton, Thomas F. *History of Jack County*. www.forttours.com/pages/saltck.asp.

"Judge David S. Hanna's Family History." http://www.perardua.net/gen/dshbook.html

"The Last Indian Raid to Hood County-The Point of Timbers Fight." Thomas T. Ewell. *Hood County History*. http://www.rootsweb.ancestry.com/~txhood/hoodcountyhistory/ewell41.htm.

Marcell, Cindy L. "Family Lines." http://freepages.genealogy.rootsweb.ancestry.com/~stumbo/pafg340.html.

"Martin, Texas," Texas Online Handbook. www.tsha.utexas.edu/handbook/online/articles/view/MM/hrmbb.html.

McConnell, Joseph Carroll. *The West Texas Frontier*. http://www.forttours.com.

"Mrs. C. C. Proctor." http://www.rootsweb.ancestry.com/~txburnet/ProctorMrsCC.html.

"Officer Down Memorial Page," http://www.odmp.org/officer/3544-sheriff-harvey-staten-cox.

"Parker County." http://familytreemaker.geneaology.com/users/r/e/i/lorene-h-reid/gene1-0005.html.

"Parker County Texas." http://www.rootsweb.ancestry.com/~txparker/history/indianraids2.html.

Roe, Mrs. James. "Cedar County."http://www.usgennet.org/usa/ne/county/cedar.

Sears, James T. "Pleasant 'Pleas' Boyd 1866." http://lipantexashistory.com/pleasant_press_boyd.html.

"Thomas Jefferson McReynolds." http://genforum.geneaology.com/mcreynolds/messages/573.html.

"Twin Oaks." http://www.mygeoinfo.com/2010/03/12/twin-oaks/.

"William Cox of Fannin County." http://freepages.family.rootsweb.ancestry.com/~texascantrells/williamcox.html.

Williams, Henry C. "Indian Raid in Young County, Texas." http://www.rootsweb.ancestry.com/txbaylor/1elmcree.html.

The Author

Gregory Michno is a Michigan native who attended Michigan State University and did post-graduate work at the University of Northern Colorado. An Award-winning author, he has written thirty articles and several books dealing with World War II and the American West. His books include *The Mystery of E Troop, Lakota Noon, USS Pampanito: Killer Angel, Death on the Hell-ships, The Encyclopedia of Indian Wars* and *Battle at Sand Creek.* He also participated in the editing and appeared in the dvd history, *The Great Indian Wars, 1540 - 1890.*

Gregory's books published by Caxton Press include *A Fate Worse than Death: Indian Captivities in the Wast, 1830 - 1885* and *The Deadliest Indian War in the West: The Snake Conflict, 1864 - 1868.*

Greg lives in Longmont, Colorado.

Index

Index

Index

Index

Index

Index

Index

Index

Other titles about
the West
from
Caxton Press

The Pony Express Trail
Yesterday and Today
by William Hill
ISBN 978-0-87004-476-2, 302 pages, paper, $18.95

The Lewis and Clark Trail
Yesterday and Today
by William Hill
ISBN 978-0-87004-439-7, 300 pages, paper, $16.95

A Fate Worse Than Death
Indian Captivities in the West
by Gregory Michno
and Susan Michno
ISBN 0-87004-473-1, 550 pages, paper, $19.95

The Deadliest Indian War in the West
The Snake Conflict 1864-1868
by Gregory Michno
ISBN 978-0-87004-460-1, 450 pages, paper, $18.95

Massacre Along the Medicine Road
The Indian War of 1864 in Nebraska
by Ronald Becher
ISBN 0-87004-289-7, 500 pages, cloth, $32.95
ISBN 0-87004-387-0, 500 pages, paper, $22.95

For a free catalog of Caxton titles write to:

Caxton Press
312 Main Street
Caldwell, Idaho 83605-3299

or

Visit our Internet web site:

www.caxtonpress.com

Caxton Press is a division of The Caxton Printers, Ltd.